European Alliances
and Alignments

§

EUROPEAN ALLIANCES
and
ALIGNMENTS
1871-1890

WILLIAM L. LANGER

HARVARD UNIVERSITY

GREENWOOD PRESS, PUBLISHERS
WESTPORT, CONNECTICUT

Library of Congress Cataloging in Publication Data

Langer, William Leonard, 1896-
  European alliances and alignments, 1871-1890.

  Reprint of the ed. published by Knopf, New York.
  Includes bibliographical references and index.
  1. Europe--Politics and government--1871-1918.
I. Title.
D397.L28 1977   320.9'4'0287   77-1767
ISBN 0-8371-9518-7

Originally published in 1931 by Alfred A. Knopf, Inc., New York

Reprinted in 1977 by Greenwood Press, Inc.

Library of Congress catalog card number   77-1767

ISBN 0-8371-9518-7

Printed in the United States of America

To my

MOTHER

in profound gratitude

Preface

ᴥ

THE SUBJECT OF PRE-WAR DIPLOMACY HAS RECEIVED A GREAT DEAL OF attention in recent years from scholars in this country as well as abroad. From the very nature of the case, however, much of the writing in this field has been devoted to the study of the origins of the war itself. Much of the literature has, in fact, been of a distinctly controversial nature, despite its technical and scientific approach. It is really surprising that so little has been done, outside Germany, with the study of European diplomacy in this period as a subject interesting and important in itself. Apart from the excellent book written by G. P. Gooch some eight years ago — that is, before the publication of most of the important material — it would be hard to mention any work in English that attempts to survey the subject in a broad general way. Even the best German works approach the subject from the standpoint of German policy rather than from the angle of general international relations, while the thorough, systematic handbook published by a group of French scholars under the direction of M. Henri Hauser (*Histoire diplomatique de l'Europe,* Paris, 1929) suffers from lack of unity and singleness of thought.

I have written this book, not with the outbreak of the World War especially in mind, but as a study of the evolution of the European states system. That is to say, I have not aimed at the production of a history of European diplomacy, properly speaking. I have not attempted to account for all the incidents which inevitably arise in the course of international relations. I have tried rather to describe and explain the broad course of development in international relations and to analyse the factors that brought about the great international groupings and alignments. In the course of my researches I have been drawn further and further away from the cheap and frequently ignorant arraignments of the " old diplomacy " which are so much in vogue at the present day. I have become less and less willing to believe that men in that day were more wicked, more unscrupulous, and more evil-minded than in our own or any other day. At bottom, it seems to me, the statesmen and governments of this period were confronted with the rapidly growing complexity of modern life, which reacted upon international affairs quite as much as upon domestic problems, if not more. The study of diplomacy, if it is to lead to anything worth while, must go beyond the mere digest or analysis of documents and negotiations. It must study the fundamental forces and the broad currents that influenced the relations of states to each other. I have made the effort, with what success remains to be seen, to take due account of economic developments, of changing military considerations, and of strong tides of national sentiment, as well as of individual leadership. Franco-German relations, the complex of problems known as the Eastern question, and the difficulties arising from European economic and political expansion were in the forefront during the years here under discussion. These the reader will find treated in considerable detail, and always with an eye to the interactions of these different problems upon the groupings of the powers. English policy, frequently hard to understand and very elusive, is usually given cavalier treatment by historians of European politics. I have at least made the effort to weave it into the general story of continental affairs and to set forth the perennial conflict between a world policy and a European policy which English statesmen more than those of any other nation were obliged to face.

Those who have worked in this field will be well acquainted with the difficulties which the subject presents. Overshadowing all other obstacles is the problem of materials. Hardly a decade ago almost nothing definitive could be said on this subject. Within the space of a few years, however, we have been literally overwhelmed by a landslide of documentary and other source material, to say nothing of a long and impressive series of monographic studies of special points. I believe that I am personally acquainted with the bulk of this material, which I have been studying uninterruptedly for more than ten years. In this book I have made full use of the documentary sources, memoirs, biographies, and correspondence, but I have also drawn freely upon whatever was suggestive or valuable in the critical work of English, French, German, Italian, and Russian scholars. No doubt some material, perhaps important, has escaped me and I shall be found guilty of inexcusable omissions. I feel certain, however, that those who are personally acquainted with this staggering mass of data, rapidly becoming too great for one human mind to grasp, will be disposed to deal leniently with me for any shortcomings of this type that may appear in this volume. I have actually made use of everything that seemed to me of real importance, I have done my best to handle this material critically, and I have tried to construct from a welter of evidence which is frequently contradictory a well-balanced, sound, and inclusive survey.

So far as possible I have attempted to spare the reader unnecessary technicalities and to make my account readable and understandable for the average educated layman. To this end I have reduced the foot-notes to an absolute minimum and have restricted them to references and citations. Where there are good English translations of books referred to, I have generally cited them in preference to the originals, thinking that they might be more readily accessible to the reader. Frequently, however, the English editions are condensed, or otherwise unsatisfactory. In such cases I have invariably referred to the original. In the brief bibliographical notes appended to each chapter I have listed such material as seemed to me most important, and have indicated, in a few words, its relative value. By no means all of the works cited in the foot-notes are listed in the bibliographical notes. These notes are intended primarily to serve as guides to further study or reading. They should have some real value, since there is, at the present time, no comprehensive bibliography of the subject available.

Professor Dwight E. Lee of Clark University was good enough to read several of the chapters dealing with the Near Eastern crisis of 1875-8 and to put at my disposal some very interesting unpublished material which he collected at the Public Record Office. Through his kindness I was able to make use also of his unpublished doctoral dissertation, which is based upon material in European archives and deals with British policy in 1878. My brother, Professor Rudolph E. Langer, of the University of Wisconsin, read practically the whole of the manuscript and made innumerable suggestions regarding style and clarity of thought. My friend and former student Mr. Walter Koetzle, of Brooklyn, took upon himself part of the tedious work of proof-reading. To all these gentlemen I am genuinely grateful for their interest and assistance. I am also deeply indebted to the Bureau of International Research of Harvard and Radcliffe for assistance which relieved me of teaching obligations for one semester and thereby enabled me to finish this volume.

WILLIAM L. LANGER

Harvard University
May 1931

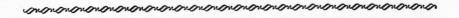

Contents

List of Maps

European Alliances
and Alignments

§

I

The Aftermath of War

⟋

WHEN PEACE WAS SIGNED BETWEEN GERMANY AND FRANCE IN MAY 1871, Europe emerged from a period of wars which resulted in a territorial revolution of far-reaching consequences. During the first half of the century the great problem had been the combating of the revolutionary movement. In a sense this phase might be described as the aftermath of the French Revolution. It came to an end with the failure of the great and impressive movements of 1848–9, which were, in a large measure, national movements. In the next period the governments themselves, despite their conservative or even reactionary character, took up the principle of nationality with all its revolutionary implications. In the brief space of fifteen years the old map of Europe was torn up and the political geography of the continent completely redrawn. This was the work primarily of Napoleon III, Cavour, and Bismarck, and it was a work of greater permanence and deeper effect than all the military conquests of the first Napoleon.

The Crimean War of 1854–6, though it was not, properly speaking, a national war, may be taken as the prelude to this period of militant and triumphant nationalism. It served to clear the atmosphere and to establish certain relationships between the European powers which continued to be of importance long after the Treaty of Paris had become only a name. The defeat of Russia by England and France meant, for one thing, the eclipse of the Tsarist Empire during the next fifteen years. On the other hand the hesitant and anomalous policy of Francis Joseph during the Crimean War led to serious estrangement between Austria and Russia and to the hostility of France towards the Habsburg Empire. The antagonism between the Kingdom of Sardinia (Piedmont) and Austria had already come to a head in the years 1848–9, but the participation of Sardinia in the war against Russia laid the basis for the future co-operation of Napoleon III and Cavour in the war of 1859. Prussia had taken no direct part in the Crimean War, but the Berlin government had abstained from an anti-Russian policy and had in this way earned the sympathy and goodwill of the Tsar, which was to be of inestimable value in subsequent crises.

The first of the truly national wars which filled the years from 1859–71 was the war of France and Sardinia against Austria. This resulted in the unification of Italy excepting for the province of Venetia and the papal city of Rome with its surroundings. There followed in 1864 the war of Austria and Prussia against

3

Denmark, and in 1866 the war of Prussia and Italy against Austria and the smaller German states. The first of these two conflicts ended in the loss of Schleswig and Holstein by Denmark; the second grew directly out of the problem of the disposal of these two provinces. By her spectacular victory over Austria in 1866 Prussia not only acquired both provinces for herself, but also forced the Habsburgs out of German affairs and established the North German Confederation under her own leadership. Prussia had further strengthened her position by numerous annexations in Germany north of the Main River, while her ally, Italy, though defeated both on land and on sea by the Austrians, was rewarded for her participation by the acquisition of Venetia.

These wars had followed upon each other at intervals of a few years. History was being made at an ever-increasing pace. Of the Crimean War it has been said that it took longer to get itself declared than any other war in history. But the next international conflicts, though their roots no doubt went far back into the past, broke upon the European world with appalling suddenness. This may have been due to the more belligerent outlook that had grown up in most countries after the long spell of international peace had been broken. It may also be explained by the greater ruthlessness, energy, and ability of men like Cavour and Bismarck, who had little in common with their more idealistic predecessors. But the rapidly changing conditions of life must have exerted a profound influence. In the old days of professional armies, inadequate transportation, and primitive supply systems there was nothing very spectacular about a declaration of war. Frequently months passed before the armies were actually on the march, and not infrequently the fighting was restricted to one campaign each year, fought during the open months when manœuvring and transportation were easiest.

All this changed after the middle of the century. The spread of ideas of equality and democracy made the transition from the professional army to the system of universal military service and the nation in arms a fairly natural one. Equality of rights logically involved equality of duties. In the same way the larger participation of the people in the affairs of government broadened the basis of interest in foreign affairs. If in the eighteenth century international relations were primarily the business of the king or his cabinet, they now became the affair of the population at large, or at least the affair of the literate and articulate part of the population. The force of public opinion and the pressure of popular sentiment became so pronounced in the period after 1849 that it soon developed into a factor of major importance in the conduct of international relations. Public opinion, as expressed in newspapers, periodicals, pamphlets, and books, might for a time be ignored, as it was by Cavour and Bismarck, but it could not be disregarded entirely. At best, governments could attempt to influence and guide it, if it became too troublesome. All the continental governments opened connexions with the press, and it frequently became difficult to decide whether it was public opinion working through the press, or the government working upon public opinion through the same channels that finally determined the course of policy. One thing, at least, is certain. The gradual popularization of government complicated international relations and introduced an accelerating element. Mob psychology and popular passion began to exert their influence. The irresistible surge of mass feeling began to hurry governments into actions which the leading statesmen, if given time, might have carefully avoided.

The growth of democracy in Europe was bound up closely with the economic changes that were taking place at the time. The so-called industrial revolution transformed the character of international relations by revolutionizing the character of warfare. Scientific development made possible new inventions in armament, while the new system of production facilitated the rapid output on a large scale of munitions and other military supplies. At the same time the improved methods of transportation, notably the railroad, paved the way for speedier concentration of large numbers of troops, for satisfactory and steady supply of the armies in the field with food, clothing, and other military necessities, and for proper communication of information between the various units of large forces. In other words, the new economic system made possible the maintenance of larger armies, accelerated their mobilization, and increased their efficiency. The nation in arms was no longer a theoretical entity. It had become a very real thing.

While the democratization of politics made international conflicts more difficult to avoid, the mechanization of warfare made the clash of arms more serious and disastrous. The governments, then, would have been negligent had they not taken every precaution and made every arrangement for an eventual crisis. Greater and greater stress was laid upon the training and equipment of the troops, and more and more attention was paid to the drafting of campaign plans. Rapidity of mobilization became a matter of supreme importance, for the first power in the field had an inestimable advantage over its opponents, and, from the standpoint of public opinion, an initial victory or defeat might decide the fate of a dynasty or a government.

Among other preparations statesmen began to devote themselves more and more to the business of finding allies, and alliances came to be the accepted thing in international relations. Such connexions between two states or even such combinations of several states were nothing new in themselves. Alliances were, in fact, as old as recorded history. But these older alliances were frequently of a religious or racial type and the combinations which led to the gradual consolidations of territory and the emergence of the modern monarchy had little in common with the combinations between the modern European states themselves. Leaving aside such vague international connexions as the Family Compact of the eighteenth century or the Holy Alliance of the nineteenth, the great coalitions of modern history were almost always made just before the outbreak of war or during the course of the conflict itself. There are few instances of alliances which extended over long periods of years and were based upon written agreements which specified in detail what should be done in certain contingencies. The easy-going nature of warfare made advance arrangements quite unnecessary, and the slowness of communication made it inadvisable to enter commitments of binding character. It was the greater pressure in international relations and the greater speed of military operations that gave rise to the necessity for permanent combinations and resulted in the gradual evolution of the great European alliance systems of the period preceding the World War. This type of international organization is one of the most striking characteristics of the period, and one which must be studied in the broad setting of European life.

After the defeat of Austria by Prussia in 1866 the situation in Europe was already so tense that serious efforts were made to build up coalitions. War between France and Prussia was regarded on both sides as inevitable, and both sides engaged in preparations, diplomatic as well as military. The Emperor Napoleon III had miscalculated badly in matters of foreign affairs. While advocating the principle of nationalism, he had failed to foresee the results to which this principle might lead. He had, in 1859, supported Sardinia against Austria with the idea of securing for his ally the Austrian provinces of Lombardy and Venetia. In return he hoped to get for France the Sardinian possessions Nice and Savoy. He had, it is true, made peace before Venetia was conquered, and the Italians never quite forgave him for his defection. But Cavour, the most adroit of statesmen, had taken the war as a starting-point for the unification of all Italy. Before his death, in 1861, the new kingdom included all of the peninsula with the exception of Venetia and Rome. Before this great work had been accomplished, French opinion had been aroused. It was realized that a united Italy on the frontiers of France constituted more or less of a danger to France herself. Many Catholics were seriously alarmed at the prospect of an assault by Italian patriots upon the remaining territorial possessions of the Pope.

Napoleon again miscalculated when he decided upon his policy in the dispute between Prussia and Austria which followed the conquest of Schleswig and Holstein in 1864. The French Emperor felt so certain that Austria would win that he actually aided the Prussians in securing the alliance of Italy. Furthermore, he made provision, by an agreement with Austria in June 1866, for the cession of Venetia to Italy and for various concessions which Austria was to make to France. But he failed to bind the Prussians by specific promises, feeling confident that the chances of a Prussian victory were very small and that Prussia, even if she won, would be so exhausted that she would be unable to resist claims that might be made upon her by France.[1]

The phenomenal victory of the Prussians at Sadowa, coming only a few weeks after the declaration of war, revolutionized the situation. Napoleon's

---

[1] See especially Alfred Stern: *Geschichte Europas*, Volume IX (Stuttgart, 1923), chapter ix; Hermann Oncken: *Napoleon III and the Rhine* (New York, 1928), *passim*.

ministers begged him to mobilize and offer armed mediation, but the Emperor was unable to bring himself to this decision and allowed the crucial moment to pass. Bismarck was permitted to reorganize Germany according to his own ideas because he was careful to limit the territorial claims of Prussia to the area north of the river Main. At the same time he kept the French Emperor in a hopeful state of mind by dangling before him the prospect of eventual territorial gains in the Rhineland or in Belgium. Once peace was concluded, however, he changed his attitude and firmly refused to consider the French claims for compensation. Even Napoleon's scheme for acquiring Luxemburg from the King of Holland was frustrated by Bismarck's uncompromising opposition. From this time on, Napoleon gave up hope of a peaceful settlement. The French as a nation had long since recognized the dangers of the Emperor's policy. The unification of Germany, much more even than the union of the Italian states, threatened to break down the paramount position of France on the continent. The cry: "Revenge for Sadowa" was heard in Paris from the day when news of the Prussian victory reached the capital. Frenchmen generally were of the opinion that the union of northern and southern Germany could not be permitted, at least not without a corresponding strengthening of France through the acquisition of territory along the Rhine.

The French attitude is understandable enough. But so is the German viewpoint. As seen by Bismarck and his fellow-countrymen the problem of German unity was a purely German matter. The French claims were regarded as unjustifiable and there was a strong feeling against making concessions. The situation was one from which it was difficult to escape without war. After 1867 both sides prepared for the conflict. Napoleon did his utmost to bring about a coalition of France, Austria, and Italy. He hoped to bring in even defeated Denmark, and his generals envisaged a plan of campaign based upon the idea of a great concentric movement directed against Prussia, much like the movement organized against Frederick the Great a hundred years before. The coalition was not completed when war broke out in 1870, but this was not the fault of Napoleon or his ministers. One of the main difficulties was that Count Beust, the Austrian chancellor, insisted that the conflict must be made to start from a Near Eastern quarrel. The Austrians felt that they could not afford, in the face of German public opinion, to take sides with the French against the Prussians, and they feared that the Hungarians, with their eyes fixed on the Russian menace, would never consent to such a policy. As for the Italians, they demanded from the beginning of the negotiations that the possession of Rome should be promised them. Regarding Rome as the only possible capital and looking upon the imperial city as the very keystone of the new Italy, they refused to compromise on this question. The Emperor, on the other hand, did not dare ignore clerical interests to the extent of abandoning what was left of the papal territories. But, despite these obstacles to a definite agreement, it was felt in Paris in 1870 that Austria and Italy could be counted upon if a crisis arose. It can hardly be doubted that, if the French had been successful in the first engagements, both Austria and Italy would really have hastened to the assistance of the victor.[1]

Bismarck did not know the details of the negotiations which went on between France, Austria, and Italy, but he could not help noticing the exchange of visits between Napoleon and Francis Joseph, or the constant coming and going of military men between Paris and Vienna and Florence. Moltke and Roon were busily preparing the Prussian army for all eventualities. Bismarck's work was the diplomatic preparation for a possible conflict. He did his best to cultivate the goodwill of Russia and thus prevent the formation of a combination between France, Austria, and Russia like the so-called Kaunitz coalition of the Seven Years' War. He even considered the possibility of an agreement between Prussia, Austria, and Russia, and on occasion thought of the inclusion of England in a great league to preserve peace.[2] But the Austrians were far too hostile and the English, led by Gladstone and a liberal ministry, were far too much wrapped up in domestic problems to have much interest in foreign affairs. Bismarck was obliged to rely upon Russian friendship, in return for which he was prepared to support the Russian aspirations in the Near East. Prussian relations with Russia remained cordial throughout this critical period. This is a point of utmost importance in the international relations of these years.

In his reminiscences Bismarck takes much credit (if one can call it that) for precipitating the war with France in 1870. He certainly encouraged the candidacy of the Hohenzollern for the throne of Spain and did little enough during the crisis of July 1870 to prevent the outbreak of hostilities. But one should bear in mind that the French government was hardly less culpable. It was no secret in Europe that the statesmen in Paris meant to get revenge for Sadowa as soon as they felt ready. The projected coalition against Prussia could hardly be called a defensive arrangement. Bismarck continually stressed the military importance of having a Hohenzollern on the Spanish throne. In other words, he regarded the Hohenzollern candidacy as a necessary counterblast to the French designs. With a friendly ruler beyond the Pyrenees, Prussia could count on the French having to leave many thousand men on the Spanish frontier in case of war on the Rhine. Viewed from this angle, Bismarck's policy was more a defensive policy than was that of the French.

Even in the crisis of July 1870 the German statesman left the initiative to the French, and the French put themselves in the wrong. Gramont, the French

---

[1] A good deal has been written on the projected Franco-Austro-Italian alliance. In addition to Stern and Oncken see Emile Bourgeois and E. Clermont: *Rome et Napoléon III* (Paris, 1907), and the bibliography of book iii; Albert Pingaud: "*Un Projet d'alliance franco-austro-italienne en 1869*" (*Revue de France*, V, pp. 416–32, October 1, 1928); Gravina: "*Una Triplice Alleanza che non fu conclusa*" (*Gerarchia*, January 1928).

[2] Walter Platzhoff: "*Die Anfänge des Dreikaiserbundes, 1867–1871*" (*Preussische Jahrbücher*, June 1922).

foreign minister, lived in the hope of re-establishing the French position on the continent. He was determined not to accept another "humiliation." When news of the Hohenzollern candidacy reached Paris, he immediately took a firm stand. His declaration in the Chamber of Deputies on July 6 practically closed the door to compromise. Bismarck himself described this action as an incredible blunder. Nevertheless, fortune was with the French. The withdrawal of the Hohenzollern candidacy was a great victory for French diplomacy, and one with which the French statesmen might well have contented themselves. But they insisted on more and demanded that King William of Prussia should write Napoleon an apology as well as promise that the candidacy would never be renewed in the future. Even the most ardent defenders of the French position find it hard to say much in justification of these unreasonable demands. There was no hope whatever that the Prussians would agree to them. On the contrary these demands gave Bismarck exactly the opportunity he wanted to put the French in the wrong and practically force them into war.

The storm broke in 1870 with amazing and alarming rapidity. There was hardly an opportunity for the neutral powers to offer mediation or to take other steps to settle the conflict. News of the acceptance of the Spanish throne by the Hohenzollern reached Paris on July 3. By July 15 war was certain, though it was not actually declared until July 19. Military events moved with similar celerity. By the first days of August the German armies were already on the march. On August 6 the first great engagements were fought. With the defeat of the French in the battles round Metz in the middle of August, and the capitulation and surrender of Napoleon at Sedan on September 2, the decision in the war had, to all intents and purposes, been reached. The French reorganized their forces and put up a valiant fight for several more months, but the result was a foregone conclusion. No war up to that time had shown so clearly the profound changes that had taken place in international relations. The French had thought they were prepared, even to the last button on the last gaiter. They

Whatever opinion historians may now hold on the question of responsibility for the war, there was little difference of opinion on this point among contemporary neutrals. English statesmen, for example, had been on cordial terms with the French for some time, but the English public had come to distrust Napoleon and his advisers. When the war broke out, Englishmen were almost unanimous in believing that the conflict had been wantonly precipitated by the French Emperor, and that the fundamental cause for the war was the French desire to re-establish French hegemony on the continent by the defeat of Prussia and the acquisition of German territory.[1]

---

[1] The best account of the English attitude is that of Kurt Rheindorf: *England und der deutsch-französische Krieg* (Bonn, 1923); but see also Dora N. Raymond: *British Policy and Opinion during the Franco-Prussian War* (New York, 1921); A. A. W. Ramsay: *Idealism and Foreign Policy* (London, 1925), chapter v; Otto Meisner: "*England, Frankreich und die deutsche Einigung*" (*Preussische Jahrbücher*, January 1928).

had confidently expected to march to Berlin. Yet their overwhelming defeat was a matter of hardly more than four weeks.

The driving power of the German armies and the decisiveness of the German victory set the world agog and gave rise to the greatest uneasiness in the governing circles of neutral countries. It was quite clear that the unification of Germany would soon be an accomplished fact, for the rulers of the South German states were no longer in a position to resist either the pressure exercised by Bismarck or the demands of public opinion. The union of the German states alone, it was clear, would inevitably lead to a serious dislocation of the balance of power. With the annexation of French territory this new state would be even further strengthened. That such annexations would be demanded by the Germans was no secret. Even before the declaration of war an important German newspaper had written (July 13) that in the event of victory it would seem impossible to every German that Strassburg should be left in French hands. After the first successes in the field the matter was taken up by the whole German press. Insistence on the cession of Alsace and Lorraine by France was nearly universal, in South Germany as well as in the north.

Bismarck himself was determined to secure the two provinces, though he was not much swayed by the sentimental arguments advanced on some sides. Questions of language and race did not appear to him decisive. He knew perfectly well that the population of these territories desired to remain French. But he, like many less interested observers, even neutrals, recognized that Alsace and Lorraine had served the French as a base for attack upon Germany, and that, strategically speaking, the two provinces were the gateway to the South German districts beyond the Rhine. At the beginning of the war the population of the Palatinate and Baden had confidently expected a French invasion, and it appears that the Prussian generals themselves were surprised that the French did not appear in the Rhineland. The panic of those days made a deep impression, and when the time to make peace came, Bismarck accepted the arguments of the soldiers. He seems to have had some doubt as to the advisability of taking Lorraine and was by no means blind to the fact that the cession of these territories would cause endless friction between France and Germany. But he regarded future war between the two countries as inevitable under all circumstances, and therefore thought it the part of wisdom to take the territory necessary for the protection of Germany.[1]

The provisional government of France, the so-called Government of National Defence, which had assumed control after the disaster at Sedan and the surrender of Napoleon, refused to look the facts in the face. During the very first days of its existence the foreign minister, Jules Favre, declared openly that France

---

[1] Johannes Haller: *Bismarcks Friedensschlüsse* (Munich, 1917); Karl Jacob: *Bismarck und die Erwerbung Elsass-Lothringens* (Strassburg, 1905); see also Bismarck's remarkably frank explanation to the French representative in August 1871 (*Documents diplomatiques français, 1871–1914,* First Series, Volume I, No. 42), and to Saint-Vallier in 1879 (ibid., II, No. 476).

would not cede an inch of her territory or a stone of her fortresses, thus more or less committing the provisional government to a war *à l'outrance*. The siege of Paris and the " People's War " in the provinces followed, but the French could hardly hope to recover militarily after the initial disasters. Their acceptance of the German terms was merely a matter of time, for even the prospects of foreign intervention in their favour were very slim. Both Francis Joseph and Victor Emmanuel would have been glad to intervene, but they no longer dared. Instead of coming to the assistance of the French the Italians consoled themselves with the occupation of Rome (September 20, 1870), thus creating a serious danger spot in Europe by putting an end to the temporal power of the Papacy. The Austrians were unable to make similar acquisitions because the Russians stood threateningly on the frontier. The defeat of France at Sedan was as much a blow at the Austrian position as the campaign of Sadowa had been a weakening of the French position. Under the circumstances the hopes of the French centred upon Russia and England.

The Russian attitude had been very favourable to the Prussians from the beginning, and it continued so until the end. The Tsar, Alexander II, revered his uncle, the King of Prussia, and insisted on standing by him, although some of his ministers called his attention to the danger of a strong Germany, and the undesirability of a complete French defeat.[1] Fortunately for Bismarck, the opportunity presented itself for bolstering up the " tacit alliance " with Russia by supporting the Tsar in his attempt to abrogate the Black Sea clauses of the Treaty of Paris (1856), which forbade Russia's maintaining a fleet or constructing fortifications in the Black Sea. The German statesman was not pleased when the Russian government announced its determination not to be bound any longer by these stipulations, but his objection was to the time chosen for this step rather than to the decision itself. Fearing greatly that war between Russia and England might result from this matter, and foreseeing the possibility of a general European war, he suggested a conference. This met eventually at London, where the representatives of the powers recognized the abolition of the Black Sea clauses, but reaffirmed the principle that an international treaty cannot be arbitrarily changed by any one of the signatory powers without the consent of the others.[2]

The power that was primarily affected by the Russian action was England, for England was directly interested in the neutralization of the Black Sea as well as in the preservation of the integrity of the Ottoman Empire. A Russian fleet in the Black Sea could at any time threaten the Turks or serve as a means for the extension of Russian influence in the Near East, a region of great

---

[1] Comte Fleury: *La France et la Russie en 1870* (Paris, 1902).

[2] *Die Grosse Politik der europäischen Kabinette, 1871–1914*, edited by Johannes Lepsius, Albrecht Mendelssohn Bartholdy, and Friedrich Thimme (Berlin, 1922–7), Volume II, chapter ix; Kurt Rheindorf: *Die Schwarze-Meer Frage, 1856–1871* (Berlin, 1925), chapter iv; Heinrich Mertz: *Die Schwarze-Meer Konferenz von 1871* (Stuttgart, 1927).

strategic importance to the English in view of their connexions with India. But the denunciation of the Black Sea clauses of the Treaty of Paris, and the eventual acceptance of this action by England, merely served to set the comparative helplessness of the latter into high relief. The country was governed at the time by a liberal ministry under the leadership of Gladstone. Attention was focused on domestic problems of great importance, such as the Irish question and matters of financial reform. Gladstone, averse by temperament to a militaristic policy or to interference in the affairs of the continent, had failed to take account of the epoch-making changes that had been taking place in Europe.

When Lord Granville took over the foreign office, on July 6, 1870, he was told by the under-secretary, Mr. Hammond, that never during the latter's tenure of office had there been so great a lull in international affairs.[1] Yet Europe stood on the threshold of a great crisis which had been coming on for years. The incident is mentioned because it throws more light upon the neglect of foreign affairs by the Gladstone ministry than could a volume of diplomatic documents. During the crucial days of 1870 the government refused steadfastly to intervene unless asked to do so by the parties to the dispute. Its sympathies were, on the whole, with Prussia, which was generally looked upon as the victim of French hostility and ambition. The conviction of the English that Napoleon was a dangerous intriguer and that Prussia was justified in meeting the French challenge was only strengthened by the publication of the so-called Benedetti Treaty, a draft agreement between France and Prussia dating from the year 1867. In this document the French had revealed their desires for Belgian territory. This was a point of great sensitivity to the English.

The English attitude, however, soon began to change. As the war progressed, the usual friction developed from the sale of arms and munitions by neutrals. Both the French and the German newspapers were full of recriminations against the English. On both sides it was felt that they were playing a dubious and not very creditable role. The Germans believed that the English could have prevented the outbreak of war if they had called upon Napoleon to halt or had threatened to intervene against him. The French, on the other hand, held that the *entente cordiale* and brothership in arms of the two countries during the Crimean War should have counted for something in determining the English attitude. Still the government at London refused to abandon the policy of non-intervention and contented itself with the formation of a league of neutrals to safeguard the interests of the powers not directly involved in the conflict.

Many Englishmen felt this policy to be unworthy of a great power and were bitter in their denunciations of Gladstone's pusillanimity. Sir Robert Morier, for example, who was at that time English minister to one of the South German courts, declared: " We sit by like a bloated Quaker, too holy to fight, but rubbing our hands at the roaring trade we are driving in cartridges and ammuni-

---

[1] Lord Edmond Fitzmaurice: *The Life of Granville George Leveson Gower, Second Earl Granville* (London, 1905), Volume II, p. 32.

tion." To Earl Russell he wrote in November 1870: " I defy any Englishman of moderate intelligence and ordinary power of judgment, who has been behind the international *coulisses* during the last six months, however boisterously hopeful his natural temperament may be, to do aught but tear his beard, strew ashes on his head and gnash his teeth. . . . We were content to do chorus off stage and to range ourselves amongst the wheezing, broken-kneed old greybeards, whose utmost feat consists in giving metrical expression to some miserable platitudes respecting the blessings of peace." [1]

These may be exaggerated statements of a forward view-point, but it is none the less true that the English attitude became more positive as the conflict progressed. With the fall of the Bonapartes after the surrender at Sedan the chief objection to the French régime was removed. At the same time the continued victories of the Germans began to create serious apprehension. It was rumoured that Bismarck was planning the restoration of the Napoleonic dynasty, and that he meant to strike a bargain with the French, by which the latter should give up Alsace and Lorraine and receive Belgium instead. The known determination of the Germans to annex the two provinces in itself called forth very adverse criticism on the other side of the Channel. Morier at first declared that " it would be unfair to ignore the fact that the demand for the Vosges frontiers is based on a perfectly justifiable sense of insecurity and that it is put forward by a people who have very recently been impressed with a sense of this insecurity." But Lord Salisbury pointed out that " the spread of education and the increased freedom of discussion have almost destroyed the healing power of time," and that " a ceded territory would be a constant memorial of humiliation." Gladstone shared this feeling. Writing to Granville in December 1870, he said: " While I more and more feel the deep culpability of France, I have an apprehension that this violent laceration and transfer is to lead us from bad to worse, and to be the beginning of a new series of European complications." A month later Morier confided to a friend: " My full conviction is that ninety-nine Englishmen out of one hundred would infinitely prefer another year or two of war with all its horrors, on condition of the Germans at last getting the worst of it, though both France and Germany were destroyed by it, to a peace concluded now which gave Bismarck what he desired." [2]

When parliament met in February 1871, the government was overwhelmed with criticism. Benjamin Disraeli, in a noteworthy speech delivered on February 9, made the following telling remarks: " This war represents the German Revolution, a greater political event than the French Revolution of last century. . . . Not a single principle in the management of our foreign affairs, accepted

---

[1] Mrs. Rosslyn Wemyss: *Memoirs and Letters of the Right Hon. Sir Robert Morier* (London, 1911), Volume II, pp. 165, 208–10.

[2] Wemyss: *Memoirs of Sir Robert Morier*, II, pp. 240–4; Lord Salisbury: " The Terms of Peace " (*Quarterly Review*, October 1870); John Morley: *The Life of William Ewart Gladstone* (New York, 1903), Volume II, p. 348.

by all statesmen for guidance up to six months ago, any longer exists. There is not a diplomatic tradition which has not been swept away. You have a new world, new influences at work, new and unknown objects and dangers with which to cope, at present involved in that obscurity incident to novelty in such affairs. We used to have discussions about the balance of power. Lord Palmerston, eminently a practical man, trimmed the Ship of State and shaped its policy with a view to preserve the equilibrium in Europe. . . . But what has really come to pass? The balance of power has been entirely destroyed, and the country which suffers most, and feels the effects of this great change most, is England."

A resolution was then brought in by Mr. Auberon Herbert to the effect that "this House is of the opinion that it is the duty of Her Majesty's Government to act in concert with other neutral powers to obtain moderate terms of peace, and to withhold all acquiescence in terms which might impair the independence of France or threaten the future tranquillity of Europe." In the course of the debate Sir Robert Peel spoke bitterly of what he described as the English policy of "selfish isolation" and the "policy of obliteration." "I must say that I look on the unification of Germany as a great peril to Europe. . . . It cannot be for the good of Europe that there should be a great military despotism in Germany, built up on the ruin and destruction of France." Another member expressed fear that Prussia and Russia had made an agreement to partition Europe at a favourable moment. "Now that Germany is united," he continued, "she would require a large seaboard, and does not this threaten danger to Holland and the Colony of Heligoland?"[1]

The resolution was voted down, but the government itself had long since come to view the situation with uneasiness, especially since the co-operation between Prussia and Russia had become so manifest in the matter of the abrogation of the Black Sea clauses. Every effort was made to arrange for the presence of a French representative at the London Conference. Bismarck refused to agree to this, fearing rightly that an attempt would then be made to introduce the question of peace terms into the discussion and to submit this problem to the judgment of an international conference. On one occasion the English seem to have considered the possibility of making an agreement with Russia by which the two powers should offer joint mediation to Germany and France.[2] However this may have been, Bismarck was certainly fortunate in avoiding intervention. Perhaps it was because he realized this that he showed himself much more ready to compromise than the French negotiators had expected. The original demand for an indemnity of six billion francs was reduced to a demand for five billion. The fortress of Belfort was left in the hands of the French, and in the final discussions a generous area round the fortress was conceded in return for slight extensions of the territory to be ceded to Germany in

---

[1] Hansard: *Parliamentary Debates*, Third Series, Volume CCIV, pp. 81–2, 396–7, 430.
[2] Rheindorf: *England und der deutsch-französische Krieg*, p. 143.

Lorraine. The Germans had come to appreciate the great value of the iron deposits in that region.

To us it seems almost incredible that a conflict of such magnitude as the Franco-German War should have remained localized. After all, the war completely destroyed the balance of power in Europe. " Europe has lost a mistress and gained a master," was the expression used by one of the diplomats. Where European politics had for centuries been based upon the principle of a weak German centre and strong French, Austrian, and Russian extremities, the tables had now been turned. France, the most important wing power, was destroyed militarily, mutilated territorially, and on the verge of anarchy so far as domestic affairs were concerned. She had failed to secure the assistance of other powers and was doomed to suffer a long period of eclipse. Whatever the sympathies of other nations, defeated France could not expect them to fight her battles, the more so when they had to reckon with the strongest military power Europe had ever known.

So for years France was left to find her own salvation. The provinces were evidently pacifically inclined, and the national assembly, elected in the spring of 1871, accepted the peace terms, though under protest. The chief of the executive power, Thiers, and the rest of the government were certainly convinced of the need of law and order for the reconstruction of the country, but the intellectual classes and the population of Paris, which had suffered acutely during the long siege, were depressed with a feeling of humiliation and defeat. Many found their sole consolation in the thought of revenge. Republican leaders, like Gambetta, fanned the flames. " France is at the mercy of Germany. We are in a state of *latent* war; neither peace, nor liberty, nor progress is possible in Europe," wrote Gambetta at the very beginning of the period, while Edgar Quinet remarked that " the surrender of Alsace-Lorraine means an endless war behind the mask of peace." [1]

Though Thiers was absolutely opposed to any policy that savoured of provocation, he was convinced that France must prepare militarily in order to be ready if the Germans should launch another attack before France could recover from her disasters. At his suggestion the various parties in the national assembly entered upon a gentlemen's agreement (the Pact of Bordeaux) to shelve discussion of the future form of government until the most important work of reconstruction had been carried through. After the suppression of the great Paris Commune in the spring of 1871 the government devoted itself to the reorganization of the army and the rebuilding of the fortresses. Every effort was made to carry out the peace terms. The indemnity was paid off as quickly as the Germans would accept it. Thiers and his associates were fairly consumed with the very natural desire to see the national territory completely freed of foreign troops. Of course the negotiations which went on constantly in regard

---

[1] Paul Deschanel: *Gambetta* (New York, 1920), pp. 140, 153; Henri Galli: *Gambetta et l'Alsace-Lorraine* (Paris, 1911).

to the carrying out of the peace terms gave rise to much friction. On the whole, however, the payments were made and the evacuation carried through as smoothly as could be expected. Both Bismarck and Thiers took a statesmanlike view of the problems that arose, and they deserve to share the credit for the peaceful solution of innumerable difficulties.[1]

The thought of another war with France haunted Bismarck from the very day when he concluded peace. He was anxious to avoid another conflict. Germany, he said, was a saturated nation, and the work of the future would be to consolidate the gains made during three wars. Unity must be more than a merely political arrangement. His was a statesmanlike attitude and one from which he did not depart during the last twenty years of his tenure of office. But he was convinced that the French would wage a war of revenge sooner or later, and he knew from experience that the other powers would not witness quietly another defeat of France or her further dismemberment. The problem of Franco-German relations was therefore always prominent in his mind. He supported Thiers and the moderate republican element in France consistently and loyally, believing them less likely to embark upon a dangerous or adventurous policy. The royalists he feared, because he thought it would be much easier for them to find allies in monarchical Europe, once they had successfully re-established the monarchy in France, than for the republicans, no matter how conservative they might be.[2]

In the meanwhile he turned his attention to the work of preparing for an eventual conflict. The German armies were kept in a high state of efficiency; that goes without saying. Germany's central position, exposed to attack from all sides, required constant vigilance and untiring devotion to problems of defence. As a result of the German victory over France the other countries on the continent speedily began the reorganization of their forces along the lines marked out by the Prussian system. French, Austrians, Russians, all introduced the principle of universal liability and carried it through with greater consistency than ever before.

With the actual military preparations Bismarck had little to do. His primary concern was with the diplomatic orientation of the new empire, and in this field he was recognized even at the time to be without a peer. With the imminent danger of another war constantly before him, and with a full realization of the changes wrought in international relations by the acceleration of mobilization and general military operations, the German chancellor had long since surveyed the European scene and considered the possibility of a future alignment of powers that would be favourable to Germany. The nations were dis-

---

[1] *Occupation et libération du territoire, 1871–1873* (Paris, 1900); *Documents diplomatiques français*, I, *passim;* Hans Herzfeld: *Deutschland und das geschlagene Frankreich, 1871–1873* (Berlin, 1924); Karl Linnebach: *Deutschland als Sieger im besetzten Frankreich, 1871–1873* (Stuttgart, 1924); Hans Goldschmidt: *Bismarck und die Friedensunterhändler 1871* (Berlin, 1929).

[2] De Roux: *La République de Bismarck* (Paris, 1915); George Rosen: *Die Stellungnahme der Politik Bismarcks zur Frage der Staatsform in Frankreich von 1871–1890* (Detmold, 1924).

trustful and unfriendly. They made no secret of their sympathy for France, and though they were not likely to make an alliance with her against Germany, they might well give her moral and perhaps material support if serious trouble arose. Above all, it was fairly clear that if a conflict broke out between any two of the major powers, the French would make use of the opportunity and take sides against Germany when the empire became involved in the dispute. The situation was so obvious that Thiers himself analysed in this way the difficulties with which Bismark was confronted.[1]

In November 1870 the English government sent Mr. Odo Russell to German headquarters in France to discuss with Bismarck the course of action to be taken in response to Russia's repudiation of the Black Sea clauses. On that occasion the German statesman told Russell that his ideal for Germany was an alliance with England and Austria rather than with Russia.[2] It is difficult to say whether this was merely a tactical move on his part or whether it was a sincere expression of conviction. No doubt there was something attractive for Bismarck in the idea of an alliance between the world's greatest military power and the world's leading naval power. Together these two nations would have been irresistible. If Austria were brought into alliance with them, Russia could be completely checkmated. She would be unable to advance in the Near East with Austria opposing her by land and England against her by sea. She would be unable to make progress even in Asia so long as Germany and Austria threatened her in the rear, on the frontiers of Poland. An alliance with France would be of little use to her, because the combined German and Austrian armies would easily be able to hold their own or even defeat their two adversaries. As a matter of fact, it was doubtful whether France, hot though her thirst for revenge might be, would agree to expose herself to defeat by Germany and to disaster at the hands of England. Such a policy would be like courting ruin, for the price of failure would take the shape of further cessions of territory in the northern departments and the sacrifice of what colonial possessions France still had.

But even if we assume that Bismarck intended his remarks to Odo Russell to be taken seriously, it must be admitted that the projected combination of Germany, England, and Austria was, in 1870, little more than a pious wish. English statesmen grew up in the tradition of England's position as a *world* power. They were, almost all of them, firm believers in the theory that England should avoid continental entanglements, except to prevent the complete domination of the continent by any one power. Isolation was still regarded as " splendid," while intervention in the affairs of others ran counter to the prevalent ideas of laissez-faire and abstention from matters which were not of direct interest to the nation. Mr. Gladstone, even more than most of his contemporaries, did homage to these principles. He had no real interest in problems of

---

[1] *Documents diplomatiques français*, I, No. 150.
[2] Fitzmaurice: *Life of Granville*, II, p. 74.

international relations, regarded England's position as blessed in her isolation, and preferred to devote himself to the pressing problems of domestic affairs. He and his friends were pacifically inclined and were anxious to reduce expenditure for armaments, thus pursuing a policy not at all in keeping with that of the continental states. England came to be looked upon as a power of secondary importance in international affairs, especially after her acceptance of a very unfavourable award in the arbitration of the *Alabama* claims. To the military states of Europe this submissiveness was looked upon_ as the most eloquent proof that England was no longer a factor to be seriously reckoned with. Bismarck is said to have declared that "he had lost five years of his political life by the foolish belief that England was still a great power."[1]

While England held aloof and showed little interest, the friendship of the Russian Tsar was still the most reliable factor in the European situation as Bismarck saw it. Germany's task from the beginning was to maintain the proper balance between Russia and England and to play off these two wing powers against each other. The other states might serve as makeweights, but so long as England and Russia were bitter rivals or enemies, it was essential that Germany should be on terms of intimacy with one or the other. The traditional connexion with Russia was, therefore, natural and logical. Bismarck was scrupulous to maintain it intact.

But the German chancellor was never content to rely upon Russia alone, for the Russian situation itself was uncertain. Ever since the Polish Revolution of 1863 Russian national feeling had been rapidly developing. Dislike of the Germans and of the new German Empire was becoming more and more pronounced. Furthermore, the position of the Russian autocracy had been badly shaken by the revolutionary movement, and there was no knowing how long the Tsar would be able to maintain his power. For these reasons Bismarck laid great stress on the desirability of good relations with Austria-Hungary. After the war of 1866 he had offered Austria very generous peace terms. The Habsburgs lost no territory and paid no indemnity, though they were obliged to sacrifice their position in Germany and thereby lose much of their prestige. In 1867 the empire had been reorganized on a dual basis, the two parts, Austria and Hungary, becoming practically independent of each other, though still connected in the person of the ruler. The international situation of the Habsburgs was actually strengthened rather than weakened by this change, for the compromise of 1867 provided for the maintenance of a common army and a common foreign policy, while at the same time it put an end to the dangerous antagonism and dissension between the German and Magyar elements within the empire.

Ever since 1867 Bismarck had made periodic attempts to win Austria over to the German side, partly because he feared that Austria would support France

---

[1] Wemyss: *Memoirs of Sir Robert Morier*, II, p. 330.

in the war which he saw coming, partly because he disliked the idea of being dependent entirely upon the goodwill of Russia. And, after all, it must be remembered that the expulsion of Austria from Germany in 1866 was regarded by many Germans as the very negation of the national ideal. Bismarck himself had the feeling that the German block, as it existed before 1866 under the German Confederation, should in some way be resurrected, if only to serve as a counterweight to the Slavic colossus in the east. The union of the new German Empire with the reorganized Austro-Hungarian monarchy would not only restore the old solidarity in defence, but establish the German influence in Europe upon a much stronger basis. Yet the Austrian Emperor, Francis Joseph, had chosen as his chancellor Count Beust, a Saxon statesman who was outspoken in his hostility to Bismarck and to the idea of German unity under Prussian leadership. For three years the idea of revenge for Sadowa was as prevalent at Vienna as at Paris. The negotiations with Napoleon III were conducted with enthusiasm.

It was not until after the German victory at Sedan that the Austrian hope of revenge disappeared and the road to an understanding between the new Germany and the Habsburg monarchy was opened. With France defeated, the Austrians were exposed to attack by victorious Germany. It was widely believed that Bismarck's next step would be the conquest of the German provinces of Austria. The Magyars in Hungary demanded close relations with the new Germany because they hated and feared the Russians. The Germans in the Austrian part of the monarchy celebrated the German victories over France with great exuberance and were so estranged from the Emperor by his policy of favouring the Slav elements in Bohemia against the Germans that there was some question whether the dominions of the Habsburgs could be kept together much longer. Even Count Beust recognized the dangers of Austria's position, exposed, as she was, to Germany on one side, to Russia on another, and to Italy on a third. Before the war between France and Prussia was over, Beust had completely changed colour and spoke sympathetically of the idea of German-Austrian friendship.

In June 1871, just after the conclusion of peace between France and Germany, the Austrian government sent to Berlin General von Gablentz, who was to pave the way for more cordial relations. Bismarck urged upon him the desirability of an understanding, especially in view of the socialist menace which loomed so large in the days of the Paris Commune. He insisted, however, that there should be no hostility to Russia in any agreement that might be come to. He was willing to promise that Germany had no designs upon Austrian territory, and declared that the German wish for good relations was sincere.

It was the first difficult step, but others followed in rapid succession. In August and September 1871 the two Emperors and their foreign ministers met at Ischl, Gastein, and Salzburg. The Austrian course had been already decided on. Beust, who was evidently not the man to inspire confidence at Berlin, was dismissed and Count Hohenwart, representative of the pro-Slav policy in Austria, was also induced to resign. Count Julius Andrássy became minister of foreign affairs, and took part in the discussions at Salzburg even before Beust's fall.

Andrássy was a Magyar to the very marrow of the bone. He had taken part in the rising of 1848 and had been condemned to death after he had already fled the country. Later on he had been pardoned by the Emperor and had taken a prominent part in the negotiations which led to the compromise of 1867. He became Hungarian prime minister and succeeded in winning the complete confidence of Francis Joseph. Like most Magyars he strongly favoured a close connexion with Germany, in view of the danger from Russia. The Magyars felt themselves stranded in the great Slavic sea of eastern Europe and saw their only hope in the alliance with Germany. Andrássy was clearly the man to carry through the new Austrian policy.[1]

Andrássy regarded the close relations between Germany and Russia with suspicion and apparently feared an eventual coalition between these two powers for the spoliation of the Habsburg dominions. His object, therefore, was to draw the Germans away from the Russians and attach them to the Austrian side. At the meeting with Bismarck at Gastein he had made use of the most persuasive arguments to enlist the support of the Germans against the Russian designs, but without success. The German chancellor was above all things anxious not to estrange Russia, and he lost no time in assuring his Russian colleague, Prince Gorchakov, that nothing had passed at Gastein at which the Russians could take umbrage.[2] But he was eager to establish close relations with Austria and welcomed the decision of the Emperor Francis Joseph to pay a visit to Berlin in September 1872. If Germany could depend upon Austrian friendship, her position in all subsequent dealings with Russia would be so much strengthened. " Only when mounted were we as tall as the Russian giant. Austria was intended to be our mount," says one of the German diplomats. By coming to Berlin the Emperor Francis Joseph would recognize the changes wrought by the late war: " The vanquished was to greet the German Emperor in his imperial capital; the middle European League, which had been destroyed in 1866, was to demonstrate anew to East and West, in a pacific but emphatic manner, its existence as an empire of seventy million." The newspapers of Vienna were full of articles on this theme and were already gloating over the set-back which was in store for Russia.[3]

[1] W. Platzhoff: " Die Anfänge des Dreikaiserbundes, 1867–1871 " (Preussische Jahrbücher, June 1922); Eduard Wertheimer: Graf Julius Andrássy (Stuttgart, 1913), Volume II, chapters i and ii; Documents diplomatiques français, I, Nos. 40, 74.

[2] Documents diplomatiques français, I, No. 76; Baron A. F. Meyendorff: "Conversations of Gorchakov, Andrássy and Bismarck in 1872 " (Slavonic Review, VII, pp. 400–8, December 1929).

[3] General von Schweinitz: Briefwechsel (Berlin, 1928), pp. 83–4; id., Denkwürdigkeiten (Berlin, 1927), Volume I, pp. 298–9; Winifred Taffs: " Conversations between Lord Odo Russell and Andrássy, Bismarck and Gorchakov in September 1872 " (Slavonic Review, VIII, pp. 701–7, March 1930); Documents diplomatiques français, I, No. 148.

But this careful plan was entirely frustrated. The Tsar, disturbed by the growing intimacy between Germany and Austria and apprehensive of further agreements that might be made during Francis Joseph's visit to Berlin, all but invited himself to the imperial reunion. He could not be refused, and so, in September 1872, the three Emperors met in the German capital, accompanied by their foreign ministers and numerous diplomats. The monarchs and their advisers were together for more than a week, but no political agreement resulted from their conferences. Everything points to the fact that all the statesmen wished to avoid definite commitments. The international situation had not become sufficiently settled. Bismarck, for example, took care never to confer with Andrássy and Gorchakov at the same time. He made no effort to elicit from the visitors any promises in regard to their attitude in the event of future complications between Germany and France, though the French were afraid that some such suggestions would be made. Not even the subject of an alliance with Austria was broached. Apparently it was felt that the effort to establish such a connexion would be premature. In Austrian military circles there was still a strong feeling against any agreement with Germany, and a pronounced sentiment for an alliance with Russia.[1] Bismarck was, therefore, content with the meeting as a demonstration of reconciliation and friendship, as an exhibition of monarchical solidarity in the face of subversive and revolutionary movements. By bringing Alexander and Francis Joseph together he strengthened Germany's position and silently warned France by showing her how isolated she was.

But the imperial heavens were not entirely unclouded. Prince Gorchakov, the Russian chancellor, was certainly jealous of Bismarck's power and uneasy about the possibility of a German-Austrian combination. In order to counteract this development he did his utmost to smooth over the differences between Russia and Austria, which centred in the Near East. Andrássy made a very favourable impression upon him. The two men discussed all matters likely to cause friction between their two countries. Gorchakov being disturbed by the supposed intrigues of the Austrians in Bosnia and Herzegovina, Andrássy assured him that the Habsburg policy was of necessity a defensive one. Austria wished nothing more than to be on good terms with Serbia, but " the extension of her frontiers which was dreamt of by the adherents of the so-called ' Greater Servia ' idea, and which would embrace Bosnia and Herzegovina as well as other districts, could not be reconciled with the standpoint of Austria-Hungary, a portion of whose subjects belong to the same race and might therefore become imbued with similar aspirations." Austria desired the preservation of Turkey as she was, and the rumours of her ambitions in Bosnia and Herzegovina were without a shadow of foundation. To which Gorchakov replied by stating

---

[1] Edmund von Glaise-Horstenau: *Franz Josephs Weggefährte: Das Leben des Generalstabschefs Grafen Beck* (Vienna, 1930), p. 176. On the meeting generally, see *Die Grosse Politik*, I, chapter v, and Wertheimer: *Andrássy*, II, chapter iii; *Documents diplomatiques français*, I, Nos. 144–9.

emphatically that Russia had no connexion with the agitation in Serbia, and that Russia too was satisfied with the *status quo* in the Near East. The two men then agreed that their governments should observe a policy of non-intervention in the Balkans and should work for the maintenance of the existing situation.[1]

This unwritten agreement between the Russians and the Austrians, though it was probably meant by Gorchakov to weaken the Austrian desire for an entente with Germany, was not of a nature to cause Bismarck much uneasiness. If the two traditional rivals could be brought together, so much the better. The danger of European war would be reduced by just so much. But Gorchakov was not content with his understanding with Andrássy. For years he had been convinced of the danger for Russia inherent in the defeat of France. He wanted to keep open the connexion with France, so that Russia, if she found herself in trouble, might reckon on a friend in western Europe. During his stay in Berlin he took great pains to assure the French ambassador that there had been no formal agreement. " There has been an exchange of views and of ideas, but no protocol; no positive agreement which could limit our freedom of action; in a word, nothing for the diplomatic archives, but the moral effect is immeasurable." [2] At the same time Gorchakov claimed to have spoken to Bismarck in favour of a conciliatory policy towards France. He made no secret of his view that Russia and Austria recognized the need for a strong France, but France must be patient and wise.[3]

It is not at all unlikely that Gorchakov touched upon Franco-German relations in his talks with Bismarck. At any rate the German chancellor knew of his Russian colleague's predilections for France, and it was probably for that reason that he approached the English ambassador and explained the nature of the meeting. " We have witnessed a novel sight today," he said. " It is the first time in history that the three Emperors have sat down to dinner together, in the interests of peace. I wanted these three Emperors to form a loving group, like Canova's three graces. I wanted them to stand in a silent group and allow themselves to be admired, but I was determined not to allow them to talk, and that I have achieved, difficult as it was, because they all three think themselves greater statesmen than they are." Andrássy he had found to be charming and intelligent, " but as for that old sot of a Gorchakov, he gets on my nerves with his white cravat and his pretensions. He brought with him some very white paper and some very black ink, together with the necessary scribes. He wanted to write, but I was deaf to these suggestions." [4]

---

[1] Meyendorff, loc. cit.; *Documents diplomatiques français*, I, No. 156.

[2] S. Goriainov: *Le Bosphore et les Dardanelles* (Paris, 1910), pp. 306–8; *Documents diplomatiques français*, I, No. 156.

[3] *Documents diplomatiques français*, I, Nos. 152, 153, 156; Taffs, loc. cit.

[4] N. Japikse: *Europa und Bismarcks Friedenspolitik* (Berlin, 1927), pp. 29–31, quoting from the British foreign office archives; Taffs, loc. cit.; Henry Salomon, in Henri Hauser: *Histoire diplomatique de l'Europe* (Paris, 1929), Volume I, p. 94, also quoting unpublished British documents, as it appears.

Andrássy was no less anxious to remove all suspicion from the minds of the English. Speaking to Russell, he declared in the warmest and most eloquent terms that all his sympathies were with England: " He sincerely regretted that her neutrality stood in the way of that intimate and active co-operation with Austria that had been the dream of his life. Now he felt that the existence of Austria depended on a cordial alliance with Germany." [1] Whether these assurances made any impression on the English foreign office we do not know. That considerable anxiety was felt in London at this imperial demonstration is certain. In fact a British squadron was sent to greet Thiers at Le Havre on September 18, much to the surprise of the French statesman. He accepted the compliment, but immediately wired to St. Petersburg to explain it and to state that for France the alliance with Russia would be more hopeful than one with England. [2]

The meeting of the three Emperors is important as a link in the story of the reformulation of European politics after the epoch-making events of the years 1866 to 1871. The result was intangible and imponderable. There was the reconciliation of the rulers, William I and Francis Joseph on the one hand, Alexander II and Francis Joseph on the other. Furthermore, there was an undeniable drawing together of Germany and Austria and of Austria and Russia. But all the leading statesmen were still lost in uncertainty, still weighed down with suspicions. Gorchakov courted Andrássy, but at the same time flirted with the French. Andrássy made up to Bismarck, but at the same time declared his affection for the English. Bismarck accepted the advances of Andrássy, but looked askance at Gorchakov and took care not to estrange the English. The English were genuinely disturbed and openly demonstrated their interest in France. The French, finally, accepted the English expressions of sympathy, but saw to it that their attitude should not be misunderstood at St. Petersburg. Obviously the international system of Europe had not yet taken definite form.

Still the League of the Three Emperors, which was foreshadowed in the Berlin meeting, was soon to become a reality. The idea was a favourite one of the Russian field-marshal von Berg, victor over the Polish Revolution and a very close friend of the Tsar. Berg had accompanied Alexander to Berlin, evidently in the hope that some progress would be made towards the realization of his plan. On this occasion he had had no success, but when the Emperor William came to St. Petersburg in May 1873, accompanied by Bismarck and Moltke, the proposed combination was again discussed. The two field-marshals worked out the text of a simple military convention, which was ratified by the two Emperors on May 6, 1873. It provided that if either of the contracting parties were attacked by another European power, the other should come to the aid of its ally with two hundred thousand men.

---

[1] Taffs, loc. cit.   [2] *Documents diplomatiques français*, I, No. 157.

Francis Joseph was asked by Alexander to subscribe to this convention in June 1873, when the Tsar came to Vienna. But the Austrian Emperor and Andrássy refused to participate, arguing that the form of the agreement was not in harmony with constitutional procedure. Thereupon Gorchakov and Andrássy drew up a convention of a much more general nature, and this was signed by the two rulers on June 6, 1873. This new agreement simply expressed the determination of the two Emperors " to prevent anyone from succeeding in separating them in the field of principles which they regard as alone capable of assuring and, if necessary, of imposing the maintenance of the peace of Europe against all subversions, from whatever quarter they may come. In case an aggression coming from a third power should threaten to compromise the peace of Europe, Their Majesties mutually engage to come to a preliminary under-standing between themselves, without seeking or contracting new alliances, in order to agree as to the line of conduct to be followed in common. If, as a result of this understanding, a military action should become necessary, it would be governed by a special convention to be concluded between Their Majesties." [1]

It will be seen that the Schönbrunn Convention of June 1873 was much less specific than the agreement concluded at St. Petersburg in May. Whereas the latter provided for definite co-operation in case of a crisis, the former involved merely a promise to take counsel and work out a military convention if action became necessary. This is quite comprehensible. There was no great outstanding difficulty in the way of close relations between Germany and Russia, and there-fore no serious obstacle to collaboration between the two nations. With Russia and Austria the situation was quite different, for these two powers were rivals in the Near East, and it was quite impossible for the Austrians to bind them-selves in advance for all eventualities. Certainly the more indefinite agree-ment of Schönbrunn met the demands of the situation more nearly than the St. Petersburg Convention. William I accepted the convention concluded by Francis Joseph and the Tsar when he, in turn, came to Vienna in October 1873. The agreement thereby became the basis for the League of the Three Emperors as it existed during the 1870's. Of the St. Petersburg Convention nothing more was heard for the time being and it is not entirely clear whether or not it was considered to be still valid. Later on, in 1881, when discussions were opened looking towards the conclusion of a formal alliance between the three govern-ments, there was some reference to the earlier agreement and at that time it was declared definitely superseded.

The connexion between Germany, Russia, and Austria as it was established by the negotiations of 1873 has often been criticized, and with some justice. It was a reminiscence of the old dynastic politics, the agreements being signed by the rulers, not by the responsible ministers. The texts, too, indicate the peculiar

---

[1] The texts of these agreements may be found in *Die Grosse Politik*, I, chapter v; in Alfred F. Pribram: *The Secret Treaties of Austria-Hungary, 1879–1914* (Cambridge, 1920), Volume II, appendix A; and in the *Krasny Arkhiv*, Volume I (1922), pp. 28–34.

dynastic nature of the understandings. What the Emperors had in mind was the principle of monarchical solidarity, which was being threatened by the revolutionary republican movement in western Europe and by the dangerous radical and socialist organizations which commonly went under the name of the *Internationale*. At bottom the League of the Three Emperors was a new Holy Alliance against revolution in all its forms. Nothing was said in any of the agreements about specific political problems. To be sure, the St. Petersburg Convention was tantamount to a Russian guarantee of the possession of Alsace and Lorraine by Germany, at least in so far as it obliged the Tsar to come to the assistance of his neighbour if the French embarked upon a war of revenge. But this provision was only implicit in the understanding. Its value might well be questioned. The more serious problem of eastern Europe, the question of the Balkans and the Ottoman Empire, was not touched upon at all, and the agreement of 1873 proved, within a few years, unable to stand the strain of an eastern crisis.

It would not be wise, however, to underestimate the value of the entente between the three eastern empires. Bismarck evidently considered it better than nothing and offered no objection to the conclusion of either the St. Petersburg or the Schönbrunn agreement. His attitude, to be sure, is not entirely clear. During the visit of William to the Russian capital in May 1873, he spoke at some length with the Russian statesmen. He told them that he was determined to repay Russia for her benevolent policy during the years preceding 1871, and that he was prepared to support Russian interests in the Orient. He felt towards England, he said, only disdain, and towards Austria only indifference. He indicated to Gorchakov his dislike of the idea of associating Austria with the agreement and expressed the desire that it be kept secret from her. The Austrians might, he remarked, reveal it to the English, and the latter would pass it on to the French.[1]

Just what value to place on these remarks of Bismarck it is very difficult to say. Most likely they were intended strictly for Russian consumption, for we know that Bismarck had been anxious to settle with the Austrians before negotiating with the Russians. Furthermore, he refused to recognize the validity of the St. Petersburg Agreement unless Austria were included, and later on he declared the German-Russian Convention to have been entirely superseded by the subsequent engagements entered into at Schönbrunn.[2] His attitude towards Austria was by no means one of indifference; neither was his attitude towards England one of disdain. It has, in fact, been suggested that he refused to sign the agreements himself because he regarded them as too anti-English. In June 1871 he had suggested the possibility of common action with England

---

[1] *Krasny Arkhiv*, I, pp. 20–6. As a matter of fact, Gorchakov himself revealed the existence of the conventions to the French ambassador before the year was out (*Documents diplomatiques français*, I, No. 247).

[2] *Die Grosse Politik*, I, Nos. 126, 128, and especially Bismarck's marginal notes in Volume III, No. 482.

against the revolutionary movements. At the very time of his visit to St. Petersburg he spoke to the English ambassador of his anxiety to maintain intimate
relations, and asserted that the League of the Three Emperors was not inconsistent with an understanding with England.[1]

Bismarck's policy in this whole negotiation can probably be understood only
if it is brought into connexion with the development of German relations with
France. At this very time important changes were taking place in the situation.
In May 1873 Thiers was obliged to resign the presidency of the republic, and
the royalists began to devote themselves to the problem of effecting a restoration
of the monarchy. At the same time the last indemnity payments were being
made and the Germans completed their arrangements to withdraw the last
troops of the army of occupation. France was regaining something of her freedom of action, and this fact alone was bound to colour the evolution of the
European states system. Thus far the European powers were groping in the
dark. In the next two years the alignment became much clearer and the policies
of the various governments became much more sharply defined.

BIBLIOGRAPHICAL NOTE

DOCUMENTARY SOURCES

Die Grosse Politik der europäischen Kabinette, 1871–1914. Edited by Johannes
Lepsius, Albrecht Mendelssohn Bartholdy, and Friedrich Thimme. Berlin,
1922–7. This huge collection of documents from the German archives is by far the
most important source for the whole period. A French translation is in process of
publication, and an English translation of selected documents is also appearing.
Volume I includes chapter i: From Versailles to the Treaty of Frankfurt; ii:
From the Treaty of Frankfurt to the Berlin Convention of October 12, 1871;
iii: From the Berlin Convention to the Versailles Convention of June 1872;
iv: From the Versailles Convention to the Evacuation of the French Territory
in September 1873; v: The League of the Three Emperors.

Ministère des Affaires Étrangères: *Documents diplomatiques français, 1871–1914.*
Paris, 1929–. This great publication, which has only just begun, will rival the
German in size and importance. The first series will cover the period 1871–1900.
Volume I of this series deals with the years 1871–5 and contains some material
of importance.

Russko-Germanskie Otnoshenia (*Krasny Arkhiv,* Volume I, pp. 1–208, 1922).
A collection of documents from the Russian archives, by no means complete, but
of considerable interest on such subjects as the Three Emperors' League.

---

[1] Hans Rothfels: *Bismarcks englische Bündnispolitik* (Berlin, 1924), pp. 13–14; Fitzmaurice:
Life of Granville, II, p. 113.

Occupation et libération du territoire. Two volumes. Paris, 1900. An important collection of material bearing on Franco-German relations 1871–3, most of which is now reprinted in the *Documents diplomatiques français.*

MEMOIRS, AUTOBIOGRAPHIES, BIOGRAPHIES, AND LETTERS

FITZMAURICE, LORD EDMOND: *The Life of Granville George Leveson Gower, Second Earl Granville.* Two volumes. London, 1905. Contains many of the letters of the foreign minister in the Gladstone cabinet. A valuable source for the study of English policy.

WEMYSS, MRS. ROSSLYN: *Memoirs and Letters of the Right Hon. Sir Robert Morier.* Two volumes. London, 1911. Morier was English minister to some of the lesser German courts, but was unusually well informed on international relations and carried on an extremely interesting correspondence.

NEWTON, LORD: *Lord Lyons.* Two volumes. London, 1913. The papers of the English ambassador at Paris.

BROGLIE, DUC DE: *La Mission de M. de Gontaut-Biron à Berlin.* Paris, 1896. Based on the papers of the French ambassador to Berlin. Important for the period 1871–3.

GONTAUT-BIRON, VICOMTE DE: *Ma Mission en Allemagne, 1872–1873.* Paris, 1906. The ambassador's own account of his mission.

GAVARD, CHARLES: *Un Diplomate à Londres. Lettres et Notes, 1871–1877.* Paris, 1897. Reminiscences of the secretary of the French embassy at London.

Denkwürdigkeiten des Botschafters GENERAL VON SCHWEINITZ. Two volumes. Berlin, 1927. The important papers of the German ambassador to Vienna during this period.

Aufzeichnungen und Erinnerungen aus dem Leben des Botschafters JOSEPH MARIA VON RADOWITZ. Two volumes. Berlin, 1925. The papers of one of Bismarck's chief collaborators.

WERTHEIMER, EDUARD: *Graf Julius Andrássy.* Three volumes. Stuttgart, 1913. The authoritative biography of the Austrian foreign minister and the most important contribution to the history of Austrian policy in this period.

GENERAL TREATMENTS OF INTERNATIONAL RELATIONS

FAY, SIDNEY B.: *The Origins of the World War.* Two volumes. New York, 1928. The best single work on the origins of the World War. Volume I deals with the period from 1871 to 1914, but the Bismarckian period is rather briefly treated.

HAUSER, HENRI: *Histoire diplomatique de l'Europe, 1871–1914.* Two volumes. Paris, 1929. The latest diplomatic history and one of the best. Written by a number of scholars under the direction of Hauser.

RACHFAHL, FELIX: *Deutschland und die Weltpolitik.* Volume I: *" Die Bismarcksche Ära."* Stuttgart, 1923. The most exhaustive treatment of the Bismarckian period, based in large part upon the German documents.

PLEHN, HANS: *Bismarcks auswärtige Politik nach der Reichsgründung.* Munich, 1920. A pioneer work, now rather out of date, but still stimulating and suggestive.

JAPIKSE, N.: *Europa und Bismarcks Friedenspolitik, 1871–1890.* Berlin, 1927. The German translation of a Dutch work which appeared in 1925. The most up-to-date account of the period.

DESPAGNET, FRANZ: *La Diplomatie de la Troisième République et le droit de gens.* Paris, 1904. One of the best conventional accounts of French diplomacy.

SCHEFER, CHRISTIAN: *D'une guerre à l'autre.* Paris, 1920. A study of French policy, but deals chiefly with colonial problems.

BOURGEOIS, EMILE, and PAGÈS, GEORGES: *Les Origines et les responsabilités de la Grande Guerre.* Paris, 1921. An uneven book, containing some material from the French archives. This book will be wholly superseded by the publication of the French documents.

REINACH, JOSEPH: *" La Diplomatie de la Troisième République "* (*Revue des sciences politiques,* Volume XLIV, January–June 1921). Adds nothing.

The Cambridge History of British Foreign Policy. Edited by Sir A. W. Ward and G. P. Gooch. Three volumes. New York, 1923. The best general account of British foreign policy, but rather weak on continental politics and problems.

RAMSAY, A. A. W.: *Idealism and Foreign Policy.* London, 1925. A conventional account of British relations with Germany and France from 1860 to 1878.

BRUGMANS, H.: *De buitenlandsche Politiek van het britische Rijk, van omstreeks 1870 tot 1914.* Leiden, 1926. A good brief account of British policy in the pre-war period.

CHARMATZ, RICHARD: *Die auswärtige Politik Österreichs im 19ten Jahrhundert.* Second edition. Leipzig, 1918. Very brief and now largely out of date.

LARMEROUX, JEAN: *La Politique extérieure de l'Autriche-Hongrie.* Two volumes. Paris, 1918. Unsatisfactory and inadequate.

KORFF, BARON SERGIEI: *Russia's Foreign Relations during the Last Half Century.* New York, 1922. A mere sketch.

ZAIONTCHOVSKI, A.: *Podgotovka Rossii k Mirovoi Voina v Meshdunarodnom Otnoshenii.* Moscow, 1926. A systematic account of Russian foreign policy in the nineteenth century, based in part upon unpublished material.

COOLIDGE, ARCHIBALD: *The Origins of the Triple Alliance.* Second edition. New York, 1926. A useful brief account of the situation in the 1870's.

SPECIAL TOPICS

PINON, RENÉ: *France et Allemagne, 1870–1913.* Paris, 1913. A conventional and now antiquated account, with a strong national bias.

GOOCH, G. P.: *Franco-German Relations, 1871–1918.* London, 1923. Easily the best account in English, well-informed and well-balanced.

HALÉVY, ELIE: "Franco-German Relations Since 1870" (*History,* April 1924). A good review of new material.

HALLER, JOHANNES: *Tausend Jahre deutsch-französischer Beziehungen.* Stuttgart, 1930. The most recent treatment and one of the most scholarly, with special emphasis on the recent period.

HERZFELD, HANS: *Deutschland und das geschlagene Frankreich.* Berlin, 1924.

LINNEBACH, KARL: *Deutschland als Sieger im besetzten Frankreich.* Stuttgart, 1924. This and the preceding are excellent studies of the Franco-German problem in the years 1871–3.

ROSEN, GEORG: *Die Stellungnahme der Politik Bismarcks zur Frage der Staatsform in Frankreich von 1871–1890.* Detmold, 1924. A careful analysis of Bismarck's attitude towards the domestic problems of France.

BECKER, OTTO: *Bismarcks Bündnispolitik.* Berlin, 1923. An excellent general account of the alliance system.

ROTHFELS, HANS: *Bismarcks englische Bündnispolitik.* Berlin, 1924. The best study of Bismarck's relations with England.

WAHL, ADALBERT: *Vom Bismarck der siebziger Jahre.* Tübingen, 1920. Primarily a study of the international aspects of the Kulturkampf.

HOLBORN, HAJO: *Bismarcks europäische Politik zu Beginn der siebziger Jahre und die Mission Radowitz.* Berlin, 1925. A valuable study of Bismarckian policy in the early 1870's, with the use of some unpublished material.

DAUDET, ERNEST: *Histoire diplomatique de l'alliance franco-russe, 1873–1893.* Paris, 1898. Still the best work on Franco-Russian relations in these years.

CURÀTULO, GIACOMO: *Francia e Italia, 1849–1914.* Turin, 1915. A conventional account of Franco-Italian relations.

SALVATORELLI, L.: "*L'Italia nella Politica Internazionale dell'Era Bismarckiana*" (*Rivista Storica Italiana,* April 1923). A general survey based primarily on the German documents.

SALVEMINI, GAETANO: "*La Politica Estera della Destra, 1871–1876*" (*Rivista d'Italia,* November 15, 1924; January 15, 1925; February 15, 1925). By far the best study of Italian policy, based in part upon unpublished material.

ITALICUS: *Italiens Bündnispolitik, 1870–1896.* Munich, 1928. A thorough scholarly study which takes account of the recent material.

HELMS, ALBERT: *Bismarck und Russland.* Bonn, 1927. A conventional doctoral dissertation.

Religion and Politics

THE WAR SCARE OF 1875

B ISMARCK WAS FIRMLY CONVINCED OF THE INEVITABILITY OF ANOTHER war between France and Germany. So were Moltke and most members of the military circle in Berlin. The soldiers took a business-like attitude towards this problem and freely discussed the advisability of waging war on France before French preparations were complete. This was the theory of the so-called preventive war, for which, from the strictly military standpoint, much could be said. Bismarck himself, just after the war, at times expressed the opinion that it would be better to strike first, once the intentions of the French were entirely clear.[1] He seems, however, to have given up this idea completely later on, and to have depended upon a clever diplomacy to deprive the French of all prospect of success.

The fall of Thiers in May 1873 was an important turning-point in international relations, for the new president, Marshal MacMahon, was a confirmed royalist who saw eye to eye with the royalist national assembly and was glad to help along the work of restoring the monarchy. The great obstacle to this restoration, however, was the traditional dissension in the monarchist camp itself. Bourbonists, Orleanists, and Bonapartists hated each other almost more than they hated the republic. Repeated efforts to bring them together had failed. But in the summer of 1873 the Bourbon and Orleans factions at last agreed to a compromise. The road was open for the accession of the Bourbon Count de Chambord, as Henry V. Then, at the last moment, the whole plan failed because Henry refused to give up the white flag of the Bourbons and accept the tricolour. The hopes of the monarchists were blasted, but it must be remembered that they still controlled the national assembly, and that President MacMahon was with them. They secured for him a seven-year lease of office, during which period he was to keep the throne warm for the Orleanist candidate, the Count of Paris.

One aspect of the conflict between legitimism and liberalism in the history

---

[1] e.g. his instructions to Waldersee, June 1871 (*Denkwürdigkeiten des General Feldmarschall Alfred Grafen von Waldersee*, Berlin, 1922, Volume I, p. 139), and his remarks to the French chargé d'affaires, Marquis de Gabriac, in August 1871 (Marquis de Gabriac: *Souvenirs diplomatiques de Russie et d'Allemagne*, Paris, 1896, pp. 138 ff.; *Documents diplomatiques français*, I, No. 42).

of modern France was the question of clericalism. The conservative elements set great store by the so-called alliance between the throne and the altar, while the liberals were firmly opposed to interference by the clericals in politics or education. This domestic problem had also an international side, especially after 1870, for the loss of temporal power by the Pope created a great stir in France. For years the French government had acted as guardian of the papal possessions. With the withdrawal of the French garrison from Rome in 1870 the powerful position of the Third Republic in Italian affairs practically disappeared. The seizure of Rome by the Italians was a blow at French power and influence as well as at French sentiment. Moderate republicans, like Thiers, were perhaps less affected by sentimental considerations, but they claimed for France, as a great Catholic power, the right to protect the personal and religious liberty of the Pope and they openly offered him an asylum in France if he decided to leave Italy. For years the French gunboat *Orénoque* lay off Civitavecchia ready to come to the assistance of the Holy Father if necessary. In view of the high tension in the relations between the Vatican and the Italian government, the claims put forward by the French might at any time lead to conflict between France and Italy.[1]

The royalists in France went much further than the moderate republicans. Like the churchmen they looked forward to the restoration of the temporal power and hoped for action when the work of re-establishing the monarchy was complete. In fact, French clerical circles and even the Pope himself took an active part in bringing about the compromise between the Bourbonists and the Orleanists in the summer of 1873, and the Count de Chambord made the statement that the two questions on which he could never yield were the questions of the white flag and the restoration of the temporal power.[2]

Thiers had initiated the policy of working for a possible alliance with Russia, Austria, or England, and he had welcomed the drawing together of any two of these powers. Such a combination might be made use of either to support the Papacy against Italy, or to serve France as a bulwark against the German menace. It was fully realized in Paris that the English could not be reckoned on for much more than a Platonic friendship, but great hopes were cherished for an eventual alliance with Russia or Austria. Even Gambetta, the most prominent republican leader, though he had little sympathy for autocratic Russia, was thoroughly in favour of an agreement with Austria, despite the illiberal and anti-national policy of the Habsburgs. In 1874 he wrote quite characteristically to a friend: " You believe in Russia; you favour an alliance with her. Well, between ourselves, let me tell you what I have in mind, something quite different: to see whether we cannot disengage Austria from the bonds that are tightening be-

---

[1] See especially Jules Favre: *Rome et la République française* (Paris, 1871); Franz Despagnet: *La République et le Vatican, 1870–1906* (Paris, 1906); *Documents diplomatiques français*, I, Nos. 6, 23, 34, 35, 83.

[2] Despagnet, op. cit., p. 32.

tween her and Prussia. Believe me, we must let twenty years elapse before we allow free play to the principle of nationality, with all the results that it entails. . . . This principle cannot but serve to upset the balance of Europe, to entangle and perplex still further the relations between the powers. . . . I prefer the European balance as conceived by diplomatists at the end of the eighteenth century, before the revolution. . . . We shall have to educate public opinion towards an alliance between France and Austria." Or again: " A Franco-Austrian Alliance might conceivably prevent war, and would in any case be the only effective means of resistance to the grasping designs of Prussia. It will be our fault if we find ourselves attacked by an Austro-Prussian combination." These words merit quotation, for they illustrate the confusion of international relations in this period. Even a radical like Gambetta could not be blind to the fact that the championing of the principle of nationality, revolutionary though the principle might be, had not led to anything but disaster for the French and a weakening of the French position. This view-point was fully shared by men like Thiers, and his policy was continued by the royalists themselves after Thiers's fall.[1]

Despite the defeat of the French in the great war of 1870-1 there was a certain strength in the French position. France still possessed a kind of mag-netic power. It was clear that neither England nor Russia would permit a further weakening of France by Germany. They had no interest in the tem-poral power of the Pope. In fact they were hostile to the papal pretensions. But they did have an interest in checking the power of the new German Empire. If Bismarck went to extremes in his relations with France, he might well find these two wing powers arrayed against him. Austria, on the other hand, was hardly in a position to come out openly against the new Germany, but the Habsburgs had a genuine interest in the settlement of the Roman question, and an entente between France and Austria on this basis was by no means outside the range of possibility.

Bismarck appreciated these factors fully. It might almost be said that he feared the France of 1873, defeated and isolated, more than he feared the France of 1869, despite the imposing façade of her power in the time of Napoleon III. It can therefore hardly be doubted that his negotiations with Russia and Austria were intended primarily to cut the ground from under the feet of the French and to prevent the two Emperors from falling under the spell of French tempta-tion. " His [Bismarck's] recent visit to Russia," wrote an English diplomat in the spring of 1873, " had been intended to awe France if possible into keeping the peace, and to dispel M. Thiers' illusions in regard to a Franco-Russian Alliance." [2]

But the German chancellor evidently did not regard the League of the Three Emperors as a sufficient guarantee. While the agreements between Germany,

[1] Deschanel: *Gambetta*, p. 220; *Documents diplomatiques français*, I, No. 241.

[2] Fitzmaurice: *Life of Granville*, II, p. 113.

Russia, and Austria were being concluded, he not only assured the English of his desire for good relations, but insisted that the new combination was in no sense inconsistent with an understanding with England. He gave his blessing to the negotiations which were opened between England and Russia in the summer of 1873 and which led to the conclusion of an agreement dealing with central Asia: the Oxus River was to be the northern boundary of a neutral Afghan state, and the Russians promised not to occupy the Khanate of Khiva. At the same time the Tsar assured the English ambassador that English suspicions of Russian designs in the Near East were unwarranted: " For his part he was convinced, and every rational man in Russia shared the conviction, that the acquisition by Russia of Constantinople would be immediately followed by the disruption of the Empire." [1]

It must not be supposed that Bismarck's attitude towards England implied an abandonment on the part of England of her traditional policy of abstention. But it did serve to remove in part the English suspicions of German policy. Much more real, however, was the rapprochement between Germany and Italy. A prominent Italian historian has compared the position of these countries in the years after 1870 with the position of strangers who enter a railroad train, look for a seat, and disturb the other passengers. The Germans could show a long ticket of military victories, which entitled them to consideration. But the Italians had no such ticket. Quite the contrary, they were suspected everywhere because of the revolutionary connexions of the movement for unification and because of their treatment of the papal question, which was looked upon as a menace to the fundamental principles of ownership and authority.[2]

The successors of Cavour in the government of Italy were men of eminently conservative temperament. That they sincerely wished to avoid trouble and to maintain the old friendship with France can hardly be doubted. But they refused to debate the Roman question with anyone. The whole problem was closely bound up with the movement for unity, and unity was to them a sacred principle. It was therefore clear from the start that so long as the French maintained an unfriendly attitude in this matter, the Italians would have to look elsewhere for support. Count de Launay, the Italian minister at Berlin, wrote in July 1871: " It is rather probable that one day or another our *good* neighbours will seek to take revenge upon us for the defeats which Germany has inflicted upon them." The newspapers began to talk of the need for friendship between Italy on the one hand, and Austria and Germany on the other. The Italian foreign minister, Visconti-Venosta, whose sympathies for France cannot be questioned, told the French minister in April 1872: " The Papacy dreams of its temporal

    [1] Hajo Holborn: *Bismarcks europäische Politik zu Beginn der siebziger Jahre* (Berlin, 1925), pp. 26–7; *The Diplomatic Reminiscences of Lord Augustus Loftus* (Second Series, London, 1894), Volume II, pp. 42 ff.; William H. Dawson, in the *Cambridge History of British Foreign Policy* (New York, 1923), Volume III, p. 75.
    [2] See especially Gaetano Salvemini: " *La Politica Estera della Destra, 1871–1876* " (*Rivista d'Italia*, November 15, 1924; January 15, 1925; February 15, 1925).

restoration only through France, and it is this hope that supports it in its ill will against Italy." In November of the same year the same Italian statesman told the Chamber of Deputies quite frankly: "Not only sentiment and community of interests, but common enemies connect us with Germany. . . . We should be culpable if we did not seek to maintain the best relations with the German government and people."[1]

Even though the connexion with Germany was recognized as desirable, it was hard for the Italian King and his advisers to carry it through. Victor Emmanuel had been eager to go to the support of Napoleon in the late war, and Bismarck had replied to the hostile attitude of the Italians by negotiating with Mazzini regarding the eventual establishment of a republic in Italy. In the spring of 1871 he had himself offered the Pope an asylum in Germany, to say nothing of friendship and alliance. But Bismarck was now only too glad to welcome the Italian advances. In both countries the fall of Thiers was looked upon as the prelude to serious complications. "The attitude of the French assembly will drive us into the arms of Prussia in spite of ourselves," said an Italian statesman to the French minister. In Germany the Italians found consolation. Bismarck promised that Germany would not support French attempts to restore the temporal power of the Pope. In fact, she would not tolerate such efforts under any circumstances. The security of Italy, the chancellor declared, is one of the true interests of German policy in Europe: "The enemies and the dangers which threaten Italy and Germany are common enemies and common dangers." An alliance between the two countries he described as "predestined."

In the spring of 1873 it was decided that Victor Emmanuel should pay a visit not only to Berlin, but to Vienna. The Italians were anxious to prevent an Austrian-French understanding, just as they were eager to secure the support of Germany against possible French designs. The visits took place in September 1873 and turned out to the satisfaction of all concerned. In Vienna the King was told that Austria would not support the papal claims, and in Berlin he was given a promise that Germany would not allow an attack upon Italy. No attempt seems to have been made to conclude a definite written agreement, and none such was necessary. But the significance of the royal visits was not overlooked in the European chancelleries. The French ambassador at Berlin reported home that the papal question and the French policy explained it all, and Thiers himself spoke of the relationship between Germany and Italy as an *"entente évidente."* In the contemporary documents there is frequent mention of the "Alliance" between the two countries. Italy was commonly included as an associate of the group of powers which had joined hands in the League of the Three Emperors.[2]

---

[1] Salvemini, loc. cit.; *Documents diplomatiques français*, I, Nos. 53, 115, 119, 120.

[2] Salvemini, loc. cit.; L. Salvatorelli: "*L'Italia nella Politica internazionale dell' Era Bismarckiana*" (*Rivista Storica Italiana*, April 1923); *Documents diplomatiques français*, I, Nos. 240, 247; Fitzmaurice: *Granville*, II, p. 114.

The religious question which lay at the bottom of the rapprochement between Italy and Germany also coloured the relations between Germany and France, especially in the years following the resignation of Thiers. In a sense the great struggle between Church and State in Prussia (the Kulturkampf), which filled the decade from 1873 to 1883, was but another aspect of Bismarck's attempt to isolate France and draw the European powers to the side of the new German Empire. The chancellor took little interest in the problems of dogma raised by the Vatican Council of 1869–70, or in the proclamation of papal infallibility. He does not, in fact, appear to have taken much part in the conduct of the struggle in Prussia itself. On occasion he actually disapproved of the steps taken by his subordinates. What interested him was the political power of the Papacy, and of this he had a high opinion and no mean fear. He maintained in the Reichstag in 1874, and the statement is repeated in his memoirs, that the Franco-Prussian War was begun by the French in agreement with the papal curia, and that the Empress Eugénie was a mere tool in the hands of the Jesuits, who were the chief protagonists of the dogma of infallibility, and the most active opponents of Protestant Prussia.[1]

Whatever truth there may have been in this assertion (Bismarck declared that he had complete proof to support it), the chancellor was moved before long to offer the Papacy friendship and support. His reasons for doing so were excellent ones and were closely bound up with the problem of German unity. The powerful Catholic Centre party in the new German Reichstag was composed primarily of separatist elements. The Bavarians had been brought into the new empire only with great difficulty; the Alsatians and Lorrainers were systematic protesters; the Poles from the eastern parts of Prussia were considered a standing menace to the new state. In other words, the larger part of the Catholic element in the empire was hostile to it, and Bismarck saw before him the danger of an alliance between these elements and the Papacy. His offers to the Pope in the spring of 1871 were made on condition that Leo use his influence to detach the Roman Catholic party in the empire from its separatist connexions. The offers were refused. Soon after, Bismarck declared war to the knife on the Centre party.[2]

The first legislation of the Kulturkampf, the first so-called " May laws," were passed in May 1873 — that is, at the very time of Thiers's fall and at the very time of the conclusion of the St. Petersburg Convention between Germany and Russia. These events were, in fact, closely related. Bismarck tried to enlist other powers in the struggle against ultramontanism and the papal pretensions, be-

---

[1] Arthur Böhtlingk: *Bismarck und das päpstliche Rom* (Berlin, 1911), pp. 135–7; *Bismarck, the Man and the Statesman* (New York, 1899), Volume II, p. 184; Robert Pahncke: *Die Parallelerzählungen Bismarcks zu seinen Gedanken und Erinnerungen* (Halle, 1913), pp. 216–17.

[2] Böhtlingk, op. cit., pp. 164 ff., 181 ff.; Georges Goyau: *Bismarck et l'église* (Paris, 1911); J. Lulvès: " *Bismarck und die römische Frage* " (*Deutsche Revue*, May and June 1916); Adalbert Wahl: *Vom Bismarck der siebziger Jahre* (Tübingen, 1920); Wemyss: *Memoirs of Sir Robert Morier*, II, pp. 251–7.

cause France championed these pretensions. He could reckon on the sympathy of Italy, on the approval of the liberal government in Vienna, and on the support of the Russian government, which had been at odds with the Papacy for some time because of the persecution of the Catholic Church in Russian Poland. In Poland as in Prussia the religious issue played a prominent role in politics. The Russian crusade against the Catholic Church was part of the crusade against Polish nationalism.

" The [German] generals tell the Emperor it would be better to fight France before she is ready than after," reported the English ambassador at Berlin to his government, " but Bismarck, who scorns the generals, advises the Emperor to fight France *morally* through Rome and the Catholic alliances against united Germany." [1] In a similar vein was the report of the French ambassador at Berlin: " It is not exactly the Catholics with whom Bismarck is angry, but the alliance which France might make with them." [2] Here is the whole thing in a nutshell. The Kulturkampf was part and parcel of Bismarck's policy to isolate France and prevent the formation of a coalition against Germany. In the summer and autumn of 1873 the German chancellor held the upper hand. He had associated Russia, Austria, and Italy with the policy of Germany, and England was not hostile. In fact, many Englishmen sympathized with Bismarck in his anti-papal policy, and there was every prospect of an Anglo-Russian understanding with respect to conflicting interests in Asia. Whatever may have been the inherent weaknesses of the system, it at least served its purpose during the most critical period, when the restoration of the monarchy in France seemed imminent and the international situation was fraught with uncertainty.

But the Three Emperors' League, flanked by Italy and England, was not a combination sufficiently strong to withstand a severe strain. Designed to keep France from finding allies and embarking upon a war of aggression against Germany, it began to crumble just as soon as the relations of Germany and France entered upon a new period of crisis. The Kulturkampf quite naturally aroused great ill will in Catholic countries, and especially in France, where the tide of clerical influence was running strong in the years 1873-5. The final evacuation of French territory by the Germans, in September 1873, enhanced the feeling of self-confidence in France and enabled the government to take a stronger stand in its relations with Germany. In August 1873 the Bishop of Nancy, whose diocese included parts of Lorraine which had been ceded to Germany, called upon the faithful to offer prayers for the return of the lost provinces to France. This appeal was read in all the churches of the diocese, even in those which had passed under German rule. In November a number of French bishops protested openly against the Prussian anti-Church legislation, the Bishop of Nîmes going so far as to refer to the Prussian tradition of " baseness and immorality." Even French writers admit that these expressions on the

---

[1] Lord Newton: *Lord Lyons* (London, 1913), Volume II, p. 29.
[2] *Occupation et libération du territoire,* I, pp. 241 ff.

part of the French clergy were inopportune and gave Bismarck a just cause for uneasiness. They did, in fact, " pass the bounds of the bitterest criticism." [1]

The German chancellor immediately insisted that the French government disavow these utterances and take the necessary steps to prevent the repetition of such incidents. The French government did what it could under the circumstances. It even appealed to the Pope to use his influence with the French clergy in the direction of moderation. But there was a limit beyond which the royalist government felt that it could not go, and the discussion between Berlin and Paris dragged on for months. The newspapers, especially on the German side, assumed a belligerent tone, and relations became tense in January 1874.[2]

The French ambassador at Berlin, who can hardly be accused of having had too much sympathy for Bismarck, believed that much of the agitation in Germany was to be attributed to the government's efforts in preparation for the coming elections and the introduction of a new military bill. When he discussed the situation with the chancellor in January 1874, he found him firm and insistent, but at the same time energetic in the declaration of his desire for good relations and in his determination to preserve peace. " Take care lest the masses become fanaticized in the name of the persecuted Catholic religion," said Bismarck, " for then the clerical party will seize control and will espouse all the quarrels of the Roman curia, and you will inevitably be drawn into a war against us. We must not allow ourselves to be taken unawares by your attack. In that case it would be better to fight in two years, in one year, than to wait for you to finish your preparations. . . . All idea of war is far from us. What profit could we derive from it? " [3]

But before Bismarck could secure the satisfaction he desired from the French government, he was obliged to let the matter drop. " It may be easy to bully and to crush France, but will it be possible to do this without raising a storm in other quarters? " wrote Lord Lyons, the English ambassador at Paris.[4] That was the great question, and the answer was unfavourable to the Germans. Bismarck was soon to learn that the powers were not prepared to see France pressed too hard, even if the fault lay with her. Bismarck's efforts to induce the other powers to follow his example and embark upon a struggle with the Church failed completely. More than that, the international alignment which he had worked out in the preceding year began to disintegrate rapidly.

The French minister of foreign affairs at this time was the Duc de Decazes, a man who was evidently bent on making the most of his opportunities to weaken the German position. Despite the reassuring reports from the ambas-

---

[1] Emile Bourgeois and Georges Pagès: *Les Origines et les responsabilités de la Grande Guerre* (Paris, 1921), p. 159; Despagnet, op. cit., pp. 39–42.

[2] André Dreux: *Dernières Années de l'ambassade en Allemagne de M. de Gontaut-Biron* (Paris, 1907), chapter i; *Documents diplomatiques français,* I, Nos. 244 ff.

[3] Dreux, op. cit., pp. 19–20; *Documents diplomatiques français,* I, Nos. 251, 263, where only Gontaut's telegram is printed.

[4] Newton: *Lord Lyons,* II, p. 50.

sador at Berlin, he decided to exploit the situation and if possible enlist the
support of Russia and Austria against Germany. The Tsar, when he was appealed to, took the matter lightly. While admitting his displeasure at the policy
of the German chancellor, he assured the French ambassador that no one
wanted war. But with Austria Decazes had more success. Austria was a Catholic
country, and felt much more directly touched by the questions at issue. Following instructions from Paris, the French ambassador at Vienna, Marquis d'Harcourt, approached Francis Joseph on the eve of his visit to Russia. He explained
that Bismarck was threatening France with war unless she joined him to
destroy the Vatican — that is, Catholicism. This, he continued, France could
not do, no matter how great the menace. The Emperor showed himself very
sympathetic, expressed his condemnation of Bismarck's action, and assured his
interlocutor that the Austrian government would not follow in Bismarck's path.

Arrived at St. Petersburg, Andrássy talked over the situation with Prince
Gorchakov. He spoke with some distrust of Bismarck's general policy and said
there was no knowing whether Germany might not, for some reason or other,
attempt some day to extend her power over the Germans of Austria. The meeting was a huge success and brought Russia and Austria much closer than they
had been for a long time. Before it was over, both Andrássy and Gorchakov
went to the French ambassador to offer him consolation. " We pray that France
may soon resume the place in the world to which she is entitled," said the
Austrian minister. " Bismarck cannot make war upon you when he has the
moral opinion of Europe against him, and he will have," declared Gorchakov.
In short, the manœuvre of Decazes was completely successful. Austria and
Russia had drawn closer to each other and they had both expressed their sympathy for France. These two powers, wrote Decazes, would serve as a counter-
weight to Germany.[1]

The bonds which held the three empires together had been loosened through
the development of the Kulturkampf and the spread of its ramifications. In the
same way the relations of Germany with Italy and England were affected.
Bismarck evidently expected the Italians to stand by him loyally in a question
where they themselves had so much at stake. He appears to have hoped for a
definite alliance with the new kingdom in the south. But the Italians held back
and pursued a very cautious policy. The danger of a monarchical restoration in
France had passed, at least for the time being. There was no urgent need for
further action by the government at Rome, and nothing was done. " We have
lost ground during the past six months," wrote the Italian ambassador at Berlin
with some regret. " It is thought here that our official circles always have too
pronounced a leaning towards France." With delight Decazes remarked the
decided easing off of France's relations to her neighbour.[2]

---

[1] *Documents diplomatiques français*, I, Nos. 271, 278, 282, 283, 284, 293; Wertheimer:
Andrássy, II, p. 110; Holborn: *Bismarcks europäische Politik*, p. 20; Dreux, op. cit., pp. 45 ff.

[2] Salvemini, op. cit., January 15, 1925, pp. 73–6; Dreux, op. cit., p. 40.

England's connexion with the continental grouping had not been a very strong one. The understanding with Russia on Asian affairs indicated a desire to smoothe out important points of friction; but even this agreement came to an early and abrupt end. In August 1873 the Russians occupied the Khanate of Khiva, which in June they had promised not to occupy. The incident was one which the English statesmen did not soon forget, but they were anxious to save the understanding with Russia, and the Tsar was invited to pay a visit to England. So far as one can judge, however, the imperial visit made no appreciable difference in the relations of the two governments. They were rapidly drifting apart. Bismarck tried hard to prevent a break, for he feared that a conflict between England and Russia would weaken the Three Emperors' League and encourage France. "Germany's European position demands that our good relations with England should not suffer by our intimacy with the two empires," he wrote somewhat later. In the meantime, however, the antagonism between England and Russia developed. The Russians made every effort to frustrate the British attempt to secure a deciding control of the Suez Canal.[1]

While England and Russia once more drifted apart, the relations of England with Germany did not remain unaffected. The English, like the Russians, were unwilling to see France entirely annihilated and they dreaded the prospect of war. For some time they had been uneasy about Bismarck's plans. What the origin of these suspicions was it is hard to say with certainty. The German Crown Princess, a daughter of Queen Victoria, was no admirer of Bismarck or his policy. She may well have had something to do with sowing the seeds of distrust. Count Beust, the old enemy of the German chancellor, was now Austrian ambassador at London and he, too, appears to have done what he could to poison the atmosphere. At any rate the depth of English distrust appears clearly enough from the diplomatic correspondence now available. It was reported to London that Bismarck wanted to unify Germany as Cavour had unified Italy — by mediatizing the reigning princes of the minor German states. " His policy is to mediatize the minor states of Germany and to annex the German provinces of Austria so as to make one great centralized Power of the German-speaking portions of Europe. To accomplish this may require another war, but it may be with Austria and not with France," wrote Odo Russell from Berlin in February 1874. "I am afraid the peace of Europe depends entirely upon the view Bismarck may take of the easiest means of bringing all German-speaking nations under one rule," reported Lord Lyons from Paris at almost the same time.[2]

The English were so apprehensive of Bismarck's plans)that on February 10,

---

[1] Holborn, op. cit., pp. 29–35; Sir Sidney Lee: *Edward VII, a Biography* (New York, 1925), Volume 1, p. 283; George E. Buckle: *The Life of Benjamin Disraeli* (New York, 1920), Volume V, p. 416.

[2] Fitzmaurice: *Granville*, II, p. 113; Newton: *Lord Lyons*, II, pp. 41, 52–5; *Letters of the Empress Frederick* (London, 1928), p. 133; Karl Klingenfuss: " *Beust und Andrássy und die Kriegsgefahr von 1875* " (*Archiv für Politik und Geschichte*, IV, pp. 616–43, 1926).

1874 Queen Victoria wrote to Emperor William in the hope of averting a crisis in Franco-German relations. " Notwithstanding an active and restless Catholic minority, the English nation, as a whole, is essentially *Protestant,* and its sympathies would be entirely with Germany in any difference with France, unless there was an appearance of a disposition on the part of Germany to avail herself of her greatly superior force to crush and annihilate a beaten foe, and thus to engender the belief that a strong and united Germany was not, after all, the expected mainstay of European peace. I need hardly say that for myself I do not share such apprehensions, but if Germany, through *incessant* provocations of a fanatical *Press* and *priesthood* in France (where, however, the Government do all in their power to keep both under control), were at last to resort to renewed war with France, this might lead to lamentable consequences, although there is nobody in doubt as to the issue, in a military sense, of such a struggle. Being sensible that the fate of Europe rests in your hands, after such unparalleled successes, I venture to express my hope that you have the power and — no doubt — also the will to be *magnanimous.*" [1]

The letter of Queen Victoria to Emperor William was certainly not meant as a threat. It was a friendly letter of warning and was undoubtedly sent in good faith. But its results can only be described as unfortunate. The French were informed of the English standpoint. Odo Russell, who was regarded as a good friend of Bismarck, said to the French ambassador at Berlin: " One cannot tell how far this man [Bismarck] may go in his pretensions. It might be necessary for the European powers to come to an understanding to stop his encroachments on the rights of liberty." Gontaut thought he even pronounced the word "league." Then, a few days later, Russell confidentially informed his French colleague of the Queen's letter to the Emperor.[2]

The French naturally received this news with elation. Evidently the situation was taking exactly the form they desired. The English action encouraged the Duc de Decazes to hope for the gradual evolution of a group of powers, a sort of league of neutrals, which would stand by France in her dispute with Germany. The tension of the winter was over, so Decazes wrote to the French representatives at the leading embassies, but France must continue to be on the *qui vive.* During the succeeding months the connexion between England and France became closer and closer. The new conservative ministry, under Benjamin Disraeli, took a much greater interest in foreign affairs than its liberal predecessor. The prime minister himself distrusted Bismarck, and looked with suspicion upon the Three Emperors' League. When the Prince of Wales came to Paris in July, he made no secret of the English view-point. Decazes hurriedly communicated his remarks to the principal embassies, adding that warnings were constantly coming to Paris from London. Not content with this, the French statesmen did their part in keeping alive the apprehensions of the

---

1 *The Letters of Queen Victoria,* Second Series (New York, 1926), Volume II, pp. 313–14.
2 Dreux, op. cit., pp. 42 ff.; *Documents diplomatiques français,* I, No. 294.

English. M. Gavard, the French chargé d'affaires at London, called the attention of the new foreign minister, Lord Derby, to the growing naval power of Germany. She had ordered three ironclads built since 1871, and these were far too heavy for use in protecting commerce. Lord Derby evidently had not realized the signifiance of this matter and went away thoughtful.[1]

The efforts of the French to destroy the connexion of England and Italy with the German group were meeting with more and more success. In the autumn the French government recalled the *Orénoque* from Civitavecchia, thus removing from Franco-Italian relations another cause for offence. In the meanwhile the Three Emperors' League was becoming more and more of a fiction. The entente between Austria and Russia was closer than ever, but Germany's relations with her two neighbours were rapidly cooling. In the autumn of 1874 there was misunderstanding with respect to the recognition of the Spanish Republic, and before long other difficulties cropped up. Curious though it may seem, the Germans had more unpleasantness with the Russians concerning affairs in the Near East than the Austrians had. Into the details of these incidents, which were in themselves devoid of all larger significance, it is unnecessary to enter here. But taken all together, they coloured the relations between Berlin and St. Petersburg to such an extent that Bismarck decided to send one of his chief assistants, Herr von Radowitz, on a special mission to St. Petersburg. He was to attempt to straighten out the misunderstandings that had arisen in regard to Serbia and Montenegro and in general to sound out the Russian attitude. When Radowitz arrived in the Russian capital, early in February 1875, he told Gorchakov frankly that Germany meant to support the Russian policy in the Near East as she had supported it theretofore. But he did not succeed in drawing out Gorchakov with respect to the ultimate aims of Russian policy, more particularly as they touched France. The assertion that Radowitz offered Russia a free hand in the Near East in return for freedom of action for Germany in regard to France, and that the Russians flatly refused to consider the offer, was current in diplomatic circles at St. Petersburg at the time of the mission and was believed by the French ambassador. But the story cannot be substantiated. It seems to have been a legend which Gorchakov himself circulated in order to set off his own virtue against the evil spirit of the German chancellor. The fact remains, however, that Radowitz did not succeed in removing the difficulties in the way of Russian-German relations.[2]

The stories of the Radowitz mission were circulated in the spring of 1875 in connexion with the famous war scare, an episode which has been much discussed by writers on all sides, but which has not even yet been completely

[1] *Documents diplomatiques français*, I, Nos. 295, 308, 309.
[2] Holborn: *Bismarcks europäische Politik zu Beginn der siebziger Jahre und die Mission Radowitz, passim; Aufzeichnungen und Erinnerungen aus dem Leben des Botschafters Joseph Maria von Radowitz* (Berlin, 1925), Volume I, chapter xiv; *Documents diplomatiques français*, I, Nos. 353, 373, 394.

clarified. In considering the incident it is essential to keep in mind two important points: the general suspicion and distrust, not to say envy, of most of the powers towards the new German Empire; and the determination of Decazes to take advantage of the situation to organize opposition to Germany. These points have already been enlarged upon, but they can hardly be overemphasized.

Towards the end of 1874 the international situation was outwardly quiet. From Berlin as well as St. Petersburg the French ambassadors reported all quiet, with no danger of war. But Prince Gorchakov was repeating his well-worn formula: "France, strong and powerful, is necessary to Europe," and "I can say only one thing, be strong, be strong." [1] Decazes had heard these exhortations often enough and was determined to test their value. At the first opportunity, he had decided, he would appeal to Europe in order to force the hands of the diplomats who were always uttering fair words, but who evaded when actions were expected of them. [2] His chance had now come, for the anti-Church legislation in Prussia had led to difficulties with Belgium. A Belgian boiler-maker had sent the Archbishop of Paris a letter in which he offered to assassinate Bismarck for sixty thousand francs. Furthermore, the Belgian clergy, like the French, made no secret of its sympathies with the persecuted German Catholics and used strong language in discussing Bismarck's policy. The German government therefore sent a note to the Belgian government, early in February 1875, suggesting the need for a revision of Belgian law in the direction of securing greater protection for foreigners and making impossible such violent attacks upon a neighbouring state.

The note to Belgium was couched in rather strong terms and is an eloquent expression of Bismarck's irritation. The difficulties which arose from the religious struggle were getting on his mind and he was nervous and excitable. His closest friends in the foreign office could hardly remember a time when it was so difficult to get along with him. He was continually talking of resigning, and his physician told him that unless he took a rest, he would soon be *un homme fini*. [3] Added to the difficulties of the struggle at home were the problems of foreign policy. Italy had refused to follow the German example or even to support it. The chancellor accused the Italians of exploiting the tension between the Prussian government and the Vatican in the hope of reaching a settlement of their own difficulties with the Papacy. "We have become altogether indifferent towards Italy," he told the Austrian ambassador. [4] The Austrians, too, showed no inclination to follow the German lead. The Russians actually opened

---

[1] *Documents diplomatiques français*, I, Nos. 343, 345, 354.

[2] Salomon, in Hauser: *Histoire diplomatique de l'Europe*, I, p. 103, quoting unpublished material.

[3] *Letters of Queen Victoria*, II, p. 394; Holborn, op. cit., p. 142; Robert, Freiherr Lucius von Ballhausen: *Bismarck-Erinnerungen* (Stuttgart, 1921), pp. 38 ff.

[4] Wertheimer: *Andrássy*, II, p. 220; Salvemini, in *Rivista d'Italia*, February 15, 1925, pp. 187–8.

negotiations with the Vatican and on March 2, 1875 came to a provisional agreement on some of the outstanding differences.[1]

Worse yet, in Bismarck's view, was the coming meeting of Francis Joseph and Victor Emmanuel at Venice. The chancellor had originally been anxious to have Emperor William present at the interview. He strongly suspected the Austrians and Italians of an effort to join hands. In view of the known attempts of the French to secure the alliance of Austria, Russia, and England, there seemed to him to be real danger of an anti-German coalition in which France would play a prominent part. At any rate the French seemed to be making substantial military preparations. It was reported that they were buying ten thousand cavalry mounts in Germany, and soon afterwards news came from Paris that the French chamber had voted, on March 13, to add a fourth battalion to each regiment of the forces. These were intended to be skeleton battalions, but the German general staff believed that in any case the new provisions would greatly strengthen the French army. Bismarck was clearly quite anxious. Just what increase of the forces was involved in the new French law it is hard to say. The Germans calculated it at 144,000 men. This the French deny. Perhaps the truth may be found in a statement of a French writer who says that the law "increased notably the strength of our army, but above all it appeared to increase it even more than it actually did." [2]

The question of the new French military law had already been discussed by the leading organs of the German press when the first of a series of noteworthy articles dealing with the general European situation began to appear in various newspapers generally regarded as inspired by the government. On April 5 the *Cologne Gazette* published a letter " from Vienna " calling attention to the dangers of " new alliances." On April 8 the Berlin *Post* printed the best-known of these articles, entitled " Is War in Sight? " The emphasis here was laid not so much on the alliances as on the danger of the French armaments. The writer came to the conclusion that war was in sight, though he admitted that the threatening clouds might yet blow over.

Both the article in the *Cologne Gazette* and the article in the *Post* were written by officials of the press bureau of the German foreign office. There is no evidence that either was instructed to sound the alarm in this fashion, though it is likely that they reflected the general feeling of the chancellor, and that the latter saw no harm in occasionally throwing a lurid light on the confused situation. In 1876 he told the Reichstag that he did not object to the article in the *Post,* but that he did not knowingly cause it to be written: " He who shouts ' Fire! ' cannot be suspected of incendiarism. Were a minister bent upon urging the country to war, he would scarcely begin by kicking up a row in the press,

---

[1] Adrien Boudou: *Le Saint-Siège et la Russie, 1848–1883* (Paris, 1925), Volume II, pp. 342–6.

[2] Bourgeois and Pagès, op. cit., p. 165.

for that would be only to call out the fire-brigade." He had no intention of
making war on France, but he had no objection to an outspoken warning, the
more so as he had just received from the general staff a report on the significance
of the new French army arrangements.[1] On the other hand the semi-official
North German Gazette on April 10 and the *Provincial Gazette* on April 14
published articles intended to reassure public opinion, though they still insisted
on the danger of the French military preparations.

Whatever Bismarck's intentions may have been — it has been thought by
some writers that he planned to make a demand on France to reduce her armaments — the events of March and April created a stir in Paris. It may be said
at the outset that the French government certainly did not want war. In fact,
the French were not prepared to wage war at that time. The Duc de Decazes
promptly made reassuring statements to the German ambassador. Gontaut, on
his return to Berlin a few days later, talked the situation over in the most
friendly way with the officials of the German foreign office. The French denied
that even a single horse had been purchased in Germany, while the Germans
explained that the prohibition of the export of horses which had been issued
was a purely economic measure. They were not satisfied by the French explanations of the military bill, but they did not press the point. There was no real
tension. Emperor William, when he returned to the capital from Wiesbaden,
made no secret of his displeasure with these newspaper manœuvres, as he described them. In conversation with the French military attaché on April 15, he
spoke of the incident as closed. On both sides the most unequivocal assurances
had been given. [2]

But the most serious part of the crisis was still to come. The Duc de Decazes
was determined to capitalize the situation, and nothing shows this more clearly
than the recently published French documents. Fair-minded Frenchmen no
longer attempt to deny the responsibility of the French foreign minister, though
they try to explain his action by his peculiar restlessness of temperament and desire to score a success.[3] When Decazes learned of the German note to Belgium,
which was obligingly communicated by the German ambassador, he immediately
saw something symptomatic in it. On the basis of very inadequate evidence he assumed that a similar summons had been sent to Italy. The German prohibition
of the export of horses simply strengthened him in the conviction that something was astir. All these events, he wrote to the ambassador at London on
March 6, " seem to be connected with a complete system of action, in the application of which it is difficult to see how far Germany, which is now putting it
into practice, may become involved in the near future." To St. Petersburg he

---

[1] Paul Wentzke: *Bismarck und der deutsche Liberalismus*, Volume II, p. 124; Adalbert Wahl:
Deutsche Geschichte (Stuttgart, 1926), Volume I, pp. 354–5; *Die Grosse Politik*, I, Nos. 160, 161.
[2] Dreux, op. cit., p. 87; *Die Grosse Politik*, I, Nos. 162, 163; *Documents diplomatiques
français*, I, Nos. 358, 359, 365, 371, 379, 381, 389, 392.
[3] See especially the well-balanced and eminently fair discussion by Salomon, in Hauser:
Histoire diplomatique de l'Europe, I, pp. 103 ff.

wrote in a similar vein, adding that if Germany followed this " system " with her usual energy and perseverance it would soon lead to serious consequences.[1]

Now, there was nothing in the situation as it presented itself in the middle of March, weeks before the appearance of the *Post* article, to justify Decazes in attributing to Bismarck " sinister designs." Even Gorchakov could not overlook this fact, and he told the French chargé d'affaires that France showed too much uneasiness. There was really no danger. But Decazes refused to be put off. He had received news from his uncle, the ambassador at Vienna, that the Germans were placing orders for cartridges and shells, and that, in the opinion of an Austrian general, they would be militarily prepared by the end of June. Without the slightest delay the French foreign minister forwarded this information to the embassies at London, Vienna, St. Petersburg, and Berlin, insisting that " it is difficult for us to avoid a certain emotion in the light of an accumulation of reports which agree in showing Prussia multiplying her military preparations and applying herself to the completion of her armaments by the end of June." [2]

The reply that came from London was that the English government saw nothing on the continent that could cause alarm for the preservation of peace, at least for the current year. But just at that time the article " Is War in Sight? " appeared in Berlin. It caused considerable consternation, not only in Paris, but in London.[3] Yet at St. Petersburg the Tsar was still unmoved. He told the French ambassador, General Le Flô, that he did not believe that the Germans wanted war. Bismarck was simply summoning up imaginary dangers to make himself seem more indispensable. France must not be alarmed: " The interests of our two countries are common interests, and if you were some day to be threatened (which I do not believe), you shall know it at once. . . . You shall know it through me." [4] Gorchakov, too, gave what consolation he could, and promised that the Tsar and he himself would use their influence in the interest of peace, during a coming visit to Berlin.

By this time, it will be remembered, very explicit assurances had been exchanged between the French and German diplomats. The whole affair was apparently satisfactorily closed. Just then a report came to Decazes from Berlin supplying him with new ammunition. The French ambassador, Gontaut-Biron, had had a long talk with Herr von Radowitz after a dinner at the British embassy on April 21. Gontaut, a very officious person, had once again gone over the French explanations, and Radowitz had declared that the Germans felt perfectly reassured for the present, though he insisted that for the future it was

---

[1] *Documents diplomatiques français*, I, Nos. 359, 362, 370.

[2] *Documents diplomatiques français*, I, Nos. 373, 374, 375.

[3] *Die Grosse Politik*, I, Nos. 164–6; the evolution of the English attitude is well brought out, with the use of unpublished materials, by Winifred Taffs: " The War Scare of 1875 " (*Slavonic Review*, IX, pp. 335–49, December, 1930).

[4] *Documents diplomatiques français*, I, Nos. 388, 393.

impossible not to be anxious. Speaking academically of the French desire for revenge, he referred to the view held by some German party-leaders that a preventive war would be justified on " political, philosophical, and even on Christian grounds."

Radowitz afterwards denied that he had made such remarks, and asserted that Gontaut, after drawing him out, had reported the conversation with many exaggerations and additions. There is some truth in this, for Gontaut in his report attributed the theory of the preventive war to Bismarck and added that Austrian and English representatives at Berlin were uneasy for fear lest the Germans might take steps to check the reorganization of the French forces. Peace would probably be preserved for a year; but then? On the whole the report was misleading, but it is certainly true, as Bismarck maintained, that Radowitz was indiscreet in his conversation with the ambassador.[1]

At the close of his famous report Gontaut had raised the question whether it would not be desirable to keep the powers informed. Decazes hardly needed this suggestion. He had already called in the representative of the London *Times* to see if the great English newspaper could not be induced to raise the hue and cry. He now showed the correspondent, M. de Blowitz, Gontaut's report. Blowitz then wrote an alarmist letter to *The Times* in which he exposed the belligerent intentions of the Germans. But the editor of *The Times* hesitated until May 6 before publishing the letter, and then accompanied it with a leading article in which he ascribed the fears prevalent in Paris to the " heated fancy of our French neighbours." [2] By that time the decision of the English government had already been made. Blowitz's claim that his letter prevented war is nothing but the product of his overdeveloped sense of self-importance.

Not content with this démarche, Decazes was preparing for his great *coup de théâtre*. To the German ambassador he expressed the wish that some common ground might be found on which the two powers could co-operate and thus lay the basis for a better understanding. He pictured the military situation of France as deplorable and declared that even in case of attack the French would not fight. They would let the Germans take Paris and would withdraw behind the Loire River. If the Germans pursued them they would retreat to the Garonne.[3] But at the same time he forwarded to London, St. Petersburg, Vienna, The Hague, Rome, and Brussels copies of Gontaut's report of his talk with Radowitz. He acknowledged the assurances given by the German ambassador and admitted that the tension was over. But the theory of the preventive war, he insisted, was held by the party which controlled the intellectual and political direction of Germany. The German government had not yet

---

[1] *Documents diplomatiques français*, I, No. 395; Dreux, op. cit., p. 90; *Die Grosse Politik*, I, No. 177; Holborn, op. cit., p. 146; Radowitz: *Aufzeichnungen*, I, pp. 318 ff.

[2] See the florid and egotistical account in *The Memoirs of M. de Blowitz* (New York, 1903), chapter v, and the amusing but keen and critical account of the incident by Charles Lowe: " A Famous War Scare " (*Contemporary Review*, July 1903, pp. 91–111).

[3] *Die Grosse Politik*, I, Nos. 167, 169.

accepted the formula, but it might do so, and then all the European powers would be in danger.[1]

The broadcasting of the Gontaut report came at a crucial moment. The English had been receiving reports of the belligerent temper prevalent in Berlin and they suspected Bismarck of designs on Belgium. It was said that Bismarck meant to annihilate Belgium as the centre of political Catholicism, and that he might divide it between France and Holland, if the former could be induced to support Germany in her struggle with the Church.[2] Then came news of conversations which the Belgian minister at Berlin, M. de Nothomb, had had with Bismarck and Moltke, during the last days of April. The chancellor had warned the Belgian diplomat that the French might invade Belgium, and Moltke had pointed out that the new French army law involved an increase of 144,000 men. " This fact," he added, " is a peremptory announcement of preparation for war; in that case we must not wait until France is ready; our duty is to anticipate her." But war must be avoided if possible, he added, and he did not believe that it would come that year.[3]

The English statesmen, who at first insisted that Austria was more menaced than France, now began to fear for Belgium and for France. On May 3, before the publication of the Blowitz letter, Lord Derby, the foreign minister, had written to the ambassador at Berlin: " Is there no hope of Russian interference to maintain peace? It cannot be the interest of Russia to have France destroyed and Germany omnipotent." Two days later he wrote the Queen that he hoped much from the Tsar's visit to Berlin, which was to take place during the next few days. Victoria herself was of the opinion that England should, with the other powers, "hold the strongest language to both Powers [Germany and France], declaring that they *must not* fight, for that *Europe* would *not* stand another war!" Disraeli agreed. "Bismarck is really another old Bonaparte again, and he must be bridled," he remarked to one of his friends. To the foreign minister he wrote on May 6: "My own impression is that we shd. construct some concerted movement to preserve the peace of Europe, like Pam did when he baffled France and expelled the Egyptians from Syria. There might be an alliance between Russia and ourself for this special purpose; and other powers, as Austria, and perhaps Italy, might be invited to accede." On the following day Lord Odo Russell was instructed " to feel his way with the Emperor of Russia, as to the desirability of some common understanding to secure the peace of Europe." [4]

It has generally been supposed that the English government acted at Berlin

---

[1] *Documents diplomatiques français*, I, No. 399.

[2] Wemyss: *Memoirs of Sir Robert Morier*, II, p. 333.

[3] *Documents diplomatiques français*, I, No. 406; Dreux, op. cit., p. 105; Newton: *Lord Lyons*, II, p. 74; *Letters of Queen Victoria*, II, p. 389.

[4] Newton: *Lord Lyons*, II, pp. 75–8; *Letters of Queen Victoria*, II, p. 391; Monypenny and Buckle: *Life of Benjamin Disraeli*, V, pp. 421–2; *Documents diplomatiques français*, I, Nos. 400, 403, 405.

at the suggestion and request of the Russian government. The documents just referred to show that this was not so. Queen Victoria's letter to Emperor William in February 1874 was an independent action, and the decision taken in May 1875 was of the same character. It is true, however, that the démarche of 1875 was greatly strengthened by the determination of the Russian government to interpose a word at Berlin, and the whole step became more serious because of the agreement of the two powers to co-operate.

When the dispatch of the Duc de Decazes, together with a copy of Gontaut's report, reached General Le Flô, the French ambassador at St. Petersburg, he went straightway to Prince Gorchakov, whom he found reclining on a chaise longue, recovering from a fall. The two men discussed the situation, and the Russian chancellor persuaded the ambassador to submit to the Tsar himself the dispatch of Decazes, the report of Gontaut, and a personal letter from Decazes to Le Flô. Of this last document there appears to be no record, but it was evidently couched in much stronger language than the official dispatch. When Gorchakov had read it, he jumped from his chair like a young man and immediately forwarded all three documents to the Tsar. This appears to have been on May 3. On the very next day Le Flô was able to report to his government the reply of Alexander. The Tsar confirmed all that he had said to the ambassador a couple of weeks before: namely, that if France were really threatened, she would know about it immediately, and from the Tsar himself. As Le Flô pointed out in his report to Decazes, this did not imply a promise to wage war in common with France, a thing which Decazes seems to have hinted at in his personal letter, but it gave France the assurance that Russia, in company with Austria (so Le Flô thought), would not allow Prussia to make war on France again simply for her own satisfaction and to escape the terror which the poor sick lion called France still inspired.[1]

The Russians were quite guarded in their promises to France, but Gorchakov at least was determined to make use of the opportunity to put Bismarck and the Germans in their proper place. There can be no doubt that he was actuated by jealousy of his "former pupil" Bismarck, and that he hoped to satisfy his notorious vanity by a resounding moral victory. He did not wish to take leave of public life like a snuffed-out candle, but like the sun, whose last rays shed a dazzling radiance over the landscape, as he himself expressed it.

It was important for the success of Gorchakov's policy that he should secure the assistance of the other powers, especially England. But that was not easy, for Russia and England had been steadily drifting apart since the Russians, by the occupation of Khiva, had broken their pledge in regard to central Asia and had resumed their advance. By the spring of 1875 a conflict between the two powers was by no means beyond the range of possibility. Bismarck, curiously enough, had done his utmost to prevent a break and had repeatedly warned

---

[1] *Documents diplomatiques français*, I, No. 404.

the English of this danger. Gorchakov himself was evidently anxious to avoid complications and had already taken the initiative by assuring the English ambassador that the idea of a Russian attack on India was absurd: " We wish to maintain the closest accord with England, and I declare to you that as long as the Emperor reigns, and as long as I am here, you may count on our good intentions — on our pacific policy. I repeat, we do not want to extend our possessions. . . . Why not believe in our sincerity? " These overtures the English followed up eagerly. Count Peter Shuvalov, the Russian ambassador at London, returned to St. Petersburg for instructions. He arrived at London again on May 8, armed with the most unequivocal promises that Russia would advance no farther in Asia and that various projects for expansion in that region had been countermanded. Not only that. He brought news of the intended intervention of the Tsar in Berlin, stated that Austria would hold the same language as Russia, asked the English government to take part in the action, and suggested that the Italians also should be brought in.[1]

But by this time instructions had already been sent to the English ambassador at Berlin. Russell was to express the opinion of the English government that France was not arming for a war of revenge and he was to offer the services of the English government in smoothing out misunderstandings. This he did on the morning of May 9 in conversation with the under-secretary of the German foreign office. On the following day the Russian Tsar and his chancellor, Prince Gorchakov, arrived in Berlin. Alexander, who had never believed seriously in the danger of a German attack upon France, was easily reassured. In fact, he said later that on his arrival he found everything quiet and nothing to pacify.

The really crucial phase of the matter, however, was the conversation between Bismarck and Gorchakov. The German chancellor was fully prepared for his Russian colleague, for Count Shuvalov, passing through Berlin a few days before, had warned Bismarck of what was coming. The discussion appears to have been a very acrimonious one. Bismarck more or less took the wind out of the Russian sails by asserting to begin with that he was actuated only by the most pacific intentions. If Gorchakov had hopes of securing from the chancellor a written promise not to attack France, he was gravely mistaken.

In the evening Russell was invited to dine with Bismarck. The English démarche had been a guarded one and had not aroused the ire of the German statesman. In fact, he thanked Russell for " the very friendly offer, which he highly appreciated as a proof of goodwill and confidence on the part of Her Majesty's Government." But before the two men parted company, Gorchakov arrived and told of having heard from London how earnestly the English government desired peace and how strongly it supported the efforts of Russia in

---

[1] Holborn, op. cit., pp. 35–7; Loftus: *Reminiscences*, II, pp. 127–30; Newton: *Lord Lyons*, II, pp. 75–6; *Letters of Queen Victoria*, II, p. 394; *Documents diplomatiques français*, I, Nos. 408, 410, 413, 426, 438.

the interests of peace. The sequence of events is not entirely clear at this point. It seems that the instructions sent to Russell and acted upon on May 9 had been drawn up before Shuvalov arrived in London with the suggestions of the Russians. This English action was very circumspect and, as aforesaid, did not offend Bismarck. Whether there was a second and stronger set of instructions sent to Russell, ordering him to support the Russian move, is not certain, though it seems very likely. At any rate, Bismarck was surprised by Gorchakov's remarks, the more so as he learned that other governments had been invited to take part in the action. To cap it all, Gorchakov could not resist the temptation of telegraphing to the Russian representatives abroad that the Tsar was leaving Berlin completely convinced of the conciliatory disposition prevalent there, which assured the maintenance of peace.[1]

It was evidently only after Bismarck realized fully the grand scale of the intervention that had been planned that he lost his temper. In his memoirs he tells of having reproached Gorchakov in the most sarcastic manner: " It was not, I said, a friendly part to jump suddenly and unexpectedly upon the back of a trustful and unsuspecting friend, and to get up a circus performance at his cost; proceedings of this kind between us, the directing ministers, could only injure the two monarchies and the two states. If he was anxious to be applauded in Paris, he need not on that account injure our relations with Russia; I was quite ready to assist him and to have five-franc pieces struck at Berlin, with the inscription: ' Gorchakov protège la France.' We might also set up a theatre at the German embassy in Paris, where he could appear before a French audience holding a placard with the same inscription, in the character of a guardian angel, dressed in white and supplied with wings, to the accompaniment of Bengal fire." [2] It is not at all unlikely that he really made remarks of this kind, for Gorchakov seemed much sobered when he spoke to the French ambassador. Bismarck, he said, was most peacefully inclined and did not share the theories attributed to Radowitz. There was no danger of war. And, he added, the French must not appear too satisfied, they must not make a parade. A few months later, after he had had time to think over his campaign, he told the French ambassador to Vienna, whom he met in Switzerland, that at bottom the whole affair rested upon suppositions which had been taken for realities, upon the reveries of military men with a plan of campaign in their heads, upon remarks awkwardly made by Berlin statesmen, and especially upon the exaggerations of the newspapers: " The cause pleaded by Russia was won in advance." He was clearly anxious not to be given too much credit in the whole affair.[3]

---

[1] *Die Grosse Politik*, I, Nos. 174–83; *Documents diplomatiques français*, I, Nos. 410, 422, 434; Newton: *Lord Lyons*, II, p. 78; P. Sabourof: " *Russie, France, Allemagne (1870–1880)* " (*Revue de Paris*, March 15, 1912). There is a good discussion of the English action in Japikse: *Europa und Bismarcks Friedenspolitik*, pp. 47 ff.

[2] *Bismarck, the Man and the Statesman*, II, p. 191.

[3] *Documents diplomatiques français*, I, Nos. 416, 418, 419, and the annexe; Hauser: *Histoire diplomatique*, I, p. 113.

The English came off somewhat easier, though Russell suspected that Bismarck "behind our backs raves like a maniac and swears he will take his revenge." But this did not disturb the English statesmen. Disraeli in particular felt that England had been very fortunate in her policy, for "what we did involved no risk and cost no trouble, while it has given us the appearance of having helped, more than we really did, to bring about the result." After all, "we must not be afraid of saying ' Bo to a goose,' " he wrote to Derby. Later on, when some friction developed between London and Berlin because of Derby's reference to the "warlike rumours" which had been spread by persons high at the German court, the Queen wrote to her daughter, the German Crown Princess: "No one wishes more, as you know, than I do for England and Germany to go well together; but Bismarck is so overbearing, violent, grasping and unprincipled that *no one* can stand it, and *all* agreed that he was becoming like the first Napoleon whom Europe had to join in PUTTING down." This statement throws a flood of light on the psychological elements that played into the crisis.[1]

The other powers had not joined England and Russia in the intervention at Berlin. Gorchakov maintained afterwards what he had told the English at the time, that "from the first period of the scare there had been a perfectly frank interchange of ideas between the Russian and Austrian Cabinets and an entente cordiale to act in common." The fact that Austria rejected the English suggestion he explained by saying that Andrássy relied upon the Tsar's success: "He [Alexander] had, as it were . . . held Austria's full powers as well as Russia's."[2] This was certainly a gross exaggeration. The truth seems to be that Andrássy stood aloof and maintained neutrality, that he was glad to see Bismarck taken down a peg by receiving a lecture, and that he was delighted to see Gorchakov take the brunt of Bismarck's indignation. It is said that when he learned of the Russian plan, he was so pleased that he jumped upon his desk and turned up on his hands three times like an exuberant and delighted child, crying: "Bismarck will never forgive that! "[3] Furthermore, when the Italians approached him for advice as to what they should do, he counselled reserve, and the Italian démarche was, in fact, taken much later, was not official, and carefully avoided the appearance of being part of a collective action.[4]

It goes without saying that Decazes was elated by the course which events had taken. On May 18 he sent a dispatch to the more important French representatives abroad in which he enlarged on the "veritable movement of the public conscience" against the German peril. He spoke with feeling of the

---

[1] Wemyss: *Memoirs of Sir Robert Morier*, II, p. 355; Monypenny and Buckle: op. cit., V, pp. 423–4; *Letters of Queen Victoria*, II, pp. 402–7; *Die Grosse Politik*, I, Nos. 184–8.

[2] Wemyss: *Morier*, II, p. 362.

[3] Wertheimer: *Andrássy*, II, p. 243.

[4] Salvemini, in *Rivista d'Italia*, February 15, 1925, pp. 192–3; *Documents diplomatiques français*, I, Nos. 411, 417, 423, 425.

action of Russia and England and took the view that the pacific assurances given by the Germans could now be regarded as something akin to an engagement to preserve the peace. Germany could now be called to account by the powers if the promise were violated. Special thanks were sent to London and St. Petersburg. In the dispatch intended for London Decazes expressed gratitude for England's part in saving France from a menacing peril, and then went on to say that Europe not only was now aware of the dangers which might arise from the restless passions which had survived the war on the other side of the Rhine, but knew also that the road was now open to a common understanding among the countries which sincerely wished to preserve the benefits of peace, and that such an understanding would be sufficient to oblige the most redoubtable military power to abandon and even disavow its projects of aggression.[1]

Decazes was certainly exaggerating, especially when he insisted on attributing to Bismarck the most sinister designs. French writers who have carefully examined the evidence have given up the idea that the German chancellor was planning to wage a preventive war. A reading of the recently published French documents should convince even the most sceptical that Decazes did not have evidence at his disposal sufficient to warrant the conclusions he reached or pretended to reach. He simply exploited the situation as it arose in the spring of 1875 and managed to play on the fears or vanities of Russia and England to such an extent that they undertook an action which assumed rather serious proportions and in some respects had rather grave consequences, especially for Russia. In speaking of the intervention a Russian diplomat once referred to its importance " as being the first indication of a *moral coalition*." [2] This appreciation is juster than that of Decazes. Bismarck had sustained a diplomatic setback, of that there can be no doubt. He himself frequently referred to the episode in later life, showing how deep was the impression it made and how much importance he attached to it. On these occasions, as in 1875, he always insisted that his attitude towards France was not *Up and at them*, but rather *Let them come on*. He did not plan to attack France. On the contrary, he appears to have cherished the idea of effecting a better relationship between the two countries.

Bismarck hoped to be able to relieve the pressure on the Franco-German frontier by diverting France to colonial activity and giving her support in all questions apart from the fundamental question of Alsace and Lorraine. In December 1873, when the relations between Germany and Italy were close, he had warned the French in no uncertain terms against taking action in Tunis, where the Italians, too, had ambitions. In January 1875, on the other hand, he wrote the ambassador at Paris, Prince Hohenlohe, that Germany had no objections to French activity in these regions: " The absorption of power which France

---

[1] *Documents diplomatiques français*, I, Nos. 427–30.
[2] Loftus: *Reminiscences*, II, p. 133.

expends and ties up there, and the difficulties which France makes for herself there, are a drain for her aggressive tendencies towards Germany." [1]

Of course this was merely an indication of a new policy. But in the midst of the crisis, in April, when the Duc de Decazes in conversation with Hohenlohe bemoaned the fact that there was no possibility of co-operation between France and Germany, the German chancellor immediately seized upon this opening. He suggested the possibility of an understanding on such questions as Africa and the Levant, Italy, Spain, and Belgium. In the last three countries a strengthening of the government's authority would be to the common good of Germany and France, and some agreement might be come to with regard to the future settlement of the papal question, assuming that the successor of Pius IX would be more ready to compromise than was Pius himself. [2] Nothing came of this advance, however. Decazes started to communicate the German proposals to the ambassador at Berlin, but the whole passage dealing with the matter was then cut out of the dispatch before it was sent. [3] Then came the intervention of England and Russia at Berlin, which made further discussion from the German side quite impossible. But the incident is of decided interest, for it shows that Bismarck, at the very time that the most reprehensible designs were being attributed to him, was beginning to feel for an understanding with France on a basis which was later accepted by Jules Ferry and became the foundation of the entente between the two countries in the years 1883-5. Bismarck's idea was obviously to divert the attention and energy of the French from the question of the Franco-German frontier and to nip in the bud a possible combination between France and one of the other great powers.

When the English ambassador at Berlin offered mediation in the Franco-German difficulty (May 9), Bismarck expressed his surprise and insisted that his government was on friendly terms with France. "As proof of friendly relations," Russell reported, "he would tell me that negotiation of a treaty or convention was under discussion between them which would tend to remove any apprehensions." [4] This was putting it rather strongly, and some writers have maintained that the understanding was not sincerely meant on either side. In support of this view a letter of June 20, 1875 from Bismarck's son Herbert to Radowitz has been adduced. In this letter Bismarck suggests, through his son, that in view of the newspaper talk of an Anglo-Russian understanding, an inspired article be published emphasizing the possibility of a Franco-German entente: "In any case, real material bases could be more easily found for co-operation between Germany and France than for co-operation between Russia and England. . . . The whole scheme [*Combination*] would certainly be ab-

---

[1] *Die Grosse Politik*, I, No. 194.

[2] *Die Grosse Politik*, I, Nos. 167 ff.

[3] *Documents diplomatiques français*, I, No. 402.

[4] Unpublished telegram quoted by Japikse: *Europa und Bismarcks Friedenspolitik*, p. 198.

surd [*unsinnig*], but the idea of an Anglo-Russian combination would be at least just as absurd." In view of the Russian machinations, continued Bismarck, it might be good policy to match the Russian soap-bubble with a German one quite as wondrous.[1]

This remarkable letter really proves very little. In the first place, it was written after the failure of Bismarck's attempt to approach France; and, in the second place, if it shows anything, it shows that the chancellor regarded an understanding with his neighbour as practically impossible. It does not prove that he looked upon it as undesirable. As a matter of fact, the idea was given another trial later, and with greater success. Of course the great obstacle to a permanent agreement was the question of the lost provinces. The French diplomats made no secret of this, and Bismarck undoubtedly appreciated it more than anyone else. But it seems certain that in April 1875 his mind was more set on reaching an agreement with France than on attacking her. It was the strategy of Decazes working on the insurmountable suspicions of the powers with respect to Bismarck and his policy that doomed the whole program to failure. The entire period from 1871 to 1875 was a formative period, during which the European states were attempting to adjust themselves to the changed conditions which resulted from a period of successive wars. Bismarck, fearful of a French attack in a short time, had attempted to build up a coalition and to isolate France. But his coalition lacked a strong foundation and was not sufficiently stable. Decazes, with a complete plan for confounding Bismarck and securing the sympathy and support of the powers, had little difficulty in playing upon their apprehensions. It was obviously not to the interest of any of the great powers to see France defeated again and completely annihilated. So they fell in with Decazes's scheme and saved France from a danger that did not exist, perhaps not even in the mind of the French foreign minister himself. Bismarck's position was, for the moment, an unenviable one. But the crisis had this one good point: it indicated the direction and strength of the various currents in European politics and thus served to clarify the general situation.

BIBLIOGRAPHICAL NOTE

DOCUMENTARY SOURCES

Die Grosse Politik der europäischen Kabinette, 1871–1914. Volume I, chapter vi: Franco-German Relations, 1873–1874; vii: The War Scare of 1875.

Documents diplomatiques français. Volume I, covering the period 1871–5.

[1] Hajo Holborn: "*Bismarck und Schuwalow im Jahre 1875*" (*Historische Zeitschrift*, CXXX, pp. 256–77, 1924).

MEMOIRS, AUTOBIOGRAPHIES, BIOGRAPHIES, AND LETTERS

NEWTON, LORD: *Lord Lyons.* Two volumes. London, 1913.

MONYPENNY, W. F., and BUCKLE, GEORGE E.: *The Life of Benjamin Disraeli.* Six volumes. London, 1910–20. Contains a mass of valuable material from the papers of the English prime minister. A source of first-rate importance.

The Letters of QUEEN VICTORIA. Second Series. Edited by George E. Buckle. Two volumes. London, 1926. Contains many entries of interest.

BLOWITZ, HENRY S.: *My Memoirs.* London, 1903. The recollections of the *Times* correspondent at Paris, who had some connexion with the events of 1875.

DREUX, ANDRÉ: *Dernières Années de l'ambassade de M. de Gontaut-Biron, 1874–1877.* Paris, 1907. Continues the story of Gontaut-Biron's embassy. Still valuable, as it contains private correspondence which is not printed in the *Documents diplomatiques français.*

Aufzeichnungen und Erinnerungen des Botschafters JOSEPH MARIA VON RADO-WITZ. Two volumes. Berlin, 1925. Very important for the history of Radowitz's mission to Russia and his conversation with Gontaut-Biron.

SABOUROF, P.: " *Russie, France, Allemagne (1870–1880)* " (*Revue de Paris,* March 15, 1912). Contains accounts of what happened in Berlin on May 10, 1875, as told to the author by the leading participants.

SPECIAL TOPICS

CURÀTULO, GIACOMO: *La Questione Romana da Cavour a Mussolini.* Rome, 1928. A brief survey of the development of the Roman question.

LULVÈS, J.: " *Bismarck und die römische Frage* " (*Deutsche Revue,* May and June 1916). A careful documented study.

JOHNSON, HUMPHREY: *The Papacy and the Kingdom of Italy.* London, 1926. A good general book on the Roman question as a problem of Italian politics.

WOODWARD, E. L.: " The Diplomacy of the Vatican under Popes Pius IX and Leo XIII " (*Journal of the British Institute of International Affairs,* May 1924). Brings together most of the recent material on the question.

LITERATURE ON THE WAR SCARE OF 1875

SCHERER, EDMOND: " *L'Alarme de 1875* " (*Revue Politique et littéraire,* August 13, 1887). Based chiefly on the revelations of General Le Flô in 1887.

GEFFCKEN, HEINRICH: " *Die russisch-französische Allianz und der Dreibund in geschichtlicher Beleuchtung* " (*Deutsche Revue,* October and December 1892). Written by a member of the circle of the German Crown Prince. Very hostile to Bismarck.

SENEX DIPLOMATICUS: *" Der Kriegslarm von 1875 "* *(Deutsche Revue,* June 1893). Thinks Bismarck regarded war as inevitable and was preparing for it.

Anonymous: " The War Scare of 1875 " *(Fortnightly Review,* December 1889). A well-informed account.

BLENNERHASSET, ROWLAND: " The Threatened War of 1875 " *(National Review,* November 1905). Adds nothing.

LOWE, CHARLES: "A Famous War Scare " *(Contemporary Review,* July 1903). A scathing criticism of Blowitz's account and an apology for Bismarck.

DAUDET, ERNEST: *" Autour de la crise de 1875 "* *(Revue des deux mondes,* April 15, 1915). The best formulation of the French view as it was before the publication of the German documents and other material.

FULLER, JOSEPH V.: " The War Scare of 1875 " *(American Historical Review,* January 1919). A very careful study, but decidedly hostile to the German view.

WAHL, ADALBERT: *Vom Bismarck der siebziger Jahre.* Tübingen, 1920. Stresses especially the connexion between the religious problem and Franco-German tension.

HERZFELD, HANS: *Die deutsch-französische Kriegsgefahr von 1875.* Berlin, 1922. On the whole the best monographic study of the crisis, though already superseded in part by later material.

SCHOCH, GENERAL G. VON: *" Der Kriegslarm von 1875 "* *(Deutsche Revue,* August and September 1922). A careful treatment, but written before the publication of the German documents.

HOLBORN, HAJO: *" Bismarck und Schuwalow im Jahre 1875 "* *(Historische Zeitschrift,* CXXX, 1924). Throws considerable light on the position of Russia and England. Based on unpublished material.

—: *Bismarcks europäische Politik zu Beginn der siebziger Jahre und die Mission Radowitz.* Berlin, 1925. A valuable contribution which completes the clarification of the Radowitz mission.

KLINGENFUSS, KARL: *" Beust und Andrássy und die Kriegsgefahr von 1875 "* *(Archiv für Politik und Geschichte,* IV, 1926). Based on material in the Austrian archives. Throws light on the intrigues of Beust and the policy of Andrássy.

LAJUSAN, ALFRED: *" L'Alerte diplomatique du printemps 1875, d'après les nouvelles publications "* *(Revue d'Histoire moderne,* October–November 1926). An excellent and fair technical discussion of the material that appeared after 1920.

JOUWERSMA, W. J.: *De duitsch-fransche Oorlogscrisis van 1875 en haar Voorgeschiedenis.* Leiden, 1928. One of the latest and most complete monographic accounts.

TAFFS, WINIFRED: " The War Scare of 1875 " *(Slavonic Review,* IX, pp. 335–49, December 1930). The first part of an extended review of the question, based upon unpublished material in the British record office and the German archives.

III

The Balkan Problem

THE INSURRECTION IN BOSNIA AND HERZEGOVINA

～

THE EXCITEMENT AND TENSION OF THE WAR SCARE HAD HARDLY SUBSIDED when the European governments found themselves confronted with a problem quite as serious and infinitely more complicated than the question of Franco-German relations. In July 1875 a rising of the Christian population took place in the province of Herzegovina, situated to the north-west of Montenegro, adjacent to Bosnia, at the very extremes of the Turkish Empire in Europe, Insurrections of this kind were by no means uncommon, but each one sent a tremor through the European chancelleries, for the general situation in the Near East was such that any local disturbance might end in a general crisis of the first magnitude. At bottom the difficulty arose from the fact that the Ottoman government controlled most of the Balkan Peninsula as well as Asia Minor, Arabia, and North Africa. By far the largest part of the population of the Balkans was non-Turk and Christian. There were Greeks, Bulgarians, Albanians, Roumanians, and Serbs, to mention only the most important racial groups. Most of these belonged to the Orthodox Greek Catholic Church, though there was a considerable Roman Catholic element in northern Albania and Bosnia, and of course a sprinkling of Mohammedans everywhere.

Prior to the nineteenth century the Turkish rule over alien peoples of Christian religion had not caused much difficulty. The Turks had shown no inclination to persecute the Christians. In fact, Mohammed the Conqueror had, in the later fifteenth century, delegated to the Greek Patriarch at Constantinople extensive civil as well as religious authority over the Christian population, and all those who professed the Greek Orthodox faith had been regarded simply as Greeks, so far as the Turkish government was concerned. There had been comparatively little contact between the government and the subject Christians, for the administration had been almost entirely in the hands of the so-called phanariot Greeks. Many of these had gone to great extremes in the direction of extortion and general oppression and had earned the cordial hatred of the non-Greek nationalities. But conditions were probably not worse than in many other parts of Europe. In the sixteenth century many prominent writers in western Europe had compared the situation of the Christians under Turkish rule very favourably with that of their own populations in the West. Even at a much later time there does not appear to have been unusual suffering on the part of the Balkan peoples. Conditions were primitive, to say the least, for the peoples of the Balkans had never been really civilized. Some, like the Bulgarians and the Serbs, had had a spectacular history and had, for brief periods, controlled most of the peninsula, but they had always been organized in a loose, tribal fashion and had had little in the way of culture to point back to. The condition of the Greeks, of course, had been somewhat different, but then, they had from the start enjoyed a rather special position in the Ottoman Empire.

The real difficulties of race and religion began to arise in the Balkans in the earlier nineteenth century, when the influence of the French Revolution and the general movement of Western ideas first made itself felt in the East. The Turkish government had been sinking into apathy for some time and had suffered severely from wars with the rising power of Russia, as well as from the conflicts of the Napoleonic period. Everywhere, throughout the immense territory, local potentates were setting themselves up as semi-independent rulers, while the pressure of international antagonisms was threatening the early disruption of the Turkish state. In the first part of the century the revolt of the Greeks, which ended ultimately in the establishment of Greek independence, marked the first real victory of nationalism and the first triumph of Western ideas. The need for reform was obvious, and ever since the end of the eighteenth century attempts had been made by the sultans to reorganize the government on a modernized basis, in order the better to assert their authority over the fractious pashas and to meet on more equal terms the impact of the great powers. It goes without saying that the earliest reforms were in the direction of military reorganization and administrative change. In these respects considerable progress was made. Mahmud II, in spite of his unsuccessful struggle with the Greeks and his disastrous war with the Russians, succeeded in reasserting the authority of the central government and in suppressing the rebellious pashas, with the exception of Mehemet Ali of Egypt.

To be sure, the work of the reforming sultans left much to be desired. It should be remembered, however, that great obstacles stood in the way of a thorough-going modernization of the Turkish system. First and foremost, the close connexion between religion and government, resulting in the complete subordination of government to the precepts of the Koran, made many measures of reform appear like sacrilege and tended to arouse the opposition of the devout. Secondly, the extent of the empire, reaching, as it did, from the Danube and Sava in the north-west to Persia, the Persian Gulf, and the Red Sea in the south-east and to Algeria in the western Mediterranean, was so great that it was almost impossible, in those days before railway and steamship transportation, to bind the outlying provinces closely to the capital. In ages past great Oriental empires like the Ottoman had usually fallen apart within a short time from the death of the founder, and the same might well have been true of the

Turkish state had it not occupied a strategic position of unusual strength and had not the rivalries of other nations served as a sort of protection. On the other hand, the interests of the powers in the Near Eastern area had become greater and greater with the development of better communications between Europe and Asia. Consequently the pressure at Constantinople, both by the governments which sincerely desired the maintenance of the empire and wished it to reform, and by those which pressed for reform in order to create difficulties for the Turkish cabinet, became so great that the Porte was usually given no time to carry through projected measures with the necessary consistency. The European powers, which had gone through the most violent struggles and acute crises in evolving the modern state, seemed to expect the Ottoman government to effect this change on the spur of the moment, though the difficulties with which it had to contend were much greater than those faced by almost any other nation.

To add to the inherent obstacles in the way of reform there came the movement of ideas from the West in the nineteenth century. The romantic movement in literature, which did so much to revive national languages as literary media and to recall to submerged nationalities the glories of their past history, led, in the second quarter of the century, to a pronounced growth of the spirit of nationalism among the Balkan peoples. The case of the Serbs is particularly instructive. They had revolted as early as 1804, and by 1830 had secured a position of autonomy within the empire. At the time this was all they desired, and Miloš Obrenovič, the first prince, was quite content to regard himself as a pasha with wide powers under the authority of the sultan. Not until after 1848 — that is, not until after the Serbo-Croat national revival was well under way — was there a genuine demand for a liberal constitutional government in Serbia and talk of complete independence. Even Alexander Ypsilanti, leader of the Greek rising in 1821, still cherished the idea of remaking the Ottoman Empire under a Russian emperor, rather than the idea of destroying it. In the minds of the earlier leaders the feeling of imperial solidarity was still so strong that they regarded the Ottoman Empire much as the peoples of the West had regarded the Holy Roman Empire.[1]

Before long, however, the idea of national self-determination and national union began to take root among members of the younger generation, many of whom had been educated in the West. The influence of the unification of Italy can hardly be overemphasized. Serbia, it was said, must be the Piedmont of the Balkans and must unite all the southern Slavs of the Balkans, and eventually those of Austria-Hungary, under one rule. In the person of Prince Michael Obrenovič(1860–8) these ideas took firm shape. When, in 1866–7, Crete rose in revolt and succeeded in securing a special position within the empire, Michael made an agreement with Roumania (May 26, 1866) to work in common for

---

[1] See especially the illuminating article of Nicholas Iorga: " *L'Origine des idées d'indépendance balkanique* " (*Le Monde slave*, IV, pp. 73–93, July 1927).

liberation from Turkish suzerainty and for complete independence. This agreement was followed at brief intervals by a Serbian-Montenegrin Treaty (September 23, 1866), a tentative Greek-Roumanian Treaty (February 1867), the crucial Serbian-Greek Treaty (August 26, 1867) and the military convention between Greece and Serbia of February 28, 1868. Under the terms of the Greek-Serbian Agreement Greece was to get Thessaly and Epirus, while Serbia was to acquire Bosnia and Herzegovina. Both sides agreed to agitate among the subject Christians and to prepare them for revolt against the Turks. Action was to be taken in 1868. Eventually, it was hoped, a Balkan confederation might be established.[1]

The plans of Prince Michael came to naught, for he was assassinated in 1868 before action could be taken. But the whole scheme indicates how far the ideas of nationality had gone in the Balkans, and how dangerous they had become for the Ottoman Empire. After all, the Western idea of nationality presupposed a territorial basis, and therefore its triumph was just as dangerous for the Turkish government as for the Austro-Hungarian or Russian governments. The result was a fundamental conflict in the ideas of reform as entertained by the liberal Turks and those put forward among the Christians. "It may be well said that the nineteenth century played a game of hide and seek with the word 'reform' as applied to Turkey," says Gabriel Hanotaux.[2] The so-called Young Turks took their ideas from the French Revolution and desired the institution of a strong centralized government which would knit the parts of the empire together more closely than ever. What the Christians desired was the very reverse. If they did not actually demand independence or union with their co-nationals outside the confines of the empire, they at least demanded a semi-independent position with complete autonomy — in other words, a large measure of decentralization. As for the European powers, they rarely specified what they meant by reform, some being more interested in the maintenance of the empire, while others concerned themselves rather with the position of the subject nationalities.

In the two provinces of Bosnia and Herzegovina the problem was particularly aggravating, for acute social problems played into the religious and racial difficulties. Being at the extreme confines of the empire, these provinces had never been much under the control of the central government. The local feudal nobility had, to a large extent, accepted Mohammedanism in order to retain its property and power and, though Serbian by race, ruled the country in the most oppressive fashion with the aid of the Janizaries, a privileged corps of troops. The peasantry was almost entirely Serbo-Croatian by race, but was

---

[1] See M. Lhéritier: " Le Traité d'alliance secret entre la Grèce et la Serbie " (Revue des Études napoléoniennes, September–October 1924); S. T. Lascaris: " La première alliance entre la Grèce et la Serbie. Le Traité de Voeslau du 26 Août 1867 " (Le Monde slave, III, pp. 390–437, September 1926), and the extensive references there given.
[2] Gabriel Hanotaux: Histoire de la France contemporaine (Paris, 1908), IV, p. 80.

divided religiously, about one third being Roman Catholic, the remainder Greek Orthodox. Insurrections were chronic during the nineteenth century, hardly a decade passing without some outbreak. Many of these risings, however, were not revolts of Christians against Turkish oppression, but of the Mohammedanized nobility against the officials of the central government. Their grievance was that the government, in attempting to improve the position of the Christians by the reform measures of 1839 and 1856, was infringing on the prerogatives of the Moslem landlords and attacking their privileges. Time and again the government was obliged to organize campaigns against them on a large scale. When their power was finally broken, in 1851, regular officials took their place in the administration. How much improvement in the position of the peasantry resulted from this change it is hard to say. During the years 1860 to 1869 the provinces enjoyed efficient and enlightened government under Osman Pasha. The British consul reported in 1871 that conditions were much better than they had been twenty-five years before; that, in fact, there had been "an immense general improvement everywhere" in Turkey since 1840.[1] But the Turkish administration was unquestionably corrupt, and there can be no doubt that only a few of the guarantees secured to the Christians by the reforms of 1856 were actually effective. The taxes were as numerous as the dues which existed in western Europe under the old régime; they were arbitrarily levied and ruthlessly collected, while the administration of justice was evidently a mockery of the word.[2]

Whether the wretched conditions in the two provinces would alone have induced the population to rise has been questioned by many writers. The inhabitants had lived for centuries under conditions which appeared to the more modern Europeans to be atrocious. Usually local disturbances ended in the migration of some fifty or a hundred people over the neighbouring frontiers, where they caused the Austro-Hungarian, Serbian, and Montenegrin governments considerable economic embarrassment. But in such cases it was not always clear whether the purpose of the migration was to escape the insufferable conditions under which the refugees claimed to be living, or whether the purpose was to stir up trouble and provoke foreign intervention. The repeated flights of merchants from Bosnia into Serbia were suspected of serving some such ulterior motive. The British consul, Mr. Holmes, could see no particular reason for the outbreak of 1875 and noted that those who first made trouble were from the "richest and most prosperous district."

But the question of Balkan unrest at this time cannot be understood

---

[1] Quoted by the Duke of Argyll: *The Eastern Question* (London, 1879), I, pp. 75–8.

[2] See William Miller: *The Ottoman Empire* (Cambridge, 1913), pp. 358 ff.; Theodor von Sosnosky: *Die Balkanpolitik Österreich-Ungarns seit 1866* (Stuttgart, 1913), I, pp. 108 ff. Good accounts of the conditions at the time may be found in A. J. Evans: *Through Bosnia and Herzegovina on Foot* (London, 1876); Dr. Josef Koetschet: *Aus Bosniens letzter Türkenzeit* (Vienna, 1905); W. J. Stillman: *Herzegovina and the Late Uprising* (London, 1877); Charles Yriarte: *Bosnie et Herzégovine* (Paris, 1876).

without reference to the activities of outside agitators. It will be remembered that the Greek-Serbian Treaty of 1867 provided specifically that subversive activity should be carried on in the Turkish provinces with the object of provoking insurrection. After the assassination of Prince Michael, in 1868, the driving power of the Serbian national movement passed from the hands of the Prince. Milan, the successor of Michael, was a mere boy, who, even after he came of age, showed little sympathy for the dangerous agitation of the patriots. But in the years from 1868 to 1875 the political situation in Serbia was very uncertain. The princely throne was unsteady and Milan himself was helpless against powerful politicians like Ristič who enjoyed the support of revolutionary and nationalist societies like the Omladina. While Milan sought support in Vienna and denounced the activities of the secret organizations, these organizations themselves continued in the tradition of Prince Michael, agitating for a crusade against the Turks and for the eventual union of all the southern Slavs under Serbian leadership. Baron Kállay, an eminent authority on Balkan affairs who was at that time Austrian representative at Belgrade, reported to his government in 1873 that "the erroneous idea according to which Serbia is called upon to play among the Slavs of Turkey the role of Piedmont is so firmly rooted in Serbia that the Serbs can no longer understand that the Slavs of the different Turkish frontiers should seek aid and protection from any state except Serbia."[1]

In much the same strain one of the Belgrade papers wrote on May 12, 1874: "Present-day Serbia is the first result of the revolutionary process of the dismemberment of Turkey; consequently it is a personified negation. . . . Her natural mission is to free her brother peoples of the Balkan Peninsula from the Asiatic yoke and to fulfil the future of all the Serbs."[2] In November of the same year the Serbian national assembly, in its address to the throne, expressed the same idea, though in veiled terms: "To direct the scattered forces of our people towards a serious common action, to reach an understanding with and to draw closer to the related peoples who have the same objectives, the same interests, and the same dangers, that is the road along which the national Skuptchina desires ardently to see its illustrious sovereign travel."[3] The Serbian national aspirations were perfectly clear, and even though the Prince may have opposed the agitation which went on about him, he could not stop it. At the time of the rising in Bosnia and Herzegovina it was commonly thought in western Europe that the whole movement was organized from outside the provinces, and that it was the result of the intrigues and machinations of Serbian revolutionaries. This may be an exaggeration, but it seems hardly doubtful that these agencies played a far from insignificant role.[4]

---

[1] R. W. Seton-Watson: "*Les Relations diplomatiques austro-serbes*" (*Le Monde slave*, III, pp. 273–88, August 1926).

[2] Nicholas Iorga: *Correspondance diplomatique roumaine sous le roi Charles I, 1866–1880* (Paris, 1923), p. 315. [3] Ibid., p. 324.

[4] Monypenny and Buckle: *Life of Disraeli*, VI, p. 35; *Parliamentary Papers, Turkey*, No. 3 (1876), pp. 39–41. See further Wertheimer: *Andrássy*, II, pp. 250 ff.; Slobodan Jovanovič: " Serbia

The Montenegrins as well as the Serbians appear to have had an active hand in the propagandist work carried on in the Turkish provinces. Nicholas I of Montenegro was a very astute and ambitious prince, who apparently cherished hopes of becoming himself the leader of the movement for southern Slav unity. At any rate he seems to have been unwilling to subordinate his own plans to those of the Belgrade government and tried to play an independent hand between Austrian and Russian influences. Whether the Montenegrin government as such carried on revolutionary propaganda in Montenegro it is impossible to say with certainty. There was no real difference between the inhabitants of Montenegro and those of the adjacent districts of Herzegovina. They were all tribesmen, wild mountaineers who were constantly fighting each other if they were not fighting the Turk. A contemporary observer notes that only those who died in their beds were mourned for. To do battle was a pastime, and to die in battle was an honour, for aiding the Herzegovinians against the Turks was regarded " partly as a sport and partly as a crusade." [1]

It is impossible to schematize the numerous tendencies and factors that entered into the development of nationalism in the Balkans at this time. Some of the southern Slav nationalist leaders, like Prince Michael of Serbia, were opposed to foreign influence and set for themselves the idea of a Balkans for the Balkan peoples. Others, like the Serbian leader Ristič, hoped for salvation through the intervention of Russia. For the Russian government the Turkish problem was *the* great problem of foreign policy. Ever since the Russian frontier had been advanced to the Black Sea, there was the economic and strategic problem of access to the Mediterranean. The Straits of the Bosporus and Dardanelles were open to merchant ships of all nations, but the Turks controlled them and could close them at any time. Besides, the Straits were, by international agreement, closed to all foreign warships in time of peace. The Black Sea, in other words, was a *mare clausum,* and the Russians felt that the very key to their house was in the hands of a foreigner. Even older than the desire to secure control of the Straits was the more sentimental aspiration of the Russians to regain control of Constantinople and place the Christian cross on the Church of St. Sophia, as well as to aid the oppressed Christians of the Balkans in their fight for liberty. It may be doubted whether these sentimental considerations played a very large role in determining Russian diplomacy, but Catherine the Great and her successors had discovered the value of the religious factor in the struggle with the Turks and had done their utmost to stir up revolt in the Balkans in order to create difficulties for the enemy. In the nineteenth century a new factor, community of race, was made use of for the same purpose.

Like other peoples the Russians had discovered their national genius. An

---

in the Early Seventies " (*Slavonic Review,* IV, pp. 385–95, December 1925). There is a good account of the Omladina in Hermann Wendel: *Aus dem südslawischen Risorgimento* (Gotha, 1921), chapter iii.
[1] Harold W. V. Temperley: *History of Serbia* (London, 1917), p. 254.

influential Slavophil movement had grown up to combat western influences and to stress the peculiar beauties of Muscovite culture. Before long, especially after the Polish rising of 1863, this movement began to take on an aggressive national tinge, which ended in the oppressive measures of Russification of the 1870's and 1880's. Another outgrowth of the movement was the so-called Pan-Slav idea, which went beyond the principle of purely Russian solidarity and preached the union of all Slavs under the ægis of Russia. This new movement took definite form in 1858, when the Slavic Welfare Society was established at Moscow. It received great impetus in 1867, when a meeting of representatives of all Slavs was held in the old Russian capital. In the three following years branches of the society were opened in St. Petersburg, Kiev, and Odessa, and in 1870 General Fadeiev, one of the leaders of the movement, published a noteworthy book which was translated into English under the title *Opinion on the Eastern Question.*

Since the ideas of western Europe in regard to Panslavism were derived largely from Fadeiev's book, it deserves a somewhat detailed examination. Apart from suggesting ways and means of effecting a cultural contact with the Slavs outside the Russian Empire, Fadeiev devoted himself chiefly to practical problems. His argument was somewhat as follows: Since the growth of national consciousness in Europe the traditional Eastern question had developed into a far more important one: namely, the Panslavic. But it was a mistake to think that Turkey, or even England or France, was Russia's chief opponent, as in the time of the Crimean War. The real obstacle in the way of the realization of the Pan-Slav program was Germanism, and more particularly the Austro-Hungarian monarchy, not only because it controlled many of the smaller Slavic nations, but because, strategically speaking, it commanded the entrance to the Balkans, the narrow pass between the Carpathian Mountains and the Black Sea. Therefore the road to Constantinople lay through Vienna, and without the defeat of Austria all thought of Slav unification would be vain. Russia desired but little for herself, but should acquire Galicia from Austria, and Bessarabia from Roumania, for these two Slavic territories separated Russia from the Slavs in the South. Once the threat of Germanism had been removed, the Slavic world could be organized as a huge confederation under the leadership of Russia. Constantinople and the adjacent territory about the Straits might be made the free city of the Slavic confederation.[1]

Even more influential in Russia was Nicholas Danilevski's book *Russia and Europe,* which appeared in 1871 and became the bible of the Panslavists. Like Fadeiev, Danilevski urged the necessity for Russia to take up the struggle against Western civilization and to assume the leadership of the weaker Slavic groups. The chief goal should be the possession of Constantinople, and the main attack should be directed against Austria and Turkey, states whose very

---

[1] See the excellent account in Alfred Fischel: *Der Panslawismus bis zum Weltkrieg* (Stuttgart, 1919), pp. 400 ff.

existence was a disgrace to the Slavic race. He then proceeded, in true Mazzinian fashion, to outline the composition of the future Slavic confederation: (1) Russia, with Galicia and the Ruthenian parts of the Bukovina and Hungary; (2) a Serbo-Croat-Slovene kingdom, to include Serbia, Montenegro, Bosnia, Herzegovina, the Banat, Croatia, Slavonia, Dalmatia, Istria with Trieste, Gorizia, and Gradisca, as well as the Slavic parts of Carinthia and Styria; (3) a Czecho-Moravian-Slovakian kingdom, to include the Slavic parts of northern Hungary; (4) a Bulgarian kingdom, with the larger part of Roumelia and Macedonia; (5) a Greek kingdom, to include Thessaly, Epirus, south-western Macedonia, the islands of the Ægean, Rhodes, Cyprus, Crete, and the Asiatic coast of the Ægean; (6) the region about Constantinople, with the capital and the territory on both sides of the Straits; (7) the kingdom of Hungary, consisting of the purely Magyar sections and part of Transylvania; (8) the kingdom of Roumania, to comprise not only Moldavia and Wallachia, but the Roumanian part of the Bukovina and half of Transylvania. The province of Bessarabia was to be transferred to Russia.[1]

To the western European of the time these plans seemed more fantastic than to our own generation, which has seen many of them realized. These far-reaching schemes appeared far more dangerous to the people of the 1870's than they seem to us of a later age when the ideas of self-determination have become current. To the western contemporaries of Fadeiev and Danilevski the Pan-Slav idea was simply one of nationalism gone wild and threatening the subversion of the whole European order. But to a large part of the intellectual element in Moscow these books made an appeal as the gospel of a new era and the doctrine of national revival. The distinction between Europeanized St. Petersburg, with its uninspired and disillusioned official classes on the one hand and the truly Muscovite elements in Moscow on the other, was frequently made by contemporary writers.[2] But even official circles were not entirely untouched by the Pan-Slav influence. In 1869 Stremouakov, the chief of the Asiatic division of the Russian foreign office, spoke of the enlargement of Serbia and Montenegro and the eventual foundation of two Bulgarian principalities. A few years later Gorchakov himself drew a rosy picture of the future of the Serbs, though he urged upon them the necessity for patience.[3]

But the most active worker in the interests of Panslavism was General Ignatiev, who became Russian ambassador at Constantinople in 1864 and in a short time had established his influence over the Sultan, Abdul Aziz, and some of the leading Turkish statesmen, like Mahmud Nedim. In his memoirs Ignatiev states his views in no uncertain terms: the aims of Russian policy in the Near East must be the abolition of the Treaty of Paris, which sealed Russia's defeat in 1856; Russian control of the Straits, direct or indirect; and the independence

---

[1] Fischel, op. cit., pp. 395 ff.
[2] See, among others, O. K. (Olga Novikova): *Russia and England* (London, 1880), chapter ii.
[3] Wendel, op. cit., pp. 325–6.

of the various Slavic peoples in the Balkans. For him, too, the chief enemy was the German-Magyar Habsburg monarchy. The extension of Austrian influence must be checked, and Russia alone must be the mistress of the Balkan Peninsula and the Black Sea.[1]

Early in 1877 there was published at London a small collection of documents entitled *Russia's Work in Turkey: A Revelation*. This was a translation of certain papers, chiefly correspondence between the Russian embassy at Constantinople and the Russian agents in the Balkans during 1872, which had supposedly come into the hands of the Turks and which appeared at Constantinople in a French edition shortly before the outbreak of war between Russia and Turkey. Although these exceedingly compromising documents have been used by reputable historians, their authenticity has been called in question and has been flatly denied by M. Nelidov, who was, at the time, secretary of the Russian embassy in the Turkish capital.[2] But even without the use of such dubious material there is no difficulty in reconstructing the work of Ignatiev. In his own memoirs he tells of his efforts to bring about the Serbian-Greek-Montenegrin alliance of 1867. As a matter of fact, the Serbs relied upon Russian help in case of dire need, though they were anxious to exclude the Russians from a share in the spoils and did not keep Ignatiev fully informed of details. It was in Bulgaria that the Russian ambassador scored most of his successes.

Prior to 1875 Bulgaria was hardly more than a name to western Europeans. It was not until the nineteenth century that a national revival took place and efforts began to be made to re-establish the identity of the people. From the middle of the century onward a number of insurrections were organized by revolutionary leaders, among whom Rakovski, an adherent of the idea of a Balkan league, was the outstanding figure. In the early stages the revolutionary movement was distinctly moderate in its aims, and the leaders in 1867 even forwarded to the Sultan a memorandum in which they suggested the establishment of a Bulgarian empire, with the Sultan as tsar and a Christian viceroy for Bulgaria proper. But later a new revolutionary committee was founded at Bucharest, and in this the Panslavic and Russian influence was predominant. It is said that by 1872 there were no less than two hundred revolutionary committees scattered throughout Bulgaria. An insurrection was started in September 1875.[3]

Meanwhile Ignatiev had thrown the whole weight of his influence on the

---

[1] " *Zapiski Grafa N. P. Ignatieva* " (*Istoricheski Viestnik*, CXXXV–CXXXVII, January-July 1914); Emmerich von Huszar: " *Die Memoiren des Grafen N. P. Ignatiev* " (*Osterreichische Rundschau*, XLI, pp. 166–74, November 15, 1914).

[2] Alexandre Nelidov: " *Souvenirs d'avant et d'après la guerre de 1877–1878* " (*Revue des deux mondes*, May 15 and July 15, 1915). See also the discussion by the Russian diplomat and historian G. Trubetzkoi: " *Les Préliminaires de la Conférence de Londres* " (*Revue d'histoire diplomatique*, XXIII, pp. 119 ff., 1909). I am unable to determine the reliability of D. Bugistre-Bellaysan: *Les Intrigues moscovites en Turquie* (Budapest, 1877).

[3] By far the best account is that of Alois Hajek: *Bulgarien unter der Türkenherrschaft* (Stuttgart, 1925), chapter xi.

Bulgarian side in the struggle of the Bulgarians in Constantinople for the administrative independence of the Bulgarian Church. It appears that the Greek Church officials outdid even the Turks so far as extortion in Bulgaria was concerned, and that the thirty thousand prosperous Bulgarians who lived in the Turkish capital felt that the expulsion of the Greeks was the most urgent need of their country. In 1870 the Bulgarian Exarchate was established, covering, territorially, not only present-day Bulgaria, but also large parts of Thrace and Macedonia. This first victory of Bulgarian nationalism was due in a large measure to the exertions of the Russian ambassador.[1]

Two years later the Turkish government brought forward a scheme for the reorganization of the empire on a federal basis. The tributary principalities, like Roumania and Serbia, were to be given a position somewhat akin to that of Bavaria in the German Empire. To this plan Ignatiev objected vigorously. Eventually he succeeded in bringing the German and French ambassadors to his side. The scheme finally fell through on this account, though the tributary states themselves refused to have anything to do with it.[2] Clearly Ignatiev was doing his utmost to keep the Ottoman Empire weak and to strengthen the insurrectionary movements among the Slavs. According to Nelidov, the secretary of the Russian embassy at the time, Ignatiev was quite ready to support the revolutionaries in Bosnia and Herzegovina, though he always feared being left in the lurch by the cautious directors of the foreign office in St. Petersburg. Sir Henry Elliot, the British ambassador at Constantinople, insisted that the rebels were encouraged by Russia in every possible way; that the leaders met at the house of Yonin, the Russian consul at Ragusa; and that they were aided by information supplied by Ignatiev himself.[3] In 1875 it was generally believed in western Europe that Ignatiev was the evil spirit of Russian diplomacy and that most of the unrest in the Balkans could be traced ultimately to his influence.

Whatever the truth may have been regarding the activities of Ignatiev and other followers of the Pan-Slav idea, there is little doubt of the responsibility of high Austrian officials for the outbreak of the insurrection in Bosnia and Herzegovina in 1875. This aspect of the problem is well worth a short digression, for it was to be of great importance in the crisis that followed. In 1866 Austria was expelled from Germany. Her interest naturally turned more and more to the Balkan area, the only region where there was still a possibility of expansion. But what the form of this expansion of influence should be was a matter of much dispute. Among the Croat leaders, who were constantly in conflict with the

---

[1] One of the best studies is by Prince Gregory Trubetzkoi: " *La Politique russe en Orient; le schisme bulgare* " (*Revue d'Histoire diplomatique*, XXI, pp. 161–98, 394–426, 1907), based upon the Russian documents; also Simeon Radeff: *La Macédoine et la renaissance bulgare* (Sofia, 1918), chapters iii and iv.

[2] N. Iorga: *Correspondance diplomatique roumaine*, pp. 95–8.

[3] Sir Henry G. Elliot: *Some Revolutions and other Diplomatic Experiences* (London, 1922), p. 207.

Hungarian government, controlled by the Magyar element, there was a strong movement in favour of a union of the southern Slavs within the Habsburg monarchy, and the reorganization of the monarchy itself on a triple rather than a dual basis. The Magyars, however, would not hear of the inclusion of more Slavs in the Habsburg state, and for that reason they were opposed to any territorial expansion in the Balkans. Their feelings were shared by the liberal elements among the Germans, who were, however, strongly interested in the economic expansion of the empire in the basin of the lower Danube and in the direction of Salonika. On the other hand the aristocratic, landholding classes in the empire, who were sympathetic towards the Slavs and favoured close relations with Russia, were out and out advocates of the movement towards the south-east.[1]

Among those who supported the idea of Austrian expansion in the Balkans the most influential group was that of the military men. From the time of the Crimean War onward these men, led at first by Radetzky, kept pointing out that Dalmatia, a narrow strip of sea-coast, was wholly cut off from the rest of the monarchy, and that it would be hard to hold it permanently unless the hinterland, Bosnia and Herzegovina, were incorporated in the empire. Furthermore, the constant unrest on the very frontiers of Austria-Hungary created an intolerable situation which must be resolutely faced and radically solved by making the necessary annexations.[2]

Andrássy had no sympathy for this view-point and, like most Magyars, was opposed to territorial expansion in the Balkans. Recognizing the danger of the agitation in Serbia and Montenegro, and being convinced that it was supported by Russia, he was very anxious to avoid complications. If Austria was to make conquests, he said in 1871, they should be peaceful ones, not warlike ones. Austria could afford to abandon the eastern part of Bosnia to Serbia, and the southern part of Herzegovina to Montenegro. It is said that in 1870, at his suggestion, the Austrian government offered to abandon two thirds of Bosnia to the Serbs, in return for Serbian neutrality in a war between Austria and any other power.[3] Andrássy's stand-point throughout was that the Habsburg monarchy did not need further acquisitions of territory, that the Ottoman Empire should be maintained as long as possible, and that a new eastern crisis should be avoided. It was this attitude that made possible the entente between Russia and Austria in the first years after 1871, which was based on the maintenance of the *status quo*. In the spring of 1874, during Francis Joseph's visit to St. Petersburg, the Austrian minister had assured Gorchakov that " he considered any annexation

---

[1] There is an admirable analysis of these various tendencies by the French consul-general at Belgrade, M. Engelhardt, a specialist on Near Eastern problems, in *Documents diplomatiques français*, I, No. 109, dated February 4, 1872.

[2] Theodor von Sosnosky: *Die Balkanpolitik Österreich-Ungarns seit 1866* (Stuttgart, 1913), Volume I, pp. 134 ff.; Wertheimer: *Andrássy*, II, pp. 256–9.

[3] Anton Freiherr von Mollinary: *Sechsundvierzig Jahre im österreich-ungarischen Heere* (Zurich, 1905), Volume II, p. 287.

of Slavic provinces to the Austro-Hungarian Empire would lead infallibly to the ruin of the empire and would therefore amount to suicide." [1]

But even Andrássy would have favoured annexation under certain circumstances. If, for example, the Ottoman Empire went to pieces, an eventuality in which he had not much faith, he would have regarded annexation as a necessary precaution. Above all he felt convinced that the road to Austrian economic and cultural expansion to the south-east must not be blocked by a greater Serbia. In speaking to Gorchakov in 1872 he had made it plain that Austria could not for a moment admit the Serbian claims to Bosnian territory. Speaking to the German ambassador at about the same time he said: "We have been thrown out of Germany, and that is well; we have lost Italy and we have become stronger as a result; we do not want to make annexations, but desire peace to defend our vital interests, which are threatened so far as our Slavic population is concerned. . . . The Christian populations of Turkey should develop in connexion with the power that is nearest them, and we are that power; we cannot allow ourselves to be encircled; for Europe it is best that we, who never can have Panslavic tendencies, should protect the Slavic states of Turkey and develop them, in order that we may, in due time, complete the civilizing work which Turkey, perhaps, is unable to fulfil." [2]

Unfortunately the military men had more influence with the Emperor Francis Joseph than did the foreign minister. Evidently with the avowed object of creating disturbances and preparing for Austrian intervention in Bosnia and Herzegovina they persuaded the Emperor to pay a long visit to Dalmatia in the spring of 1875. For more than a month the imperial party travelled along the Turkish frontier, receiving delegations of various kinds, but especially Catholic leaders from the two provinces, who looked to Francis Joseph for salvation. The effect of such a demonstration was perfectly clear to anyone acquainted with the complicated conditions in the Balkans. Austrian historians themselves admit that in all likelihood the Emperor's visit to Dalmatia set the spark that led to the conflagration in Herzegovina in July 1875. From the start it was noted abroad that the Roman Catholic element, which on previous occasions had remained quiet, took a prominent part in the movement. That Francis Joseph himself regarded the whole insurrection merely as the first step on the road to Austrian annexation is shown by the fact that in July 1875 he appointed General Mollinary commander of the corps assigned for the invasion of Bosnia, which was to take place if the Turks were unable to maintain themselves. The provinces must not be allowed to fall into the hands of others, said the Emperor, meaning the Serbs. [3] Furthermore, the Austrian officials in Dalmatia, many of

[1] *Documents diplomatiques français,* I, No. 306.

[2] Schweinitz: *Denkwürdigkeiten,* I, pp. 296–7. On Andrássy's attitude, see further Wertheimer, op. cit., II, pp. 259–60; Mollinary, op. cit., II, p. 287.

[3] Mollinary, op. cit., II, pp. 281, 288; Edmund von Glaise-Horstenau: *Franz Josephs Weggefährte: Das Leben des Generalstabschefs Grafen Beck* (Vienna, 1930), pp. 179–88; Oskar Freiherr

whom were Serbo-Croats by race, lent aid and comfort to the rebels and gave asylum to the refugees from the very start. In most of the Dalmatian towns there were committees which took care of the needs of the insurgents.[1]

The Eastern question had long been a welter of conflicting interests and aspirations, religious, political, military, and economic, but in this latest phase it had become even more involved through the spread of ideas of nationalism and race solidarity. These ideas, victorious in Italy and Germany, were so fraught with danger, not only for the Ottoman Empire, but for the Habsburg Empire as well, that any disturbance in this area immediately became a matter of grave importance. As soon as it became evident that the insurrection was spreading and that the Turks could not immediately suppress it, the powers began to consider ways and means of dealing with the situation.

It is clear that neither Andrássy nor Gorchakov welcomed the recurrence of the Balkan problem at this time. The Austrian minister, evidently not entirely initiated into the plans of the military circles, hoped that the Turks, if given the necessary support by the powers, might settle the problems raised by the insurrection without causing serious changes. The greatest chance for a pacific settlement lay, he thought, in the institution of necessary reforms.

Tsar Alexander was quite in sympathy with this approach to the problem. In February 1875 he had told Radowitz that he desired the maintenance of the *status quo* in the East, not because he regarded it as an ideal situation, but because he was convinced that a change would lead to unpredictable complications for the whole world. Who should have Constantinople, and who should rule over the restless chaos of peoples now united under the Turkish sceptre? It would be best, he continued, if the three empires co-operated in preventing the situation in the East from becoming troublesome.[2]

Of course the temptation for the Russian statesmen was very great. They could hardly resist the opportunity for carrying their traditional policy a step further. In August 1875 Gorchakov began to talk of securing for the revolted provinces an autonomous position like that of Roumania. Baron Jomini, a high official of the foreign office and a close friend of Gorchakov, was more outspoken yet. He discussed the situation with the secretary of the French embassy, M. Laboulaye, in language strongly reminiscent of the famous conversations between Nicholas I and Lord Seymour on the eve of the Crimean War. " Will it not be better," said Jomini, " to open our eyes at once and recognize that the time is near when the incapacity of the Turkish government must inevitably bring about its ruin? Is not its bankruptcy the most certain sign of its decrepitude? In order not to be taken by surprise Europe must, without delay, look to those

---

von Mitis: *Das Leben des Kronprinzen Rudolf* (Leipzig, 1928), pp. 274 ff., 323; August Fournier: *Wie wir zu Bosnien kamen* (Vienna, 1909), p. 14; *Documents diplomatiques français,* II, No. 2.

[1] W. J. Stillman: *Herzegovina and the Late Uprising* (London, 1877), pp. 2–7; Wertheimer, op. cit., II, pp. 257 ff.; Sosnosky, op. cit., I, pp. 127 ff.; Hermann Wendel: *Der Kampf der Südslawen um Freiheit und Einheit* (Frankfurt, 1925), pp. 328 ff.

[2] Holborn: *Bismarcks europäische Politik und die Mission Radowitz,* p. 101.

naturally appointed as its heirs." Thereupon he proceeded to outline a future federal organization of the Balkans, with Constantinople, a free city, as capital.[1] This was the Pan-Slav program all over again, while Gorchakov's suggestion, made in November 1875, that Austria and Russia should occupy the insurgent provinces jointly, represented an effort to make a business deal, which Andrássy rejected.[2]

In this earlier stage of the question Andrássy managed to secure for Austria the lead in the action of the European powers. Bismarck had no direct interest in the Near Eastern problem and indicated his willingness to subscribe to anything that Austria and Russia might determine upon. Even England followed the lead of Vienna, for, like Austria, she had a pronounced interest in the maintenance of the integrity of the Ottoman Empire, though there was not much inclination in London to support the Turks for their own sake, as at the time of the Crimean War. Lord Derby had, in fact, expressed himself in unmistakable terms to the German ambassador, in January 1875, to the effect that the Turkish rule was rapidly collapsing and that little could be done to maintain it.[3] Lord Salisbury, the secretary of state for India in the Disraeli cabinet, shared this view and later made the statement that in 1854 England had put her money on the wrong horse. Disraeli himself had no illusions on the subject of Turkish rule and was constantly casting about for some way of taking a more active part in the larger questions of European politics. Though England was not directly affected by the developments in the Balkans, and Disraeli had little sympathy for national movements, the Near East had become increasingly important for England since the opening of the Suez Canal, in 1869. The acquisition of a controlling share of the stock of the Suez Canal Company by the purchase of the shares of the impecunious Khedive of Egypt, in November 1875, was a masterstroke on the part of the English prime minister and illustrated the English interest in the most important route to the East. The prime minister and many Englishmen with him still feared the prospect of an eventual possession of Constantinople and control of the Straits by Russia and saw in the Balkan uprising merely another instance of Russian intrigue working through Serbian or Montenegrin agitators.

For the English the most desirable solution would have been the suppression of the insurrection by the Turks themselves, without outside interference. Disraeli complained bitterly in his letters that "the want of energy at Constantinople is superhuman," and referred to "this dreadful Herzegovina affair, which, had there been common energy, or perhaps pocket money even, among

---

[1] Hanotaux, op. cit., IV, p. 70; in speaking to the French ambassador, Jomini was more circumspect (*Documents diplomatiques français*, II, No. 2).

[2] Wertheimer: *Andrássy*, II, pp. 274 ff.; id., "*Neues zur Orientpolitik des Grafen Andrássy, 1876–1877*" (*Historische Blätter*, I, pp. 252–76, 448–63, 1921), p. 259. He told the French ambassador that Austria wanted no territory (*Documents diplomatiques français*, II, No. 25).

[3] Holborn, op. cit., p. 95; see also the admirable analysis of the English view in *Documents diplomatiques français*, II, No. 12.

the Turks, might have been settled in a week." [1] But the Turks failed to move energetically and some action by the powers became inevitable. In this step Disraeli was obliged to join, for, though he was moved by the deepest distrust of the Three Emperors' League, England was powerless to stand against so imposing a combination. "Unless we go out of our way to act with the three Northern Powers, they can act without us, which is not agreeable for a state like England," he wrote to one of his friends.[2]

So Andrássy had his way. The first move of the Three Emperors' League was to induce the Turks to send a commissioner into the provinces to investigate the situation. At the same time Austria, Russia, and Germany instructed their consuls to attempt mediation. France and Italy did likewise, while England took part reluctantly. Nothing came of these first efforts. The consuls interviewed some of the rebel leaders, but failed to get a very clear picture of what the difficulty really was. According to the British consul, Mr. Holmes, the rebels "repeatedly declared that they were and wished to remain faithful subjects of the Sultan (taking off their caps at the mention of his name), but that His Majesty was deceived by his pashas, and could not be aware of their condition." In the consul's opinion the trouble was all due to Serbian agitation, yet "almost to a man the population would refuse to be annexed to Servia or Austria; and they have never dreamed of independence. They also wish to be Turkish subjects, but to be governed with justice and peace on an equality in law with their Mussulman compatriots." [3] In other words, the consuls heard chiefly local grievances and carried away the impression that real reforms by the Turkish government might yet save the situation. But these reforms would have to be thorough-going. The insurgents demanded either autonomy under a Christian prince or an occupation by foreign powers until justice had been done them.[4] Instead of this a decree of the Sultan on October 2 promised only alleviations of taxation, religious freedom, and equality before the law, all of them concessions which had been promised many a time before without having ever materialized.

The insurrection, therefore, went on and spread rapidly. In fact, there was an attempted rising in Bulgaria in September, which boded no good for the future. Andrássy, who had rejected the Russian suggestions for autonomy or joint occupation, felt the necessity for imposing a program of reform upon the

---

[1] Monypenny and Buckle: *Life of Benjamin Disraeli*, VI, pp. 11–13.

[2] Ibid., VI, p. 13; R. W. Seton-Watson: "Russo-British Relations during the Eastern Crisis" (*Slavonic Review*, III, pp. 423–34, December 1924), pp. 426–31. But to Queen Victoria he wrote at the same time that there was no reason to suspect the three empires (Buckle: *The Letters of Queen Victoria, 1862–1878*, II, p. 421). For a competent discussion of English policy see Rudolf Liebold: *Die Stellung Englands in der russisch-türkischen Krise von 1875–78* (*Wilkau, 1930*).

[3] Quoted by the Duke of Argyll, op. cit., pp. 149–50, from the British Blue Books. See also *Aktenstücke aus den Korrespondenzen des K. und K. gemeinsamen Ministeriums des Äusseren über orientalische Angelegenheiten, 16 Mai 1873–31 Mai 1877* (Vienna, 1878).

[4] See Miller, op. cit., pp. 360–1; Carl Ritter von Sax: *Geschichte des Machtverfalls der Türkei* (second edition, Vienna, 1913), pp. 401 ff.

Porte. But the Sultan, when he got wind of the intentions of the powers, decided to act himself. Foreign interference in the domestic affairs of the empire he was determined to reject. " That would be like committing suicide, and I prefer to die on my throne," he told the Russian ambassador.[1] So on December 12, 1875 a firman announced the introduction of reforms in the whole Turkish Empire. It was an old method of dealing with discontent in special provinces and was designed primarily to prevent the interference of the powers. But this reform project was simply a new edition of an old program: judicial reform, reorganization of taxation, equality of opportunity in government service, improvement of agriculture, industry, and commerce, etc.

It was obvious that this half-hearted effort on the part of the Porte would have no effect on the particular problem at issue, and Andrássy continued to work out his own reform plan unmoved. On December 30, 1875 it was communicated to the powers which had signed the Treaty of Paris of 1856 and had thereby become guarantors of the independence and integrity of the Ottoman Empire. The so-called Andrássy Note demanded complete religious freedom, abolition of tax-farming, a guarantee that the revenue of the provinces should be spent for local needs, improvement of agrarian conditions, and, finally, the establishment of a mixed commission, composed equally of Mohammedans and Christians, to supervise the working of these reforms. Though the note was accepted by the other powers and was communicated to the Porte on January 31, 1876, and though the Turkish government accepted the reform program almost *in toto,* the whole action fell through, because the insurgents themselves rejected the concessions, on the plea that they were inadequate without a guarantee by the powers.

Both Tsar Alexander and Gorchakov, as well as Andrássy, appear to have entertained high hopes that a reform program, supported by the six powers, would solve the question. But Bismarck was, from the very beginning, full of doubt. He was in no way directly interested in the problem and had no intention of becoming involved in its complications. Yet a question of so great importance to at least three of the leading European nations would of necessity influence their relations to each other, and in the general alignment of the powers Bismarck took a supreme interest. On a later occasion he once spoke of Alsace and Lorraine on the one hand and the Eastern problem on the other as the two foci of all conceivable continental complications.[2] At the very beginning of the crisis he had called the attention of the Emperor to the advantageous aspect of the problem. The other powers would now, for a time, direct their attention and concentrate their policies on other questions than that of Franco-German relations.[3] The dangers involved in general European complications

---

[1] *The Diplomatic Reminiscences of Lord Augustus Loftus* (Second Series, London, 1894), II, p. 142.

[2] *Die Grosse Politik,* VI, p. 76.

[3] Bismarck: *Gedanken und Erinnerungen,* I, p. 260. See Hans Rothfels: *Bismarcks englische Bündnispolitik* (Stuttgart, 1924), p. 27.

might be exploited in the interests of Germany. That is, a constellation of powers might result of which Germany could take advantage to safeguard herself against France.[1]

Anticipating the probable failure of the Andrássy Note, Bismarck could also foresee the eventual clash of Russian and Austrian interests. In the event of such a conflict it was quite clear that the English would sympathize with the Austrians rather than with the Russians, and it was highly probable that Germany would have to choose between the two antagonistic groups. This making of a choice between his two neighbours Bismarck was very anxious to avoid. He desired to maintain his triangular rampart and thus keep France isolated. If he turned Russia away and sided with Austria, it was almost certain that Russia would appeal to France, and Germany would then have enemies on two fronts. Yet Bismarck regarded the existence of the Austrian Empire as a primary German interest, and though he did not make a choice between Austria and Russia before he was obliged to do so, he must have turned over the various possibilities in his mind even at this time. At any rate, while anxious to maintain the peace and to preserve the solidarity of the three empires, he began tentatively to sound out the attitude of the powers and to consider various possible combinations.

After the intervention of England in behalf of France in May 1875, Bismarck thanked the English and expressed his pleasure that they were again taking an interest in continental affairs. The possibility of bringing in England as a counter-weight to Russia already loomed up before him. The purchase of the Suez Canal shares, in November 1875, was added evidence of Disraeli's imperialistic leanings and interest in foreign relations. Bismarck knew that the English prime minister had little use for the Three Emperors' League, and that he had only reluctantly joined the three powers in their efforts to settle the Near Eastern difficulty. As for the Andrássy Note, Disraeli, in contrast to Lord Derby, the foreign minister, was opposed to joining in the action, and most of his colleagues in the cabinet supported him. England would probably have refused her co-operation had it not been for the fact that the Turkish government itself asked that the English government associate itself with the others, in order not to leave the field clear for Austrian-Russian action. Disraeli felt that the English could not be more Turkish than the Sultan, but the whole attitude of the cabinet was unfavourable and the matter was treated in a very dilatory way.[2]

Realizing England's growing interest in European international relations, and bearing in mind the possibility of future complications, Bismarck approached Lord Odo Russell, the ambassador at Berlin, on January 2, 1876. He expressed his astonishment that a power so vitally interested in the Near

---

[1] *Denkwürdigkeiten des Botschafters General von Schweinitz* (Berlin, 1927), I, p. 318.

[2] Monypenny and Buckle, op. cit., VI, pp. 18–19; Seton-Watson, in the *Slavonic Review*, III, pp. 657–8, March 1925; *Documents diplomatiques français*, II, No. 32.

East should be so hesitant in setting forth its views. He himself would be glad to know the ideas of the English government in regard to the Andrássy Note before he gave his own reply. Indeed, he desired a " frank and frequent " exchange of views with the English cabinet so that he might regulate his own policy accordingly as far as possible, and he would be glad to find an opportunity of cementing the good relations between the two governments even more firmly by co-operating with England in Turkish affairs, if difficulties should arise. He did not agree with those who said, " Things are too bad to last so any longer." In his opinion Turkey might yet be kept together with a little goodwill, but goodwill depended on mutual forbearance and cordial co-operation. He did not put much store by the administrative reforms proposed in the Andrássy Note. The important question was to know what the ambitious politicians of Austria and Russia were secretly contemplating. The peace of Europe depended on the maintenance of good relations between Russia and Austria, and Gorchakov was acting cordially with Andrássy. But there were ambitious men in Russia and Austria who might interfere. Andrássy might be swept aside and the annexationists might triumph in Vienna. Besides, Bismarck could not afford to let Austria and Russia become too intimate behind Germany's back. He wished to avoid causing a quarrel by taking sides.

Russell explained the reticence of his government by saying that so far Germany had left the solution of the problem to Austria and Russia, and there seemed to be no occasion for an exchange of opinion between London and Berlin. England was primarily interested in safeguarding the route to India, and the eventual annexation of the insurgent provinces by Austria might be the least objectionable solution from the English view-point. Of course, Russia might then seek to regain Bessarabia by way of compensation. But the English ambassador, in reporting to his government, expressed the opinion that Bismarck meant what he said about an understanding. The German chancellor, he thought, had begun to feel isolated since Austria and Russia had become so intimate.[1]

Lord Derby, in reply, expressed the desire of the English government to co-operate with Germany in Turkish affairs, but reserved an expression of opinion until he had consulted his colleagues. Russell himself did not think that there was any need for an immediate reply, for Bismarck's offers of friendship were intended to come into play when his present allies began to quarrel and prepare to fight, perhaps in the spring.[2] Under the circumstances Derby allowed the matter to rest. We have no evidence that he consulted Disraeli, though

---

[1] The German account is contained in a letter from Bülow to Münster, January 4, 1876, the date of the conversation being erroneously given as January 3. My account is based primarily upon Russell's telegram and dispatch of January 2 and a dispatch of January 3, abstracts of which were taken from the Record Office by Professor Dwight E. Lee of Clark University and kindly placed at my disposal.

[2] Derby's dispatches of January 6; Russell to Lord Tenterden, January 8 (unpublished); *Die Grosse Politik*, IV, p. 3, note.

Lord Lyons learned of the affair, probably from Russell. His reaction is very instructive. All he could see was that Bismarck was trying to separate England and France: " The despatch looks as if Bismarck were preparing for a quarrel with Russia. . . . Like everybody else, he feels sure that if there is a quarrel between Russia and Germany, France will side with Russia. In order to prevent his enemy from being all-powerful at sea, he must have the English fleet not merely neutral, but on his side. The only advantage he can offer to England is support on the Eastern Question, and it is on this question that he would have the best chance of embroiling her with Russia." [1]

That Bismarck had France at the back of his mind there can be no doubt, but the English ambassador at Paris was misled by his own suspicions when he thought that the chancellor intended to start trouble. From the German documents it is clear that trouble was exactly what he wished to avoid, and that therefore he aimed not at the separation of England and France, but at the continuance of a certain intimacy between them, so that England might act as a brake on French policy. His desire to prevent complications comes out clearly enough in his conversation with the Russian ambassador a few days later. Here again he talked of feasible solutions of the problem, suggesting the possibility of a settlement on the basis of the acquisition of Bosnia by Austria and of Bessarabia by Russia. England would make no trouble about " such bagatelles " if she could be given security in respect to the Suez Canal. He himself would be prepared to act as mediator between the interested powers and would be willing to prepare the English cabinet in order to secure its eventual agreement.[2]

But Gorchakov, like the English statesmen, was suspicious lest Bismarck be contemplating some action against France. He had not given up hope for the success of the Andrássy Note and evidently preferred to deal directly with the Austrian minister. The German chancellor's efforts, therefore, proved to be vain. Yet a good deal depended upon the action he had attempted to initiate and he soon returned to the charge. Being ill, he asked the English ambassador to call on him on February 1. The upshot of the conversation can best be given in Russell's own words: " Prince Bismarck spoke earnestly and impressively of the importance he attached to a timely understanding between our two governments. He begged I would again assure Your Lordship that Germany having no direct interests in the East, he is willing to further the interests of the friends of Germany who will support him in maintaining the peace of Europe. Believing as he does that England is the Power most directly and sincerely interested in the maintenance of peace he anxiously desires and solicits a thorough understanding with Her Majesty's Government, so as to be well prepared before complications arise, to give his full support to the peace policy of England in the East. England desires, and Germany requires peace, while Austria

---

[1] Newton: *Lord Lyons,* II, p. 96.
[2] Goriainov: *Le Bosphore et les Dardanelles* (Paris, 1910), pp. 314 ff.

and Russia have conflicting interests in the East, which may at any moment lead to sudden and serious differences between them, — when Germany, unable to agree with both, or to stand aloof and be neutral, may have to take sides; and in so doing a previous knowledge of the views of Her Majesty's Government would enable him, by adopting those views and making them his own, to secure beforehand the moral support of England, in seeking to keep the peace between Austria and Russia in Turkey." The danger of Andrássy's being over-ruled by the military circles in Vienna he regarded as a serious matter.[1]

This appeal was too urgent to be ignored. Russell himself was strongly in favour of a mutual understanding and urged his government to accept the offer. Queen Victoria was even more outspoken. She believed in the sincerity of Bismarck's desire for an understanding and in the honesty of his wish for peace: " The Queen therefore thinks that it is of the utmost importance that we should accept the proffered aid of Germany, a strong state whose interests are the same as ours and whose whole policy can or should seldom be opposed to that of an English Government. . . . The Queen considers that the importance of establishing a link between the two countries cannot be overrated, and desires earnestly to impress upon Lord Derby the necessity of authorising Lord Odo Russell to enter into free and unrestricted communication with Prince Bismarck upon Eastern Affairs." [2]

Disraeli was no less enthusiastic: " If this practical good understanding with Germany be accomplished, it will place our external relations on a rock, and England will again exercise that influence which, of late years, has so pain-fully and mysteriously disappeared." He was convinced, so he wrote the Queen, of " the absolute necessity of frankly and definitely co-operating with the offers and overtures of Prince Bismarck." [3]

But Lord Derby was still circumspect. He proposed to meet Bismarck's overtures in a spirit of cordial friendship, but he feared that " more may be intended by this communication than meets the eye. [Lord Derby] cannot possess implicit confidence in Prince Bismarck's desire of peace, remembering the events of last spring. And he would like to see more clearly than he does what assistance England is expected to give in return for that which is of-fered." [4] He therefore wrote to Russell pointing out that, from the English standpoint, any disturbance in the territorial *status quo* would be " unadvisable and dangerous," because one change would lead to another and there would be no knowing where the policy of annexation would end. England desired no " exclusive alliances." Her principal object was the maintenance of peace, which might under certain circumstances be promoted by " concerted action " and " cordial understanding " between England and Germany. But this line of

---

[1] Russell dispatch, February 1, 1876 (unpublished), for which I am indebted to Professor Lee.
[2] Buckle: *Letters of Queen Victoria,* II, pp. 443–4.
[3] Ibid., p. 444.
[4] Monypenny and Buckle, op. cit., VI, pp. 20 ff.

policy would be possible only after Bismarck's motives were better known. Russell was to invite Bismarck to make a full disclosure of his intentions and ideas.[1]

Now, this was certainly turning the tables on the German chancellor. His stand had always been that Germany had no interests in the East, but was anxious to maintain the peace between the powers that did have interests. He had offered to support the English peace program if the English would put it forward. In reply Derby talked about alliances and tried to get Bismarck to advance a policy. It was only natural, under the circumstances, that the German statesman should have received the English answer with coolness. All he had asked for, he told Russell, was the faculty of exchanging ideas confidentially with the English government in case of danger. The general aspect of affairs was now satisfactory, and Andrássy's position no longer appeared to be seriously menaced. But he still thought that England and Germany were the two powers best able to prevent mischief if things took a threatening turn. "England had a legitimate right to the road to India, which Germany cordially supported, and both wished for nothing but peace in the East." There were two ways of dealing with the problem, as he saw it. First all the powers should agree to work cordially to maintain the territorial *status quo*. But if quarrels should arise — for example, if Montenegro claimed more territory and was supported by Russia and opposed by Austria — and England and Germany could not find a pacific solution, then a second plan should be resorted to. "It consisted equally in agreeing and working cordially together to maintain the peace of Europe, not by upholding the territorial *status quo,* but by amicably settling what should be done with Turkey to satisfy the Powers concerned, instead of going to war about it." He would be the last to stand in the way of any reasonable settlement, the more so as Germany was satiated and had no claims of her own. In order to secure the friendly co-operation of France and Italy he would be willing to meet their wishes half-way, "whatever they were." But all he had wanted for the present "was the power to communicate freely and frankly with Your Lordship when he saw rocks ahead, and the assurance that he might reckon on the co-operation of Her Majesty's Government in trying to steer clear of them."[2]

Russell did not believe that Bismarck had in mind any "positive or fixed plan of action," but that he wanted to be ready for any contingency, as he dreaded too great intimacy between Austria and Russia. More important yet, perhaps, was Bismarck's fear that Austria and Russia might fall out. This comes out clearly enough in the correspondence quoted above. The chancellor was not fishing for an alliance with England. What he was after was the conversion of the English and then the Russians to the idea of a settlement based on partition

---

[1] Derby to Russell, February 12 and 16, 1876 (unpublished, but referred to by N. Japikse: *Europa und Bismarcks Friedenspolitik,* p. 59). See also the discussion of this episode in Rothfels, op. cit., pp. 28–31; and Friedrich Frahm: "*England und Russland in Bismarcks Bündnispolitik*" (*Archiv für Politik und Geschichte,* VIII, pp. 365–431, 1927), pp. 379 ff.

[2] Russell to Derby, February 19, 1876 (unpublished).

of the Ottoman Empire if the reform program failed. Austria and the other powers could be squared if England and Russia agreed. This solution would have avoided the later conflict between England and Austria on the one hand and Russia on the other and would thus have obviated the danger of a Franco-Russian alliance against Germany. The failure of the scheme, the importance of which can hardly be exaggerated, was due entirely to Derby's insuperable suspicion. In the spring of 1876 it was still generally believed that Bismarck was a wolf in sheep's clothing, and that to deal with him meant to be duped by him.

Meanwhile the insurrection continued and the fighting became more and more ferocious. By March 1876 it was estimated that about 156,000 refugees from the provinces had passed the frontiers into Montenegro, Serbia, and Austria-Hungary. In both Serbia and Montenegro popular feeling was running higher and higher. Neither Prince Milan nor Prince Nicholas desired war, either for financial or for political reasons, but it took the most vigorous warnings from the powers to prevent the rulers from being carried away by the popular enthusiasm. So critical had the situation become that further action on the part of the powers was imperative, and, at the suggestion of Gorchakov, a meeting of the foreign ministers of the three empires was arranged for May 1876, to take place at Berlin. Andrássy arrived a few days earlier than Gorchakov and went over the situation with Bismarck. Just what passed between the two statesmen has never become known, but it appears that the German chancellor, convinced that the policy of reform was mistaken, did his utmost to convert Andrássy to the idea of annexations at the expense of the Ottoman Empire.[1]

Much the same ideas seem to have occupied the Russian chancellor. When he arrived in Berlin, he brought with him a scheme for an Austrian-Russian understanding to meet the situation if the dissolution of Turkey could no longer be avoided. Of the details of the scheme we have no knowledge. Andrássy is said to have admired it as a masterpiece of the diplomatic art, but of course it ran counter to the very principles of his policy. He therefore set himself the task of winning over Gorchakov to his own view-point and did finally succeed, by the lavish use of flattery, in converting the Russian minister. As Gorchakov complained later, the famous Berlin Memorandum of May 12 was an Austrian rather than a Russian product.[2]

In a sense the Berlin Memorandum was merely an elaboration of the Andrássy Note, though it went much further in its demands. In the first place it called for an armistice of two months, during which peace was to be made between the Turkish government and the insurgents, on the following terms: (1) the government to provide means sufficient to settle the refugees in their homes; (2) the distribution of these means to be effected through a mixed commission, with a Herzegovinian Christian as president; (3) Turkish troops to be concentrated in a few specified places; (4) the Christians to retain their arms for

---

1 Wertheimer: *Andrássy*, II, p. 296.
2 Wertheimer: *Andrássy*, II, pp. 297–8; Hanotaux, op. cit., IV, p. 100.

the time being; (5) the consuls of the powers to watch over the application of the reforms and the repatriation of the refugees. The note ended with a veiled threat: " If, however, the armistice were to expire without the effort of the powers being successful in attaining the ends they have in view, the three imperial courts are of the opinion that it would become necessary to supplement their diplomatic action by the sanction of an agreement, with a view to such efficacious measures as might appear to be demanded in the interest of general peace, to check the evil and prevent its development." Gorchakov himself admitted that he was responsible for this " tail-end," which was all that was left of the program of action he had brought to Berlin.[1]

Like the Andrássy Note, this new reform project had been worked out by the representatives of the three empires, in the expectation that the other powers would subscribe to it. The ambassadors of England, France, and Italy were thereupon called together, and the memorandum was read to them. Gorchakov expressed the hope that a favourable reply might be received before the imperial statesmen left Berlin, which was to be only two days later. France and Italy did, in fact, accept the program, but the English refused to follow the lead of the others. In part the English attitude was due to perfectly understandable objections to the program, which was all in favour of the insurgents. For example, Lord Derby wrote to Odo Russell, how could the Porte grant an armistice while the insurrection was receiving support from Serbia and Montenegro? An armistice might simply give the rebels time to strengthen their position. Furthermore, Lord Derby doubted whether the Turkish government could find the money to re-establish the refugees. " The distribution of relief by such a commission as is contemplated would be little better than a system of indiscriminate alms-giving." " The concentration of the Turkish troops in certain places would be delivering up the whole country to anarchy, particularly when the insurgents are to retain their arms." " The consular supervision would reduce the authority of the Sultan to nullity." Above all, the concluding paragraph of the memorandum was thoroughly inacceptable; it would render the whole negotiation between the government and the rebels abortive, " for it could not be supposed that the insurgents would accept any terms of pacification from the Porte in face of the declaration that if the insurrection continued after the armistice, the Powers would intervene further." [2]

The position of the English government was a sound one, but its refusal to accept the memorandum was based on larger and more general considerations rather than on these concrete objections. Disraeli had looked upon the meeting in Berlin with great distrust, and the tactless manner in which the program had been presented to the ambassador, with the request for a reply in two days, simply enraged the English minister. England, he felt, was being asked " to sanction them putting a knife to the throat of Turkey, whether we like it or

---

[1] Schweinitz: *Denkwürdigkeiten*, I, p. 330.
[2] British Blue Book, No. 275.

not." To the Russian ambassador he complained with biting sarcasm that England was being treated as though she were Montenegro or Bosnia.[1] In the words of the English ambassador to Constantinople: " There it was — flung at us as an intimation of the decision of the three Emperors, to which, indeed, we might give our adhesion, but without a hint that any amendment would be listened to." [2] Queen Victoria feared that the attitude of her government might encourage the Turks, and that in this way England might " precipitate rather than prevent the catastrophe," but Disraeli was unmoved and the cabinet supported him.

The failure of the Berlin Memorandum marks a turning-point in the history of the crisis. Gorchakov, who had reckoned confidently on the acquiescence of the English, was enraged, and threatened to let matters take their course. He could no longer restrain Serbia and Montenegro, he told the English ambassador, and there could be no doubt that if these two states took action against the Turkey, " the insurrection would assume much larger proportions, and a flame would be kindled in Bulgaria, Epirus, Thessaly and Albania, which the Porte, with its weakened resources, would be unable to extinguish; and the Christian Powers of Europe, awakened by public opinion to the call of humanity, would have to interpose to arrest the effusion of blood." [3] At first he tried to induce the other powers to act without England and to submit the memorandum to the Sultan in the form of a collective note, but finally he was dissuaded by Andrássy and Bismarck from embarking upon so hopeless an undertaking. There can be no doubt that the set-back suffered by the Russian chancellor in the whole matter of the memorandum had much to do with his attitude in the succeeding months.[4]

Bismarck, on the other hand, seems to have derived considerable satisfaction from the discomfiture of Gorchakov, whose intervention in Berlin in May 1875 he had never forgiven. " He fell into a fit of laughing at Gortchakoff," reported the English ambassador at Berlin.[5] At the same time he was greatly pleased by the attitude of London, which marked the return to an active policy and promised to supply a counter-weight to the Russians. Early in June he reopened discussions with the English, though only indirectly. The German Crown Princess, a daughter of Queen Victoria, reported to her mother that it was Bismarck's wish " that England should entirely take the lead in the Oriental question, and that he was quite ready to follow and back up whatever England proposed." [6] Disraeli replied that he was ready to co-operate with the German chancellor, but had no suggestions to make at the moment. In fact, he was well satisfied with

---

[1] Monypenny and Buckle, op. cit., VI, pp. 22 ff. Seton-Watson, in the *Slavonic Review*, III, pp. 664–5; Schweinitz: *Denkwürdigkeiten*, I, p. 330.

[2] Sir Henry Elliot: *Some Revolutions*, p. 209.

[3] Blue Book, No. 250.

[4] Wertheimer, op. cit., II, pp. 302–3; *Documents diplomatiques français*, II, Nos. 51, 55.

[5] Monypenny and Buckle, op. cit., VI, p. 32.

[6] Buckle: *Letters of Queen Victoria*, II, p. 464; Monypenny and Buckle, op. cit., VI, p. 32.

his action and with the general situation. The decided stand of the cabinet in the question of the memorandum had put it back on the political map. Not only had Bismarck renewed his overtures, but even the Russians were now full of protestations of goodwill. Gorchakov defied anyone to prove that during the twenty-one years of the Tsar's reign " the action and attitude of His Majesty had been anything but transparent with truth, like crystal." All that Russia asked for the provinces was administrative, not political, autonomy. Disraeli denied all distrust of Russia and expressed his willingness to consider any proposal coming directly from St. Petersburg. He admitted that the eventual disappearance of Turkey in Europe was inevitable, and that the insurgents would not be satisfied with anything less than independence. A certain amount of blood-letting seemed to be necessary. Europe could take counsel if the rebels were defeated. Count Shuvalov, the Russian ambassador, insisted that Russia desired to improve the conditions of the Christians without bringing on war.[1]

All this was merely academic discussion, and Gorchakov was probably right in suspecting Disraeli of working for the complete break-up of the connexion between Austria and Russia. For the time being, the situation was chaotic, for since the first days of May events had been taking place which were to change the entire complexion of affairs. On May 6 the German and French consuls at Salonika had been murdered by an infuriated Moslem mob which demanded the surrender of a Christian girl converted to Islam. On May 10 a demonstration of the softas, or theological students, in Constantinople, led to the overthrow of the Grand Vizier, Mahmud Nedim, and the formation of a new cabinet, in which Midhat Pasha, the intellectual leader of the reforming or Young Turk party, had a seat. On May 30 the Sultan Abdul Aziz was declared deposed and Murad V, a liberal-minded prince, called to the throne. During the same month of May a revolution was attempted in Bulgaria, which ended in the famous " Bulgarian horrors."

These stormy events in the Ottoman Empire are not without significance for the story of the Eastern crisis. They mark the rising tide of Turkish and Moslem sentiment against the insurgent Slavs and against the great powers who were interfering on their behalf. The softas in Constantinople were generally regarded as the chief supporters of conservatism and orthodox Mohammedanism. If they helped to lift Midhat Pasha and his reforming friends into power, it was chiefly because they had come to recognize the utter incompetence of the Sultan and the unpatriotic policy of Mahmud Nedim, who was so completely under the thumb of Ignatiev and the Russians that he was called *Mahmudov*. The whole change in régime forecast the rule of the Young Turks, with their program of reform for the whole empire and administrative centralization, which was in direct opposition to the demands of the revolted provinces.

---

[1] Seton-Watson, in *Slavonic Review*, III, pp. 669–75; Monypenny and Buckle, op. cit., VI, pp. 34–5; *Documents diplomatiques français*, II, No. 69.

In the same way the murder of the consuls at Salonika and the suppression of the insurrection in Bulgaria may be taken as evidence of the growing feeling of Turkish national resistance to the attacks made upon the empire. The situation in Bulgaria was particularly instructive. Attention has already been called to the awakening of national consciousness in the Bulgarian provinces and to the revolutionary work carried on there under Russian inspiration. Reference has also been made to the abortive rising of September 1875, when Botjev, the revolutionary leader, declared of the Bosnian insurrection "that is the spark which will set the whole Balkan Peninsula in flames; now is the time to lay the Turkish monarchy in ruins." The rebels had relied upon Serbian help and had gone so far as to make plans for the burning of Constantinople, Adrianople, Sofia, and other places. As a result of this attempted revolution the Turkish officials had proceeded with rigour and had quartered troops on the country. A new uprising was planned for May 1876, and the "apostles" of revolution once more began their work. A wildly romantic meeting or general assembly was held in April 1876, and decided on a great *levée en masse,* which was to culminate in the burning of the larger cities. Owing to treason on the part of a few Bulgarians, the rising began in the last days of April. Even the most friendly writers admit that the revolutionaries cut down helpless and unarmed Turks in the most ruthless fashion. Conditions had not changed since the time of the Greek insurrection earlier in the century. The authorities, lacking a sufficient number of regular troops to deal with the situation, armed the Moslem population and called upon the irregular forces, bashi-bazouks and Circassians. With their aid the uprising was put down in an orgy of incendiarism and bloodshed. Just how many people lost their lives during these horrible conflicts has never become known. The first investigators, MacGahan of the *Daily News* and the American Mr. Schuyler estimated 15,000 killed and 79 villages destroyed. Mr. Baring, acting somewhat later for the British government, thought about 12,000 had been killed and 60 villages destroyed. Bulgarian historians have put the loss of life at 30,000 to 60,000, one even at 100,000.[1] It appears, however, that even the first reports were exaggerated, since neither MacGahan nor Schuyler was thoroughly familiar with the eastern languages, and both were therefore obliged to rely largely upon interpreters and upon the representative of the Russian embassy, Prince Tseretelev, who had received orders from Ignatiev as to what he should report.[2]

In any case, the powers found themselves confronted by an increasingly serious situation just as the concert of Europe had been broken up by England's defection. Henceforth a more uncompromising attitude was to be looked for

---

[1] The best account is in Hajek, op. cit., pp. 249–93. The Russian influence is discussed at length by Sir Henry Elliot, op. cit., pp. 255–68; and by D. Bugistre-Belleysan: *Les Intrigues moscovites en Turquie* (Budapest, 1877). See also H. S. Edwards: *Sir William White* (London, 1902), pp. 97 ff.

[2] Alexander Nelidov, in the *Revue des deux mondes,* May 15, 1915, p. 331; Evelyn S. Schaeffer: *Eugene Schuyler, A Memoir* (New York, 1901), pp. 63 ff.

from the Turks. Taken by and large the change in the situation was pure gain for the English. Disraeli had originally feared that Ignatiev would induce Abdul Aziz to call the Russian fleet to Constantinople to protect him from his subjects, and it was probably this fear, rather than mere anxiety for the safety of the Europeans, that led to the concentration of British ships at Besika Bay, at the mouth of the Dardanelles. " If England had accepted the Berlin Memorandum," wrote the prime minister to the Queen on May 29, 1876, " Constantinople would, at this moment, have been garrisoned by Russia, and the Turkish fleet have been placed under Russian protection." [1] As it was, the British premier could now regard the Three Emperors' League as being " as extinct as the Roman Triumvirate," and the English influence as in the ascendant at Constantinople, where Midhat and his friends looked to Sir Henry Elliot rather than to Ignatiev for counsel and support. To be sure, news of the Bulgarian atrocities had not yet reached London.

BIBLIOGRAPHICAL NOTE

DOCUMENTARY SOURCES

Accounts and Papers. State Papers. There is a long series of voluminous Blue Books dealing with the Eastern problem in this period. They will be found in the series for 1876, Volume LXXXIV; 1877, Volumes XC, XCI, XCII.

Aktenstücke aus den Korrespondenzen des K. und K. gemeinsamen Ministeriums des Äusseren über orientalische Angelegenheiten vom 16 Mai 1873 bis 31 Mai 1877. Vienna, 1878. The Austrian Red Book on the subject, containing some interesting material.

Documents diplomatiques. Affaires d'Orient, 1875, 1876, 1877. Paris, 1877. The French Yellow Book dealing with the crisis.

Die Grosse Politik der europäischen Kabinette, etc. Volume II, chapter x (The Eastern Crisis, 1876).

Documents diplomatiques français. Volume II (Paris, 1930), covers the years 1875 to 1879.

"Unprinted Documents. Russo-British Relations during the Eastern Crisis." Edited by R. W. Seton-Watson (*Slavonic Review,* Volumes III and IV, 1924–6). Important correspondence taken from the Russian embassy archives at London.

Correspondance diplomatique roumaine sous le roi Charles I. Edited by Nicholas Iorga. Paris, 1923. Contains some very interesting reports from Roumanian agents at the Balkan capitals.

---

[1] Buckle: *Letters of Queen Victoria,* II, p. 455; Monypenny and Buckle, op. cit., VI, pp. 29–30.

MEMOIRS, AUTOBIOGRAPHIES, BIOGRAPHIES, AND LETTERS

MONYPENNY, W. F., and BUCKLE, G. E.: *The Life of Benjamin Disraeli.* Volume VI, *1876–1881.* London, 1920.

BUCKLE, G. E.: *The Letters of Queen Victoria.* Second Series, *1862–1878.* Two volumes. London, 1926.

LOFTUS, LORD AUGUSTUS: *Diplomatic Reminiscences, 1862–1879.* Second Series. Two volumes. London, 1894.

ELLIOT, SIR HENRY: *Some Revolutions and Other Diplomatic Experiences.* London, 1922. Valuable for the study of the situation in the Near East. Elliot was English ambassador at Constantinople.

MIDHAT BEY, ALI HAYDAR. *Midhat-Pacha; sa vie, son œuvre.* Paris, 1908. English translation, London, 1903. The standard life of the Young Turk leader. Important for the study of the developments in Turkey and the Turkish attitude.

SCHWEINITZ, GENERAL VON: *Denkwürdigkeiten.* Two volumes. Berlin, 1927.

WERTHEIMER, EDUARD: *Graf Julius Andrássy.* Three volumes. Stuttgart, 1913. One of the most important sources for this period, especially with reference to Austrian policy.

Aus dem Leben König Karls von Rumänien. Four volumes. Stuttgart, 1897. Volume III contains interesting papers dealing with the Balkan situation at this time.

"ZAPISKI GRAFA N. P. IGNATIEVA o prebvanii v Konstantinopolie v *1864–1874*" (*Russkaia Starina,* XLV, No. 4, April 1914). The first part of Ignatiev's memoirs, dealing with the first decade of his ambassadorship.

"ZAPISKI GRAFA N. P. IGNATIEVA" (*Istoricheski Viestnik,* Volumes CXXXV–CXXXVII, January–July 1914). Deals with the period 1874–7.

MONOGRAPHIC STUDIES

MARRIOTT, J. A. R.: *The Eastern Question.* Oxford, 1917; third edition, 1924. A brief, conventional survey.

DRIAULT, EDOUARD: *La Question d'Orient.* Eighth edition. Paris, 1921. The best general survey in French, but quite out of date so far as the later period is concerned.

SAX, CARL RITTER VON: *Geschichte des Machtverfalls der Türkei.* Second edition. Vienna, 1913. One of the best accounts of the decline of the Ottoman Empire.

ARGYLL, DUKE OF: *The Eastern Question.* Two volumes. London, 1879. On the whole the best single contemporary study, based in large part on the British Blue Books.

BAMBERG, FELIX: *Geschichte der orientalischen Angelegenheit.* Berlin, 1892. At one time the standard treatment of the period between 1856 and 1878, but now out of date.

TYLER, MASON W.: *The European Powers and the Near East, 1875–1908.* Minneapolis, 1925. A reconsideration of the problem in the light of later source material, but incomplete and inadequate.

GORIAINOV, SERGE: *Le Bosphore et les Dardanelles.* Paris, 1910. Really a study of Russia's Eastern policy, based in large part upon unpublished material.

FOURNIER, AUGUST: *Wie wir zu Bosnien kamen.* Vienna, 1909. Based upon unpublished Austrian documents and therefore of prime value.

SOSNOSKY, THEODOR VON: *Die Balkanpolitik Österreich-Ungarns seit 1866.* Two volumes. Stuttgart, 1913. The best account of Austrian policy, though now somewhat antiquated.

FLIEGENSCHMIDT, MAXIMILIAN: *Deutschlands Orientpolitik im ersten Reichsjahrzehnt.* Berlin, 1912. A careful study, but now out of date.

FISCHEL, ALFRED: *Der Panslawismus bis zum Weltkrieg.* Stuttgart, 1919. The best single account of the Pan-Slav movement.

ENGELHARDT, EDOUARD: *La Turquie et le Tanzimat.* Two volumes. Paris, 1884. Still one of the best studies of the reform movement in Turkey.

WENDEL, HERMANN: *Der Kampf der Südslawen um Freiheit und Einheit.* Frankfurt, 1925. An excellent study of the renaissance of the Balkan states.

HAJEK, ALOIS: *Bulgarien unter der Türkenherrschaft.* Stuttgart, 1925. A splendid scholarly account of the Bulgarian movement.

LASCARIS, S. T.: *La Politique extérieure de la Grèce avant et après le Congrès de Berlin.* Paris, 1924. The best account of Greek policy in this period.

SETON-WATSON, R. W.: " *Les Relations diplomatiques austro-serbes* " (*Le Monde slave,* III, pp. 273–88, August 1926). Based on material from the Austrian archives.

GAULD, WILLIAM A.: " *The ' Dreikaiserbund' and the Eastern Question, 1871–1876* " (*English Historical Review,* pp. 207–22, April 1925).

JOVANOVIČ, SLOBODAN: " *Serbia in the Early 'Seventies* " (*Slavonic Review,* IV, pp. 384–95, December 1925).

IORGA, NICHOLAS: " *Origines des idées d'indépendance balkanique* " (*Le Monde slave,* IV, pp. 73–93, July 1927).

TRIVANOVITCH, VASO: " *Serbia, Russia, and Austria during the Rule of Milan Obrenovitch* " (*Journal of Modern History,* III, June 1931). Primarily an analysis of the memoirs of Ristič and other Serbian sources.

LIEBOLD, RUDOLF: *Die Stellung Englands in der russisch-türkischen Krise von 1875–78.* Wilkau, 1930. A substantial doctoral dissertation and the best systematic study of British policy. The author has not, however, made use of the important Russian documents published by Seton-Watson.

IV

The Balkan War and the Conference at Constantinople

ᴐ

A
TTENTION NOW CENTRED ON THE ACTION OF SERBIA AND MONTENEGRO.
At Belgrade there had been a pronounced war movement ever since the
autumn of 1875, which had been checked only by the dismissal of Ristič,
the former regent and the leader of the nationalist element. Prince Milan, who
was opposed to an adventurous course, was, however, unable to enforce his
view against the agitation of the Pan-Serbian organizations like the Omladina
and against the intrigues of the Panslavic agents. As early as April 1876 war was
practically decided on, and when Ristič returned to power, on May 5, it became
almost a certainty.[1] The Prince had his choice between war and revolution. In
fact, it was said that the nationalist organizations would depose him and call to
the throne either Prince Peter of the rival dynasty of the Karageorgevič or
Prince Nicholas of Montenegro. Under the circumstances the European governments made desperate efforts to prevent the outbreak of hostilities. Andrássy
suggested to Gorchakov that Russia and Austria intervene militarily, but the
Russian government insisted on a policy of non-intervention and proposed that
the two revolted provinces be given an autonomous status like that of Roumania,
while Serbia and Montenegro should receive rectifications of their frontiers. To
this, again, Andrássy would not listen. He pointed out that to grant such
autonomy would simply be to invite a similar demand from all the other Slavic
provinces of the Ottoman Empire. Besides, there was no homogeneity in the
population of the provinces and they would simply fall into anarchy. The Mohammedans and the Christians would devour each other like the two lions in
the story, until only the tails were left.[2]

No agreement being possible between the powers, Serbia and Montenegro
drifted into war. To be sure, the Russian government repeated its warnings at
Belgrade, but the Russian consul-general played a double role. While he communicated the official warnings, he advised Serbia, in his capacity of a " friend,"

---

[1] *Aus dem Leben König Karls von Rumänien* (Stuttgart, 1897), III, pp. 15, 21, 24; Edouard
Driault and Michel Lhéritier: *Histoire diplomatique de la Grèce*, Volume III (Paris, 1925), pp. 382,
385–6.
[2] Wertheimer: *Andrássy*, II, pp. 309–14; Seton-Watson in *Slavonic Review*, III, p. 679;
Monypenny and Buckle, op. cit., VI, pp. 34–5; *Documents diplomatiques français*, II, No. 72.

to go to war.[1] On June 22 Prince Milan wrote at great length to the Grand Vizier that the Serbian people, "the most zealous apostles of the integrity of the Ottoman Empire," recognized the need of bringing their interest into accord with the general interest of the empire and the demands of European policy. He therefore proposed that Serbia "second" the efforts of the Porte to re-establish quiet by sending her own troops into Bosnia. At the same time Ristić wrote suggesting that the administration of Bosnia be confided to Serbia in return for an increased payment of tribute. These proposals were, of course, rejected, and on June 30 Milan issued a proclamation of war. Although he referred in this document to the "high mission which Providence has entrusted to us of representing civilization and liberty in the Orient," the Prince curiously enough still stuck by the fiction of maintaining the Ottoman Empire: "Do not forget that we remain faithful to the principle of the integrity of the Ottoman Empire as long as the resistance of the imperial army does not force us to make the success of our holy cause dependent on the arbitrament of the sword."[2]

Of the nature of the struggle there could be not the slightest doubt, in spite of the disarming declarations of the Serbian Prince. General Chernaiev, a prominent Panslavist, who had left the Russian army to come to the assistance of the Serbs, was made commander-in-chief and issued a proclamation in which he stated openly: "We are fighting for the sacred idea of Slavdom. . . . We are fighting for freedom, the Orthodox cross, and civilization. Behind us stands Russia. If fickle fortune should desert us, this holy ground will be drenched with the costly blood of our Russian brothers, and these hills and ravines will resound for the last time with the clash of arms and the thunder of cannon. If we, wading in blood to our shoulders, are unable to open the doors to freedom and civilization, the iron hand of Russia will break them open, and over the corpses of our enemies, amid the applause of the free peoples of Europe, we shall cry in a loud voice: Long live freedom, long live the Slavic idea!"[3] The excitement in Serbia was so great that observers on the spot took it as ample evidence that the country as well as the national assembly desired war. "The idea which animates all minds," wrote the Roumanian representative, "is to withdraw from Turkish domination their Yugoslav brothers of the Balkan Peninsula. Their aim is reunion, for the moment under two sceptres and finally under one. . . . This is a war to the death between the southern Slavs and the Turks. . . . It is a war of race and religion. Whatever the official protocols may say, it is Russia that gave the impetus to this movement and continues to support it. . . . Today the idea of a throne for a Russian prince, reuniting the southern Slavs of the Balkan Peninsula, is the silent aspiration and the ultimate hope of all these populations."[4]

---

[1] Jovanovič, in the *Slavonic Review*, IV, p. 395; Elliot, op. cit., p. 215.

[2] Texts in Benoît Brunswik: *Recueil de documents diplomatiques rélatifs à la Serbie* (Constantinople, 1876), pp. 70 ff.

[3] Fischel: *Der Panslawismus*, pp. 412–13.

[4] Iorga: *Correspondance diplomatique roumaine*, pp. 128–9.

The enthusiasm of the southern Slavs found its counterpart in the awakened national spirit of the Turks. Volunteers in such large numbers flocked to Constantinople to join the army for the forthcoming campaign that the war department could not take care of them. Here, too, the war was regarded as a life and death struggle, and before long it appeared that the moribund Turkish Empire, if properly keyed up and inspired, was not yet unequal to the struggle with its insurgent subjects. Just as the Bulgarian rising had been put down in a torrent of blood, so were the Serbs now rapidly defeated in a series of engagements. By September 1 Chernaiev, who had unwisely divided his forces, was obliged to give up the idea of further invasion. The Montenegrins, however, managed as usual to hold their own and even to take the offensive against the enemy.

The declaration of war by Serbia and Montenegro served as an incentive to the Panslavists in Russia to redouble their efforts. More than ten years before this the discarded rifles of the Russian army had been sent to Serbia. During the summer of 1876 the Russian enthusiasts developed a feverish activity, in which the Tsarina and the Tsarevich assumed prominent roles. Not only were subscriptions for the Red Cross solicited by aristocratic ladies in the public places of the cities, but volunteers began to leave for the scene of action, financed by the Society for Slavic Welfare. In July the Roumanian representative at Belgrade reported that five hundred thousand rubles ($250,000) had been given by Russia to the Serbs and three hundred thousand to the Montenegrins, and in September he wrote that "Belgrade is literally inundated by Russians," who were arriving by hundreds. The sums sent from Russia he estimated at twenty million francs ($4,000,000). Aksakov, the leader of Pan-Slavs, admitted in November 1877 that his society had sent some three million rubles ($1,500,000) in money and five hundred thousand rubles' ($250,000) worth of goods to the Balkans, and in the course of the war some four thousand Russian volunteers appear to have joined in the crusade.[1]

Under the circumstances the possibility of Russian intervention, even against the desires of the Tsar, became steadily greater. Gorchakov, who had come to Berlin in May with a program of partition of the Ottoman Empire, was anxious not to be unprepared in the hour of Slavic victory, which he confidently expected. He therefore welcomed the suggestion, which seems to have been made by the Emperor William, that he discuss the situation with Andrássy. For it was clear to the Russian chancellor that Austria would be the great obstacle to the realization of Slavic aspirations and that it would be impossible for Russia to invade the Balkans unless Austria could be squared. Otherwise the Austrian army might, at the crucial moment, cut the Russian lines of

---

[1] Iorga: *Correspondance diplomatique roumaine,* pp. 314, 372; Olga Novikova: *Russia and England,* chapter iii, *passim;* Loftus: *Diplomatic Reminiscences,* Second Series, II, p. 171; Fischel: op. cit., p. 413; Schweinitz: *Denkwürdigkeiten,* I, pp. 340 ff., etc. Nelidov, op. cit., p. 335, admits that he transmitted to Belgrade all the news of the Turkish armies that he could get at Constantinople. See also H. S. Edwards: *Sir William White* (London, 1902), pp. 94 ff.

communication by closing the narrow passage between the Carpathians and the Black Sea. Russian writers have again and again stressed the immense importance of Austrian neutrality for Russia.[1]

On July 8, 1876 the Russian and Austrian ministers met at Reichstadt, Bohemia, and discussed the situation. The outcome was an informal agreement, which Andrássy dictated immediately afterwards to the Russian ambassador, under the title *Résumé de pourparlers secrets de Reichstadt,* and which Gorchakov also appears to have dictated to one of his secretaries. The form of the record is of considerable importance, because on a later occasion there was some dispute between the two statesmen as to what had actually been agreed upon, and the Austrian and Russian texts, which have been published since the World War, are at variance the one with the other on several points.[2]

Leaving aside minor questions, however, the basis of the understanding was the idea of common action, whatever the outcome of the struggle between the two principalities and the Ottoman Empire might be. But the agreement had no bearing on a possible future Russian-Turkish war, as stated in many books. Gorchakov and Andrássy agreed to insist on the re-establishment of the *status quo ante bellum* if Serbia and Montenegro were defeated. In that event Austria and Russia would insist that Bosnia and Herzegovina be organized on the basis of the program embodied in the Andrássy Note and the Berlin Memorandum. In other words, the Turks were not to be allowed to derive any advantage from an eventual victory. On the other hand, if Serbia and Montenegro were victorious, Austria and Russia were to co-operate to regulate the territorial changes. According to the Austrian version, "it was agreed that Serbia should obtain an extension of territory in the Drina region of Bosnia, at the same time as in that of Novi-Bazar in Old Serbia and in the direction of the Lim. On her side Montenegro should be rounded out by the annexation of a part of Herzegovina adjoining her territories; she should obtain the port of Spizza as well as an aggrandizement in the region of the Lim, in such a way that the tongue of land which now stretches between Serbia and Montenegro should be divided between the two principalities by the course of the river. The rest of Bosnia and Herzegovina should be annexed to Austria-Hungary." According to the Russian text the two contracting powers agreed not to favour the establishment of a large Slavic state, but "Montenegro and Serbia may annex, the former Herzegovina and a port on the Adriatic, the latter some parts of Old Serbia and of Bosnia.

---

[1] e.g., Anon. (Elie Cyon): "*La Guerre russo-turque d'après des documents inédits*" (*Nouvelle Revue*, IV, pp. 473–507, June 1, 1880), based upon the papers of the Grand Duke Nicholas.

[2] The Austrian text in A. F. Pribram: *The Secret Treaties of Austria-Hungary, 1879–1914* (Cambridge, 1921), II, p. 188; the Russian text in the *Krasny Arkhiv*, I, p. 36 (1922). The best discussions of the agreement are by Wertheimer, op. cit., II, pp. 321 ff., on the Austrian side, and by Goriainov: op. cit., pp. 318, 329. The discrepancies in the two texts were first pointed out and explained by G. H. Rupp: "The Reichstadt Agreement" (*American Historical Review*, XXX, pp. 503–10, April 1925). See also R. W. Seton-Watson: "Russian Commitments in the Bosnian Question" (*Slavonic Review*, VIII, pp. 578–88, March 1930).

But in that case Austria may annex Turkish Croatia and some parts of Bosnia contiguous to her frontiers, the line of demarcation to be agreed upon later."

Here lay the root of the misunderstanding. The Austrians thought that in case of a victory of the Christians the larger part of Bosnia and Herzegovina should fall to the Dual Monarchy. The Russians understood that the larger part of these two provinces was to go to the principalities, and that Austria should get only a relatively small part of Bosnia. There are other points of difference in the two texts, but in general it was agreed that Russia should get Bessarabia and some extension of her frontier in Asia Minor on the Armenian side. If the Ottoman Empire in Europe should collapse entirely, Bulgaria and Roumelia (according to the Austrian text, Albania also) might form autonomous states (according to the Russian text, independent principalities). Greece might make annexations in Epirus, Thessaly, and Crete. Constantinople and the vicinity might be made a free city.

Both parties left Reichstadt very well satisfied, because each thought he had made a good bargain. Andrássy's reform policy having failed, he had been forced to accept the Russian partition policy or else leave the Russians a free hand. He now believed that he had made adequate provision against the formation of a large Slav state on the Austrian frontier, not only by curtailing the eventual annexations to be made by Serbia, but by securing for Austria the larger part of the two provinces. Gorchakov, to be sure, had had to make sacrifices, but he was, so he thought, abandoning only a fraction of Bosnia to Austria in order to secure the rest for the Slav principalities. In addition there was the prospect for Russia of regaining Bessarabia and of seeing Bulgaria and Roumelia established as autonomous or even independent principalities.

Gorchakov's position was, for the time being, a strong one, for, having squared the Austrians, he now had only the opposition of the English to fear. When the Serbs declared war on Turkey, the danger of active English intervention became really serious. The German ambassador reported Disraeli and his friends talking as though war with Russia and an English occupation of Constantinople were inevitable.[1] The English prime minister was disgusted by the " unjustifiable " and " infamous " invasion of the Serbs, who, he felt sure, would never have dared move unless supported by Russia.[2] But almost immediately a great change took place in the position of the English government. News of the Bulgarian massacres, which had occurred in the earlier part of May, began to appear at last. The government was accused of having attempted to withhold the facts, and the English ambassador at Constantinople especially was believed to have been shielding the Turks. As a matter of fact, he appears to have been quite innocent; the delay in the transmission of the news was due chiefly to the reprehensible conduct of the English consul-general at Constantinople.[3]

---

[1] Wertheimer, op. cit., II, p. 314.
[2] Monypenny and Buckle, op. cit., VI, pp. 36–7.
[3] Full details in Sir Henry Elliot, op. cit., pp. 260 ff.; Monypenny and Buckle, op. cit., VI,

The English public was prepared to make the most of the reported atrocities. Sympathy with the Turk had disappeared and the feelings of Crimean War days were a thing of the past. In large part this was due undoubtedly to an outraged sense of humanitarianism, but it should not be forgotten that more sordid motives played a part. Since 1856 both the British and the French had been doing a rushing financial business with the Turkish government. One loan had been floated after another on terms most favourable to the lenders. In one case the issue price was as low as 43.5, and the average was about 60. The interest was usually five or six per cent, and the brokers took a commission of six or seven per cent. So profitable was the business that the Ottoman Bank was able to pay a dividend of twelve to thirteen per cent over a period of years. By 1875 more than one billion dollars had been loaned to the Turkish government. The annual service on such a huge debt was quite beyond the capacity of a comparatively primitive financial organization, and before long the government, which had been raising new loans in order to pay the interest on the old, was confronted with bankruptcy. Ignatiev advised Mahmud Nedim to meet his problem by suspending payments, for he saw here an excellent opportunity to undermine the Anglo-French influence at Constantinople. In any case, the Ottoman government in October 1875 announced payment in cash of only half the interest coupons, and in March 1876 passed the coupons of the 1858 loan and deferred the payments on the loans of 1869 and 1873.[1]

The news of the Bulgarian atrocities, then, came just at a time when many people in England had already lost all sympathy with the Turks and their government. As further details reached London, a tremendous agitation began to develop, which by the end of the summer had reached unheard-of proportions. Gladstone, leader of the opposition, saw his opportunity to exploit the situation for political purposes and published, on September 6, his famous pamphlet *Bulgarian Horrors and the Question of the East,* of which it is said that forty thousand copies were sold in a short time. The pamphlet, with its bitter arraignment of the Turks, was really an attack on the English government, which was supposed to be supporting them. Gladstone admits in his brochure that Serbia had " no stateable cause for war," but, he continued, " there are states of affairs, in which human sympathy refuses to be confined by the rules, necessarily limited and conventional, of international law." England should recognize this and give up her distrust of " the standing hobgoblin of Russia." " I say the time has come for us to emulate Russia by sharing in her good deeds, and to reserve our opposition until she shall visibly endeavour to turn them to evil account." The Turks, he maintained, " were, upon the whole, from the

chapter ii; Sir Edwin Pears: *Forty Years in Constantinople* (New York, 1916), chapter ii; Marquis of Zetland: *Letters of Disraeli to Lady Bradford* (London, 1929), II, pp. 69 ff., 75–7.

[1] The most recent account and one of the best is by Donald C. Blaisdell: *European Financial Control in the Ottoman Empire* (New York, 1929), pp. 1–80. On Ignatiev's influence, see further; " *Aus dem politischen Nachlass des Unterstaatssekretärs Dr. Busch* " (*Deutsche Rundschau,* XXXV, pp. 368–406, December 1908).

black day when they first entered Europe, the one great anti-human specimen of humanity. Wherever they went, a broad line of blood marked the track behind them; and, as far as their dominion reached, civilization disappeared from view." Yet Gladstone did not by any means forget himself to the extent of demanding that the Turks be expelled from Europe, as many writers seem to believe. " As regards the territorial integrity of Turkey, I for one am still desirous to see it upheld," he said. All he asked was that the Turkish administration be excluded from Bosnia, Herzegovina, and Bulgaria. In other words, administrative autonomy was to be the goal. " Let the Turks now carry away their abuses in the only possible manner, namely by carrying off themselves. Their Zaptiehs and their Mudirs, their Bimbashis and their Yuzbachis, their Kaimakams and their Pashas, one and all, bag and baggage, shall, I hope, clear out from the province they have desolated and profaned." It should be noticed that this eloquent and oft-quoted passage refers merely to Bulgaria and merely to the Turkish officials in Bulgaria, and that it was in no sense intended to be a demand for the ejection of the Turks from Europe.[1]

The Gladstone pamphlet was only the most spectacular episode in the great anti-Turk agitation which swept through England. When a Bulgarian delegation arrived in London, the government could not avoid receiving it. The delegates themselves seem to have been unable to understand the indescribable enthusiasm of the population. It has been estimated that no less than two hundred and sixty-eight meetings were held in favour of the Bulgarians.[2]

It was only natural that the Russians should deduce from this vigorous anti-Turk movement that the English government would be quite unable to take a strong stand against the Russian policy in favour of the southern Slavs. That some action would have to be taken became perfectly clear after the defeat of Chernaiev on September 1 and the appeal of Prince Milan for intervention. The powers, therefore, proposed that the Porte grant an armistice of one month "with a view to the immediate discussion of conditions of peace." This proposal the Turks regarded quite naturally as wholly to the advantage of Serbia. They were ready to grant an armistice, but only together with a preliminary agreement as to the terms of peace. The powers were not obliged to wait long to find out what these terms would be: the Prince of Serbia was to come to Constantinople to renew his homage; certain Serbian fortresses were to be reoccupied by Turkish troops; the Serbian army was to be limited to ten thousand men; the Serbian militia was to be disbanded entirely; and Serbia was to pay either an increased tribute or a war indemnity. The terms were hard. No question about that. But they were mild compared to the terms that were to have been imposed on the Porte in case of a Christian victory.

---

[1] The sense is clear from the context, but see also Monypenny and Buckle, op. cit., VI, p. 61; John Morley: *Life of Gladstone* (London, 1903), Volume II, pp. 551 ff.; Gladstone's letter in *The Times*, September 10, 1876.

[2] Hajek, op. cit., pp. 303 ff. There is an excellent account of the agitation in Rudolf Liebold: *Die Stellung Englands in der russisch-türkischen Krise von 1875–78* (Wilkau, 1930), pp. 45 ff.

None of the powers regarded the projected Turkish peace terms as at all acceptable, and Russia saw here her opportunity of utilizing the anti-Turkish sentiments of Europe to organize a general crusade against Russia's traditional enemy. From England nothing was to be feared for the moment. Under pressure of public opinion the English government had practically adopted the earlier Russian program, and was willing to support the demand for peace on the basis of the *status quo ante bellum,* administrative autonomy for Bosnia and Herzegovina, and some similar arrangement for Bulgaria. Disraeli himself had come to see that the policy of non-intervention had gone bankrupt, and agreed with Andrássy that there was no alternative between the reform notes of the winter and spring, and the " solution " of the Eastern question. He no longer believed that the " solution " could be prevented, and foresaw the eventual invasion of the Balkans by Russia and Austria and a division of the spoils between them. Under the circumstances he thought it would be better for England to join and even assume the leadership: " Constantinople with an adequate district should be neutralised and made a free port, in the custody and under the guardianship of England, as the Ionian Isles were." [1] Lord Salisbury believed that " the Turk's teeth must be drawn even if he be allowed to live," and that, since the British lion, whose nerves were not so good as formerly, had been driven half mad by the Bulgarian stories, " no arrangement will be possible which does not in some form administratively detach the revolted provinces from the Government at Constantinople." To attain this end peacefully the best method would be to come to an early understanding with Russia, and to stop hanging on to the coat-tails of Austria, whose tremors England had no reason to share. Disraeli himself had come to see the need for an understanding with Russia.[2]

Clearly there was nothing threatening in the English attitude, and Gorchakov for the time being had a free hand. But Gorchakov had no very definite idea as to how to attack the problem. In August he had suggested to Bismarck the convocation of a European congress or conference to deal with the situation. In this Bismarck was to take the initiative. But the German chancellor was unalterably opposed to being sent to the firing line. He suspected that his Russian colleague was moved less by the hope of effecting a general agreement than by the desire to preside at a congress and appear in the eyes of Europe as a prince of peace. At any rate he was determined not to put himself in the awkward position of having to choose between the conflicting views and interests of Austria and England on the one hand, and of Russia, probably supported by France, on the other. He refused Gorchakov's suggestion, but decided to send General von Manteuffel to the Tsar, who was attending the manœuvres at Warsaw.

---

[1] Disraeli to Derby, September 4, 1876 (Monypenny and Buckle, op. cit., VI, p. 52).
[2] Lady Gwendolen Cecil: *Life of Robert Marquis of Salisbury* (London, 1921), II, pp. 84–6; Monypenny and Buckle, op. cit., VI, p. 71; Buckle: *Letters of Queen Victoria,* II, p. 478.

Manteuffel was given a letter from the Emperor William to the Tsar, in which the German ruler stressed the fact that Germany's attitude would always be determined by the memory of Russia's benevolent attitude during the years from 1864 to 1870. Both the Tsar and Gorchakov, however, made it clear that they expected a more pronounced stand in favour of Russia. Finally Alexander himself approached General von Werder, the special military plenipotentiary at the Russian court, with the question whether Germany would remain neutral if Russia became involved in war with Austria. Bismarck was much taken aback both by the form and the content of this inquiry, for at this very moment a Russian emissary was at Vienna engaged in negotiations. The German chancellor had been informed by this time of the Reichstadt agreement and had gathered from it that Russia and Austria had settled their problem. Thus far the question of a possible war between Russia and Austria had not been mentioned at all. The Russian request does, in fact, strike one as extraordinary, but it appears that the Emperor William, by constantly harping upon the service performed by Russia for Germany in the period before 1870, and Manteuffel, by his assurances to the Tsar at Warsaw, had given the impression that Germany was prepared to take the Russian side and was merely waiting to be asked.

For Bismarck the question was an exceedingly awkward one, for it involved making a choice between Russia and Austria, the very thing that he was anxious to avoid. The Russians, however, were unwilling to accept an evasive reply, and finally Bismarck recalled from leave General von Schweinitz, the ambassador to Russia, and sent him to Livadia, in the Crimea, where the Russian court was staying. The German chancellor's reply to the Russian inquiry was that Germany would, in case of war between Russia and Turkey, use her influence with Austria to maintain peace. If a break between Austria and Russia were to take place, that in itself would be no reason for Germany to give up her neutrality. On the other hand, it would not be to Germany's interest if, in such a war, Russia's position as a great power were fundamentally or permanently injured, or if the independence of the Austrian monarchy or its position as a European power were imperilled. In his memoirs Bismarck puts the thing picturesquely: "We could indeed endure that our friends should lose or win battles against each other, but not that one of the two should be so severely wounded and injured that its position as an independent great power, taking its part in the councils of Europe, would be endangered." [1]

This was one of the cardinal points in Bismarck's policy, and one which he maintained throughout the rest of his political career. For him the position of Austria as a great power was a primary German interest, an idea which he expressed over and over again. It is rather peculiar, then, to note that he suggested

---

[1] *Bismarck, the Man and the Statesman*, II, p. 234. On this whole important episode see the documents in *Die Grosse Politik*, II, Nos. 229–53; Schweinitz: *Denkwürdigkeiten*, I, pp. 349 ff.; Schweinitz: *Briefwechsel*, I, pp. 115 ff.; *Documents diplomatiques français*, II, Nos. 83, 91; and the discussion in Albert Helms: *Bismarck und Russland* (Bonn, 1927), chapter vi.

to Schweinitz the possibility of an agreement with Russia if the latter were willing to guarantee the German possession of Alsace-Lorraine. The German ambassador actually raised the point in talking to Gorchakov, but the Russian chancellor put it off by saying that such a guarantee would be of no use to Germany, for formal treaties had a very small value. Historians have differed much in their interpretation of this episode. There seems to be no doubt that Bismarck toyed with the idea of an agreement with Russia, not against Austria, but against France. To one of his confidants he remarked at this time: " During these Eastern troubles the only question that might crop up for us would be that of having Russia guarantee us Alsace and eventually to use this combination to belabour the French thoroughly once again." [1] But he did not think the Emperor could be converted to this idea, and he probably knew that the Russians would not entertain it. Schweinitz, in fact, was not authorized to conclude a formal agreement. On later occasions he reminded the Russians of his offer of October 1876 and of the way he had been " snubbed " by Gorchakov, but this was a purely tactical matter, the chancellor's object being to show the Russians that they had had their chance and had passed it by. Surely it can hardly be imagined that Bismarck seriously entertained the plan of allying with Russia against Austria.[2]

Although the Tsar did not conceal his disappointment at the German reply, and Gorchakov put himself out to show the German ambassador his extreme dissatisfaction, it is very doubtful whether the Russians had seriously expected to receive the permission of one of their colleagues in the Three Emperors' League to make war on the other. Nothing shows this more clearly than the mission of General Sumarokov-Elston to Vienna at the very time of the negotiation with Germany. What the Russian general proposed to the Austrians was that Russia should occupy Bulgaria while Austria occupied Bosnia and the great powers sent their fleets to the Bosporus. In this way the Turks might be compelled to accept the decisions of Europe. The letter of the Tsar to Francis Joseph in which these proposals were laid down was communicated to the other governments, a really unprecedented procedure. The Russian object was to reestablish in this way a European concert against Turkey. But the scheme, like Gorchakov's earlier efforts to unite the powers against the Turks, was doomed to failure. The Austrians made it clear that they could not tolerate political autonomy for Bosnia and Herzegovina, and that they objected to the occupation of Turkish territory. Once the troops of the powers had marched in, it would be almost impossible to withdraw them again or to leave the Christian populations at the mercy of Turkish promises. A long correspondence followed between

---

[1] Lucius von Ballhausen: *Bismarck-Erinnerungen*, p. 93.

[2] Later references to this subject in *Die Grosse Politik*, III, No. 455; V, Nos. 991, 992. See also Volume II, No. 252 and note, and the discussion of the whole problem by Graf Max Montgelas: " *Bismarck und Schweinitz* " (*Die Kriegsschuldfrage*, VII, pp. 47–63, January 1929), p. 58; and in Helms, op. cit., chapter vi.

Alexander and Francis Joseph, but the Austrian Emperor throughout maintained his stand. He could not be expected to join in forcing the Porte to accept a solution which was distinctly not to the interest of the Dual Monarchy.[1] The other powers showed no greater inclination to support the Russians. In fact, the Sumarokov mission was taken as further evidence, if such were needed, that Russia was determined to act.

Andrássy was much exercised by these developments, especially as he feared that Italy might join Russia, and that thereby Austria might be exposed to an attack from the rear. He tried to square the Italians by suggesting that they take Tunis as compensation for eventual Austrian expansion in Bosnia.[2] More important yet, he sent Baron Münch to consult with Bismarck, immediately after the departure of Sumarokov-Elston. Münch had several interviews with Bismarck at the chancellor's estate at Varzin and set forth the seriousness of an eventual Russian occupation of Bulgaria. Bismarck did not consider this so disastrous a prospect. The Austrians could occupy Bosnia, and, above all, they could rely upon the opposition of England to the Russian scheme. Austria and England should stand shoulder to shoulder. Münch then broached the subject of an eventual alliance between Austria and Germany to keep Italy quiet, but Bismarck refused to entertain the Austrian suggestion, just as he had refused to consider the Russian. If the alliance were to be made, he said, the Russians would interpret it as directed against themselves. He was unwilling to do anything that would change Germany's status from that of a peaceful power to that of a warlike one. He had rejected the Russian suggestion because it involved hostility to Austria. In the same way he would have to reject the Austrian suggestion because it involved hostility to Russia.[3]

In the midst of the general uncertainty all eyes were turned to Berlin. The Russians foresaw the necessity of taking action eventually and had sounded the German chancellor as to his attitude. The Austrians, fearing the Russian plans, had done likewise. Now the English, too, were to follow suit. Disraeli was thoroughly upset by the news of the projected action of Russia in Bulgaria. This action, if actually carried out, would seriously affect England's position by threatening the road to the East. There was no use talking about taking Egypt, for the Russians could advance by way of Constantinople and Asia Minor and attack the Suez Canal from Syria. Then even the English fleet would be of no

---

[1] The fullest account is in Wertheimer, op. cit., II, pp. 341 ff.; see also *Documents diplomatiques français*, II, Nos. 88, 92.

[2] I am relying on a manuscript history of Italian foreign policy shown me by Professor Gaetano Salvemini. The French fears of such a bargain appear in *Documents diplomatiques français*, II, Nos. 116, 122.

[3] Wertheimer: " *Neues zur Orientpolitik des Grafen Andrássy* " (*Historische Blätter*, I, pp. 269–73, 1921). This phase of Austrian policy is also treated by Otto Lange: *Die Orientpolitik Österreich-Ungarns vom Ausgleich bis zum Berliner Kongress* (Berlin, 1926), of which only the chapter dealing with the period from the Reichstadt agreement to the mission of Schweinitz to Livadia has been published.

use: " Constantinople is the key of India, and not Egypt and the Suez Canal." All talk to the contrary was mere " moonshine." [1] Disraeli was already considering the possibility of sending an English force to occupy the lines of Constantinople and the Dardanelles, though Lord Derby was flatly opposed to any military measures' being taken. The one redeeming feature of the situation was that the rumours of the Russian plans were bringing about a reversion of feeling in England. " England looks upon the proposed occupation by Russia as a real Bulgarian atrocity," wrote Disraeli.[2] Gradually fear of the Russian designs was overcoming the spirit of crusade in favour of the Christians.

Disraeli made one last effort to prevent a crisis. The English ambassador to Constantinople was instructed to urge the Porte to grant an armistice, and to threaten to leave the Turks to their fate if they remained obdurate. It was hard for the Turks to yield. The reforming element, with its nationalistic tendencies, was now in complete control. On August 30 Midhat and his friends had deposed Murad V on the plea of insanity. His successor, Abdul Hamid II, was expected by the reformers to realize their constitutional and national aims. Sentiment in Constantinople ran high. Why should the victorious Turks accept conditions favourable to the defeated Christians? In the capital posters were set up threatening the ministers with impalement if they accepted conditions other than that Serbia, Montenegro, and Roumania should become provinces of the reorganized Turkish Empire.[3] And yet the ministers thought it best to yield to the English representations. On October 10 they agreed to an armistice of five or six months. Since the original English request had been for an armistice of not less than one month or six weeks, the English raised no objection. Neither did the other great powers, except Russia, which backed Serbia in the demand for a short armistice, the Serbs insisting that they could not tolerate a Turkish occupation of their territory throughout the winter.

No progress, then, had been made towards solving the Eastern imbroglio or towards removing the threat of Russian action. As a last resort Disraeli decided to approach Bismarck for aid. On October 16 the London *Times* published a leading article which may have been inspired: " One plain word from Bismarck would stop Russia even on the brink of the abyss into which a very little more pressure would make her plunge." This word could be uttered in a friendly way and would be to Bismarck's own advantage, for if war broke out, France might be tempted by the offer of an attractive alliance from Russia. *The Times* therefore suggested " a cordial alliance between Germany and England for the purpose of making the requisite changes in Turkey." On the very next day Disraeli wrote to the Queen, to Derby, and to Salisbury suggesting an agreement with Germany on the basis of the *status quo:* " This would make us easy about Constantinople and relieve Bismarck of his real bugbear, the eventual

---

[1] Monypenny and Buckle, op. cit., VI, pp. 84, 100.
[2] Ibid., p. 79.
[3] Iorga: *Correspondance diplomatique roumaine,* p. 383.

alliance of England and France, and the loss of his two captured provinces."
This indication of Disraeli's willingness to guarantee to Germany the possession
of Alsace and Lorraine was a noteworthy departure, and there is no knowing
what Bismarck's reaction might have been if the proposal had actually been
made. All we know is that the British ambassador confined himself to a request
for Bismarck's suggestion as to a possible solution. The chancellor was not in
Berlin, and the inquiry was forwarded to him at Varzin.

The English request, as it reached him, was not of the kind that required
an immediate answer, nor could it appear to the German chancellor as anything
but a renewed attempt to induce him to take the initiative. He therefore prefaced his instructions to the German foreign office with a restatement of the
German view. It would be erroneous, he argued, to suppose that human wisdom
could discover a formula to settle the problem. There were here conflicting
interests on the part of the powers, and only if they made concessions to each
other could a clash be avoided. For Germany to suggest these concessions or
to press them upon the powers would simply mean that she would assume the
odium for an unpopular solution, and this she could not afford to do, since she
had no direct interest in the matter. In his view the whole Ottoman Empire as a
political institution was not of sufficient value to justify the civilized peoples
of Europe in ruining themselves by wars to uphold it. Peace might be maintained and the problem settled at Turkey's expense. If Russia went to war with
Turkey, Austria would do wisely if she remained neutral and occupied Bosnia.
England should occupy Egypt and Suez and reach an agreement with Russia
about Constantinople, by which the Turkish capital and its environs, as well as
the Straits, would remain under Ottoman sovereignty. Russia apparently did not
intend a permanent occupation of Bulgaria, but desired primarily the acquisition of Bessarabia. A possible antagonism between England and France in
regard to Egypt might be obviated by assigning Syria to France. Far from being
a bugbear to Germany, the friendship of England and France was positively
valuable to her, for the one power would act as a check upon the other, and
there was no real danger that the English would ever go to war to help the
French reconquer Alsace and Lorraine.[1]

Bismarck described this projected program as a picture of fancy (*Phantasie-
gemälde*), but it was really an unusually revealing presentation of the policy he
had been suggesting since January. European peace, his greatest interest, could
best be secured by satisfying the interested powers at the expense of Turkey, a
state which was hardly worth preserving. Of course this program was not submitted to the English ambassador in all detail, but Russell was told that the German chancellor " failed to understand what interest England had in risking a
second time to dissolve the European Concert for the sake of the Turkish Empire, which peace could not long keep together, and war must inevitably break

---

[1] *Die Grosse Politik*, II, No. 250.

up. . . . Believing England to be the Power most likely and best able to promote peace in Europe, he had begged at the commencement of the crisis to be allowed to support her efforts to find a pacific solution of the Eastern problem. Events had not justified his hopes and expectations. . . . He was the first to acknowledge the vital interest of England in Egypt, Asia and India, he could appreciate the wish of England to prolong the Sultan's rule on the Bosphorus, but he failed to see what interest England had to defend north of the Balkans that could be dearer to her than peace. It was his earnest wish to join hands with England for the maintenance of peace, but public opinion in Germany would not support a war policy for the Sublime Porte who was no longer able to supply the just demands of her Christian subjects for a civilized administration in accordance with modern requirements."

Russell's comment on this statement left no doubt that he had understood Bismarck's point: " The impression left on my mind," he wrote home, " is that Prince Bismarck wishes for a more lasting settlement of the Turkish Question than he suspects Her Majesty's Government are prepared to sanction. He thought that a mere 'replastering' of the edifice as originally proposed by Prince Gortchakow would not last many months, — and when he offered his support and co-operation to England, he fancied that the purchase of the Suez Canal shares indicated a tendency to secure the road to India, and arrest the progress of Russia in the East. He then hoped to realize, with the consent of England, his favourite scheme of inducing Austria gradually to extend her dominions over European Turkey, and of keeping Russia in check with the help of England and Austria combined. Events have not taken the course he expected, England has not annexed Egypt, and has not opposed the progress of Russia, so he turns to the rising sun in the East, and hopes to get through Russia what he had hoped to obtain through England, — i.e. a more thorough and lasting settlement of the ever-recurring Turkish Question, and the extension of Austrian rule in Eastern Europe." [1] In other words, Bismarck's solution was based upon the idea of partition, and this, he realized, the English would be unwilling to accept. Since there was no prospect of doing business with London, he would have to fall back upon the Russian policy of enlisting the powers in a joint action against the Turks.

Meanwhile things had been going from bad to worse in the Balkans. The Turks had continued their campaign against the Serbs and during the last days of October had inflicted another crushing defeat upon them. The road to Belgrade lay open and the Turks showed no inclination to retard their advance. In Russia indignation, fanned by the Panslavists, had been rising higher and

---

[1] Russell to Derby, October 23, 1876. This document is unpublished, and I am indebted to Professor D. E. Lee for an abstract of it. See further Monypenny and Buckle, op. cit., VI, pp. 81–2; Buckle: *Letters of Queen Victoria*, II, pp. 489–93, 495, 502–3. A detailed discussion of the episode may be found in Heinrich Prosch: " *Ein englischer Bündnisfühler im Jahre 1876* " (*Historische Vierteljahrschrift*, XXIV, No. 4, pp. 588–607, 1929).

higher. Ever since the first set-backs suffered by the Serbs late in August, the movement had become a danger to the government. The diplomats, many of them, had no sympathy with the agitation and regarded it as a menace. Count Shuvalov, the ambassador at London, spoke of the volunteers who had hurried to Serbia as a " band of revolutionaries, ambitious agitators, members of secret societies, and the very scum of Russia." But the Tsar and the government felt helpless. Alexander is said to have written his uncle, Emperor William, that he had received personal menaces, and that he could no longer resist what Ignatiev, himself a Pan-Slav, described as the " national conscience." [1]

The Tsar, forced to do something, finally took the bull by the horns. On October 31 Ignatiev handed in to the Porte a forty-eight-hour ultimatum demanding an armistice of six weeks for the Serbs. Under threat of the severance of diplomatic relations the Porte yielded. The uncertainty of the past two months came to an end. What the Porte had objected to was the suspension of hostilities before knowing what peace terms would be accepted. In suggesting a six months' armistice the Turkish government had evidently hoped to evade a European conference to discuss the peace terms, as proposed by the powers. Now, however, the short armistice had been granted, and it was to be expected that the powers would proceed to the conference.

England did, in fact, issue invitations to a conference to be held at Constantinople, to which special plenipotentiaries should be sent. The situation was a peculiar one. Turkey had won the war against one of her tributary states. Now the powers were to assemble at the Turkish capital to arrange terms to the advantage of the rebels. It may be argued that the oppression of the Christians made the case a special one, but it should not be forgotten that the Russian crusade in Poland since the suppression of the great rising of 1863 was hardly more edifying. The difficulty with the Turks was at bottom due to the fact that they were unable to defend themselves against the great powers, and that their territorial position was so strong in a strategic sense that more than one of the powers had long been casting covetous eyes on parts of the empire. Disraeli's remark, somewhat later, that Lord Salisbury had been sent to the conference " to keep the Russians out of Turkey, not to create an ideal existence for Turkish Christians," is as illuminating as it is frank.[2]

In spite of the fact that a conference was agreed to by the powers, none of them had much confidence in its success. The Russians had by this time decided ·on taking action and had begun active preparations for war. To be sure, the Tsar told the British ambassador on November 2 that " he desired no conquest, that he aimed at no aggrandizement, and that he had not the smallest wish or intention to be possessed of Constantinople," but at the same time he made it clear that unless Europe were ready to proceed with firmness and energy, he

---

[1] *Documents diplomatiques français,* II, Nos. 80, 81, 91, 94, 100.
[2] Monypenny and Buckle, op. cit., VI, p. 111.

would be obliged to act alone.[1] Even before the ultimatum had been dispatched to the Porte, a great war council had been held at Livadia, and the Grand Duke Nicholas had been designated as commander-in-chief. The goal of the campaign, he was told, would be Constantinople. Nicholas and the military men favoured immediate action, in view of the fact that only four army corps could be spared and it would be necessary to attack before the enemy had time to prepare. But the acceptance of the armistice by the Porte put an end to these plans for the time being.[2]

That the great powers were not in a very pacific frame of mind was shown by the speeches delivered by Disraeli at the Guildhall on November 9 and by the Tsar at Moscow on November 10. " Although the policy of England is peace," said Disraeli, " there is no country so well prepared for war as our own. If she enters into a conflict in a righteous cause — and I will not believe that England will go to war except for a righteous cause — if the contest is one which concerns her liberty, her independence, or her empire, her resources, I feel, are inexhaustible. She is not a country that, when she enters into a campaign, has to ask herself whether she can support a second or a third campaign. She enters into a campaign which she will not terminate till right is done." The Tsar had no knowledge of this speech when he delivered his own on the following day, though the two sound much like an exchange of challenges. " My ardent wish is for a peaceful agreement," said Alexander. " Should we not obtain from the Porte such guarantees for carrying out the reforms we have a right to demand, I am firmly determined to act independently; and I am convinced that the whole of Russia will support me, should the honour of Russia require it, and that Moscow will set the example." Within a week the Russian government ordered the mobilization of four corps of the active army and two corps for observation, in all one hundred and sixty thousand men. The Russians were determined to force acceptance of their demands by " material coercion " in the form of an occupation of Bulgaria.[3]

Lord Salisbury had been selected as the English plenipotentiary to the conference, and he left for Constantinople towards the end of November. Like most of the European statesmen he had no confidence in the success of the meeting, which he considered a " comedy " involving " seasickness, much French, and failure." [4] On the way to the Turkish capital he stopped at Berlin and Vienna to confer with Bismarck and Andrássy. He found the German chancellor very pessimistic, but very anxious to avoid a general European struggle. He felt that the Russians would take action, for, he remarked to one

---

[1] Loftus. *Diplomatic Reminiscences*, II, pp. 183–4; Seton-Watson, in *Slavonic Review*, IV, pp. 194–5, June 1925; Schweinitz: *Denkwürdigkeiten*, I, p. 361; Wertheimer: *Andrássy*, II, p. 352; Goriainov, op. cit., p. 325; *Die Grosse Politik*, II, Nos. 254, 255.

[2] (Cyon:) " *La Guerre russo-turque* " (*Nouvelle Revue*, IV, p. 480, June 1, 1880).

[3] *Documents diplomatiques français*, II, Nos. 112, 113.

[4] Cecil: *Salisbury*, II, p. 90.

of his intimates, they were in the position of the man who, having ordered a steak, will eat it because he has paid for it, even though his appetite has passed. The Russians, having made great preparations, would go to war.[1] But, he said to Salisbury, even in the event of a Russian-Turkish war a general conflagration need not follow. England should not act precipitously and should not move until the Russians had at least crossed the Balkan Mountains. Even then she should first occupy Turkish territory as a guarantee. Egypt or even Constantinople would serve the purpose. With the Russians in Bulgaria and the Austrians in Bosnia, an agreement between the three powers could then be arranged. Much the same language was held by Andrássy, who had been informed of what had been said in Berlin.[2]

Meanwhile, however, Disraeli had been taking precautions, just like the Tsar. On October 29 a group of English officers had been sent out by the war office to examine the defences in Thrace, from the Black Sea westward, and to investigate " all matters required . . . in the event of a British force being sent to hold [Constantinople]." Colonel Home, one of the members of the commission, later on drew up memoranda for Lord Salisbury as to steps to be taken " in case of its becoming necessary for Great Britain to secure guarantees, of England occupying the Dardanelles permanently on both the European and Asiatic sides." [3] In short, the English government had been envisaging exactly the measures which Bismarck proposed.

It appeared soon afterwards that there was no occasion for the alarm felt in Russian and British governmental circles. Salisbury, on arriving at Constantinople, got in touch with Ignatiev, and before long the two diplomats were working together in harmony. Various explanations have been advanced to account for this strange phenomenon. According to Sir Henry Elliot, Salisbury's colleague, the English minister was quite ignorant of conditions in Turkey and fell under Ignatiev's influence. The secretary of the Russian embassy tells us that Ignatiev put himself out to win Salisbury by " flattery and by intelligent and specious technical explanations and statistical data." [4] There is no doubt that Salisbury did not share Elliot's distrust of the Russian ambassador, but it is also true that he had long felt the necessity for an understanding with Russia. He had less fear of the Russian hobgoblin and more sympathy for the Balkan Christian than had Disraeli.[5] Above all, he was anxious to avoid a Russian occupation of Bulgaria.

[1] Lucius von Ballhausen, op. cit., p. 94.

[2] Cecil: *Salisbury*, II, pp. 96 ff.; *Die Grosse Politik*, II, Nos. 263, 264; Wertheimer: *Andrássy*, II, pp. 362 ff.; Radowitz: *Aufzeichnungen*, I, pp. 363–4; *Documents diplomatiques français*, II, No. 121.

[3] From a memorandum by J. L. A. Simmons, dated October 2, 1877, in the Simmons Papers, F. O. 358, for which I am indebted to Professor D. E. Lee.

[4] Elliot: *Some Revolutions*, pp. 276 ff.; Nelidov, in the *Revue des deux mondes*, XXVIII, pp. 18 ff., July 15, 1915.

[5] Cecil: *Salisbury*, II, *passim;* Seton-Watson, in *Slavonic Review*, IV, pp. 447, 452, 453, December 1925.

Be that as it may, the two men lost no time in working for a compromise. Gorchakov certainly hoped that through the conference the question could at last be Europeanized, and that, even if the Turks refused the projected program, the powers would either act or give Russia a mandate to act.[1] But the Russians desired to avoid a humiliation and insisted that the powers draw up the terms first, without the co-operation of the Turks. To this Salisbury finally agreed, and the preliminary conferences began on December 11. Ignatiev succeeded in throwing the emphasis of the discussions on the Bulgarian question, rather than on the problem of peace between Turkey and Serbia or on the question of the status of Bosnia and Herzegovina, though these last were the ostensible agenda. On the other hand Ignatiev gave up the original Russian demand that Bulgaria be occupied by Russian troops, and agreed to an administrative division of Bulgaria. Briefly stated, the delegates agreed that peace should be made with Serbia on the basis of the *status quo ante,* excepting for a rectification of the frontier in Serbia's favour. Montenegro was to receive the conquered districts of Herzegovina and northern Albania. Bulgaria, by which was meant roughly the region under the religious jurisdiction of the Bulgarian exarch, was to be divided into an eastern and a western province (the twin-vilayet scheme). Bosnia and Herzegovina were to be united as one province, and each of the three provinces mentioned was to receive not only a governor-general (a Christian in the two Bulgarian provinces), appointed for five years by the Porte with the approval of the powers, but also a provincial assembly. A police force was to be established in the provinces, to be composed of Moslems and Christians in the ratio of the populations belonging to each confession. Seventy per cent of the income of the provinces was to be devoted to local expenditure, and European commissions were to supervise the introduction of these reforms. Curiously enough, this reform scheme, especially as it applied to Bulgaria, was in large measure the work of the American consul-general at Constantinople, Eugene Schuyler, who had investigated conditions in Bulgaria after the massacres and who was invited by Ignatiev to draw up a constitution which would serve as a basis of discussion.[2]

These terms were described as the "irreducible minimum" which the powers would accept. By the time they were drawn up and the first plenary session called on December 23, it was already clear that they would be rejected. The Turks had, from the beginning, opposed the idea of a conference. Feeling against foreign intervention in the domestic affairs of the empire had become very strong and was as firmly rooted among the Christians as among the Moslems of Constantinople. The convocation of a meeting in the capital to

---

[1] Nelidov, op. cit., pp. 18 ff.; Seton-Watson, op. cit., p. 450.

[2] Evelyn Schaeffer: *Eugene Schuyler* (New York, 1901), pp. 85, 91 ff.; I. E. Gueshov: "*Zapiski na edin Osoden*" (*Periodichesko Spisanie*, No. 36, pp. 941–68, 1891). The delimitation of the Bulgarian provinces is discussed by William A. Gauld: "*The Making of Bulgaria*" (*History*, X, pp. 26–35, April 1925).

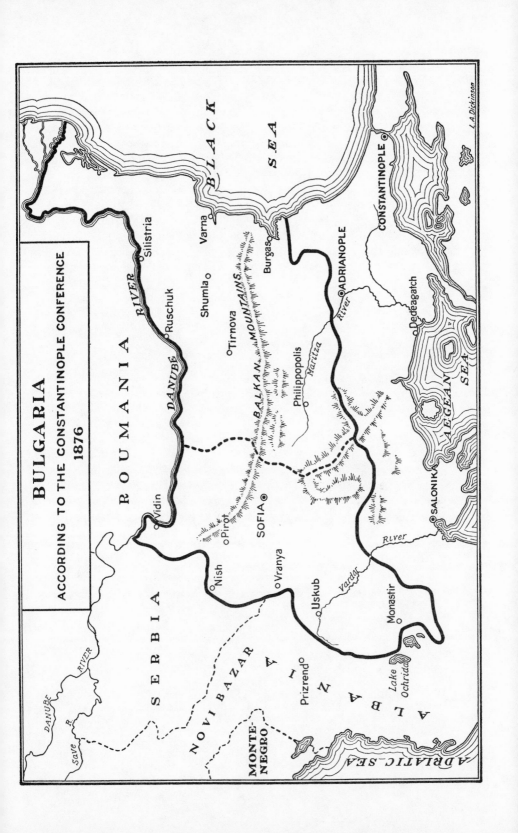

BULGARIA

ACCORDING TO THE CONSTANTINOPLE CONFERENCE

1876

L.A.Dickinson

BLACK SEA

CONSTANTINOPLE

AEGEAN SEA

ADRIATIC SEA

ROUMANIA

SERBIA

NOVI BAZAR

ALBANIA

MONTE-NEGRO

DANUBE RIVER

DANUBE

Silistria

Ruschuk

Shumla

Tirnova

Varna

Burgas

ADRIANOPLE

Dedeagatch

Maritza River

Philippopolis

BALKAN MOUNTAINS

Vidin

Pirot

SOFIA

Nish

Vranya

Uskub

Vardar River

River

Monastir

SALONIKA

Lake Ochrida

Prizrend

DANUBE RIVER

SAVE R.

discuss internal affairs was regarded as a national affront, the more so as the Turks themselves were excluded from the preliminary sessions. In order to counteract the plans of the powers Midhat Pasha and his reforming friends had been working very hard to draft a constitution for the whole empire. The publication of the outlines of this document on October 12 was meant as a warning to the powers and as a reply to the suggestion of an international conference to discuss the peace terms to be granted the Serbs. On December 20, 1876 Midhat had been made grand vizier. He had a surprise in store for the conference. When the first plenary session was opened, on December 23, a cold, raw, rainy day, the discussions of the delegates were disturbed by salvoes of artillery. By way of explanation, Safvet Pasha, the Turkish foreign minister, addressed the meeting as follows: " A great act, which is at this moment being accomplished, has just changed a form of government which has lasted 600 years. The constitution with which His Majesty the Sultan has endowed his Empire has been promulgated. It inaugurates a new era for the happiness and prosperity of his people." [1] This was the famous constitution of 1876, the work of Midhat Pasha, which introduced a form of limited monarchy, based upon western models, with a guarantee of civil liberties and an elected parliament. The very first article of this constitution stated: " The Ottoman Empire comprises present territory and possessions, and semi-independent provinces. It forms an indivisible whole, from which no portion can be detached under any pretext whatever." This was defiance hurled at the delegates to the conference, a reply to the terms which had been " flung " at the Turks, as Sir Henry Elliot put it.

When the disturbed delegates were told by Safvet Pasha that in his view the work of the conference had become superfluous since the constitution guaranteed liberties to the whole empire, his remarks were the equivalent of an announcement that the Turks would reject the recommendations of Europe. This was what actually happened. The next problem was how to save the situation. The Russian view was that united pressure should be brought to bear upon the Porte, and this procedure even Salisbury favoured. But his hands were tied. The British government informed him that it would " not assent to, or assist in coercive measures, military or naval, against the Porte." There cannot be the slightest doubt that the Turks learned of the English opposition to strong-arm methods at a very early date, probably through the British ambassador, Sir Henry Elliot, who was thoroughly out of sympathy with Salisbury's procedure and with the decisions arrived at under Russian leadership. Midhat Pasha himself says: " Turkey was not unaware of the attitude of the English government towards her; the British cabinet had declared in clear terms that it would not interfere in our dispute. . . . We knew still better that the general interests of Europe and the particular interests of England, were so bound up in our dispute

---

[1] *British State Papers. Turkey*, No. 2 (1877), p. 228.

with Russia, that, in spite of all the declarations of the English cabinet, it appeared to us to be absolutely impossible for her to avoid interfering sooner or later in this Eastern dispute." [1]

Under the circumstances there was nothing for the delegates to do but to reduce the "irreducible minimum" and submit to the Porte what was described as the "quintessence" of the demands of the powers. The Turks were told that their rejection of these modified demands would lead to the withdrawal of the ambassadors, though this did not necessarily mean rupture of diplomatic relations. But even these reduced terms were inacceptable to the Turks, because they still involved foreign interference in the domestic affairs of the empire. The delegates were prepared to withdraw the demand that the governor-generals of the Bulgarian provinces should be Christians and were ready to agree that only the selection of the first governor should require the approval of the powers. The demand for European supervision of the reforms was retained. The Duke of Argyll, who was one of the most persistent champions of the cause of the Balkan Christians, says that "it is only fair towards Turkey to admit that the proposals of the powers, even in their ultimate and most modified form, were such as no government could admit, if it pretended to real and substantial independence and if any choice were left to it in the matter." [2]

In spite of this the new Sultan, Abdul Hamid, appears to have favoured acceptance; at least he told Lord Salisbury and others that he would make his peace with the powers, excepting for the fact that he feared deposition by his ministers. [3] Even Midhat is said to have been in favour of some concession and further negotiation with the powers, but by this time public spirit had been aroused to such an extent that there was no going back. On January 18 a large assembly of notables was convened in the capital. Among the two hundred persons summoned there were some sixty Christians, including representatives of the Greek Patriarch and of the Armenian Patriarch. Midhat explained that the acceptance of the terms submitted by the powers would involve an infringement of the independence of the empire, but that rejection of the terms might lead to war at a time when the national finances were chaotic and the empire isolated. But the assembly was immovable. Even the Greek and Armenian representatives made wildly enthusiastic speeches, most of which hinged on the theme that it would be better to die in honour than to live in dishonour. Rarely had public spirit risen so high in Constantinople. Nationalism had become a force with which the government had to reckon. Nothing shows more clearly than the firm support given the government by the Greeks and Ar-

[1] Midhat Pasha: "The Past, Present and Future of Turkey" (*Nineteenth Century*, III, pp. 981–1000, June 1878); Cecil: *Salisbury*, II, p. 118; *Documents diplomatiques français*, II, No. 129.
[2] Duke of Argyll: *The Eastern Question*, I, p. 336.
[3] Seton-Watson, in *Slavonic Review*, December 1925, p. 459; *The Memoirs of Ismail Kemal Bey* (London, 1920), p. 136; *Denkwürdigkeiten des Marschalls Izzet Pasha* (Leipzig, 1927), p. 79.

menians that at bottom the whole problem of the Balkans was at this time not so much a religious as a national and racial one.[1]

On January 20, 1877 the abortive conference was brought to a close. During the next few days the various ambassadors departed, leaving chargés d'affaires to transact current business. Lord Salisbury had not been entirely free from suspicion as to the motives of the Russians, and thought that they had made so many concessions in the knowledge that the Turks would reject them and would in this way shoulder the odium for a break with the powers.[2] But before the end of the conference he had come to believe that the Russians were sincere in their desire for a pacific settlement, and that Bismarck was responsible for the failure of the meeting, because of the intransigent attitude he had assumed towards the Turks.[3] This impression was shared by other delegates and appears to have originated with Ignatiev. It was propagated by the Duc de Decazes, who tried to utilize the conference as a basis for an entente with Russia and England which would isolate Germany. The French plenipotentiary, Comte de Chaudordy, had sided demonstratively with Ignatiev and Salisbury on every point, and Decazes himself was busy pointing out to Lord Lyons that the German chancellor's policy was to break down the incipient Anglo-Russian-French combination by attacking France.[4] Gorchakov, dissatisfied with the way things had gone, joined his efforts to those of the French minister and began to accuse Bismarck of being the guilty one. Had he supported the Russians loyally at Constantinople, things would have turned out quite differently. The newspapers took the cue from the foreign offices, and before long Europe was flooded with articles accusing the Germans of underhanded opposition to the Russian desires.[5]

The war scare of the month of January 1877 was not unlike that of the spring of 1875, though it is less well known. On both occasions Bismarck was alarmed by reports of French efforts to build up a coalition against Germany. In both cases the military men in Berlin were faced with the fact of French military increases or dispositions. In January 1877 news reached the German general staff of troop concentrations on the Russian-German frontier and of the massing of French cavalry in the departments adjacent to the German border. Efforts were made to reply to these dislocations by strengthening the German frontier troops, but it seems that Emperor William objected to any arrangements that might cause uneasiness in Paris. From Moltke's military memoranda we know that the German general staff in January and February worked on plans of campaign against France and Austria combined, as well as against France and

---

1 Ali Haydar Midhat Bey: *Midhat-Pacha* (Paris, 1908), pp. 103 ff.; *Memoirs of Ismail Kemal Bey*, pp. 133–4, 139; Busch: " *Die Botschafterkonferenz in Konstantinopel* " (*Deutsche Rundschau*, CXLI, pp. 12–28, October 1909); Comte de Moüy: *Souvenirs* (Paris, 1909), chapter ii.

2 Cecil: *Salisbury*, II, p. 120; Buckle: *Letters of Queen Victoria*, II, p. 507.

3 Salisbury to Derby, January 11, 1877 (unpublished).

4 Unpublished reports of Lord Lyons; *Documents diplomatiques français*, II, Nos. 126, 127, 131, 138.

5 Details in Schweinitz: *Denkwürdigkeiten*, I, pp. 378 ff.

Russia. It is impossible to say whether this was routine work or whether it was inspired by the political situation. At any rate it was believed by military men that the French would be able to operate in Alsace and Lorraine within five days of the outbreak of the war and that Metz was seriously threatened.[1]

At the beginning of the tension Thiers, in conversations with the German ambassador, had asserted categorically that the French had no warlike intentions. But it was difficult to know how well he was informed of his government's plans and policies. The German statesmen, too, gave unequivocal assurances. Yet the strain in relations continued for weeks, accompanied by bitter newspaper recriminations on both sides. Neither from the German nor from the French material is it possible to derive a very clear idea of what was at the bottom of the whole affair. At any rate the tension was not relaxed until, towards the end of March, Bismarck had a talk with the French ambassador, in the course of which he told him that the Germans would always say what the English had said at the battle of Fontenoy: "You fire first, Messieurs les Français." The German Emperor finally agreed to the necessary strengthening of the German forces, and late in April, just as war broke out between Russia and Turkey, even Moltke declared himself satisfied. The conflict between Mac-Mahon and the French Chamber, which came to a head on May 16, 1877, served to revive anxiety for the future. It was not until the formation of a thoroughly republican ministry in December that Franco-German relations became more stable and cordial.[2]

In January, after the failure of the Constantinople Conference, the international situation was still utterly chaotic. Bismarck, genuinely alarmed by reports of French advances to Austria, realized the need for action in that direction. Though he had scrupulously avoided committing himself to either Russia or Austria in the autumn of 1876, he now proposed to the Emperor the idea of an organic alliance with Austria, hoping at the same time that England would be friendly to such a combination. Russian threats, he argued, were forcing Germany, against her will, to seek alliances among all states excepting France and Russia, even if these alliances involved sacrifices on Germany's part.[3]

What advances Bismarck actually made to Austria we do not know, but it is certain that Andrássy reassured him in regard to the Austrian attitude and reasserted his intention of standing by his agreement with Germany and Russia.[4] Of his proposals to the English we cannot be certain either. The ambassador at Berlin reported a conversation which he had with the chancellor on

---

[1] Graf Moltke: *Die deutschen Aufmarschpläne, 1871–1890* (Berlin, 1929), pp. 62 ff.; *Die Grosse Politik*, I, No. 202; Russell to Derby, January 25, 1877 (unpublished).

[2] On Franco-German relations during this period see *Die Grosse Politik*, I, Nos. 201–4; Hohenlohe: *Denkwürdigkeiten*, II, pp. 207 ff.; *Documents diplomatiques français*, II, Nos. 134–7, 142, 145, 147, 149, 161, 162, 164, 172, 180, 187, 188, 197, 198; Dreux: *Dernières Années de l'ambassade de Gontaut-Biron*, pp. 264 ff.

[3] Schweinitz: *Briefwechsel*, pp. 125–6; id., *Denkwürdigkeiten*, I, p. 383; Busch, in *Deutsche Rundschau*, November 1909, pp. 207–8.

[4] Russell to Derby, January 25, 1877 (unpublished).

January 16, 1877. Bismarck asked what England would do now that the conference had failed. Russell replied that he thought England would do nothing, which the chancellor agreed would be the safe course, since there was nothing to be done. He believed that Gorchakov was anxious to avoid war, probably for fear lest control of affairs should pass to the Russian war office. If a conflict did result, it would probably be hard to localize it, for Russia would attempt to draw in other states. He regretted not having been consulted by any power excepting Austria since the conference had opened, and was sorry to see the French trying to set Russia against Germany. But the German and Russian governments had long been friends, and Russia should not be misled into thinking that she could no longer rely on Germany. He meant to give Russia moral support and disprove the calumnies of the hostile Russian press, and he had succeeded in bringing the Austrians and Russians together again. Russell took away the impression that Bismarck, in his anxiety to avoid a Franco-Russian alliance, would accord Russia " somewhat more than benevolent neutrality." [1]

But there is another report from Russell, the authenticity of which cannot be proved, though it bears several marks of genuineness. This document appears in the Russian correspondence and seems to have been communicated to Shuvalov by his friend Lady Derby, through whom many English secrets apparently became known to the Russians. According to this report, Bismarck said to Russell that the rapprochement of France and Russia might induce the former to invade Alsace-Lorraine with an army of five hundred thousand men, which could be mobilized in five days. The German army could not be prepared in less than ten days and he would therefore be obliged to advise the Emperor to take military measures immediately. These measures would be restricted to the collection of munitions of war at Metz and Strassburg and to the reinforcement of the garrisons. No doubt they would be interpreted in France as measures of provocation and would create a great deal of excitement in Europe. If war were to follow, what would be the attitude of England? Would she offer her mediation to preserve peace? In a later conversation he put the matter even more bluntly and asked Russell to sound his government as to the conclusion of an offensive and defensive alliance against France. The ambassador expressed doubts whether his government would consider such a proposal, but agreed to communicate with London. From veiled references in the English sources it appears that some such proposal was brought before the cabinet and rejected.[2]

---

[1] Russell to Derby, January 16, 1877 (unpublished). The strength of the entente between the three empires is attested by Gorchakov's remarks to the French ambassador (*Documents diplomatiques français*, II, No. 129).

[2] Seton-Watson, in *Slavonic Review*, IV, pp. 737–8, 746, March 1926. See also the cryptic references in Cecil: *Salisbury*, II, p. 127; *Gathorne-Hardy, a Memoir* (London, 1910), II, p. 15; Goriainov, op. cit., p. 339. The French government received reports of this move from General Le Flô on February 3 and seems also to have been told something by Lord Derby. But it is hard to make much sense out of Decazes's enigmatic dispatch to Harcourt (*Documents diplomatiques*

If such proposals were actually made to the English government, their rejection was almost a matter of course. In the first place the English statesmen strongly suspected Bismarck of trying to fish in the troubled waters, and in the second place they were firmly convinced of the Russian desire for peace. Salisbury was ready to come to an understanding with Russia, and even Disraeli believed that knowledge of the Russian desire to avoid war had helped to stiffen the back of the Turks: " Russia would give a good deal to get out of the scrape into which her blustering has entrapped her; and the Porte knows this, and seems resolved to make the Emperor and his princely minister eat the leek: very difficult to digest, if not impossible."[1] The Russian ambassador himself informed Lord Derby that negotiations were in progress between Russia and Austria, but Andrássy continued to deny this, and the English foreign minister, far from being alarmed at the prospect of renewed action by the three Emperors to the exclusion of England, preferred to centre his suspicions upon Bismarck and to maintain his view that the German chancellor was trying to drive the Russians into war with Turkey in order that he might have a free hand to deal with France. To avoid such a calamity, which, most likely, would involve the greater part of Europe in conflict, the English statesmen, at least Derby and Salisbury, were anxious to go half-way to meet the Russians.[2]

Of the pacific inclinations of the Russians after the failure of the conference there can be no doubt whatever. None of the European chancelleries questioned them, nor are they hard to understand. The Tsar and Gorchakov from the start had been bent on bringing about united action by the powers and united pressure upon the Turks, with an eventual European mandate for Russian action. Even Ignatiev admitted that the favourable moment for war had passed with the summer of 1876, when Europe was outraged by the Bulgarian massacres and was in a crusading spirit. The Tsar had been carried away in November by a wave of Panslavic enthusiasm and had made some belligerent utterances, but all that had passed. By the beginning of the new year it had become plain that the Turks would not yield without a struggle and that the Porte would have Turkish public opinion behind it. Besides, it was impossible to begin a campaign against the Turks in mid winter. In any case, the Russian government had got over its belligerent propensities and was clearly ready to retreat if a golden bridge were built for the operation.[3]

---

français, II, No. 141). There is a discussion of the question by Frahm, in Archiv für Politik und Geschichte, VIII, p. 378 (1927), but Frahm had not seen the Russian reports or the French documents.

[1] Monypenny and Buckle, op. cit., VI, p. 112.

[2] Derby to Salisbury, January 15, 1877; Derby to Loftus, February 21, 1877 (unpublished). See also William A. Gauld: " The ' Dreikaiserbündnis ' and the Eastern Question, 1877–1878 " (English Historical Review, October 1927, pp. 561–8); Monypenny and Buckle, op. cit., VI, p. 126; Cecil, op. cit., II, p. 130; Seton-Watson, in Slavonic Review, IV, p. 747.

[3] Monypenny and Buckle, op. cit., VI, p. 126; Busch, op. cit., pp. 26–7; " Poyezdka Grafa N. P. Ignatieva po evropeiskim stolitzam " (Russkaia Starina, XLV, Nos. 3 and 4, March–April 1914); Documents diplomatiques français, II, No. 139.

Judged from the international standpoint, the Russian position was anything but strong. If war were declared against the Turks, it was quite conceivable that Bismarck might seize the opportunity to square accounts with the French, and there was always the knotty problem of the Austrian attitude. Ever since the Sumarokov mission to Vienna the Russian government, anticipating the probable failure of the Constantinople Conference and the eventual collapse of the concert of Europe, had been negotiating with Andrássy to determine what the attitude of the monarchy would be if Russia were obliged to take action against the Turks. It had soon turned out that Andrássy meant to drive a hard bargain. In the course of the negotiations a dispute arose as to how much of Bosnia had been reserved for Austria under the Reichstadt Convention and whether Bosnia included Herzegovina. The Austrian minister insisted upon the larger part of both provinces and refused to modify his demand that Serbia and Montenegro should be excluded from the scene of military operations. " The co-operation [of Russia] with Serbia and Montenegro would transform the European action into a Slavic movement, the Christian and humanitarian aim would become a one-sided Orthodox aim, and the war would turn into a revolution."

The Russians were helpless, and in the end were obliged to accept the Austrian terms unless they wished to retreat entirely from their previous position in the whole Eastern question. Finally, on January 15, 1877, the so-called January Convention or Treaty of Budapest was signed by the two powers. Austria agreed in this treaty that if the Constantinople Conference should fail and war between Russia and Turkey should ensue, she would preserve an attitude of benevolent neutrality and would attempt to paralyse all efforts at intervention or collective mediation by other powers. On the other hand Austria was to choose the moment and the mode of the occupation of Bosnia and Herzegovina. She was not to extend the radius of her military action to Roumania, Serbia, Bulgaria, and Montenegro, while Russia was not to extend the radius of her action to Bosnia, Herzegovina, Serbia, and Montenegro. Serbia, Montenegro, and part of Herzegovina were to form a neutral zone, though Serbian and Montenegrin troops were to be allowed to engage in joint action with the Russians outside their own territory. The consequences of the war and the territorial modifications which might result from an eventual dissolution of the Ottoman Empire were to be regulated by a special convention, to be concluded at once.[1]

The " additional convention "—that is, the political agreement, without which the military convention of January 15 was invalid—was not actually concluded until March 18, though it was antedated to January 15. It really represented a return to the Reichstadt program, with some modifications. Gorchakov was anxious to restrict its application to the event of the actual

---

[1] Text in Pribram, II, pp. 190 ff.; on the negotiations see Wertheimer: *Andrássy*, II, pp. 384 ff.; Wertheimer, in *Historische Blätter*, I, pp. 450 ff.; Goriainov, op. cit., pp. 327 ff.

dissolution of the Ottoman Empire, but Andrássy insisted that it should apply equally to the changes wrought by a Russian victory over Turkey. In either case Austria was to annex Bosnia and Herzegovina, excepting for the strip of territory which ran between Serbia and Montenegro (the Sanjak of Novi-Bazar). Russia was to have Bessarabia and the frontier of 1856. The two governments agreed also to lend each other diplomatic assistance if the territorial modifications resulting from a war or from the dissolution of the Ottoman Empire should give rise to a collective deliberation of the great powers. Furthermore, the agreement excluded the eventual formation of a large state, Slavic or other; Bulgaria, Albania, and the rest of Roumelia might be constituted as independent states; Thessaly, part of Epirus, and Crete might be annexed to Greece; Constantinople and its environs might become a free city.[1]

It will be seen that in the course of these negotiations Andrássy was able to force the acceptance of almost all his demands, and this simply because the Russians, for military reasons, could not consider a campaign in the Balkans while Austria was hostile. But the Austrian terms were so unfavourable to Russia that for her to fight under these conditions would be to fight for Austria rather than for herself. The Russians, then, were anxious to find some other way out, and the English were ready to entertain suggestions.

Gorchakov began the action with a Russian circular dated January 31, which tried to represent the Turkish rejection of the demands of the powers as an affront to Europe and asked the various governments directly what they proposed to do under the circumstances. The English rejected the idea that an insult had been offered by the Porte, but were glad to seize the opportunity offered by Midhat Pasha's fall from power on February 5 and by the conciliatory advances of his successor. Count Peter Shuvalov, the Russian ambassador at London, began negotiations with Lord Derby for the drafting of a protocol, which, it was hoped, would save the face of Europe, ameliorate the lot of the Christians without offending the Porte, and at the same time lead to demobilization on both sides. Meanwhile Count Ignatiev was sent to the West, ostensibly to visit an oculist in Paris, but in reality to win the support of the various governments for the Russian program. If the protocol proved a failure, the Russians hoped at least to secure a European mandate for separate action.

Ignatiev's reputation was too bad to make him a help in the negotiations, and the English statesmen looked upon his coming with horror. But Shuvalov and Derby finally managed to reach an agreement on the protocol, which was signed in London during the last days of March by the representatives of all the powers. The protocol reaffirmed the interest of the powers in the amelioration of the condition of the Christian populations and in the reforms to be introduced in Bosnia, Herzegovina, and Bulgaria. It took cognizance of the peace concluded by the Porte with Serbia on March 1. The Turkish government

---

[1] Text in Pribram, II, pp. 198 ff.; on the negotiations see especially Wertheimer, in *Historische Blätter*, I, pp. 456-ff.

was invited to consolidate the peace by putting its armies on a peace footing and by taking in hand the reforms which had been promised. The powers proposed to watch carefully, by means of their representatives, the manner in which the promises of the Porte were carried into effect. If their hopes should again be disappointed, they declared, such a state of affairs would be incompatible with their interests and those of Europe generally. In that case they reserved to themselves further consideration as to the means best fitted to secure the welfare of the Christian populations and the interests of general peace.[1]

It was a curious document, to say the least. Disraeli maintained he could not quite make head or tail of it. It certainly was a distinct toning down even of the "quintessence" of the demands of the powers as presented by the Constantinople Conference and was so far removed from the conditions laid down by the Berlin Memorandum that the earlier program was no longer recognizable. Yet even on this mild program England and Russia were not in complete agreement. Derby added a declaration that, since the English government had signed only in the interests of general peace, the protocol should be regarded as null and void unless reciprocal disarmament on the part of Russia and Turkey were attained. Shuvalov, on the other hand, declared that if Turkey concluded peace with Montenegro, and if she accepted the advice of the powers, and if she were willing to put her forces on a peace footing, then she might send a special envoy to the Tsar to treat of Russian disarmament, to which the Russian government would consent, provided no further massacres took place. In other words, the English refused to recognize the protocol unless both sides disarmed, while the Russians made disarmament on their part conditional on the previous disarmament of the Turks and the fulfilment of other terms. Even then the Turks were to be humble and send an envoy to beg the Tsar for favours. It was almost a foregone conclusion that the Porte would reject the protocol. On April 9 the Turkish government protested against the tutelage and supervision which the demands of the powers would impose upon her, and appealed to the provisions of the Treaty of Paris, which guaranteed the independence and integrity of the Ottoman Empire.

The London Protocol had contemplated further negotiation between the powers in the event of rejection of the program by the Turks. But no move was made by the Russian government to reopen the discussion. The full mobilization of the forces was immediately taken in hand. The Tsar had lost patience, and Gorchakov had become convinced that the Russians could count only on God and their own good sword.[2] The neutrality of Austria, which was an "absolute condition" of Russian military action, had been secured through the agreements with Vienna, and the season for campaigning was now open. On April 24 the Tsar declared war on Turkey. In a memorandum to the powers

---

[1] On the Ignatiev mission see his memoirs: "*Poyezdka Grafa N. P. Ignatieva po evropeiskim stolitzam*" (*Russkaia Starina*, XLV, Nos. 3 ff., March–September 1914).

[2] Goriainov, op. cit., p. 344.

he still insisted that his object was solely to secure the execution of the decisions of all Europe — that is, to bring about forcibly an amelioration of the lot of the Christians.

The negotiations of almost two years had proved futile. But it must be admitted that the situation had, from the beginning, been unusually difficult. The fundamental problems of Turkish government, and the interests of the powers in the Near East, had been complicated by the underground activities of foreign agents and the subversive agitation of revolutionary committees in the Christian provinces. According to Turkish writers, the religious element was quite secondary, for the Turkish population suffered almost as much as the Christian from the abuses of a corrupt administration. What distinguished this crisis from earlier Eastern crises was the nationalist factor, which lay at the very bottom of the propaganda carried on in the revolted sections and which may be taken as the real explanation of the declaration of war by Serbia and Montenegro. It was this same rising spirit of nationalism which impelled both the Russian and the Turkish policies. The governments were almost helpless in the face of it. It seems fairly clear that Midhat Pasha was anxious to avoid extreme measures, but he was unable to check the movement which he himself had fostered. As for the Sultan, he considered himself doomed if he accepted a program that involved foreign interference and supervision of Turkish affairs.

In Russia the situation was similar. Neither the Tsar nor Gorchakov desired war against the Porte. What they wanted was a European crusade in favour of the Christians, or, failing that, combined action by the powers of the Three Emperors' League. The Tsar explicitly denied that he had a quarrel with the Turks. The problem, he maintained, was a European one. But, like the Sultan, he was carried away by the nationalist deluge. His government could not prevent the departure of volunteers or the subvention of the Serbs and Montenegrins. The connexion of the whole Panslavic movement with the revolutionary currents in Russia was a matter to be carefully considered. In March 1877 Aksakov made a speech in Moscow that served as a warning. The insane pacifism of Russian diplomacy, he said, threatened to make Russia accept all the insults offered her by the Turks. The Russian blood spilled on the battlefields of Serbia was as unavenged as though it had been the blood of Hottentots. The higher circles of Russian society were morally corrupt, but the will of the people would be strong enough to tear asunder the bonds of treason and take up the struggle against the infidel. The report of the speech was immediately suppressed, but the government knew what it meant. There was no turning back.

While eastern Europe was being swept by the rising tide of national feeling, it cannot be said that much statesmanship was shown by the chancelleries of the West. Andrássy, wholly on the defensive, stuck by the outworn reform program; and when this proved impracticable, he contented himself with securing territorial compensation in return for Austrian neutrality in a Russian-Turkish war. In England there was little enough sympathy for the Turk, but the cabinet and the party in power were determined to maintain the integrity of the Ottoman Empire against Russian designs. Disraeli favoured strong action from the beginning, not only for the protection of British interests, but also for considerations of prestige. The Three Emperors' League was quite as much of a bugaboo for him as Russian intrigue. But Disraeli's political thinking was scrappy and incoherent, and he was constantly faced with the anti-Turkish sentiment in the country, as well as by dissension in the cabinet. Only Bismarck showed sound judgment and clear vision. For him the best solution would have been an all-round compromise between the interested parties — a compromise based on the partition of Turkey in Europe. The Ottoman Empire, he believed, was not worth maintaining, and it would in any case be better to sacrifice it than to jeopardize peace between the great powers. He himself had no interest in the question, but was genuinely anxious to avoid a European war, because a large-scale conflict might always end in Germany's becoming involved. Consequently he did his best to maintain the Three Emperors' League and smooth out the differences between Russia and Austria. But he firmly refused to choose between them. The weakness of the combination he recognized from the very start; hence his repeated approaches to England, which show that he was all too ready to consider an Anglo-German-Austrian combination — that is, a combination of the "saturated" powers — as a substitute for the traditional Three Emperors' League. But the distrust of Bismarck's policy was still too great. All sorts of sinister designs were still being attributed to him in London. The same distrust characterized the relations of the other powers. Not even Austria and England, whose interests were similar, were able to overcome this obstacle. In the end Bismarck was probably glad to see the war between Russia and Turkey, because it reduced the danger of an Austro-Russian conflict and promised to hasten the collapse of the Ottoman Empire. This would clear the way for the program of partition, which Bismarck regarded as the most satisfactory solution of the entire problem.

BIBLIOGRAPHICAL NOTE

DOCUMENTARY SOURCES

Accounts and Papers. State Papers. The Blue Books dealing with this period will be found in the series for 1877, Volumes XC, XCI, XCII, and 1878, Volume LXXXI.

Actenstücke aus den Korrespondenzen des K. und K. gemeinsamen Ministeriums des Äusseren über orientalische Angelegenheiten vom 16 Mai 1873 bis 31 Mai 1877. Vienna, 1878.

Documents diplomatiques. Affaires d'Orient, 1875, 1876, 1877. Paris, 1877.

Die Grosse Politik der europäischen Kabinette. Volume II, chapter x (The Eastern Crisis, 1876); xi (The Constantinople Conference, the London Protocol, and the Russian-Turkish War).

Documents diplomatiques français. Volume II. Paris, 1930. Covers the period 1875-9.

"Unprinted Documents. Russo-Turkish Relations during the Eastern Crisis." Edited by R. W. Seton-Watson (*Slavonic Review,* III and IV, 1924-6).

"*Russko-Germanskie Otnoshenia*" (*Krasny Arkhiv,* I, pp. 10 ff.). Gives the Russian texts of the Austro-Russian agreements.

MEMOIRS, AUTOBIOGRAPHIES, BIOGRAPHIES, AND LETTERS

Monypenny, W. F., and Buckle, G. E.: *The Life of Benjamin Disraeli.* Volume VI. London, 1920.

Buckle, G. E.: *The Letters of Queen Victoria.* Second Series. Two volumes. London, 1926.

Cecil, Lady Gwendolen: *Life of Robert Marquis of Salisbury.* Two Volumes. London, 1921. One of the most important sources for the study of English policy.

Hardy, A. E. G.: *Gathorne Hardy, First Earl of Cranbrook.* Two volumes. London, 1910. Based on the papers of the war minister in Disraeli's cabinet.

Edwards, H. Sutherland: *Sir William White.* London, 1902. The biography of a noted English diplomat. Especially interesting on the events in Serbia and the history of the Constantinople Conference.

Elliot, Sir Henry: *Some Revolutions and other Diplomatic Experiences.* London, 1922. The account of the English ambassador at Constantinople and second plenipotentiary to the conference.

Schaeffer, Evelyn S.: *Eugene Schuyler.* New York, 1901. The biography of the American consul-general at Constantinople. Interesting on the Bulgarian massacres and the Constantinople Conference.

Midhat Bey, Ali Haydar: *Midhat-Pacha.* Paris, 1908. One of the most valuable accounts from the Turkish side.

Schweinitz, General von: *Denkwürdigkeiten.* Two volumes. Berlin, 1927. Of great value for the study of German-Russian relations.

—: *Briefwechsel.* Berlin, 1928. Supplements the preceding.

Wertheimer, Eduard: *Graf Julius Andrássy.* Three volumes. Stuttgart, 1910-13.

Moüy, Comte Charles de: *Souvenirs et causeries d'un diplomate.* Paris, 1909. Moüy was secretary of the Constantinople Conference and gives a very good picture of this episode.

Busch, Dr.: *" Aus dem literarischen Nachlass."* Edited by Ludwig Raschdau (*Deutsche Rundschau,* October and November 1909). The papers of a German expert on Eastern affairs, especially interesting for the period of the Constantinople Conference.

(Cyon, Elie de:) *" La Guerre russo-turque d'après des documents inédits"* (*Nouvelle Revue,* June 1, 1880). A valuable contribution, based on the papers of the Grand Duke Nicholas and throwing light on the Russian policy in the autumn of 1876.

Nelidov, Alexandre: *" Souvenirs d'avant et d'après la guerre de 1877–1878 "* (*Revue des deux mondes,* May 15, 1915). The memoirs of the secretary of the Russian embassy at Constantinople.

" Poyezdka Grafa N. P. Ignatieva po evropeiskim stolitzam pered voinoi 1877–1878 " (*Russkaia Starina,* March–September 1914). Gives Ignatiev's account of his journey to the Western capitals in the spring of 1877.

Ristič, Jovan: *Diplomatska Istorija Srbije za vreme srpskič ratova za osloboene u nezavisnost, 1875–1878.* Belgrade, 1896–8. The important memoirs of the Serbian statesman.

SPECIAL TOPICS

Wertheimer, Eduard: *" Neues zur Orientpolitik des Grafen Andrássy 1876–1877 "* (*Historische Blätter,* Nos. 2 and 3, pp. 252–76, 448–63, 1921–2). Uses material from the Austrian archives and contributes considerably to the clarification of the Austrian policy in the autumn of 1876.

Frahm, Friedrich: *" England und Russland in Bismarcks Bündnispolitik "* (*Archiv für Politik und Geschichte,* VIII, pp. 365–431, 1927). One of the best studies of Bismarck's policy.

Helms, Albert: *Bismarck und Russland.* Bonn, 1927. The most recent monographic study of Russian-German relations in the Bismarckian period. Adds nothing of importance.

Prosch, Heinrich: *" Ein englischer Bündnisfühler im Jahre 1876 "* (*Historische Vierteljahrschrift,* XXIV, No. 4, pp. 588–607, 1929). Deals at length with the English soundings in the autumn of 1876.

Rupp, George H.: *" The Reichstadt Agreement "* (*American Historical Review,* XXX, pp. 503–10, April 1925). Analyses the Russian and the Austrian texts and tries to explain the differences.

Andréadès, A.: *" La Politique orientale anglaise avant et pendant le Congrès de Berlin "* (*La Vie des peuples,* VII, pp. 877–919, August 10, 1922). Primarily an analysis, but a keen one, of the biographies of Disraeli and Salisbury.

Seton-Watson, R. W.: *" Russian Commitments in the Bosnian Question "* (*Slavonic Review,* VIII, pp. 578–88, March 1930). Discusses the Reichstadt and

January conventions between Austria and Russia, making use of some unpublished material.

LIEBOLD, RUDOLF: *Die Stellung Englands in der russisch-türkischen Krise von 1875-78*. Wilkau, 1930. A detailed and reliable account of British policy. The best monographic study of the subject.

V

The Russian-Turkish War and the Congress of Berlin

～

WARS BETWEEN RUSSIA AND TURKEY WERE NO NOVELTY IN EUROPEAN history. Since the time of Peter the Great there had been one of these conflicts every twenty or twenty-five years. But Russia had rarely entered upon the campaign under such favourable political conditions as in 1877. Of the military aspects little need be said. Frederick the Great once remarked that wars between these two antagonists were wars of the one-eyed against the blind, and the war of 1877–8 in no way disproved the dictum. Russia was in poor financial condition and the great army reforms were only a few years old, so that the new system was not yet in running order. The Grand Duke Nicholas, who was given supreme command, proved himself incompetent. During the whole campaign there was nothing in the way of real leadership on a grand scale.

The financial position of the Turks was worse even than that of the Russians, and it will remain for ever a mystery how the war was paid for without raising a foreign loan. In point of armament the Turks had several advantages. They possessed at this time the finest navy they had had since the time of Suleiman, a force said by some to have been second only to that of England. Abdul Aziz had made a hobby of this fleet, which was under the command of Hobart Pasha, an Englishman in the Ottoman service. Though the fleet was never really utilized to the full during the war, it did retain control of the Black Sea and in this way forced the Russians to confine their operations to the land. The Turkish armies were well equipped with modern weapons, far superior to those of the Russians, while the valour of the Turkish rank and file, when properly led, was notorious. Even in matters of leadership the Turks had the advantage. Osman Pasha's defence of Plevna was one of the most brilliant military feats of modern warfare and one of which the Turks had every reason to feel proud. But, as in most Turkish wars, there was no unity of command and no real plan of campaign. The generals in the field were constantly receiving conflicting orders from the capital, and the work of the various commanders was never properly co-ordinated by a competent central control. In the end the Russian colossus demoralized and crushed its opponent by sheer weight and pressure.

In April 1877, however, it was generally believed that the Russian forces were greatly superior to the Turkish in every respect, and a brilliant, speedy victory was looked for. The Western powers watched the conflict with the greatest interest, for the Russians had practically a free hand. Turkey was completely isolated, and there was no chance of a repetition of the Crimean War. Germany was benevolently neutral towards Russia, and before the war was long under way the Russian authorities themselves recognized that the attitude of the German government was all that could be asked for. Austrian neutrality, which was more important than anything else for the Russians, had been secured by the January Convention. The price had been high, but Austrian abstention was hardly less than a *sine qua non* for waging the war at all. Italy's position was not wholly clear at this time, but Italy was not a sufficiently important factor to decide the course of European diplomacy. France, on the other hand, could be reckoned on for a benevolent attitude. Her policy had usually been one of opposition to Russian control in the Near East, but since 1870 she had been obliged to follow a policy of reserve, and the Russophil proclivities of the Duc de Decazes were sufficient assurance that no course hostile to Russia would be followed.

There remained, of the great powers, only England, and England was apt to be unfriendly, to say the least. Indeed, it was England that, together with Russia, had come to play the leading role in the whole Near Eastern problem, so that the history of the crisis began to centre more and more on the relations between these two countries. Once Russia had declared war, the English government lost no time in making its views known. While none of the other powers troubled to reply to the Russian circular in which it was said that the Tsar felt convinced, as he embarked upon war, that he was serving not only Russian interests, but the interests of Europe, the English government promptly protested against the Russian assumption of a European mandate. According to the British view, Russia had separated herself from the concert of Europe, and in going to war was violating the stipulation of the Treaty of Paris which guaranteed the independence and territorial integrity of the Ottoman Empire. In so doing she was not serving the interests of Great Britain or of the other powers.

But Disraeli was by no means satisfied with mere polemics. In the opinion of the military experts, the Russians would be able to reach Constantinople in fourteen or fifteen weeks after crossing the Prut River into Roumania. It was further reported that the Russian Baltic fleet had been sent to the Mediterranean, and that operations against Egypt were being planned. The prime minister was greatly exercised, and the letters of the Queen strengthened him in his conviction that something must be done to protect English interests. "It is not a question of upholding Turkey; it is a question of Russian or British supremacy in the world," wrote Victoria.[1]

---

[1] Monypenny and Buckle, op. cit., VI, pp. 132–3.

Under the circumstances Disraeli favoured a temporary occupation of the Dardanelles Peninsula by England, as a "material guarantee" against a Russian occupation of Constantinople. But this suggestion was not well received by the cabinet, which did not consider the danger quite so pressing. It was finally agreed to send a note of warning to Russia before deciding on definite action. On May 6 the government sent a dispatch which Disraeli himself described as "the charter of our policy." Russia was warned against attempting to blockade the Suez Canal and against occupying Egypt, even though only temporarily for purposes of war. The English government, the note continued, "are not prepared to witness with indifference the passing into other hands than those of its present possessors of a capital [Constantinople] holding so peculiar and commanding a position. The existing arrangements, made under European sanction, which regulate the navigation of the Bosphorus and Dardanelles appear to them wise and salutary, and there would be, in their judgment, serious objections to their alteration in any material particular." [1]

Count Shuvalov, the Russian ambassador at London, was deeply impressed with the danger of English action and regarded these points as the "Breetish torpedoes." [2] He therefore asked permission to go to St. Petersburg and lay the situation before the Russian government. On his way he stopped at Berlin and discussed matters with Bismarck. Russia would do well, he told the German chancellor, if she concluded a moderate peace after a few initial victories. Autonomy for Bulgaria, acquisitions for Montenegro, and the retrocession of Bessarabia to Russia would be sufficient. Bismarck agreed with him as to the wisdom of this course of action and expressed his readiness to support the program of what he called "la petite paix."

Hardly had Shuvalov left the German capital when Bismarck approached Lord Odo Russell, suggesting that England take Egypt and mentioning even Syria, Crete, and Cyprus as possible compensation for Russian gains. Tripoli might be turned over to Italy, and Tunis be left to France. Divide Turkey and satisfy everyone was the chancellor's solution, one which he had proposed before and one which he was still willing to press. Apparently he was deeply concerned by the prospect of a Russian-English clash, which might well end in a general cataclysm. This disaster he was anxious to avoid at all costs. He told Russell that "he would give his last effort to bring about a cordial and intimate understanding between England and Russia to which Germany would become a party," and asked him to tell Lord Derby "of his earnest, sincere, and anxious desire to bring about an intimate and lasting alliance between England and Germany." [3]

---

[1] Monypenny and Buckle, op. cit., VI, pp. 135 ff.; Buckle: *Letters of Queen Victoria*, II, pp. 529–35; Cecil: *Salisbury*, II, p. 139; Seton-Watson, in *Slavonic Review*, V, December 1926, pp. 416–22; Goriainov, op. cit., pp. 345 ff.; *Documents diplomatiques français*, II, No. 171.

[2] Loftus: *Diplomatic Reminiscences*, II, p. 218.

[3] I am relying here upon an unpublished thesis, based upon English archive material, by Dr. Dwight E. Lee, entitled: "British Policy in the Eastern Question, 1878." The reports of Russell

That Bismarck was sincere in his desire for an understanding between England and Russia can no longer be doubted. In a memorandum dictated at this time he explained that if England had Egypt, and Russia were in control of the Black Sea, both would be content with the *status quo* for a long time, but would still be rivals to an extent that would keep them from joining coalitions against Germany. In case of war between Russia and England he was determined to mediate and settle the problem at the expense of Turkey.[1] But his policy was entirely misunderstood in England, and his offers of support were viewed with the deepest suspicion. The English statesmen firmly believed that Bismarck was trying to push them into war with Russia and that he was manœuvring to get a free hand for war with France or else for the realization of his supposed designs on Holland. If England wants Egypt, said Disraeli, she does not require the suggestion or the permission of Prince Bismarck.[2] Not long afterwards he is reported to have vented his spleen in speaking to the Austrian ambassador: " I find him [Bismarck] everywhere in my way. . . . The man is a European nuisance. My quarrel is much less with Russia than with Bismarck, and I am resolved to thwart him." [3]

Bismarck, seeing that nothing could be done with the English, withdrew from active participation in negotiations and allowed matters to take their course. Meanwhile Shuvalov had persuaded the Russian government of his own view. He found the upper classes in St. Petersburg foaming at the mouth whenever the English were mentioned, but the government was genuinely anxious to avoid a clash.[4] He therefore returned to London with a favourable reply to the English note of May 6. In a letter to Lord Derby, dated May 30, Gorchakov gave assurances that the Russians would not blockade or interrupt navigation in the Suez Canal, nor bring Egypt within the radius of military operations. So far as Constantinople was concerned, without being able to prejudge the course or issue of the war, the imperial cabinet repeated that the acquisition of that capital was excluded from the views of the Tsar, and recognized that in any case the future of Constantinople was a question of general interest, which could not be settled except by a general understanding. In regard to the Straits, it was important that this question should be settled by a common agreement on equitable and efficiently guaranteed bases.

The Russian reply was vague, both as to Constantinople and as to the Straits,

---

are dated May 19, 21, 27, 1877. On Shuvalov's mission see also Schweinitz: *Denkwürdigkeiten*, I, pp. 427 ff. The substance of Bismarck's talk with Russell may be found in Sir Horace Rumbold: *Further Recollections of a Diplomatist* (London, 1904), pp. 103–4, under date of June 1, 1877.

[1] *Die Grosse Politik*, II, No. 294.

[2] Buckle: *Letters of Queen Victoria*, II, pp. 541–2, 546, 549, 550; *Die Grosse Politik*, II, Nos. 294–5; *Documents diplomatiques français*, II, No. 165.

[3] Wertheimer: *Andrássy*, III, p. 50.

[4] Schweinitz: *Denkwürdigkeiten*, I, p. 425. The French government, unnerved by the prospect of a Russian-English conflict, did its utmost to secure a satisfactory declaration from the Russians (*Documents diplomatiques français*, II, Nos. 165, 168, 169, 177, 178).

but the real Russian policy was elucidated for Shuvalov in a memorandum of the same date drawn up for his personal use. In this document Gorchakov pointed out that Russian assurances in regard to Constantinople referred only to taking possession or to permanent occupation. Russia could not bind herself not to carry out a temporary occupation and must reserve this right even though only for use as a threat against the Turks to force them to make peace. The Straits agreements should be revised in such a way as to guarantee Russia against attack in the Black Sea in time of war. Russia was anxious for an agreement with England and was prepared for moderate peace terms if the Turks sued for peace before the Russian armies crossed the Balkan Mountains. These terms would be: autonomy for Bulgaria north of the Balkan Mountains; regular administration for the other Christian provinces, to be guaranteed by the powers; Serbia and Montenegro to receive augmentations of territory; Bosnia and Herzegovina to be given institutions compatible with their conditions; the future of Roumania to be regulated by general agreement; Russia to receive Bessarabia and Batum; Roumania to be compensated for Bessarabia by receiving part of the Dobruja; Austria to be given compensation, if demanded, in Bosnia and Herzegovina.[1]

When Shuvalov presented these terms to the English, on June 8, they failed to make a noticeable impression. They were regarded as too harsh to be submitted to the Turks, and, like most Russian assurances and promises, were viewed with great suspicion. Disraeli was still in favour of protecting English interests by an occupation of the Dardanelles or by sending the British fleet to Constantinople. Several of his colleagues objected to this course, but agreed that an understanding with Austria would strengthen the English position. On May 19, even before Shuvalov's return from St. Petersburg, Derby had approached Count Beust, the Austrian ambassador, with the suggestion that the two nations act in concert, especially in the event of a Russian advance on Constantinople. English ships might take Austrian troops to the Turkish capital.

The Austrian reply was cool. Andrássy pointed out that Austria and England could always force the Russians to withdraw from Constantinople, once they were in the city. Instead of accepting the English proposal the Austrian minister suggested an understanding regarding the changes that could or could not be permitted in the final settlement. Austria could not accept any one of the following seven points: (1) that the exclusive protectorate over the Balkan Christians should be conceded to any one Christian power; (2) that the definitive peace settlement should take place without the participation of the powers signatories of the Treaty of 1856; (3) that Russia should acquire territory on the right bank of the Danube; (4) that Roumania should be incorporated with Russia or made dependent upon her; (5) that a prince of either the Austrian or

---

[1] Seton-Watson, in *Slavonic Review*, V, pp. 422–7, December 1926; Goriainov, op. cit., p. 349; Wertheimer, op. cit., III, pp. 36–7.

the Russian reigning family should be established on a Balkan throne; (6) that Russia should occupy Constantinople; (7) that a large Slav state should be established in the Balkans at the expense of the non-Slav elements, or that the reorganization should go beyond the granting of autonomy to the present provinces, under a native prince.

The English government was well enough satisfied with this program, but believed that it did not go far enough. What was wanted was common action in the existing crisis. The entente with Austria was a question of decisive importance, Disraeli told the Austrian ambassador. Russia should not be allowed to cross the Balkans, and if she did, England and Austria should take guarantees. England should send the fleet to Gallipoli, while Austria should invade Roumania and eventually Serbia. Would Austria join England in preventing the occupation of Constantinople?

To this Andrássy replied that he was not worried about the Russians crossing the Balkans. He had no objection to the English occupation of Gallipoli, and he would regard the retention of Constantinople by Russia as a *casus belli*. There was not much consolation for the English in the Austrian stand, but Andrássy refused to go further. So far the Russians had not gone back on their agreements with Austria, and there was no reason for his antagonizing them. The English suspected that a bargain had been made between the two empires, but since Andrássy could not be induced to come out and make a stand against Russia, they had to content themselves with what he was ready to offer. The two governments therefore agreed to an exchange of declarations of policy on the basis of the seven points proposed by the Austrian minister. This was accomplished by a dispatch of Andrássy, dated July 26, and the reply of Derby, dated August 14. It was a purely negative agreement and laid down no special course of action for the event of its violation. Disraeli described it as a " moral understanding." More could not be said for it.[1]

While these negotiations were in progress, the Russian army was marching through Roumania. The position of this state was a very peculiar one, in so far as it was technically part of the Ottoman Empire and had been declared to be such by the new Turkish constitution of December 1876. It was clear, however, that the Roumanians would never fight for the Turks. The real question for them was what should be their attitude towards Russia. Not having a direct interest in the conflict, the Roumanian government would have preferred to stand aloof, but this was impossible, for the Turkish control of the Black Sea made the road through Roumania the only one available for a Russian advance. Discussions were carried on by the two governments from September 1876 until April 16, 1877, when a convention was concluded which gave the Russians

---

[1] Lee MS.; Monypenny and Buckle, op. cit., VI, pp. 140, 144, 147, 171; Wertheimer: *Andrássy*, III, pp. 29–39; Seton-Watson, in *Slavonic Review*, V, pp. 428–33, December 1926. The reports of Shuvalov were full and accurate, showing that he had excellent sources of information as to what was going on in the cabinet.

the right of transit through Roumanian territory. The whole arrangement was unsatisfactory from the view-point of the Roumanians, for they were quite aware that Russia, in case of victory, would demand the retrocession of Bessarabia. On this account they would have preferred either to stay out of the conflict altogether or else to take part with the Russians and so share in the spoils. Apparently the Russians feared that this might lead to Roumanian aggrandizement at the expense of the southern Slavs, and therefore the aid of the Roumanians was rejected. The only consolation for the Roumanians lay in the Russian pledge " to maintain and to protect the actual integrity of Roumania." From the documents, however, it appears that the statesmen at Bucharest were by no means deluded with respect to the question of Bessarabia, and that consequently they drew but little comfort from the Russian promises. The government actually declared war on Turkey and proclaimed the independence of Roumania on May 21, after the Turks had bombarded a Roumanian town.[1]

The Russian armies effected the crossing of the Danube on June 23, without meeting much opposition from the Turks. The advance was immediately pushed with great energy. A flying column under General Gourko pushed south through the Balkan Mountains and on July 19 occupied Shipka Pass. The rapidity of the Russian advance to the mountains was very spectacular and was viewed with the greatest alarm in England. Disraeli was convinced more firmly than ever of the necessity for occupying the Dardanelles and was fortified in his opinion by the deluge of hysterical letters he received from Queen Victoria. But some of the members of the cabinet were not so panic-stricken. According to the Russian ambassador, whose excellent source of information appears to have been Lady Derby, the cabinet disliked " this conspiracy between a half-crazy woman and a minister who had once possessed genius but had now degenerated into a political clown." [2] Finally, however, it was agreed to warn Russia against an occupation of Constantinople. On July 21 the cabinet made a decision to declare war on Russia if the Russians occupied the Turkish capital and did not make arrangements to retire immediately. On July 27 a report arrived from Layard, the ambassador at Constantinople, saying that the Russians would be at Adrianople soon and that they would probably advance on Gallipoli. The Sultan was already planning to retire to Brusa, on the Asiatic side. This news was so serious that on the following day Layard was asked to induce the Sultan to invite the British fleet to come up to Constantinople. But before this

---

[1] An excellent account, based on the Roumanian *Documente Oficiale* (1878), may be found in Adolphe d'Avril: *Négociations relatives au Traité de Berlin* (Paris, 1886), book vi. The more important sources are the notes of King Charles I: *Aus dem Leben König Karls von Rumänien* (Stuttgart, 1897), III, *passim;* Iorga: *Correspondance diplomatique roumaine;* Nelidov: " *Souvenirs,"* in the *Revue des deux mondes,* XXVIII, July 15, 1915. See also R. Rosetti: " Roumania's Share in the War of 1877 " (*Slavonic Review,* VIII, pp. 548–77, March 1930).

[2] Seton-Watson, in *Slavonic Review,* V, pp. 430–1, December 1926. See also Monypenny and Buckle, op. cit., VI, pp. 142–8; Buckle: *Letters of Queen Victoria,* II, pp. 539–50.

important step became necessary reports arrived of the first serious set-back suffered by the Russians in the European theatre of war.[1]

On July 19, the very day of the occupation of Shipka Pass by General Gourko, the Turkish general, Osman Pasha, arrived at the fortress of Plevna, coming from the Serbian front in five night marches. The Russians had taken inadequate measures to mask the forts south of the Danube and now had a strong force on their right flank. An attempt to dislodge Osman on July 20 failed, and ten days later an organized attack was repulsed with heavy loss. At about the same time Gourko met with reverses at the hands of the Turks and was obliged to give up his attempt to campaign south of the mountains. In Asia Minor, too, the initial Russian advance was being checked.

These military events completely changed the complexion of affairs. Andrássy considered the mobilization of two divisions and in a ministerial council on July 31 developed the idea that advantage should be taken of Russia's plight. He favoured cutting Russia's communications with the Balkans by throwing a strong force across the narrow passage between the Carpathians and the sea. But the military men, most of whom advocated an understanding with Russia, raised numerous objections to the brave course suggested by the foreign minister. This difference of opinion continued to afflict Austrian policy throughout the critical year that followed, and it is therefore extremely difficult to assess accurately the factors that decided the Austrian action or inaction at any particular time.[2]

The English, who, in the days of the initial Russian advance, had privately dispatched an officer to blow up the defence guns of the Dardanelles if necessary, were immensely relieved by the Russian set-back. There was, for the present, no immediate threat either to the Dardanelles or to Constantinople. In fact, it seemed fairly certain that the Russians would require a second campaign to win a decisive victory. The appearance of Colonel Wellesley, the English military attaché with the Russian armies, served to reassure the English statesmen even more. The Tsar, who had begun to lose his original confidence and enthusiasm, had agreed that Wellesley should return to London to quiet the fears of his government. The Colonel discussed the situation at great length with Disraeli and Derby and also with the Queen. Though the apprehension at London had been greatly allayed, Disraeli and the Queen decided, without consulting Derby, to make doubly sure. Wellesley was sent back to Russian headquarters with an unofficial but very plain-spoken warning to the Tsar against prolonging the conflict or planning a campaign for the following year.[3]

---

[1] Lee MS.; Monypenny and Buckle, op. cit., VI, pp. 150–60; Seton-Watson, in *Slavonic Review*, V, pp. 433–4.

[2] Wertheimer: *Andrássy*, III, pp. 46–8; Edmund von Glaise-Horstenau; *Franz Josephs Weggefährte* (Vienna, 1930), pp. 193–4.

[3] Monypenny and Buckle, op. cit., VI, pp. 173 ff.; *Letters of Queen Victoria*, II, pp. 560–5; Colonel F. A. Wellesley: *The Russians in Peace and War* (London, 1905), chapter xx; Sir Arthur Hardinge: *The Life of Henry Howard Molyneux Herbert, Fourth Earl of Carnarvon* (London, 1925), II, p. 362.

The remainder of the summer passed in relative calm, for the Russians were in a bad way. Earlier in the war they had rejected the aid of Roumania, but now they were only too glad to accept it. In fact, they made vigorous attempts to induce the restless Greeks to assist them. But the government at Athens held back, partly because of English pressure, partly because of fear of the Turkish fleet.[1] Meanwhile the Russian armies were held up at Plevna. A third assault, on September 7, was repulsed with great bloodshed, and General Todleben, the famous defender of Sebastopol in 1855, had to be called to organize a regular siege. Under these circumstances the governments of Vienna and London were able to get breathing-space. Disraeli still urged the need for precautionary measures to meet future developments, but nothing definite was done.

On December 10 Osman Pasha, in danger of starvation, made a vigorous attempt to break through the lines which invested Plevna, but, being outnumbered almost three to one, he was doomed to failure from the start. The valiant Turkish commander was repulsed and obliged to surrender. The greatest obstacle to the Russian advance was thus overcome, and the war of movement could be resumed. Gourko had already begun the advance on Sofia, a city which he took during the first days of January, while other detachments were beginning to pour over the higher passes of the mountains.

The ultimate capitulation of Plevna had been expected for some time, because it was quite evident that no relief would reach Osman Pasha. In anticipation of the great event the Tsar had communicated to the German and Austrian Emperors the general outlines of the peace which he hoped to impose upon the Turks. The projected terms called for the creation of an autonomous, tributary Bulgarian state as large as that provided for by the Constantinople Conference, and for the occupation of the new state by Russian troops for two years. Bosnia and Herzegovina were to be organized along the lines agreed upon by the Constantinople Conference, and Austria was to participate in the control of the two provinces much as Russia planned to do in Bulgaria. Reforms were also to be provided for the other Christian provinces. Roumania, Serbia, and Montenegro were to be made independent. Russia was to receive Bessarabia and to dispose of the conquered territory in Asia Minor. The Straits were to remain closed to foreign warships in time of peace, but the riparian states of the Black Sea were to have the right to pass single ships through the Straits with the authorization of the Porte in each instance. Provision was also to be made for the payment of a money indemnity by the Turks. The peace treaty was to be made by Russia and Turkey, but the powers were to be permitted to concert methods of developing the stipulations relating to general interests.[2]

---

[1] S. T. Lascaris: *La Politique extérieure de la Grèce avant et après le Congrès de Berlin* (Paris, 1924), pp. 85–7.

[2] Seton-Watson, in *Slavonic Review*, VI, pp. 427–8, December 1927; Wertheimer: *Andrássy*, III, pp. 56 ff.

These terms could hardly inspire much confidence for the future in either London or Vienna. The English had not been directly informed, but had derived a fairly accurate idea of the Russian intentions from the Russian press. For them the idea of opening the Straits to Russian warships on any condition except that of complete reciprocity was intolerable. To the Austrians the creation of a large Bulgarian state appeared as a direct challenge to earlier engagements and a serious menace to the security of the monarchy. The uneasiness in London had been growing for some time and was further enhanced by the report from Constantinople that the Turks were inclined to yield to the Russian demand for the opening of the Straits unless England came to the aid of the Porte.[1] Fortunately the Turks themselves had come to realize the danger of their position. On December 12 they asked the powers to mediate. The request was couched in very arrogant terms and made a bad impression on the European governments. Its chances of success were completely ruined when Bismarck refused absolutely to take part in such a move, on the plea that Russia did not desire mediation in the hour of victory and that he had no intention of throwing obstacles into her path to please the Turks.[2]

Disraeli, however, was determined to take a strong stand at any cost. On December 13 a note was handed to the Russian ambassador warning the Russian government that an occupation of Constantinople or the Dardanelles, even though temporary and for purely military purposes, might oblige the British government to take measures of precaution. The Queen urged her prime minister to be firm. " England will never stand to become subservient to Russia, for she would then *fall down* from her high position and become a *second rate Power*," she wrote on December 13. To be sure, there were six or seven parties in the cabinet, as Disraeli put it,[3] but in spite of the lack of harmony among the members of the government, the prime minister came before his colleagues on December 14 and asked that parliament be summoned before the usual time, that a vote of money for increases in the land and sea forces of the empire be requested, and that mediation be undertaken.

Not only Lord Derby, but also Lord Salisbury was opposed to this policy, which, he insisted, would end in an alliance with the Turks. There were several heated cabinet meetings, but Disraeli finally won his point by threatening to resign. Austria was then invited to join in a note to Russia offering mediation before the Balkans were crossed. In accordance with the Russian declaration of June 8 it was assumed that peace on moderate terms (*la petite paix*) would be acceptable. It may well be doubted whether Russia would have entertained the suggestion that she accept in December what she had offered to accept in June. The English had refused to press *la petite paix* on the Turks while they were victorious, but were anxious to save them from complete disaster in the days of

---

[1] Lee MS. Report from Layard, December 10, 1877.
[2] *Die Grosse Politik*, II, Nos. 297–9.
[3] Monypenny and Buckle, op. cit., VI, p. 194; Hardinge, op. cit., II, p. 364.

defeat. As a matter of fact, however, the Austrians themselves refused to act on these lines, for even the program of June 8 was regarded in Vienna as impractical and dangerous in so far as it would involve a Russian occupation of Bulgaria. Andrássy was anxious to avoid British mediation. It would be better, he argued, to let the Turks get the Russian terms and then have them appeal to the powers to bring about a reduction.[1] He therefore contented himself for the present with a pretty stiff rejoinder to the letter of the Tsar to Francis Joseph, in which the Russian terms had been communicated. In this reply it was pointed out that the Turkish Empire had not met a natural death, and that therefore the Russian program was untenable. The Austrian government insisted on having a voice in the peace settlement and reminded the Russian cabinet of the arrangements that had been made as to Bosnia and Herzegovina. Above all, vigorous objections were raised to the Russian plans for a great Bulgaria.[2]

The English prime minister, however, was determined to make an effort to bring about peace negotiations, even without the aid of Austria. Fear of an understanding between the three empires was deeply rooted in the minds of the English statesmen, and they were in constant dread lest they should be presented with a *fait accompli* against which they could do nothing. At just this time, on December 24, the Turks appealed to England to mediate. The opportunity was seized by the English government. Russia was informed of the desire of the Turks for peace. The Tsar refused mediation, even though disguised, and referred the Turks to the commander in the field, who was empowered to discuss an armistice. The granting of the armistice, however, was to be conditional upon previous acceptance of preliminary peace terms. These terms were communicated to the Grand Duke Nicholas on December 29, and the Russian tactics were explained two days later to the commander-in-chief as well as to the ambassador in London. The Russian government intended to drag out the negotiations for the armistice until after January 17, when the English parliament was to meet and when the situation would have become clarified. Even then the Turks were first to accept vague and elastic preliminary terms. Russia would not admit foreign intervention, but recognized the principle of deliberation and sanction by the powers of such clauses as touched general interests. Gorchakov thought he could rely upon Germany and Austria and believed that England, though she might stage a few demonstrations, would be unable to do more. Never had the alliance of the Three Emperors been more complete, Gorchakov told the French ambassador. " I can assure you that there is not even the semblance of a rift." [3]

The Turks, disappointed in their hopes of English aid to secure an armistice,

---

[1] Lee MS.; Monypenny and Buckle, op. cit., VI, pp. 200–6; Cecil, op. cit., II, pp. 163 ff.; Hardinge, op. cit., II, pp. 364 ff.

[2] Wertheimer: *Andrássy*, III, pp. 58 ff.

[3] Seton-Watson, in *Slavonic Review*, pp. 430–3; Goriainov, op. cit., p. 359; Cyon in *Nouvelle Revue*, IV, pp. 759 ff., June 15, 1880; *Documents diplomatiques français*, II, No. 232.

had no other course open to them but to follow the Russian directions. On January 9 they appealed to the Russian commander for an armistice and were told of the conditions under which it would be granted. But it was not until ten days later that the Turkish delegates arrived with full powers to treat. Meanwhile the Russian advance continued and the excitement in the European capitals ran high. Queen Victoria repeatedly pressed upon her ministers the need for action, and wrote to Disraeli on January 10: " She feels she cannot remain sovereign of a country that is letting itself down to kiss the feet of the great barbarians, the retarders of all liberty and civilization that exists. . . . Oh, if the Queen were a man, she would like to go and give those Russians, whose word one cannot believe, such a beating! We shall never be friends again till we have it out. This the Queen feels sure of." [1]

Disraeli hardly needed prodding. Alarming telegrams were coming from Constantinople, reporting that the Turks felt unable to defend Adrianople or the lines of the Gallipoli Peninsula, and that the situation was critical. The prime minister therefore decided to ask the cabinet to send the fleet up to the Turkish capital. His colleagues, however, refused to agree to more than that the Sultan's permission should be asked to have the fleet anchor within the Straits, and that Russia should be asked for assurances that she would not occupy the Dardanelles. Orders to the fleet were avoided because, at the crucial moment, assurances came from St. Petersburg that Gallipoli would not be occupied unless the Turks concentrated there. The Sultan, too, was hesitant about inviting the British fleet, fearing the reaction of such a step upon Russia.[2]

Disraeli's next step was to reopen discussions with Austria, in an attempt to effect concerted action against the Russians, who, to all appearances, were conducting the negotiations with the Turks in the greatest secrecy and planning to present the powers with a *fait accompli*. The Austrian ambassador was asked whether his government was prepared to play the *grand coup* and mobilize. In that case England would take equivalent action. Apparently Disraeli brought before the cabinet a proposal for a defensive alliance with Austria to extend over a term of years. But nothing could be got out of Andrássy. Personally he favoured vigorous action and advocated a concentration of forces in Transylvania, as in 1855. This would force the Russians to evacuate the Balkans. But the military men pointed out insuperable obstacles to such a policy. After days of debate no decision was come to.

So Andrássy told the English ambassador that he was profoundly disappointed with the address from the throne on the opening of the British Parliament on January 17. In the nature of the case he was obliged to prevent a break with Russia if it were at all possible. He was anxious enough for the English to move and send the fleet to Constantinople, but, he explained, Austrian mobi-

---

[1] Monypenny and Buckle, op. cit., VI, p. 217.
[2] Monypenny and Buckle, op. cit., VI, pp. 218–20; Cecil, op. cit., II, pp. 186–7; Hardinge, op. cit., II, pp. 372–4; *Gathorne-Hardy*, II, pp. 46–7.

lization was so expensive that it could not be undertaken unless absolutely imperative. To the English suggestion of identic notes to Russia warning her against the continued occupation of Bulgaria, or the occupation of the shores of the Bosporus, the Sea of Marmora, or the Dardanelles, he replied that such a move might give rise to the impression that England and Austria objected only to these acts and accepted the rest of the Russian program.[1] The negotiations with Austria were as unsatisfactory as ever. Both powers were opposed to the Russian advance, but the Austrians were unable to act or unwilling to do so until they were certain that Russia would go back on her agreements. Besides, they were less interested in the Straits problem than in the Bulgarian. Each of the two powers was willing to follow the lead of the other, but neither was prepared to take the initiative.

The alarming thing in these days was the rapidity of the Russian advance to the Straits and Constantinople. The Turkish capital was in a veritable panic. On January 19 the Sultan asked that the English fleet be prepared to come through the Straits if Russia advanced on Gallipoli. The Grand Duke Nicholas, who had received orders to abstain from an attack on Gallipoli, was pressing upon the Tsar the urgent necessity for occupying the Turkish capital in order to coerce the Turks into acceptance of the Russian terms. There was, in fact, a strong feeling in Russia that the occupation of Constantinople would be the only fitting close to the war.[2] Under the circumstances the English government, still hoping that vigorous action might influence the Austrians favourably, decided on January 23 to send the fleet to the Turkish capital, though this decision resulted in the resignation of Lord Derby, the foreign minister, and of Lord Carnarvon, the colonial minister. But after the orders to proceed had already been sent, reassuring telegrams regarding the nature of the preliminary peace terms arrived from Constantinople. Layard reported that the Straits question was to be settled by "the congress and the Emperor of Russia." This seemed satisfactory enough, and the English cabinet, already fearful of the effect which Derby's resignation might have, especially in parliament, decided to recall the fleet. It turned out shortly afterwards that Layard's telegram was based on a misunderstanding and that the Russian terms called for a settlement of the Straits question by the Sultan and the Emperor of Russia. But it was clearly impossible for the government to change its mind again and send the fleet forward once more. As it was, this famous incident threw a rather lurid light on the indecision of the cabinet and in no way served to strengthen the British position.[3]

---

[1] Monypenny and Buckle, op. cit., VI, pp. 225–7; Hardinge, op. cit., II, p. 375; *Letters of Queen Victoria*, II, p. 596; Wertheimer, *Andrássy*, III, p. 61; Lee MS.; *Gathorne-Hardy*, II, p. 47; Glaise-Horstenau, op. cit., pp. 197–8.

[2] Schweinitz: *Denkwürdigkeiten*, II, p. 6; Cyon, loc. cit., pp. 765–7; Goriainov, op. cit., p. 361.

[3] Monypenny and Buckle, op. cit., VI, pp. 227–31; Cecil, op. cit., II, pp. 191–3; Hardinge, op. cit., II, pp. 376 ff.; *Gathorne-Hardy*, II, pp. 47–9. The French representative at Constantinople reported much as Layard did (*Documents diplomatiques français*, II, Nos. 232, 233).

The Russian terms were communicated to England and Austria on January 26. They did not differ materially from those which had been outlined by the Tsar early in December and showed no trace of moderation as a result of English or Austrian agitation. In London some consolation was derived from the fact that the question of the Straits was reserved for a later understanding. On the whole, the Russian program was harder on the Austrians than on the English, and for the moment the Vienna government, which had been trying to burden the English with the initiative, was obliged to take the lead.[1] Andrássy made no secret of his feeling that Austria had been deceived and duped by the Russians, and declared his determination not to accept conditions which affected European or Austrian interests unless the powers gave their assent. He even went so far as to ask the English for armed aid to combat such a one-sided peace, but now the English refused to move.[2] Derby had been induced by his colleagues to re-enter the cabinet after the orders to the fleet had been countermanded, and it went without saying that he would continue to oppose a forward policy. Meanwhile the Turkish delegates accepted the Russian terms on January 27, and the armistice was signed on January 31.[3]

In accordance with his view that the Russian terms must be submitted to the judgment of the powers or Austria would go to war, Andrássy on January 28 suggested the convocation of a conference. Gorchakov, in replying to the Austrian objections, stated without equivocation that the preliminary terms were merely provisional so far as Europe was concerned, and agreed to a meeting to discuss the European aspects of the peace settlement. During the next weeks, then, the negotiations for the conference occupied the attention of the various governments. None of the powers was at first very favourably disposed towards the Austrian suggestion. Gorchakov would not hear of a meeting of the powers at Vienna and preferred some small German resort, like Baden-Baden. In any case, he desired a formal congress in which the foreign ministers of the various states should take part. The English, on the other hand, were filled with distrust and suspected a coalition of the three empires which would leave England isolated and helpless. Only after considerable pressure by Andrássy and only after Austrian promises of co-operation with England did the London cabinet agree. Bismarck was lukewarm, but was ready to accept the conference if it promised to prevent a break. He even agreed eventually to have the conference at Berlin, though he was fully aware of the danger involved and realized that the powers who left the meeting dissatisfied would put the blame on Germany. In the meanwhile he attempted to bring about conversations *à trois* at Vienna between Andrássy and the Russian and German ambassadors. In this way he hoped that the difficulties could

---

[1] Monypenny and Buckle, op. cit., VI, pp. 231–3; Wertheimer, *Andrássy,* III, p. 69; Lee MS.

[2] *Die Grosse Politik,* II, No. 303; Wertheimer, *Andrássy,* III, p. 70; Monypenny and Buckle, op. cit., VI, p. 237.

[3] Cyon, loc. cit., p. 767.

be overcome through direct negotiation between the members of the Three Emperors' League.[1]

The armistice terms agreed upon by the Porte provided for Russian occupation of Turkish territory almost to the lines of Bulair in the direction of the Gallipoli Peninsula, and almost to the Chatalja lines outside Constantinople. Consequently the Russian advance continued during the first weeks of February. But the terms of the armistice had not yet been officially communicated to the powers, and the Russian action therefore appeared very ominous. In England the war spirit rose day by day, and before long the country resounded with the tune of the well-known jingo song:

> We don't want to fight, but by jingo if we do,
> We've got the men, we've got the ships, we've got the money too.

The cabinet was in almost daily session, discussing the question of sending the fleet to Constantinople and the problem of foreign co-operation in a move to check Russia. The Turkish capital was at the mercy of the enemy, and all direct wires had been cut. On February 8 the cabinet decided to send up the fleet and to invite other neutral powers to join in the step. The great aim of the English government was to "Europeanize" the action against Russia. At the same time parliament granted a credit of six million pounds for preparations. Admiral Hornby, in command of the fleet lying outside the Dardanelles, was immediately ordered to advance and was informed that the English ambassador at Constantinople had been instructed to get the Sultan's permission. But when the fleet reached the first stopping-place in the Straits, the town of Charnak, no permission had arrived. After waiting for several hours, Hornby returned with his ships to Besika Bay. The trouble was that the Sultan had been warned by the Grand Duke Nicholas that if the British fleet came up, the Russians would occupy the capital. Abdul Hamid, therefore, was anxious to avoid the appearance of the fleet.

Even at the time of the first fleet episode, in January, the British government had exposed itself to ridicule with its orders and counter-orders. In the House of Commons the following ditty had been devised to fit the situation:

> When Government ordered the fleet to the Straits
> They surely encountered the hardest of fates;
> For the order, scarce given, at once was recalled,
> And the Russians were not in the slightest appalled.
>   And everyone says, who has heard the debates,
>   "It's the Cabinet now, not the fleet, that's in straits."

Clearly the government now had to go through with the operation or run the risk of becoming the laughing-stock of Europe.

---

[1] See especially *Die Grosse Politik*, II, chapter xii (A); *Documents diplomatiques français*, II, Nos. 236 ff.

On February 12 Hornby received instructions to proceed without permission and to return fire on the Turkish forts if his ships were fired on and hit. A few of the ships were left off Gallipoli to guard the approach to the Dardanelles. The others proceeded to the Princes Islands, just off Constantinople, where they anchored on the morning of February 15. The Grand Duke Nicholas had been given a free hand and had been told to use his judgment about the occupation of the capital, but there was evidently some delay and considerable misunderstanding about his instructions, and furthermore the Turks had thrown up defences, so that the occupation would not have been so easy as a few weeks before. In any case the Russians did not advance beyond the town of San Stefano, some ten miles from the capital, while the English fleet was withdrawn to Mudania, on the Asiatic side of the Sea of Marmora, after several earnest appeals from the Sultan to Queen Victoria.[1]

In these days peace hung by a hair. The European world was deluged with all sorts of alarming rumours. It was said that the Russians were demanding the surrender of a number of the best Turkish ships, and that they would occupy the Ottoman capital after all. The English position was rather ridiculous, even after the arrival of the fleet at Constantinople. There had been too much indecision, and the continent was not yet convinced that England would fight. In the critical days before Hornby appeared at the Princes Islands placards had been posted on the British embassy at Constantinople: "Lost — between Besika Bay and Constantinople — one fleet. Reward to anyone furnishing information."[2] England was becoming a butt for the ridicule of other nations, and Bismarck himself said that if he had made such brave speeches as Disraeli, he would have drawn the sword long before. To the Prince of Wales, during the latter's visit to Berlin, he once again expounded his theory of a settlement based on partition. If he were English prime minister, he said, he would withdraw the fleet from the Sea of Marmora and send it to Egypt instead.[3]

Disraeli felt the anomaly of the English position very keenly and was determined to put an end to the uncertainty at any cost. Not only was the fleet sent up in spite of Turkish objections, but Layard was instructed to purchase the best ships of the Turkish navy, if possible. Lord Napier was appointed commander-in-chief, and General Wolseley chief of staff of an eventual expeditionary force. Russia was warned that if Constantinople were occupied without the Sultan's consent, the English ambassador would be withdrawn from St. Petersburg.

---

[1] Monypenny and Buckle, op. cit., VI, pp. 241–4; Cecil, op. cit., II, pp. 197–8; *Documents diplomatiques français*, II, No. 246; Busch, in *Deutsche Rundschau*, XXXVI, pp. 216 ff., November 1909; Evelyn S. Schaeffer, op. cit., pp. 113 ff.; Cyon, loc. cit., pp. 769–70; Goriainov, op. cit., p. 364; Egerton: *Admiral Sir G. T. Phipps Hornby* (London, 1896); Sir William L. Clowes: *The Royal Navy* (London, 1903), VII, pp. 294 ff.; Schweinitz: *Denkwürdigkeiten*, II, pp. 9–10.

[2] Schaeffer: *Eugene Schuyler*, p. 115.

[3] Egon C. Corti: *Alexander von Battenberg* (Vienna, 1920), p. 33; Sir Sidney Lee: *King Edward VII* (London, 1925) I, p. 432; Buckle: *Letters of Queen Victoria*, II, p. 608.

At the same time negotiations were once again carried on with Austria. The Austrians, like the French and the Italians, had held out some hope that they would join in a naval demonstration at Constantinople, ostensibly to protect their nationals in a crisis. But they had failed, at the last moment, to co-operate. It was now proposed by the English government that a loan should be granted the Austrian government, provided it would mobilize three hundred thousand men and join England in sending identic notes to Russia warning her that neither England nor Austria would go to a conference unless the Russians retired from Constantinople or placed Gallipoli and the Straits fortresses in English or neutral custody. Andrássy once more demanded vigorous measures in the form of mobilization, but found it impossible to overcome the objections of the military men. On February 16 it was decided not to mobilize. Andrássy's problem was to secure Austrian interests without a war. Vienna circles were suspicious of English policy. Besides, the influential military element at the Austrian court objected vigorously and on principle to the idea of war against Russia.[1]

In the meanwhile Disraeli was busy elaborating further measures for the preservation of English interests in the Mediterranean. One of these was the formation of a Mediterranean league to oppose the advance of Russian influence. On March 2 the prime minister brought before the cabinet the question of the organization of such a group of nations, to include Italy, Greece, and probably Austria and France, " to secure the trade and communications of Europe with the East from the overshadowing interference of Russia." Though Derby was not favourably disposed towards such far-reaching plans, it was decided to approach Italy. Both Disraeli and Salisbury felt certain that if one power agreed, the others would join, and the Italians had expressed themselves so strongly in opposition to the Russian pretensions that there seemed more prospect of success in that direction than in any other. Instructions were sent to Rome on March 13, but in the interval the Depretis cabinet had fallen. The new Cairoli ministry, in which Count Corti was foreign minister, was less inclined to take a prominent part in the Eastern imbroglio, and so, on March 29, the English proposal was rejected.[2]

More important than these vague schemes of a Mediterranean coalition were the concrete measures which Disraeli had in view. Ever since November 1877 he had been considering the desirability of acquiring, perhaps by purchase from the Porte, a naval base in the eastern Mediterranean. We are told by Lord Salisbury's biographer that he, too, had been revolving in his mind some such measure, and that he had, ever since the Constantinople Conference, considered Cyprus as a possible base. It is an actual fact that at the end of the conference

---

[1] Wertheimer, *Andrássy*, III, p. 76; Glaise-Horstenau, op. cit., pp. 199 ff.; Monypenny and Buckle, op. cit., VI, pp. 248–51; Lee MS.

[2] Dwight E. Lee: " The Proposed Mediterranean League of 1878 " (*Journal of Modern History*, III, pp. 33–45, March, 1931). The chief sources are Francesco Crispi: *Memoirs* (London, 1912), II, pp. 95–7; Luigi Chiala: *Pagine di Storia Contemporanea* (Turin, 1892), I, pp. 294–6; Monypenny and Buckle, op. cit., VI, pp. 253–5.

he had sent Colonel Home to examine and report on Rhodes, Cyprus, and Egypt. Home visited the first two places and was then recalled. The question of securing a naval base was first brought before the cabinet on February 27, and, like all other proposals for vigorous action, met with the opposition of Derby. Nevertheless the cabinet adopted the proposal " provisionally and hypothetically " on March 8. Various places were mentioned as desirable, such as Mytilene in the Ægean; St. Jean d'Acre on the Syrian coast, and a port on the Persian Gulf. With three such stations the road to India would be secure, no matter what the outcome of the existing crisis.[1]

Measures of precaution had, in the meantime, become even more urgent, for on March 3 the Russians and the Turks had signed the peace treaty of San Stefano. The terms were not officially notified to the powers until after the exchange of ratifications, on March 23, but they were known unofficially even before they were signed. The treaty had been negotiated by General Ignatiev and was an eloquent expression of Pan-Slav aspirations. Andrássy, in fact, spoke of the Russian program as an " Orthodox Slavic sermon." It is hardly necessary here to review all the clauses of the treaty. The crucial points were these: Montenegro was to be considerably enlarged and given the port of Antivari on the Adriatic; her status was to be that of complete independence. Serbia, too, was to be made completely independent and to receive an increase of territory towards the south-east; Roumanian independence was to be recognized, while Russia reserved the right to cede to Roumania the Dobruja district, in return for the cession of Bessarabia to Russia. Bosnia and Herzegovina were to be granted the reforms proposed by the Constantinople Conference, with some modifications. Thessaly, Epirus, and the other Christian provinces of Turkey in Europe were to receive an organization like that of Crete. Turkey was to pay almost one and a half billion rubles of indemnity, but in lieu of one billion one hundred thousand rubles Russia agreed to accept the cession of the Dobruja and the islands of the Danube delta, and in Asia Minor the towns of Ardahan, Kars, Batum, and Bayazid. Of the Straits little was said, except that, even in time of war, neutral merchant ships going to and from Russian Black Sea ports should be allowed to pass through the Straits unmolested.

But the most important and interesting part of the treaty referred to Bulgaria, the territory on which the chief hopes of the Pan-Slavs had been centred. The preliminary terms of peace, signed on January 31, had provided for a Bulgarian state not smaller than that projected by the Constantinople Conference. Under the terms of the San Stefano Treaty the new Bulgaria was to be an autonomous state under an elected prince, was to be tributary to the Sultan and to be occupied by fifty thousand Russian troops for about two years. Territorially it was to be considerably larger than the Bulgaria proposed in December 1876 and was to have an Ægean seaboard. The line was to start on the coast

---

[1] Monypenny and Buckle, op. cit., VI, pp. 251–5; Cecil, op. cit., II, p. 214; Simmons Memorandum, dated October 2, 1877 (unpublished).

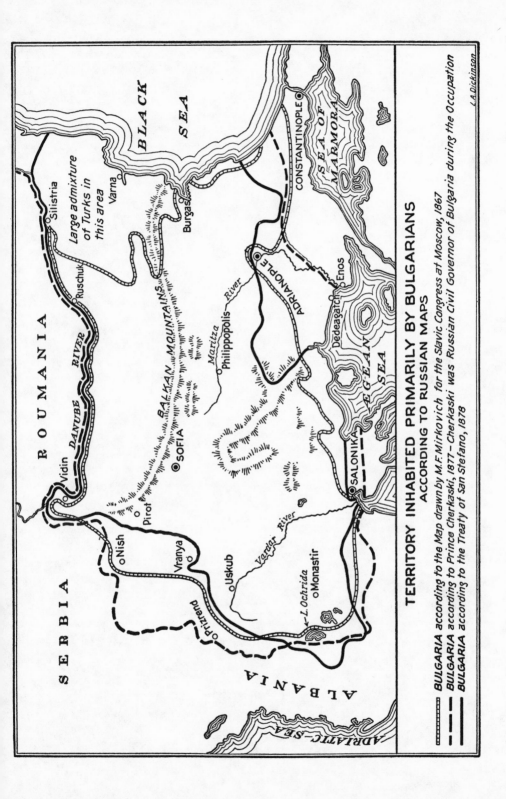

TERRITORY INHABITED PRIMARILY BY BULGARIANS
ACCORDING TO RUSSIAN MAPS

— BULGARIA *according to the Map drawn by M.F.Mirkovich for the Slavic Congress at Moscow, 1867*

.... BULGARIA *according to Prince Cherkaski, 1877 – Cherkaski was Russian Civil Governor of Bulgaria during the Occupation*

— — — BULGARIA *according to the Treaty of San Stefano, 1878*

J.A.Dickinson

SERBIA

ROUMANIA

BLACK SEA

Vidin

Silistria

Large admixture of Turks in this area

Varna

Ruschuk

DANUBE RIVER

Burgas

BALKAN MOUNTAINS

Pirot

SOFIA

Philippopolis

Maritza River

ADRIANOPLE

CONSTANTINOPLE

SEA OF MARMORA

Nish

Vranya

Uskub

Vardar River

Monastir

L. Ochrida

prizrend

SALONIKA

Dedeagatch

Enos

EGEAN SEA

ALBANIA

ADRIATIC SEA

of the Black Sea just north of Karaman and run thence north-west to Silistria, follow the Danube up-stream to beyond Vidin, run from there in a broken line south-westward to include the entire territory around Lake Okhrida, thence eastward to strike the sea at the mouth of the Vardar River. Salonika and the peninsula of Chalcidice were not included, but east of the peninsula the line ran along the Ægean coast to beyond the mouth of the Mesta River, turned northward and then eastward, passing just north of Adrianople, making a considerable dip to the south and then continuing to the Black Sea.

This line remained, even after the Treaty of Berlin, the ideal of the Bulgarians and therefore played an important role in the later history of the Balkans. It was certainly a daring demarcation from the political standpoint, for the Bulgaria created by the Treaty of San Stefano was a state far larger than any other in the Balkans at that time. It was therefore in contradiction to the provisions of Russia's agreements with Austria. Under the peace terms the Turks were left with only a few isolated bits of territory in Europe: namely, Thrace, the Chalcidian Peninsula and Salonika, Thessaly and Epirus, Albania, and the strip of land between Serbia and Montenegro. Communication with most of these territories would have been possible only by sea.

Yet in judging the provisions of the Treaty of San Stefano as they touched Bulgaria it must be remembered that the new Bulgaria did not differ very much from the two Bulgarian vilayets envisaged by the Constantinople Conference in 1876–7. The conference had used the recently published Kiepert map, the best ethnographic map of the Balkans available at that time. This Kiepert map represented not only scientific investigation by the map-maker, but a general consensus of opinion among ethnologists. On accompanying pages of this book there are freely drawn reproductions of ethnological maps made by Pan-Slav writers and other maps published by leading authorities in western Europe. There are no striking differences between these various products. All agree that most of Macedonia was primarily inhabited by Bulgarians. Bulgarian scholars have had no trouble in finding numerous quotations from contemporary travellers testifying to this same fact. Taken by and large, it is clear that Ignatiev in drawing the frontier of the new Bulgaria might have gone even further than he did. He followed not only the work of the Constantinople Conference, not only the theories of the Pan-Slavs, but also the best contemporary evidence of a scientific character. Here and there he overstepped the bounds somewhat, especially in advancing the boundary to the Ægean Sea, but on the whole the new Bulgaria had a sound national basis.[1]

But the rights of the Bulgarian nationality did not concern either Andrássy

[1] For contemporary evidence see especially N. Mikhoff: *La Bulgarie et son peuple d'après les témoignages étrangers* (Lausanne, 1918) and the second volume: *Bulgarien und die Bulgaren im Urteil des Auslandes* (Sofia, 1929). Many maps are reproduced in D. Rizoff: *Die Bulgaren in ihren historischen, ethnographischen und politischen Grenzen* (Berlin, 1917). There is some discussion of the Bulgarian boundary problem in William A. Gauld: "*The Making of Bulgaria*" (*History*, X, pp. 26–35, April 1925).

or Disraeli nearly so much as the question of power and the problem of Russian influence. There were people, to be sure, who argued that the new states would be anxious to assert themselves, and would by no means accept the tutelage of Russia without question. The larger they were, the better able they would be to resist Russian encroachments. Bismarck himself doubted whether Russia would gain by the destruction of the Turkish Empire and the creation of Slavic states in the Balkans. The statesmen at Vienna and London were, however, unmoved by these arguments. Though the crucial question of the Straits was not raised by the Treaty of San Stefano, it was felt that the new Bulgarian state would be a mere outpost of Russia on the Ægean, and, furthermore, that the advance of Russia in Armenia would be the first step in Russia's progress towards the Gulf of Alexandretta. The English had by this time become so firmly set on an anti-Russian course that they no longer wavered in their opposition to the Russian policy. Andrássy felt that Austria was directly menaced by the projected creation of a large Slav state, not so much because it reached the Ægean, though that was bad enough, but because it extended so far to the west. His discussions with the Russian ambassador, Novikov, and the German ambassador, Stolberg, had come to nothing. The Austrian minister had expressed his willingness to have Bulgaria made independent, provided the limits of the new state were reduced. The Russian representative had shown no inclination to yield, excepting possibly on the question of the duration of the Russian occupation. On March 6, therefore, Andrássy issued invitations to the powers to attend a congress to be held at Berlin.[1]

The powers accepted this proposal as offering the only hope of a pacific solution. France, to be sure, found some difficulty in deciding to go to Berlin. The last congress on the Eastern question had been held at Paris, in the most glorious days of the Second Empire. To go to Berlin was, in a sense, to recognize that the centre of gravity had shifted from the French to the German capital. Fortunately the decision was made somewhat easier by the improved relations between Germany and France. In the elections for the chamber in October 1877, the French republicans had won an overwhelming victory, thus putting an end to the movement for a royalist restoration. MacMahon was, from that time until his resignation in 1879, a mere figure-head, and the real force behind the government during the following years was Gambetta. Bismarck had always preferred the republican form of government in France, because he felt that a republic would of necessity remain isolated in monarchical Europe. He had every reason to be pleased with the new régime. In the republican cabinet the portfolio for foreign affairs had been given to M. Waddington, a Protestant of English extraction, whose very selection served as an announcement that the new government would not pursue a policy favourable to the Papacy. At the same time Gontaut-Biron, the ambassador to Berlin, who was intensely

---

[1] *Die Grosse Politik*, II, Nos. 325, 328, 329; *Documents diplomatiques français*, II, Nos. 255, 256, 261.

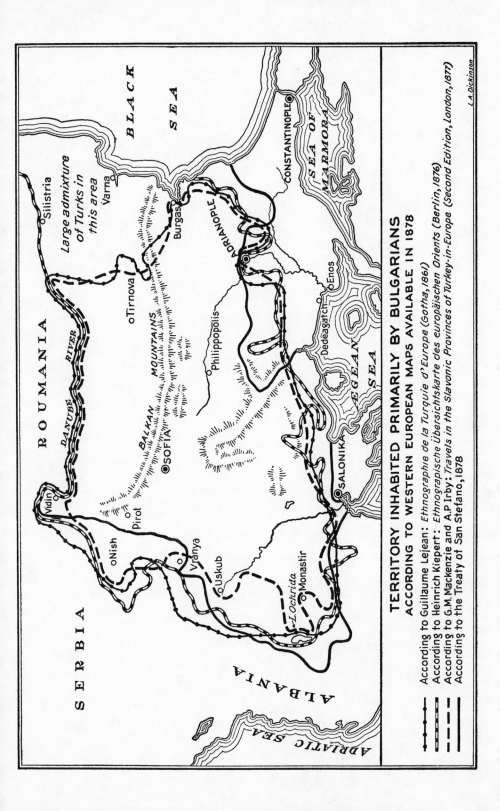

L.A. Dickinson

TERRITORY INHABITED PRIMARILY BY BULGARIANS

ACCORDING TO WESTERN EUROPEAN MAPS AVAILABLE IN 1878

According to Guillaume Lejean: *Ethnographie de la Turquie d'Europe (Gotha, 1861)*
According to Heinrich Kiepert: *Ethnograpische Übersichtskarte des europäischen Orients (Berlin, 1876)*
According to G.M. Mackenzie and A.P. Irby: *Travels in the Slavonic Provinces of Turkey-in-Europe (Second Edition, London, 1877)*
According to the Treaty of San Stefano, 1878

BLACK SEA

SEA OF MARMORA

AEGEAN SEA

ADRIATIC SEA

ROUMANIA

SERBIA

ALBANIA

CONSTANTINOPLE

Silistria

Large admixture of Turks in this area

Varna

Burgas

ADRIANOPLE

oTirnova

Enos

DANUBE RIVER

Philippopolis

Dedeagatch

BALKAN MOUNTAINS

SOFIA

SALONIKA

Vidin

Pirot

Nish

Vranya

Uskub

Monastir

L. Ochrida

disliked by Bismarck, was recalled and replaced by the Comte de Saint-Vallier, a very moderate and conciliatory personality. The new ambassador was received with great cordiality in Berlin, and the tension between the two governments was so far relieved that during the winter of 1877-8 negotiations were carried on for a visit which Gambetta was to pay to the chancellor. The great French leader was the apostle of revenge, but he had become convinced that the " radiant aurora of right " was dawning on the " monster," and that the time had come for France to "formulate her legitimate claims clearly." The interview was fixed for April 30, but at the last moment Gambetta withdrew. He had, apparently, convinced himself that he would have to return with " empty hands." [1]

In spite of the failure of the projected meeting between Gambetta and Bismarck, relations between the two countries continued to be cordial, and when the French government accepted the invitation to the Berlin Congress, it made no reservation excepting that only such questions as had arisen from the war should be discussed. The French government was anxious not to have such problems as those of Egypt, Syria, Tunis, and the Holy Places brought before the congress.[2] The English government, on the other hand, was very hesitant about deciding to attend the congress. A meeting at Berlin, it was felt, would have a far too Russophil tone, and England might find herself faced with a program previously concerted between the three empires. When the decision to attend was finally reached, important reservations were attached to it. It was to be understood that all questions touched upon in the Treaty of San Stefano should be considered suitable for discussion by the congress, and that no modification of the state of affairs previously established by the treaties should be admitted as valid without the assent of the powers. Every article should be submitted to the congress, " not necessarily for acceptance, but in order that it may be considered what articles require acceptance or concurrence by the several powers and what do not."

Gorchakov had, long before, recognized the right of the powers to pass upon such articles as were of European interest and, in reply to the English reservations, promised to communicate the whole treaty of peace to the various governments before the meeting of the congress. Each of the powers might reserve to itself " full liberty of appreciation and action." The English government thereupon inquired whether the Russian cabinet was willing to consider the communication of the treaty to the powers as the equivalent of its submission

---

[1] Hanotaux, op. cit., IV, pp. 254 ff.; Joseph Reinach: *Vie politique de Léon Gambetta* (Paris, 1918), pp. 245 ff.; Henri Galli: *Gambetta et l'Alsace-Lorraine* (Paris, 1911), chapters v, vi. The correspondence is conveniently translated and presented in de Roux: *La République de Bismarck* (Paris, 1915), pp. 63 ff. On Gontaut and Saint-Vallier see André Dreux: *Dernières Années de l'ambassade de M. de Gontaut-Biron* (Paris, 1907), chapter viii, and Ernest Daudet: *La Mission du Comte de Saint-Vallier* (Paris, 1918), chapter iii; *Documents diplomatiques français*, II, Nos. 197, 198, 222, 237, 259; *Die Grosse Politik*, III, Nos. 650-4.

[2] *Die Grosse Politik*, II, No. 339; d'Avril: *Négociations relatives au Traité de Berlin*, pp. 279-81; *Documents diplomatiques français*, II, Nos. 262, 265 ff.

to the congress, but the Russian government refused to accept this interpretation. It was willing to leave " to the other powers the liberty of raising such
questions at the Congress as they might think fit to discuss, and reserved to
itself the liberty of accepting or rejecting the discussion of these questions." On
the surface it is difficult to see any substantial difference in the views of the
two foreign offices. The English wanted the congress to decide what questions
were of European interest and therefore desired to have the treaty submitted to
the congress. The Russians were willing to submit the treaty to the individual
powers, allow them to bring any point before the congress, and then let the
congress decide whether they were fit subjects for discussion. In the end it all
came to the same thing, for it was agreed that decisions at the congress should
not be by majority vote, and that therefore no one power could be outvoted.
Russia, then, was not binding herself in advance to accept the definitions of the
congress. At bottom the dispute was a test of strength and a matter of prestige.
In Russia the submission of the treaty to the congress was looked upon as a
humiliation. Perhaps the English intended it to be so. They were determined
to bring Russia before a European Areopagus to answer for her sins.[1]

As a result of the difference between England and Russia regarding the
competence of the congress, the prospects of a European meeting appeared very
black at the end of March. The Russians determined to make a last effort to
settle with the Austrians and in this way isolate England and reduce her to
impotency. On March 25 General Ignatiev arrived in Vienna. His discussions
with Andrássy are more or less shrouded in mystery to this day, and it
cannot be said with certainty just what the course of the argument was. It
seems that Ignatiev began by explaining that the Treaty of San Stefano had been
concluded with full consideration for the previous agreements with Austria.
Austria's objection to a large Slavic state had been taken by the Russians to refer
only to Serbia and Montenegro. After all, the outlines of the new Bulgaria had
been fixed by the Constantinople Conference in 1876. They were not the expression of a Russian desire to establish a great Slavic outpost in the Balkans, but
merely to create a state based upon ethnographic considerations.

Andrássy replied to these arguments by reading Ignatiev the January Convention of 1877. He told him that Austria would not be content unless the occupation of Bosnia and Herzegovina were agreed to by Russia, unless the
acquisitions of Montenegro towards the east were pared down and Montenegro
and Serbia left separated by the Sanjak of Novi-Bazar, and unless the Bulgarian
frontier were pushed back so as to leave most of Macedonia in Turkish hands.
The occupation of Bulgaria by Russian troops should be limited to six months.

The Austrian desires as they affected Bosnia and Herzegovina did not cause
difficulty, for the Russians had already resigned themselves to Austrian occupation or even annexation of these provinces. But the other demands of An-

---

[1] Monypenny and Buckle, op. cit., VI, pp. 257–60; Goriainov, op. cit., pp. 371–3; *Die Grosse
Politik*, II, Nos. 337, 343, 350, 356, 358, 361, 366–8. A good summary in d'Avril, pp. 331–8.

drássy were of a far more serious nature. It is known that he had worked out a plan by which he hoped to build up Austrian political influence and economic control of the whole western Balkan area and open up a road to Salonika. He claimed that Ignatiev had offered these territories (Albania and Macedonia) and suggested the erection of a new principality under Austrian influence. Ignatiev, on the other hand, accused Andrássy of wanting to acquire this area for Austria. The truth seems to be that Andrássy had no desire to annex even Bosnia and Herzegovina, but that he did wish to keep the region to Salonika free for Austrian economic expansion. For that reason he was determined not to allow the Montenegrin gains to extend so far east that the principality could join with Serbia and thus block the road to the south-east. For the same reason he was determined that Macedonia should be excluded from the new Bulgaria. The whole problem is of great importance not only for the study of the crisis of 1878, but for the subsequent history of Austrian policy. At the time of the Ignatiev mission there was much acrimonious discussion as to what had actually been said. The mission failed. Its only result was to generate greater friction between the two rival powers.[1]

Disraeli, too, had decided upon further measures. On March 27 he laid before the cabinet three proposals: that the reserves should be called out; that troops should be summoned from India; and that these troops should occupy some station or stations in the eastern Mediterranean. It appears that Cyprus and Alexandretta were meant by this last proposal, and that they were actually mentioned in the cabinet meeting. With these two stations the English would be able to block the eventual advance of the Russians from Armenia across Asia Minor to the Gulf of Alexandretta. The cabinet agreed to call out the reserves and accepted in principle the proposal to bring Indian troops to occupy the needed stations. Derby, however, objected vigorously and handed in his resignation, which was accepted. Since only the decision to call out the reserves was made public, it was believed that he had resigned on this score alone. In reality he was out of sympathy with the whole Disraelian program and had done little in the way of constructive work since his earlier resignation in January. The Queen regarded his going as " an unmixed blessing," and the cabinet now felt free to pursue a firmer policy. Lord Salisbury, who succeeded Derby as foreign minister, was in agreement with the prime minister and there was every indication that, after all its tergiversations, the government would take a strong and consistent stand.[2]

The new foreign minister made his début with a famous circular, dated April 1. The outlines of this important document appear to have been drawn

---

[1] Wertheimer, op. cit., III, pp. 90–3; Die Grosse Politik, II, Nos. 371, 376, 377, 380, 393; Documents diplomatiques français, II, Nos. 284, 291, 294, 295, 296; Glaise-Horstenau, op. cit., p. 204.
[2] Monypenny and Buckle, op. cit., VI, pp. 262–71; Cecil, op. cit., II, pp. 218–19; Gathorne-Hardy, II, pp. 56 ff.; Die Grosse Politik, II, No. 375.

up immediately after Derby's resignation, but there is little doubt that it was Salisbury himself who gave it final form and who was responsible for its clear and incisive character. The circular restated England's view-point in regard to the congress and set forth the objections to the various stipulations of the San Stefano Treaty. "But," it continued, "their separate and individual operation, whether defensible or not, is not that which should engage the most earnest attention of the signatory powers. Their combined effect, in addition to the results upon the Greek population and upon the balance of maritime power which have already been pointed out, is to suppress, almost to the point of entire subjection, the political independence of the government of Constantinople. The formal jurisdiction of that government extends over geographical positions which must, under all circumstances, be of the deepest interest to Great Britain. . . . It cannot be otherwise than a matter of extreme solicitude to this country that the government to which this jurisdiction belongs should be so closely pressed by the political outposts of a greatly superior power that its independent action, and even existence, is almost impossible. These results arise not so much from the language of any single article in the treaty as from the operation of the instrument as a whole. A discussion limited to the articles selected by any one power in the congress would be an illusory remedy for the danger to English interests and to the permanent peace of Europe which would result from the state of things which the treaty proposes to establish."

This exceedingly clear formulation of the English view did much to put an end to the general uncertainty and made a profound impression on Europe. To be sure it was not a positive program that Salisbury outlined. Gorchakov complained quite rightly that the English had stated what they did not want, but had not revealed what they did want. The same feeling was shared by Shuvalov, the Russian ambassador at London, who believed war almost inevitable after this inflexible expression of opposition. He immediately approached Salisbury and invited him to state just what England wanted. The English minister replied that he was not yet ready to present the English demands.[1]

The English were much worried by the mission of Ignatiev to Vienna and the danger of an agreement between Russia and Austria which would leave England isolated. They determined to redouble their efforts to reach an agreement with the Viennese government, in order to make resistance to the "subterranean peace" overwhelming. There was a lively exchange of notes between London and Vienna during the month of April, though the efforts of the English government proved abortive. Andrássy continued to evade, and stressed the question of the Russian occupation of Bulgaria, the necessity for maintaining adequate communication between Constantinople and the remaining possessions of the Sultan in Europe, and the need for restricting the expansion of Montenegro. On April 20 Salisbury put the question squarely to his Austrian

---

[1] *Die Grosse Politik*, II, No. 379; Buckle: *Letters of Queen Victoria*, II, p. 611.

colleague: Would Austria be ready to insist on the restriction of the new Bulgaria to the region north of the Balkan Mountains? Andrássy refused to treat any one question separately and submitted the Austrian program, much in the form of the demands made upon Ignatiev. The Austrian occupation of Bosnia was included in this program, and a long memorandum set forth the reasons why Austria regarded this step as indispensable. In regard to the southern frontier of Bulgaria Andrássy was still unwilling to commit himself, probably because he still hoped for a longitudinal rather than a latitudinal division. By this time the English were disgusted, and the negotiations lapsed.[1]

But the English statesmen had not staked all their money on one horse. In view of the vacillation of Austrian policy, they probably had little hope of success in that direction. At any rate, they had taken good care to keep the wire to St. Petersburg intact. On April 4 the English ambassador at Berlin was instructed to approach Bismarck and find out whether he would be willing to act as mediator in effecting the withdrawal of the Russian army and the English fleet from the vicinity of Constantinople.[2] In a famous speech made on February 19 the German chancellor had defined his position as that of the " honest broker " who really desired to bring the transactions to a successful close. In view of the acute danger of war he was only too ready to remove the most menacing factor, the possibility of a clash of arms at the Turkish capital. He therefore accepted the idea as his own and undertook to mediate. The English were anxious to have the fleet retire, for it was no longer of much use. The admiral on the spot had declared that he could not enter the Black Sea unless the Bosphorus could be kept open for wooden transports.[3] The Russians were no less eager to withdraw from their exposed position, for the Turks were assembling troops in and about the capital and were erecting earthworks. The negotiations continued throughout April, but here, too, the powers failed in their attempt to come to an agreement. It was understood that the Russians should withdraw to Adrianople and that the English fleet should return to Besika Bay, but owing to the difference in time between rail transportation and travel by sea, and because of the unwillingness of each party to retreat first, the negotiations came to nothing. The army and the fleet were not withdrawn until after the Congress of Berlin. It will be for ever a source of wonder that no " untoward event " took place. As Lord Charles Beresford put it: " If even a midshipman had lost his temper, he might have run the country into war." [4]

The negotiations for the withdrawal of the forces, even though they failed, afforded a convenient bridge to direct discussions between the English and Russian governments. These had been envisaged by the English cabinet for

---

[1] Lee MS.; *Die Grosse Politik*, II, No. 400; William A. Gauld: " The Anglo-Austrian Agreement of 1878 " (*English Historical Review*, XLI, pp. 108–12, January 1926).

[2] Lee MS.; *Letters of Queen Victoria*, II, pp. 612–13; Cecil, op. cit., II, p. 242.

[3] *Letters of Queen Victoria*, II, pp. 613–14; Newton: *Lord Lyons*, II, p. 134.

[4] Clowes, op. cit., p. 298. On the negotiation see especially *Die Grosse Politik*, II, Nos. 381 ff.; *Documents diplomatiques français*, II, Nos. 289 ff.

some time and had only been deferred pending the negotiations with Austria. Salisbury's idea was to follow a policy of " compensatory provisions." That is, a diminution of Russian preponderance in European Turkey in order to ensure a modicum of independence to the Turkish government was to be secured by England's abandonment of her uncompromising opposition to Russian conquests in Asia. But the Russian advance in Asia was to be counterbalanced by obtaining for England a concession of comparable importance from the Sultan.[1] The announcement on April 17 that seven thousand Indian troops had been ordered to Malta was intended in part to impress the continent with England's inexhaustible supply of men, and in part as the first step towards the eventual occupation of Cyprus. On the very next day Salisbury explained to the German ambassador the desirability of settling outstanding questions between the powers concerned before a congress was actually convened. As soon as it became evident that the negotiations with Austria would fail, the English minister took up the suggestion made by Shuvalov, that England and Russia should attempt to reach an understanding.

On May 8 the Russian ambassador left London to return to St. Petersburg and lay the English demands before his government. These demands were essentially the same as those set forth in the Salisbury circular. England objected to the San Stefano Treaty because it admitted a new naval power to the Ægean, because it threatened with extinction the non-Slav populations of the Balkans, and because it placed the Porte so much at Russia's mercy that it could no longer discharge with independence the political functions assigned to it. Bulgaria must be restricted in size, and the Asiatic annexations of Russia must be reconsidered. As for the Straits, England would prefer to have them opened completely.[2]

On his way to St. Petersburg Shuvalov stopped to consult Bismarck, to whom he communicated the English memorandum. The German chancellor was not a little surprised to learn of this development and apparently had some apprehension lest eventually Austria should find herself isolated. He still regarded the Three Emperors' League as more valuable for Germany than the possible alliance with England and urged upon Shuvalov the desirability of an agreement between Russia and Austria.[3]

In the Russian capital the ambassador found affairs in a chaotic condition. Gorchakov, an octogenarian, was in very poor health and hardly able to keep up with developments, though he refused to relinquish his control. The deciding influence was that of Ignatiev, the maker of the San Stefano Treaty. Taken by and large, however, military and governmental circles were distinctly in favour

---

[1] Cecil: *Salisbury,* II, p. 239.

[2] Lee MS. Memorandum of May 3, 1878.

[3] Hanotaux, op. cit., IV, p. 339, based upon the unpublished memoirs of Shuvalov. See also Bismarck's note to Bülow, May 7, 1878, printed in Manfred Müller: *Die Bedeutung des Berliner Kongresses für die deutsch-russischen Beziehungen* (Leipzig, 1927), p. 16, note.

of some peaceful arrangement. The condition of the troops was wretched, and the revolutionary movement was becoming more and more menacing. The Grand Duke Nicholas, the Grand Duke Michael (commander-in-chief in the Caucasus), the minister of war, and the minister of finance were all agreed that it would be impossible to continue the war, let alone to undertake a new conflict with England. The Tsar himself urged Shuvalov to make use of his influence with Bismarck to get the congress arranged for and to effect an agreement with England which would isolate Austria.[1]

When Shuvalov returned to London on May 23, he was the bearer of conciliatory proposals. Russia was prepared to have the Bulgarian frontier pushed back from the Ægean and delimited in the west in such a way as to exclude non-Bulgarians. Furthermore, Bulgaria should be divided into two parts, with the Balkan Mountains as the boundary. The northern part should enjoy political autonomy under a prince, the southern part administrative autonomy under a native prince chosen with the assent of Europe for a period of five to ten years. Russia desired the withdrawal of the Turkish army from the southern part, but was ready to leave to the decision of the congress the question of when and how the Turkish government might send in troops to defend the Balkan frontier. The other European powers should be permitted to join Russia in organizing the government of the Christian provinces remaining to the Porte. In Asia, Russia was ready to restore Bayazid to the Turks. By implication Russia insisted on the retention of Kars and Batum in Asia, as well as on the retention of the clauses of the Treaty of San Stefano dealing with Bessarabia and the acquisition of Antivari by Montenegro. Russia expressed also a decided preference for a longitudinal division of Bulgaria.[2]

Both the Queen and Disraeli were distrustful of the Russian proposals and objected to them, but Salisbury favoured them and was insistent. After some negotiation as to details, an agreement was reached on May 24, though it was not actually signed until May 30. The English demand for a division of Bulgaria by the Balkan Mountains was upheld, and the definition of the southern and western frontier was agreed to in a general way. England accepted the Russian view with respect to the acquisitions of Montenegro and Serbia, as well as the annexation by Russia of Bessarabia, Kars, and Batum. The problems of billeting Turkish troops in southern Bulgaria, of European participation in the organization of the two Bulgarias, of the Russian occupation of Bulgaria, of Russia's right of way through Roumania, and of the Straits regulations were left open for further discussion at the congress. England accepted the formula proposed by Bismarck for the invitations to the congress, which read: " In accepting the invitation the various governments agree to admit and participate in the free discussion of the entire content of the Treaty of San Stefano." This

---

[1] Hanotaux, op. cit., IV, p. 340; John F. Baddeley: *Russia in the " Eighties "* (London, 1921), pp. 368–70, based upon Shuvalov's own account.

[2] Lee MS.; *Letters of Queen Victoria*, II, pp. 621–2; *Die Grosse Politik*, II, No. 410.

satisfied the English demand for consideration of the treaty as a whole and met also the Russian objection to submitting the treaty to the congress for judgment. The invitations to the congress were issued on June 3 and were accepted by all the powers signatories of the Treaty of Paris in 1856.[1]

The English government had accepted the Russian advance in Asia Minor, in spite of the threat involved to the British position in India. The reason for this was simple, for during Shuvalov's absence Salisbury had made preparation for the erection of "another dyke behind the shattered Turkish breakwater." After various places, such as Mytilene, Lemnos, Alexandretta, Acre, Crete, Haifa, and Alexandria, had been considered, the government had finally decided on the acquisition of Cyprus, which Disraeli described to the Queen as "the key of western Asia." On May 10 the outlines of an agreement had been sent to Mr. Layard, the ambassador at Constantinople, with instructions to proceed with the negotiations as soon as word arrived from London. The cabinet approved of the projected convention on May 16, and as soon as it became clear that Russia would insist on the retention of Kars and Batum, Layard was instructed, on May 23, to submit the draft agreement to the Sultan, who was given forty-eight hours to take it or leave it. In view of the English threat to desist from further opposition to the Russian advance and from further efforts to postpone the partition of his empire, the Sultan made no objection, and the convention was signed in due form on June 4. It provided that if Russia retained Batum, Ardahan, or Kars, the British government would defend by force of arms the Sultan's Asiatic possessions against any fresh Russian attack. In order to execute this engagement England was to be allowed to occupy and administer the island of Cyprus, paying annually to the Sultan the excess of income over expenditure. The Sultan further agreed to introduce necessary reforms, to be decided on later by the two powers, for the protection of his Christian and other subjects in these Asiatic territories.[2]

The series of agreements concluded by England was completed on June 6 by the signature of the convention with Austria. This had come about with remarkable rapidity, considering how long it had been in the air and what efforts had been made by the English to effect it. On May 8 the Russians submitted at Vienna their reply to the demands made upon Ignatiev. Russia was willing to divide Bulgaria into a western and an eastern part, with boundaries roughly like those laid down by the Constantinople Conference. The powers were to be allowed to participate in the organization of these two Bulgarias, which were to be autonomous, but tributary. Austria was to be allowed to occupy Bosnia and Herzegovina and was to be free to make such economic ar-

---

[1] Lee MS.; Cecil, op. cit., II, p. 258; *Die Grosse Politik*, II, Nos. 419, 426, 427; Monypenny and Buckle, op. cit., VI, p. 294; Goriainov, op. cit., pp. 373 ff.

[2] Cecil, op. cit., II, p. 263–71; Monypenny and Buckle, op. cit., VI, pp. 291, 293, 295–8. The instructions to Layard have recently been published by Sir James Headlam-Morley: *Studies in Diplomatic History* (New York, 1930), pp. 199–200, and pp. 207 ff. (Salisbury's exposition of motives).

rangements with Serbia and western Bulgaria as were necessary to guarantee communications from Salonika to Mitrovitza, and an eventual railroad junction through Serbia. But Montenegro was to retain the area assigned to her by the Treaty of San Stefano, and the territory lying between Serbia and Montenegro (the Sanjak of Novi-Bazar) was to be divided between them. In return for these concessions Austria was to promise to support Russia at the congress and remain neutral if the war were reopened or extended.[1]

The object of the Russians in offering these concessions was to separate England and Austria. It was the same aim they were pursuing by their negotiations with England. Andrássy, however, regarded these terms as even worse than those offered earlier. The junction of Serbia and Montenegro was particularly ominous and appeared like a plan to exclude Austria entirely from access to the Balkans. Andrássy's position was far from enviable, for he had learned from Bismarck of the English negotiations with Shuvalov and had every reason to fear that Austria would be left out of account. He therefore expressed great eagerness to reach an agreement with England, along the lines marked out by Salisbury in the previous negotiations. Austria would support the English stand in respect to the restriction of Bulgaria if England would support Austria in the question of Bosnia and Herzegovina and the problem of Montenegro.

Salisbury, however, now held the whip hand and decided to await the return of Shuvalov. Andrássy's sudden realization " of the imprudence and wickedness of separate negotiations " with Russia only amused him. The Austrian minister went so far as to enlist Bismarck's influence, in order that Austrian interests might not be overlooked in the negotiations between Salisbury and Shuvalov. As a matter of fact, the Queen was anxious lest England and Austria should become separated, and Salisbury, in his discussions with Shuvalov, was "very careful to keep as much as possible on the same ground as the Austrians." As soon as the convention with Russia had been arrived at, instructions were sent to the ambassador at Vienna to proceed with the negotiations. The draft agreement provided that the two powers should urge at the congress that the autonomous Bulgaria should not extend south of the Balkan Mountains. The rest of the territory assigned to Bulgaria by the Treaty of San Stefano should be subject to provisions securing to the Sultan adequate political and military supremacy to guard against invasions or insurrections. The two powers would also urge that the Russian occupation south of the Danube should be limited to six months, and passage through Roumania to nine months, the occupying force to be restricted to twenty thousand men. The powers were to take part in the organization of the Sultan's remaining European provinces. England would support any proposal with respect to Bosnia which Austria might make at the congress. After some discussion of details the agreement was finally signed on June 6. In part because of domestic difficulties, in part because of his desire to play off one side against the other and commit himself to neither, Andrássy

---

[1] *Die Grosse Politik*, II, No. 404; Wertheimer: *Andrássy*, III, p. 98.

had come to play a rather sorry role. The leadership in the action against Russia had long since passed to the English.[1]

The congress, which convened at Berlin on June 13, was one of the most brilliant political assemblies of modern times, not unworthy of comparison with the congresses of Vienna and Paris. Most of the leading statesmen of Europe were present, though for a time it seemed as though Disraeli and Gorchakov would be prevented from attending on account of bad health. Bismarck, too, had been suffering from illness for a long time, but he came to Berlin full of determination and energy. According to custom, he was elected president of the congress, and throughout the course of the transactions he left no doubt as to who was the dominating figure and influence. It is said that he appropriated the phrase attributed to Louis XIV and declared: " Le congrès, c'est moi." [2] At any rate, the members of the congress were agreed that without him the meeting might well have ended in failure. During the various sessions he was rigorous in his insistence that irrelevant discussion be dispensed with and that an agreement on disputed points be reached with the greatest dispatch. Outside the formal sessions he was intensely active in furthering the negotiations between the parties concerned, and in pressing on for a compromise when the situation became critical. His complete impartiality cannot be better illustrated than by the fact that he was afterwards accused by each side of having favoured its opponent. The chancellor was assisted by von Bülow, the German secretary for foreign affairs, a charming and sympathetic figure, and by Prince Hohenlohe, the ambassador to Paris, one of the most attractive personalities in European diplomatic circles.

The English plenipotentiaries were Disraeli, Salisbury, and Lord Odo Russell, the ambassador to Berlin. Of these men little need be said beyond a few words regarding the part they played at Berlin. Disraeli was very deficient in his knowledge of French and had to be induced by his colleagues to speak English. It was feared that he would expose his country to ridicule if he attempted to use French, so he was told that the congress would be greatly disappointed not to hear so great a master of oratory speak in his native tongue. This language difficulty no doubt acted as a considerable obstacle to Disraeli, but he played a leading role nevertheless. Bismarck, who appears to have been less favourably impressed with Salisbury than he had been in 1876, found Disraeli interesting and attractive. The two had many long discussions, which both seem to have enjoyed. The English minister listened in astonishment to his colleague's " Rabelaisian monologues," and to his " endless revelations of things he ought not to mention." The chancellor, in turn, found his earlier distrust of Disraeli rapidly changing to admiration for the English statesman's brilliance and energy. " The

---

[1] Lee MS.; *Die Grosse Politik*, II, Nos. 410, 412, 417; Cecil, op. cit., II, pp. 256 ff.; *Letters of Queen Victoria*, II, pp. 620–3; Wertheimer: *Andrássy*, III, pp. 98–100; *Documents diplomatiques français*, II, Nos. 297, 304, 305; Gauld, in *English Historical Review*, XLI, pp. 108–12, January 1926.
[2] H. S. Edwards: *Sir William White* (London, 1902), p. 154.

old Jew, he is the man," he is reported to have said; and after the congress he regularly kept a picture of Disraeli on his dresser. Salisbury's role at the congress was by no means so spectacular, though in reality he did most of the work on the English side and was largely responsible for the settlement.

Prince Gorchakov had been unable to resist the temptation to appear in so distinguished a company, though his attendance proved to be a drawback rather than an advantage. "There is no doubt the presence of Gorchakov materially complicates matters and that if some kindly fit of gout would take him off we should move much faster," wrote Salisbury on the second day of the congress.[1] The trouble was that Bismarck was filled with enmity against the old man, whom he had never forgiven for his part in the action of 1875. The more influential the position of the German chancellor became, the more he was filled with rancour. The historical sources for the events of these years literally bristle with references to Bismarck's resentment and to his determination to take revenge. An added difficulty arose from the fact that Gorchakov had been ill for months and that he had taken relatively little part in the negotiations since the beginning of the war with Turkey. The Treaty of San Stefano had been concluded by Ignatiev, more or less over the head of the chancellor, just as the agreement with England had been primarily the work of Shuvalov. Under the circumstances Gorchakov was anxious to avoid shouldering the responsibility for a disastrous settlement. Disraeli describes him as a "dear old fox, who seems melting with the milk of human kindness."[2] Of his suavity and charm there can be no question, but this made no impression upon Bismarck, who was "brutally frank" by contrast. Neither did Gorchakov's interference in the course of the negotiation, and his opposition to the policy of Shuvalov, help the Russian cause. Shuvalov, the second plenipotentiary, was in reality the leader of the Russian delegation, for the third plenipotentiary, Count Oubril, Russian ambassador to Berlin, was a mediocre diplomat and a person whom Bismarck distrusted. On the other hand, Shuvalov was a favourite with both the English and the Germans, who admired not only his ability, but his great good sense, his desire for peace, and his readiness for reasonable compromise.

Of all the delegates at the congress Count Andrássy was undoubtedly the most picturesque. His exotic, gypsy-like appearance and the brilliance of his uniforms made him the point of attraction in every assembly. With Bismarck he was a great favourite, partly, no doubt, because of his pronounced pro-German policy. But Andrássy did not play a very prominent part at the congress. His aim was primarily to secure Bosnia and Herzegovina for his country, and the question was full of difficulties, both domestic and international. There was much opposition both in Austria and Hungary to the policy of including more Slavs in the empire, and consequently the foreign minister had not been able to follow Bismarck's advice and occupy the territory before the congress

---

[1] Cecil, op. cit., II, p. 281.   [2] Monypenny and Buckle, op. cit., VI, p. 328.

met. In fact, he was obliged to try to get from the powers an invitation to occupy the provinces. "I have heard of people refusing to eat their pigeon unless it was shot and roasted for them," said Bismarck; "but I have never heard of any one refusing to eat it unless his jaws were forced open and it was pushed down his throat." [1] This uncomfortable situation had no doubt influenced Andrássy's policy during the spring of 1878. At any rate, he had been left behind by the English and the Russians and saw no other mode of procedure than to sail the Austrian ship in the wake of the British man-of-war. From the very start he offered his support to the English delegates, and throughout the congress he stood by them loyally. His was a sensible, though hardly an inspiring, part. His colleague, Count Károlyi, the popular Austrian ambassador at Berlin, provided the social activity, while Baron Haymerlé, a professional diplomat, supplied the expert advice.

France was represented by her foreign minister, M. Waddington, and her ambassador to Berlin, Count Saint-Vallier, both men of attractive personality and moderate, sound views. Waddington was distinctly a representative of the French upper middle classes and impressed the aristocrats as a pronounced bourgeois, but Saint-Vallier was a member of the nobility and maintained the French tradition in diplomacy. Both men were popular at the congress and enjoyed Bismarck's friendship. Though France had pursued a policy of neutrality throughout the Eastern crisis and was determined to stick by this policy at the congress, there was ample opportunity to work as mediator, and the French plenipotentiaries ably seconded Bismarck's efforts to effect a peaceful solution.

The first Italian plenipotentiary was Count Corti, the foreign minister. The second was Count de Launay, the ambassador at Berlin. Corti was an experienced diplomat with a wide experience in Eastern affairs. Though not at all attractive to behold, he was a man distinguished by his saneness and balance. He represented the foreign policy of Cavour and his successors rather than that of the more radical and nationalistic Left, which had come into power in March 1876. Corti was determined to come away from the congress with clean hands, and he worked at all times in a conciliatory way, eager to avoid complications for his country and for Europe.

The Turks were rather unfortunate in their choice of delegates. They did not want to burden a pure Turk with the responsibility for a disastrous settlement, and consequently sent Caratheodory Pasha, a typical phanariot Greek, as chief of the delegation. Caratheodory was an able and sensible person, but the Turkish position was a very unpopular one at the congress, and his role was therefore a rather pathetic one. Bismarck lost no opportunity to snub the Turkish representatives in the most ruthless fashion and to make clear to them that the con-

---

[1] Cecil, op. cit., II, p. 281. The same story is told in the correspondence of the Italian delegate, Count Corti (see E. Conte Corti alle Catene: "*Bismarck und Italien am Berliner Kongress 1878*," in *Historische Vierteljahrschrift*, XXIII, pp. 456–71, May 1, 1927).

gress had been convened, not to save territory for the Turks, but to preserve the peace between the powers. The Turks should be grateful for every modification of the Treaty of San Stefano and should not make trouble by asking more. It may be that the chancellor's attitude was in part due to the third Turkish delegate, Mehemet Ali Pasha, who had commanded one of the armies during the war. Mehemet appears to have been of Huguenot ancestry, but was born in Germany. He had escaped from a ship at Constantinople while still a boy, had adopted Mohammedanism, and had been brought up by Ali Pasha, one of the ablest grand viziers of the mid-century. The idea of a German posing as a Turk and representing the Turkish cause was too much for Bismarck, who treated the general with the greatest disdain. The second Turkish delegate was Sadullah Bey, ambassador at Berlin.

It has often been said that the Congress of Berlin was at bottom a farce, because all the decisions had been made beforehand and the delegates merely signed their names to earlier agreements. Bismarck would have been only too glad if this had been true. He was anxious to get the thing over with and had hopes at first that all could be settled in a week or ten days. As a matter of fact, it turned out that the questions that had been left to the decision of the congress were numerous and difficult. The agreements made beforehand were all of a vague nature, and all of the powers chiefly concerned were determined to get what they could out of the congress. On more than one occasion there was danger that the meeting would break up, and Bismarck's greatest skill was required to bring about a compromise. His procedure was invariably to submit questions to the congress and after a brief discussion refer them to the interested powers for private negotiation. Little is to be learned from the official protocols, excepting the final decisions, but fortunately there is a wealth of material in the way of correspondence and memoirs, so that the history of the gathering can be written with some assurance.

To review in detail the course of the negotiations is hardly necessary for the purpose of this book. The success or failure of the meeting at all times hinged upon a few crucial questions, of which the Bulgarian problem was the most difficult. According to Disraeli, it was the real point for which the congress was assembled, and upon its treatment depended whether there should be a Turkey in Europe or not.[1] For that very reason Bismarck had put it first on the agenda. Disraeli at the opening meeting demanded the withdrawal of the Russian troops from the vicinity of Constantinople, on the plea that they were a menace to the general peace and a danger to the success of the congress. Bismarck suggested that the matter be left for direct negotiation between the English and the Russians, but in the interval between the first and second sessions he exerted himself to persuade the Turks to surrender the fortresses of Shumla and Varna, or at least the latter, to the Russians, such surrender having been made a

---

[1] Monypenny and Buckle, op. cit., VI, p. 321.

condition for the Russian withdrawal. The Turks, however, refused, and no decision was come to until weeks later. But the question was not brought before the congress again.[1]

The discussion of the problems of Bulgaria, properly speaking, began at the second session, on June 17. The Anglo-Russian Agreement had laid down only the general lines of the settlement, and there still remained such questions as those of the actual frontier between the two Bulgarias, the right of the Sultan to fortify the frontier and occupy the southern province, the name of the southern part, the length of the Russian occupation, etc. The problems were knotty enough in themselves, but their solution was greatly endangered by the publication of the Anglo-Russian Agreement in the London *Globe* on June 14. This revelation was due to a subordinate clerk in the English foreign office, named Marvin, but it never could be shown whether he had been bought by the Russians or whether his action was due to purely financial considerations. At any rate, the publication of the agreement made a profound impression in England. For the government it was only one side of a settlement, the Cyprus Convention being the other. But the Cyprus Convention was still a deep secret, and there was a loud outcry in England against the concessions which had been made to Russia. The result was that Disraeli, who had never been favourable to the settlement with Russia, became more and more stiff in his attitude, while Gorchakov, on his side, began to speak of Shuvalov as a traitor and to make it clear that he would not be associated with the concessions made to the English.

The wide divergence of views and the unwillingness of both sides to yield came out clearly in the second session, and Bismarck therefore deferred discussion. The question was not actually settled until the sixth session, on June 26. In the interval the congress went through its greatest crisis and came near breaking up. After the first private discussions between the English and the Russians, to which the Austrians were admitted by their own request, the situation looked very black. "The Russians are wriggling a good deal on the subject of the military occupation of the southern province," wrote Salisbury, "and some time may be required in order to persuade them to be skinned quietly." At the same time Disraeli told Count Corti, evidently in the hope that he would report to Bismarck, that he took "the gloomiest view of affairs," and that if the Russians refused to accept the English proposals, he would wreck the congress.[2] The Russians had accepted the line of the Balkan Mountains as the frontier between the two Bulgarias and had agreed to the name "East Roumelia" for the southern part. They would have preferred "South Bulgaria," but this emphasis on the Bulgarian nature of the country did not appeal to the English. Shuvalov had once, in disgust, suggested calling the two parts "satisfied Bulgaria," and

---

[1] Hajo Holborn: *Aufzeichnungen und Erinnerungen aus dem Leben des Botschafters Joseph Maria von Radowitz* (Stuttgart, 1925), II, pp. 40 ff.; Carathéodory Pacha: *Le Rapport secret sur le Congrès de Berlin* (Paris, 1919), pp. 85 ff.; *Documents diplomatiques français*, II, No. 317.

[2] Cecil, op. cit., II, p. 283; Monypenny and Buckle, op. cit., VI, p. 323.

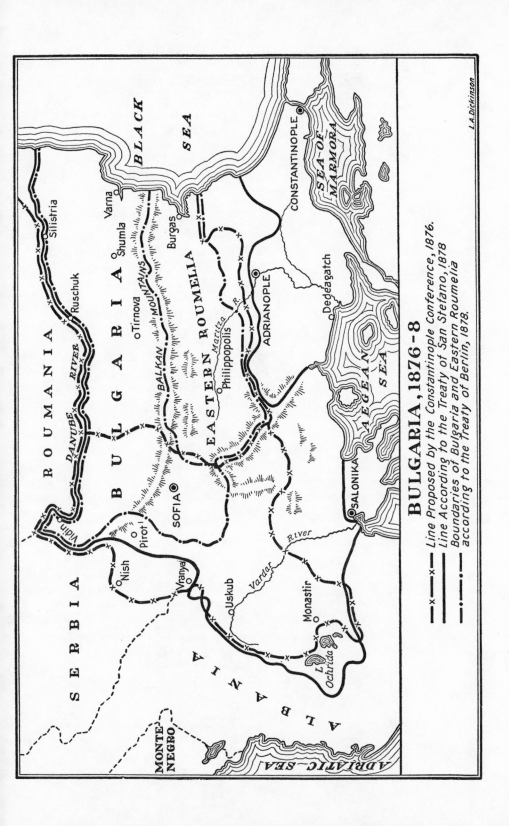

I.A.Dickinson

BULGARIA, 1876-8

×—×—× Line Proposed by the Constantinople Conference, 1876.
————— Line According to the Treaty of San Stefano, 1878
·—·—· Boundaries of Bulgaria and Eastern Roumelia
————— according to the Treaty of Berlin, 1878.

"discontented Bulgaria," but he yielded to the English on this point. The real difficulties arose from the attempt to define the "line of the Balkans" and from the English demand that the Sultan should have political and military control in the southern province (East Roumelia). According to the English view, the line of the Balkans would leave Varna outside the new Bulgaria, as part of East Roumelia. In the west, where the Balkan Mountains fork, the northern fork was to be the boundary of the new Bulgaria, leaving the Sanjak of Sofia to East Roumelia.

Shuvalov flatly refused to accept so serious a restriction of the new state or to entertain the idea of Turkish political and military control in East Roumelia. He therefore referred back to St. Petersburg for instructions in the matter. By June 21 the prospect was very dark. Disraeli, it is said, gave orders to have a special train in readiness for his departure from the congress. On learning of this danger Bismarck, who had little use for such theatrical methods, decided to intervene. He called on Disraeli to find out if the English demands had the character of an ultimatum. The English prime minister was firm, but apparently agreed to yield on some points. The demand for Varna and the Sanjak of Sofia for East Roumelia was dropped, and in return the Russians agreed to the exercise of political and military control by the Sultan in East Roumelia and to some curtailment of this province in the west. There were still extended discussions on special points, especially with reference to the presence of Turkish troops in East Roumelia. With French mediation it was finally decided that the Sultan might garrison troops on the frontier between East Roumelia and Bulgaria, but not billet them on the population. Public order was to be secured by the use of militia, account being taken of the religion of the inhabitants in each locality. The governor-general might call in troops if the internal or external security of the province were menaced, but in that case the Porte should be obliged to notify the representatives of the powers not only of the step taken, but of the reasons for it. The Russian occupation of Bulgaria was to be limited to nine months. The consuls of the powers were to be associated with the Russian commission in the organization of Bulgaria, while in East Roumelia the organization was to be carried out by a European rather than by a Russian commission.[1]

The next question of major importance to come before the congress was the disposition of Bosnia and Herzegovina, which was taken up in the session of June 28. Great efforts had been made by the Austrians to come to a separate agreement with the Porte, but these had ended in failure. In the earlier days of the congress Andrássy had made a deal with the English, elaborating the agreement of June 6. The Austrian chancellor promised his support in the Bulgarian

---

[1] Monypenny and Buckle, op. cit., VI, pp. 321 ff.; Cecil, op. cit., II, pp. 283 ff.; Carathéodory Pacha, op. cit., pp. 85 ff.; Radowitz, op. cit., II, pp. 42 ff.; Hohenlohe: *Denkwürdigkeiten*, II, pp. 236 ff.; *Documents diplomatiques français*, II, Nos. 319 ff.; Busch, in *Deutsche Rundschau*, XXXVI, pp. 361–80, December 1909; A. N. Cummings: "The Secret History of the Treaty of Berlin" (*Nineteenth Century*, LVIII, pp. 83–90, July 1905).

question, in return for which the English were to propose the occupation of Bosnia and Herzegovina by Austria. From the English view-point it was highly desirable that this step should be taken with the approval of the Turks, but all last-minute efforts made to secure the assent of the Porte had failed. When Salisbury made the proposal that Austria occupy the two provinces, Bismarck seconded the suggestion, and the other powers raised no objection. It was not until later, and outside the congress, that the Turks came to an agreement with the Vienna government on this matter.

It seems rather peculiar that the Austrians should have asked for occupation rather than for annexation. In the discussions of the spring of 1878 reference was made at times to occupation, at times to annexation, and it was not quite clear just what Andrássy wanted. The limitation of the demand to occupation was undoubtedly due to opposition in the monarchy itself and to the desire to placate the Turks, but consideration for the Italians played perhaps an even greater role. The party of the Left, which had come into power in Italy in 1876, was more radical and nationalistic than the Right, which had followed the tradition of Cavour. Almost immediately the agitation for unredeemed Italy (*Italia Irredenta*) had begun to spread throughout the peninsula, the government doing little or nothing to discourage it. What was meant by *Italia Irredenta* were the provinces of Trentino and Trieste, which were still under Austrian rule. Relations between the Austrian and Italian governments had soon become tinged with distrust and suspicion, and the Austrian government had been forced, throughout the Eastern crisis, to make allowance for the possible hostility of Italy. Andrássy had tried to divert the attention of his neighbours to other fields, and soon after the Reichstadt meeting, on August 9, 1876, he had suggested to the Italian ambassador that Italy might find compensation in Tunis for the eventual annexation of Bosnia and Herzegovina by Austria. The Italians, however, had no mind for such exploits, which would bring down upon them the wrath of the French. In September and October of 1877 Francesco Crispi, president of the Italian chamber, and one of the leaders of the Left, had made a tour of the European capitals in an effort to win support for the Italian aspirations. But he met with no encouragement. Bismarck was willing to negotiate with Italy an alliance against France, but he would not hear of opposition to Austria. His advice was that Italy should take Albania if Austria annexed Bosnia and Herzegovina.

Count Corti, the Italian foreign minister and first plenipotentiary to the congress, had accepted office only with the greatest reluctance. The prime minister, Benedetto Cairoli, was a passionate patriot, several of whose brothers had lost their lives in the wars against Austria. Corti made it perfectly clear that he would not be associated with an irredentist policy and went to Berlin only on condition that Italy should pursue a policy of neutrality and should avoid putting herself in opposition to the rest of Europe. There was nothing final about the Austrian occupation of the provinces; in fact, the sovereignty of Turkey was explicitly recognized. So Corti voted in favour of the proposal, though only with reluctance. It was certainly the only sensible thing to do, though the policy was so unpopular in Italy that the foreign minister resigned soon after the congress was over.[1]

The Asiatic problem had supposedly been settled in the Anglo-Russian Agreement, the understanding being that Russia, while returning Bayazid and the Alashkerd Valley to Turkey, should retain Kars and Batum, in exchange for concessions in the Bulgarian question. It was apparently this part of the agreement of which Disraeli had never entirely approved. At any rate he seized upon the phraseology (Russia was to "occupy" Batum) to extract further advantages if possible. The agitation in England following the publication of the agreement with Russia only strengthened him in his determination, and he is reported to have said that he was going to Berlin in order to prevent Salisbury from making too extensive concessions. He would never agree to the abandonment of Kars and Batum to Russia.[2]

Salisbury himself seems to have come to the conclusion that Batum should not be abandoned so easily. It was the only good port on the east side of the Black Sea, though its value was greatly exaggerated, in Salisbury's opinion. Nevertheless, public sentiment on the subject might be put to good use. The Cyprus Convention was deficient in so far as it did not enable England to use her naval force in the Black Sea against Russia. Therefore Salisbury decided to threaten the Russians with a change in the Straits regulations if she did not give up Batum. He even went so far as to propose to the Porte an agreement under the terms of which the Sultan should not offer forcible opposition to the passage of the English fleet through the Straits if, Russia having acquired Batum, the English government should consider the presence of a naval force in the Black Sea expedient to protect the Turkish territories. The Porte rejected this proposal, and the British cabinet was rather dubious about it, but the foreign minister decided to make some modification of the Straits settlement in any case. In view of the ambiguity of the stipulations of 1841 and 1856, the English government, while accepting their renewal, was to declare that in so doing it was entering into an agreement with the Sultan alone and that it reserved to itself the right of assisting him with the fleet whenever it considered his independence threatened.[3]

---

[1] *Memoirs of Francesco Crispi* (London, 1912), II, pp. 10–86, and the devastating criticism of his account by Gaetano Salvemini: "*Alla Vigilia del Congresso di Berlino*" (*Nuova Rivista Storica,* IX, pp. 72–92, 1925), based upon unpublished documents. See further the two articles based upon the Corti papers, by Count Egon C. Corti: "*Il Conte Corti al Congresso di Berlino*" (*Nuova Antologia,* CCXL, pp. 361 ff., April 16, 1925), and "*Bismarck und Italien am Berliner Kongress 1878*" (*Historische Vierteljahrschrift,* XXIII, pp. 456–71, May 1, 1927); Michele Rosi: *I Cairoli* (Bologna, 1929), Volume I, chapter xiv.

[2] Report of the German ambassador, June 19, quoted from the German archives by Müller, op. cit., p. 35, note.

[3] Lee MS.; Cecil, op. cit., II, pp. 289 ff.

In the actual negotiations with Shuvalov Salisbury hinted that England would demand the opening of the Straits if the Russians insisted on retaining Batum. If Russia would consent to the establishment of a separate khanate to include Batum, England would accept the *status quo* in regard to the Straits. At this point the negotiations became confused through Gorchakov's insistence on treating the question with Disraeli. The latter is said to have offered to content himself with the establishment of Batum as a free port. It appears that Bismarck had some share in bringing about this result, and that he brought pressure to bear upon Disraeli by threatening to close the congress unless the English yielded. However this may have been, the Tsar agreed to make Batum a free port, and therewith the question was solved without reference to the discussions between Salisbury and Shuvalov. The English foreign minister tried to insert something about Batum being " disarmed " and " exclusively commercial," but Gorchakov persuaded Disraeli that *"essentiellement commercial"* was the same thing as *"exclusivement commercial."* Further irritation was caused by obscurity in the agreement between Gorchakov and Disraeli regarding the frontier. The English understood that the Lazi, a Mohammedan tribe that protested against annexation to Russia, should be left with Turkey. But in the session of July 9 it turned out that the English had the Russian secret map, and the Russians the English map, so the dispute started anew. In the end a line half-way between the extremes was agreed to.[1]

Lord Salisbury had decided to make a declaration in regard to the Straits, irrespective of the fate of Batum. He therefore rose, during the session of July 11, and announced that, since the Treaty of Berlin involved changes in an important part of the Treaty of Paris and since the stipulations regarding the Straits in the Treaty of London might become subject to difference of opinion, " the obligations of His Britannic Majesty in respect to the closure of the Straits are limited to an engagement to the Sultan to respect in this regard the independent determinations of His Majesty in conformance with the spirit of existing treaties."

In effect this meant that the Sultan might call up the British fleet whenever he saw fit, or give permission for the passage of English ships whenever he chose. If other powers made similar declarations, the whole régime of closure would be at an end. In order to prevent such a development, which might easily have resulted in the opening of the Straits, Shuvalov on the following day declared to the congress that in the opinion of the Russian delegates " the principle of the closure of the Straits is a European principle, and that the stipulations laid down in this matter in 1841, 1856, and 1871, now confirmed by the Treaty of Berlin, are obligatory upon all the powers, in conformance to the letter of the existing treaties, not merely towards the Sultan, but also towards

---

[1] Cecil, op. cit., II, pp. 286 ff.; Monypenny and Buckle, op. cit., VI, pp. 337 ff.; Hanotaux, op. cit., IV, pp. 353 ff.; Wellesley: *With the Russians in Peace and War*, pp. 294 ff; Baddeley: *Russia in the " Eighties,"* pp. 370–2. The last three references are based on Shuvalov's accounts.

all the powers signatories of these transactions." This meant the insistence by Russia upon the international, multilateral character of the Straits settlement, as against the attempt of the English to make the Straits agreements appear as bilateral obligations. Neither side of the question was argued, so that the whole matter, one of the most important problems of European international relations, was left vague and undecided.[1]

The leading affairs of the congress had been settled when the Batum question was disposed of, but one of the most dramatic episodes was yet to take place before the delegates departed. It will be remembered that for the English statesmen the concessions made to Russia were inextricably bound up with the Cyprus Convention, which was to compensate them for any loss of English power resulting from the Russian advance in Armenia. The Cyprus Convention was entirely dependent upon Russia's retention of Kars, Ardahan, or Batum and consequently had to be kept secret until final disposition of the Asiatic questions had been made. After the revelation of the Anglo-Russian Agreement in the *Globe* there was great danger that the secret would leak out. As a matter of fact, it did leak out at Constantinople. Andrássy seems to have had news of it as early as June 9, and by June 23 it was known unofficially to most members of the congress.[2] Neither the Russians nor the Germans could have been surprised by it, for Salisbury had hinted quite broadly, even before the meeting of the congress, that England might have to take " precautions " in the event of a Russian advance in Asia. But the question was a serious one and was greatly complicated by the refusal of the Turks to issue a firman, or order, permitting the English to occupy the island immediately. It was only after threats by Lord Salisbury that the island would be occupied without a firman that the Sultan finally yielded, on July 6.[3] It was high time, for the Batum question was just being settled, and the members of the congress were about to disperse. All that remained to be done was to break the news to the powers, of whom, in this instance, France was the most important. Broad hints of the English plans had been dropped to the French as far back as April 5, and the French government had expressed its disapproval of any such step — in fact, of the whole system of compensations. Waddington had agreed to come to the congress only on condition that the questions of Egypt, Syria, and the Holy Places should not be discussed, and that the meeting should confine itself to problems arising from the treaty of peace between Russia and Turkey. Having great interests in the Mediterranean, France was unlikely to accept the English step without protest. The question had exercised the English statesmen even

---

[1] Goriainov, op. cit., p. 381; Grigore Dendrino: *Bosporus und Dardanellen* (Berlin, 1915), chapter v; Nicolas Dascovici: *La Question du Bosphore et des Dardanelles* (Geneva, 1915), chapter iii, section v; Sir James Headlam-Morley: *Studies in Diplomatic History* (New York, 1930), pp. 235–7.

[2] Lee MS.; Müller, op. cit., p. 15, note.

[3] The negotiations are reviewed in detail by Lee, MS.

before the signature of the Cyprus Convention. Lord Lyons, the ambassador at Paris, was certain that the French would take a stiff attitude, though Salisbury hoped they " would confine themselves to epigram." [1]

Bismarck, who had for a long time been urging a settlement of the Eastern question on a basis of compensation at the expense of Turkey, apparently suggested to the English the possibility of squaring the French by leaving them a free hand in Tunis. There is some evidence that this mode of procedure was decided on by the chancellor and the English delegates during the early days of the congress. At any rate Salisbury hurried to see M. Waddington on the evening of July 6, just as soon as the necessary arrangements had been made at Constantinople. The French foreign minister appeared to be very much upset, but was soon calmed when Salisbury indicated to him that England would not raise obstacles in the way of a French occupation of Tunis. "You cannot leave Carthage in the hands of the barbarians," he is reputed to have said. Bismarck, too, said to the French minister: " Why do you not go to Carthage? " and Waddington was evidently prepared to take the English and the Germans at their word. But in Paris the suspicion was too great, and nothing was done for the time being.[2]

Tunis was the bait that had been dangled before the Italians time and time again, both by the Austrians and the Russians in their efforts to enlist the government at Rome either for or against the Austrian acquisition of Bosnia and Herzegovina. But the Italians had rejected these offers for fear of complications with France, and nothing had been said since April 1878, when England began to work out the Cyprus project. Count Corti was left to learn of the Cyprus Convention on the morning of July 8, when the agreement was announced in the newspapers. It is true that Bülow, the second German plenipotentiary, replied to Corti's complaints by saying that Italy might take Tunis, though there is no satisfactory evidence that Bismarck did likewise. It may be that Bülow's statement was due to ignorance on his part of the understanding between Bismarck and Salisbury. As for the English foreign minister, his only reply to the remonstrances of his Italian colleague was that the Mediterranean was large enough for all. There is some evidence that he had discussed with Waddington the possibility of quieting Italy by assigning Tripoli to her, but it is not clear that Tripoli was actually mentioned by Salisbury in his conversations with Count Corti. However that may be, Waddington returned to Paris contented to have Tunis in his pocket, while Corti returned to Rome with hands that were not only clean, but empty.[3]

---

[1] Newton: Lord Lyons, II, pp. 141, 144–5; Documents diplomatiques français, II, Nos. 283, 285, 304.

[2] Full details in W. L. Langer: " The European Powers and the French Occupation of Tunis, 1878–1881 " (American Historical Review, XXXI, pp 55–78, October 1925); Documents diplomatiques français, II, Nos. 325 ff.

[3] For details, see Langer, op. cit.; Rosi: I Cairoli, I, pp. 298–9; II, pp. 273 ff.; Documents diplomatiques français, II, No. 330.

Of the minor questions dealt with by the congress little need be said. The independence of Roumania, Serbia, and Montenegro was agreed to, and the acquisition of Bessarabia by Russia was also accepted. In return, Roumania was given the district known as the Dobruja, south of the Danube delta. Serbia was given an extension of territory to the south-east, and the congress decided that Montenegro should have the seaport town of Antivari on the Adriatic. The problem of Greece, however, caused considerable difficulty, for the Greeks, who had threatened to go to war with the Turks in the spring of 1878, had been kept quiet by general promises on the part of England that something would be done to realize the Greek aspirations. England had, in fact, done all that was possible to induce the Turks to make concessions, even before the meeting of the congress, but the Porte had been adamant in its refusal. At the congress the Greek desires were regarded with sympathy not only by England and Austria, who aimed at playing off the Greek influence against the Slav in the Balkan Peninsula, but also by France and Italy. On June 29 the Greek delegates were admitted to the congress to present their case in regard to the provinces of Epirus and Thessaly. But the English were unable to go too far in favour of Greece without losing their influence at Constantinople, and consequently the congress went no further than to invite the Turkish government to come to an agreement with Greece in regard to the rectification of the frontiers. The powers were prepared to offer their mediation to effect this result. It was a vague and unsatisfactory settlement, which was to cause much trouble later. The root of the difficulty lay in the fact that the powers had so many other interests to further that the Greek question could not be given full consideration.[1]

The congress came to a close on July 13, and the delegates returned home, some satisfied, others profoundly disappointed. Disraeli and Salisbury had greater reason for self-congratulation than any of the others, and the prime minister was justified in announcing with pride that he had brought his country peace with honour. The crisis had, in fact, ended with an unqualified success for the English. The powerful continental combination known as the Three Emperors' League, which always threatened to leave England isolated and to throw her back on the support of a weakened France or a struggling Italy, had been rent asunder by the rivalry of two of its members. Austria, indeed, had been forced to take issue openly with Russia, and in the last count had been obliged to seek salvation through British support. To be sure, the victory had long been in doubt. The English policy in the time of Derby's administration of the foreign office had been anything but impressive. His weakness and passive resistance almost drove his colleagues to distraction. Contending with him was like fighting a feather-bed, to use one of Salisbury's figures. Only after his going could the English policy pass from the negative to the positive stage; only then could it be definitely formulated and consistently carried through.

---

[1] Lascaris, op. cit., part ii; *Documents diplomatiques français*, II, Nos. 323 ff.

The association of Disraeli and Salisbury proved to be one of the most fortunate in the history of British diplomacy, for the one supplied the vision and energy, while the other conducted the actual negotiations with the greatest good sense and the finest appreciation of the value of compromise. Russia could hardly have been more effectively checked even by war. The Turkish Empire in Europe had been preserved as a viable factor in the international situation, while the huge Bulgaria of San Stefano had been pushed back over the Balkans. What gains Russia had made in Asia Minor had been counterbalanced by the revived alliance of England with Turkey and by the establishment of British control, first in the Suez Canal, and then in the island of Cyprus. The British route to the East was more effectively secured than could have been expected, and the British position in the Mediterranean was stronger than it had ever been since the time of Napoleon III and the construction of the canal at Suez. In the broader sense England had once more appeared as a decisive force in continental affairs and had made clear to the powers that she still valued her European position in spite of her larger world interests.

The victory of England spelled the defeat of Russia, and Russia had never since the time of Catherine the Great suffered so terrible a diplomatic set-back. It must be admitted, however, that the fault lay largely with the Russians themselves. At the outset they placed too much confidence in the Three Emperors' League. They deluded themselves with the idea that Austria could be outplayed and that Germany would support the Russians to the detriment of the Austrians. England they treated from the start as a negligible quantity. The lesson of the Berlin Memorandum was entirely lost upon them, and they drew very erroneous conclusions from Salisbury's anxiety to reach a compromise at the Constantinople Conference. Worse yet, the Tsar and his advisers were weak enough to allow themselves to be carried away by the Pan-Slav agitation and evidently hoped to divert attention from the domestic crisis by engaging in a crusade against the Turk. But Europe did not accord the Russians a mandate. Instead, Europe held Russia strictly accountable, and before the campaign was really under way, the Russians had been forced to accept numerous limitations upon their action, through obligations entered into with both Austria and England. But the crowning folly was the attempt to evade these obligations in the hour of victory. Whatever may have been the real explanation for the wondrous San Stefano Treaty, it would be hard from a political standpoint to defend it. The Russians themselves recognized that their victory over the Turks had been too complete, and Gorchakov was forced to agree to the revision of the peace terms by a European congress even before the peace was concluded.

The result was that Russia, exhausted and unable to back up her decisions, was in no position to present Europe with a *fait accompli*. Austria and England each demanded the stipulated pound of flesh. Bismarck refused to go beyond the role of honest broker, and even France, under the new republican régime, showed greater inclination to support the English than to stand by the Russians.

The Congress of Berlin was humiliating and disastrous. It really appeared that Russia had fought a great and difficult war in order to secure advantages for Austria and England. Even the opening of the Straits for Russian warships had not been attained. In the view of Russian governmental circles, this aim was far more important than the liberation of the Christians from the Turkish yoke or even the planting of the Orthodox cross on the Church of St. Sophia. To have attained it would have been ample compensation for all the sacrifices of a long and costly war, says Goriainov, the great Russian authority on the question.[1] But from the earliest weeks of 1878 it had become obvious that all Russian hopes of this kind would be blasted, and the question had been shelved for fear lest the English might press their demands for complete opening of the Straits to the warships of all nations. Salisbury's declaration on this subject at the congress was in itself a serious undermining of the Russian position. In the end Russian diplomacy had nothing to show but the retrocession of southern Bessarabia and the acquisition of a strip of Armenia in return for a costly campaign, the advance of Austria in Bosnia, and the British occupation of Cyprus. Even the Pan-Slavs could draw no satisfaction from the course of events, for the independence of Serbia and Montenegro was greatly outweighed by the reduction of Bulgaria by about three fifths. In fact, the Berlin Treaty was the complete negation of Pan-Slav aspirations as expressed in the Treaty of San Stefano.

Since the publication of Wertheimer's exhaustive biography of Andrássy the legend of the Austrian minister's pre-eminent statesmanship has become firmly rooted. A close examination of the source material published during the past decade, however, makes the earlier estimate quite untenable. Andrássy began by staking everything on the possibility of inducing the Turks to introduce reforms under the direction of the powers. There is no evidence that he had any appreciation for the rising nationalist movement in the Ottoman Empire itself, or that he was able to assess properly the obstacles in the way of reform. For him the root of the whole international difficulty lay in England's desertion of the concert of Europe. In trying to make the best of a bad situation he sold Austrian neutrality to the Russians in return for the eventual annexation of Bosnia and Herzegovina, provinces which he did not really want and which both German and Magyar public opinion was opposed to annexing. The opposition of the military men made war against Russia almost impossible. When the Russians flaunted their engagements to Austria, Andrássy's only hope was the hope of salvation through others, for that was the idea underlying his appeal for a European congress. Had he frankly come to an agreement with England, much might have been accomplished with less effort, but he was distrustful of "perfidious Albion" and almost till the last minute negotiated with the Russians in the hope of saving what he could from the wreckage. The Russians treated the Vienna government cavalierly throughout, with the result that

---

[1] Goriainov, op. cit., pp. 373 ff.

Andrássy had to be glad of England's firm stand. At the Congress of Berlin the Austrian minister did hardly more than play second fiddle to the English. There was nothing of "*grande politique*" about the acquisition of Bosnia and Herzegovina. The Turks had flatly refused their permission, and Andrássy almost humbly asked for occupation, for fear that a demand for annexation would arouse the opposition, not only of the Turks, but of the Italians.

For Bismarck the final settlement was a mixed blessing. To be sure, he had the satisfaction of seeing the policy he had advocated so long in vain finally secure general acceptance. From the very start he had made his own opinion clear. Those people "down there," the semi-barbarous Balkan peoples and the Turks as well, were not worth a deluge of blood in Europe. The preservation of peace among the great powers was the primary consideration, and this, he believed, could be best attained by a policy of reciprocal compensation for all concerned. Germany wanted nothing herself, but Bismarck was willing to act as the honest broker for the others. His earlier suggestions had been rejected with horror and suspicion of his ulterior motives. Even in March 1878 Disraeli had written irritably to the Queen: "A policy of partition is very simple, and does not require much genius to devise." [1] Perhaps so, but in the end all the powers accepted it as the only possible solution. As Sir Charles Dilke so cleverly put it: "The labours of the Berlin Congress, or its festivities, so confused the minds of the plenipotentiaries that they have never been clear who offered what to whom; but it at least seems plain . . . that a great deal of offering of other people's property took place." In the words of Count Corti, the Italian foreign minister: "Everybody was telling everybody else to take something which belonged to somebody else." [2]

The "somebody else" at whose expense the peace was to be secured was invariably the Turk. Bessarabia, Armenia, Bosnia, Herzegovina, and Cyprus, to say nothing of Roumania, Serbia, and Montenegro, were all parts of the Ottoman Empire prior to 1878. To satisfy France the English and Germans dangled Tunis before the dazzled eyes of Waddington, and Tunis also owed allegiance to the Porte. The Tripoli and Albania that were mentioned at one time or another as possible compensation for Italy were parts of the empire. In other words, sections of the empire were lost at the congress, and the eventual loss of other areas was already decided upon. Disraeli proudly insisted afterward that this was not partition, but merely dismemberment. Technically he may have been right. Practically it made little difference to the Turks. The policy was a ruthless one, but it had the great advantage of simplicity, and, after all, Bismarck may have been right, and with him the statesmen who finally adopted his program. The peace of Europe was more

---

[1] *Letters of Queen Victoria*, II, p. 608.

[2] Sir Charles Dilke: *Europe in 1887* (London, 1887), p. 27; Gwynn and Tuckwell: *The Life of Sir Charles Dilke*, I, p. 334.

worth saving than the Ottoman Empire, which at the time seemed unable to cope with its problems and had been for years a menace to European tranquillity.

The other side of the sheet was not so attractive to Bismarck, for the Eastern crisis had ended in the collapse of the Three Emperors' League, his cherished "triangular rampart." Worse yet, it had forced the German government into a position of resistance to Russian hopes and expectations and had thereby cast a dark shadow over Russian-German relations. The only consoling features were the corresponding changes in the position of Austria and England. The estrangement between Russia and Austria was far greater than that between Russia and Germany, and consequently Austria became in the future more dependent than ever on Germany. More significant even than this was the reappearance of England on the continental stage, an event of supreme importance from Bismarck's standpoint, for it liberated him from complete dependence on the Three Emperors' League and opened up the prospect of a combination with England and Austria as an alternative to the Eastern orientation. The great crisis had thrown the European system into the melting-pot. After the experience of 1875 Bismarck had no need to regret it. He had had his opportunity to prove that his policy was no longer a warlike one, and that the preservation of peace was his highest aim. With new friendships he could start in the following years upon the construction of his own system.

Like most great peace treaties from Westphalia to the present, the Berlin Treaty has been subjected to scathing and devastating criticism, and it has been all too frequently pointed out that its most important provisions were torn up in a very short time. With the advantage of hind-sight it is always easy for posterity to pick the flaws and defects in the work of statesmen of the past. But in justice to them one must view the situation as it presented itself in their own time. Bismarck himself never regarded treaties as eternal settlements, but rather as arrangements based upon the understanding that things remained as they were, *rebus sic stantibus*. The world constantly changes, and readjustments become necessary periodically. The Berlin Treaty was framed to meet a particular and very dangerous situation and was designed to keep the peace between the great powers.

It is perfectly true that this was done, not only at the expense of the Turks, but also at the expense of the Balkan peoples. The Bulgarian settlement was not a good one if one approaches it from the strictly nationalist view-point. Neither was the occupation of Bosnia and Herzegovina by Austria, or the forced retrocession of southern Bessarabia to Russia, or even the English occupation of Cyprus. To attribute these provisions to the blindness or ill will of the statesmen assembled at Berlin would, however, be puerile. They could hardly be expected to understand the working of the spirit of nationality in a region which was all but unknown. The very name *Bulgaria* was practically unheard of in Europe prior to 1875, and few experienced travellers had a direct acquaintance with the conditions existing in the fastnesses of the mountains. Excepting for the people of the Gladstonian persuasion in England, there were not many persons who were moved by the plea of Christian suffering. There was nothing resembling the Hellenistic movement of the earlier part of the century. In fact, the liberation of the Christians from the Turkish yoke sounded entirely too much like a Panslavic slogan concealing more sordid Russian ambitions. Why, it was asked, were the Russians so concerned with the lot of the southern Slavs when at the very same time they were oppressing other fellow Slavs in Poland in the most ruthless way? In other words, the mistakes made by European statesmen were due to pardonable ignorance rather than to malice, and there was more excuse for them than for some of the later peacemakers. After all, an ideal territorial settlement is a chimera, and the Balkan settlement of the present day is in many ways not much better than that laid down in the Treaty of Berlin.

BIBLIOGRAPHICAL NOTE
(SUPPLEMENTARY TO THE BIBLIOGRAPHY OF CHAPTER II)
DOCUMENTARY SOURCES

Accounts and Papers. State Papers: 1878. Volumes LXXXII, LXXXIII.

Actenstücke aus den Korrespondenzen des K. und K. Ministeriums des Äusseren über orientalische Angelegenheiten vom 7 April 1877 bis 3 November 1878. Vienna, 1878.

Actenstücke in orientalischen Angelegenheiten. Präliminarfriede von San Stefano. Congress-Protokolle und Vertrag von Berlin. Vienna, 1878.

Documents diplomatiques. Affaires d'Orient. Congrès de Berlin. Paris, 1878.

Documenti Diplomatici concernenti gli affari d'Oriente. Rome, 1878.

Ministerul affacerilor Straine. Documente Oficiale. Bucharest, 1878.

Die Grosse Politik der europäischen Kabinette, 1871–1914. Volume II.

Documents diplomatiques français, Volume II (Paris, 1930).

"Unprinted Documents. Russo-British Relations during the Eastern Crisis." Edited by R. W. SETON-WATSON. *Slavonic Review,* V, pp. 413–34; VI, pp. 422–34 (1926–7).

Le Rapport secret sur le Congrès de Berlin, addressé à la Porte par Carathéodory Pacha. Edited by BERTRAND BAREILLES. Paris, 1919.

Correspondenta Generalului Iancu Ghica. Edited by GENERAL R. ROSETTI. Bucharest, 1930. The important correspondence of the Roumanian representative at Russian headquarters from April 1877 to April 1878.

MEMOIRS, AUTOBIOGRAPHIES, BIOGRAPHIES, AND LETTERS

GLAISE-HORSTENAU, EDMUND: *Franz Josephs Weggefährte* (Vienna, 1930). Adds some valuable points to the story of Austrian policy.

MOÜY, CHARLES DE: *Souvenirs et causeries d'un diplomate*. Paris, 1909. The reminiscences of one of the secretaries at the Berlin Congress.

RADOWITZ, JOSEPH MARIA VON: *Aufzeichnungen und Erinnerungen aus dem Leben des Botschafters Joseph Maria von Radowitz*. Edited by Hajo Holborn. Two volumes. Stuttgart, 1925. The notes and memoranda of the first secretary of the congress, and one of the most valuable sources for the inside history of the negotiations.

WELLESLEY, COLONEL F. A.: *With the Russians in Peace and War*. London, 1905. The story of the English military attaché to Russia, with some information on his mission in 1877.

CRISPI, FRANCESCO: *Memoirs*. Collected and edited by T. Palamenghi-Crispi. Three volumes. London, 1914. Important for the history of Italian foreign policy, but a work that must be used with caution.

ROSI, MICHELE: *I Cairoli*. Two volumes. Bologna, 1929. Based on the Cairoli papers. Important for Italian policy.

HOHENLOHE-SCHILLINGSFÜRST, FÜRST CHLODWIG ZU: *Denkwürdigkeiten*. Two volumes. Stuttgart, 1907. English translation. Notes of the third German plenipotentiary to the congress, full of revealing items.

(CYON, ELIE DE:) *" La Guerre russo-turque d'après des documents inédits "* (*Nouvelle Revue*, IV, pp. 738–74, June 15, 1880). Of greatest importance for the crisis of March 1878.

NELIDOV, ALEXANDRE: *" Souvenirs d'avant et d'après la guerre de 1877–1878 "* (*Revue des deux mondes, 6ième période*, Volume XXX, pp. 241–71, November 1915). The last instalment of the Russian diplomat's memoirs, with some light on the crisis of 1878 and the Congress of Berlin.

BUSCH, DR.: *" Aus dem literarischen Nachlass des Unterstaatssekretärs Dr. Busch."* Edited by L. Raschdau. (*Deutsche Rundschau*, CXLI, pp. 361–80, December, 1909). Throws interesting light on the history of the congress.

CUMMINGS, A. N.: *" The Secret History of the Treaty of Berlin "* (*Nineteenth Century*, LVIII, pp. 83–90, July 1905). Giving a late account of the congress by Disraeli's secretary.

Poyezdka Grafa N. P. Ignatieva *po evropeiskim stolitzam pered voinoi, 1877–1878* (*Russkaia Starina*, XLV, Nos. 3–9, March–September 1914). Of great interest for the history of Russian diplomacy and the making of the Treaty of San Stefano.

168 BIBLIOGRAPHICAL NOTE

MONOGRAPHIC STUDIES

GAULD, WILLIAM A.: " The ' Dreikaiserbund ' and the Eastern Question, 1877–1878 " (*English Historical Review*, XLII, pp. 561–8, October 1927).

—: " The Anglo-Austrian Agreement of 1878 " (*English Historical Review*, XLI, pp. 108–12, January 1926).

IORGA, NICHOLAS: " *La Guerre de 1877–1878* " (*Revue d'Histoire moderne*, III, pp. 81–102, March–April 1928).

SALVEMINI, GAETANO: " *Alla Vigilia del Congresso di Berlino* " (*Nuova Rivista Storica*, IX, pp. 72–92, January–February 1925).

ANDRÉADÈS, A.: " *La Politique orientale anglaise avant et pendant le Congrès de Berlin* " (*La Vie des peuples*, VII, pp. 877–919, August 10, 1922).

LIEBOLD, RUDOLF: *Die Stellung Englands in der russisch-türkischen Krise von 1875–78*. Wilkau, 1930. The best monographic study of English policy.

HEADLAM-MORLEY, SIR JAMES: *Studies in Diplomatic History*. New York, 1930. Contains chapters on the Straits question and on the British acquisition of Cyprus.

LEE, DWIGHT E.: " The Proposed Mediterranean League of 1878 " (*Journal of Modern History*, III, pp. 33–45, March 1931).

SPECIAL LITERATURE ON THE CONGRESS OF BERLIN

AVRIL, ADOLPHE D': *Négociations relatives au Traité de Berlin*. Paris, 1886. Still one of the most useful books, reviewing the negotiations of 1875–8 as they appear in the various contemporary documents.

BRUNSWIK, BENOÎT: *Le Traité de Berlin annoté et commenté*. Paris, 1878. A thorough critical work on the text.

BONGHI, RUGGIERO: *Il Congresso di Berlino e la Crisi d'Oriente*. Milan, 1878. An admirable book, written by one of the leading Italian statesmen and throwing much light especially on the Italian position.

HANOTAUX, GABRIEL: *Histoire de la France contemporaine*. Four volumes. Paris, 1903–9. The chapter on the Berlin Congress is of special value because Hanotaux made use of the unpublished memoirs of Shuvalov.

LORD, ROBERT H.: " The Congress of Berlin " (in Hazen, Thayer, and Lord: *Three Peace Congresses of the Nineteenth Century*. Cambridge, Mass., 1917).

MUNRO, HENRY F.: *The Berlin Congress*. Washington, 1918. Prepared for the American State Department, and dealing primarily with the organization and procedure of the congress.

WOODWARD, E. L.: *The Congress of Berlin, 1878*. London, 1920. In Peace Handbooks, No. 154. Prepared for the British foreign office. A good brief sketch, but now somewhat antiquated through the appearance of new material.

Müller, Manfred: *Die Bedeutung des Berliner Kongresses für die deutsch-russischen Beziehungen.* Leipzig, 1927. A very careful and thorough study of the congress, based upon all the recent material. The best analysis available.

Larmeroux, Jean: *L'Autriche-Hongrie au Congrès de Berlin, 1878.* Paris, 1915. Really a study of Austrian policy throughout the crisis, but quite incomplete and inadequate.

Medlicott, W. N.: "The Berlin Treaty: Fifty Years Afterwards" (*Quarterly Review,* CCLI, pp. 1–18, July 1928). Deals largely with the aftermath of the settlement.

Corti, Count Egon C.: "*Il Conte Corti al Congresso di Berlino*" (*Nuova Antologia,* CCXL, pp. 351–61, April 15, 1925).

—: "*Bismarck und Italien am Berliner Kongress*" (*Historische Vierteljahrschrift,* XXIII, pp. 456–71, May 1, 1927). These two articles are of prime importance for the study of Italian policy.

Chastel, Comte A. du: *Les Événements d'Orient et le Congrès de Berlin de 1878.* Tournai, 1908.

Anuchin, Dmitri N.: *Berlinski Kongres 1878 goda.* St. Petersburg, 1912.

VI

The Problem of Security

THE AUSTRIAN–GERMAN ALLIANCE AND THE ALLIANCE OF THE THREE EMPERORS

WHILE THE ENGLISH STATESMEN RETURNED TO LONDON AFTER THE congress well satisfied and convinced that they had brought back "peace with honour," the Russians felt correspondingly disillusioned and depressed. Whatever gains they had made through the decisions of the congress, the fact remained that the Treaty of Berlin was unimpressive as compared with the Slavic peace of San Stefano. The Pan-Slav elements in Russia lost no time in voicing their dissatisfaction. In a famous speech delivered before the Slavic Welfare Society of Moscow on July 4 — that is, even before the congress had completed its labours — Aksakov had indulged in a violent tirade against the activities of the Russian diplomats, whom he described as the "true nihilists" of Russia: "Beaconsfield stamped his foot, Austria held up a threatening finger, Russian diplomats were terrified, and all was surrendered. . . . The congress is nothing more or less than an undisguised conspiracy against the Russian people, a conspiracy plotted with the concurrence even of the Russian representatives themselves." The attack was a telling one and apparently wounded the vanity of Gorchakov very deeply. Shuvalov maintained afterward that the Russian chancellor wilfully withdrew from the work of the congress whenever it was clear that Russia stood to lose, and that he reported separately from his colleagues, criticizing their policy to the Tsar.[1]

Whether or not this was the truth, there can be no doubt that Russian opinion was much wrought up over the outcome of the holy crusade against the Turks. The more loudly and eloquently the English proclaimed their victory, the more irritated were the Russians. Lord Salisbury diagnosed the situation correctly when he wrote to Odo Russell late in July 1878: "It is one of the misfortunes of telegraphic communications that no Treaty of Peace can ever be generally popular, because, directly that A knows that B is pleased, he thinks that B is likely to be the best judge, and he is proportionately displeased." In other words, the very efforts of the statesmen to make the settlement palatable to their countrymen led to new friction.[2] So far as the Russian public could see,

---

[1] *Die Grosse Politik*, III, No. 440.   [2] Cecil: *Salisbury*, II, p. 327.

the country had been unjustly deprived of the fruits of its efforts and sacrifices by the combined action of England and Austria. Of Germany little was said, and Bismarck was hardly mentioned by the press.[1] But the diplomats, who were anxious to exonerate themselves of responsibility, found it much more convenient to lay the blame on Bismarck, who owed Russia so much and had done so little to help her out of her dilemma. Shuvalov, on his return to St. Petersburg after the congress, found the Tsar convinced that the whole meeting had been " a European coalition against Russia under the leadership of Prince Bismarck," whose aim had been to secure all possible advantages for Austria.[2] Though the ambassador did his utmost to convince the Tsar of his error and adduced concrete evidence of Bismarck's intervention in favour of Russia on several crucial occasions, he did not succeed in convincing Alexander entirely.

The disappointment of the Russians was only natural. It did not of necessity imply a fundamental estrangement from the Germans. In fact, the acerbity soon passed out of Russian-German relations again, and the representatives of the powers settled down to the work of the commissions which had been appointed to decide the outstanding questions of evacuation, administration, and boundary delimitation. But here again the Russians found cause for complaint, for the English and the Austrian delegates regularly voted together, and more often than not the French representative joined them. Bismarck, who had no direct interest in the questions at issue, attempted at first to co-operate with his two eastern neighbours, and on occasion went so far as to support the Russians against the other powers. But their critical attitude soon convinced him that supporting Russia was a thankless task, and by October 1878 he had come to the conclusion that the policy could not be continued at the expense of a quarrel with England.[3]

The Russian position at the end of 1878 was, therefore, by no means an enviable one. Not only were England and Austria consistently opposing the Russian views, but Germany, too, had become estranged. At home the rising tide of Nihilism made the situation exceedingly insecure and dangerous. Russia was well-nigh isolated, and isolation inevitably breeds suspicion and anxiety in the power that is subjected to it. Before long the Russians found further grounds for distrust of their German neighbour. The rigorous German quarantine regulations designed to prevent the spread of the plague from Russia to western Europe created much irritation in January 1879,[4] while the publication of an Austrian-German Agreement abrogating Article V of the Treaty of Prague appeared to supply all needed justification for the theory of German

---

[1] See the illuminating discussion by Irene Grüning: *Die russische öffentliche Meinung und ihre Stellung zu den Grossmächten, 1878–1894* (Berlin, 1929), pp. 54 ff.

[2] *Die Grosse Politik*, III, Nos. 440, 441; Freiherr von Mittnacht: *Erinnerungen an Bismarck. Neue Folge* (Stuttgart, 1905), pp. 9 ff.

[3] Müller: *Die Bedeutung des Berliner Kongresses*, pp. 61 ff., which is based upon unpublished documents from the German archives.

[4] General von Schweinitz: *Denkwürdigkeiten*, II, pp. 40–4.

ingratitude and for the rumour of a rapprochement between Germany and Austria.

This article of the treaty which ended the Austrian-Prussian conflict in 1866 envisaged the eventual retrocession to Denmark of part of northern Schleswig provided a plebiscite indicated the desire of the inhabitants to return to their former allegiance. The plebiscite had never been held, for reasons which need not be entered upon here. But the non-execution of the treaty left the future uncertain and opened the door to all sorts of intrigues and manœuvrings. Bismarck had long been anxious to free himself from this fetter and had, on various occasions, sounded Andrássy as to the possibility of abrogating Article V. Nothing had come of the negotiations until the spring of 1878, when Andrássy suddenly expressed his readiness to meet the wishes of the chancellor. Obviously the plan of the Austrian minister was to ingratiate himself with Bismarck at a time when German support against Russia was particularly needed. An agreement was come to on April 13, 1878, but was kept secret at Bismarck's request in order not to arouse the suspicions of the Russians. Later in 1878, however, the German chancellor was prepared to make the substance of the treaty known, in the hope of definitely ending the agitation carried on in Denmark. Andrássy consented to the step, but desired that the agreement be post-dated so as to avoid the appearance of Austria's having purchased German support at the Berlin Congress by concessions in the North-Schleswig question. The agreement was finally signed and ratified in January 1879, though it was dated October 11, 1878. On February 4 it was published.[1]

The Russians, of course, did not know that the Austrian-German Agreement had been concluded in April 1878, but at bottom it did not make much difference whether the Austrian concession took the form of an advance payment or not. Assuming that the agreement was come to after the Congress of Berlin, the Russian government and press immediately raised the question as to what Bismarck had paid in return. It was even suggested that he had promised support for Austrian aspirations in the direction of Macedonia.[2] It is not necessary to lay over-much stress on this particular point, although the Russian court took a direct interest in the Danish claims. What must be stressed is the fact that here the Russians seemed to have concrete evidence of an Austro-German pact and therefore real justification for their suspicions. The hostility of the press began to turn from England and Austria to Germany, and there was even some talk of the desirability of an eventual agreement with France.

By this time Bismarck had already lost patience. He had tried to hold the balance even between Austria and Russia at the time of the Berlin Congress,

1 *Bismarck und die nordschleswigsche Frage, 1864–1879* (Berlin, 1925); P. Ingwersen: *Der Artikel V des Prager Friedens* (Flensburg, 1918); Aage Friis: *" Ophaevelsen af Pragfredens Artikel 5"* (*Tilskueren*, February 1921); id., *" Die Aufhebung des Artikels V des Prager Friedens"* (*Historische Zeitschrift*, CXXV, pp. 45–62, 1921); *Documents diplomatiques français*, II, Nos. 370, 377–9, 382, 389.
2 *Documents diplomatiques français*, II, No. 383; Grüning, op. cit., pp. 60 ff.

and if he departed at all from his role of "honest broker," it was rather in favour of Russia than of Austria. He was convinced that the Tsar had come out of the crisis much better than he had a right to expect after the ridiculous Treaty of San Stefano, and on later occasions he often maintained that he had conducted himself at the congress as though he had been the fourth Russian plenipotentiary. It therefore appeared to him that his neighbours were consciously seeking to pick a quarrel. The Three Emperors' League, he told the Austrian ambassador in January 1879, could function only if based upon a complete understanding between the three Emperors. But the Tsar himself had become unreliable and unaccountable. Consequently he had told Andrássy during the preceding autumn that Austria should seek to effect a rapprochement with England, for Russia would be unable to resist England and Austria acting together.[1]

A profound change had been taking place in the mind of the German chancellor since the congress. During the preceding years he had been opposed in principle to all general alliances and had taken the view that treaties should be concluded just prior to the action which they were intended to influence.[2] That is to say, he did not favour fixed agreements of a general nature and was unwilling to go beyond agreements *ad hoc,* concluded when the probable course of events could already be foreseen. Now, however, he had changed his mind, evidently under pressure of the developments since the congress and because of the restlessness of the Russians. He frequently maintained later that the idea of an agreement with Austria had been in his mind ever since her defeat in 1866, and he told the French ambassador in November 1879 that from that time on his "constant effort had been to sew up the fabric which had been torn and to re-establish friendly relations with Prussia's former associate in the German Confederation."[3]

Such statements *ex post facto* must, however, be viewed with great reserve, for Bismarck had an irresistible tendency to dramatize his actions. Of greater importance is the evidence that can be adduced to show that he had begun to familiarize himself with the idea by the beginning of 1879. During the month of January he spoke of the subject in unmistakable terms to Freiherr von Franckenstein, one of the members of the Reichstag. "Germany and Austria united," he said, "would be the best guarantee of peace for Europe; he had always thought so and would always think so. . . . Even a constitutional connexion between Germany and Austria was conceivable. . . . If Germany and Austria were united, they would be, together, a match for any enemy, France or Russia."[4] A month later he was complaining bitterly of the Russian accusa-

---

[1] Bismarck: *Die gesammelten Werke.* Volume VIII. *" Gespräche "* (Berlin, 1926), pp. 293 ff.

[2] See, for example, his remarks to Baron Münch in October 1876 (Wertheimer, in *Historische Blätter,* I, p. 272, 1921), and his remarks to Schweinitz in the latter's *Denkwürdigkeiten,* I, p. 362.

[3] Comte de Chaudordy: *La France en 1889* (Paris, 1889), pp. 253 ff. Saint-Vallier's report is now printed in full in *Documents diplomatiques français,* II, No. 476.

[4] Heinrich von Poschinger: *Fürst Bismarck und die Parlamentarier* (Breslau, 1896), II, pp. 315 ff.

tions against him, and pointing out that the attitude of the Russians served to make Germany's relations with Austria more intimate.[1] And when Schweinitz came to Germany early in April, he found the chancellor opening up " entirely new and terrible horizons." Speaking to the ambassador, Bismarck said that the constant coquetting with France on the part of Gorchakov, the endless armaments of Miliutin, the advanced-guard position of the Russian cavalry on the German frontier, and the violent language of the St. Petersburg and Moscow press had convinced him that Russia could no longer be relied upon. Not even Russia's ruler could be depended upon to the same extent as before. " Therefore one could not, for the sake of the uncertain friendship of Russia, antagonize the other powers, especially England and Austria. On the contrary, a closer understanding with the latter must be striven for, and this should be developed into an organic relationship that could not be dissolved without the consent of the parliamentary bodies." [2]

Lord Salisbury was not far from wrong when, in May 1879, he expressed the opinion that " all Bismarck is doing looks like clearing the decks for action." [3] Of course he had no belligerent intentions, but it is clear from his conversation with Schweinitz that he had practically made up his mind regarding his future course. In fact, it may be said that his remarks to the ambassador epitomized the whole policy which led to the alliance with Austria. Here one finds all the complaints which crop up again and again in the subsequent months, and here is the fundamental program that was to be realized before the year was out. No wonder that he spoke so definitely to the French ambassador in June, pointing out that the intimacy between Germany and Austria " is and will be more and more the basis of my policy." " I desire," he continued, " that there should be between us [Germany and Austria] not a single point of disagreement, and to this I attach so great a value that I am prepared to make real sacrifices to bring it about. . . . The existence and the integrity of the Austrian Empire are for us the first conditions of security." [4]

It does not follow from this that the chancellor had definitely decided to back Austria against Russia. Indeed, he told the French ambassador on this same occasion that, while he regarded the Three Emperors' League as having ceased to exist, he regretted the fact and would like to revive it. The dominant idea in his mind seems to have been not one of antagonizing Russia, but one of defending Germany and Austria against Russia. After all, he was quite clear in his mind, even in 1876, that Germany could not afford to see Austria completely

---

[1] Müller: *Bedeutung des Berliner Kongresses*, pp. 89–90.

[2] Schweinitz: *Denkwürdigkeiten*, II, p. 60. At this very time the French ambassador reported continually on Bismarck's irritation and fear lest Russia attack Austria (*Documents diplomatiques français*, II, Nos. 406, 409, 411).

[3] Cecil: *Salisbury*, II, p. 362.

[4] *Documents diplomatiques français*, II, No. 440. A part of this very interesting report was published in Emile Bourgeois and Georges Pagès: *Les Origines et les responsabilités de la Grande Guerre* (Paris, 1921), pp. 368 ff.

defeated and deprived of her position as a great power. If that were to happen, the Habsburg Empire would undoubtedly be disrupted, and even if Germany were strengthened by the acquisition of the German provinces of the empire, she would find herself alone between the powerful Tsarist Empire on the one side and a vengeful France on the other. The idea of reviving the defensive union of central Europe as it had existed prior to 1866 was, therefore, a fairly obvious one.

But the question arises immediately whether the central powers were actually menaced in 1879, as Bismarck asserted. No doubt the reorganization of the Russian army had been proceeding apace since 1871, under the energetic direction of Miliutin, who was known to entertain no friendly feelings towards Germany and Austria. Furthermore, it is true that Russian troops were constantly being transferred from the more fertile interior sections to the areas along the German and Austrian frontiers. The German military authorities themselves felt quite certain that Germany would be more than a match for the Russians, and the relations of the German government to the French government were better than they had been at any time since 1871, so that there was relatively little danger at the time of a Franco-Russian combination. The danger to Germany, if there was one at all, was an indirect one, involved in the danger to Austria.

But the evidences of hostile Russian designs against Austria are hardly more convincing than the evidences of Russian preparations against Germany. To be sure, the Pan-Slav elements were agitating uninterruptedly and talking of the road to Constantinople passing through Vienna. But Russia was quite clearly unprepared to embark upon another war, and the rapid spread of Nihilism and terrorism more than offset the impetus of Panslavism. Bismarck himself described Russia to General Chanzy in the spring of 1879 as a country in full process of decomposition.[1] The remark was probably intended as a veiled warning against French tendencies towards an alliance with Russia, but this does not deprive it of all force. That Russia was rapidly sinking into the slough of revolution was an opinion commonly held at the time. Under the circumstances the Tsar could hardly hope to embark upon an aggressive policy unless he had the support of France.

Bismarck, in making the decisive change in his policy, appears to have been less influenced by the fear of an actual attack by Russia upon Germany or upon Austria than by the fear that Russia herself would succeed in building up a coalition. For in spite of the unusually good relations existing between Germany and France, the chancellor never could get rid of the nightmare of an eventual Franco-Russian alliance. The articles in the Russian press suggesting such a combination aroused his anxiety and he instructed one of his agents, Moritz

---

[1] *Documents diplomatiques français*, II, No. 398; E. Daudet: *La Mission du Comte de Saint-Vallier* (Paris, 1918), p. 108.

Busch, to write an adequate reply.[1] Not only that; he began to suspect that the high tone of the Russians might be due to an agreement reached between St. Petersburg and Vienna. This, if extended to include France, would amount to the revival of the famous " Kaunitz Coalition " of the Seven Years' War.[2]

To provide against these possible combinations the chancellor appreciated the opportunity offered by the international alignment in the summer of 1879. England and Austria had been working together systematically in all matters pertaining to the execution of the Treaty of Berlin and to the Near East generally. In the same way England and France had been co-operating, especially in the regulation of the Egyptian question, and France had loyally supported the English policy in the Balkans as well. In August 1879 Andrássy went so far as to hint to Bismarck that England, France, and Austria were bound to act together against Russia in the Near East. The chancellor was probably not far from wrong when he told Saint-Vallier in June that Russia was impatient of the Anglo-French entente, of the good relations existing between Paris and Berlin, and of the intimacy between Germany and Austria. The combination had all the characteristics of the coalition against Russia in the Crimean War, and the Russians were justified in feeling that they were being isolated.[3] If the Germans could associate themselves with this Western alignment, they would have nothing to fear from the Russian policy, for they would be able to turn the tables completely on their neighbour and would succeed in erecting an insuperable barrier against the Russian advance. To Bismarck, at any rate, it was clear that Germany could no longer play the part of the " honest broker " or avoid all obligations of a larger nature. Commanding the central position on the continent, she had to keep an alert watch to both the west and the east. The first step to obtain security would be to establish a satisfactory connexion with the other central power, in order that the inside lines might be strengthened for the event of an attack on either or both fronts.

The great obstacle to the realization of the new Bismarckian program was the Emperor William I, a convinced proponent of the traditional friendship with Russia and a man deeply sensitive of the family tie between the Hohenzollerns and the Romanovs. As early as January 1879 Bismarck was complaining that the Kaiser objected to his using strong language in dealing with Russia.[4] It was an attitude that was perfectly well known and with which the German statesman had to reckon. It accounts in a large measure for the fact

---

[1] Kurt Köerlin: Zur Vorgeschichte des russisch-französischen Bündnisses 1879–1890 (Halle, 1926), p. 34; Bismarck: Werke, VIII, p. 305.

[2] Hohenlohe: Denkwürdigkeiten, II, p. 275; Schweinitz: Briefwechsel, I, p. 150; Wertheimer, Andrássy, III, pp. 221, 238; Lucius: Bismarck-Erinnerungen, pp. 173 ff.; Karl Schünemann: " Die Stellung Österreich-Ungarns in Bismarcks Bündnispolitik " (Archiv für Politik und Geschichte, VI, pp. 549–94, 1926).

[3] Wertheimer: Andrássy, III, p. 238; Documents diplomatiques français, II, No. 440; and the Saburov Memorandum of August 1879, in the Krasny Arkhiv, I (1922), pp. 78 ff.

[4] Bismarck: Werke, VIII, p. 293.

that no action was taken for months after the chancellor had come to a decision as to the course he would pursue. But before long the Russians themselves were to extricate him from his dilemma. Early in August the Russian chargé d'affaires at Berlin called the attention of the German foreign office to the fact that the German representatives on the Balkan commissions were regularly voting with Austria and against Russia. He asked that Germany continue the work of mediation which she had initiated at the Berlin Congress. Bismarck, who was taking the waters at Kissingen, wrote to the foreign office instructing it to receive the Russian request with coolness and pointing out that Germany had placed herself unreservedly at the service of Russia during the congress, but had in no sense earned her gratitude thereby. Germany must now take greater consideration of the other powers and not expose herself to their hostility in matters which were of no direct interest to Germany herself. Bismarck's conversations with the Russian diplomat, Saburov, at this very time, show how much irritated he was by the impatient and unreasonable attitude of the Russians. The violent press campaign which broke out simultaneously had all the characteristics of invective inspired by the governments. The German papers attacked Gorchakov, the Russian papers denounced Bismarck. It was a veritable " War of the Chancellors," as a French diplomat put it.[1]

More serious by far than this initial passage at arms was the report of a conversation between the Tsar and Schweinitz, which reached Bismarck within the next few days. The Tsar spoke in a mild tone and without threatening, but his words were weighty enough. After complaining of the German attitude he went on to say that if the century-old friendship was to continue, the Germans must change their ways: " This will end in a very serious fashion." [2] Not content even with this, Alexander wrote a personal letter to his uncle the German Emperor, repeating his grievances and bitterly accusing Bismarck of throwing into the scales the weight of his personal resentment against Gorchakov. " The consequences," he added, " may be disastrous for both countries." [3]

Matters had gone far. Bismarck had already instructed his subordinates at Berlin to call to the Emperor's attention the implications of the Russian attitude. He now pointed out himself that if the Emperor were to reply in the same fashion, war would undoubtedly result.

The moment was a crucial one, for it had just become known that Andrássy, who had been ill all summer, had decided to resign. Bismarck feared at first that the Austrian minister was being forced out of office by the military group about the Archduke Albrecht, which had always been hostile to Prussia and had advocated an agreement with Russia. For all the German chancellor

---

[1] J. Y. Simpson: *The Saburov Memoirs* (Cambridge, 1929), pp. 50–5; *Krasny Arkhiv*, I (1921), pp. 64 ff.; Bismarck: *Werke*, VIII, p. 323; *Documents diplomatiques français*, II, Nos. 457, 462.

[2] *Die Grosse Politik*, III, No. 443; Schweinitz: *Denkwürdigkeiten*, II, pp. 64 ff.

[3] *Die Grosse Politik*, III, No. 446. Bismarck's assertion to Saint-Vallier (*Documents diplomatiques français*, II, No. 476) that a similar letter was written to Francis Joseph cannot be substantiated from other evidence.

could know, the disappearance of Andrássy might be the first step in the re-orientation of Austrian policy in the direction of an alliance with Russia and France. Under the leadership of Count Taaffe the domestic policy of the Austrian government was already turning from the German groups to the Slavic elements.[1] If Bismarck's idea of an agreement with Austria was to be carried out, it would have to be done immediately and on the strength of the menacing language of the Russians. He therefore urged the Emperor to remain firm, for any sign of yielding would serve only to reinforce the position of the hostile elements in Russia. At the same time he stressed the importance for Germany of cultivating closer relations with Austria and asked permission to visit Andrássy at Vienna, before his own return to Berlin.

The Emperor objected strenuously to the chancellor's projected journey to the Austrian capital, on the plea that this would appear like a demonstration against Russia. It was clear from the start that he would resist the new policy step by step. Bismarck's greatest efforts during the next six weeks were devoted to convincing his sovereign. His draft of the reply to be sent to the Tsar was couched in the most moderate language, stressing the fact that the Emperor still regarded the friendship with Russia as a "sacred legacy." In the end this expression proved to be an excellent weapon in the hands of William during his conflict with the chancellor, who found that he had overshot the mark in his effort to reconcile the old man to a policy which was fundamentally antipathetic to him. In the meanwhile Bismarck and Andrássy met at Gastein on August 27 and 28. We have no direct information of what passed between the two statesmen, but from references to the meeting in later documents it appears that Andrássy assured his interlocutor that there was no Austrian-Russian agreement and that even the Archduke Albrecht had become wholly converted to the idea of an alliance with Germany. He himself was ready to remain in office until an agreement had been concluded, if the prospect were such as to warrant this procedure. Bismarck evidently spoke about the situation as it existed before 1866, when the German Confederation bound the various German states together in a defensive pact. He recognized that this situation could not be revived *tel quel,* but he proposed a general defensive alliance directed against aggression by any other power or powers and secured by constitutional provisions. Andrássy, however, indicated that for Austria an alliance which might in any way be interpreted as directed against France would be impossible, for, he said, England would not approve of such an arrangement. He was, therefore, opposed to the idea of a general defensive agreement, though he was quite ready to consider a defensive alliance directed against Russia, provided always that the Emperor Francis Joseph would consent.[2] It would appear from later statements that something was also said about the desirability of associating England with the projected pact, but the evidence

---

[1] Wertheimer: *Andrássy,* III, pp. 214, 221, 231; Schünemann, loc. cit.
[2] *Die Grosse Politik,* III, Nos. 449, 455, 458; Wertheimer: *Andrássy,* III, pp. 221, 238–40.

on this point is so vague and inconclusive that it must be used with the greatest caution.

Bismarck had every reason to feel satisfied with the result of his conference with Andrássy, for he had received not only assurances as to Austria's position, but also expressions of willingness to enter upon definite engagements with Germany. But he knew from the beginning that the greatest task would be to convert his own Emperor to his point of view. On August 31 he dispatched from Gastein the first of an extended series of long memoranda designed to convince William that the situation demanded the policy suggested. As models of political writing and as specimens of close and cogent reasoning these reports and memoranda are without equals in the literature of modern diplomacy. They show once again how complete was Bismarck's mastery of the statesman's art and how deep his insight into the workings of the European states system. And yet the historian cannot accept these documents at face value, for it must always be remembered that they were specially designed for the mentality of the Emperor. Many of the arguments are arguments *ad hominem* and cannot, therefore, be taken as irrefutable proof of the chancellor's real intentions or views.

The very first of the appeals to the Emperor reviewed the whole international situation. Bismarck stressed the fact that Russia could no longer be depended upon, and that not even the Tsar's friendship for his uncle could be trusted too far. Therefore Germany should conclude a defensive alliance with Austria which would give her the same protection she enjoyed in the days of the German Confederation. Russia could not find in this arrangement anything offensive, for it would simply be the revival of an earlier combination, and Russia could join at any time if she wished. In fact, the agreement would be of service to her in so far as it would draw Austria away from a possible anti-Russian coalition of the western powers. From the German standpoint the alliance with Austria had become an absolute necessity, not only for her own protection against Russia, but also for the purpose of preventing Austria from drifting into the arms of France. The Austro-German combination would, in the last count, serve even as a barrier to an eventual Franco-Russian alliance, because, in the first place, Russia would hesitate before taking action against a united central Europe, and because, secondly, the combination of Germany and Austria would be so strong that England would join it, thus making it almost impossible for France to take the side of Russia in a future conflict.[1]

Brilliantly though the argument was presented, the Emperor William would have none of it. He had never been convinced of the unfriendliness of the Tsar and now had evidence to prove that he was right. For the Tsar had by this time come to see the error of his ways and had already made advances to his uncle. This change of mind was perhaps due to the influence exerted by Saburov, who had spoken at length with Bismarck at Kissingen and had handed to the Tsar a long and interesting memorandum setting forth the

---

[1] *Die Grosse Politik,* III, No. 455.

impending danger of Russia's finding herself isolated. Russia, he argued, must not reckon too strongly on the continuance of the Franco-German antagonism, for Bismarck might at any time effect a reconciliation with France by abandoning to her either part of Lorraine, or Belgium, or Holland. By remaining faithful to the traditional friendship with Germany the Tsar would make a Franco-German settlement unnecessary and would therefore be able to capitalize the Franco-German tension.[1] Alexander was much impressed with this reasoning and indicated his approval.[2] He then proceeded to the army manœuvres, which were being held in Poland, and was delighted to find there Field-Marshal von Manteuffel, who had been sent by the German Emperor to greet his fellow sovereign. Manteuffel had frequently been sent on confidential missions of this kind, though he had no special diplomatic skill. He received the Tsar's explanations quite uncritically and supported the Tsar's suggestion that the Emperor himself should come to Poland to talk over the situation. Alexander was quite prepared to go to Germany, so he said, but the danger of Nihilist and socialist plots made this course inadvisable.

The members of the German foreign office were, one and all, firmly opposed to the Emperor's desire to accept his nephew's invitation. Bismarck took the same attitude, but before he could communicate with his sovereign, the latter had already made up his mind, and resisted all efforts to move him. On September 3 the two monarchs met at Alexandrovo, in Poland, not far from the German frontier. The two men, who were sincerely attached to each other, had no difficulty in coming to an understanding. The Tsar explained his letter and maintained that he and he alone was responsible for it. No threat was intended, and he now realized that he had committed a bad blunder. There was nothing he desired more than the continuance of the Three Emperors' League, though Austria, in all conscience, had not treated Russia very well.

The Emperor was much touched by Alexander's reference to the " sacred legacy" and accepted the Tsar's explanations at their face value. In his view the whole difficulty was to be traced to the recklessness of the Russian press, which, he was glad to learn, had been called to order by the government. Miliutin, with whom the Emperor spoke on the following day, assured him that the Russian military concentrations were due to the fact that Russia was threatened by an Anglo-Austro-French coalition and was therefore obliged to take all precautions. William appears to have been satisfied with these assurances. In fact, before leaving Alexandrovo he conferred upon Miliutin a high German order, despite the fact that the war minister was generally regarded as the very soul of the anti-German party at the Russian court.[3]

The Alexandrovo meeting made the task of securing the Emperor's

---

[1] J. Y. Simpson, op. cit., pp. 56 ff.; *Krasny Arkhiv*, I (1921), pp. 78–84.

[2] Schweinitz: *Denkwürdigkeiten*, II, p. 72; *Die Grosse Politik*, III, No. 461.

[3] *Die Grosse Politik*, III, Nos. 457, 460, 465, 466; Wertheimer: *Andrássy*, III, p. 251; Radowitz: *Aufzeichnungen*, II, pp. 90–1; *Documents diplomatiques français*, II, Nos. 461, 462, 473.

approval for a defensive alliance with Austria infinitely more difficult, for he was sincerely convinced that the Tsar desired to continue the old friendship and could not free himself from the feeling that he would be committing perfidy if he supported a convention directed against his friend. He would rather retire from the throne, he declared, than make himself responsible for a dishonourable act. Bismarck might discuss with Andrássy what action should be taken in certain eventualities, but he must not ask for the Emperor's consent to negotiate an alliance. Had he not himself always taken the view that agreements except for specific, limited purposes should be avoided? Bismarck's oft-repeated arguments made little impression upon him. The chancellor insisted that the projected understanding did not involve hostility to Russia, and that it was the intention of Andrássy and himself to cultivate good relations with the Tsar. But the Emperor felt that any such combination would, in the end, turn against Russia, and he strongly suspected Bismarck of trying to win him over to the idea of a coalition between Germany, Austria, France, and England, of which Russia would be the victim. Bismarck categorically denied this allegation and continued to stress his conviction regarding the unreliability of the Russians. At just this time he learned of Russian soundings in Rome in the spring of 1879 and of further approaches made to the French by General Obruchev, who attended the French manœuvres in August 1879. From all the scattered references to this episode that can be found in the sources it appears that the advances, if there actually were any, which Waddington denied, were unofficial and extremely vague. In the *Documents diplomatiques français* there is no evidence of these soundings — in fact, no reference excepting Bismarck's own allusion in his talk with Saint-Vallier. It may well be doubted whether Bismarck himself took them seriously, but, as he told Hohenlohe, the news came very opportunely and furnished him with a powerful argument for his debate with the Emperor.[1]

After the Crown Prince, the German ambassador at Paris and even Moltke had been enlisted by Bismarck to bring pressure upon his sovereign, William finally agreed that Bismarck should discuss with Andrássy, at Vienna, the bases of a general defensive alliance, in which Russia should not be specifically mentioned. The Emperor, in fact, hoped strongly that the agreement might be communicated to the Russian Tsar in advance. Bismarck, meanwhile, had already outlined the text of the agreement and had forwarded it to the German ambassador at Vienna, Prince Reuss. Andrássy in turn had drawn up a draft embodying the Austrian view. On September 22 Bismarck arrived in Vienna, loudly acclaimed by the population. For two days he conferred with Andrássy, and when he departed for Berlin, the two statesmen had come to an understanding. The discussion hinged upon the question whether the alliance should be of a general or of a specific nature, for the earlier suggestion of Bismarck, that the alliance should be supported by constitutional provisions, was dropped at Andrássy's request, evidently for fear of opposition in the Austrian parliament.[1] In respect to the question of a general treaty Andrássy's position had been made clear from the beginning. He was unwilling to assume the obligation of supporting Germany in the event of a French attack and feared that any treaty in general form would be immediately interpreted as directed against France. This might lead France to seek protection in the arms of Russia and would, in any case, meet with the disapproval of England. Bismarck himself seems to have been convinced of the greater desirability of an alliance in which Russia was specifically envisaged, but he was bound by the instructions of the Emperor and was therefore obliged to defend his view to the very limit.

Andrássy was adamant in his determination not to accept the suggestion of Bismarck, and so the German chancellor was obliged either to yield or to give up the idea of a treaty entirely. Andrássy later described to a friend the dramatic last act of the conference. The German chancellor, he said, suddenly arose from his seat and came so close that one could almost hear him breathe. The two men looked each other steadfastly in the eye, and Bismarck began: " All I can say is: consider carefully what you do. For the last time I advise you to give up your opposition." Then, almost threatening: " Accept my proposal, else . . . else I shall have to accept yours." " But," added Bismarck laughingly, " it will cause me a damned lot of trouble." [2]

The alliance text on which Bismarck and Andrássy had come to an agreement at Vienna did not differ materially from the draft worked out and submitted by Andrássy beforehand. It provided that if either of the contracting powers were attacked by Russia, its ally should come to its assistance with all its forces, and that neither should conclude a separate peace. If either contracting power were attacked by any other power, its ally should observe at least a benevolent neutrality. In the event of Russia's coming to the assistance of the attacking power, Article I should apply; that is, each contracting power should be obliged to come to the assistance of the other with all its forces. The treaty was to run for five years and was to be kept secret. Both powers expressed the hope that the Russian armaments would not prove to be menacing, but agreed that in the contrary case they should regard it as their duty to inform Tsar Alexander confidentially that an attack upon either Austria or Germany would be regarded by these two powers as directed against both.[3]

Bismarck had good reason to anticipate trouble in the final negotiation of the treaty, for the draft as he had accepted it was directly contrary to what the

[1] Brauer, Marcks, Müller: *Erinnerungen an Bismarck* (Stuttgart, 1915), p. 333; Eduard Heller: *Das deutsch-österreichisch-ungarische Bündnis in Bismarcks Aussenpolitik* (Berlin, 1925), pp. 44 ff.
[2] Wertheimer: *Andrássy*, III, p. 284; see also *Die Grosse Politik*, III, Nos. 481 ff.
[3] *Die Grosse Politik*, III, No. 485. The Andrássy draft is printed in Heller, op. cit., pp. 126 ff.

Emperor desired and was clearly in conflict with the instructions which Bismarck had taken to Vienna. The struggle between the monarch and his minister reopened immediately upon the latter's return to Berlin. The chancellor was thoroughly exhausted and became very bitter as the discussion continued. The difficulties which rulers placed in the way of their ministers when the latter tried to serve their country almost tempted him to become a republican, he complained. His greatest task had always been to protect the Emperor against himself. Bismarck had always known in three minutes what he wanted, but the Emperor was always on the wrong tack and obstinately refused to be moved.[1]

While the Emperor William, at Baden-Baden, still resisted the importunities of his chancellor and the representatives of the foreign office who were in his entourage, Bismarck resorted to heroic measures. On September 28 he called a meeting of the ministers and explained the situation to them. It was one of his most masterly surveys of the European scene. Tracing the idea of an Austro-German alliance back to the days of 1866, he pointed out that the high tone of the Russian press had led him to suspect that some sort of agreement already existed between Russia and Austria. Andrássy had reassured him on this point and had expressed his willingness to conclude a defensive arrangement. An offensive-defensive agreement would have been undesirable, for it would have led to trouble with Italy and would have involved Austria in the Alsace-Lorraine question. But if the defensive agreement against Russia were not concluded, Austria might be driven into the arms of Russia or France and the coalition of the Seven Years' War might be revived. On the other hand, if an alliance were concluded with Austria, England would be brought to the side of the allied powers. The Emperor's opposition, he said, was quite unreasonable; he was misrepresenting the situation and maintaining that Bismarck wanted to conclude an alliance with Austria, England, and France against Russia. The chancellor then appealed to the ministers to support him in his determination to resign if the Emperor persisted. All those present upheld his decision and in this way supplied him with a powerful weapon against his sovereign.[2]

Bismarck himself refused to go to Baden-Baden to lay the situation before William, for he feared that the demands of respect would make it impossible for him to have his say. Letters would at least have to be read to the end, he said. But even the letters failed to convince the Emperor, whose firm opposition and forceful arguments were truly remarkable for a man of eighty-two. The points he made could not be wholly disregarded, for his position was, in many respects, well taken. He could not see why the alliance with Austria could not be extended to include Russia and in this way made to strengthen the Three

---

[1] Mittnacht: *Erinnerungen*, pp. 15 ff.; A. von Scholz: *Erlebnisse und Gespräche mit Bismarck* (Stuttgart, 1922), pp. 12 ff.

[2] The best account in Lucius, op. cit., pp. 173 ff. and in Radowitz, op. cit., II, pp. 99 ff. See also *Die Grosse Politik*, III, No. 487.

Emperors' League, which William still regarded as valid between Germany and Russia. In any case, he could not see why Germany should be obliged to support Austria if she were attacked by Russia, while Austria was not obliged to come to the assistance of Germany in the event of aggression by France. Bismarck, he thought, was relying altogether too much upon the continuance of the moderate Waddington régime in France. The real danger for Germany lay in the direction of France, and the conclusion of a separate agreement against Russia would be certain to bring Russia and France together.

Never in the seventeen years during which William and Bismarck had worked together had they found themselves so completely in conflict, not even during the critical days following Sadowa. The Emperor felt throughout that the chancellor was simply taking advantage of the Tsar's blunder in writing the famous letter of August 15, in order to force upon his master the alliance with Austria, which he had been preparing for some time. Even then, he said to Schweinitz, Andrássy had not gone half so far as Bismarck wished. But there was nothing to do. Bismarck threatened to resign, and the other ministers were ready to follow him. The Emperor had to yield, for, as he said, in the last count Bismarck was more necessary to Germany than he.[1] But he yielded step by step. When he finally agreed to the alliance with Austria, he insisted that the Tsar should be informed of it before it was signed. This, however, Andrássy refused to permit. It required what amounted to an ultimatum from Bismarck to induce the old ruler to give his consent on October 5. The treaty was signed on October 7 at Vienna, but even then the conflict between the Emperor and his chancellor continued. William insisted upon notifying the Tsar, now that the treaty had been signed, while Bismarck took the view that the agreement had no validity until ratified. In the end the Emperor had to yield on this point also, and the ratifications were exchanged on October 17, 1879.

The period between Bismarck's return from Vienna and the actual signing and ratifying of the pact was filled not only with the conflict just described, but also with two interesting episodes which are of more than academic interest and have a direct bearing on the development of the situation. The first of these concerned the relationship between Germany and England. The details are not entirely clear, but there is some evidence in the sources that the position of England occupied the attention of both Bismarck and Andrássy from the very beginning. The Austrian minister argued that he could not accept an agreement which appeared in any way directed against France, because England would be estranged by such a policy. Bismarck saw the force of the argument and referred repeatedly in his conversations to the fact that the alliance with Austria would bring England to the German side, even though indirectly. How seriously the German chancellor regarded this aspect of the problem of security may be deduced from the fact that, even before he went to Vienna, he

---

[1] Schweinitz: *Denkwürdigkeiten*, II, pp. 76-7. The Kaiser's criticisms appear clearly from his marginal notes on Bismarck's letter from Vienna (*Die Grosse Politik*, III, No.. 482).

had Count Münster, the German ambassador at London, informed of the situation by the foreign office. The ambassador was further instructed to approach Disraeli and elicit a statement of England's probable policy in the event that Germany became involved in a conflict with Russia through refusal to support the latter further in her Eastern policy. Only consideration for the interests of Austria and England could induce Germany to oppose the Russian desires in a question which did not directly touch German interests.[1]

Count Münster, who had been spending a vacation in Germany, hurried back to his post, but most of the English ministers were away from London, and it was only on September 26 that the ambassador was able to visit the English prime minister at Hughenden. We have reports of the conversation from both men, but the accounts diverge in many particulars, so that it is impossible to form a just estimate of what actually transpired. Each asserted that the other came forward with proposals of the gravest character. But certain facts stand out clearly enough and enable the historian to form a reasonably sound conclusion as to the general trend of the discussion. Münster enlarged upon the unsatisfactory state of Russian-German relations and recalled the earlier approaches of Bismarck to England, which were rejected by Lord Derby. Germany had, in this way, been thrown back upon the Three Emperors' League, but this combination had now become impossible. The Russian complaints of German policy were false and were mere pretexts: " Russia is preparing to attack Austria; the peace of the world will be disturbed; it is in the nature of things that it will not be a localized war; it will be a great and general war. Peace is necessary to Germany; no country desires or requires peace more. To secure it she proposes an alliance between Germany, Austria, and Great Britain." But before broaching this project to the Emperor, Bismarck desired to know what the reaction of Disraeli would be.

Disraeli received the suggestion very sympathetically. He admitted that England needed and desired allies, in order to be able to take an active part in European affairs. The policy of non-intervention had proved to be detrimental to England's real interests. " The most natural allies for England are Germany and Austria," he went on. He would gladly enter into an alliance with Germany. But the root of the matter lay in the attitude of France and the possibility of a Franco-Russian combination. Any step that would appear hostile to France would be viewed with suspicion in England.

Münster replied that Bismarck had foreseen this difficulty, but " that the alliance he contemplated would not be incompatible with cordial relations with France." In fact, German relations with France were of that description, and there was no danger of French aggression so long as the republican régime continued to maintain itself. Disraeli agreed to this and added that in any case France would not move against Germany if she knew that her action would bring England upon the scene. If England and Germany were united, " the

---

[1] *Die Grosse Politik*, IV, No. 710.

two leading features of such co-operation would naturally be, to guard Germany from such aggression, and to support in the Levant, and in the East generally, the policy and interests of England." " If Prince Bismarck is willing to help us in the Orient, and there the interests of England go hand in hand with those of Austria, we will guarantee that France shall not move, in case such a policy were to involve Germany in a conflict with Russia. We will in that case keep France quiet, you may depend upon us." [1]

The foregoing account has been collated from the reports of the two statesmen and represents the elements which these reports have in common. It is clear from what has been said that Münster, who was outspokenly Anglophil, had either consciously or unconsciously departed from the letter of his instructions. What Bismarck had desired was a statement of English policy in the event of a Russian-German conflict. Münster had allowed the conversation to depart from this simple question and drift into the domain of general Anglo-German relations, with special reference to France. The conversation had not supplied Bismarck with an answer to his question, and he noted upon Münster's report: " Is that all? " In replying to Münster, on October 8, he pointed out that the English statement was inadequate, and repeated that unless English aid were certain, Germany would have to avoid a conflict with Russia in matters concerning the Near East. Münster was not to take up the question again.[2]

The remarkable thing about the negotiation was the willingness of Disraeli to guarantee Germany against French attack if Germany became involved in war with Russia. He did, in fact, want the alliance with Germany and Austria, which fitted in very well with his general policy. Before 1878 the Three Emperors' League had been a veritable bugaboo to him, for it practically excluded England from the discussion of continental affairs. Now that the league was, to all intents and purposes, a thing of the past, he was quite prepared to turn the tables upon Russia and give English backing to an anti-Russian coalition. Before the conversation with Münster he had written to the Queen that he was not at all certain that Germany would come to the aid of Austria in the event of a Russian attack, because fear of France would deter her. " England may become dictator in this position." [3] If Münster had put Bismarck's question to Disraeli fairly and squarely, there can be little doubt that the English prime minister would have given a favourable reply. He was, in fact, more whole-heartedly behind the idea of an alliance with Germany than either the Queen or Lord Salisbury. The Queen was very anxious not to antagonize France: " If we ally ourselves with Germany and Austria, France

---

[1] Monypenny and Buckle, op. cit., VI, pp. 486–9 (Disraeli to the Queen, September 27, 1879); *Die Grosse Politik*, IV, No. 712 (Münster to Bismarck, September 27, 1879).

[2] *Die Grosse Politik*, IV, No. 713. By far the best discussion of this important episode is that of Hans Rothfels: *Bismarcks englische Bündnispolitik* (Berlin, 1924), pp. 45 ff. The divergent views and interpretations of historians are admirably summarized in Arnold O. Meyer: *Bismarcks Friedenspolitik* (Munich, 1930), Appendix I.

[3] Buckle: *Letters of Queen Victoria*, III (London, 1928), p. 46.

might join with Russia and Italy, which would be very serious." [1] Salisbury, on the other hand, could not entirely shake off his distrust of Bismarck. Is the German chancellor forcing the offensive upon Russia, as he had forced it upon others in the period before 1870, he asked. "It will be very difficult for us not to go to Austria's assistance if she is seriously attacked by Russia, no matter how the attack comes about." But what will be the effect upon England's relations to France? [2]

Disraeli's reply to the foreign minister's hesitation was quite characteristic. Even if Bismarck were playing his own game, he argued, this might be England's game as well, at the moment. After all, there was general apprehension of Russia in England. "I believe," he wrote, "that an alliance between the three powers in question, at this moment, might probably be hailed with something like enthusiasm by the country." It might be possible to come to an agreement with Germany and Austria on some specific matter, in order to conceal the larger purpose. [3]

In the meanwhile the English statesmen were waiting for a reply from Bismarck, which did not come. On October 13 Münster spoke to Salisbury of the German alliance with Austria, which was practically assured, and expressed the hope that England would approve and would use her influence to prevent France from joining Russia in any attack. But he did not get beyond generalities, and Disraeli became impatient. He suggested that Salisbury take the initiative and reopen the subject. The matter should be fathomed, even if it were necessary to scare Bismarck with the spectre of an eventual English-French-Russian combination. Salisbury thereupon invited Münster to Hatfield and discussed the situation with him. The ambassador could say nothing, except that he had never received a reply from Bismarck. Besides, Russia had poured water into her wine, and there was, therefore, no need to hurry. Salisbury then volunteered an expression of the English view-point: "That Austria's position in Europe was a matter in which we took deep interest, and considered essential: that, if Russia attacked Germany and Austria, Germany might rely on our being on her side. I said, 'I suppose the service you would want of us would be to influence France and Italy to observe neutrality.' He replied that was their object: that Metz and Strasburg made them tolerably safe from all attack on the south part of the frontier; but that they were open through Belgium and they wished to feel confident that we should not tolerate an attack through Belgium. Of that, I said, he might feel confident; and I was pretty sure that we could prevent any French Government from joining Russia against him; but that he might rely on our goodwill and assistance in the contingency of an attack on Austria and Germany." [4]

---

[1] Monypenny and Buckle, op. cit., VI, p. 489.   [2] Cecil: *Life of Salisbury*, II, p. 365.
[3] Monypenny and Buckle, op. cit., VI, pp. 489–90; Cecil, op. cit., II, p. 366.
[4] Monypenny and Buckle, op. cit., VI, pp. 490–1; Cecil, op. cit., II, pp. 367–8; *Die Grosse Politik*, IV, Nos. 714, 715.

No document reveals more clearly the distortion of the negotiations. Münster left the English under illusions as to Bismarck's aims and still maintained that it was the French aspect of the problem that interested the Germans primarily. The curious thing is that Salisbury voluntarily offered the assurance of English aid in case of a Russian attack upon Austria or Germany. This was exactly what the chancellor had originally desired, and yet nothing was done to take up the negotiations again or to develop them. The reasons why Bismarck should have opened the question and then dropped it are shrouded in mystery. The first step was apparently due to his fear that the pourparlers with Austria might become known in Russia and lead to an act of desperation. In other words, the original sounding was intended as a measure of precaution. But why were the negotiations dropped? No doubt Bismarck was disappointed by Münster's first report, but this was no reason why the discussion should have been discontinued.

Various explanations have been offered, some of which seem to be pertinent. We do not know when Münster's report of September 27 reached the chancellor, but at the meeting of the council of September 28 he spoke of England as supplementing the alliance with Austria: " England would be like a third member of the alliance, with or without a treaty." In other words, the need for a formal agreement with England no longer appeared to be pressing. Besides, it is possible that he lacked faith in the continuity of English policy, considering the constant party changes. Yet again, he was anxious to conduct the negotiations with his friend Disraeli, whom he knew to be sympathetic. But the English minister had insisted from the start that the foreign minister, Lord Salisbury, and the Queen should be initiated into the negotiations, and Münster had been obliged to give in on this point. That Bismarck was somewhat suspicious of Salisbury there can be no doubt. " Since the Congress of Berlin I distrust that obstinate and clumsy lay clergyman called Salisbury," he had said to the French minister some months before.[1] Possibly he may have feared that through Salisbury the negotiations might become known to the French and the Russians. It may also be that the pourparlers were discontinued because the chancellor, meeting with forceful opposition from the Emperor to a defensive alliance with Austria against Russia, realized that his master would never approve of an even more formidable coalition against his neighbour. He already suspected Bismarck of harbouring some such design and would certainly have fought the idea with the greatest vigour.

One other explanation that has been offered to clarify Bismarck's attitude in this important matter is worth mentioning. It has been suggested that the chancellor, knowing of Andrássy's objection to committing himself to a general treaty that would envisage France as well as Russia, decided to circumvent this difficulty by turning the tables on the Austrian minister. Andrássy argued that England would object to any agreement directed against France, and that Austria could not afford to estrange England. Bismarck therefore attempted to

---

[1] *Documents diplomatiques français*, II, No. 369; Bourgeois and Pagès, op. cit., p. 367.

bring England into the alliance, so that he could disprove Andrássy's statement. When he discovered, however, that the Austrian minister would not consent to a general defensive treaty in any case, the negotiations with England lost all point, and so he dropped them.[1]

The chief objection to this explanation is that it assumes that Bismarck really worked for an alliance which would apply to France as well as to Russia. Now, as a matter of fact, he put forward this idea because he knew that the Emperor was insistent on this point. Surely he would have liked some such agreement himself, but he appears to have been convinced that it was a hopeless desire. He did not exert himself to the utmost to bring Andrássy round, despite his arguments in that direction. After all, it will be recalled that even in the instructions to Münster there was talk of English support against Russia, not against France. And it must be remembered that German relations with France were at this time better than they had ever been since 1870. While Bismarck had talked for months about the necessity for making some arrangement to meet the challenge of the Russians, he never spoke of the need for an agreement to protect Germany against French attack. Quite the contrary; he loyally supported the French in their Tunisian policy and gave the utmost encouragement to the work of the Anglo-French combination in the Egyptian question. " I consider the alliance of France and England the best guarantee I could wish for the peace of Europe and the security of Germany," he had told the English ambassador in March 1879; " for the more closely you are united, the better chance we Germans have of enjoying good relations with you both." [2] That these were not empty words was shown by the whole history of German policy during this decisive year. Perhaps it would not be saying too much to assert that Bismarck dropped the negotiations with England because they threatened to take a more anti-French turn than he desired. This may seem incredible, but it does appear that at this particular time the English were less anxious to maintain the entente with France, which turned on the Egyptian question, than Bismarck was to have that combination continued.

Something can be said for all the explanations that have been discussed, but at bottom Bismarck's policy appears to have been determined by more immediate and simple considerations. He had sounded England because he feared the possibility of Russian action when the negotiations became known. But before any reply had been received from Münster, the situation had taken an unexpected turn. On September 27 the newly appointed Russian ambassador to Constantinople, Peter Saburov, arrived in Berlin, followed soon after by Prince Orlov, the Russian ambassador at Paris. Saburov had already discussed the international situation with Bismarck at Kissingen in July and August. He had at that time become convinced of the dangers of Russian policy. Through his

---

[1] This view is advanced and developed by S. Skazkin: *Konets avstro-russko-germanskogo soiuza* (Moscow, 1928), Volume I, pp. 94–102.

[2] *Documents diplomatiques français*, II, No. 390.

able memorandum to the Tsar he had helped to bring about a change of heart in Alexander. This initial success had been followed up with Saburov's visit to Livadia in September. In the course of long discussions the Russian diplomat had carried the council of ministers and the Tsar with him and had secured instructions for a new visit to Germany. The instructions hinged upon the danger of trouble in the Near East and the fear that Russia would find herself isolated. Of all possible allies Germany seemed the most promising, for Germany might serve as a check on the Austrian-English advance in Turkey. Russia could not allow the extension of Austrian influence beyond the provisions of the Treaty of Berlin; neither could she tolerate a permanent occupation of the Straits by England. If a conflict should arise between Russia and Austria, Germany could be of service to Russia by keeping the struggle localized. Similarly, in the event of a clash between England and Russia, Germany could deprive England of a continental ally by forcing Austria to remain neutral. The first step would be to sound Bismarck and to reassure him in regard to Russia's intentions.[1]

These instructions are of great interest, because they outline a complete policy and because they indicate the fundamental needs and desires which underlay the Russian position. When Saburov arrived in Berlin, Bismarck spoke sneeringly to his friends of the honeyed words which now emanated from Muscovite circles. This change of heart he attributed to the suspicion that Germany and Austria were about to conclude an agreement by which they guaranteed each other's territory. He was too much of a statesman, however, to deny the Russian diplomats a full hearing. In fact, he discussed the situation with Saburov for fully three hours and explained to him that the negotiations with Austria were the result of his nightmare of coalitions. It might be true that the famous letter of August 15 was merely the letter of a nephew to his uncle, " but it is a nephew whose every gesture represents a force of two million bayonets." It had therefore been necessary for him to make sure of Austria: "I wished to dig a ditch between her and the western powers," he said charitably. But now that Austria was prevented from taking arms against Russia, in company with the English and French, he would be glad to proceed to the re-establishment of the Three Emperors' League, " the only system offering the maximum of stability for the peace of Europe."

Saburov dealt with the delicate situation very adroitly. Recognizing the futility of arguing against the German-Austrian accord, he indicated the readiness of his government to accept such an understanding provided it were purely defensive. Indeed, Russia would be prepared to enter as a third party into a combination and promise to respect the territorial integrity of the Habsburg

---

[1] Simpson, op. cit., pp. 66 ff.; Skazkin, in his excellent monograph, used only the extracts from Saburov's memoirs, published in 1917–18, but he adds somewhat through the use of unpublished Russian material.

monarchy if the latter would promise not to extend her influence in the East beyond the provisions of the Treaty of Berlin, excepting with the consent of Russia.

The important thing for Saburov was to prepare the way for an agreement with Germany, and he therefore laid the emphasis rather upon other aspects of the European situation. Bismarck left no doubt that he would consider nothing beyond a defensive understanding, but he was ready to admit that Russian action in the Straits to prevent England from placing her sentinels there might be construed as a defensive action on Russia's part, " for an empire like Russia cannot let herself be cooped up by England in the Black Sea." In other words, the German chancellor indicated his readiness to support the Russians against the English in the Near East and in this way gave Saburov an opening to make more specific proposals. What Russia desired to avoid, said the Russian diplomat, was a war with England for control of the Straits. Her object was to prevent the occupation of the Straits by England, and all territorial changes in Turkey without the previous consent of Russia. In the same way the ultimate object of Germany must be to prevent a war with France for the recovery of Alsace and Lorraine. Germany's aim must be to leave France without an ally if she moved to attack Germany. Here, certainly, was the basis for an agreement. Germany could engage to remain neutral in an Anglo-Russian conflict and could promise to prevent, if need be by force, any other power from joining England. Russia, on the other hand, would agree to remain neutral in a war between France and Germany and would prevent any other power from joining France. Bismarck seemed to be quite taken with the idea and appeared anxious not to have the agreement put off. The details, of course, were left to further discussion.[1]

For Bismarck the Saburov mission was a great victory. He had argued with the Emperor and had tried to point out to him that the Austro-German alliance would bring the Russians round, and now his forecast had come true. Not that he had much faith in the assurances of the Russians. He still believed them liars. But he regarded a war with Russia as a serious calamity, no matter what the outcome, for there was nothing for Germany worth getting, even in case of victory. In crucial matters the chancellor generally had at least two strings to his bow. Therein lay his superiority as a statesman. So it was in this instance. While envisaging the possibility of drawing England to the side of Germany and Austria in the event of a Russian attack, he had, from the start, considered the possibility of Russia's revising her policy and returning to the system of the Three Emperors' League. What he wrote to the Emperor in this matter can hardly be taken as conclusive evidence, for it may have been intended simply to pacify the old man. But as early as September 14 he had told the ambassador

---

[1] Simpson, op. cit., pp. 70–83; Radowitz, op. cit., II, pp. 97–8, 102; Lucius, op. cit., p. 176; Wertheimer: *Andrássy*, III, pp. 292–3; Skazkin, op. cit., I, pp. 110 ff.

to Paris, Prince Hohenlohe, that his idea was to conclude a defensive alliance with Austria "inside the Three Emperors' League." [1]

He therefore received the Russian overtures with great cordiality. " The great powers of our time," he said to Orlov, " may be compared to travellers, unknown to each other, whom chance has brought together in the same railroad coupé. They watch each other, and when one of them puts his hand into his pocket, his neighbour gets ready his revolver in order to be able to fire the first shot." Orlov replied that the neighbour may only have wished to draw out his handkerchief, and that suspicion as well as lack of foresight may lead to error.[2] The chancellor, however, went on to complain of the Russian concentrations in Poland and of the reputed soundings in Paris. Asked whether he had gone to Vienna to conclude an offensive and defensive alliance against Russia, Bismarck replied that, on the contrary, he had gone in order to keep Austria from projects hostile to Russia. To Saburov he said: " I wanted to put a gulf between her [Austria] and the Western powers." He had found the Emperor Francis Joseph animated by the most friendly feelings towards Russia, and Austria and Germany had simply signed a protocol containing a mutual engagement not to take part in any menacing steps against Russia, if there should be disagreement between Russia and the powers who had signed the Treaty of Berlin. The League of the Three Emperors continued to exist, he said, so far as the Emperor William and the Tsar were concerned, and Francis Joseph desired nothing more than the resumption of the complete understanding between the three courts. The Three Emperors' League, he was convinced, was " the only system offering the maximum of stability for the peace of Europe." [3]

The Russian overtures were not followed up for the time being. Bismarck's desire, it appears, was to gain time until the situation had calmed down and until Europe had had an opportunity to accustom itself to the new Austro-German combination. The Emperor wrote to the Tsar on October 20 indicating what had taken place and making it perfectly clear that if the revolutionary plans of the Panslavists and Nihilists were to lead the Russian government into difficulties with other countries, the Tsar would find " solidarity of resistance " in Austria and Germany. Alexander's reply was anxiously awaited in Berlin, but it turned out to be extremely moderate. Bismarck's discussions with Saburov and Orlov had evidently made a deep impression upon the Tsar, who wrote to his uncle, the German Emperor, that his personal confidence had not been shaken by what had taken place, and that he was happy to say that there was nothing in the political transaction between Germany and Austria that was contrary to his desires. In associating himself with the accord arrived at by Germany and Austria he desired to regard it as a return to the complete

---

[1] Hohenlohe, op. cit., II, p. 274.
[2] *Krasny Arkhiv*, I (1922), pp. 86 ff.
[3] *Krasny Arkhiv*, I (1922), pp. 86 ff.; J. Y. Simpson, op. cit., loc. cit.

understanding between the three Emperors, which had rendered such great service to Europe.[1]

In other directions the chancellor was no less lavish in his assurances. Both he and Andrássy had been very anxious not to antagonize the French, and during the negotiations at Vienna Bismarck had made the most solemn declarations to the French ambassador that there was nothing hostile to France in the plans of Austria and Germany.[2] Later on, Bismarck continued his efforts to quiet the apprehensions of his neighbour. To Saint-Vallier in November he gave a detailed if somewhat coloured and distorted account of what had transpired, assuring him that the steps taken were absolutely limited to Russia and did not envisage any other power, least of all France, so long as France had at her head a government composed of statesmen in whom Germany had complete confidence. What Germany desired above all things was peace. She was entirely in sympathy with the Anglo-French entente, for England in strengthening France also restrained her, and France, in her turn, acted as a check on England: "Our agreement with Austria, to my mind, is the complement of your agreement with England." [3]

While reassuring the French and mollifying the Russians, Bismarck was careful to avoid either estranging or encouraging the English in any way. When Lord Salisbury, in his speech at Manchester on October 16, referred to the reports of a defensive alliance between Germany and Austria as " good tidings of great joy " to all who valued the peace of Europe and the independence of nations, he brought down upon himself not only the criticism of those who resented his irreverence, but also the anger of Bismarck. It was not his idea that Russia should be enraged by having the new arrangements flaunted before her. This was made quite clear when Baron Haymerlé, Andrássy's successor at the Austrian foreign office, proposed that England be asked to " support " the principles of the alliance. The German chancellor objected to this procedure, on the plea that it would estrange Russia. Indeed, it was the Austrian government which first communicated the fact of the alliance to the English foreign minister on October 27. Salisbury stated in reply that the agreement would be received in England with " great gratification " as a pledge of peace.[4]

Looking back, during the last months of the year 1879, Bismarck saw the whole development of this crucial period as a perfectly logical and inevitable one. Speaking to Lord Dufferin in December, he explained how the agreement with Austria had brought about a complete change of heart in the Russians. Saburov had come to him assuring him that the new arrangement was the thing he most desired. " He could not have been more affectionate had we been about to marry our son and daughter," said Bismarck. He had explained to

[1] Die Grosse Politik, III, Nos. 509, 512; Wertheimer: Andrássy, III, pp. 294 ff.
[2] Documents diplomatiques français, II, Nos. 467, 468; Wertheimer: Andrássy, III, p. 308.
[3] Documents diplomatiques français, II, No. 476; Chaudordy: La France en 1889, pp. 268 ff.
[4] Cecil, op. cit., II, pp. 369–70; Monypenny and Buckle, op. cit., VI, p. 491.

the Russian ambassador frankly about his visit to Vienna and had said to him: "I regarded you as a dear friend with whom I was taking a solitary walk and who suddenly had gone mad. I rushed off to provide myself with a pocket pistol, and now I am come back to continue my walk with you in the same amicable manner, but in a more comfortable state of mind as to my own safety." [1] In other words, the alliance with Austria was entirely precautionary and did not imply hostility to anyone. Bismarck had supplied himself with this weapon to defend himself, if need be, against his demented Russian friend. He was now ready to continue on his previous course, which lay along the road of the Three Emperors' League. In the West he looked to the friendship of England to protect him against eventual danger from France, just as in the East he relied upon the connexion with Austria to keep the Russians in order. England could help to preserve the peace by continuing her entente with France, and Germany, too, hoped to maintain cordial relations with her neighbour. "As long as we are friends and act together in the East," he told Lord Dufferin, "France is unlikely to fall into the hands of Russia, but if we shake her off like a woman of doubtful virtue, into the arms of Russia she will go."

These conversations are of more than passing interest, because they illustrate the evolution of the Bismarckian policy. Here was one of those rare statesmen who could view a given situation from all conceivable angles and adjust his own actions to meet a large variety of contingencies. In speaking to Andrássy one side of the problem was stressed, while in the discussions with the Emperor other aspects were set into high relief. In conversation with the Russians he represented the ultimate goal of his efforts as the re-establishment of the Three Emperors' League, the "triangular rampart" that was to maintain the peace of the continent and uphold conservative principles against revolutionary agitation. The French and the English, on the other hand, found the chancellor emphasizing the need for a dam to hold in check the rising tide of Panslavism and Nihilism and heard him dilate on the need for maintaining the Anglo-French entente, an arrangement which would deter each of its members from dangerous adventures. It will not do to accept any one of Bismarck's statements as the true exposition of his policy. What he aimed at was rather a system of checks and balances. Germany desired peace, because she had nothing to gain by war and needed peace to consolidate what she had gained by war in the past. But Germany lay embedded in the very heart of Europe. Any war between the great powers would, almost of necessity, involve her sooner or later. Therefore Bismarck desired peace for the continent. If England or any other power liked to have a little "sporting" war or two in distant parts, that was one thing. An Afghan conflict or a native rising in Zululand left the German chancellor quite unmoved. What concerned him was the continent and the

---

[1] Sir Alfred Lyall: *The Life of the Marquis of Dufferin and Ava* (London, 1905), I, p. 305. The same story, with variations, in Hohenlohe, op. cit., II, p. 280, and in Schweinitz: *Denkwürdigkeiten*, II, p. 80.

questions that reacted upon the continental situation. But throughout he aimed at holding the balance between West and East and at upholding the commanding position of Germany by playing off the one against the other.

The Austrian-German Alliance of 1879 lay almost in the nature of things. It was, for example, the logical completion of the work of German unification begun in the 1860's. The solution may not have been ideal, but it was the only feasible one, and it once more established the German bloc in central Europe, prepared to hold the inner lines against attack, as in the days of the German Confederation. In a short time the new combination was to become the kernel of the whole Bismarckian system. Till the collapse of the Habsburg and Hohenzollern empires in 1918 it was to continue unchanged. All other arrangements centred about it. It was the very mainspring of the Bismarckian and Wilhelminian policy. That it met the desires of the Germans in both empires there can be no doubt, for it fulfilled as well as possible the old dream of the Great Germany of 1848. Of course it was not above criticism. The Emperor William in 1879 pointed out some of its fundamental weaknesses and foresaw some of its defects. It may be questioned whether the situation in 1879 justified so radical a departure from the earlier Bismarckian policy of a free hand, and whether there was sufficient justification for so far-reaching an innovation. What cannot be denied is that the Russian Tsar and his advisers had more or less run amuck and were, for the moment at least, a menace to the peace of Europe. The concentration of large masses of troops, the merciless press warfare were characteristic of the new age and made the situation more critical and dangerous. That Bismarck had long envisaged something like a return to the defensive arrangement provided for by the defunct constitution of the German Confederation is reasonably clear. He saw Europe in ferment and observed the nations gravitating into various constellations. Germany could not afford to stay out, so he seized the first opportunity to realize his plans and anticipate those of the other powers. He certainly appreciated the inner weakness of the Habsburg monarchy, but as between Russia and Austria was there much to choose? The Tsarist Empire in 1879 seemed nearer revolution and dissolution than did the Habsburg Empire, for it was racked with revolutionary movements and social unrest. Very likely the chancellor appreciated also the danger of Germany's becoming involved in the problems of Austrian policy in the Near East. But he argued that Austria, as the weaker of the allied powers, could be led by Germany; and, after all, an alliance with Russia would almost certainly have raised the same question, for the Tsar would have had no interest in an agreement which did not involve some sort of support for Russian aspirations in the Balkans. There is really little use in applying hind-sight to problems of this kind. For Bismarck the alliance of 1879 was not only logical, but necessary. That he built upon it an imposing system of international agreements which preserved the peace of Europe for many long years is a fact that cannot be argued away.

The conclusion of the alliance with Austria left Bismarck in something of a dilemma. His relations with England were very good and the Franco-German tension had all but disappeared. With the close friendship of England and Austria the Russians were, in point of fact, effectively isolated, and Germany had become more or less identified with the western powers. But Bismarck was embarrassed by the advances of the Russians, who were fully cognizant of the dangers of the situation and were anxious to continue the discussions begun by Saburov in September 1879. The constant dread of an English attack on the Straits almost forced upon the Russians the desire for an agreement with Germany, the only power which could prevent England from finding a continental ally.[1] This pressure from the Russian side Bismarck could not afford to ignore, for large numbers of troops were concentrated in Poland, and the chancellor could not forget that his eastern neighbour was a formidable military power. During the first months of 1880 there was not a little acrimonious debate between the Russian and German governments in respect to these concentrations, and there was some fear that war might result from the unwillingness of the Tsar to relocate his forces. Bismarck admitted that the concentrations had little military significance, but laid stress on the psychological aspect of the problem.[2]

In the very midst of these acrid disputes the Russian advances were resumed by Saburov, who discussed the bases of an agreement with Bismarck in a series of important conferences between January 31 and February 7, 1880. The German and the Russian accounts of these conversations vary considerably in the details, but certain points stand out clearly enough. In the first place, Bismarck had evidently lost interest in the idea of a Russian-German treaty designed to protect the two contracting powers against coalitions. Such an arrangement, he pointed out, might in certain eventualities involve an attack upon Austria. If news of such an understanding were to become known in Vienna, it would result in a revival of Austrian fear and distrust. " Austria will instinctively begin anew to seek Western alliances, and the results so laboriously secured by Germany will be lost." Russia should realize that it would not be in her interest to embroil Germany and Austria: " You too often lose sight of the importance of being one of *three* on the European chess-board. That is the invariable objective of all the cabinets, and of mine above all others. Nobody wishes to be in a minority. All politics reduce themselves to this formula: to try to be one of three, so long as the world is governed by the unstable equilibrium of five great powers. That also is the true preservative against coalitions." For example, when Gorchakov had once entertained the idea of a close entente with England, the German chancellor, so he said, would have been willing to join as a third. But he had become convinced that the scheme was chimerical. The antagonism between England and Russia in the Near East was still too acute. In the meanwhile he

---

[1] Simpson, op. cit., pp. 88 ff. (Saburov memorandum on the Straits question).

[2] Simpson, op. cit., pp. 97–105; Schweinitz: *Denkwürdigkeiten*, II, pp. 92–108; *Letters of Queen Victoria*, III, p. 74.

had become converted to the idea of a triple entente between Germany, Russia, and Austria.

Saburov denied that Russia harboured designs hostile to Austria, or that he intended to propose any aggressive combination. Though he apparently accepted the idea of a triple entente, he clearly would have preferred the separate agreement with Germany which had originally been proposed. After all, the chief problem for Russia centred upon the question of the Straits. The point at issue was one of Russian-English relations rather than one of Russian-Austrian. Since the English declaration at the Berlin Congress Russia was exposed to the danger of having an English squadron appear in the Black Sea whenever the English government chose to send it. In the event of war between Russia and England would the Turkish government have the right, as a neutral power, to allow an English fleet to enter the Black Sea? Bismarck thought not, for the Straits were so narrow that, in his opinion, they would have to be regarded as territorial waters, which Turkey, as a neutral, could not allow to be violated. In other words, Bismarck was prepared to accept the Russian view on the Straits question, but he still showed the same hesitancy about making this the basis for a separate agreement between Russia and Germany. Saburov, on the other hand, was ready to consider the inclusion of Austria in the agreement, provided Russia could secure her interests in the Straits. But he preferred an understanding with Germany and avoided showing much enthusiasm for the Bismarckian solution. The chancellor, anxious lest he had appeared too eager, closed the conversation by expressing doubt whether an arrangement could be come to with a timid minister like Haymerlé, the successor of Andrássy, or with Gorchakov, who was still nominally Russian minister for foreign affairs.

In the second important conference between the two men, on February 5, Bismarck returned with more vigour to the idea of a triple understanding. Even Russia's objectives — protection against coalitions and maintenance of the principle of the closure of the Straits — could be more easily attained by including Austria in the bargain. In a treaty between Germany and Russia alone, Germany would be able to bind herself only against France, not against Austria. To be sure, no real coalition could be built up against Russia unless France were a party to it, so that a German promise to keep France out of a coming struggle would give Russia " moral certainty " that a coalition would not be possible. " But the mathematical certainty will only be secured by attracting Austria into this system. Forming a permanent coalition ourselves, we shall have no fear of one against us." The same arguments would apply to the Straits problem: " What will Germany be able to do by herself to prevent the violation of the Straits? She can protest, write notes, but her army will not be able to swim to London or pass over the body of Austria to go to fight in the Straits. The question changes in aspect if one can interest Austria in it. She is in a better position to threaten Turkey and compel her, in concert with Russia, to fulfil her obligations of neutrality." Saburov saw the uselessness of arguing the point and therefore confined himself to the remark that his instructions did not envisage an agreement to include Austria, and that he would have to refer home. He left with Bismarck a memorandum setting forth the Russian view of the Straits question and agreed to draw up a tentative project of agreement between the three powers.

The draft in question was handed to the chancellor on the following day. It defined the objectives of the three powers as follows: for Russia, to obtain security in the Black Sea; for Austria, for the present, to assure herself of the new position she had gained in the Near East; for the future, the certainty that no changes should be made in the *status quo* of Turkey in Europe without her consent; for Germany, to establish on a permanent basis a European system favourable to her security and to the maintenance of peace; for all three powers, a guarantee against the danger of coalitions. These principles were to find expression in the recognition of the Russian view of the Straits conventions. The three powers would concert measures to prevent an infraction of the Straits agreements by the Turkish government. In the second place, Russia would recognize the position acquired by Austria in the Near East, and the three powers would agree that no modifications should be made in the territorial *status quo* of Turkey without their consent. Finally, the contracting powers would promise each other benevolent neutrality if one of them became involved in war, and would see to the localization of the conflict.

Bismarck approved of the project in a general way, but expressed the desire for a provision for mediation in the event of a dispute between any two members of the entente. He thought also that, out of consideration for Austria, the Straits problem should not be pushed so far into the forefront. On the whole, however, he saw here the possibility of an understanding the object of which would be to protect the " flabby parts " of the three empires. A tentative agreement having been reached between the two negotiators, Saburov left for St. Petersburg to lay the new proposals before his government.[1]

At the Russian foreign office there was considerable difference of opinion as to what should be done about Bismarck's proposals. The old chancellor, Prince Gorchakov, took no part in the discussions. His first assistant, Giers, lacked the necessary authority to enforce his own view-point. The conflict was one between Saburov and the powerful war minister, Miliutin. Of the two Saburov favoured a more active policy. Russia, he argued, should embark upon an aggressive policy in central Asia, in order to divert England from the Near East. Austria, left to her own resources, would then be willing to come to an agreement with Russia, especially if favourable terms were offered. According to Saburov, the interests of Russia in the Near East were of a double nature. The problem of security in the Black Sea brought her face to face with England, while the desire to emancipate the southern Slavs led to conflict with Austria. Much had been done for the Balkan Slavs during the recent wars, and, since Russia could

---

[1] These discussions are dealt with at length in Simpson: *The Saburov Memoirs*, pp. 110–122, and in Skazkin, op. cit., pp. 132 ff. For the German side see *Die Grosse Politik*, III, Nos. 515–18.

not pursue both aims at the same time, this aspect of her policy should be relegated, for the time being, into the background. " In other words," he said, " let us be less Slav and more Russian." " As soon as our policy ceases to be inspired by Pán-Slav ideas," he wrote somewhat later, " I believe we can be satisfied if we succeed in assuring the independence of the small states already created or to be created in the Balkans. . . . Within these limits everything that we can accord Austria in the way of advantages to her political and commercial influence in these countries will be for us so many means for disinteresting her in the purely Russian side of the Eastern question, as the late Emperor Nicholas, of glorious memory, defined it when he demanded for Russia the key to her house." Therefore an agreement should be made with Austria based on the delimitation of spheres of influence in the Balkans: Constantinople for Russia, Salonika for Austria, as suggested by Bismarck. Once England had been diverted to central Asia, and Austria had been disinterested, it would be easy to conclude an alliance with Turkey which would restore the system of Nicholas I, the system of the Treaty of Unkiar Skelessi (1833) and what amounted to a Russian protectorate.

This view was vigorously combated by Miliutin, who was opposed to any forward policy and objected to abandoning the Balkan Slavs to either Austria or Turkey. Russia's immediate aim, he believed, should be to secure from Germany and Austria a guarantee against the disturbance of the *status quo* or any infringement of it by England. As an eventual solution of the Eastern question Miliutin envisaged a Balkan confederation to include not only the Slavic states, but also Roumania, Albania, Greece, and even the Adrianople vilayet of Turkey, with Constantinople. The Sea of Marmora and the Straits could be neutralized and placed under international control.

Miliutin's policy was clearly determined by the unpreparedness of Russia in a military sense and by the acute fear of action by England. These considerations were so important that even Saburov could not ignore them. It was therefore decided to secure the support of Germany and if possible of Austria for the maintenance of the principle of closure of the Straits as an international obligation. If Bismarck could bring the Austrians to accept the Russian view in this matter, so much the better. If, on the other hand, the Austrians refused to come into the entente, Bismarck would be angry with them: " The seed of distrust will have been sown, and Germany, by a natural reaction, will once more remove the principal centre of her political affinities from Vienna to St. Petersburg." In other words, Russia had everything to gain and nothing to lose by acceptance of the Bismarckian formula.[1]

Once this decision had been reached, Saburov hastened back to Berlin with the consent of the Tsar for the negotiation of an *entente à trois*. But he found the German chancellor preoccupied. Bismarck was not ready to be stampeded

---

[1] Skazkin, op. cit., pp. 132–45, 155; Simpson: *The Saburov Memoirs*, pp. 123–7.

by the Russians and was anxious not to compromise his relations with other powers. After his conversations with Saburov early in February, he had spoken to one of his military friends, General Waldersee, in a way that revealed his difficulties. He was firmly determined, he said, never again to make a separate agreement with Russia. A triple agreement might, however, be considered. But of triple agreements he would still prefer one with Austria and England to one with Russia and Austria. The relations with England were very good, and England would be ready to attack Italy if the latter were to turn against Austria.[1] In other words, German policy had become identified with that of the western powers to such an extent that Bismarck saw no real advantage in a reorientation, especially as he distrusted the Russian military party and was uneasy about the concentrations in Poland. Then again, the attitude of the Austrians had to be taken into account. Bismarck had been urging Haymerlé to take a very strong stand against the violent irredentist agitation in Italy. He could not forgive the Italians for having lent a sympathetic ear to the Russian advances in August 1879 and denounced them as trouble-makers. " They have such a large appetite," he said, " and such poor teeth." [2]

But Haymerlé had resolutely refused to adopt the menacing attitude which Bismarck recommended. To clear the situation he sent his friend Count Kálnoky to Berlin. The Austrian diplomat arrived in the German capital on February 7, just as Saburov was leaving for St. Petersburg. He urged the view of his government upon Bismarck and pointed out that the policy of Vienna was to let the Italian problem come to a head. Austria's chief purpose, he went on, was still "the permanent blocking of Russia." This involved, quite naturally, the maintenance of close relations with England. In fact, Haymerlé proposed that England should be further initiated into the Austro-German alliance " in order to obtain promises or declarations pledging England, in case of a conflict with Russia . . . to use her direct pressure, or, should occasion arise, a naval demonstration to prevent Italy from attacking us." Bismarck's viewpoint was diametrically opposed to that of the Austrians. For him the Italians were like jackals who, " with furtive glance, rove restlessly hither and thither, instinctively drawn on by the odour of corruption and calamity — always ready to attack anybody from the rear and make off with a bit of plunder." They should, he thought, be reprimanded and humiliated. Threats of the restoration of the temporal power of the Pope or of the Bourbons would serve the purpose. As for England, there would be no use in making further advances. England would hold Italy in check in any case.[3]

Bismarck's own uncertainty and the wide divergence between his views and

---

1 Waldersee: *Denkwürdigkeiten*, I, pp. 200 ff.

2 See the evidence in W. L. Langer: " The European Powers and the French Occupation of Tunis " (*American Historical Review*, January 1926, p. 253), and *Documents diplomatiques français*, II, Nos. 369, 440.

3 A. F. Pribram: *The Secret Treaties of Austria-Hungary, 1879–1914*, II, pp. 5–6.

those of the Austrians threatened to place him in a very awkward position. But the general European situation was suddenly and completely changed by the fall of the Conservative ministry in England and the advent of Gladstone and the Liberals to power (April 1880). The new prime minister's views on foreign politics were perfectly well known. He had denounced the policy of his predecessor in the Near East in the most unequivocal terms, and had no sympathy for the Turks. If anything, he was inclined to co-operate with the Russians in furthering the cause of the smaller nations of the Balkans. Furthermore, his lack of sympathy for the Habsburg monarchy had just been published to the world in the most extraordinary manner. In an election speech at Edinburgh on March 17 he had declared that "Austria has been the unflinching foe of freedom in every country of Europe. . . . There is not an instance — there is not a spot upon the whole map where you can lay your finger and say: ' There Austria did good.' "

Of Gladstone's hopes and desires there could be no doubt. Bismarck feared that the overturn in England would lead to much unrest in Europe and would give rise to false hopes in Russia and among the small nations of southern and eastern Europe. He already saw Gladstone stirring up revolution in all the corners of Europe, wrote Saburov.[1] But on second thought he recognized that the dangers of the situation should not be overemphasized. The interests of a country like England were too great to make a serious diversion of policy possible. England's policy must always be determined by her anxiety for India and by the necessity of keeping open the road to the East. Even if England and Russia were to come to an agreement, and Italy were to join them, this combination would not seriously endanger Germany, for it would menace the French position in the Mediterranean and might lead to an understanding of France with Austria and even Germany. Germany could offer something — not Alsace-Lorraine, but something else, he was not sure what. At any rate, France and Austria could easily effect an understanding at Italy's expense.[2]

With his usual alertness Bismarck began to examine the change of front with a view to extracting some good from it. Fortunately for him the French and Russian governments had just fallen out, because of the refusal of the French to arrest Hartmann, who was accused of the attempt to blow up the Tsar's train in 1879. In this way the danger of a Franco-Russian understanding was removed, at least for the time being. As for the English side, it was clear that Lord Granville, the new foreign minister, would act as a brake on the aspirations of his chief, and that the cooling of Anglo-Austrian relations would make Haymerlé more tractable in regard to an agreement with Russia. To the Austrian minister's objection that support of the Russian policy in the Straits would be contrary to English interests and would therefore spoil the chances

---

[1] Simpson, op. cit., p. 128.

[2] E. C. Corti: *Alexander von Battenberg* (Vienna, 1920), pp. 91–2; Busch: *Bismarck, Some Secret Pages of his History* (London, 1898), II, pp. 430–1.

of an alliance with England, the German chancellor replied that the latter could no longer be regarded as a possible ally, and that in any case the Russian desires in the Straits were purely defensive.[1]

Bismarck's estimate of the probable course of English policy turned out to be correct. From the start Granville wrote to the Queen that he would " impress upon Russia that while we wished to be on good terms with her, we could not make any concessions, which perhaps they might expect." " The policy of the Government," he explained, " is to press, in concert with Europe, for the full execution of the conditions of the Treaty of Berlin." [2] Gladstone was induced to write what amounted to an apology to the Austrian government for his past utterances, and Lord Odo Russell was instructed to communicate to Bismarck the desire for continued close relations with Germany as well as the approval of the new English government of the alliance between Germany and Austria. Bismarck accepted this declaration for what it was worth, but indicated to the English ambassador that he would be willing to re-establish the Three Emperors' League if the peace party were to regain the ascendancy in Russia. Russell reported that since the fall of the Conservative ministry the German chancellor had been lending a more favourable ear to the Russian approaches, though he preferred England as an ally.[3]

But the immediate effect of the political overturn in England was that the Russian-German negotiations were shelved for several months, pending the clarification of the international situation. During the summer of 1880 the attention of the European foreign offices was concentrated on the Near Eastern question and the attempt of the English government to enlist the support of the powers for a policy of coercing Turkey into making the territorial concessions to Montenegro and Greece which had been provided for by the Treaty of Berlin. The details of the dispute need not be entered into here. So far as Montenegro was concerned, the question hinged upon the opposition of Albanian tribes to their proposed transfer. Religious as well as racial differences played a part in the conflict, which was waged on the one side by the Montenegrins, on the other by the so-called Albanian League, a union of tribes which was probably encouraged by the Ottoman government. In the Greek question greater territories were at stake, for the Greeks demanded Epirus and Thessaly, while the Turks temporized and resisted the cessions envisaged by the Treaty of Berlin. Efforts of the powers to mediate had ended in failure, and by the summer of 1880 there was serious danger of war between the Greeks and the Turks. A conflict in that part of the world was always a dangerous thing and a menace to the general peace of Europe.

The first move on the part of the Gladstone government was to propose a

---

[1] Simpson, op. cit., pp. 132–5.
[2] *Letters of Queen Victoria*, III, pp. 90, 93.
[3] Morley: *Life of Gladstone*, III, p. 8; Fitzmaurice: *Life of Lord Granville*, II, pp. 209, 211–12; *Die Grosse Politik*, IV, No. 716.

conference to settle these two thorny questions. The conference actually met at Berlin on June 16 and finally came to an agreement regarding the solution of the matter. It was decided that Montenegro should receive the town of Dulcigno and a strip of coast-line in lieu of the disputed territory. This settlement, however, proved to be no more successful than the arrangements suggested earlier, so that in September the powers joined in a naval demonstration off the coast at Dulcigno. The demonstration came to nothing, for the Turks refused to budge, and the Montenegrins, who were outnumbered, did not dare attack. Of the powers, only England and Russia were prepared for coercive measures. Bismarck had made it clear from the start that the German government, while willing to show the German flag, would not participate in an aggressive action. The result was that the concert of Europe became a laughing-stock, and the powers might as well have sent six washing-tubs with flags attached to them, to borrow an expression of Lord Salisbury. The question dragged on for some weeks while the English were attempting to win over the other powers to a policy of coercion. Gladstone suggested the occupation of the customs houses at Smyrna, and there was even some talk of sending the fleet to the Dardanelles or to the Golden Horn. But the Queen was unalterably opposed to any move that might lead to war with the Turks, and Austria's objections to further pressure were supported by both Germany and France. The danger of complications was so great, and Bismarck appears to have dreaded a possible Anglo-Russian-Italian combination so much, that he exercised all his great influence at Constantinople to induce the Sultan to yield. It was not until the end of November, however, that a Turkish force under Dervish Pasha subdued the forces of the Albanian League, which threatened to become dangerous for the Turkish government itself. Dulcigno was then handed over to the Montenegrins.[1]

While these events were taking place, the negotiations between Germany and Russia were resumed. Bismarck was clearly alarmed by the turn of affairs and by the readiness of the English to play into the hands of the Muscovites. Time and again he spoke of Gladstone as a " crazy professor " and included him as a player in the " revolutionary quartet on the G string," of which Gorchakov, Garibaldi, and Gambetta were the other members.[2] He therefore, in August, summoned Prince Hohenlohe, the secretary for foreign affairs, to Kissingen and gave him instructions for reopening the discussions with Saburov. An accord between Russia and Austria in Eastern affairs, he said, was essential. This agreement would have to secure for Russia a favourable settlement of the Straits question. The Turks would have to be enticed into accepting such a

[1] The best general account is that of Sax: *Geschichte des Machtverfalls der Türkei*, pp. 463–71. See also Busch: " Die Durchführung der Berliner Kongressakte, 1880–1881 " (*Deutsche Rundschau*, CXLVII, pp. 222–48, May 1911); Arthur D. Elliot: *The Life of George Joachim Goschen* (New York, 1911), I, pp. 200–3; Fitzmaurice: *Life of Granville*, II, pp. 216–21; Simpson, op. cit., pp. 156–60.

[2] Conversations with Cohen (Bismarck: *Gesammelte Werke*, VIII, pp. 378–90, *passim*).

solution, which, after all, would be the best safe-guard of Turkish sovereignty. But the Porte would first have to yield on the Montenegrin question, accept the union of Bulgaria and Eastern Roumelia, and recognize the definitive surrender of Bosnia and Herzegovina.[1]

It should be noted that Bismarck had now decided to extend the basis of the discussion, his reason being, apparently, to quiet the fears of the Austrians and make them more favourably disposed. In the first days of September the chancellor received Baron Haymerlé, the Austrian foreign minister, at Friedrichsruh and immediately took up the plan which he had already suggested to Saburov. He was able to tell Haymerlé that the Russians had no idea of hastening the union of Bulgaria and Eastern Roumelia, and succeeded in extracting from his Austrian colleague the statement that the Austrian government might eventually agree to the union. On the other hand, Haymerlé showed little interest in the problem of the eventual annexation of Bosnia and Herzegovina. Austria, he said, regarded these two provinces as irrevocably hers, whatever the form of her tenure. What interested him chiefly was to check the Bulgarian propaganda in Macedonia, which would lead in the end to war with the Turks and eventual Russian intervention.[2]

The substance of Haymerlé's remarks was communicated to Saburov, who suggested to his government a conciliatory reply: the eventual union of Bulgaria and Eastern Roumelia should not extend to Macedonia, and Russia would be willing to join Austria in making remonstrances against Bulgarian propaganda in Macedonia, if that should become necessary. The Russian government was determined not to extend the provision of the Treaty of Berlin relating to the Sanjak of Novi-Bazar, the narrow passage between Montenegro and Serbia which the Austrians had the right to garrison, but not to administer. Nothing was said of this in the Russian reply, because the object of the negotiations was to establish points of agreement rather than points of divergence.[3]

Bismarck's stand had become more definite since the Dulcigno demonstration had clarified the English policy. Gladstone, supported by the radicals in his party, had taken the lead in an action which might end with war against Turkey and the eventual collapse or partition of the empire. No matter what the conditions under which this conflict was waged, it would be contrary to the interests of Austria and indirectly deleterious to the position of Germany. If the Ottoman Empire were to break up, Bismarck told the English ambassador in October, his own solution of the problem would be a peaceful division of influence in the Balkans between Austria and Russia. The former should have the preponderant influence in the western half of the peninsula, as far as the Ægean, while the latter should have a free hand in the eastern half, as far as the Straits. Germany could act as mediator between the two. As for England, her interests

---

[1] Simpson, op. cit., p. 143.
[2] Simpson, op. cit., pp. 145–7; Die Grosse Politik, III, No. 520.
[3] Simpson, op. cit., pp. 147–55; Skazkin, op. cit., pp. 139 ff.

were in Egypt and Asia, and those of France were in Syria and Tunis. An illuminating statement indeed, which indicates the extension of the program of 1878 and is one of Bismarck's earliest suggestions of a peaceful division of influence in the Balkans, an idea which was to become the guiding principle of his Near Eastern policy during the next decade.[1]

But Bismarck, though he considered the eventual disruption of the Ottoman Empire, was sincerely anxious to avoid a premature catastrophe. He desired the maintenance of peace and especially the avoidance of a conflict between Austria and Russia. It was therefore necessary to encourage the moderate element in Russia, of which Saburov was the representative, and to strengthen it against the Pan-Slav and revolutionary element, which would embark on subversive agitation against Austria in the Balkans and might in the end ally itself with French republicanism and Italian, Spanish, or even English radicalism.[2] He therefore warned the English, indirectly, not to reckon on hostility between Germany and Russia. He told Lord Odo Russell that " he wished to remain, as in the past, the friend of Russia; that his alliance with Austria offered no hindrance to this, and that he intended, if the case arose, to support very fully the interests that Russia possesses in the Eastern question." [3]

In order to put his plans into effect, the German chancellor invited Saburov to visit him at Friedrichsruh late in November. The conversation began in a general way, Bismarck recalling his discussions with Haymerlé, who " seemed like a schoolboy impatient to get out of school " and who evidently feared losing the Austrian monopoly of German friendship. But Germany had an interest in Russia as well as in Austria: " Our interest demands that neither Russia nor Austria should be *completely* crippled. Their existence as Great Powers is equally necessary to us." If there were perspicacious statesmen at Vienna, he " would not have hesitated to draw on the map of Europe a line of demarcation between the interests of Austria and ours [Russia's], and that to the satisfaction of both parties," Saburov reported him as saying. But Haymerlé was timid, and therefore Russia and Germany would have to be content with an entente which would keep Austria from joining a new coalition like that of the Crimean War. " I flatter myself," continued the German statesman, " on having been the first, in Europe, to break with that old tradition with which the western powers have inoculated all the cabinets: namely, that Constantinople in the hands of Russia would be a European danger. I consider that a false idea, and I do not see why an English interest must become a European interest." [4]

The two men then took out the project of a triple agreement, which had been drawn up in February and which had been approved by the Tsar. With

---

[1] Fitzmaurice: *Life of Granville*, II, p. 225. So far as I know, Bismarck first suggested this solution to Saburov in September 1879 (Skazkin, op. cit., p. 135).

[2] *Die Grosse Politik*, IV, No. 719 (November 7, 1880).

[3] Simpson, op. cit., pp. 167–70 (November 28, 1880).

[4] Simpson, op. cit., pp. 171–7; Skazkin, op. cit., pp. 142–3.

this as a basis a new draft was worked out along much broader lines. The old provision for mediation by one of the three powers in case of a dispute between the other two was retained, as was the clause providing for friendly neutrality in the event of one of the contracting parties finding itself compelled to be at war with a fourth power, excepting Turkey. Russia promised to respect the interests arising from the new position assured to Austria by the Treaty of Berlin and defined by her convention with Turkey concerning the occupation of certain Ottoman territories (Bosnia and Herzegovina). Modifications of the territorial *status quo* in Turkey should take place only after agreement between the three powers. None of them would send troops into Turkey in Europe, Roumania, Serbia, or Montenegro without the agreement of the other two parties. If one of them were to feel compelled to go to war with Turkey, she would consult her allies beforehand as to the eventual results of the war. The three governments recognized the principle of the closure of the Straits as laid down in the treaties on this subject. They promised to watch in common that Turkey should make no exception in favour of any government by lending the Straits to the military operations of a belligerent power. In case of infringement, or in order to prevent infringement, the three courts would warn Turkey that they would consider her as having put herself into a state of war with regard to the party injured and as having deprived herself of the benefits of security assured her by the Treaty of Berlin.[1]

With this draft Saburov hastened to St. Petersburg, where the matter was carefully considered and some minor changes proposed. In the meanwhile Haymerlé had got wind of the negotiations. He began to complain bitterly of the Russian policy in the Balkans. If Russia were really well-disposed, she should put an end to the endless intrigues against Austria in the Near East. Bismarck admitted that the fundamental antagonism of Austrian and Russian interests in that part of the world could hardly be entirely removed, and he also admitted the danger of being deceived by the Russians. But in any case the danger would be less with a formal treaty than without one, and the old maxim that the better is the enemy of the good should not be forgotten. Haymerlé reluctantly expressed his willingness to enter upon a limited agreement in regard to the East. Russia should promise not to further the union of Bulgaria and Eastern Roumelia and should not oppose the eventual annexation of Bosnia and Herzegovina.[2]

As soon as the Russian ambassador returned to Berlin, early in January 1881, discussions opened on the question of approaching Austria. The project had been approved by the Tsar, with some slight changes, and was now communicated to the Emperor William, who was greatly pleased with the prospect of re-establishing closer relations with Russia. It was finally decided to submit the project to Vienna as coming from Germany alone. It was at first planned to

---

[1] Simpson, op. cit., pp. 177–9.
[2] *Die Grosse Politik*, III, Nos. 520–2; Skazkin, op. cit., pp. 148 ff.

inform Haymerlé of the step to be taken, but to submit the draft to Francis Joseph through the Grand Duke of Saxe-Weimar, thus anticipating the unfavourable influence of the minister upon the sovereign. The Grand Duke, however, refused this unusual mission, so that the draft was communicated to Haymerlé and Francis Joseph almost at the same time. With the projected text went a letter from Emperor William to Francis Joseph, in which it was argued that the Russian initiative indicated Russia's pacific intentions. The treaty would guarantee Germany against Russian participation in a French attack and would guarantee Austria against Russian participation in an Italian attack. Without hope of Russian assistance neither France nor Italy would dare take action. Furthermore, the treaty would make Russian action in the Near East dependent on previous agreement with Germany and Austria. So far as the Straits were concerned, the treaty would simply reaffirm the international agreements on the subject.[1]

The reaction of Francis Joseph to the proposal laid before him was distinctly favourable, but he was a constitutional monarch and refused to ignore the advice of his minister. Haymerlé himself did not dare speak out boldly in his communications to Bismarck. He was, in fact, in a difficult position, for the forward policy of the English government in respect to the Greek-Turkish dispute still threatened the peace of the Near East. Austria could not afford to expose herself to an Anglo-Russian action, which Bismarck, curiously enough, was now supporting, evidently as a manœuvre to force Haymerlé into acquiescence. The Austrian statesman was likely to find himself between two stools if he rejected the German proposals, and yet he saw many objections to this course. The whole project went far beyond his conversations with Bismarck at Friedrichsruh in September and did not remove his suspicions of Russian designs, especially in Roumania. At bottom he could not get over the feeling that he was losing the position of sole friend of Germany. It could not be denied that Russia and Germany could always come to an agreement about the Near East much more easily than could Russia and Austria. This meant that Austria would always be at a disadvantage in the Three Emperors' League, and Germany would impose Russia's wishes upon her.[2]

So Haymerlé temporized and played for time while Bismarck and Saburov waited impatiently at Berlin. "Haymerlé," said Bismarck to Goschen, the English ambassador at Constantinople, as the latter passed through Berlin, "is so timid that he says 'no' three times in the morning when he wakes up, lest he should have committed himself to something in his dreams." "One would think," remarked Saburov to the chancellor, "that Germany and Russia were lying in wait for Austria in a corner of the woods." "And that in order to give her our purse," added Bismarck.[3]

---

[1] *Die Grosse Politik*, III, No. 524; Simpson, op. cit., pp. 184–92.
[2] Simpson, op. cit., pp. 198 ff.
[3] Elliot: *Life of Goschen*, I, p. 214; Simpson, op. cit., p. 210.

The question had become an urgent one for Bismarck, for in the Near East the war clouds were massing upon the horizon. A conflict between the Greeks and the Turks seemed imminent and the powers, unable to agree on measures of coercion, had no means of making the decisions of the Berlin Conference of June 1880 acceptable to either party. The concert of Europe had become ludicrous, and no serious attention was paid in Constantinople to the innumerable suggestions and proposals or to the ultimata that emanated from the various chancelleries. Gladstone, whose failure offered the opposition in parliament rare material for attack, found himself reduced to appeal to Bismarck to take the matter in hand. Finally Goschen was sent to Berlin to discuss the question before he went on to Constantinople. The German chancellor agreed to co-operate in a scheme by which the ambassadors at the Porte should come to a decision as to the territory to be ceded by the Turks, after which the decision should be forced upon the Greeks and Turks in turn. The time had come for business-like measures, and sentimental considerations should be put aside. "When I hear of the sufferings of a Negro in China or in some other remote part of the world, I may mention him in my prayers, but I cannot make him an object of German policy," said the chancellor.[1]

As a matter of fact, the ambassadors at Constantinople did not hold to the plan suggested, for they admitted the Turks to their deliberations. After much wrangling, however, the powers finally agreed to a line of demarcation by which Turkey was to cede to Greece in Thessaly and Epirus less territory than had been contemplated by the Treaty of Berlin and much less than had been envisaged by the fantastic decisions of the Berlin Conference of 1880. The Greeks protested, but were obliged, in the end, to yield. The interesting point for this study is the co-operation of Bismarck with the English to effect a settlement. The chancellor's purpose seems to have been, in the first place, to avoid a conflict; in the second, to prevent an ultimate Anglo-Russian combination; and, in the third place, to save ⌐ladstone from a complete debacle. He acted thus, not because he loved Gladstone or the Liberals, but because he feared that the return of the Conservative party, with its Austrophil sentiments, would strengthen the resistance of Haymerlé to the proposed agreement with Russia.[2] In any case, Bismarck could not wait indefinitely for Haymerlé's decision. He warned the Austrian minister early in March that rejection of the proposed treaty would be at his own risk. The two important points were those dealing with neutrality and with the Straits. On these items he must have a definite yes or no. Under pressure Haymerlé was forced to yield, though he reserved the right to make minor changes.

Hardly had the Austrian minister been brought to agreement when the whole project was, for a moment, placed in jeopardy by the assassination of

[1] Busch, in *Deutsche Rundschau*, May 1911, p. 245.

[2] Simpson, op. cit., p. 192; Fitzmaurice: *Granville*, II, p. 226; Elliot: *Goschen*, I, pp. 212 ff. See also S. T. Lascaris: *La Politique extérieure de la Grèce*, chapter vii, part iii.

Tsar Alexander II, on March 13, 1881. The new sovereign, Alexander III, was known not to share the Germanophil sentiments of his father, yet almost immediately he notified his approval of what had been done and his desire that the agreement should be realized. Still, the new Tsar's refusal to continue with the reforming program of General Loris Melikov indicated a break with the domestic policy of his predecessor. Bismarck had no sympathy with the constitutional experiment in Russia, but the extreme conservative influences around Alexander III, men like Tolstoi and Pobiedonostsev, were known for their dislike of things German. The situation in Russia was anything but clear.

For some weeks the representatives of the three powers were engaged in the dreary work of redaction and in the drawing up of a list of points on which agreement had been reached, the so-called " current account." The only question which caused serious difficulty arose from the desire of the Austrians to keep open the road to Salonika and their insistence on the right to annex, eventually, not only Bosnia and Herzegovina, but also the Sanjak of Novi-Bazar. This right the Russians were unwilling to recognize, though they had informally accepted such action in earlier agreements with Austria. Bismarck did his best to mediate and finally threatened to leave on vacation before the negotiations were brought to a close. In the end the point was left indefinite and referred to the declaration of the Russian and Austrian plenipotentiaries at the Congress of Berlin.

The treaty was finally signed at Berlin on June 18, 1881. The first three articles were substantially like those worked out by Bismarck and Saburov in December 1880, excepting that the provision for mediation by the third power in a dispute between the other two was omitted and there was no obligation to refrain from sending troops into European Turkey, Roumania, Serbia, or Montenegro. Other articles provided that the treaty should remain in force for three years. Bismarck would have preferred a longer term, but left Haymerlé to settle the point. " When Austria has worn that flannel next to her skin for three years, she will no longer be able to discard it without running the risk of catching cold," he said. It was further stated that the treaty should be kept secret, both its existence and its contents. It was, in fact, so successfully concealed from the public that it did not become known until after the World War. A further article provided that the agreements of 1873 should be replaced by the new treaty.

The special points of the agreement were consigned to a protocol. Austria reserved the right to annex Bosnia and Herzegovina whenever she deemed such action opportune. The Sanjak of Novi-Bazar was left subject to earlier arrangements. The three powers promised to employ their efforts to dissuade the Turkish government from occupying Eastern Roumelia or the Balkans, on the understanding that Bulgaria and Eastern Roumelia should abstain from provoking the Porte by attacks against other provinces of the Ottoman Empire (Macedonia). The three contracting powers stated further that they would not oppose the eventual reunion of Bulgaria and Eastern Roumelia, " should this question happen to arise by force of circumstances." In general, they would instruct their representatives in the East to endeavour to smooth out their differences by friendly explanations, and, in case of failure, to refer the matters in dispute to their governments.[1]

The negotiations for this Alliance of the Three Emperors were long and arduous, and the basis of discussion was frequently shifted. Originating as a projected Russian-German agreement of security, it was expanded to include Austria and finally was further extended into a settlement of various crucial questions of Austro-Russian rivalry in the Balkans. Saburov had, from the beginning, been the driving force behind the project. Bismarck had been rather lukewarm at the start and had hesitated about sacrificing his connexion with the western powers for a new agreement with Russia. Gradually he had come to see the advantages of a triple agreement, and from that time on he had refused to consider a separate entente with Russia. With the development of English policy in the Near East the treaty had become for him one of great importance and he had thrown himself into the negotiations with his accustomed energy. Haymerlé's attitude remained unchanged throughout, not only because of his timidity and lack of vision, but because of his fear that Austria would be eclipsed by Russia in the affections of Germany.

And yet the great importance of the treaty cannot be denied. In the Bismarckian policy it was second in importance only to the alliance with Austria. For the duration of the agreement it definitely orientated the German policy to the eastward. The advantages of this orientation were obvious. Bismarck himself summarized them in his letter to the Emperor: the treaty established monarchical solidarity against revolutionary and subversive movements; it served to preserve the peace between Austria and Russia and so spared Germany the thankless task of taking sides against one or the other of her neighbours; and, above all, it guaranteed Germany against an alliance between Russia and France, which gave it an inestimable value in the eyes of Bismarck.

Saburov, too, felt that the agreement was of fundamental importance for Russian policy: Russia, which had been isolated and exposed to a hostile coalition in 1879, was now no longer in danger, for she had insinuated herself into the Austro-German Alliance. Furthermore, her action in the Near East was no longer paralysed as it had been, for the eventual reoccupation of Eastern Roumelia by the Turks was now hardly possible, and both Germany and Austria had agreed to the eventual union of Bulgaria and Eastern Roumelia. But the greatest immediate gain from the alliance, so far as Russia was concerned, was the practical guarantee against attack in the Black Sea. The most desirable solution of the Straits problem for her would have been control of Constantinople and the Straits by actual territorial occupation. This point is brought out

---

[1] The final negotiations and texts in Simpson, op. cit., pp. 233–55; Skazkin, op. cit., pp. 170 ff.; *Die Grosse Politik*, III, Nos. 528–31; Pribram: *Secret Treaties of Austria-Hungary*, I, pp. 36–50.

in all the Russian memoranda of the period. But this solution was, at the time, patently impossible. Neither was there any prospect that the powers would consent to the opening of the Straits to Russian warships while they remained closed to the craft of the other nations. The Russian position at the time was of necessity a defensive one. Far from trying to extend their privileges, the Russian statesmen were intent on preventing the English from extending theirs. Consequently the reaffirmation of the principle of the closure of the Straits was of the greatest value for Russia. In the event of a conflict with England either in the Near East or in Central Asia, Russia could be sure that she would not be attacked in her most vulnerable spot, the Black Sea. A repetition of the Crimean War was beyond the range of possibility.

As for Austria, it must be admitted from the beginning that her gains from the treaty were less impressive than the gains of the other two partners. Haymerlé could see only that the exclusive alliance between Germany and Austria was being more or less emasculated, and it was necessary for Bismarck to give Austria a written declaration to the effect that the new agreement could under no circumstances prejudice the Austro-German Alliance of 1879, that the earlier treaty remained binding, and that it continued to determine the relations of Austria and Germany without undergoing any limitation or alteration in any point whatsoever.[1] And yet it must be conceded that Haymerlé pressed the point somewhat too persistently. In the Europe of that day no power could hope to monopolize the support of another. It was unreasonable to suppose that Bismarck would for ever tie himself to the chariot-wheels of Austrian policy. The same holds true of Haymerlé's complaint that the agreement would not remove the fundamental antagonism of Austria and Russia in the Balkans. Of course not, for this antagonism was inherent in the nature of things. As Bismarck said, one could hope only for a mitigation of the rivalry, and a treaty was better than nothing. After all, the new alliance did, for the time being, remove the likelihood of open conflict in the Near East, it did give Austria a guarantee against a possible Russian-Italian attack, and it did enable Austria to consolidate her position in the Balkans by the eventual annexation of Bosnia and Herzegovina, while it left the road to the Ægean open through the Sanjak of Novi-Bazar. Taken by and large, the agreement secured to all three of the contracting parties substantial gains. It is easy to point out its fatal weakness — the continuation of Austrian-Russian rivalry in the Balkans, even though latent — but one must not leave out of account the fact that the treaty helped to take the edge off this antagonism. Thereby it served not only the interests of the three parties, but the cause of general peace. Its conclusion was an achievement of real statesmanship and an important step in the evolution of the Bismarckian system.

---

[1] Ministerial declaration of May 18, 1881, (Pribram, op. cit., I, p. 33).

BIBLIOGRAPHICAL NOTE

DOCUMENTARY SOURCES

Die grosse Politik der europäischen Kabinette, 1871–1914. Berlin, 1922–7. Volume III, chapter xiii (The Austro-German Alliance of 1879) and chapter xiv (The Three Emperors' Alliance of 1881); Volume IV, chapter xxi (The Relations between England and Germany in the Years 1879–1885).

Documents diplomatiques français, Volume II. Paris, 1930. Covers the period to 1880.

PRIBRAM, ALFRED F.: *The Secret Treaties of Austria-Hungary, 1879–1914.* American edition by Archibald Cary Coolidge. Two volumes. Cambridge, 1920. Volume I contains the texts of the Austro-German Alliance and the Alliance of the Three Emperors.

" Russko-Germanskie Otnoshenia" (*Krasny Arkhiv,* I, pp. 1–208. Moscow, 1922). Contains the Russian text of the Alliance of the Three Emperors.

Accounts and Papers. State Papers. 1878–1879, Volumes LXXVII, LXXIX–LXXXI. 1880, Volumes LXXVIII, LXXX–LXXXII. 1881, Volumes XCVIII and C. These volumes of British documents contain the negotiations respecting the determination of the Montenegrin and Greek frontiers.

Documents diplomatiques. Affaires de Montenegro. Nos. 1 and 2. Paris, 1880. *Négociations relatives à la rectification des frontières de la Grèce.* Paris, 1880. *Affaires de Grèce en 1880.* Paris, 1881. Voluminous collections of French documents dealing with the Montenegrin and Greek problems.

MEMOIRS, AUTOBIOGRAPHIES, BIOGRAPHIES, AND LETTERS

MONYPENNY, W. F., and BUCKLE, G. E.: *The Life of Benjamin Disraeli.* Volume VI. London, 1920.

CECIL, GWENDOLEN: *Life of Robert Marquis of Salisbury.* Volume II. London, 1921.

ELLIOT, ARTHUR D.: *The Life of George Joachim Goschen, First Viscount Goschen.* Two volumes. London, 1911. Important for the history of the Greek and Montenegrin questions.

FITZMAURICE, LORD EDMOND: *The Life of Lord Granville.* Two volumes. London, 1905.

NEWTON, LORD: *Lord Lyons.* Two volumes. London, 1913.

WERTHEIMER, EDUARD: *Graf Julius Andrássy.* Three volumes. Stuttgart, 1910–13. One of the most important sources for the history of the Austro-German Alliance.

BISMARCK, PRINCE OTTO VON: *Gedanken und Erinnerungen. Anhang.* Stuttgart, 1901. The supplementary volumes of Bismarck's reminiscences contain some interesting correspondence in regard to the Austro-German Alliance.

Schweinitz, General von: *Denkwürdigkeiten.* Two volumes. Berlin, 1927.

Radowitz, Joseph Maria von: *Aufzeichnungen und Erinnerungen.* Edited by Hajo Holborn. Two volumes. Berlin, 1925.

Simpson, J. Y.: *The Saburov Memoirs, or Bismarck and Russia.* Cambridge, 1929. This is by far the most important single source for the history of the negotiation of the Alliance of the Three Emperors.

—: " Russo-German Relations and the Sabouroff Memoirs " (*Nineteenth Century*, LXXXII, pp. 1111–24, December 1917, LXXXIII, pp. 60–76, January 1918). These articles are an abstract of the Saburov memoirs and are therefore entirely superseded by the foregoing title.

Marczáli, J.: " *Zur Geschichte des deutsch-österreichisch-ungarischen Bündnisses* " (*Deutsche Revue,* 1906).

Doczi, Ludwig: " *An der Wiege des Dreibundes* " (*Neue Freie Presse,* October 13, 1904). " *Andrássy und Bismarck* " (ibid., December 2, 1906). These articles are based upon personal recollections and information from Andrássy.

Hohenlohe-Schillingsfürst, Fürst Chlodwig zu: *Denkwürdigkeiten.* Two volumes. Stuttgart, 1907.

Busch, Dr.: " *Die Durchführung der Berliner Kongressakte, 1880–1881* " (*Deutsche Rundschau,* CXLVII, pp. 222–48, May 1911). Diaries of the German under-secretary of state, in charge of Eastern affairs.

GENERAL TREATMENTS OF THE ALLIANCES AFTER 1878

Gooch, G. P.: *History of Modern Europe, 1878–1919.* Still one of the best general accounts, though now somewhat out of date.

Becker, Otto: *Bismarcks Bündnispolitik.* Berlin, 1923. On the whole the best brief account of the alliance system from the German standpoint.

Granfelt, Helge: *Das Dreibundsystem, 1879–1916.* Stockholm, 1924. A careful and impartial study, covering the period 1879–90. The second volume has not yet appeared.

Japikse, N.: *Europa und Bismarcks Friedenspolitik.* Berlin, 1927. An excellent brief treatment, by a Dutch scholar.

Noack, Ulrich: *Bismarcks Friedenspolitik und das Problem des deutschen Machtverfalls.* Leipzig, 1928. The latest large-scale treatment, but a book that must be used with some care, as it expounds a theory and is rather unbalanced.

Platzhoff, Walter: *Bismarcks Bündnispolitik.* Bonn, 1920. An early, but very stimulating essay.

Meissner, H. O.: " *Bismarcks Bündnispolitik, 1871–1890* " (*Preussische Jahrbücher,* 1923). Primarily an examination of the German documents.

Rachfahl, Felix: *Deutschland und die Weltpolitik.* Stuttgart, 1923. The most exhaustive treatment, but rather warped in its view-point.

MEYER, ARNOLD O.: *Bismarcks Friedenspolitik*. Munich, 1930. The most up-to-date sketch of the Bismarckian system.

STOLBERG-WERNIGERODE, ALBRECHT, GRAF ZU: *Bismarcks Bündnissystem und seine Lehren*. Berlin, 1930. A reliable introductory survey.

MONOGRAPHIC STUDIES

HELLER, EDUARD: *Das deutsch-österreichisch-ungarische Bündnis in Bismarcks Aussenpolitik*. Berlin, 1925. By far the best monographic treatment of the Austro-German Alliance, based in part upon unpublished material from the Austrian archives.

GRÜNING, IRENE: *Die russische öffentliche Meinung und ihre Stellung zu den Grossmächten, 1878–1894*. Berlin, 1929. A careful and valuable study of the evolution of Russian public opinion in matters of foreign relations.

MÜLLER, MANFRED: *Die Bedeutung des Berliner Kongresses für die deutsch-russischen Beziehungen*. Leipzig, 1927. Especially valuable for the analysis of the Russian-German estrangement after 1878.

FRIIS, AAGE: " *Die Aufhebung des Artikels V des Prager Friedens* " (*Historische Zeitschrift*, CXXV, pp. 45–62, 1921). The best account of this interesting point.

KOERLIN, KURT: *Zur Vorgeschichte des russisch-französischen Bündnisses 1879–1890*. Halle, 1926. Discusses the soundings of the Russians in Paris in 1879.

ROTHFELS, HANS: *Bismarcks englische Bündnispolitik*. Berlin, 1924. The best account of the Anglo-German negotiations in 1879.

TAUBE, ALEXANDER VON: *Fürst Bismarck zwischen England und Russland*. Stuttgart, 1923. A general treatment of Bismarck's relations to Russia and England.

FESTER, RICHARD: " *Saburow und die russischen Staatsakten über die russisch-deutschen Beziehungen von 1879–1890* " (*Die Grenzboten*, LXXX, No. 16, April 20, 1921). Primarily a translation and summary of the Simpson articles in the *Nineteenth Century*.

KRATCHOUNOF, K.: *L'Alliance des Trois Empereurs*. Sofia, 1924. A brief, conventional, monographic treatment of the Alliance of the Three Emperors.

MEDLICOTT, W. N.: " Diplomatic Relations after the Congress of Berlin " (*Slavonic Review*, VIII, pp. 66–79, June 1929).

SCHÜNEMANN, KARL: " *Die Stellung Österreich-Ungarns in Bismarcks Bündnis-politik* " (*Archiv für Politik und Geschichte*, VI, pp. 549–94, 1926). A valuable critical article, which should be read in connexion with Heller's book. The author makes use of some unpublished material.

SKAZKIN, S.: *Konets avstro-russko-germanskogo soiuza*. Volume I, *1879–84*. Moscow, 1928. Easily the best monographic treatment of the Three Emperors' Alliance. The author makes use of all published material and draws heavily also upon unpublished material in the Russian archives.

VII

The Triple Alliance

I T CERTAINLY COULD NOT BE CLAIMED THAT THE ALLIANCE OF THE THREE Emperors settled the Balkan problem which had been so half-heartedly disposed of at the Congress of Berlin. Before many years had passed, this intricate complex of questions once again focused the attention of the European statesmen and brought the continent to the verge of a great general war. And yet the Alliance of the Three Emperors served a very useful purpose, for it established a truce between the two antagonists, Austria and Russia, and in this way gave Europe a breathing-space, an opportunity to direct its energies into other channels. The centre of gravity in the years from 1881 to 1885 shifted from the East to the West. The relations between the European powers were influenced by their conflicting interests in the colonial field. In rapid succession the problems of European control in Tunis and Egypt followed upon one another, and before the year 1885 was reached, Bismarck had succeeded, by exploiting the international situation, in laying the foundations of the German colonial empire.

There was nothing abrupt or surprising in the increased activity of the powers outside Europe, though the development of expansive tendencies became of greater and greater significance for the history of the European nations from year to year and gradually transformed the very basis of international relations. By 1880 the great changes wrought by the industrial revolution were making themselves keenly felt. The practical monopoly of the English in the supply of manufactured goods was already a thing of the past, and some of the continental states had, even before this, reached the self-supporting stage so far as this is possible at all under the modern economic system. For many years countries like England and France had been exporting the products of their factories, and by 1880 there was already a pronounced international competition in the field of foreign investment. France, for example, was sending large blocks of capital abroad and held a considerable stake in countries like the Ottoman Empire and its Egyptian dependency. This is not the place to examine minutely the theories and manifestations of what has come to be known as *economic imperialism,* but the general facts must be borne in mind, while a review of the developments in specific crucial instances will serve to illustrate the problem in its practical aspects.

Take the Tunisian question, for example. Technically speaking, this North

African territory was part of the Ottoman Empire. But the connexion had always been tenuous, and a native dynasty had controlled the country since the early eighteenth century. Tunis, like Algeria, served as headquarters for Mediterranean pirates in the early nineteenth century, and it was probably due primarily to the warlike proclivities of the population that the country was not conquered. The French had begun the conquest of Algiers in 1830, but had found the task so arduous that no serious thought was given to extending the new colony to the eastward, though geographically Tunis is only an extension of Algeria. Nevertheless the French influence was strong at the court of the native prince, or bey. Only the English representative appeared as a serious competitor, his object being to prevent further stretches of the Mediterranean littoral from falling into the hands of the French.

After 1860 the question underwent a distinct change. The Italians, who could be found in some numbers in all the Mediterranean countries, began to establish themselves in Tunis, which was just across the sea from Sicily. By 1880 it is said that there were no less than twenty thousand Italians settled in the territory, while there were only about two hundred Frenchmen. This flow of population was accompanied by a growing agitation in Italy for the acquisition of Tunis, which, according to the nationalist writers, was part of the old Roman Empire, which the new unified Italy was to revive in a modern form. Even in 1870 the Italian government had been tempted to take advantage of France's disasters to seize the territory of the Bey. On that occasion it was only the unveiled threat of the French provisional government that deterred Victor Emmanuel from taking action.

Apart from sentimental considerations, it was the proximity of Tunis and the opportunity for settlement of colonists that made the country attractive to the Italians. The French already possessed Algeria and were not embarrassed by a surplus population at home. For them Tunis was important rather for strategical purposes and as a field for economic investment. " Tunis," said the Duc de Decazes in 1876, " is the very entry to Africa and is the opening to our Algerian possessions. We could not tolerate the establishment of any European power there without danger to the security of our colony, and we should be obliged, in such a case, to engage in a struggle of extreme gravity or suffer a situation in which we should bear the burden of arrangements by which others would profit." [1] The English interest was of the same general nature, and before long the representatives of these two powers developed a feverish activity. In a remarkably brief space of time backward Tunis was " opened up " to European enterprise. The Bey, like most Oriental rulers, was a spendthrift when he had the money to spend, and thus gave European business interests exactly the opportunity which they needed. They supplied him with the necessary funds to build splendid palaces and elaborate barracks, requiring only his signature on a loan contract and a return for the accommodation in the form of concessions.

---

[1] *Documents diplomatiques français*, II, Nos. 116, 122, 216, 217, 221, 300.

Attention has already been called in an earlier chapter to the extortionate conditions under which the first loans to the Ottoman Empire were floated. Of the Tunisian loans the terms were even more exorbitant. The interest varied from twelve to fifteen per cent, and the brokers' commissions not infrequently devoured a third or a half of the return. For example, a consolidation loan floated on the Paris exchange for a sum of thirty-five million francs brought the Bey a net return of only about six million, while greatly enlarging the interest on his indebtedness. The financial burden could be alleviated only by increasing the national income through additional taxes, but resort to this dangerous expedient often resulted in outbreaks of the population, which, in turn, cost more money to suppress.

By 1869 the financial condition of the Bey had become desperate, and an international commission was then established to consolidate the debt and arrange for its service. On this commission the English, French, and Italian interests were represented, though most of the debt was in the hands of French creditors. In the meanwhile the policy of peaceful penetration had been scoring one success after another. The French had secured a monopoly of the telegraph lines in the country, while the English held a concession for an important railroad from the city of Tunis to Goletta. After 1870 the Italians joined in the struggle for opportunities and before long took the place of the English as the chief competitors of the French. The interests of the powers were growing by leaps and bounds, while the Bey and his government could no longer meet their obligations. It was clear that the question of Tunis was reaching an acute stage. The final disposition of the territory could not be postponed for very much longer.

It will be recalled that this problem of Tunis played into the general discussions at the Congress of Berlin. Not that it was brought up in open meeting. On the contrary, it was mentioned only in secret conclave and in hushed tones. But the upshot of the negotiations was that a free hand in Tunis was offered to the French plenipotentiary, M. Waddington, by Lord Salisbury, Lord Beaconsfield, and Prince Bismarck. For the English the sacrifice was necessary, since they had to buy off French opposition to the Cyprus Convention by some appropriate concession. Bismarck supported the English plan, in part because he had for some time advocated a settlement of the Near Eastern problem on the basis of territorial cessions at the expense of Turkey, in part because he was anxious not to estrange the French or drive them into the arms of Russia. In any case, Waddington returned home from the congress with " Tunis in his pocket." [1]

If the French minister had had his own way, the occupation of Tunis would probably have taken place before the end of the year. But Waddington found

---

[1] This account of the Tunisian question is based upon the author's articles: " The European Powers and the French Occupation of Tunis " (*American Historical Review*, October 1925, pp. 55–78, and January 1926, pp. 252–65). See also *Documents diplomatiques français*, II, Nos. 325, 330–2, 334, 336.

little sympathy in Paris for his plan. The leaders of the Republican party, notably Gambetta, were irreconcilably opposed to embarking upon colonial adventures. They did not trust the offers that came from the " monster " in Berlin and suspected that an attempt was being made to divert the attention and the energies of the French nation from the " hole in the Vosges." It was Gambetta's firm conviction that the first and most sacred duty of the country was to prepare for the day when the two lost provinces could be recovered for the motherland.[1]

Meanwhile the Italians had got wind of what had transpired at Berlin. There was no definite proof that Tunis had been assigned to France, but the fact was strongly suspected. The whole weakness of the Italian policy at the congress now appeared. Attention had been centred on the question of securing compensation for the expansion of Austria in the Balkans. Until the very meeting of the congress the hope had been entertained that somehow or other Austria could be induced to make concessions in Italia Irredenta, the Trentino and Trieste. As a matter of fact, Andrássy never had the slightest intention of ceding an inch of territory to the Italians. He had time and again offered them his support for aspirations in the Mediterranean, but, as aforesaid, the Italian government concentrated on the question of making gains in Europe and did not follow up the suggestions as to Tunis. The result was that the Italian plenipotentiary, Count Corti, came back from the congress with clean hands, which were also empty. The indignation in Italy was so great that Corti was almost stoned in the streets and soon after resigned his position as foreign minister.

Benedetto Cairoli, the prime minister, was a member of a famous Lombard patriot family. Together with his four brothers he had fought in the wars against Austria, and he still bore the scars of warfare. Of his patriotism and fervour there could be no doubt whatever, but those who knew him were almost unanimous in describing him as utterly devoid of sound judgment and statesmanship. The chances of acquiring the Trentino and Trieste had practically vanished with the Congress of Berlin, but the Cairoli government did nothing to suppress the irredentist agitation, if it did not actually encourage it. The only result of the demonstrations, however, was that the tension between Austria and Italy soon reached the breaking-point, while in Europe generally Italy was looked upon as a pretentious disturber of the peace. " Why on earth should Italy demand an increase of territory? " said a Russian diplomat to Bismarck. " Has she lost another battle? " This reference to Italy's repeated ill fortune on the field of war shows the characteristic mixture of irritation and scorn with which the other governments viewed the new kingdom.[2]

---

[1] Waddington's idea was to establish a French protectorate and occupy several strategic points. See his correspondence with the French consul-general Roustan, in *Documents diplomatiques français*, II, Nos. 337, 339, 340. See also D'Etournelles de Constant: *La Politique française en Tunisie* (Paris, 1891), p. 172.

[2] In addition to evidence quoted in my articles, see, on Italian policy, Michele Rosi: *I Cairoli* (Bologna, 1929), chapters xiv, xv, a defence of Cairoli's policy, based on his unpublished papers.

To allow dangerous and useless demonstrations against Austria to continue was bad enough, but Cairoli and his friends did not stop there. His party strongly favoured close relations with democratic France, but was unwilling to see the sister Latin nation steal a march on Italy in Tunis, for which Italy herself cherished strong aspirations. Immediately after the congress the government took up the problem. Signor Maccio, a very determined man, was sent to Tunis as consul and before long became involved in a truceless struggle with his French colleague, M. Roustan, who was no less energetic. In the next few years one dispute between France and Italy followed another until the French government brought the episode to a close by invading and occupying the country.

The conflict was really a hopeless one so far as the Italians were concerned, for the French had much greater resources, financial and military, at their disposal, and, what was more, they had the other great powers behind them. Waddington had taken the precaution of securing from Salisbury written confirmation of the Berlin bargain and he found Bismarck as well-disposed as ever. The German chancellor took the view consistently that it would be to Germany's interest if the French became involved in colonial enterprises and found compensation for their losses in Europe by acquiring new territories in Africa. In other words, by diverting the activities of the powers to extra-European fields he would be able to reduce the pressure on the continent. If, beyond this, the various nations came into conflict on colonial issues, so much the better for Germany. The danger of hostile coalitions would be reduced by just that much. So when the French ambassador, Count Saint-Vallier, came to him in January 1879 to sound out his attitude, the German chancellor gave all possible encouragement. " Well," he exclaimed, " I think the Tunisian pear is now ripe, and the time has come for you to pick it; the insolence of the Bey has acted like the August sun on this African fruit, which may well rot or be stolen by another if you leave it on the tree too long." [1]

This very eagerness on the part of Bismarck acted as a deterrent rather than a stimulus upon the French statesmen. Gambetta and his friends were more firmly convinced than ever that the German chancellor had some ulterior motive, and that his object was to sow dissension between France and Italy. Waddington, who understood Bismarck's policy perfectly, was anxious to proceed, but, in view of the opposition at home, was obliged to give up the idea of military action. Under the circumstances the Bey evaded all suggestions made by Roustan.[2] For the time being, the question hung fire. The year 1879 was filled with the threat of war in eastern Europe. It will be remembered that in August and September unofficial soundings were taken by the Russians in Paris

---

[1] *Documents diplomatiques français*, II, Nos. 366–9; Bourgeois and Pagès: *Les Origines et les responsabilités de la Grande Guerre* (Paris, 1921), pp. 192, 365, 368; Ernest Daudet: *La Mission du Comte de Saint-Vallier* (Paris, 1918), pp. 88–94; *Die Grosse Politik*, III, Nos. 655–6.
[2] *Documents diplomatiques français*, II, Nos. 372, 375, 376, 381, 449.

and Rome. Waddington himself reported these advances to the Germans, while the Italians, on the other hand, seem to have considered the Russian offers quite seriously until they were warned off in unmistakable terms by the English government. The reaction of this incident upon Bismarck was of importance, for he was now more than ever determined to support the French, while his rage against the Italians knew no bounds. Throughout the summer of 1880 he loyally supported the French government in the long-drawn negotiations concerning the Greek frontier, as well as in the Moroccan question, which was being discussed by an international conference at Madrid.[1] So far as Tunis was concerned, his attitude continued to be one of benevolence and cordial goodwill.

Cairoli took no account of this general European alignment, although the Italian ambassadors repeatedly warned him not to precipitate a crisis. With supreme nonchalance he allowed Italian interests to continue the competition with the French. The two governments clashed in the matter of the Tunis-Goletta railway, which the English owners had offered for sale. By the lavish use of money the Italian Rubattino Company finally secured the line, after which the Italian parliament passed a bill granting the new owner an annual subvention. The incident led to a sharp exchange of notes between Paris and Rome, and the French would probably have proceeded to take action in the summer of 1880 had it not been for the opposition of prominent French leaders and for the coolness of the new liberal government in England, which recognized the commitments of Salisbury only with grudging reluctance. Even so, Freycinet, the French premier, appears to have considered the establishment of a protectorate just before his ministry fell from power, in September 1880.[2]

The Italian government was not unaware of the danger, and hinted that the course of Italian policy would be changed if the French proceeded with their plans.[3] General Cialdini, the Italian ambassador to Paris, was deeply impressed with the danger of French action, and finally, at a conference on August 26, 1880, persuaded the incredulous Cairoli that an effort should be made to effect an understanding with Germany and Austria. Count Maffei, the secretary-general of the Italian foreign office, turned his efforts to the same end, speaking in the most violent terms of the French procedure. After the conference he called in the Berlin correspondent of the influential Italian newspaper *Diritto*, a certain Gronert Goercke, and apparently authorized him to make unofficial advances to Bismarck. The journalist sent the chancellor an account of the proceedings of the conference, indicating that it was hoped by the Italians that an alliance would be repaid by the cession of the Trentino by Austria. It so hap-

---

[1] The details may be read in R. H. Wienefeld: *Franco-German Relations, 1878–1885* (Baltimore, 1929), chapter iii.

[2] Freycinet: *Souvenirs*, p. 168; D'Etournelles de Constant: *La Politique française en Tunisie* (Paris, 1891), p. 172, note.

[3] Andrea Torre: " *Come la Francia s'impadroni di Tunisi* " (in Giacomo Curàtulo: *Francia e Italia, 1849–1914*, Turin, 1915).

pened that Baron Haymerlé was visiting Bismarck at Friedrichsruh during these very days (September 3–4). Bismarck read him the letter and apparently found the Austrian minister not wholly averse to following the matter up. But Bismarck himself showed no inclination to help the Italians out of their difficulties. He wrote Gronert Goercke that the road to Berlin lay through Vienna, and refused to act as intermediary. When the journalist appeared at the German foreign office shortly afterwards, he was turned away with the remark that his advances, to have real value, had better come from the Italian government officially and through the regular channels.[1]

Haymerlé, however, consulted the Italian ambassador to Vienna as soon as he had returned to the capital. Count Robilant replied that he knew nothing of Gronert Goercke and thought he was probably " an intriguing adventurer." In writing to his government he pointed out that the central powers showed no " great desire for our company " and that therefore it would be more dignified to retain freedom of action. Thereupon Gronert Goercke was disavowed and the matter was dropped. Cairoli, it seems, had been only half convinced to begin with, while Depretis, one of the most influential Italian leaders, shared the premier's scruples about setting forth upon a road that would definitely lead away from France.[2]

The failure of the unofficial approaches to Germany and Austria left the Italians at sea. It was agreed between Cairoli and Cialdini that, for the time being, a policy of the " utmost coldness and indifference " should be followed in the relations with France, but the fiery Italian premier could not long abstain from activity. Early in November he instructed Cialdini to open negotiations with the French in regard to a concession for a telegraph line from Sicily to Tunis. Cialdini's remonstrances were of no avail, and the matter was pressed by the Italian government. The result might easily have been foreseen. Every move made by the Italians created uneasiness in Paris and convinced even the most reluctant Frenchman that something would soon have to be done to bring the matter to a close. It was not surprising that Saint-Vallier again appeared at Friedrichsruh to enlist Bismarck's support. The German chancellor enthusiastically promised all possible assistance, short of military measures, and agreed to warn the Italians that he disapproved of their policy.[3]

The French still hesitated, for there was little sentiment in Paris in favour of colonial adventure, and much disagreement in government circles as to what should be done. President Grévy maintained that Tunis was not worth a ten-centime cigar; Jules Ferry, the prime minister, and Barthélemy Saint-Hilaire,

---

[1] On the important Belgirate conference see Torre, loc. cit., which is based on Cialdini's papers and corrects the account in Chiala: *Pagine di Storia Contemporanea*, II, pp. 222–4. Rosi: *I Cairoli*, II, pp. 54 ff., adds nothing. There is no evidence in the Austrian records of Gronert Goercke's mission (Pribram, op. cit., II, p. 8), but it is discussed in Crispi: *Memoirs*, II, pp. 118–19, and there are German papers on the subject (*Die Grosse Politik*, III, p. 183, foot-note).

[2] Chiala, op. cit., II, p. 224; Crispi, op. cit., II, p. 119.

[3] Bourgeois and Pagès, op. cit., p. 203; Hohenlohe: *Denkwürdigkeiten*, II, pp. 306–7.

the foreign minister, were anxious to avoid complications; and Gambetta still felt certain that some arrangement could be come to. He sent his friend Baron de Billing to Rome to see if the whole business could not be " chloroformed." A real effort was made by de Billing to put an end to the Franco-Italian antagonism. It was agreed that both consuls, Roustan and Maccio, should be replaced by less aggressive men.[1]

But before the recall of the consuls could be announced, a new incident rendered futile Gambetta's well-intentioned effort to dispose of the question. On January 10, 1881 Maccio appeared at Palermo to greet King Humbert. With him was the brother of the Bey and a delegation of Italians resident in Tunis. High-sounding speeches were made and the Italian press took care to point out the political significance of the visit. These demonstrations, naturally, had an electrifying effect in Paris. Even Gambetta was forced to admit that action was imperative. Efforts appear to have been made almost immediately to induce the Bey to sign a treaty with France and accept some form of protectorate. For unknown reasons the Bey refused to entertain these questionable proposals.

It was too late for the French government to turn back. In Paris it was generally felt that military action of some kind had become necessary, while an acute controversy with the English concerning the claims of one of their citizens in Tunis made it clear that they might make trouble in the future. Towards the end of March, therefore, Ferry took advantage of a raid by frontier tribesmen into Algeria. There was nothing unusual about these raids. There had been over two thousand of them between 1870 and 1881. They were inevitable among a people organized on a primitive tribal basis. Not even French writers take the famous Krumir raid of March 1881 very seriously. Its importance lay solely in the fact that it served as a convenient French pretext for a punitive expedition. The French chamber voted the credits for an expeditionary force on April 7, and the invasion began soon after. Since the Bey had no armed forces of consequence, the French expedition was merely a " military promenade," which ended on May 12 with the signature of the Treaty of Bardo and the establishment of what amounted to a protectorate by France.

That the French were able to carry through the occupation of Tunis without calling forth European complications was due in very large part to Bismarck's attitude. During April he urged them to go ahead and not bother about the Italians.[2] Under the circumstances the desperate appeals of the latter to England, Turkey, Austria, and even Germany were of no avail. Lord Granville, to be sure, was intensely irritated by the French action and was sorely tempted to accept the Italian suggestions for co-operation. He actually went so far as to draft a dispatch to Germany and Austria in an effort to raise the concert of Europe against France. From this course he was dissuaded by Gladstone and

---

[1] Le Baron Robert de Billing, Vie, Notes, Correspondance (Paris, 1895); Chiala, op. cit., II, pp. 262–5.

[2] Hohenlohe, op. cit., II, p. 310; Lucius von Ballhausen, op. cit., p. 207.

Dilke, who probably realized the futility of such last-minute action.[1] The Sultan, too, encouraged by the attitude of the English, was only too ready to do something to save the territory over which he claimed a nominal control. He went so far as to threaten to send a squadron to Tunis, but was deterred by the threats of the Paris government and the sharp warnings that came from Berlin.[2] In other words, Bismarck kept the ring while the French settled the matter to their own satisfaction. The Italians found themselves completely isolated. Cairoli at first consoled himself with the declarations of the French foreign office that no military occupation or annexation was intended, and wilfully ignored the fact that Barthélemy Saint-Hilaire said nothing of a protectorate and warned the Italian ambassador that France would be forced to regulate her conduct by the events.[3] When it was too late, the Italian premier realized how helpless he was. His inexcusable and almost insane policy of the previous two years had found a fitting close. There was little enough sympathy for the Italians in Europe, and such as there was could not find expression in concrete measures so long as Bismarck stood by the French.

Over and over again the German chancellor has been accused of having staged the Tunisian episode with the object of creating friction between France and Italy. It is, of course, a fact that this was the result of the French occupation. For almost twenty years there was acute tension in the relations of the two powers with each other. Bismarck had quite enough vision to foresee this outcome, and no doubt it played some part in determining his policy.[4] But it would be quite erroneous to picture the great German statesman as basing his own position primarily on a policy of creating ill will and antagonisms among other nations. In the course of his long tenure of office after 1870 he was more active in the work of mediation than in the sowing of discord. At times he made use of international rivalries, of course, but the creation of dissatisfaction was not his chief aim. In the Tunis question, for instance, it is perfectly clear that he worked almost exclusively with France in view. He had too low an opinion of the Italians to care very much what they did or where they stood. He encouraged France and supported her chiefly because he honestly desired to find for her some compensation for the losses of 1870–1 and because he saw that it was to the interest of Germany to divert the attention of the powers as much as possible from continental questions to extra-European fields where Germany had nothing to lose.[5]

[1] Newton: *Lord Lyons*, II, p. 241; Gwynn and Tuckwell: *Life of Sir Charles Dilke*, I, p. 380; Fitzmaurice: *Life of Lord Granville*, II, pp. 234–5; the Anglo-Italian negotiations are discussed at length in Rosi: *I Cairoli*, II, chapter xix, *passim*.

[2] Constant, op. cit., pp. 124–8; Daudet, op. cit., pp. 210–17; Hanotaux, op. cit., IV, pp. 654 ff.

[3] Torre, loc. cit., pp. 113–17.

[4] Lucius von Ballhausen, op. cit., p. 212; Moritz Busch: *Bismarck, Some Secret Pages of his History*, II, p. 475.

[5] See, e.g., Busch, op. cit., II, p. 122; *Die Grosse Politik*, III, chapter xx, *passim;* IV, No. 723; *Documents diplomatiques français*, II, No. 368.

But for the Italians the Tunisian episode was painfully revealing. The party of the Left, which had been in power since 1876 and had been the driving force behind the irredentist movement, had regarded good relations with France as one of the most important planks in its platform. Many members of the party were Neapolitans and Sicilians who were only half converted to the monarchical form of government. Some had been members of Garibaldi's famous Thousand in 1860 and had not entirely recovered from their earlier radicalism and republicanism. They had no sympathy with the "autocratic" empires, but looked for inspiration to the French Republic, which, since 1879, had passed completely under the control of the republican parties. Of Cairoli it has been said that he "lived in a world of continuous hallucination."[1] His hallucination was his unshakable belief that the French republican government would never do its Latin neighbour so mean a turn as to snatch away Tunis. This was the view of numerous radical deputies in Italy who constantly egged on the prime minister and who, therefore, were at least in part responsible for the disastrous outcome.

Men like General Cialdini and Count Maffei saw more clearly than Cairoli and his associates. Long before the occupation of Tunis was an accomplished fact, they had warned against too great faith in the French and had urged the necessity of enlisting the support of the central powers. After the failure of the first unofficial advances made through Gronert Goercke they continued their efforts in this direction. The evidence at our disposal is, however, so fragmentary that it is hardly possible to reconstruct the story of these negotiations. It appears that Herr von Keudell, the German ambassador at Rome, was a warm protagonist of the idea of an agreement between Italy and the central powers. Returning to his post in mid-October 1880, he had a conversation in Vienna with Baron Haymerlé, from which it appeared that the Austrian minister laid some store by the cultivation of better relations between Italy and the central powers. A neutrality treaty between Italy and Austria would, he said, be well worth while and would guarantee Austria against attack in the rear if she became involved in war with Russia. Possibly some consideration of Italian interests in the Mediterranean could be given in return. The time had not yet come for discussing a formal treaty, but the idea should not be discouraged.[2]

Bismarck showed no interest whatever in these suggestions. He was convinced that the Italians were pursuing a double-faced policy, that they were thoroughly unreliable, and that any agreement made with them would be lived up to only if it suited their interests. Without any guarantee of fulfilment such an agreement would be "absolutely worthless" for the preservation of peace. Ever since Crispi's mission in 1877, he told the French ambassador, he had lost all faith in the Italians. It would take a full page, reported Saint-Vallier, to record all the cutting remarks with which the chancellor flayed the Italian policy.[3]

---

[1] Torre, loc. cit., p. 109.   [2] *Die Grosse Politik*, III, Nos. 533, 534.
[3] *Die Grosse Politik*, III, No. 535; *Documents diplomatiques français*, II, Nos. 369, 440, etc.

In spite of this uncompromising stand on the part of the chancellor, Keudell seems to have continued his activities at Rome and to have encouraged the Italian statesmen to hope that an agreement between Italy and Austria would be welcomed in Berlin and would lead to an Italian-German treaty. With his approval Crispi secured permission from Cairoli to explore the ground. A secret agent named Hirling was entrusted with the mission and was sent to Vienna in January 1881 with oral instructions, which had been drawn up with Maffei's collaboration. The basis selected for negotiation was " respect for the *status quo* in the Orient as established by the Treaty of Berlin." Austria was to be kept from further expansion in the Balkans and especially on the shores of the Adriatic.

Hirling met with a better reception from Haymerlé than had been accorded Gronert Goercke by Bismarck. The Austrian minister eagerly welcomed the idea of a reciprocal assurance of neutrality in the event of attacks by foreign powers, and expressed the opinion that such an agreement could easily be reached. While reserving her freedom of action in Bosnia and Herzegovina, Austria was prepared to declare her intention of respecting scrupulously the *status quo* in the East: " She will not push forward to Salonika or into Albania, where she will carefully maintain the *status quo.*" At the same time Austria was ready to respect Italy's legitimate ambitions as a great maritime power: " She therefore not only will refrain from placing obstacles in Italy's way, but will derive satisfaction from the extension of her sphere of power in the Mediterranean, provided the *status quo* in the Adriatic remain intact and this sea be not converted into an Italian Lake. Influenced by these sentiments, Austria-Hungary will gladly accept any arrangement that may advance the interests of Italy in regard to the Tunisian question, and further the possible acquisition of Tripoli." [1]

Considerable interest attaches to these earlier exchanges between Rome and Vienna. They show, in the first place, that Haymerlé was quite prepared to come to some arrangement with the Italians, and that he was willing to make decided concessions by giving assurances in regard to Austrian policy in the Balkans and by promising support of Italian aspirations in North Africa. Having no faith in Russia, he had no enthusiasm for the idea of a new alliance of the three empires and would have preferred a treaty of neutrality with Italy so that Austria might be secure on her southern frontier if she became involved in war with Russia. Cairoli would have done well to follow up these earlier advances, for an alliance with Austria and perhaps with Germany would have changed the European alignment profoundly and might have given a very different turn to the Tunis question. But neither Cairoli nor Depretis had much sympathy for the policy advanced by Crispi and Maffei. They were still optimistic about Tunis, they were still unwilling to renounce all hope of securing the Trentino and Trieste, and they were still averse to the abandonment of the

---

1 Pribram, op. cit., II, pp. 8–9; Crispi, op. cit., II, pp. 119–22.

traditional policy of friendship with France. Even after the French occupation of Tunis the Italian leaders of the Left were unable to bring themselves to a reorientation of the national policy. Depretis continued to oppose a plan which would cause still greater estrangement between France and Italy, and appears to have wished to draw a veil over the Tunis episode.[1]

There was something incredibly doctrinaire about this attitude of Depretis. He did not, at first, seem to appreciate what a profound impression the French occupation of Tunis had made upon the Italian public. Clemenceau, the French radical leader, gauged the situation more accurately when he declared that the Treaty of Bardo had changed the diplomatic position of France to her own disadvantage, and that it had profoundly modified the diplomatic order of Europe. In Italy public feeling ran so high that Cairoli was obliged to resign. His whole group was pretty well discredited and the monarchy itself began to suffer from this colonial setback, following so soon upon the national reverse at the Congress of Berlin. An attempt was made to set up a ministry under the lead of Sella, one of the ablest men of the more conservative Right, but the country was in no mood for a cautious or circumspect policy. The extreme radicals and republicans threatened to seize power, a step which would have resulted inevitably in the overthrow of the monarchy and probably in an irredentist war against Austria. In the face of the radical menace Depretis, who had been minister of the interior under Cairoli, hastily formed a new cabinet, in which Pasquale Mancini became minister for foreign affairs.

Depretis was a prince of opportunists, in domestic as in foreign affairs. His policy, when a difficult question of international relations arose, was to put up his umbrella and wait for the storm to pass. So he himself put it. Being convinced of the desirability and possibility of maintaining close relations with France, and fearing the power of the Francophil radical group, he turned a deaf ear to all suggestions of a reorientation of Italian policy. Mancini shared the views of his chief, so there could, for the time being, be no thought of resuming the pourparlers with Austria.

And yet the country was in a furor. The French action was a hard blow to Italian pride, a blow that smarted more and more as time went on. In the middle of June there were serious anti-French outbreaks in Genoa, Milan, and Turin, which were meant as a reply to the attack upon Italian labourers at Marseilles by French troops returning from Tunis. In the Italian parliament, too, there was an outspoken demand for a new departure in foreign policy, while the press became vociferous in its outcry against the policy of the free hand which Cairoli had followed.

It was on May 29, 1881 that Sonnino, a prominent member of the parliamentary centre, published his famous article in the *Rassegna Settimanale,* in which he urged the necessity for closer relations with the central powers and England. First of all, he asserted, Italy must resolutely put aside the question

---

[1] Crispi, op. cit., II, p. 123; *Die Grosse Politik,* III, No. 536; Chiala, op. cit., III, p. 13.

of irredentism. The possession of Trieste was of supreme importance to Austria and was, at the same time, of interest to Germany, for Trieste was the most convenient port for the commerce of her interior regions. The population of the city was mixed, and to demand it as a right would be an exaggeration of the principle of nationality. As for the Trentino, it was certainly Italian, but the interest which Italy had in possessing this district was small compared to the value of Austrian friendship. " This friendship represents for us the free dis-position of all our forces on land and sea; it represents the authority of our word in the European concert. . . . Friendship with Austria is, for us, an indis-pensable condition for a conclusive and effective policy." Of equal necessity was friendship with England, which was just as much threatened as Italy by French preponderance in the Mediterranean. But the great object of Italian policy should be a closer accord with the central powers: " No conflicts of interest separate us from Germany, while many common interests unite us; primarily, the preservation of peace and the curbing of France's lust for power. As soon as we have removed the causes of distrust existing towards us in Austria, the accomplishment of an alliance with Germany will meet with no obstacle. Our diplomacy must accordingly remove every suspicion that our policy might be disadvantageous to the former power, in order to win for us her friendship. Isolation means annihilation." [1]

Sonnino by no means stood alone with his views. Some of the most influen-tial organs of the press joined in the demand for a rapprochement with the central powers, and Benedetto Croce is certainly right when he says of the Triple Alliance: " The truth is that the treaty was concluded as a result of the irresistible pressure of public opinion, led by deputies, senators and publicists of the greatest influence, including survivors of the Mantuan trials and of the Austrian prisons, like Cavalletto and Finzi, who all alike advised and urged it." [2] The Italians themselves, later on, preferred to give other explanations, but the evidence is irrefutable.

The Depretis ministry was finally obliged to yield to this popular pressure and to accept the suggestion of Baron Blanc, the secretary-general of the foreign office, that the King pay a visit to Francis Joseph at Vienna. The idea was first broached in the Austrian press, but was put in such a way that it seemed like an official pronouncement. Mancini allowed himself to be hurried into making a decision and did not even consult Count Robilant, the ambassador to Vienna, who favoured an agreement, but objected to Italy's throwing herself at the Austrians and therefore opposed the visit at that time. He tried to dissuade Mancini and Depretis from accompanying the King, on the plea that their presence would give the visit far too serious a complexion. Neither Depretis nor his foreign minister, however, relished the idea of being left out of the picture. From October 27 to 31 Humbert and his two chief advisers were in

---

[1] Chiala, op. cit., III, pp. 20–4.
[2] Benedetto Croce: *A History of Italy, 1871–1915* (New York, 1929), p. 121.

Vienna as the guests of Francis Joseph. After their departure even Robilant had to admit the unqualified success of the visit, though there had been no discussion of the great issue. The Austrians made no advances and were not in a position to negotiate, for Haymerlé had died a short time before and his successor had not yet been appointed.[1]

It is said that the Italian ministers went to Vienna prepared to offer the Austrian government a treaty by which the two powers should guarantee each other's territories, but that they said nothing because no opening was given them.[2] Whether or not this was so, the Italian foreign office made no further overtures during the succeeding weeks. Meanwhile some very important changes took place in the general European situation.

On November 14, 1881 Gambetta formed his first and only cabinet. He had been the power behind the government for several years, but personal jealousies and President Grévy's dislike of the popular tribune had prevented his assumption of power. The new cabinet was generally called "the Great Ministry," though Gambetta himself was the only great figure in it. His closest friends deserted him at the last moment and he was obliged to choose his colleagues chiefly from the ranks of subordinates and government clerks. Still, Gambetta himself was an impressive figure, and his advent to power sent a thrill through the European chancelleries. Here at last was the man who had galvanized France into resistance in 1870, who had made himself the champion of the lost provinces, and who had become the incarnation of the spirit of revenge. In a famous speech at Cherbourg, in August 1880, he had declared his faith in "immanent justice" that would right the wrong done in 1871. In an election address at Belleville one year later he had defined his policy as one which would aim at being on good terms with all the members of the European concert, but at the same time he had expressed his belief and hope that he would see the day when, by the majesty of right, truth, and justice, France would recover her separated brothers.[3]

In France Gambetta's enemies published a pamphlet entitled: *Gambetta c'est la guerre,* of which over one hundred thousand copies are said to have been distributed. It was generally felt that an era of active foreign policy was inevitable. The conservatives had taken the stand that since the victory of republicanism the best course for France would be one of abstention, because the republic was too weak to play a prominent role. The radicals, on the other hand, had put forward the argument that France should refrain from activity abroad because she had enough to do at home, and affairs beyond her frontiers

---

[1] The most complete account is in Chiala, op. cit., III, pp. 84–125. On Robilant see also Raffaele Cappelli: "La Politica Estera del Conte di Robilant" (Nuova Antologia, LXXII, pp. 3–10, November 1, 1897).

[2] Pribram, op. cit., II, p. 11.

[3] Joseph Reinach: Le Ministère Gambetta (Paris, 1884), pp. 375–6. There is a good account of the Cherbourg episode, by an eyewitness, in Henri Galli: Gambetta et l'Alsace-Lorraine (Paris, 1911), pp. 199–200.

were none of her business. But a Gambetta ministry without a determined foreign policy and perhaps war was almost unthinkable. Europe in general was on tenter-hooks, not quite knowing when or where the lightning would strike.

Curiously enough, Bismarck appears to have been less upset than other statesmen by Gambetta's advent to power. These two strong men had a peculiar attraction for each other. Bismarck had evidently hoped that Gambetta would pay him a visit in the summer of 1881 during his tour of the North German seaports. Nothing had come of it, but the German chancellor was determined to continue on the road he had marked out for himself. To Prince Hohenlohe, the ambassador at Paris, he said, in October 1881, that Germany could only be pleased if France found satisfaction elsewhere than on the Rhine. So long as France had no allies, there was no danger for Germany. Germany could defeat France, even if England were on the French side. But no matter who became minister in France, Germany's pacific policy would not be altered, even if that minister were Gambetta.[1]

As a matter of fact, the French army was still in poor shape, in spite of the efforts that had been made to purge and reorganize it after the republican victory of 1879. Lord Lyons, the English ambassador at Paris, was of the opinion that " certainly Gambetta would not find the nation in heart to follow him in defying Germany." [2] The estimate was probably correct. It is certain that Gambetta did not seriously consider making war on Germany, and Bismarck no doubt realized this and made due allowance.

In Italy, however, the ministerial changes in France caused the greatest uneasiness, for Gambetta was looked upon as the embodiment of aggressive French nationalism and republicanism. His advent to power, it was thought, would undoubtedly encourage the Italian radicals and republicans and further endanger the monarchy. The situation was particularly serious because radical agitators had already made a good deal of trouble. Fervent haters of the Papacy and all that it represented, they had resumed with new vigour their demonstrations against the Church. The smouldering passions of the anti-clericals led to a violent outburst on the night of July 12–13, when the remains of Pius IX were transferred to the Church of San Lorenzo, in accordance with his last will. The papal authorities had intended the ceremony to be secret, but the news leaked out and many thousands of people turned out for the occasion. Most of those in the crowds were, no doubt, devout Catholics, but a group of radicals took an all too active part in the proceedings, followed the hearse with imprecations, attempted to stop the procession, and even threatened to throw the corpse into the Tiber. The police contingent was wholly inadequate and apparently made no great effort to preserve order.[3]

---

[1] Hohenlohe: *Denkwürdigkeiten*, II, p. 319.   [2] Newton: *Lord Lyons*, II, p. 264.

[3] By far the best account is in Giuseppe Manfroni: *Sulla Soglia del Vaticano* (Bologna, 1925), Volume II, chapter xii. Manfroni was a government official and liaison officer between the government and the Vatican.

The anti-papal outbreak of July 12–13 was a matter of the most serious nature, for it revealed to the world that the Pope was exposed to the most outrageous humiliation, to put it mildly. In the Vatican itself there was a general panic, and some of the Pope's more irreconcilable advisers urged him to leave Rome and Italy and go into voluntary exile. We now know that rumours then current were substantially correct and that Leo did actually and seriously consider departure. This comes out clearly from his correspondence with Francis Joseph at the time.[1] The Italian government, getting wind of the deliberations which were taking place at the Vatican, became seriously alarmed, but hardly dared to deal firmly with the vigorous radicals. The question raised by a clerical paper whether Italy was ruled by a parliamentary government or by the Free Masonic Orders was not wholly inappropriate.

Throughout the autumn of 1881 the storm raged in Rome. The radicals organized a strong movement for the abolition of the law of guarantees, by which the Italian government had defined the position of the Pope. Some talked of blowing up the Vatican with dynamite and of perpetrating other atrocities. The clericals replied with all sorts of denunciations, which the Pope himself supported in his allocutions. His Holiness even went so far as to say that stones had been thrown at the remains of Pius IX. He bitterly decried the "pestiferous and insane doctrines" of the sects. Pilgrims who came to Rome did what they could to give vent to their sentiments. At the tomb of Victor Emmanuel II they shouted: "Long live the Pope King!" a cry which was positively anathema to the patriots.[2]

The government was almost helpless before this great tumult. Whatever course it took, it was bound to expose itself to violent attack and possibly to revolution. If it gave way to the radicals, the monarchy would be abandoned to its fate, or the Pope, fleeing from Italy, might be brought back in the train of foreign armies. It is more than likely that knowledge of Leo's correspondence with Francis Joseph was responsible for the hasty decision of King Humbert and his advisers to visit Vienna and for their readiness to consider a treaty of mutual guarantee with Austria. Such an arrangement would disarm the Austrian government and secure for the Italian cabinet Austrian support against future attempts to restore the temporal power. For that very reason, no doubt, the Austrians were reticent and evasive. In any case, the monarchy was in worse repute than ever with the radicals after the King's return. They called him "the Austrian colonel" and plastered the walls of Rome by night with posters accusing Humbert of Savoy of being no longer an Italian.[3]

The revolutionary agitation in Italy was not at all to Bismarck's liking, for it touched upon some of his own most troublesome problems. Ever since the

---

[1] Francesco Salata: *Per la Storia Diplomatica della Questione Romana* (Milan, 1929), pp. 134 ff.; Manfroni, op. cit., II, p. 60.

[2] Manfroni, op. cit., II, pp. 60–9.

[3] Ibid., II, p. 67.

introduction of the new tariff in 1879 had broken the ranks of the National Liberal party, he had lacked a firm supporting majority in the Reichstag and had been obliged to rely, more or less, upon the conservatives and Catholics. It was necessary for him, therefore, to put an end to the struggle with the Church and to bring the Kulturkampf to a close. Since the advent of Leo XIII desultory negotiations had been carried on with the Papal See, in an effort to reach some compromise. The latest move of Bismarck in this direction had been the mission of Kurd von Schlözer to the Pope in July and August 1881. The mission was secret, and almost nothing is known of it, but it appears that Schlözer suggested to His Holiness that the German government, while retaining the May laws on the statute books, would abstain from enforcing them rigorously. To these proposals Leo replied that pardon should be granted the persecuted German bishops, that the German legation at the Vatican should be re-established, and that the May laws should eventually be revised.[1]

Whether Bismarck liked these terms or not, he was soon forced to accept them at least in part, for after the elections of October 27 his parliamentary position was worse than ever. Arrangements were made for the reopening of the legation at the Vatican, and the chancellor himself made every effort to ingratiate himself with the clericals. Speaking in the Reichstag on November 29, he referred in unvarnished terms to the situation in Italy: " The idea of a republic haunts many Italian minds. . . . Can you give a guarantee for the future of the country, especially if God does not preserve the dynasty, which depends on only a few persons? . . . The road which Italy has travelled towards this goal in the last twenty years, is it not visible, and the goal itself (I do not maintain that it will be reached), is it not recognizable? Has not the centre of gravity shifted, from one ministry to the other, more and more to the left, so that now it cannot slide further to the left without falling into republican territory? " Hardly were these words spoken when a series of articles began to appear in the Berlin *Post,* an organ which frequently published inspired material. It can hardly be doubted that the substance of these articles came from an authoritative source, for they fitted in too well with the general policy of the chancellor at this time. Lucius reports him in these days as full of consideration for the Pope, at the expense of the Italian government, and notes, on December 8, 1881, that he was repeatedly emphasizing the necessity for making peace with Rome.[2]

The articles of the *Post* took as their starting-point a clerical pamphlet which had just appeared in Paris under the title: *La Situation du Pape et le dernier mot de la question romaine.* The argument put forward in this publication was that the position of the Pope in Rome had become untenable, and that his departure was therefore merely a question of time. The law of guarantees had

---

1 Kurd von Schlözer: *Letzte römische Briefe, 1882–1894* (Berlin, 1924), p. 5; Hohenlohe, op. cit., II, p. 319; Lucius von Ballhausen, op. cit., p. 213.

2 Lucius von Ballhausen, op. cit., pp. 218–19.

become ineffective, and should be re-established by the combined action of the powers. A sensible solution of the Roman question would be the transference of the Italian capital to Florence, where it had been from 1860 to 1871, and the return of the city of Rome and the port of Civitavecchia to the Pope.

The writer in the *Post* agreed that the position of the Pope had become untenable, for in the city of St. Peter the Pope could not appear on the same footing as unbelievers of all sorts, atheists and Jews. But how was the Pope to recover sole possession of Rome? The answer was: by voluntary exile. His departure from Rome would lead to the victory of radicalism and would result in the establishment of an atheistic republic. Even if these changes eventually gave rise to a reaction and to the revival of the monarchy, the restored ruler would be obliged to recall the Pope on much more favourable conditions. A second article in the series argued that the time had come for the Papacy to make a decision: either it must make vigorous efforts to effect a reconciliation with the government, or else it must leave Rome. If the Pope took his departure, Italian public opinion would soon realize that Italy had been harmed more than the Pope himself, because, whatever the Italians might say about the Roman question, this problem was an international one which concerned all states with a Catholic population. Finally, in the third article of the series the question was asked how long Europe could avoid a settlement in common of this question and whether Europe could continue to leave the matter to the two powers most directly concerned, the Papacy and the Kingdom of Italy. The writer denied that he was trying to bring about European intervention to restore the temporal power, but insisted that the Pope could put before the Italian government the question whether it would assure him a better position on Italian soil or whether it would oblige him to leave Italy altogether.[1]

The articles in the *Post* appeared on December 1, 10, and 17 and, following so closely upon Bismarck's disparaging remarks in the Reichstag, created consternation in Italian government circles. The general situation led to a heated debate in the chamber on December 6. Sonnino insisted that the visit to Vienna should now be followed by a definite agreement, not only with Austria, but with Germany. The idea of an alliance with France should be given up entirely. Minghetti supported this view and pointed out that Italy must give the powers guarantees of stability and safety: "The best reply to Bismarck's utterances will be deeds." Mancini had evidently been forced to come to the same conclusion. In his reply he indicated the intention of the government to cultivate closer relations with Vienna and Berlin and establish with the central powers "common action in European politics."[2]

The critical stage had certainly been reached and the Italian government had come to the parting of the ways, for while the prospect of the Pope's leaving

---

[1] These articles are reprinted in full in Bastgen: *Die römische Frage* (Freiburg, 1919), III, pp. 20–7; on pages 256 ff. a number of other important press utterances are reproduced.

[2] Chiala, op. cit., III, pp. 176–88.

Rome opened up a vista of international complications, news came that Gambetta was considering sending a special agent to the Italian capital to attempt a rapprochement between France and Italy and to keep Italy from joining the central powers. Mancini was apparently still hesitant and was supported by Robilant, who thought that negotiations with Vienna would be premature. Blanc, on the other hand, exerted himself to the utmost to bring about the realization of his plan: " I believe there is no time to be lost in driving in with heavy blows the nail that was set at Vienna," he wrote Robilant.[1]

Not content with these efforts, Blanc went so far as to approach both the German and the Austrian ambassadors with a view to determining whether advances made by the Italian government would be favourably received. In his conversations he laid great stress on the danger to which the monarchy was exposed and to the uneasiness of many of the more conservative Italians in regard to Gambetta's approaches. What he desired was some sort of treaty of territorial guarantee.

The soundings of the Italian secretary-general were received with different feelings in Berlin and Vienna. Bismarck, while admitting the value of treaties of guarantee in general, still maintained his earlier view-point that an agreement with Italy would be a one-sided pact, for there was no certainty that a new Italian ministry would be able to live up to its obligations, and it seemed more than doubtful whether Italy would ever actually take the field against France. Kálnoky, the new Austrian foreign minister, on the other hand, was deeply impressed with the dangers which threatened the Italian monarchy. It could not be a matter of indifference to the other monarchies, he argued, that one throne after another should be overturned and a group of Latin republics arise in Europe. At the same time, there could be no doubt that the fall of the monarchy in Italy would jeopardize the position of the Papacy in Rome. Such an event would raise unforeseeable difficulties for Austria. Still, he found no particular advantage in a treaty of guarantee, for Italy was not really threatened by any foreign power; neither did he believe that much faith could be placed in Italian promises of support.[2]

Kálnoky's attitude made a deep impression on Bismarck, for it revealed to him how much store the Austrians put by the establishment of good relations with their southern neighbour. He therefore modified his attitude. Writing to the German ambassador at Vienna on December 28, he pointed out that a treaty of guarantee would involve a guarantee by Austria and Germany of the Italian possession of Rome. This action would not be wholly without danger for any state with a large Catholic population. But doubts on this point would be removed if the Italian government succeeded in coming to an arrangement with the Pope by which the latter would be enabled to live independently and

---

1 Ibid., III, pp. 226, 234, 235. On French pressure and influence see also Blanc's letter of March 1888 to Sir Charles Dilke (Gwynn and Tuckwell, op. cit., I, p. 478).
2 *Die Grosse Politik*, III, Nos. 538–40; Pribram, op. cit., II, pp. 11–12.

in dignified fashion in Rome. The German chancellor agreed with his Austrian colleague respecting the danger to which the Italian monarchy was exposed, though he doubted whether the overthrow of the monarchy would necessarily jeopardize the Pope's position. The old liberal idea of an Italian federation under the presidency of the Pope might prove workable and it was conceivable that the Pope might make better arrangements with a group of Italian republics than with the monarchy. In any case, a republicanized Italy would seek a close and permanent connexion with France. Therefore he thought it would be unwise to reject offhand any overtures which the Italians might make. An agreement with them might cause international tension, but this could be overcome so long as Austria and Germany maintained close relations with Russia. His advice, therefore, was that the Austrians should not decline straightway any proposal that might strengthen the position of the King of Italy, but should express a wish for the establishment of a *modus vivendi* agreeable to the Pope. If serious negotiations were then opened, the assumption of obligations by Austria and Germany should be made dependent on the duration of their existing relations with Russia. Kálnoky assented to these arguments, in a general way, though he could not see how the settlement of the Roman question could be brought about.[1]

These preliminary exchanges of opinion between Berlin and Vienna have been entered into at some length because a full appreciation of them is necessary for an understanding of the subsequent negotiations. Several points stand out very clearly: For example, the usual explanation of the Triple Alliance as a direct result of the French occupation of Tunis should be put aside. That event certainly estranged France and Italy, but it did not expose Italy to the danger of a French attack. Even Italian historians admit that Italy was not really menaced, and that was also Kálnoky's opinion.[2] The important thing was that the Tunis affair showed Italy the completeness of her isolation and thereby gave rise to agitation for an agreement with the central powers. But it cannot be doubted that neither Depretis nor Mancini had any use for this solution. Nothing was done, as a matter of fact, until the Roman question came to the fore in July, and the Italian government was confronted with the danger of international action in what it considered a domestic matter. These events explain the precipitous visit to Vienna and the readiness of the Italian ministers to negotiate a treaty of guarantee. It is important to note that they put forward the idea of a treaty of guarantee rather than of a treaty of neutrality. The former would have assured them in regard to the Roman question. Had they been apprehensive of a French attack, they would have been eager for a neutrality treaty or something stronger yet. On the other hand, a treaty of guarantee could hold no attraction for either Austria or Germany. For them it would only mean awkward complications. That is why nothing was done. That is why the

---

[1] *Die Grosse Politik,* III, Nos. 541–2; Pribram, op. cit., II, p. 12.
[2] Chiala, op. cit., III, p. 79; *Die Grosse Politik,* III, No. 540.

Italians temporized until, in December 1881, the whole papal question came up in its most acute form.

In his Christmas allocution to the assembled cardinals Leo XIII declared the existing situation to be absolutely incompatible with the freedom and dignity of the Papal See and demanded the restoration of the temporal power. Bismarck believed that this uncompromising pronouncement might make the Italian government more eager than before to find support among the powers and might lead to concrete proposals. The German chancellor was right. On December 30 the Austrian ambassador was able to report that the King, assuming the initiative, had induced his ministers to take a definite step forward. The Italian ambassadors at Vienna and Berlin had been instructed to inform the governments to which they were accredited that, "without regard to specific questions," the King wished to join hands with Germany and Austria-Hungary and was ready to come to an understanding with the central powers even if the obligations which they had assumed towards other powers stood in the way of concluding an alliance with Italy.[1]

We do not know just how these instructions were carried out or what response they evoked, but it seems that Count de Launay, the ambassador at Berlin, found the Germans still distrustful, while Count Robilant, at Vienna, appears to have hung back and postponed action, on the plea that the Italian government was too radical to please the Austrian, and that Italy should not throw herself at the Austrians.[2] In conversation with Kálnoky on January 18, he confined himself to generalities, expressing the desire of his government to make an alliance with Germany and Austria and to strengthen relations with those countries by engagements of a more precise nature. But he did not formally propose an alliance or even say whether the Italian government had in mind a treaty of guarantee or a treaty of neutrality. Kálnoky replied in equally vague terms, harping on the theme of monarchical solidarity, but referring to his distrust of written secret treaties and indicating his doubt as to the seriousness of Depretis.[3]

Count de Launay, the Italian ambassador at Berlin, was one of the most enthusiastic proponents of an agreement. In conversation with Bismarck he not only expressed the readiness of his government to enter upon binding engagements, but invited the chancellor to draft an alliance between Italy and the central powers or even with all the three empires together. Bismarck, however, refused as firmly as ever to act as mediator, repeating that the key to the German door was to be found in Vienna, and stressing, like Kálnoky, the difficulties of drawing up a secret treaty with a parliamentary government. "In a country where the king goes about in civilian clothes, his position of command cannot be counted on," he remarked.

---

[1] Pribram, op. cit., II, pp. 12–13.
[2] Chiala, op. cit., III, pp. 255–7; Cappelli, loc. cit., p. 5.
[3] Pribram, op. cit., II, pp. 13–14; Die Grosse Politik, III, No. 543.

So the negotiations made little progress. Robilant evidently had instructions, but refused to carry them out, thereby creating considerable tension in the relations between himself and Mancini. Finally, on February 19, Kálnoky took the initiative and questioned Robilant about his supposed instructions. The conversation took an academic turn. Eventually the ambassador came forward with his proposal for a treaty of guarantee. This suggestion the Austrian minister flatly refused to entertain. The territories of the three powers, he said, were of such an extent that no parliamentary minister could lightly assume the responsibilities arising from such a territorial guarantee. Undoubtedly there was something in this argument, but we know from the correspondence between Vienna and Berlin that Kálnoky's real objection to a treaty of guarantee arose from the fact that the Austrian government wished to avoid a recognition of the possession of Rome by the Italian government. This, of course, was just what the Italians were angling for. So the situation reduced itself to this: Kálnoky refused the suggestion of a guarantee treaty, while Robilant rejected his interlocutor's proposal of a neutrality treaty, on the ground that no profit for Italy could be discerned in it. Kálnoky's emphasis on the value of Austrian neutrality for Italy in case of a Franco-Italian war brought no response from Robilant — another indication that the danger of French aggression played almost no part in the matter. So the conversation ended with some discussion of a possible general agreement providing for mutual support and common action in questions that might arise. What was meant here was evidently joint action in Balkan affairs and support for Italian activities in the Mediterranean.[1]

There was not much prospect of agreement after these preliminary exchanges. The starting-points chosen by the Italians and the Austrians were so far apart that it seemed unlikely that they would eventually meet. The one party desired a treaty of guarantee which the other refused to give. The second offered a treaty of neutrality which appeared to the first quite useless. In the meanwhile, however, events were taking place in Europe which distinctly affected the negotiations because they served to modify the views of the German chancellor. In order to understand this development a brief digression is necessary.

Bismarck once said that Gambetta's advent to power would act on the nerves of Europe like a man beating a drum in a sick-room. He himself had taken the new ministry philosophically, relying on the inability and unwillingness of the French people to embark on an adventurous policy. But on the other powers the cabinet change in France in November 1881 did have a nerve-racking effect. The governments were worried for fear lest the delicately adjusted international balance should be upset, while the radicals and revolutionaries everywhere took heart. As a matter of fact, Gambetta himself recognized that the time was not ripe for attempting to conclude definite alliances, but he did,

---

[1] Pribram, op. cit., II, pp. 14–16; *Die Grosse Politik*, III, Nos. 545–7; Chiala, op. cit., III, pp. 263–5.

during his brief tenure of office, make strenuous efforts to cultivate useful friendships and thus prepare the way for the future. We know for an actual fact that his ultimate goal was the conclusion of an agreement with England and Russia. In other words, he already envisaged the so-called Triple Entente of later years, which was to prove fatal to German preponderance in Europe. It was in accordance with this policy that he made efforts to conclude a commercial treaty with England and to strengthen the principle of joint action in the Egyptian question, which was becoming more and more critical. It was also in accordance with this policy that he chose as his collaborators men of royalist views, like General Miribel, and sent to Russia as ambassador Count Chaudordy, one of his ablest assistants.[1]

Gambetta's attempt to draw closer to Russia may appear rather ludicrous to the present generation, which knows of the alliance between Russia, Germany, and Austria concluded in June 1881. But, as a matter of fact, this treaty had by no means clarified the atmosphere completely. The new Tsar, Alexander III, had long been an adherent of the nationalist doctrine, and he had among his advisers men like Miliutin and Ignatiev and Pobiedonostsev, who were the strong men of the Slavophil and Panslavic groups. Gorchakov was in retirement, and died in 1882. His successor, Giers, held a purely subordinate position until his formal appointment as minister of foreign affairs in April 1882. At best he was primarily a bureaucrat. Under the circumstances he could not hope to compete with Ignatiev, who was minister of the interior. The upshot of it all was that the future development of the situation in Russia was obscure. Bismarck had engineered a meeting between the Tsar and the German Emperor at Danzig in September 1881 and had tried hard to point out to the Russian autocrat the extent of the revolutionary danger and the necessity for the monarchies to stand together. But the Danzig meeting had little effect. Ignatiev gave free rein to the nationalist agitation in Russia, and, together with Michael Katkov, the great editor of the *Moscow Gazette,* exercised a decisive influence on the Tsar. For a time it seemed more than likely that Ignatiev would be appointed foreign minister.

This situation caused Bismarck great uneasiness. The Panslavic group in Russia was filled with hatred of Austria, and indirectly of Germany, the ally and supporter of Austria. It followed naturally from this that many members of the group were generally sympathetic to the idea of a rapprochement with France, the natural ally of Russia against the central powers. They even converted the Tsar in some measure to this view. Alexander was deeply impressed with Gambetta's appointment of men like Miribel and Chaudordy, and, though he could not sympathize with the republican form of government, with its characteristic instability, he was not wholly blind to the desirability of close relations with France. General Chanzy, leaving his St. Petersburg post in

---

[1] Freycinet: *Souvenirs,* pp. 108–11, 175, 182; Reinach: *Le Ministère Gambetta,* pp. 408–10; Deschanel: *Gambetta,* pp. 286, 303.

December 1881, was able to report that his audience with the Tsar had left with him the impression that the Russians were well-disposed to maintain close connexions with France, that they had confidence in the republic, and that it depended upon the French themselves whether relations continued friendly.[1]

During a visit which General von Schweinitz paid to Bismarck in the last days of October 1881, the chancellor spoke of the possibility of war with Russia and France. The future of Russian policy remained uncertain throughout the winter. Then, in January and February 1882, a crisis was reached. General Skobelev, hero of the war of 1877-8, and victor over the central Asian tribesmen in the battle of Geok-Tepe (January 1881), arrived in Paris in January 1882. The general was known to be one of the most prominent Pan-Slavs and was, perhaps, the most popular man in Russia at the time. Everyone knew and admired the " White General," who had all the dash and personal charm of the traditional hero. It was therefore natural that his words should arrest the attention of Europe.

Skobelev's visit to Paris was not a chance occurrence. Even before he left Moscow, he made a resounding speech denouncing the oppression of the Slavic peoples by the Germans. It was the time of the great insurrection against Austrian rule in Bosnia and Herzegovina, and Skobelev was probably expressing the feelings of all Pan-Slavs when he told the German military attaché that the Austrian shots echoed in his own breast. Russia would, he said, be driven eventually to acts of desperation. In Paris the general made no formal address, but he spoke to a group of Serbian students in very strong terms. Europe, he declared, was in imminent danger of a great war, for Austria was trampling underfoot the provisions of the Treaty of Berlin, and Germany was doing nothing to hold her back: " The Slavs must struggle unceasingly. It is a long and arduous contest between two civilizations; it is going on in every Slavonic land, but if we are true to ourselves, in the end we shall be victorious."

There was much dispute as to what further statements the general made. The sympathetic part of the French press reported his saying that the German was the enemy of the Russian and the Slav: " A struggle is inevitable between the Teuton and the Slav. It cannot be long deferred. It will be long, sanguinary, and terrible, but I have faith that it will culminate in the victory of the Slav." Whether these were his actual words is a question of no consequence. Skobelev's admirers admitted that they represented his views, and they were hailed with enthusiasm by the group of French publicists who agitated for an alliance between France and Russia.

Gambetta fell from power on January 26, before the White General made his resounding utterances. Whether he had anything to do with the visit it is hard to say. It is fairly clear, however, that his friend Madame Adam (Juliette

---

[1] Edmond Toutain: *Alexandre III et la République Française* (Paris, 1929), pp. 7-11; Hanotaux, op. cit., IV, p. 739; Schweinitz: *Denkwürdigkeiten*, II, pp. 173, 178.

Lamber), one of the leading protagonists of a Franco-Russian alliance against the Germans, was involved in the plans. Gambetta and his followers evidently appreciated the danger of so downright a challenge of the Germans and toned down their enthusiasm. But Gambetta met Skobelev privately at the home of General Galiffet. On this occasion the White General spoke his mind freely and proposed an alliance between France and Russia. Both Gambetta and Galiffet asserted that they rejected the idea. However this may have been, Skobelev was disappointed by Gambetta's reticence, though it is said that the French leader thanked him for his speech and declared that it had filled " all hearts with patriotic ardour and had roused hopes of a Franco-Russian alliance." To one of his closest friends Gambetta confessed that Skobelev's idea was to " let loose upon Germany all the warlike peoples of Asia and to crush Germany under the weight of these galloping nomad hordes." [1]

Skobelev had no official mission, and his opinions were, technically speaking, private opinions. But these facts were of no importance, because the situation in Russia was so confused and the general was so popular that there was no knowing whether he would not turn out to be the leader of a movement that would carry the country with him. Pobiedonostsev, the teacher and adviser of Alexander III, warned his sovereign of the dangerous popularity of the hero, who was supported by Ignatiev, the powerful Pan-Slav leader and minister of the interior. In a sense Skobelev and his friends were a menace to the Russian autocracy itself. For this reason the Emperor William and Kálnoky were outraged by his utterances and wanted to demand that the Russian government disavow and reprimand him. Russian diplomats appreciated the dangers of the situation and feared the consequences. But Bismarck felt that it would be dangerous to magnify the affair by insisting on satisfaction, which would only make Skobelev a martyr. He abstained from official protests, but in private he spoke of the general in scathing terms. At the same time he mobilized the German press. He instructed his henchmen to make the Russian hero ridiculous and to warn the Tsar against allowing such lack of discipline in the army. Eventually Giers induced the Tsar to recall Skobelev from Paris, but even then the general took his time about going home. On his way he stopped at Warsaw and made yet another speech, this time appealing to the Poles, as fellow Slavs, to stand by their Russian brothers against the growing power of Germanism. It was only then that he was reprimanded by the Tsar and told to abstain from further political pronouncements. In April Giers was formally appointed minister for foreign affairs, after the German ambassador had used all his influence in that direction. In June Ignatiev was dismissed from the post of minister of the interior. The struggle between the Pan-Slavs and the

---

[1] Henri Galli: *Gambetta et l'Alsace-Lorraine*, p. 242; *Die Grosse Politik*, VI, No. 1210. On Skobelev see especially Olga Novikova: *Skobeleff and the Slavonic Cause* (London, 1883), part II, chapter iii; and Mme Adam: *Le Général Skobeleff* (fifth edition, Paris, 1886), chapter vi.

moderate elements in the diplomatic service came to a temporary close. Before the year was out, both Gambetta and Skobelev were in their graves.[1]

Before the Russian scene began to clear, the international situation seemed very disheartening, at least as viewed from Berlin and Vienna. Skobelev's speech in Paris was made on February 17. On February 28 instructions were sent from Berlin to the ambassador at Vienna. In these instructions Bismarck approved entirely the stand taken by the Austrian foreign minister with respect to the Italian proposal for a treaty of guarantee. He advised Kálnoky " to turn a deaf ear as long as possible to everything concerning the Pope." On the other hand, the general situation was such that the chancellor now felt more inclined to enter upon a written agreement with Italy. He realized that this could not be done without making concessions, and he therefore advised Kálnoky not to stand too firmly by the idea of a neutrality treaty plain and simple. Clearly such an agreement would not satisfy the Italians. Yet if the Italians were left to themselves, they might be tempted to enter into an " active alliance " with France, in return for a guarantee of the possession of Rome. To forestall this, the central powers should consider whether it would not be well to give Italy assurances of support in case of an unprovoked attack by France. The offer should be made on the basis of reciprocity, partly to save Italy's self-respect, partly in the interest of the central powers themselves. Italy would be of little help for action outside her own borders, but it was of importance to the central powers to be assured against attack from the south in the event of a war on two fronts. The agreement could no longer be made dependent on the relations between Germany and Austria and Russia, for there was no telling what the outcome of the conflict of forces in Russia would be.[2]

This dispatch marks an entirely new departure in the negotiations. It was bound to meet with a favourable response in Italy. Baron Blanc, in fact, was so anxious for an understanding that he had already assured the Austrian ambassador that " the question of Rome had no bearing on the positive agreement which the Italian government wished to conclude with Austria-Hungary," and that what was wanted was an alliance similar to the Austro-German Alliance, which would go hand in hand with an Italian policy of conciliation and friendship towards France.[3] In this way Blanc tried to dispel the suspicions of Kálnoky and Bismarck. Both sides had approached nearer the goal.

For about two weeks, however, little progress was made, since the divergence in view between influential members of the Italian government made it im-

---

[1] Schweinitz: *Denkwürdigkeiten*, II, pp. 186, 194; Waldersee: *Denkwürdigkeiten*, I, pp. 219–20; E. V. Tarle: "*Ryech Gen. Skobeleva v Parishe v 1882 goda*" (*Krasny Arkhiv*, No. xxvii, 1928, pp. 215–25). There is a detailed discussion, based in part on unpublished German papers, by Hans Herzfeld: "*Bismarck und die Skobelev-Episode*" (*Historische Zeitschrift*, CXLII, pp. 279–302, 1930).

[2] *Die Grosse Politik*, III, No. 548; Pribram, op. cit., II, p. 18.

[3] Pribram, op. cit., II, p. 17.

possible to decide on the proposals which Italy should make. Blanc seems to have favoured an oral and informal agreement in general terms, by which the contracting parties should, in case of common danger, come to a closer understanding and, in case of necessity, take such measures as might be necessary for lending each other assistance. Depretis, on the other hand, was cool towards the whole project and finally insisted on a defensive treaty of neutrality which should be limited in scope to a war with France.[1] Eventually the discussion ended in a compromise. On March 19 the Austrian ambassador was able to telegraph to Vienna the substance of the proposals that would be made. In the meanwhile Kálnoky, who did not like the idea of an alliance specifically directed against French action, insisted that for Austria the chief enemy was Russia, and that therefore the provision for support against unprovoked attack should be made general. In anticipation of the Italian proposals he drew up a draft treaty for his own guidance. He had, from the start, suspected the Italians of having secret commitments to Russia and intended to get light on this subject by confronting them with concrete terms.

On March 22 Count Robilant finally came forward with the Italian proposals. First of all he resurrected the matter of a treaty of guarantee, but, finding Kálnoky immovable on this point, he proceeded to discuss a treaty of neutrality. Simple neutrality, however, would be insufficient. Italy, to be sure, had only one dangerous neighbour, France, but France was not only dangerous as a military power; she was also a menace to the monarchical interests and the social order of Italy. Therefore what Italy wanted was a treaty couched in the following terms: In the event that France, under no matter what pretext, should attack Italy without provocation, the two other powers should pledge themselves to furnish assistance to the attacked party with all their forces. The same obligation should rest upon Italy in the event of an unprovoked attack by France upon Germany. In case of war between the two empires and Russia, Italy should remain benevolently neutral, but she should take active part on the side of her allies if France entered into action. Should one or more of the contracting parties become otherwise involved in war, the others should observe benevolent neutrality, and, if occasion should arise, come to a further agreement with regard to furnishing aid.

These proposals were so closely in accord with the suggestions that Bismarck had made to Kálnoky a few weeks before that one can hardly escape the conclusion that they were inspired by the German ambassador. If so, they indicate that the chancellor was now eager to come to an agreement. Kálnoky received the Italian advances with reserve, though he was pleased to note that they did not involve Austria in a possible conflict between Germany and France. He did not raise the question of Italian support of Austria if the latter were attacked by Russia, probably because he did not want to introduce Italy to the

---

[1] Pribram, op. cit., II, pp. 19-20.

Balkan field, and perhaps because he shared Bismarck's view that the chief object of the central powers should be "to save Austria's fighting forces rather than to secure Italy's."[1]

From this point onward the negotiations moved quickly. The matters under discussion were chiefly questions of redaction. Into the details of all the drafts and counter-drafts, the proposals and counter-proposals, it is unnecessary to enter, since there were no fundamental questions of principle involved. The chief points of interest were three: firstly, Robilant's repeated efforts to smuggle in "as contraband," to use Kálnoky's expression, some guarantee of Rome; secondly, Mancini's attempt to extend the agreement so as to secure for Italy support in her Mediterranean policy; thirdly, the Italian suggestion that a protocol be added making possible the admission of England to the alliance, or at least providing for her acceptance of the neutrality formula. The request for a guarantee of Rome was, of course, rejected. The same was true of the proposal for an extension of the agreement, for the central powers felt that Italy was getting the chief benefit from the treaty as it was, and her colonial ambitions were so extensive that they would soon lead to complications with other states, notably France, if they were encouraged. Most important and interesting was the point concerning England. The central powers fully understood the Italian position and realized that Italy and England had a common interest in checking French expansion in the Mediterranean. That Italy could on no account afford to arouse the hostility of England was also clear, for her long sea-coast was peculiarly exposed to naval attack. But Kálnoky and Bismarck were agreed that the Italian desire could not be entirely satisfied. They feared that the English radicals in Gladstone's cabinet, friends of France like Dilke and Chamberlain, would report the whole treaty to Paris if they knew about it. On the other hand, they were willing to include in the agreement a declaration that it was not directed against England, and this was actually done.

During the last weeks of the negotiations Bismarck made every effort to have the thing wound up. Time and again he wrote to Vienna stressing the fact that in an alliance with Italy the form of the agreement was of relatively little importance. The main thing was to have the agreement and to secure Italian neutrality. As he said on a later occasion, he would be satisfied if, during a European war in which the central powers were involved, "one Italian corporal with the Italian flag and a drummer at his side should take the field on the western front (against France), and not on the eastern front (against Austria)." Just as he had argued a year before that Russia, however untrustworthy, would be less likely to take hostile action if a treaty existed than if nothing bound her, so now he argued from a purely negative standpoint. Ger-

---

[1] Pribram, op. cit., II, p. 28. We are dependent for our knowledge of the negotiations entirely upon Pribram, op. cit., pp. 3–43; *Die Grosse Politik,* III, chapter xv; and Chiala, op. cit., III, pp. 265–320. Detailed references appear, therefore, to be superfluous.

many and Austria did not need Italian help and did not expect it. All they wanted was the assurance that Italy would not be antagonistic and in that way tie up valuable Austrian forces on the Austro-Italian frontier. Under such pressure from the German chancellor the last difficulties were soon overcome, and the treaty was signed on May 20, 1882.

Although the final version did not differ in any essential point from the draft suggestions made by Robilant, it may be desirable to recapitulate the terms here. The curious thing about the text is the preamble, which states that the rulers of Austria, Germany, and Italy, " animated by the desire to increase the guarantees of peace, to fortify the monarchical principle, and thereby to assure the unimpaired maintenance of the social and political order in their respective states, have agreed to conclude a treaty which, by its essentially conservative and defensive nature, pursues only the aim of forestalling the dangers which might threaten the security of their states and the peace of Europe." This declaration is interesting not only for its stress on the desire to fortify the monarchical principle, but also for its emphasis on the maintenance of the social and political order. In a sense this last phrase might be interpreted as a tacit recognition of the possession of Rome, and it was no doubt in reliance upon this preamble that Italian statesmen later on repeatedly stated in public utterances that the treaty guaranteed the status of Rome. However that may be, the rest of the text secured the same end in practice, even though indirectly.

Article I stated that the contracting parties promised each other peace and friendship, and that they would enter into no alliance or engagement directed against any one of them. They engaged further to exchange ideas on political and economic questions of a general nature which might arise, and they promised mutual support within the limits of their own interests.

Article II declared that if Italy were attacked by France without provocation, Germany and Austria would come to Italy's assistance with all their forces. Italy was similarly obliged to come to the assistance of Germany if the latter were attacked without provocation by France.

Article III provided that if one or two of the contracting parties, without provocation on their part, were attacked or engaged in war with two or more great powers not members of the alliance, the non-attacked member or members of the alliance should come to the aid of the other or others.

Article IV specified that if a great power non-signatory to the treaty should threaten the security of the states of one of the contracting powers, and the threatened party should find itself forced to make war, the other two parties should observe a benevolent neutrality, while reserving the right to take part in the war on the side of their ally if they should see fit to do so.

Article V stated that if the peace of any of the contracting parties should be threatened as foreseen in the preceding articles, the parties to the treaty should take counsel together in ample time as to military measures to be taken with a view to eventual co-operation. In case of common participation in war they engaged not to conclude an armistice, peace, or treaty except by common agreement.

Article VI provided for secrecy as to the contents and the existence of the treaty. Article VII fixed its duration at five years. Article VIII dealt with ratification.

A word of explanation should be given in regard to Articles III and IV. Article III was obviously intended to provide for a Franco-Russian war against the central powers and was designed to assure Italy's co-operation on the side of the allies of 1879. Article IV envisaged primarily a war of Germany or Austria with Russia and secured Italy's benevolent neutrality for such a conflict.

The Triple Alliance continued in existence until 1915 and was therefore one of the most stable and important of the European alignments. Its actual terms were not known until after the World War. Consequently there was a good deal of speculation as to its contents. The very fact that Italy and Austria had at last come together in an agreement stimulated the curiosity of historians and of the politically-minded public. As a matter of fact, however, the treaty in itself was not so important as many have thought, certainly not in this first period. Bismarck and Kálnoky were under no illusions about the value of Italian support and were interested only in keeping Italy from joining their enemies. The treaty gave them the assurance that Italy would not join a hostile combination, and that she would not attack Austria in the rear in case of war between Austria and Russia. Italian writers frequently argued that Italy derived very little benefit from the agreement, and Depretis apparently did not believe, even when the treaty was signed, that it was worth while or that the advantages would outweigh the disadvantage involved in estranging France.[1]

There is some truth in the argument, for Italy got from the treaty what she did not really need: namely, a promise of support in case of French attack. There was no danger of such a contingency arising at the time. In fact, the Italian and French governments signed an important commercial treaty just five days before the secret treaty of the Triple Alliance was concluded. The real Italian desires for a guarantee of Rome and for support in colonial policy were satisfied only indirectly, through the preamble and the vague second part of Article I. Still, the papal question was solved for the Italian government, no matter how indirectly, for the treaty obviated the danger that Austria or Germany would take steps to restore the temporal power, and provided for support if France should attempt any such action.

Leo XIII understood the significance of the Austro-Italian rapprochement, even if he did not know the terms of the treaty. He was so discouraged and disheartened by the negotiations that Francis Joseph found it advisable to send Baron Hübner, the famous Austrian diplomat, on an extended special mission to the Vatican. Hübner found the Pope in desperate straits. Leo insisted that

---

[1] Chiala, op. cit., III, p. 318.

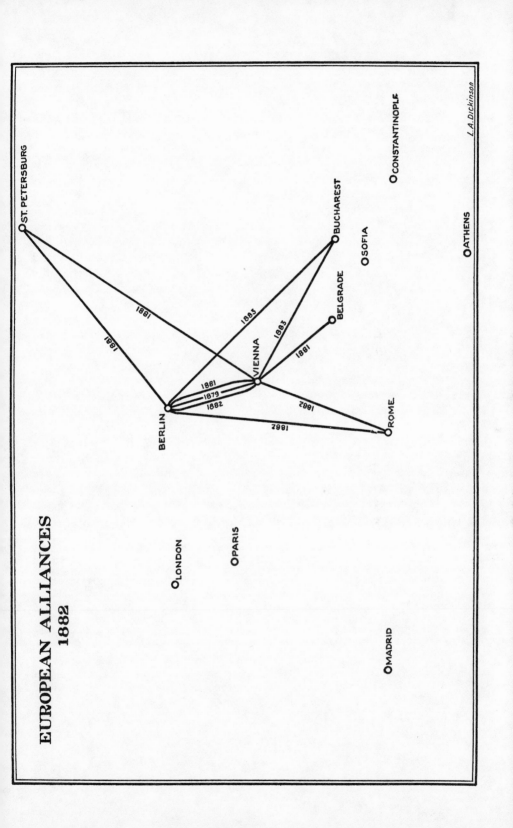

EUROPEAN ALLIANCES
1882

ST. PETERSBURG

BUCHAREST

CONSTANTINOPLE

SOFIA

BELGRADE

ATHENS

VIENNA

BERLIN

ROME

LONDON

PARIS

MADRID

1881

1881

1883

1883

1881

1881

1879

1882

1882

1882

L.A.Dickinson

in order to live properly at Rome it was necessary for him to leave and then return with the aid of foreign rulers, who ought to understand that their cause and his were one and the same. He had not set a definite date for his departure, but Hübner had a hard time convincing His Holiness that he should contemplate leaving Rome only as a last desperate resort.[1] In the long run, therefore, the Italians secured from the treaty all they could reasonably expect, even though they were denied the satisfaction of having a guarantee black on white.

BIBLIOGRAPHICAL NOTE

DOCUMENTARY SOURCES

PRIBRAM, ALFRED F.: *The Secret Treaties of Austria-Hungary, 1879–1914.* Cambridge, 1920. Contains the texts of the Triple Alliance and the account of the negotiations from the Austrian side.

Die Grosse Politik der europäischen Kabinette, 1871–1914. Volume III, chapter xv, contains the German documents dealing with the Triple Alliance of 1882; chapter xx deals with the Franco-German relationship from 1878 to 1885.

Documents diplomatiques français, Volume II. Paris, 1930. Contains a number of documents on the Tunis question in the period prior to 1880.

Documents diplomatiques. Affaires de Tunisie, 1870–1881. Paris, 1881.

Documents diplomatiques. Affaires de Tunisie. Supplément, Avril–Mai, 1881. Paris, 1881.

Accounts and Papers. 1881. Volume XCIX. *Tunis,* Nos. I, II, III, IV.

BOURGEOIS, EMILE, and PAGÈS, GEORGES: *Les Origines et les responsabilités de la Grande Guerre.* Paris, 1921. Contains documents on Franco-German relations. Now superseded.

MEMOIRS, AUTOBIOGRAPHIES, BIOGRAPHIES, AND LETTERS

FREYCINET, CHARLES DE: *Souvenirs, 1878–1893.* Paris, 1913.

CRISPI, FRANCESCO: *Memoirs.* Edited by T. Palamenghi-Crispi. London, 1912. Volume II contains important information on the earlier part of the negotiations.

SCHWEINITZ, LOTHAR VON: *Denkwürdigkeiten.* Two volumes, Berlin, 1927. Important for the Russian side of the situation.

T'SERCLAES, MONSIGNOR DE: *Le Pape Léon XIII.* Paris, 1894. The most authoritative biography of the Pope, so far as it goes.

---

[1] Salata: *Storia Diplomatica della Questione Romana,* pp. 142–54.

MANFRONI, GIUSEPPE: *Sulla Soglia del Vaticano, 1870–1901.* Two volumes. Bologna, 1920. Interesting and important memoirs of an Italian official on duty at the Vatican.

SCHLÖZER, KURD VON: *Letzte römische Briefe.* Stuttgart, 1924. The letters of the German minister at the Vatican. Not of much importance for the period prior to 1882.

DESCHANEL, PAUL: *Gambetta.* New York, 1920. The best brief biography of the great French leader.

ROSI, MICHELE: *I Cairoli.* Two volumes. Bologna, 1929. Based on the unpublished Cairoli papers and on other Italian diplomatic documents.

SPECIAL LITERATURE ON THE TRIPLE ALLIANCE

CHIALA, LUIGI: *Pagine di Storia Contemporanea.* Volume III: *La Triplice e la Duplice Alleanza, 1881–1897.* Second edition, Turin, 1898. Still the best account from the Italian side, written in part with the use of Robilant's papers.

ITALICUS: *Italiens Dreibundpolitik, 1870–1896.* Munich, 1928. The most recent scholarly account and one of the best, based upon all the available material. Orthodox in approach and interpretation.

SALVEMINI, GAETANO: "*La Triple Alliance*" (*Revue des nations latines*, July 1916). Does not enter into detail on the making of the alliance.

SULLIOTTI, A. I.: *La Triplice Alleanza, 1882–1915.* Milan, 1915. Chiefly war propaganda.

SINGER, ARTHUR: *Geschichte des Dreibundes.* Leipzig, 1914. Valuable for chronology and press comment.

FRAKNOI, WILHELM: *Kritische Studien zur Geschichte des Dreibundes.* Budapest, 1917. A very careful analysis, published before the actual text and correspondence had become known.

COOLIDGE, ARCHIBALD CARY: *The Origins of the Triple Alliance.* Second edition, New York, 1926. One of the best accounts in English, with critical notes on the recent source material.

MENDELSSOHN BARTHOLDY, ALBRECHT: "*Der Dreibund in der europäischen Politik*" (*Archiv für Politik und Geschichte*, June–July 1924).

STIEGLITZ, BARON DE: *L'Italie et la Triple Alliance.* Paris, 1906.

SILVA, PIETRO: *Come si formò la Triplice.* Milan, 1915.

SPECIAL LITERATURE ON THE ROMAN QUESTION

BASTGEN, HUBERT: *Die römische Frage.* Three volumes. Freiburg, 1919. An extremely useful source book.

CLAAR, MAXIMILIAN: "*Italien, der päpstliche Stuhl und die Lösung der römischen Frage*" (*Zeitschrift für Politik*, IX, pp. 321–70, 1916). Surveys the problem from 1870 to the World War.

CuRÀTULO, GIACOMO: *La Questione Romana da Cavour a Mussolini.* Rome, 1928. A general survey.

JOHNSON, HUMPHREY: *The Papacy and the Kingdom of Italy.* London, 1926. An introductory account.

PESARO, A. A. DI: *" La Diplomazia Vaticana e la Questione del Potere Temporale "* (*Rassegna Nazionale,* May 1, 1890, pp. 3–129). An exhaustive critical study of high merit.

SALATA, FRANCESCO: *"La Questione Romana e la Triplice Alleanza"* (*Nuova Antologia,* March 1, 1923, pp. 49–63). Chiefly a study of the Austrian and German revelations.

—: *Per la Storia Diplomatica della Questione Romana.* Milan, 1929. Valuable for the correspondence of the Austrian representatives at the Vatican during this period.

WOODWARD, E. L.: " The Diplomacy of the Vatican under Popes Pius IX and Leo XIII " (*Journal of the British Institute of International Affairs,* May 1924).

BOURGEOIS, EMILE: *" Les Origines de la Triple Alliance et la question romaine"* (*Revue de Paris,* January 1, 1926, pp. 37–58). Based primarily on the German and Austrian material.

LULVÈS, J.: *" Bismarck und die römische Frage"* (*Deutsche Revue,* June, 1916, pp. 289–303).

RUBBA, DOMENICO DI: *Bismarck e la Questione Romana nella formazione della Triplice.* Santa Maria Capua, 1917. Now out of date.

SPECIAL LITERATURE ON THE TUNIS QUESTION

LANGER, W. L.: " The European Powers and the French Occupation of Tunis, 1878–1881 " (*American Historical Review,* XXXI, pp. 55–79, 251–65; October 1925, January 1926).

CONSTANT, D'ETOURNELLES DE: *La Politique française en Tunisie.* Paris, 1891. The standard French account.

CHIALA, LUIGI: *Pagine di Storia Contemporanea.* Volume II. *Tunisi.* Second edition, Turin, 1895. The best Italian account.

PLEHN, HANS: *" Die Methoden der französischen Politik bei der Erwerbung Tunesiens"* (*Zeitschrift für Politik,* VII, pp. 1–48. 1914).

HOFSTETTER, BALTHASAR: *Die Vorgeschichte des französischen Protektorats in Tunis bis zum Bardovertrag.* Bern, 1914.

LULVÈS, J.: *" Auf welche Weise machte sich Frankreich zum Herrn von Tunis? "* (*Deutsche Revue,* February 1915, pp. 125–42).

TORRE, ANDREA: *" Come la Francia s'impadroni di Tunisi "* (*Rivista di Roma,* April–May 1899). A very important contribution, based upon the correspondence of General Cialdini.

LEBON: " *Les Préliminaires du Traité de Bardo* " (*Annales des sciences politiques,* 1893, pp. 403 ff.). Based upon new material from the French archives.

SPECIAL TOPICS

REINACH, JOSEPH: *Le Ministère Gambetta.* Paris, 1884. Still the best treatment of the Gambetta ministry, by one of Gambetta's closest friends.

TOUTAIN, EDMOND: *Alexandre III et la République française.* Paris, 1929. Contains some interesting material on the background of the Franco-Russian Alliance.

GALAVRESI, GIUSEPPE: *Italia e Austria, 1859–1914.* Milan, 1922. Contains a good chapter on the irredentist movement.

CURÀTULO, GIACOMO: *Francia e Italia, 1849–1914.* Turin, 1915. Conventional.

WIENEFELD, ROBERT H.: *Franco-German Relations, 1878–1885.* A minute, exhaustive study, but suggests no new approach.

HERZFELD, HANS: " *Bismarck und die Skobelev-Episode* " (*Historische Zeitschrift,* CXLII, 1930, pp. 279–302). Based in part on unpublished German documents. Interesting on the international aspect of the question.

VIII

The Egyptian Question and the British Occupation

⌇

O N JULY 11, 1882, A BRITISH SQUADRON BOMBARDED ALEXANDRIA; ON September 13 General Wolseley defeated the Egyptian army at Tel el Kebir; shortly afterwards the British forces entered Cairo, and the occupation of Egypt began. These events were not only crucial in the development of the perennial Egyptian question; they were also of capital importance in the history of European international relations. The key position of Egypt, located on the cross-roads between Asia and Africa and lying athwart the line of communication between Europe and the East, seems so obvious to the present generation that it appears incredible that it should not have been realized by the statesmen of the earlier nineteenth century. Yet it took the expedition of Napoleon to Egypt in 1798 to bring the English government to an appreciation of the strategic significance of the Nile land. Even then there appears to have been little desire in London to seize control of the territory, which was under the suzerainty of the Ottoman Sultan. The English policy was rather a negative one, aimed at keeping the French out and maintaining the overlordship of the Turk, rather than at establishing the authority of the British crown.[1] At any rate, the French forces were eventually driven out, and before the end of the Napoleonic period Mehemet Ali, greatest of all Egyptian rulers in modern times, had established himself as governor of the country, acknowledging the suzerainty of the Porte and paying tribute to the Sultan. During his long rule, which lasted until 1848, the country was completely remade and to a large extent modernized, while Mehemet was able through war and diplomacy to establish the office of viceroy as a hereditary possession of his family.

The expulsion of Napoleon's troops from Egypt in 1801 did not, however, mark the end of the French influence. On the contrary, Mehemet Ali relied very largely on French officials and teachers to assist him in the military and economic development of the country. Their cultural and even political influence was never stronger than during his reign. In 1840 the least adventurous of French kings, Louis Philippe, allowed himself to be dragged to the very verge of war in defence of the Viceroy against the Turkish Sultan. As the

---

[1] The international aspects of the question in this period are competently discussed in the recent book by Shafik Ghorbal: *The Beginnings of the Egyptian Question and the Rise of Mehemet Ali* (London, 1928).

M. de Freycinet has aptly said, from the time of Napoleon onward France was never indifferent to the affairs of Egypt, not for a single day. At times it even seemed to her that her prestige in the world was to be measured by the role which she played on the banks of the Nile.[1]

It was only natural that the construction of the Suez Canal, which had been considered by Napoleon and had been urged by the followers of Saint-Simon, should have been undertaken by the French engineer Ferdinand de Lesseps, a close friend of Mehemet Ali's son and successor, Mohammed Said. When the canal was finally opened, in 1869, the whole Eastern question was revolution-ized, for the new line of communication through the Mediterranean and Red seas was so obviously superior, economically speaking, to the route round the Cape of Good Hope that it was merely a matter of time before the trade from Europe to the East was diverted to the new water-way.

In retrospect it seems hardly believable that British statesmen of the earlier nineteenth century should have offered systematic opposition to the construc-tion of the canal, even after the dangers of navigation in the Red Sea had been largely obviated by the advent of the steamboat. And yet the English through-out this period showed more interest in the possible construction of railroads through the Euphrates Valley to the Persian Gulf than in the opening of a water route by way of Suez. Apparently the British policy, especially in the time of Lord Palmerston, hinged upon the idea that the canal would lead only to the eventual loss of Egypt by Turkey, England's protégé, and to the strengthening of the French position in the Mediterranean and the East. It would not do to have Marseilles nearer the sources of Eastern supply than Liverpool.[2] But, the canal once opened, trade soon chose the shorter and more economical route. In 1870, 486 ships, totalling more than 650,000 tons, passed through the canal. In the succeeding years the figures rose with amazing rapidity until in 1882 the route was being used to capacity. At that time more than 3,000 ships, totalling over 7,000,000 tons, made use of the new water-way, and of these over eighty per cent were of English registry.

Under the circumstances the English policy was bound to change, for the Suez Canal had, in spite of the attitude of the English government, become one of the most important links, if not *the* most important, in the chain of imperial communications. Disraeli, the great exponent of British imperialism, saw this clearly enough and was determined to act if the occasion presented itself. He had not long to wait, for the Egyptian ruler, Ismail, found himself compelled, in 1875, to offer for sale his shares in the stock of the canal company, in order to meet his financial obligations. Ismail has gone down in history with the epithet " the Spendthrift " attached to his name. During his rather brief rule, from 1863 to 1879, he did, in fact, run the finances of the Egyptian

---

[1] Charles de Freycinet: *Souvenirs, 1878–1893* (Paris, 1913), p. 215.

[2] The best general treatment of the problem of British communications with the East is that of Halford L. Hoskins: *British Routes to India* (New York, 1928).

government into the ground. The funded debt left him by his predecessor amounted to only about three million pounds. Under Ismail it rose to sixty-eight million, without mentioning the substantial floating debt, which brought the total to some ninety million pounds, a tremendous sum for a country of five million inhabitants, with an annual revenue of about eight million pounds.

There can be no doubt, however, that the current judgment of Ismail requires some revision. Much of the money borrowed during his reign was devoted to commendable and promising enterprises. A goodly sum went to the construction of the Suez Canal, which, far from benefiting Egypt, deprived her of much trade that had formerly passed over the land route from Alexandria to Suez. Other large sums went to the construction of over 8,000 miles of irrigation canals, of almost 1,000 miles of railroads, of 5,000 miles of telegraph lines, of more than 400 bridges, of harbour works at Alexandria, of lighthouses, and so on. These expenditures alone have been estimated to have come to forty-six million pounds, and to them must be added the sums devoted to the establishment of about 4,500 elementary schools. Even the huge sums paid as bribes to the Sultan of Turkey and his ministers cannot be regarded as wasted money, for Ismail, by the use of these Oriental methods, obtained concessions which greatly strengthened his own position in Egypt and advanced the country considerably along the road to independence. Even so unfriendly a critic as Edward Dicey has said: " In common justice it must be admitted that, if the Khedive had not indulged in any ambitious schemes or embarked in any extravagant expenditure, Egypt would never have obtained her present prosperity and security." [1]

In Ismail's own time the results were already obvious. During his reign the population increased from 4,833,000 to 5,518,000, and the foreign trade of Egypt rose by leaps and bounds. The imports, which in 1863 amounted to £1,991,000, came to £5,410,000 in 1875, while the exports increased from £4,454,000 to £13,810,000 during the same years. No wonder that the Alexandria correspondent of the London *Times* could write in January 1876: " Egypt is a marvellous instance of progress. She has advanced as much in seventy years as many countries have done in five hundred." [2]

Mr. Stephen Cave, the English paymaster-general, who was sent in 1876 to investigate the financial situation of Egypt, reported that " the expenditure, though heavy, would not of itself have produced the present crisis, which may be attributed almost entirely to the ruinous conditions of the loans raised for pressing requirements, due in some cases to causes over which the Khedive had little control." [3] This statement strikes at the root of the problem and is well worth a bit of elaboration, for the financial history of Egypt prior to 1875

---

[1] Edward Dicey: *The Story of the Khedivate* (London, 1902), p. 110.

[2] See especially Theodore Rothstein: *Egypt's Ruin* (London, 1910), pp. 34–6; George Young: *Egypt* (New York, 1927), pp. 82 ff.

[3] *Egypt*, No. 7 (1876).

is particularly instructive of the methods of modern imperialism. Ismail and Egypt were systematically victimized by the money-sharpers and jobbers whose headquarters were at Alexandria. The Khedive's European training and his love for petty bargaining could not save him from their clutches. As Lord Cromer himself says: " The maximum amount of harm is probably done when an Oriental ruler is for the first time brought into contact with the European system of credit. . . . During the early years of his [Ismail's] rule, Egypt must have been an earthly paradise for all who had money to lend at usurious rates of interest, or third rate goods of which they wished to dispose at first rate prices." [1]

What happened in Egypt in these years has been aptly described as " a case of financial robbery such as had never been heard of before, except in the case of Turkey." Adventurers of the most questionable type flocked to Egypt like vultures to feed on the spoils. Whereas there had been only about 3,000 foreigners in Egypt in 1836, there were 100,000 in 1870. Under the capitulations these foreigners were all outside the jurisdiction of the native courts and subject only to consular control. Many of them lived and grew rich in the smuggling business. Tobacco and opium were brought in in large quantities, and the foreign consuls, of whom there were about seventeen, invariably protected their nationals against interference. It should be added that foreigners were completely exempt from taxation, and that this ideal situation, which, it has been estimated, cost the Egyptian government about £500,000 annually, continued until 1876, when fourteen of the powers agreed to the establishment of mixed tribunals in Egypt.

The Levantines who were not engaged in smuggling were mostly either concession-hunters or bankers, and in these roles they frequently acted as agents or go-betweens for outwardly more respectable concerns in Paris and London. These " jackals of finance," as Dicey calls them, frequently sought concessions, not in order to make a reasonable profit on them, but in order to bring suit against the government in case of the slightest failure to live up to the terms. In constructing the harbour works of Alexandria British contractors overcharged about eighty per cent. Instances of less impressive graft were legion. But the great opportunity for profits came in furnishing the Khedive with the funds he required for his extensive innovations. The great Jewish banking-houses of Paris and London — the Rothschilds, Frühlings, Oppenheims, and Bischoffheims — floated the loans with heavy discount and took for themselves a fancy commission. The interest was usually six or seven per cent, but for the Egyptian government it invariably amounted to upward of twelve or thirteen per cent, running as high as twenty-five or twenty-seven per cent. Sir Charles Rivers Wilson, who probably knew more of Egyptian finance than any man in his day, says that none of the loans of Ismail cost him less than twelve per cent. In the great loan of 1873 the Khedive got, instead of the

---

[1] Earl of Cromer: *Modern Egypt* (New York, 1908), Volume I, pp. 58–9.

face value of £32,000,000, only about £19,000,000, and a large part of this in depreciated treasury notes. In order to meet the mounting charges for debt service Ismail soon had to resort to short-term loans, which offered the sharks in Alexandria their golden opportunity. Borrowing the money in Paris or London for three to six per cent, they took from Ismail interest varying from twelve to twenty per cent. Under such circumstances it does not take long for a government to get into the habit of incurring new indebtedness in order to meet the service of the old. It has been estimated that by 1882 Egypt had paid in interest a sum equal to the total capital lent her, plus interest at six per cent. Yet her total indebtedness was still £90,000,000 of which no more than two thirds had ever found their way into the Egyptian treasury.[1]

While the financial cliques of Alexandria, Paris, and London were battening on the exorbitant commissions and attractive returns from the jobbings in " Egyptians," the palmy days of Ismail's reign had already come to a close and he was rapidly drifting into bankruptcy. Having sold the interest coupons on his 177,000 shares of Suez Canal stock, he was soon obliged to cast about for a purchaser of the shares, in order to find money to meet an interest charge of some three million pounds, payable in December 1875. This was Disraeli's opportunity and he seized it with alacrity. Through an arrangement with the Rothschilds, who took a commission of two and a half per cent, he was able to secure the necessary sum while parliament was not in session. The transaction was carried through with the greatest secrecy and was not announced until the deal was completed.[2]

As a result of this clever move the Egyptian loan of 1873, which was quoted in London at 54 on November 15, rose to 73 by November 30, indicating a handsome profit for those who were in the know. But it would be erroneous to overemphasize the financial aspect of the transaction. The Khedive's holdings did not give England a controlling share of the canal stock, though they made her the chief single stockholder and gave her in practice a determining voice in the councils of the company. For Great Britain's imperial position the significance of this fact cannot be stressed too persistently. The canal was of supreme political and strategical importance, and it is on this aspect of the purchase that the chief emphasis must be laid. Speaking in parliament on February 21, 1876, Disraeli said: " I have never recommended and I do not

[1] The literature on Egyptian finance prior to 1875 is quite extensive. In addition to the British Blue Books see T. Faucon: La Ruine de l'Égypte (Paris, 1873); J. C.: Histoire financière de l'Égypte depuis Said Pacha, 1854–1876 (Paris, 1878); J. Seymour Keay: Spoiling the Egyptians (London, 1880); J. MacCoan: Egypt as it is (London, 1877); M. G. Mulhall: " Egyptian Finance" (Contemporary Review, October 1882). The best recent accounts are those of Rothstein: Egypt's Ruin (London, 1910); Sabry: La Génèse de l'esprit national égyptien, 1863–1882 (Paris, 1924); Leland H. Jenks: The Migration of British Capital to 1875 (New York, 1927), chapter x; Mohamed H. Haekal: La Dette publique égyptienne (Paris, 1912).

[2] See especially Charles Lesage: L'Achat des actions de Suez (Paris, 1906), to be supplemented by Monypenny and Buckle: Life of Disraeli, Volume V, chapter xii, and Documents diplomatiques français, II, Nos. 13 ff.

now recommend this purchase as a financial investment. . . . I do not recommend it either as a commercial speculation. . . . I have always and do now recommend it to the country as a political transaction, and one which I believe is calculated to strengthen the empire." Writing on the day when the purchase was announced, and carrying the same idea somewhat further, *The Times* said: " The public, both of this and other countries, will look to this important act of the British government rather in its political than its commercial aspects. It will be regarded as a demonstration, and something more: a declaration of intentions and a commencement of action upon them. . . . It is impossible to separate in our thoughts the purchase of the Suez Canal shares from the question of England's future relations with Egypt, or the destinies of Egypt from the shadows that darken the Turkish Empire. . . . Should insurrection, or aggression from without or corruption within bring a political as well as financial collapse of the Turkish Empire, it might become necessary to take measures for the security of that part of the Sultan's dominions with which we are most nearly connected." [1]

Here you have the gist of the whole problem. With a great interest in the Suez Canal the English government had naturally a profound concern for the condition of the country through which the canal flowed. Bismarck saw this and once spoke of England's needing Egypt as she needs her daily bread. Egypt, he continued, is like the spinal cord of the empire, which connects the backbone with the brain.[2] These considerations certainly did not escape English statesmen. Lady Gwendolen Cecil, indeed, tells us that her father, Lord Salisbury, " from his first occupation with the question, seems to have had no doubt as to what must be its ultimate issue, and at the outset was prepared actively to promote it." [3] Disraeli undoubtedly shared the conviction, though he kept his ideas to himself. It is worth noting, however, that immediately after the purchase of the canal shares Mr. Stephen Cave was sent to Egypt to investigate the financial situation, though the Khedive had asked only for the appointment of two officials to participate in the work of the department of finance. The veil of mystery that has rested over this Cave mission has not been lifted by Mr. Buckle in the last volumes of the standard life of Disraeli. It has long been believed, however, that there was something more than the ostensible purpose behind it, and in Egypt it was generally thought that Cave's investigation was the prelude to a British occupation. If this was so, the idea was dropped, either because public opinion in England was not prepared for so radical a solution, or because the general international situation at the time of the Balkan crisis was regarded by Disraeli as unfavourable.[4] After all, the Egyptian

---

[1] Quoted by Rothstein, op. cit., p. 8.
[2] Conversation with Busch, June 9, 1882 (Busch: *Bismarck,* III, p. 52).
[3] Cecil: *Life of Salisbury,* II, p. 329.
[4] This matter is dealt with at length by Dicey: *The Story of the Khedivate,* pp. 133 ff., and by Rothstein, op. cit., pp. 12 ff.

question could not be divorced from general European politics. It must be remembered that in the spring of 1876 the British government felt itself isolated in the face of the three imperial governments which were, so it seemed, attempting to solve the Balkan problem according to their own ideas. Under the circumstances it was of the utmost importance for England to maintain the friendly relations with France which had already found expression during the war scare of 1875.

" As to our policy — the defence of it lies in a nutshell," wrote Lord Salisbury in retrospect a few years later to one of his political friends. " When you have got a neighbour and faithful ally who is bent on meddling in a country in which you are deeply interested — you have three courses open to you. You may renounce — or monopolise — or share. Renouncing would have been to place the French across our road to India. Monopolising would have been very near the risk of war. So we resolved to share." [1] The British policy during the following years, therefore, was one of co-operation with France and the recognition of what was called " parity of influence." The arrangement was not wholly satisfactory to either side, and British statesmen were constantly haunted by the idea that circumstances might force them to take a stronger line and separate action. Salisbury steadfastly refused to make a definite engagement with France recognizing parity of influence and told the French foreign minister, Waddington, in September 1878, that, while England had no intention of establishing an exclusive footing in Egypt, she must not be held to any promise if the Turkish Empire went to pieces. " As matters now stand, we have no choice but to admit some sort of parity of influence between England and France," he wrote to Disraeli. " But the state of affairs may change and it may suit us at some future period to push ahead; and then any obligatory engagement would be highly inconvenient." [2] On the other hand, Freycinet, in his memoirs, expresses the opinion that from the French standpoint the condominium of England and France was a mistake, and that complete freedom of action would have served French interests more effectively.

Into a detailed account of the working of the Anglo-French policy it is hardly necessary to enter here. A brief outline of the course of events will suffice for the purposes of this study. Returning to the report of Mr. Cave, the interesting point is that the situation of Egypt, from the financial standpoint, was pictured by the English investigator as being by no means desperate. " Egypt," says the report, " is well able to bear the whole of her present indebtedness at a reasonable rate of interest; but she cannot go on renewing floating debts at 25% and raising loans at 12 or 13% to meet these additions to her debt." Still, the report made much of Ismail's extravagances and served to undermine what little credit he had left.

Hardly was the report published when the Khedive, on April 8, 1876,

[1] Cecil, op. cit., II, pp. 331–2.
[2] Ibid., II, pp. 332, 334; Documents diplomatiques français, II, No. 342.

suspended payment of treasury bills. On May 2, under the influence of French and Italian advisers, he established the Public Debt Commission (*Caisse de la Dette Publique*). On May 7 he announced the unification of the entire debt at ninety-one million pounds, with interest at six per cent, plus a sinking fund of one per cent. This arrangement caused consternation in London, for it favoured the holders of the floating debt, who were mostly French and Italians, at the expense of the holders of the consolidated debt, who were mostly English. The English government and the bondholders refused to name a representative to sit on the commission, and soon afterwards negotiations were opened between Mr. Goschen, as agent for English interests, and M. Joubert, as agent for the French. Goschen succeeded in having some of the earlier loans, which were floated in England, excluded from the general funded debt. For them the original interest rate was retained. It was also arranged that European controllers-general should be named, one to supervise income, another to watch over expenditure. The Khedive, who was quite helpless, was obliged to accept the Goschen-Joubert suggestions and issued a decree to that effect in November 1876.

The Goschen-Joubert inquiry and the so-called Goschen Decree, by which its recommendations were accepted, were of considerable importance, for they established Anglo-French co-operation. The Paris government had from the start taken its stand firmly behind the bondholders, a fact which Freycinet bemoans in his memoirs. The English government, on the other hand, carefully abstained from interfering officially. This was true after the Goschen mission as well as before. The government refused to name either a commissioner of the public debt or a controller-general. Goschen was invited by the Khedive to make suggestions, which were later accepted. But one must not be misled by this attitude on the part of the government. Goschen worked with the unofficial approval of the English ministers, and he was justified in telling the bondholders on his return: " When we went to Egypt we found France and England not united, but struggling for different financial schemes; we have left English influence and French influence both working together to support the scheme which we have propounded." [1] Freycinet dates the Anglo-French condominium from the institution of this decree.

But the arrangements made by the representatives of the English and French investors, attractive as they were from the standpoint of London and Paris, were hardly workable in Egypt. The obligations of the Khedive's government were, to be sure, met with the greatest punctuality during 1877, but only at the cost of the most ruthless taxation and oppressive extortion. The country suffered severely, the more so as the Nile floods were irregular and the year was a bad one for the crops. What happened, therefore, was that

---

[1] Arthur D. Elliot: *Life of George Joachim Goschen* (New York, 1911), Volume I, chapter v. A full account of these developments may be found in Cromer, op. cit., I, pp. 12 ff.; Rothstein, op. cit., pp. 24 ff.; Freycinet: *La Question d'Égypte* (Paris, 1905), pp. 154 ff.

£7,473,000 out of the total revenue of £9,543,000 went to the service of the debt. After payment of the regular tribute to the Sultan and the dues on the canal shares which had been sold to England the government had left something over a million pounds for the administration of the country. Of course this situation could not last, no matter how ready the bondholders were to insist on their pound of flesh.

It was at this very time, in April 1877, that Nubar Pasha, the Egyptian statesman of Armenian birth who had been most instrumental in getting the mixed tribunals established in Egypt, but who had fallen into disgrace, appeared in London. His object was to bring about intervention in Egypt and, if possible, to induce the English to establish a protectorate, as a counter-weight to the threatening Russian advance in the Balkans and in Asia Minor. Nubar found much sympathy for his idea in official circles, but the members of the ministry turned a deaf ear, evidently because they were more anxious than ever to avoid a falling out with France. The sole evidence of Nubar's efforts was to be found in the active campaign begun by Edward Dicey in the *Nineteenth Century*. With information supplied by Nubar the English journalist advanced one argument after another to show the hopelessness of a satisfactory settlement with Ismail and the necessity for England to protect her route to India.[1]

As the only way out of the impasse another commission of inquiry was decided upon at the beginning of 1878. The French government having been most insistent on the ability of the Egyptian government to pay and having capitulated entirely to the bondholders, the presidency of the commission was given to M. de Lesseps. In reality, however, the chairmanship devolved upon the vice-president, Sir Charles Rivers Wilson, under whose leadership the commission demanded and secured the widest powers and applied the most rigorous methods. The report of the commission was ready in August 1878. It turned out to be a merciless indictment of Ismail and an unqualified condemnation of the system of personal rule. The Khedive was called upon to turn over responsibility to his ministers. He reluctantly called Nubar Pasha to form a cabinet, in which Wilson himself became minister of finance, while a Frenchman, Blignières, became minister of public works. The road was now free for the flotation of another loan by the Rothschilds, the Khedivial estates serving as security.[2]

The experiment of the "responsible ministry" did not turn out to be very successful. It was, after all, primarily "the substitution of the bondholders' absolutism for that of the Khedive," as Rothstein puts it rather bluntly.[3] The chief purpose of the ministry was to regulate affairs in such a way that the

---

[1] See especially Edward Dicey: *England and Egypt* (London, 1881), pp. 19–20, and his *Story of the Khedivate*, pp. 166 ff. The German ambassador's very interesting reports of his conversations with Nubar at this time may be found in *Die Grosse Politik*, II, Nos. 290, 294, 295.

[2] The most complete account of the work of the commission may be found in C. Rivers Wilson: *Chapters from my Official Life* (London, 1916), chapters xi–xiv.

[3] Rothstein, op. cit., p. 62.

money could be found to pay the European investors. In the interest of greater efficiency numbers of Europeans were brought in to act as officials, all of whom enjoyed attractive salaries, while the native officials went unpaid for a year or eighteen months. The ministry carried this type of economy too far, however, when it placed twenty-five hundred officers of the army on half pay, although their salaries were already far in arrears. This move led to a military demonstration in February 1879, during which the lives of Nubar and Wilson were for a moment endangered.

Whether the Khedive was in any way connected with this demonstration we need not investigate here. It would appear that he had no part in the action of the army, but he naturally had little sympathy for the Nubar-Wilson combination, had abstained from all participation in the affairs of government, and very likely had intrigued against his ministers, as Lord Cromer asserts. At any rate, the incident of February gave him an excellent opportunity to step forward once more, to declare that the ministry enjoyed neither his own confidence nor that of the country, and to replace it with a native cabinet under Sherif Pasha, in April 1879. The new government was to be responsible to a Chamber of Notables, elected by the population. It is hardly to be supposed that Ismail was interested in the establishment of free institutions for their own sake. Lord Cromer is probably right in saying that the free institutions were intended to be an instrument by which the Khedive could regain his personal power, of which he had been deprived by foreign interference. It may also be that his object was to drive a wedge into the Anglo-French entente, for the French government, which had urged upon Ismail the Goschen-Joubert decree and all later schemes and had appointed Blignières officially, was bound to take the Khedive's *coup d'état* as a direct affront, while the British government, which was not officially involved, would be less likely to offer strong opposition.

However that may have been, the Khedive's move nullified the importance of a new financial scheme which the commission of inquiry had worked out and which was completed just as the so-called " European ministry " was overthrown. Ismail was free now to produce a plan of his own, which involved the reduction of the interest on the unified debt from seven to six per cent, the payment in cash of fifty-five per cent of the floating debt (the remainder to be paid in two and a half years), and the assignment of four million pounds annually to administrative purposes.

Before the British and French governments had time to reach an agreement as to the course to be pursued under these changed circumstances, the diplomatic world was surprised on May 18 by a vigorous protest from the German government against the new financial scheme of Ismail. Austria came out with a similar protest, but it was not until June 8 that England and France followed suit. This spectacular move on the part of Bismarck has given rise to much conjecture regarding the motives which lay behind it. The German interests in Egypt were insignificant at the time, and the chancellor's policy could hardly be accounted for as a stroke in behalf of German investors.[1] Lord Salisbury and others thought the only plausible explanation could be found in the desire of the chancellor to protect the interests of his banker friend Herr Bleichröder.[2] But this naïve idea is hardly tenable. Bismarck was not the man to pursue a personal policy of this sort. His action was no doubt influenced by considerations of general politics. Ever since 1875 he had been suggesting to England the occupation of Egypt, either as a counter-weight to Russian gains in the Balkans or Asia Minor, or to eventual French gains in Tunis. In the spring of 1879, however, his relations with Russia were becoming very tense. To suggest that at such a crucial moment he would have aimed at setting England and France by the ears, as has frequently been maintained, would be to deny him even average ability in statesmanship. It is clear from the German documents that while the German chancellor may have desired a certain amount of rivalry and tension between England and Russia or between England and France, he also desired to prevent such tension from leading to war.[3]

The situation in the spring of 1879 threatened to end in the rupture of the Anglo-French condominium, for the English were clearly unwilling to act as vigorously in behalf of the bondholders as were the French. " It may be quite tolerable and even agreeable to the French government to go into partnership with the bondholders; or rather, to act as Sheriff's officer for them," wrote Lord Salisbury to Lord Lyons. " But to us it is a new and embarrassing sensation. Egypt can never prosper as long as some 85% of her revenue goes into paying interest on her debt. We have no wish to part company with France; still less do we mean that France should acquire in Egypt any special ascendancy; but, subject to these two considerations, I should be glad to be free of the companionship of the bondholders." [4] Bismarck's surprising intervention was clearly designed to encourage the English and to anticipate a split in the Anglo-French entente which would have driven France into the arms of Russia. This comes out clearly enough in the assurances which the German government gave to both the English and French governments that there was no intention of infringing in any way on the political field where the Anglo-French entente functioned.[5]

The united front presented by the powers certainly did much to hearten the English. Salisbury, who was convinced that there could be no " decent " government in Egypt until Ismail himself was overthrown, joined France in advising the Khedive to abdicate. The other powers followed suit and finally appealed to the Sultan to depose the Egyptian ruler. On June 26, 1879 the

[1] See especially Mathilde Kleine: *Deutschland und die ägyptische Frage, 1875–1890* (Greifswald, 1927), chapter i.

[2] Cecil, op. cit., II, p. 353.

[3] See, for example, *Die Grosse Politik*, II, No. 294; III, No. 661; Lyall: *Life of Lord Dufferin*, I, p. 309; *Documents diplomatiques français*, II, Nos. 390, 403, 408, 440, 476.

[4] Cecil, op. cit., II, p. 352.

[5] *Documents diplomatiques français*, II, Nos. 408, 430, 440.

Sultan informed Ismail of his deposition in a novel fashion by sending him a telegram addressed to the "Ex-Khedive Ismail Pasha."[1]

The new Khedive, Tewfik Pasha, was honest and well-intentioned, but he lacked the personality and strength of his father. With the example of Ismail before him, he made no effort to resist the demands of the foreign powers, but did as he was told. In September 1879 the controllers-general were re-established, with the important additional provision that they should not be removed again without the consent of England and France. In other words, the British government now followed the example of France and openly took part in the work of securing the interests of the bondholders. Lord Salisbury had his misgivings, and thought that it would be safer and more effective to work as "wirepullers" rather than as ostensible rulers, but of the two evils, foreign ministers or controllers, the latter was certainly the lesser.[2]

During the winter and spring the attention of the European world was centred on the work of financial reorganization, which could now be carried through without opposition. An international commission, on which England and France had double representation, went over the entire situation and presented a report which was embodied in the law of liquidation of July 17, 1880. With certain modifications this law remained the financial charter of Egypt. The entire indebtedness of the country was rearranged in certain categories, and the interest was reduced. On the other hand, the revenue was estimated at a low figure, with the provision that all surplus should be devoted to the redemption of the debt, so that the interests of the bondholders were amply cared for. Under this law the financial aspect of the Egyptian question was effectively settled, and in the succeeding period this problem played a less significant part in the development of the situation.

With a total debt of about ninety-eight million pounds, financial soundness could be maintained in Egypt only by the practice of rigid economy. The policy pursued by the controllers-general, however, did not in any way interfere with the more than one thousand European officials who drew an annual salary of some three hundred thousand pounds. It affected rather the Egyptian population generally, and more particularly the army officers of the lower grades, who were natives, in contrast to the higher officers, who were of Turkish or Circassian race. One would think that the outbreak against Nubar and Wilson in February 1879 should have shown the danger of rousing the anger of the troops, but it did not. The officers continued to receive cavalier treatment, their discontent grew, and before long they were to appear as the leaders of the opposition.

It would be erroneous, however, to regard the troubles which arose in Egypt in 1881 and 1882 purely as a mutinous movement of discontented officers. This view was commonly held in western Europe at the time, and even Lord

---

[1] New material in *Documents diplomatiques français*, II, Nos. 407, 432–9.
[2] Cecil, op. cit., II, pp. 355. 359.

Cromer, writing in 1908, thought that the disorders were attributable chiefly to a clique of military agitators. That this view is mistaken there can now be little doubt. Lord Morley, in his biography of Gladstone, admits that the powers misunderstood the nature of the movement: "They perceived in it no more than a military rising. It was in truth national as well as military; it was anti-European, and above all, it was in its objects anti-Turk."

In order to understand this first Egyptian national movement one must remember that Mehemet Ali had, in the earlier part of the century, endowed Egypt with a political individuality and had enabled her to play a part in European history quite out of proportion to her actual strength and resources. One must also remember the influence of the numerous Frenchmen who were in the service of Mehemet and his successors and who brought to Egypt something of the western European outlook. Furthermore, the deciphering of the hieroglyphs, the establishment of museums, the development of Egyptology, all these factors contributed to the growth of a national consciousness among the members of the rising generation. Ismail, who put over a hundred thousand children into elementary schools, unquestionably furthered the process of national revival. By 1875 Cairo had become the intellectual centre of Islam. The great University of Al Azhar, with its fifteen thousand students, was a rallying-point for those with national aspirations as well as for those with religious ideals.

The great leader of early Egyptian nationalism in the 1870's was Jemmal ed Din, an Afghan by birth who had come to Constantinople in 1870 and had served as a member of the Turkish council on public instruction. His great idea was to bring Islam into harmony with modern thought and to identify it with science and progress. Forced to leave the Turkish capital because of the opposition to his teachings of the reactionary Sheikh ul Islam and the ulemas, Jemmal came to Cairo in 1871 and soon assumed the leadership of the religious and political renaissance. His doctrine has been described as a sort of political Panislamism. Arguing that the Christian states excused the attacks and humiliations which they inflicted on the Moslem states by pointing to the " backwardness" of the latter, he pointed out that the Christian states nevertheless prevented in every possible way the efforts made by " backward " states in the direction of reform. Therefore the Moslem states must unite in a great league for self-protection and must acquire the technique and secrets of European power. Among other things a constitutional form of government must be introduced.

The effects of Jemmal's teaching were soon to be seen. Impressed, no doubt, by the experiments of Midhat Pasha in Turkey and the introduction of a Western constitution in 1876, and influenced further by the religious and racial aspect of the Russian-Turkish War, in which some thirty thousand Egyptian troops took part, the followers of Jemmal developed an ardent activity in the years 1877–8. A native press sprang up, and before long something resembling a national, constitutional party appeared on the scene. Of course, one must not look for absolute unity of purpose or for consistency in a rudimentary move-ment of this sort. Religious, political, and social factors were all intertwined in it, and within the group itself there were ill-concealed contradictions and antagonisms. The ecstatic partisanship of European Arabophils, like Wilfrid Scawen Blunt, harmed the movement perhaps more than it helped it, for by idealizing it these men made it rather ridiculous in the disillusioned eyes of the Westerner. It is fairly clear, however, that the religious element played a rela-tively unimportant role. There was not much of the antichristian crusade in the activities of the national group. The movement was, in fact, directed prima-rily against the domination of the country by foreign interests, against the personal rule of Ismail, and against the monopoly of office and social position by the Turkish and Circassian elements.[1]

The demonstration against Nubar and Wilson in February 1879 may be taken as the first overt act on the part of the opposition. The Chamber of Notables, which was summoned by Ismail for his own purposes, submitted demands in the spring of 1879 which could hardly have been inspired by the Khedive or have met with his approval. Powers analogous to those of a Eu-ropean parliament were demanded for the chamber, in addition to a liberal electoral law and a responsible ministry. To represent the chamber as a mere tool in the hands of Ismail is certainly to misunderstand the whole situation. The chamber, relying no doubt on the army, was in opposition not only to the European domination, but also to Ismail himself. Ismail tried to use the anti-foreign aspect of the chamber's demands to re-establish his personal power. As it happened, the conflict between the Khedive and the chamber was prevented only by his own deposition.

The events of June 1879 did not, however, settle the problem, for they only re-established the foreign influence on a firmer basis. In September 1879 the opposition organized a secret national party at Helouan, near Cairo. At this time the military and civil elements were already working in unison. The mani-festo of the group, drawn up in November, declared in so many words that "the party cannot consider the government constituted by foreign influence as the expression of the desires and needs of the country." The public debt was to be guaranteed by the nation, but foreign control was to be tolerated only on an international basis and only as a special and temporary arrangement to supervise the service of the debt.[2]

The organization of the opposition offered at least some possibility of redress against the arbitrary actions of Tewfik and his foreign mentors. When, in

---

[1] Although W. S. Blunt's *Secret History of the English Occupation of Egypt* (London, 1907) must be used with caution, much can be learned from it in regard to the nationalist movement, because of Blunt's close contacts with the leaders. One should also consult A. M. Broadley's *How We Defended Arabi and his Friends* (London, 1884). By far the best general account, and one on which I have relied heavily, is M. Sabry's *La Génèse de l'esprit national égyptien, 1863–1882* (Paris, 1924), which makes use of much unpublished material bearing on the movement and its leaders.

[2] Sabry, op. cit., pp. 173–4.

January 1881, a native officer was removed from his position and replaced by a Circassian, the officers of several regiments, led by Ahmed Arabi, protested. Summoned to a conference with Osman Rifki, the minister of war, who was a Circassian, they suspected a plot and arranged for their deliverance, in case of necessity, by their own troops. It had been planned, in fact, to court-martial them, but the interference of the troops saved the officers, who now demanded the dismissal of the minister of war. The Khedive was helpless and was consequently obliged to yield. He appointed as war minister Mahmud Pasha Sami, one of the nationalists and perhaps the ablest and most energetic of the whole group. A commission was established under the presidency of Arabi himself to investigate the situation of the army and to suggest reforms. The essential demands of the army, for increased pay and equality of opportunity, were granted without opposition on the part of Tewfik.

And yet the situation did not quiet down. The Khedive was afraid to proceed against the army, which became more and more insubordinate, while the army officers themselves feared for their position and their lives. Finally, after continued friction, Tewfik summoned up all his courage, dismissed Mahmud Sami, and announced the transfer of the most disaffected regiments from Cairo to Alexandria. This step led to the great demonstration of September 9, when the regiments, under Arabi's leadership, marched to the palace and submitted to the frightened Khedive three far-reaching demands: the dismissal of the ministers, the convocation of the chamber, and the increase of the army to eighteen thousand men. When the Khedive agreed to the first two demands and promised to refer the third to Constantinople, he practically resigned power into the hands of the opposition. The army, and with it the national movement, was well on the way to complete victory.

All these happenings served to make the position of the foreign control a very painful one. The Khedive, on whom so much depended, was at the mercy of the army. The opposition demanded a modification of the existing arrangement which had put Egypt under foreign tutelage. It was perfectly clear that, as the Alexandria correspondent of *The Times* reported, the movement of the army had no other object than the destruction of European interference with Egyptian administration.[1] A conflict was inevitable, for, to speak with Lord Morley, " the law of liquidation — whatever else we may think of it — at least made the policy of Egypt for the Egyptians unworkable." [2]

In France there was some inclination to adopt the nationalist movement and to pose as the champion of popular aspirations. But this tendency did not meet with the approval of the governing circles, which were strongly influenced by bankers and financiers. " All we could see in Egypt," complains Freycinet, " was debtors; a single interest dominated everything, and that was the interest of the European creditors." [3] The British government, now in the hands of the

---

[1] Quoted by Rothstein, op. cit., p. 133. [2] Morley: *Life of Gladstone*, III, p. 76.
[3] Freycinet: *La Question d'Égypte*, p. 194.

Liberal Gladstone ministry, with Lord Granville as foreign minister, had no particular policy and would gladly have accepted the mission of Turkish troops to restore order. But this solution was made impossible by the vigorous opposition of the French, who had to consider the possible effect of such a move on the populations of Tunis and Algeria. When the Sultan finally did send two commissioners, the English joined the French in sending a warship to Alexandria by way of persuading the Turkish agents to return home. So far as one can detect, the only result of this interlude was that it brought the various opposition groups in Egypt into closer union than ever, in view of the danger of foreign intervention.

The general uncertainty in the situation was brought to a rather abrupt close when Gambetta, who came into power in November 1881, assumed the initiative and proposed vigorous action on behalf of Tewfik, who, it was believed, would be dethroned by the national party or would fall wholly under the influence of the chamber, which was to meet on December 23. The idea of intervention on behalf of the Khedive was not a new one. Lord Lyons had written home as early as September 30 suggesting this very course: " I think the best thing to be done is to take an opportunity of distinctly manifesting at Cairo the continuance of the Anglo-French understanding. If we let either the Egyptians or Foreign Powers suppose they can upset that, we shall not be able to maintain the English and French controllers, and if they disappear the financial prosperity will disappear with them, and we shall have the bondholders, French and English, on our backs again." [1]

The line of argument used in this letter probably underlay Gambetta's policy also. At any rate, the vigorous French statesman was able to convince his English friends of the necessity for doing something, and Lord Granville accepted the draft of a note which was handed to the Khedive by the British and French consuls-general on January 8, 1882. This has gone down in history as the Gambetta Note. In it the two governments declared that they considered the maintenance of the Khedive on the throne " as alone able to guarantee, for the present and future, the good order and development of general prosperity in Egypt," and that the two governments, " being closely associated in the resolve to guard by their united efforts against all cause of complication, internal or external, which might menace the order of things established in Egypt, do not doubt that the assurance publicly given of their formal intentions in this respect will tend to avert the dangers to which the Government of the Khedive might be exposed, and which would certainly find England and France united to oppose them."

This threatening note, which specifically mentioned the chamber as one of the dangers menacing the Khedive and his cabinet and was therefore a slap in the face for the nationalist party, could have been effective only if the two governments had been willing to follow up the threat with coercive action.

---

[1] Newton: *Lord Lyons,* II, pp. 258–9.

Gambetta was evidently prepared to go the limit and thought the English would do likewise. Granville had made a reservation to the effect that the note should not be taken as committing the English government to any particular mode of action, but Gambetta understood this to imply that action of some sort would be taken if necessary. When it turned out that such was not the case, and that Granville intended the whole thing as a platonic demonstration of moral support, the two governments appeared simply ridiculous.[1]

Far from attaining any positive gains through the issuance of the note, France and England only weakened the Khedive and his government. Coming at a time when there was no real danger of revolution or disturbance, the joint action of the powers was looked upon in Egypt as unwarranted interference and dictation. Sir Edward Malet, the English representative, wrote in alarm in the days following the submission of the note: " The communication has, at all events temporarily, alienated from us all confidence. Everything was progressing capitally, and England was looked on as the sincere wellwisher and protector of the country. Now, it is considered that England has definitely thrown in her lot with France, and that France, from motives in connection with her Tunisian campaign, is determined ultimately to intervene here." Furthermore, as Malet reported on the following day: " For the moment it has had the effect to cause a more complete union of the national party, the military, and the Chamber, to unite these three in a common bond of opposition to England and France, and to make them feel more forcibly than they did before that the tie which unites Egypt to the Ottoman Empire is a guarantee to which they must strongly adhere to save themselves from aggression." [2]

Another important result of the Gambetta Note was that it brought the European powers upon the scene once again. Thus far Bismarck had supported the actions of England and France, because he needed the Anglo-French entente and desired to prevent France from drifting into dependence on Russia. But in June 1881 the signature of the Alliance of the Three Emperors had alleviated the Russian-German tension, and Bismarck's interest in the Anglo-French entente was diminished accordingly. The Gambetta Note seemed to indicate Anglo-French action in Egypt at an early date. It was only reasonable to suppose that in this action Gambetta and France would play the leading role. Such an increase in French prestige and strength could not be to Germany's interest, so Bismarck, much as he despised the weakness and vacillation of the Gladstone government, determined to build a golden bridge over which Granville could retreat. As early as January 10, 1882 the French chargé d'affaires in Berlin reported that conferences between the representatives of Germany, Russia, Austria, and Italy were taking place. On February 2 these discussions ended, when the states in question submitted to the Sultan identic notes in which they expressed the opinion that the *status quo* in Egypt, as established by

---

[1] An excellent discussion in Freycinet: *La Question d'Égypte,* pp. 206 ff.
[2] Quoted by Cromer, op. cit., I, pp. 228–9.

the firmans of the Sultan and by European agreements, should be maintained and that it could not be modified without previous understanding between the great powers and the suzerain.

Bismarck and Granville were agreed that Anglo-French action would be dangerous to European peace, and that Egypt might in the end prove to be the Schleswig-Holstein of the Western powers, as the German chancellor put it. He therefore urged upon the English minister the desirability of not antagonizing the Turkish government further by repeated demands for reform in Armenia. What England should do, he said, was to appeal to the Sultan to restore order in Egypt. Such a procedure would avoid conflict with other powers and would, at the same time, leave the innocuous Turks as the guardians of the British route to India. Granville, however, could not quite bring himself to taking up this suggestion, the more so as he knew that the French were unalterably opposed to it. He therefore did the next best thing and decided to internationalize the question — that is, to work out a program in consultation with the other powers. Gambetta would hardly have consented to this, but the fall of his ministry on January 30 brought in a Freycinet cabinet. The new premier was much more disposed to adopt the suggestion.[1]

" As far as can be gathered, the attitude of both governments was the reverse of heroic. The British government was anxious to hand over its responsibility to other parties, and the French government was not disposed to take any initiative at all," says Lord Newton in a summary of the situation which is only too accurate.[2] Bismarck could hardly believe that a great power like England could be ruled with such complete lack of foresight. He felt that England under Gladstone could no longer be reckoned one of the important and certain factors in European politics.[3] Fortunately Freycinet agreed to consultation with the other powers, and negotiations could begin for the convocation of a conference to consider the question, if the necessity for actual intervention arose. The form of intervention, whether by Turkish troops under conditions laid down by the powers, or by an Anglo-French force operating under a European mandate, was reserved for future discussion.

For the time being, there appeared to be little danger of disorder in Egypt, for the Chamber of Notables, which had met on December 26, was distinctly moderate in its attitude. The Khedive himself seemed to be favourably disposed towards it and submitted a draft of an organic law or constitution which was the subject of debate during the whole month of January. The most difficult point to settle was the future control over the budget. The chamber insisted that, while the engagements and obligations of the government and the rights and powers of the foreign controllers should be unequivocally recognized, it should have the right to vote at least that part of the budget that pertained to

---

[1] *Die Grosse Politik,* IV, Nos. 723–5; Fitzmaurice: *Life of Lord Granville,* II, pp. 259–60; Freycinet: *La Question d'Égypte,* pp. 217 ff.; Newton, op. cit., II, pp. 271–7.

[2] Newton, op. cit., II, p. 277.   [3] *Die Grosse Politik,* IV, No. 725.

the administration of the country and had nothing to do with the service of the debt. The representatives of England and France at Cairo and Lord Granville himself were rather inclined to take a sympathetic attitude and to accept these reasonable demands of the chamber, but the two controllers-general, Sir Evelyn Baring and M. de Blignières saw nothing but the possible danger to the interests of the bondholders. They were supported in their obstinate attitude of refusal by Gambetta himself.

Among the leaders of the nationalists it was felt that in the matter of budget control the ministry was too much under the influence of the controllers, and the chamber therefore requested the Khedive to summon a new ministry. Tewfik, who had no means of resisting the constitutional movement, supported as it was by the army, was obliged to yield. On February 5 the new ministry, under Mahmud Pasha Sami, took office. In this ministry Arabi appeared as minister of war, while the rest of the cabinet also was composed of nationalists. Yet it speaks well for the nationalist leaders that this cabinet, which has been called the Ministry of National Defence, was, from the very start, quite as moderate as its predecessor. There is no satisfactory evidence to support the assertion sometimes made [1] that Mahmud Sami meditated the overthrow of the Khedive, the ejection of the foreign controllers, and the establishment of an Egyptian republic with himself as president. On the contrary, he asserted and reasserted in the most positive manner the intention of the government to respect its obligations and to support the arrangements made for the service of the debt. There was little of arbitrary military despotism about this régime. In fact, during February and March the situation was calmer than it had been for a long time. There was every indication that the new ministry would progress in safe and sane fashion.

Despite the moderation of the nationalist ministry, the representatives of the powers could not throw off a feeling of uneasiness. What would be the ultimate effect of the new movement upon the financial arrangements that had been worked out? By many it was felt that sooner or later an effort would be made to throw off foreign domination and dictation, and that, in order to safeguard the interests involved, some sort of intervention would become necessary. Lord Cromer expresses the attitude of the European agents on the spot when he says: "The financial interests concerned were so great, and the risk that financial disorder would eventually have led to anarchy was so considerable, that it may well be that armed intervention of some sort would ultimately have become an unavoidable necessity." [2] It is certainly clear from the British Blue Books that men like Sir Edward Malet, the British consul-general, were in no way favourable to the new régime. They regularly and faithfully reported home every little disturbance in the country and continued to talk about the "anarchy" prevalent throughout the land, and the evils of "military domination." So

[1] e.g., by P. G. Elgood: *The Transit of Egypt* (London, 1928), p. 70.
[2] Cromer: *Modern Egypt*, I, p. 233.

persistent were these reports that Lord Granville finally proposed to the French government that the Sultan be invited to send a general to Egypt to restore discipline in the army, the Turkish representative to be accompanied by two colleagues, one English and one French.[1]

Considering the existing uncertainty and uneasiness, it is not to be wondered at that the powers seized the earliest opportunity to take a hand in affairs. The opportunity was furnished by Arabi himself. In the first months of 1882 he promoted hundreds of native Egyptian officers, at the same time retiring some of the Turkish and Circassian officers who had held high rank. This was, of course, a sort of political revenge, for the native officers had never been allowed to rise above the rank of colonel, while the Circassians secured all the attractive positions. Naturally the Circassian military did not relish the policy of the new ministry. There was threatening language used in their circles, and it may well be, as the government asserted, that there was a plot on foot to assassinate Arabi. On April 12 the cabinet arrested a number of officers, who were tried by a court martial, over which, curiously enough, a Circassian presided. On May 2 forty officers, including Osman Rifki, former minister of war, were condemned to exile for life to the farthest limits of the Sudan, a judgment which was almost the equivalent of the death-sentence.

In order to be valid this sentence required the approval of the Khedive. Instead of consulting with his ministers, who, incidentally, favoured simple banishment from Egypt as an appropriate penalty, Tewfik appealed to the English and French consuls for advice, and then to the representatives of the other powers. Eventually he approached even the Sultan, on the plea that Osman Rifki held rank in the Turkish army and hence could not be degraded without the Sultan's consent. The whole object of Tewfik seems to have been to rid himself of the nationalist ministry and regain personal control through foreign aid. The danger of foreign intervention seemed slight to the Khedive, who was clearly relying on his ability to play one power off against the other.

Anyone could see that the Khedive, by appealing to Europe, was precipitating a conflict with his nationalist ministers. Some, like Sir Edward Malet, evidently thought that the policy was a good one, and that the time had come to cut the Gordian knot: "I venture to observe that in considering the form in which the sentence of the court-martial should be dealt with by the Khedive, the bearing of the general situation should be taken into account. It should be remembered that the present Ministry is distinctly hitherto bent upon diminishing the Anglo-French protection, and that, as a matter of fact, our influence is daily decreasing. It will not be possible for us to regain our ascendancy until the military supremacy which at present weighs upon the country is broken. The Minister for Foreign Affairs told me this morning, unofficially, that the Government would resist the arrival of Turkish Commissioners by force, and he begged me to use my influence to prevent this complication. I

---

[1] Cf. *Egypt*, No. 7 (1882), *passim*.

believe, however, that some complication of an acute nature must supervene before any satisfactory solution of the Egyptian question can be attained, and that it would be wiser to hasten it than to endeavour to retard it, because the longer misgovernment lasts the more difficult it is to remedy the evils which it has caused." [1]

It is surprising that such an outspoken report should ever have found its way into a published Blue Book. Of course, the views of Malet were not the views of the British foreign office, but it was inevitable that, under the influence of such expressions of opinion, the policy of the British government should have become affected. The complications envisaged by Malet were not slow in supervening. The Egyptian ministry regarded the Khedive's appeal to foreign powers as a very serious departure, which it was, and summoned the chamber without consulting Tewfik. Thus was created what Freycinet describes as a "revolutionary situation." It was clear that the nationalist leaders were bent on the deposition of the Khedive.[2] In Paris as well as in London it was felt that something must be done promptly to put an end to the revolutionary movement. Freycinet, while anxious to work in consonance with the other powers, suggested that England and France, whose preponderant rights had been recognized by the other governments, should send squadrons to Alexandria. Since the two powers did not have a European mandate, it was agreed that they should not land troops. If debarkation of an armed force were to become necessary, Freycinet was willing to have the Turks summoned, provided always that they acted under Anglo-French control and for a specific purpose.

This policy, it must be confessed, was a rather involved one, for the question of how and when Turkey should intervene was left quite uncertain, much to the distress of the English, the Khedive, and the Sultan. The reason for this was the obstinacy of the French, who wished to avoid Turkish intervention at any cost. Clearly the naval demonstration was intended, from the first, not so much to initiate occupation of the country, or even to protect the foreigners, as to intimidate the ministry. The French and British consuls were instructed to recognize as legal no authority other than that of Tewfik and to advise the Khedive " to take advantage of a favourable moment, such, for instance, as the arrival of the fleets, to dismiss the present Ministry." But Tewfik lacked the necessary courage, and the consuls themselves felt that it would be dangerous for him to take too strong a line. It was not until various efforts had been made to induce Arabi and other leaders to leave the country that the consuls finally demanded the resignation of the ministry. The cabinet resigned under protest, but the Khedive was unable to find another to take its place. The officers demanded Arabi's reinstatement, and Tewfik, who could count neither on action by the French and English nor on intervention by the Sultan, was forced to

---

[1] Malet to Granville, May 7, 1882 (*Egypt*, No. 7, 1882, p. 107).

[2] Cromer, op. cit., I, p. 265; Sir Auckland Colvin: *The Making of Modern Egypt* (London, 1906), p. 11; and others.

yield. On May 28 Arabi returned to office. His position was stronger than ever, while that of Tewfik had been tremendously weakened. Apparently his fate was sealed, for his appeals to foreign nations had not as yet led to action in his favour from any direction, and on this lack of agreement among the powers the nationalists obviously relied.

The Western powers now found themselves obliged to do something. The Sultan was ready enough to send commissioners and troops to Egypt to restore the Khedive's authority under Turkish suzerainty. This would have been the most acceptable solution from the British view-point. But the French still objected to all proposals of this nature and finally suggested the convocation of an ambassadorial conference at Constantinople to discuss the ways and means of Turkish action. The Sultan, however, disliked the idea of European supervision and managed to drag out the negotiations for the conference so that it did not meet until June 23. In the meanwhile he had sent a mission under Dervish Pasha to Egypt, apparently with the idea of negotiating with all parties and strengthening Turkish authority in every possible way. On the plea that he must await the results of this mission the Sultan finally refused to take part in the Constantinople Conference.

As a matter of fact, the ambassadorial conference did not play an important part in deciding the outcome of the Egyptian crisis.[1] While it debated, events in Egypt were forcing action. Since the arrival of the squadrons at Alexandria and the intervention of France and England to force the resignation of Arabi, public opinion had become more and more excited and more and more outspoken on the subject of foreign interference. On June 12 anti-foreign riots broke out in Alexandria, which led to the death of some fifty Europeans. The exact reasons for the outbreak have never been determined. Arabi and his friends have been blamed for it by some writers, though evidently without any serious justification. Those who attribute it to the secret action of the Khedive, working through the governor of Alexandria, are able to make out a much stronger case. It is not unlikely that Tewfik hoped in this way to force action by the squadrons on his own behalf.[2] Immediately after the riots he came down to Alexandria to be under the protection of the squadrons. At the same time thousands of Europeans left the country.

The situation had by this time become really serious, for anti-foreign outbreaks, sometimes coloured with religious fanaticism, began to take place in other localities. The Khedive being powerless, Arabi was now practically dictator. He succeeded in restoring order and quiet in Alexandria, but he also began to make preparations for defence against action from without. From

---

[1] The work of the conference is studied in great detail by Sayed Kamel: *La Conférence de Constantinople et la question égyptienne en 1882* (Paris, 1913).

[2] The evidence is discussed in detail by Blunt: *Secret History*, pp. 497–534, and Rothstein, op. cit., pp. 196 ff. The accusations against Arabi were pretty thoroughly exploded at his trial, later in 1882.

the beginning of June onward the Egyptians started work on fortifications and earthwork defences at Alexandria. The operations were suspended a few times, but always recommenced. It seems that the earthworks were never of great importance in a military sense. "It cannot be said that the defences were of a formidable nature," remarks Sir William Laird Clowes. "Judging from the manner in which Seymour ordered them to be attacked, he must have despised them." [1] But Admiral Seymour seems to have chafed at remaining inactive and appears to have had his own ideas as to the solution of the Egyptian question. He evidently magnified the importance of the forts and batteries and represented them to the government as a formidable menace to the safety of the squadron. On July 3 he was instructed to prevent continuance of the work and if neces-sary to destroy the earthworks and silence the batteries.

The European governments were informed of this decision, and the French government was invited to co-operate. This Freycinet refused to do, on the plea that a bombardment would constitute an act of war, and the French govern-ment could not declare war without the consent of the chamber; furthermore, such action would be contrary to the engagement entered into by the powers represented at the conference, not to take separate action excepting to protect nationals; finally, the French could not see that the bombardment would be anything but a menace to the European element in Alexandria so long as the ships were unable to land a force of troops. So the French ships were withdrawn to Port Said. On July 10 Admiral Seymour sent an ultimatum to the Egyptians, and on July 11 he started at seven in the morning to bombard the forts. They could offer no serious resistance, and by four in the afternoon they were destroyed. Fires broke out in the city, due either to the gun-fire of the English ships or to incendiarism. The result was that a considerable amount of damage was done to European property. It was not until some days later that a landing force arrived to join the squadron, and men could be put ashore to restore order.

The military and naval authorities were desirous of landing a force from the very beginning, but Gladstone regarded this course as objectionable because it involved the "assumption of authority" and would have been "grossly dis-loyal" in the face of Europe and the conference. Lord Cromer scathingly dis-misses the quibbling of the English statesman and points out that the bom-bardment in itself was enough of an "assumption of authority," an opinion to which one can hardly help subscribing. [2] After the bombardment of Alexan-dria the conference at Constantinople became quite futile, for while it was debating the conditions under which the Sultan should be invited to intervene and all the other modalities of action, the need for immediate measures had become imperative. No doubt the English statesmen would still have preferred to see the Sultan do the work under European direction, but the chances that

---

[1] Sir William Laird Clowes: *The Royal Navy*, Volume VII (London, 1903), p. 326.
[2] Cromer, op. cit., I, p. 298.

Abdul Hamid would agree to the terms of the powers were very uncertain, and the situation called for urgent measures. The fundamental difference of view in this matter arose from the fact that the Sultan wished to act in his capacity as suzerain, while the powers desired him to act as the mandatory of Europe.

"The history of the next two months may be summarized in a single sentence," says Lord Cromer. "England stepped in, and with one rapid and well-delivered blow crushed the rebellion." [1] English opinion was, in fact, very much aroused and was loudly demanding action. Even Gladstone, averse as he was to foreign adventure, was obliged to announce that England would seek the co-operation of Europe, but that " if every chance of obtaining co-operation is exhausted, the work will be undertaken by the single power of England." Parliament voted the necessary credits, and arrangements were made for military operations.

The most urgent problem was that of the Suez Canal, which was being threatened by desert tribes. The mere presence of light ships of war in the canal was not enough to put a stop to these threats. It was necessary to land a force of troops. This, of course, involved the violation of Egyptian territory. But even the French were willing to overlook this point, provided they could secure themselves by obtaining from the conference a mandate to act in the name of Europe. Together with the English, the French indirectly requested such a mandate. But the powers refused to bind themselves so formally. They were willing to give England and France or any other power a blank cheque to do what was deemed necessary to protect their interests, but they would not agree to approve in advance the measures to be taken.

This attitude on the part of the powers, led by Germany, raised serious difficulties for the French government. The chamber on July 29 defeated the ministry by a huge majority, Clemenceau expressing the prevalent attitude of the deputies in the eloquent words: " In truth, it seems that somewhere there is a fatal hand preparing a terrible explosion in Europe. Who will venture to assume responsibility for what is about to happen? Who will dare say that on the day of the diplomatic settlement of the Egyptian question it will be better for France to be alone with England and quarrelling with Europe than to be with the whole of Europe demanding a legitimate share of influence on Egyptian territory? . . . Gentlemen, the conclusion to be drawn from all that is happening is this: Europe is covered with soldiers; everyone is waiting, all the powers are reserving their liberty of action for the future; reserve the liberty of France as well."

The fall of the Freycinet government, so far as the Egyptian question was concerned, meant simply that France would not participate in any military operations, not even the occupation of a few posts along the canal. It did not mean that the French intended to obstruct the action of the English. On the contrary, they were anxious to see the Egyptian revolution suppressed and

---

[1] Cromer, op. cit., I, p. 300.

order restored. They offered the English their best wishes for early success. " Panislamism is a factor of great weight in the future," said President Grévy, " and I consider it of the highest importance that there should be no doubt, even for a moment, that Musulman or Arab troops cannot resist Europeans in the field." In much the same sense Duclerc, the successor of Freycinet, said, in congratulating the English government on its victory, some weeks later: " The sober good sense of France felt that the success of England against Arabi was also a solid gain to the rulers of Algeria." [1]

The English at the moment really had a free hand. There was no danger of serious obstacles being placed in their path. Nevertheless it was decided to invite Italy to join in the operations, first to protect the canal, then to participate in the campaign against Arabi. The suggestion seems to have come from Gladstone, the avowed friend of the Italians. It did not appeal either to the Queen or to Granville. The Italian government, however, refused to accept the invitation, on the plea that the Turks had now at last joined the conference and had agreed to the proposal of the powers that Turkish troops should be dispatched. The real reason for the rejection of the English offer by the Italians seems to have been that they feared the ire of the French, and felt that they could not rely on much support from Bismarck in a question which did not interest Germany directly. From the Italian standpoint the decision of the government was undoubtedly a grave one, but in the general setting of the Egyptian problem it does not loom very large. Granville was delighted by the Italian refusal and carefully abstained from bringing pressure.[2]

The Turks having finally signified their willingness to send troops, the English were now obliged to take this point into consideration. It seems perfectly clear that they were not anxious for Turkish help, but they opened negotiations as to details. The Turks as usual tergiversated till the favourable moment had passed. The fact that an agreement was come to just as the battle of Tel el Kebir was fought, on September 13, has led some writers to assert that Lord Dufferin, the English ambassador to the Porte, drew the Turks on until it was too late for them to take part. This accusation has been warmly disputed by Dufferin's biographer, who quotes a letter of Dufferin in which he says: " From first to last we have run as straight as a die; but the truth is, as I have myself told them, the fatuity of the Porte has been so beyond belief, and so contrary to their own obvious interests that people are forced to attribute the results which have accrued to the diabolic astuteness of the British ambassador. Our Government really wanted the Convention (in spite of the inconvenience which might be occasioned by the presence of Turkish troops in

---

[1] Cromer, op. cit., I, pp. 305–6; Newton: *Lord Lyons*, II, p. 293.

[2] Fitzmaurice: *Granville*, II, p. 271; Newton: *Lord Lyons*, II, p. 294; Buckle: *Letters of Queen Victoria*, III, pp. 312–13; Gwynn and Tuckwell: *Sir Charles Dilke*, I, pp. 473–4, 477–80; *The Memoirs of Francesco Crispi*, II, chapter iii; T. Palamenghi-Crispi: *L'Italia Coloniale e Francesco Crispi* (Milan, 1928), chapter ii.

Egypt) from considerations of general European policy; but it was necessary in order to minimize the ill consequences of the Turks being in Egypt, to let them go there under pretty stringent conditions." [1] Over against this we have the statement of Major Swaine, the military secretary of the commander of the English forces in Egypt, to the effect that Granville wired asking what would be the latest date on which the Turkish troops should reach the scene. To this General Wolseley replied: "Wait and see the result of my operations up to September 13 before fixing any date for the Turks to join me." This reply was repeated to Lord Dufferin, who, after the battle of Tel el Kebir, wrote to Swaine: "Please thank Sir Garnet Wolseley for his telegram from Ismailia. It enabled me to temporize with the Turk until he spitted himself on his own foil." [2]

The campaign of Tel el Kebir need not detain us. Though greatly outnumbered, Wolseley won an easy victory on September 13 and, driving the remnants of Arabi's forces before him, entered Cairo on September 15. The collapse of the Egyptian army was so complete that it has frequently been stated that it was arranged beforehand with Arabi. Freycinet repeats the story, which hardly seems likely. It is very possible, however, that Wolseley profited from the reports of Egyptian traitors. At any rate, it is strange that he knew long beforehand the exact date on which the engagement would be fought, and that all his arrangements were carried out to the letter. [3]

With the defeat of Arabi and the collapse of the nationalist and revolutionary movement the most acute phase of the Egyptian question came to an end. The British were in occupation, though they could hardly have said themselves how they had managed to get there. That they did not want to intervene militarily in Egypt is perfectly clear. That they did not want to become involved in complications for the sake of the interests of European investors is also fairly clear. The English government would have preferred to have Egypt under Turkish suzerainty, guarding the important route to India. But the financial investments led to foreign interference of one sort or another, and gradually this interference assumed an official form. When it resulted in the formation of an Egyptian national group and the organization of a military movement, the governments were almost forced to do something. That their preoccupation with financial interests blinded them to the real nature of the national movement cannot be denied and is not denied, even by men like Freycinet and Lord Cromer. But the liberalism of the English ministers forbade their drawing the natural conclusions. There was nothing heroic about their

---

[1] Lyall: *Lord Dufferin*, II, pp. 20–9; Harold Nicolson: *Portrait of a Diplomatist* (Boston, 1930), pp. 29 ff.

[2] Major-General Sir Leopold V. Swaine: *Camp and Chancery in a Soldier's Life* (London, 1926), pp. 144–5. Sir James Headlam-Morley: *Studies in Diplomatic History* (New York, 1930) has some doubts as to the sincerity of the English offers to Turkey.

[3] The most recent account of the campaign, based on Wolseley's papers, is in Sir F. Maurice and Sir George Arthur: *The Life of Lord Wolseley* (London, 1924), chapter vii.

policy. They were frightened by Gambetta, who really knew what he wanted, but they got along admirably with Freycinet, who was just as much at sea as they were themselves.

From the time of Freycinet's advent to power, in February 1882, the keynote of the Anglo-French policy was the internationalization of the Egyptian question. The difficulty of applying this principle lay in the desire of the English to leave intervention to the Turks as the mandatories of Europe, and in the fact that the French wanted above all to keep the Turks out of Egypt and to secure a European mandate for England and France. Neither side wanted to go on alone. In their anxiety to conceal the rift in the Anglo-French entente the ministers on both sides muddled along, never knowing just where it would all lead, constantly turning to this or that expedient, appealing to the powers, and so on. The result was that they both failed to bring the matter to a satisfactory conclusion. The French, who had been more disposed to intervene than the English, did not take part in the operations of July to September 1882. The English, who were opposed to Anglo-French intervention, to say nothing of separate action by England, eventually found themselves alone in occupation of the country. One cannot speak of statesmanship in a case like this. It is only with the exercise of their imaginative powers that English writers themselves are able to construct a " policy " out of the helpless flounderings of the English ministers in the spring of 1882.

The remarkable thing is that an operation of such international importance as the occupation of Egypt should have been carried through by the English without creating difficulties with the other powers. That the powers did not all approve of what was being done is certainly true. Russia and Italy, for example, were clearly hostile to the English policy. But they were kept in line by Bismarck, whose own policy in this matter was certainly not spectacular, though it was of supreme importance. When the chancellor first took an active part in the negotiations, in 1879, it was, as aforesaid, primarily with the object of preventing a split in the Anglo-French entente, which might have led to the eventual drifting together of France and Russia. But in 1882, after the conclusion of the Alliance of the Three Emperors, he had less reason for fear on this score. His great dread then was that the weak Gladstone ministry would be dragged into action by the vigorous determination of Gambetta, and that the position of the French would be far too much strengthened. He therefore did what he could to help the English, though he avoided estranging the French. He ruined the forward policy initiated by Gambetta by mobilizing the continental powers and protesting against a change in the *status quo* without consultation with the suzerain power. He urged the intervention by the Turks as the most acceptable and most logical solution, but he continued to support all proposals made by England and France jointly with regard to the methods of action. It is certainly not true that Bismarck worked for a break between England and France or that his aim was to smash the understanding between them in order to isolate France. Freycinet admits this without hesitation, and adds that the estrangement of the two powers came about through mistakes over which Bismarck had no control.[1]

But when the two powers did begin to part company, when the French abstention from the bombardment of Alexandria made it increasingly evident that the French government would not act, the chancellor gave England his whole-hearted support. He would not agree to a European mandate for England and France, but he proclaimed Germany's disinterestedness and gave all the powers a free hand. England enjoyed his " moral support " in every way. Just before the battle of Tel el Kebir he sent his son Count Herbert to London to convey his best wishes. The German interest in Egypt, Count Herbert was instructed to say, was so small that no settlement would be of as great weight as the chancellor's desire for friendly relations with England. Reporting the conversation to Queen Victoria, Lord Granville went on to say that Count Herbert stated " that his father would not oppose even annexation, and that France would not do so, the influence of the financial world was so great over the present government. But, if he were in our place, he should avoid annexation, which, although it would not be opposed, would leave a fruitful source of quarrel with the French, who would not forget it. He thought that we were entitled to settle matters, so as to retain a real preponderance. . . . He should, in our place, cover up the preponderance with every form that would make it less irritating to the *amour propre* of the French. He also thought it would be wise to use the Turk, who should be placed as much as possible in the position of a landholder who has given us the leasehold; that he thought a rupture with Turkey would be a great misfortune both as regards Mohammedans and as regarded Europe."

This report tallies with the German documents available for the period and makes Bismarck's policy perfectly clear. It explains, furthermore, why the English with their uncertain policy were able to carry through an operation of such moment without meeting serious opposition. The benevolent attitude of the French was, of course, of great importance, but it was equally important that the other powers should maintain an attitude of abstention. Bismarck may be truly said to have kept the ring for the English and to have made the occupation of Egypt possible.[2]

---

[1] Freycinet: *Souvenirs, 1878–1893*, p. 243; see also the considered opinion of Sir James Headlam-Morley: *Studies in Diplomatic History* (New York, 1930), p. 60, foot-note.

[2] Granville's report, quoted above, is in the *Letters of Queen Victoria*, III, p. 332. Cf. the documents in *Die Grosse Politik*, IV, Nos. 727–30; Gwynn and Tuckwell: *Sir Charles Dilke*, I, pp. 470–1; Fitzmaurice: *Granville*, II, pp. 268–9, 273; and the dispatch of Bismarck to Prince Reuss, printed in Rothfels: *Bismarcks englische Bündnispolitik*, pp. 134–5.

BIBLIOGRAPHICAL NOTE

DOCUMENTARY SOURCES

Accounts and Papers. State Papers. There is a long series of Blue Books covering this period. These form the most important single collection of source material and are the basis of the more extensive secondary accounts. They will be found in *Accounts and Papers for 1876,* Volume LXXXIII; *1877,* LXXXVIII; *1880,* LXXIX; *1881,* XCVIII; *1882,* LXXXII and LXXXIII.

Documents diplomatiques. Affaires d'Égypte. There are six volumes of the French correspondence, which, next to the British material, is the most voluminous. These six volumes cover the period 1878–82.

Documents diplomatiques français. Volumes I and II. Paris, 1930. These recent French documents contain some material on the Egyptian question, but nothing of importance.

Libro Verde. Gli Affari d'Egitto. Volumes of Italian documents on this question were published in 1879 and 1882.

MEMOIRS, AUTOBIOGRAPHIES, BIOGRAPHIES, AND LETTERS

CROMER, LORD: *Modern Egypt.* Two volumes. London, 1908. Really a study of the question from the documents, but containing also the impressions of the British controller and later consul-general. This is the classic account of the crisis, but it should be read in connexion with critical works in order to counteract the apologetic element.

FREYCINET, CHARLES: *Souvenirs, 1878–1893.* The memoirs of the French premier who was chiefly responsible for French policy in 1882.

MALET, SIR EDWARD: *Egypt, 1879–1883.* London, 1909. The reminiscences and impressions of the English consul-general. Does not contain much that is revealing.

DES MICHELS, JULES A.: *Souvenirs de carrière, 1855–1886.* Paris, 1901. Recollections of the French consul-general. Interesting rather for the earlier years of the crisis.

BLUNT, WILFRID SCAWEN: *Secret History of the English Occupation of Egypt.* Two volumes. London, 1907. Full of interesting information on Arabi and his circle, but essentially uncritical. A book which should be used with caution.

WILSON, SIR C. RIVERS: *Chapters from my Official Life.* London, 1916. The memoirs of the controller-general. Not very informative, excepting for the history of the Commission of Inquiry.

ZANANIRI, GASTON: *Le Khédive Ismail et l'Égypte.* Alexandria, 1923. The most recent biography of the Khedive.

FITZMAURICE, LORD EDMOND: *The Life of Lord Granville.* Two volumes. London, 1905. The standard life of the English foreign minister.

NEWTON, LORD: *Lord Lyons*. Two volumes. London, 1913. The life and letters of the English ambassador to Paris.

SPECIAL STUDIES OF THE EGYPTIAN QUESTION

FREYCINET, CHARLES DE: *La Question d'Égypte*. Paris, 1905. One of the best general studies. Based in large part upon the French documents, it should be read in conjunction with Cromer.

MILNER, SIR ALFRED: *England in Egypt*. London, 1892. An excellent presentation of the official view. Now largely superseded by Cromer.

ROTHSTEIN, THEODORE: *Egypt's Ruin*. London, 1910. An exceptionally able study, which rather overdoes the factor of financial interest, but which should be read as an antidote to the accounts of Cromer and Milner.

BIOVÈS, ACHILLE: *Français et Anglais en Égypte, 1881–1882*. Paris, 1910. An admirable review of the subject, and the best specialized treatment.

LEGER, EUGÈNE: *La Question d'Égypte et l'occupation anglaise*. Paris, 1902. A doctoral dissertation.

VELAY, ETIENNE: *Les Rivalités franco-anglaises en Égypte, 1876–1904*. Toulouse, 1904. Another doctoral dissertation.

CHARLES-ROUX, JULES: *L'Isthme et le Canal de Suez*. Two volumes. Paris, 1901. The most extensive and on the whole the best historical treatment of the canal.

PEMEANT, G.: *L'Égypte et la politique française*. Paris, 1909.

HAGEN, MAXIMILIAN VON: *England und Ägypten*. Bonn, 1915. Really a study of Bismarck's policy. An admirable essay, though now somewhat out of date.

KLEINE, MATHILDE: *Deutschland und die ägyptische Frage, 1875–1890*. Greifswald, 1927. Primarily based upon the German documents. The best study of the German policy.

CHARLES-ROUX, FRANÇOIS: " *Allemagne, Angleterre et Égypte en 1877–1878* " (*L'Afrique française*, Volume XXXVIII, Supplement, March 1928, pp. 175–80).

—: " *L'Allemagne et les questions de Tunisie, du Maroc et de l'Égypte de 1879–1884* " (*L'Afrique française*, Volume XXXVIII, Supplement, June 1928, pp. 345–55). This and the preceding article are hardly more than analyses of the German documents, written by the foremost authority in France.

HAEKAL, MOHAMED HUSSEIN: *La Dette publique égyptienne*. Paris, 1912. The most recent systematic and scholarly treatment of the financial aspect of the Egyptian question, though it does not add materially to our previous knowledge.

IX

Colonial Activity and the Isolation of England

W HEN THE BRITISH TROOPS MARCHED INTO CAIRO IN SEPTEMBER 1882, the government had no intention of leaving them there longer than was necessary to restore order and to re-establish the authority of the Khedive. Suggestions that Egypt should be annexed were not seriously entertained. In fact, the suzerainty of the Porte was recognized, and responsible officials stated repeatedly in public that the occupation was purely temporary. An indefinite occupation, said Gladstone on August 10, 1882, " would be absolutely at variance with all the principles and views of Her Majesty's government, and the pledges they have given to Europe, and with the views, I may say, of Europe itself." On November 14, after the battle of Tel el Kebir, he again declared that the occupation was merely provisional. In a circular to the powers, dated January 3, 1883, Lord Granville reiterated the position of the government and stated once more that the cabinet was desirous of withdrawing the forces as soon as the state of the country permitted. There is no need to multiply instances. Suffice it to say that Madame Adam, writing in 1922, succeeded in finding no less than sixty-six declarations of this kind in the period from 1882 to the date of her book.[1]

It must not be assumed that these statements were made in bad faith. But they were, from the start, elastic. How was one to know when the state of the country permitted evacuation or when the authority of the Khedive had been re-established? Men like Gladstone and Granville undoubtedly intended to give these declarations a generous interpretation, but they would certainly have met with determined opposition from the more imperialistic element in the Liberal party, to say nothing of the Queen and the Prince of Wales. The Queen was anxious that the government should not bind itself to effect an early withdrawal, and the Prince wrote to Wolseley after Tel el Kebir: " After this campaign we must for ever keep a strong hold over Egypt, as our interests are too great ever to be lost sight of again." In February 1883 Victoria wrote to Lord Granville: " The Queen feels very anxious that nothing should be said to

---

[1] Mme Juliette Adam: *L'Angleterre en Égypte* (Paris, 1922), p. 73. Mme Adam reprints most of the important declarations, and Blunt also has collated them in the introduction to Rothstein's *Egypt's Ruin*.

fetter or hamper our action in Egypt; we *must* have a firm hold on her *once for all.*" [1]

Before appreciable progress had been made with the administrative reorganization of Egypt, even Gladstone and Granville came to see the impossibility of an early evacuation. In August 1881 a religious leader named Mohammed Ahmed had proclaimed himself Mahdi in the Sudan and before long had brought most of the country under his control. Egyptian expeditions were sent out against him, but were invariably defeated. The crowning disaster came in November 1883, when an Egyptian force commanded by General Hicks was annihilated near El Obeid. It was now decided to abandon the Sudan; in January 1884 General " Chinese " Gordon was sent out to evacuate the garrison at Khartoum. But Gordon was soon cut off and besieged by the enemy. A relief expedition under Wolseley was dispatched in August 1884, but before the town could be reached, it had fallen into the hands of the Mahdi. Gordon himself met his death in the disaster (January 26, 1885).

The situation in the Sudan in the years from 1883 to 1885 was such that it was hard to predict the future. The British government felt obliged to postpone all thought of evacuation and to devote itself to the pressing problems which were continually arising. This, in turn, led to a growing tension between the English and the French. The government at Paris was eager to know just when the evacuation of Egypt would be carried out. As early as September 1882 the question had been put to the English cabinet. As it became increasingly clear that withdrawal could not be looked for in the immediate future, the feeling that France had been duped began to spread, the more so as the English government insisted on the abolition of the dual control, despite the strong protests that came from Paris.

From the end of 1882, therefore, it can be said that the Anglo-French entente had come to an end, and this was a fact of the greatest importance for the general international relations of Europe. Till this time the two powers had usually felt a certain community of interest as against the coalition of the Three Emperors. The western European block was now dissolved. For twenty years a fierce antagonism replaced the former cordiality. The result was a foregone conclusion. The eastern European combination and its leader, Prince Bismarck, were in a much stronger position than before, while both France and England were obliged to shift for themselves and make the best terms possible with their opponents. The German chancellor can hardly be burdened with the responsibility for the rupture of the Anglo-French entente. That he took advantage of it can not be held against him. It has been aptly said that in him personal ability was reinforced by luck: his opponents always made exactly the mistakes which were necessary for the success of his game. [2]

---

[1] *Letters of Queen Victoria*, III, pp. 334, 407; Lee: *Edward VII*, Volume I, p. 459.
[2] Schweinitz: *Denkwürdigkeiten*, II, p. 212 (September 18, 1882).

The English statesmen saw clearly enough that friendship with Germany was absolutely essential as the entente with France gradually weakened and finally broke up.[1] But in the cultivation of German friendship they showed themselves even less adroit than in the handling of the Egyptian question. They forgot that they were dealing with Bismarck, and that they could not expect from the German chancellor a policy based on sentiment. In January 1883 the English ambassador at Berlin wrote home that " the key to Bismarck's policy is to be sought in the true interests of Germany, and that those interests require the maintenance of the Anglo-French alliance and of intimate relations between England and Germany." A short time before, the chancellor had remarked to Prince Hohenlohe that Germany could stand by quietly " if the English and French locomotives collided somewhere." [2]

These statements simply indicate the view of the situation taken by Bismarck. His own position was unassailable. He had no desire to foment friction between the two Western powers; in fact, he believed that the one acted as a salutary check on the other. But if they were to collide, no German interests would demand that he take action to prevent the collision. Indeed, the outbreak of a conflict would only drive England further into dependence upon German goodwill, and France would be completely isolated.[3]

The situation as it was created by the occupation of Egypt was, therefore, this: Bismarck, who held the balance, had supported the English policy loyally, and he was prepared to do so in future. But he expected a *quid pro quo;* he felt that he was entitled to cordial support in matters of importance to Germany which did not seriously affect British interests. Specifically, he expected the English government to look benevolently upon the German efforts to acquire colonial possessions and establish an overseas empire.

Prior to this period Bismarck had described himself as " not a colonialist " and had likened German colonies to the silken sables on the back of a Polish noble who had no shirt beneath.[4] These utterances have been quoted by many writers, frequently with considerable astonishment. As a matter of fact, the attitude of Bismarck was by no means unusual. On the contrary, it was shared by the governing classes of most countries in the period prior to 1870 and was quite in consonance with the teachings of the Manchester free-traders. The old mercantilist conception of colonies and their importance to the mother country had been completely exploded. The idea that colonies, like fruit on the tree, would drop off as soon as ripe, was generally accepted without much question. The English governing classes firmly believed that the great white colonies like Canada, South Africa, and Australia would soon demand independence, and the prospect was not regarded with fear or even regret. According to the

---

[1] *Die Grosse Politik,* IV, No. 730; Fitzmaurice: *Granville,* II, p. 273.

[2] Fitzmaurice, op. cit., II, p. 273; Hohenlohe: *Denkwürdigkeiten,* II, p. 328.

[3] Bismarck's remarks to Cohen, May 12, 1882 (Bismarck: *Gesammelte Werke,* VIII, p. 448).

[4] Busch: *Bismarck, Some Secret Pages,* I, p. 552.

principles of free trade, the mother country would lose nothing but her responsibilities. These were the days when even Disraeli could speak of the colonies as "a millstone round our necks," and could write, as he did to Lord Derby in 1866: "Power and influence we should exercise in Asia; consequently in Eastern Europe, consequently also in Western Europe; but what is the use of these colonial deadweights *which we do not govern?* . . . Leave the Canadians to defend themselves; recall the African squadron; give up the settlements on the west coast of Africa; and we shall make a saving which will, at the same time, enable us to build ships and have a good Budget." [1] In the years before 1870 the great English colonies were given self-government, and the English garrisons were withdrawn. The colonies were well on the road to independence, and the Gladstone cabinet of 1868–74 was generally suspected of trying to hasten the disruption of the empire. Far from attempting to extend their dominions, the English statesmen, and the French statesmen as well, regarded expansion more or less with horror. What additions were made to the English and French overseas possessions were made by force of circumstances or by the initiative of military and naval officers on the spot; hardly ever by the will of the government.

But the days when Cobden could denounce the "bloodstained fetish of Empire" came to a very abrupt end. As industrialism took firm root and developed on the continent, the economic supremacy of England became threatened, in spite of the much vaunted principles of free trade. The 1870's saw the swing of continental Europe from free-trade principles to protection; the continental market began to close against England. At the same time the new industrial nations began to feel the pressure of over-production and to seek outlets for their surplus goods. The greatly improved means of communication opened up the more remote parts of the world. It was clear, as Sir John Seeley expressed it, that " science has given to the political organism a new circulation, which is steam, and a new nervous system, which is electricity. These new conditions make it necessary to reconsider the whole colonial problem." [2] Furthermore, the danger arose that the colonies, if they were let go, would fall into the hands of some other European power and would then be closed to general trade. The American Civil War showed only too clearly how dangerous it was for a modern industrial state to be dependent on a foreign power for the supply of an essential raw material, like cotton.

In the years 1868 to 1872 there grew up in England a movement which became known later as the Imperial Federation Movement. Its purpose was not originally to work for the federation of the parts of the British Empire, but simply to protest and combat the supposed intention of the Gladstone ministry to break up the empire. Prominent men in the movement, like the historian Froude, recognized clearly enough the dangers of the situation, and expressed

---

[1] Monypenny and Buckle, op. cit., III, p. 385; IV, p. 476.
[2] Seeley: *The Expansion of England* (London, 1883), p. 85.

doubts as to the continued economic supremacy of England. The dream of England as the workshop of the world " is already a dream of the past . . . the singularity of our position has gone," wrote one of the advocates of the imperial connexion.[1] The almost phenomenal success of the movement, and the growth of the Royal Colonial Institute, which came under the new influence soon after its founding in 1868, shows that the new imperialism struck a sympathetic chord in the hearts of Englishmen. When Disraeli, in his famous Crystal Palace speech of 1872, ranged himself on the side of the imperialists, the first critical period of the movement came to an end. It was obvious that the disruption of the empire could no longer be thought of. It was only a matter of time before the movement for the preservation of the empire became a movement for expansion. As early as 1870 Ruskin had said in his inaugural lecture at Oxford: " This is what she [England] must do, or perish: she must found colonies as fast and as far as she is able, formed of her most energetic and worthiest men; — seizing every piece of fruitful waste ground she can set her foot on, and there teaching these her colonists that their chief virtue is to be fidelity to their country, and that their first aim is to be to advance the power of England by land and sea."[2]

Of course it was not to be expected that men like Gladstone should suddenly reverse the views and policies which they had cherished for many years. Gladstone remained to the end the opponent of expansion, except in cases of urgent necessity. Even Disraeli has been denied by some writers the distinction of leading in the new imperialist crusade. He was, in fact, more interested in the Near and Middle Eastern problem and was a jingoist almost more than an imperialist in the modern sense. At no time did he show genuine interest in the great white colonies of the empire or in the African possessions of the crown.[3]

In the meanwhile, however, the ideas which had made their appearance in England began to take root on the continent. Of France relatively little need be said, for in 1870 the weak and scattered possessions of the new republic were regarded with frank hostility by the great majority of the French people. The colonial trade was only six hundred million francs per year, of which one third was in the hands of foreigners, while the colonies cost the government annually thirty million francs.[4] French statesmen generally had no use for the colonies and were passionately opposed to further expansion. So long as their eyes were riveted on the German menace, and their thoughts concentrated on the lost provinces, it was regarded almost as treason to suggest the dissipation of French

---

[1] D. Grant: Home Politics, or the Growth of Trade (1870), quoted in the excellent book of C. A. Bodelsen: Studies in Mid-Victorian Imperialism (New York, 1925), on which I rely to a large extent. But see also R. L. Schuyler: " The Climax of Anti-Imperialism in England " (Political Science Quarterly, XXXVI, December 1921, pp. 537–61), much of whose materials and conclusions has been taken over by Bodelsen.   [2] Quoted by Bodelsen, op. cit., p. 105, note.

[3] Bodelsen discusses the question at some length, op. cit., pp. 120 ff.

[4] Marcel Dubois and Auguste Terrier: Les Colonies françaises (Paris, 1902), p. 374.

forces outside of Europe. France, it has been said, was suffering from " acute national myopia "; while gazing at the blue line of the Vosges, she became entirely blind to world movements.[1]

France was certainly less affected by the great economic changes that were coming over Europe than were, for example, England and Germany. She had no surplus population to export and was not sufficiently industrialized to feel keenly the pangs of over-production. At worst she faced the problem of exporting surplus capital, which accumulated the more rapidly as so little of it, relatively speaking, was reinvested in domestic enterprises. Yet the theory of modern economic imperialism was formulated by Frenchmen as clearly as by any others and was acted upon by a few prominent leaders. Paul Leroy-Beaulieu, the French economist, published in 1874 his great work *De la colonisation chez les peuples modernes,* which had a profound influence, more almost outside France than at home. In the preface he declared colonization to be one of the highest functions of those societies that have reached an advanced stage of civilization. But in the preface of the 1882 edition he went much further. He there stressed the importance of colonization, especially for France. This, he maintained, had nothing to do with her lack of surplus population, for "the true sinews of colonization are capital funds rather than emigrants." Colonization, he declared, " is for France a question of life and death: either France will become a great African power, or in a century or two she will be no more than a secondary European power; she will count for about as much in the world as Greece and Roumania in Europe."

The ideas of Leroy-Beaulieu were vigorously supported by certain French statesmen, like Waddington and even Gambetta, who asked the deputies in December 1881: " Do you not feel that the peoples are suffocating on this old continent? " But the great proponent of overseas expansion was Jules Ferry, the founder of the modern French colonial empire. He not only led the French to Tunis, against the desires of a large part of the chamber and the majority of the country, but assumed a leading role in the imperialist activity of the years 1883 to 1885.

Ferry's views were eloquently expressed in his speeches and writings. They deserve quotation as classical expressions of the new outlook in Europe. " This is not a question of the immediate future, but of a future fifty or a hundred years hence, of the very future of the country, of the heritage of our children, of the bread of our workers." " Is it not clear that the great states of modern Europe, the moment their industrial power is founded, are confronted with an immense and difficult problem, which is the basis of industrial life, the very condition of existence — the question of markets? Have you not seen the great industrial nations one by one arrive at a colonial policy? And can we say that this colonial policy is a luxury for modern nations? Not at all, messieurs, this

---

[1] Stephen H. Roberts: *History of French Colonial Policy, 1870–1925,* (London, 1929), Volume I, pp. 11–12.

policy is, for all of us, a necessity, like the market itself." " Today, as you know, the law of supply and demand, freedom of exchange, the influence of speculations, all these move in a circle which extends to the ends of the world." " Colonies are for rich countries one of the most lucrative methods of investing capital. . . . I say that France, which is glutted with capital and which has exported considerable quantities, has an interest in looking at this side of the colonial question. . . . It is the same question as that of outlets for our manufactures." " Colonial policy is the offspring of industrial policy. For rich states in which capital is abundant and is rapidly accumulating, in which the manufacturing system is continually growing and attracting, if not the most numerous, at least the most alert and energetic part of the population that works with its hands, in which the country-side is obliged to industrialize itself in order to maintain itself, in such states exportation is an essential factor of public property. . . . The protective system is like a steam-boiler without a safety-valve, unless it has a healthy and serious colonial policy as a corrective and auxiliary. . . . European consumption is saturated: it is necessary to raise new masses of consumers in other parts of the globe, else we shall put modern society into bankruptcy and prepare for the dawn of the twentieth century a cataclysmic social liquidation of which one cannot calculate the consequences." [1]

In Germany the pressure of modern economic development had made itself felt at an early date. Indeed, it may be said that the whole modern system of economic nationalism and protection goes back to the classic work of Friedrich List: *Das nationale System der politischen Ökonomie*, which was first published in 1841. Though the ideas of List found many adherents and were accepted in more or less modified form by historians like Droysen and Treitschke, the tide of free-trade doctrine continued to rise in Germany until after the founding of the empire. In the meanwhile German industry and commerce grew by leaps and bounds. Merchants and traders from Hamburg and Bremen began to appear on the coasts of Africa and in the Pacific. Missionaries, who went out by the hundreds, generally managed to combine trading activities with their spiritual duties and established important economic interests in remote parts of the world. By the 1880's about fifteen German firms had sixty factories on the west coast of Africa, while the missionaries had some hundreds of stations. In the Pacific the German firm of Goddefroy enjoyed a practical monopoly of the Samoan trade, and Germans were heavily interested in the Fiji and other islands.[2]

---

[1] Speeches of October 11, 1883, December 11, 1884, and July 28, 1885; preface to *Le Tonkin et la Mère-Patrie* (1890). These extracts are all given in Dubois and Terrier, op. cit., pp. 401 ff., but see also Alfred Rambaud: *Jules Ferry* (Paris, 1903), chapter xxvii; Roberts: *History of French Colonial Policy*, I, pp. 15 ff.; Leonard Woolf: *Empire and Commerce in Africa* (London, n.d.), pp. 25 ff.; and the excellent brief account in Parker T. Moon: *Imperialism and World Politics* (New York, 1926), pp. 43 ff.

[2] J. Scott Keltie: *The Partition of Africa* (London, 1893), pp. 169 ff. On the history of German colonial development see T. Sommerlad: *Der deutsche Kolonialgedanke und sein Werden im 19ten*

The extension of German interests abroad necessarily involved new claims on the imperial government. Before long the missionaries and traders were clamouring for protection and agitating for annexation of this or that territory by the home government. At the same time there was a growing demand for the development of German sea-power. "For a young people," said Prince Albert of Prussia, "there is no prosperity without expansion, no expansion without an overseas policy, and no overseas policy without a navy." [1]

Bismarck was ready enough to provide naval protection for German commerce, and considerable progress was made during the 1870's in building up a cruiser force.[2] But of colonial annexations he would hear nothing. All the proposals and suggestions for expansion which came to him (and they were many) were rejected on the plea that the new empire must first be consolidated, that it needed its strength for home problems, that Germany could not afford to antagonize other states, and that there was no really popular demand for expansion in Germany itself. This does not mean that Bismarck lacked understanding for the problem. It means only that he did not consider it urgent, and that he did not feel that Germany was sufficiently prepared for a policy of overseas activity. In 1876 he explained to the German merchant Lüderitz that he had studied the question for some years and had concluded that " a great nation like Germany could not, in the end, dispense with colonies; but, much as he favoured in principle the acquisition of colonies, he hesitated to embark upon colonial enterprise without adequate preparation and without a definite impulse from the nation itself." Furthermore, the international situation was unfavourable at the time. Perhaps in nine or ten years something could be done.[3]

In the following years Bismarck initiated various measures to protect German traders and concluded a series of commercial treaties with the rulers of the most important areas of German enterprise. Apparently his interest in colonies and his realization of their importance grew with his conversion to the principles of protection, while the high-handed attitude of England in annexing the Fiji Islands and refusing to settle the claims of the Germans interested there showed him how unsatisfactory was an arrangement which left German commerce at the mercy of foreign goodwill. The Fiji episode seems to have reacted forcefully on German public opinion as well, for " the whole tone of the communications of the British foreign office on the subject revealed the fact that the colonial aspirations of Germany were either unknown in that

Jahrhundert (Halle, 1918); Maximilian von Hagen: *Bismarcks Kolonialpolitik* (Stuttgart, 1923); and especially the thorough recent study of Mary E. Townsend: *The Rise and Fall of Germany's Colonial Empire* (New York, 1930), chapter ii.

[1] Quoted by Townsend, op. cit., p. 57.

[2] Raimund Foerster: *Politische Geschichte der preussischen und deutschen Flotte bis zum ersten Flottengesetz von 1898* (Dresden, 1928), chapter ii.

[3] Hagen, op. cit., p. 52; Townsend, op. cit., p. 68; Helmuth Rogge: " *Bismarcks Kolonialpolitik als aussenpolitisches Problem* " (*Historische Vierteljahrschrift*, XXI, pp. 304–33, 423–43. 1923–4), p. 312.

quarter or not taken seriously."[1] At any rate, a concerted agitation for the establishment of colonies was now started in Germany, by men like Friedrich Fabri and Wilhelm Hübbe-Schleiden. The former, in an effective, popularly written volume: *Bedarf Deutschland der Kolonien?* (1879), set forth the principal economic considerations, such as the rising tide of emigration from Germany, which came to about two hundred thousand annually, and stressed the need for colonial markets and new fields of investment. Hübbe-Schleiden, on the other hand, devoted his book, *Deutsche Kolonisation* (1881), to the cultural and political side of the problem, decrying the cosmopolitanism of free-trade principles and preaching a healthy, national world policy.[2] The agitation thus started gave rise to the establishment of a Colonial Society (*Kolonialverein*) in 1882 and the publication of the *Kolonialzeitung* in 1884. By 1885 the organization had over ten thousand members, and it might be said without exaggeration that the strength of numbers and organization of the colonial movement in Germany was in advance of similar movements in any of the other countries.

As a matter of fact, Bismarck, supported by a surge of public opinion, played the leading role in the great outburst of imperialism which filled the years from 1883 to 1885. If you accept the doctrine of imperialism and expansion as it was advanced at that time, there is no denying that Germany's needs were greatest. She needed areas for colonization unless she were willing to continue to export population to American and other foreign shores. She needed markets for her growing industrial output, and she needed sources for raw materials. France, on the other hand, needed fields for foreign investment, but nothing more. Ferry, already somewhat discredited by the occupation of Tunis, fought an uphill battle throughout. The plea of future needs was not very convincing to the French. If they tolerated his policy for a time, it was chiefly as a matter of national pride. France could not afford to be left behind and believed, with Seeley, that " the same inventions which make vast political unions possible, tend to make states which are on the old scale of magnitude unsafe, insignificant, second-rate."[3] England, on the other hand, played a passive or negative role throughout these years. The Gladstone government, still clinging to the ideas of an age that was past, faced with a rather formidable movement for strengthening the bonds between the mother country and the great dependencies and anxious to withdraw from the Egyptian imbroglio into which it had blundered, was not likely to look for further adventure. The question here was what would be the attitude of the English government towards the imperialistic enterprises of countries like Germany and France.

The immediate impetus to colonial activities in the years here under discussion undoubtedly came from the great explorations in Africa in the middle of

---

[1] Keltie, op. cit., p. 171.

[2] These works are ably analysed by Hagen, op. cit., pp. 21 ff., and by Townsend, op. cit., pp. 77 ff.

[3] *The Expansion of England*, p. 85.

the century and from the schemes advanced by King Leopold II of the Belgians. Until about 1850 Africa could be truly called the Dark Continent. The state of geographical knowledge of this vast area could still be adequately described in the words of the eighteenth-century poet who said:

> Geographers, in Afric maps
> With savage pictures fill their gaps;
> And over uninhabitable downs
> Place elephants, for want of towns.

All this was changed in the thirty years from 1850 to 1880, during which Barth, Vogel, Rohlfs, Nachtigal, and Duveyrier explored the Sahara and the Sudan; Baker, Speke, Grant, and Schweinfurth opened up the region of the great lakes; Livingstone investigated the Zambezi basin; and Stanley solved the key problem, the mystery of the Congo. Most of these explorers, and many others of lesser note, came back from their travels with dramatic stories of cannibals and with horrible tales of slave-trading, but they came back also with glowing reports of the great economic possibilities of the countries they had traversed. Europe rapidly succumbed to a veritable " Africa fever," and the great continent was everywhere spoken of as " a second India," a land of promise.[1]

At the time, Africa was still an open field for European enterprise. If you exclude Egypt and north-west Africa, regions which were really part of the Mediterranean basin, the South African settlements were the only ones of real importance. Only about one tenth of the area of Africa was claimed, and the claims of powers like Portugal were nebulous in the extreme. England and France had various trading posts along the coast. The great interior plateaux had only just been explored, and offered a free field. Leopold of Belgium saw here his great opportunity. Even before his accession to the throne, in 1865, he had travelled widely in northern Africa as well as in India and had made himself a leading exponent of imperialism. " The sea bathes our coast, the world lies before us," he had written in 1861. " Steam and electricity have annihilated distance, all the non-appropriated [?] lands on the surface of the globe can become the field of our operations and of our success." [2]

By 1876 Leopold's attention had become focused on Africa. He had taken the first step towards the realization of his plans by inviting to Brussels a large number of distinguished geographers, travellers, and explorers to discuss the possibility of organizing the further opening of Africa " to civilization " on an

---

[1] See especially Paul Darmstaedter: *Geschichte der Aufteilung und Kolonisation Afrikas*, Volume II (Berlin, 1920), pp. 22 ff.

[2] Paul Crokaert: *Brialmont* (Brussels, 1925), p. 420. Similar utterances may be found in Max Büchler: *Der Kongostaat Leopolds II* (Zurich, 1912), Volume I, pp. 35 ff., and in A. J. Wauters: *Histoire politique du Congo belge* (Brussels, 1911), pp. 8 ff. See also Emile Banning: *Mémoires politiques et diplomatiques. Comment fût fondé le Congo belge* (Paris, 1927), and Comte Louis de Lichtervelde: *Leopold II* (New York, 1929).

international basis. The Brussels Conference was a distinct success and resulted in the foundation of the International Association for the Exploration and Civilization of Central Africa. Each national group was to form a national committee and carry on its part of the work under the program of the association. The executive committee, however, was to be in Brussels, under the eye of Leopold.

As a matter of fact, the association as such did not accomplish much. The French and German groups established a number of stations in Africa, but the English refused to be associated with the larger movement. The greater part of the actual work done was done by the Belgian group, which, like the others, put the national aspect above the international. Scholars are pretty generally agreed that the association was meant from the beginning to be a mere cloak for the schemes of the Belgian King, who had failed to interest his own countrymen in imperialistic enterprises and could hardly hope to attain his end openly in the face of the opposition of the greater powers.

At this time Leopold was still interested primarily in East Africa. But Stanley's exploration of the Congo basin in 1876-7 led him to see the great possibilities of the central region of the continent. He immediately attempted to enlist the services of Stanley when the latter returned to Europe. The explorer would have preferred to have England take the lead in the coming scramble, but the English government, like the country at large, did not show much interest, and so, in the autumn of 1878, Stanley accepted the offer of Leopold on behalf of the Committee for the Study of the Upper Congo, a new Belgian-Dutch organization, under Leopold's direction, which was nominally associated with the International Association. The object of the committee was to establish stations and to study the ways and means of opening up the Congo basin by railways, steamships, or otherwise. Stanley returned to the Congo in 1879 and remained there, with a brief interlude, until 1884, furthering the work of the Belgian syndicate, which in 1882 changed its name to that of International Association of the Congo.

Stanley, like other agents of Leopold and the organizations through which he worked, was bound to absolute secrecy. But it is not surprising that other governments began to suspect ulterior motives behind the loud declarations of international co-operation in the task of civilizing Africa. The French government, at least, regarded the activities of Leopold and Stanley with some uneasiness and almost immediately sent out the great explorer Savorgnan de Brazza to push forward from Gabun to the Congo and establish the French claims to the north bank of the great river. This is hardly the place to enter upon a detailed discussion of the highly dramatic rivalry between De Brazza and Stanley, or, indeed, to follow minutely the story of the founding of the Congo State. The important point is that the projects of Leopold opened up the whole African question. Partition of the continent could not be far off, and the government that hesitated would soon be left behind.

In dealing with the fate of the great Congo basin neither Leopold nor the French government had to reckon with opposition from any great power. The English were still indifferent; only the Portuguese put forward claims, and these were poorly founded and extremely indefinite. The real antagonism in the matter of the Congo came only when the English began to champion the Portuguese claims. But by that time, by 1884, the English had already become seriously involved in colonial disputes with the Germans.

The international position of Germany was an unusually strong one in 1883, for the situation on the continent was secured by the Three Emperors' Alliance and the Triple Alliance, while the English were more or less dependent on German goodwill for the successful handling of the Egyptian problem. Bismarck therefore decided to make use of his advantages to secure for Germany a part of the colonial spoils. He resumed negotiation on the German claims which had arisen out of the English annexation of the Fiji Islands, and pressed them with greater vigour than before. At the same time he invited the trading centres to make suggestions as to better methods of protecting trade interests in Africa. When, in November 1882, the well-known merchant Lüderitz asked for protection for his settlements in south-west Africa, the chancellor encouraged him and promised action.

But he did not want to fly in the face of the English, who had, however, refused in 1880 to give protection to German interests in that region excepting in the vicinity of Walfish Bay. On February 4, 1883 Bismarck inquired of the English whether they exercised any authority over the Angra Pequena region. If not, Germany intended to afford her subjects in that region the protection which they needed. To this courteous inquiry the English government replied evasively. The German request for information conveyed the impression that Germany had not the least design of establishing a foothold in south-west Africa and preferred to leave the responsibility of protection to England. The English were therefore much surprised when the agents of Lüderitz established themselves at Angra Pequena and hoisted the German flag. When Bismarck inquired what were the English claims to this area, the reply came from London that the English government regarded any claim to sovereignty over areas between Portuguese territory in the north and the territory of Cape Colony on the south as an infringement of England's legitimate rights. In view of the previous correspondence between the two governments this reply is almost inexplicable. The German chancellor was certainly justified in asking, rather irritatedly, by what right the British advanced their claim. It may be supposed that the English statesmen found it rather difficult to find a satisfactory answer to this pertinent question. Evidently they had been acting all along with the idea of saving the feelings of the Cape government. At any rate, the German demand was referred to the colonial office and from there was sent on to the Cape. Owing to local difficulties, no reply was given until May 29, 1884, at which time the Cape government recommended the annexation of all territory as far as Walfish Bay—that is, including Angra Pequena. But Bismarck had already anticipated this move. On April 24 he had declared the Lüderitz settlements under German protection.

By this time the relations between the two governments had already become strained and tense, for the German chancellor had come to believe that the English were unwilling to allow the Germans a fair chance in the colonial field. Recognizing the hopeless isolation of England, Bismarck attempted to bring the London foreign office to its senses. While stiffening his attitude in the matter of the Fiji claims, he also tried by persuasion to secure the cordial support of the English. In a crucial dispatch of May 5, 1884 to the German ambassador at London (Count Münster) the German chancellor set forth his view-point: "Owing to her geographical position, England is in no serious danger from any Power except from France in Europe, and in Asia from Russia. France, however, should she adopt a menacing attitude towards England, would require at the very least the certainty of German neutrality, and Russia also must have an eye to the attitude of Germany, should she really wish to move against England, whether in India or Constantinople. We believe, therefore, that our attitude—I will not say towards England herself, with whom we should not think of quarrelling—but our attitude to her enemies or rivals is of more importance to British policy than the possession of Heligoland and all the trade rivalry of German and British firms in distant seas. England can secure for herself the continuance of our active support for her political interests through sacrifices, which she would hardly feel."

In order to understand the full significance of this extract, it must be added that Bismarck suggested the cession by England of the little island of Heligoland in the North Sea as an indication of her desire for good relations, at the same time pointing out the value of Germany's continued support of English policy in Egypt. Heligoland was of little value to England, but was of great interest to Germany in view of the projected canal from the North Sea to the Baltic. General von Caprivi, the chief of the admiralty, was particularly anxious to secure this island outpost and had persuaded Bismarck of its importance. Taken by and large, it seemed to the chancellor that his suggestion should appeal to the English, whose international position at the moment was far from satisfactory. " In making these proposals," Bismarck went on to say in his dispatch to Münster, " we seem, in my opinion, to be offering rather than demanding a sacrifice, for the support, which we can and eventually shall give to England, is worth in reality more than Heligoland, Fiji and Little Popo, put together." [1]

Nothing came of this advance of Bismarck's, excepting an acrimonious discussion which left its traces for a long time in the traditions of the British foreign office. Lord Fitzmaurice, in his biography of Lord Granville, says that

---

[1] This dispatch is in *Die Grosse Politik*, IV, No. 738. I quote the English translation of E. T. S. Dugdale: *German Diplomatic Documents*, Volume I (London and New York, 1928), pp. 170 ff.

Bismarck referred to it in a speech before the Reichstag on March 2, 1885. As a matter of fact, Bismarck made no reference to this document at the time; neither was it published in the German White Book on Angra Pequena, as Sir Eyre Crowe maintained in a memorandum of 1907, which will be referred to presently. What happened was this: Bismarck referred to his instructions to Münster when he discussed the situation with the English ambassador in January 1885. Lord Ampthill reported to his government, and Lord Granville took up the matter with Count Münster. The German ambassador stated that the instructions of May 5, 1884 had been revoked in a later dispatch of the same month. Thereupon Gladstone, in a speech delivered on March 12, 1885, suggested that Bismarck had forgotten the fact that Münster had been instructed to defer his communication. The English government then published Ampthill's report of his conversation with Bismarck in a Blue Book, without asking the permission of the German government.

Yet Bismarck, when he called Münster to account, was told by the ambassador that he had followed instructions to the letter. The chancellor had not recalled the instructions of May 5, 1884. The trouble was that Münster, who had no sympathy whatever for the colonial agitation in Germany, but was a warm advocate of the idea of securing Heligoland, had raised only the question of the eventual cession of the island in his conversations with Granville. Bismarck, seeing that Münster completely misunderstood his object, reprimanded him and pointed out that Heligoland was of secondary importance. What he really wanted to know was whether " England is inclined, in her present situation, in return for our firm offer of greater support than before for British policy, to satisfy our overseas grievances by ceasing to place hindrances in the way of the legitimate enterprises of German nationals." Münster, he said, would have been justified in expressing astonishment that England was attempting to apply a sort of Monroe Doctrine to Africa, as indicated by her attitude in the Angra Pequena question. " Supposing it to be really our intention to establish colonies, how can Lord Granville contest our right to do so at the very moment when the British government is granting an unlimited exercise of the same right to the government at the Cape? This naïve egoism is in itself an insult to our national feeling, and you will please point this out to Lord Granville. The ' quod licet Jovi,' etc., cannot be applied to Germany. The game of hide and seek with the colonial office and the appeal on account of the independence of the British colonies, are merely an evasion, so long as these colonies remain under the protection of the mother country, when their policy brings them into contact with foreign powers." [1]

Münster, when called to account in the spring of 1885, maintained that he had actually called the attention of Lord Granville to the possible consequences of the English policy. But even if he did, it is clear that the misunderstanding which arose was at least in part due to his awkward handling of the matter

---

[1] *Die Grosse Politik,* IV, No. 743.

and to his lack of appreciation of the issues involved. It appears that on one occasion he actually invited the English to proceed to the establishment of a protectorate over Angra Pequena.[1] On the other hand, the following considerations must be borne in mind: The English statesmen were hardly in a position to follow up Bismarck's offer even if they were so inclined; for there was considerable opposition to making concessions to Germany in colonial matters. Gladstone and Granville were quite willing to regard the German aspirations indulgently, but the younger and more radical leaders of the party, the imperialists like Dilke and Chamberlain, were dead against such a policy.[2] Furthermore, the English government was confronted with the protests of the colonial governments, which were in favour of annexing everything, if only to keep out new-comers. The Australians were even less reasonable on this score than the South Africans. Fearing possible French or German designs on the Pacific islands, they wanted to annex or declare a protectorate over New Guinea, the New Hebrides, Samoa, and all the islands north and north-east of New Guinea. Lord Derby, the colonial secretary, who had no sympathy for what looked like a Monroe Doctrine in the Pacific, referred scathingly to these colonial aspirations: " I asked them whether they did not want another planet all to themselves? and they seemed to think it would be a desirable arrangement if only feasible. The magnitude of their ideas," he wrote to Queen Victoria's secretary, Sir Henry Ponsonby, "is appalling to the English mind. . . . It is hardly too much to say that they consider the whole Southern Pacific theirs *de jure*. . . . It certainly is hard for four millions of English settlers to have only a country as big as Europe to fill up." [3]

The whole incident of May 1884 was most unfortunate for Anglo-German relations. The thought of it rankled for a long time in the minds of those concerned. In a famous memorandum of 1907 Sir Eyre Crowe, an important official of the foreign office, recalled the matter and referred to it as evidence of Bismarck's " disregard of the elementary rules of straightforward and honourable dealing." He admitted that the desires entertained by the Germans were not seriously antagonistic to British policy: " Most of the territory ultimately acquired by Bismarck had at some previous time been refused by England, and in the cases where British occupation had lately been contemplated, the object had been not so much to acquire fresh provinces, as to prevent their falling

---

[1] Herbert Bismarck to his father, June 24, 1884, printed in Rothfels: *Bismarcks englische Bündnispolitik*, p. 82, note. Rothfels discusses the episode in detail, but see also Rogge: " *Bismarcks Kolonialpolitik als aussenpolitisches Problem* " (*Historische Vierteljahrschrift*, XXI, pp. 318–19); Walther Stuhlmacher: *Bismarcks Kolonialpolitik* (Halle, 1927), pp. 40 ff.; and, above all, the keen analysis by Friedrich Thimme: " *Das Memorandum E. A. Crowes vom 1 Januar 1907* " (*Berliner Monatshefte*, VII, pp. 732–68, August 1929) and " *Das ' berühmte Schwindeldokument' E. A. Crowes* " (ibid., pp. 874–9, September 1929).

[2] Gwynn and Tuckwell: *The Life of Sir Charles Dilke*, II, chapter xxxvii; Lee: *Edward VII*, Volume I, p. 480; Paul Knaplund: *Gladstone and Britain's Imperial Policy* (London, 1927), pp. 155–7.

[3] *Letters of Queen Victoria*, III, p. 432.

into the hands of protectionist France, who would inevitably have killed all British trade." The trouble, as he saw it, was with Bismarck's tactics, especially with his systematic misleading of the British ambassador at Berlin, who insisted to the last that Bismarck had no interest in colonies and was simply utilizing the public demand for purposes of parliamentary manœuvres. Crowe then dilates on Bismarck's deception of the Reichstag and the German people by publishing in a White Book a dispatch to Münster which had never been communicated to the British foreign office.[1]

Now these assertions will not hold water. Later on, when Bismarck had become disillusioned about the colonial experiment, he did say that he had pursued his colonial policy for opportunist reasons. He had hoped that the Germans would have some understanding for it and would support it. At that time everyone was so wrapped up in party politics that he believed a colonial policy would divert attention from all the petty wrangling.[2] It may well be that Lord Ampthill derived the impression from Bismarck's utterances that the domestic side of the situation was what interested him most. But how, after the exchange of notes in the spring of 1884, the English government could still misunderstand the German attitude and still take the matter lightly is quite beyond comprehension. Dilke admitted to Herbert Bismarck in the spring of 1885 that there was no excuse whatever for the blundering of the government. As for the story of Bismarck's deception in the matter of the dispatch, that has been completely exploded.[3] It is hard, in fact, to exonerate Crowe from the charge of wilfully misrepresenting the facts. One of his own colleagues, Lord Sanderson, felt keenly the injustice of the accusations brought forward in the memorandum. On the margin he noted: " If the mere acquisition of territory were in itself immoral, I consider that the sins of Germany since 1871 are light in comparison to ours. . . . It has sometimes seemed to me that to a foreigner reading our press the British Empire must appear in the light of some huge giant sprawling over the globe, with gouty fingers and toes stretching out in every direction, which cannot be approached without eliciting a scream." The sentiment was aptly expressed by a member of a deputation from South Africa who concluded an address to the late Lord Salisbury with the remark: " My Lord, we are told that the Germans are good neighbours, but we prefer to have no neighbours at all."

Whatever may have been the rights and wrongs in this dispute between the English and German governments, the attitude of the British statesmen was a mistaken one, especially when viewed from the standpoint of practical politics. At the time, Bismarck held the whip hand, and he was determined to make the utmost use of it if necessary to gain his point. The key to an understanding of

---

[1] *British Documents on the Origins of the War,* edited by G. P. Gooch and Harold Temperley, Volume III (London, 1928), pp. 408–9.

[2] Ferdinand Philipp: *Bismarck-Gespräche* (Dresden, 1927), p. 105.

[3] Especially by Thimme, loc. cit.

the international situation must be sought in the position of England. As a great sea-power with extensive overseas possessions she was the neighbour of every country accessible by sea and was, *ipso facto*, constantly exposed to friction with these other countries and in danger of finding a combination of powers directed against her.[1] This was the price which England was obliged to pay for her greatness, and under normal conditions the inevitable dangers of her position could be counteracted by a skilful diplomacy which depended upon the principle of maintaining the balance of power. But the years 1883–4 were not normal. The world was carried away by an orgy of imperialism and expansion. England immediately felt the increased pressure. She was soon at serious odds not only with the Germans, but with the French, who had ambitions in Madagascar as well as on the African continent, and with Russia, who was pressing forward in central Asia. The idea of these powers co-operating against their common opponent was the most natural idea in the world. When the English statesmen stood up to Bismarck, they were practically inviting him to organize a coalition against England, a coalition so strong that it could not be resisted for very long.

After the renewal of the Three Emperors' Alliance in 1884, Bismarck could count on Russia, Austria, and Italy as allies. Germany's relations with Turkey were closer than they had been for some time,[2] and the visit of King Alfonso of Spain to Germany, followed by the return visit of the German Crown Prince to Spain in the autumn of 1883, had made it plain that the Spanish government, too, desired to be identified with the continental group.[3] If Bismarck could succeed in establishing close contact with France and induce the French government to pursue a common policy directed against England, the iron ring would be completed. England would be helpless when opposed by a united continent.

The idea of a Franco-German entente is likely to strike the student of pre-war diplomacy as rather incredible and even anomalous, and yet Bismarck's plan was actually put into practice during the years 1884 and 1885. As a matter of fact, the idea is not so incongruous when one remembers that relations between the two countries had been distinctly good ever since the coming into power of the republican groups in 1877. Gambetta, the recognized leader of the revenge movement, had died in 1882, and the prime minister, Jules Ferry, though a Lorrainer by birth, took a very different view of the situation. To suppose that he really desired an alliance with Germany, or that he actually ignored the problem of the lost provinces, would, of course, be as naïve as it would be unjust. Ferry's friend and collaborator, the historian Alfred Rambaud,

---

[1] The point is well developed in the memorandum of Sir Eyre Crowe, quoted above, pp. 402–3.

[2] See Hajo Holborn: *Deutschland und die Türkei, 1878–1890* (Berlin, 1926), pp. 33 ff.

[3] Albert Mousset: *L'Espagne dans la politique mondiale* (Paris, 1923), chapter ii; Hohenlohe: *Denkwürdigkeiten*, II, p. 344; Bismarck: *Gesammelte Werke*, VIII, pp. 493–6; Waldersee: *Denkwürdigkeiten*, I, pp. 229–31.

is right in denying this accusation in the warmest terms.[1] The situation was simply this: Ferry, who was one of the most convinced proponents of the new imperialism, saw as clearly as did Bismarck that England was the great obstacle to the expansion of the continental countries. Realizing that the dreams of recovering Alsace and Lorraine could not, for a long time at least, be translated into practice, he believed that the wisest thing to do would be to co-operate with Germany for the attainment of certain specified colonial aims, while reserving the larger and more knotty problems for the future. Ferry accepted the advances of Bismarck and worked cordially with the chancellor, but he did so with his eyes open and without committing himself too far. Few of the statesmen of the Third French Republic have shown the same breadth of view and the same lack of prejudice.[2]

It was easy enough to find common ground for Franco-German action, once the principle of co-operation had been agreed to. Egypt was one of the most obvious. Indeed, the international aspect of this problem, as established by the law of liquidation of 1880, was such that the powers could cause England endless difficulty by raising awkward objections, especially in financial matters. Before long the troublesome Egyptian question became a veritable sword of Damocles suspended over the heads of the English statesmen.

The years 1883-4 were among the most trying in the history of the British occupation. As Lord Milner says: "Everything, yes, absolutely everything, seemed bent upon going wrong at one and the same time. Alike in military matters, in diplomacy, and in politics, Great Britain was simply haunted by the Egyptian Question."[3] But worst of all was the financial crisis, which could not be solved without some co-operation from the powers. By 1884 the financial difficulties of the Egyptian government, bad enough before the occupation, had become very much greater because of the expenses of the campaign of 1882 and the outlay for the armies in the Sudan. In addition, an award of some four million pounds for damages resulting from the burning of Alexandria had been handed down by an international commission. As a result a deficit of almost a million pounds was in prospect for the year 1884. In the meanwhile, however, the share of the revenue assigned to the service of the debt was in a most prosperous state and promised a surplus of four hundred thousand pounds, which, under the terms of the law of liquidation, would be devoted to the repurchase of unified stock, no matter what the other needs of the country might be. Something, clearly, had to be done, and the main question the

---

[1] Rambaud: *Jules Ferry*, p. 395.

[2] On the Franco-German entente see the essay by G. P. Gooch: *Franco-German Relations, 1871–1914* (London, 1923); the article by Elie Halévy: "Franco-German Relations since 1870" (*History*, Volume IX, new series, pp. 18–29, April 1924); and more recently Johannes Haller: *Tausend Jahre deutsch-französischer Beziehungen* (Berlin, 1930), chapter vii. A detailed monographic study has been written by Robert H. Wienefeld: *Franco-German Relations, 1878–1885* (Baltimore, 1929).

[3] Alfred Milner: *England in Egypt* (London, 1892), pp. 90–1.

English government had to decide was who should be sacrificed, the bondholders or the English taxpayers. It was no longer a question of the bondholders
as against the Egyptian population, for the English government was now before
the alternatives: reduce the rate of interest or bear the costs of the army of
occupation.[1]

The English statesmen decided to sacrifice the bondholders if they could.
In April 1884 they invited the powers to a conference at London to consider
the possibility of changes in the law of liquidation. Ferry agreed to attend only
after the British, by an exchange of notes, had promised to evacuate Egypt by
1888, " provided that the powers were of the opinion that the evacuation could
take place without compromising the peace and order of Egypt." The conference then opened at London on June 28. But it never ran a successful course,
and broke up early in August. The trouble was with the English proposals,
which called for the reduction of the interest on the unified debt by one-half
per cent, the floating of a new loan of some eight million pounds to cover the
new indebtedness, and the meeting of the new interest charges by the transfer
of surplus income from the assigned revenues to administrative expenditure.
This plan was firmly opposed by the French, who objected to " cutting the
coupon." The important thing, however, was that France was consistently
supported by Germany and most of her friends, so that the conference was
bound to fail. When it came to a close, the new Franco-German combination
had won a resounding victory. The English were left in their dilemma, and
might with profit have reflected on the kaleidoscopic changes of the international scene.

The Egyptian question was a powerful weapon in the hands of France and
Germany and could be effectively wielded to make the English modify their
attitude of opposition to the colonial aspirations of other nations. It left the
French and Germans in a stronger position to press their claims in Africa and
elsewhere. In fact, at the very time of the Egyptian negotiations Bismarck and
Ferry united in a direct action designed to solve the Congo problem to their
own satisfaction.

The activities of Stanley, serving as Leopold's agent, had immediately
aroused the most serious apprehensions of the French. De Brazza had been
sent out to head off Stanley and had, in fact, established the French in a strong
position. But the feverish haste with which the various explorers concluded
treaties with the native chiefs aroused the suspicions of the Portuguese government, which claimed the whole Congo region on the basis of priority of discovery. These nebulous claims of Portugal, a power wholly discredited by the
laxity of her colonial system, would probably have caused little trouble had it
not been for the fact that the English, recognizing at last the significance of
the problem and fearing lest the French might secure control of the mouth of

---

[1] Childers to Baring, February 26, 1884 (Spencer Childers: *The Life and Correspondence of
the Right Hon. Hugh C. E. Childers,* London, 1901, p. 201).

the great river and shut it to British commerce, had taken up the suggestions made by the Portuguese government in November 1882 that an Anglo-Portuguese agreement be reached. This agreement was to define the territorial claims of the Portuguese and at the same time to guarantee the free navigation of the Congo. The details of the negotiations need not detain us. The discussions dragged on for some time, but finally ended with the signature of the treaty on February 26, 1884.

This Anglo-Portuguese Treaty, which recognized Portugal's rights to the mouth of the Congo, immediately raised a storm of protest in English commercial circles and in parliament. Worse yet, it brought the French upon the scene, and the French were supported by Bismarck. In view of the delicate international situation and the sorry plight of England with respect to the Egyptian imbroglio, Gladstone and Granville were unable to hold out. The treaty with Portugal was abandoned on June 26, 1884, after German sovereignty at Angra Pequena had been recognized by England a few days earlier. When, in July, the attempt of the Cape government to annex south-west Africa led to further bitter recriminations from Bismarck, the English government was obliged to yield on this point too. The Germans hoisted the flag on August 22. One month later the English formally recognized German sovereignty over this vast territory.[1]

The English had yielded all along the line. It was the only thing they could do under the circumstances, and the British surrender is not to be wondered at. What does seem incredible is the complete lack of understanding shown by Lord Granville in this period. The failure to grasp the connexion of the Egyptian problem with the colonial question, the whole clumsy attempt to settle the Congo problem by the roundabout route via Portugal, the unbelievable ineptitude with which the south-west African situation was handled — all this put the British foreign office in a discreditable light. It may be true that Bismarck did not keep the British ambassador fully informed as to his schemes, and it may be true that the British government was actually misled in regard to German activities in the Cameroons and New Guinea. Such a policy did not enhance the glory of Bismarck, though it was common enough on the part of other governments as well; but it does not excuse the English statesmen either. Their lack of foresight and failure to appreciate the situation is so obvious that it cannot be explained away. The English press itself refused to follow the lead of the government. Charles Lowe, who was at that time the Berlin correspondent of *The Times,* says that few writers did not admit that Bismarck had a real grievance against the British government, " for it had been clearly guilty of apathy and neglect, of blindness and vacillation, of dawdling, shilly-shallying, discourtesy and downright dog-in-the-manger conduct." There was nothing heroic or even graceful in its surrender. If anything, it was ludi-

---

[1] Fitzmaurice: *Life of Granville,* II, pp. 352–9; *Die Grosse Politik,* IV, Nos. 745 ff.

crous. *Punch* represented the situation accurately enough in a little imaginary dialogue: " Prince Bismarck: ' We have helped you in Egypt, why not oblige us in Fiji? ' Lord Derby: ' We can't do it.' Lord Granville: ' We won't do it.' Prince Bismarck: ' But you *must* do it.' Lord Granville: ' Very well, we will then.' " [1]

The English statesmen had got themselves into a serious and dangerous scrape, for Bismarck, having tasted the sweets of victory, had no intention of letting matters rest where they were. General von Schweinitz, who visited him during the last days of July 1884, came away with the impression that Bismarck was aiming at nothing less than a *Continental System,* similar to the one projected by Napoleon I, though on a different basis.[2] It was in pursuance of this idea that he negotiated with the French in August, his object being to lay the bases for close co-operation in the further treatment of the Egyptian and colonial questions. Ferry accepted the German proposals almost immediately, and on August 24 Baron de Courcel, the French ambassador at Berlin, was back in the German capital with the approval of his government for the program of co-operation. The two powers were to act together in securing freedom of commerce in west Africa, as well as in the solution of the Egyptian question. The entente was complete and signified a great rapprochement, as Hohenlohe remarked.[3]

Bismarck received Courcel on August 26, at Varzin. The conversation before long took a general turn, the chancellor declaring that he had long desired a rapprochement with France, but that mutual distrust had thus far prevented its realization. Courcel was evasive and the subject was dropped. The entente remained, for the present, a specific understanding relating to African and other colonial questions. Its first fruit was the international conference which met at Berlin in November to discuss the Congo problem. This meeting had practically been arranged by Germany and France, the English receiving an invitation without being drawn into the confidential discussions.

While the relations between Germany and England were going from bad to worse, while one government was bitterly accusing the other of unfairness and at the same time trying to steal a march on its rival in various disputed colonial fields, Bismarck continued his efforts to draw the French more closely to the side of the continental coalition. After the meeting of the three Emperors at Skierniewice in September, the chancellor called upon the French ambassador and gave him positive assurances that the imperial combination was in no sense directed against France. He then went on to expound his plan of a Franco-German agreement: "What I want is to establish a sort of equilibrium on the sea, and France has a great role to play in this matter if she is willing

---

[1] Charles Lowe: *The Tale of a* Times *Correspondent* (London, 1928), p. 205.

[2] Schweinitz: *Denkwürdigkeiten,* II, p. 283.

[3] Hohenlohe: *Denkwürdigkeiten,* II, p. 351. See also Bourgeois and Pagès: *Origines et responsabilités de la Grande Guerre* (Paris, 1921), pp. 208–9; *Die Grosse Politik,* III, Nos. 680 ff.

to concur in our views. Men spoke formerly of a European equilibrium; it's an eighteenth-century expression. But I think it is not obsolete to speak of the equilibrium of the seas. I repeat, I do not want war with England; but I want her to understand that if the navies of the other nations unite, they will counterbalance her on the ocean and will compel her to consider the interests of others. To do this she must accustom herself to the idea that a Franco-German alliance is not an impossibility."

The idea of such an alliance against England was not new. Napoleon I and Napoleon III had envisaged it. Clearly it would be to France's advantage to encourage the increase of the German navy, as a counter-weight to England. Of course, if the French were unwilling to take up the idea, so much the worse for them. Bismarck's position was so secure that he could easily make up with England: " I do not fear the opposition of the English," he said to Courcel; " in view of the embarrassment into which their action in Egypt has placed them, they have need of us; one can bargain with them." [1]

The idea of a maritime league directed against England may at first appear somewhat fantastic, but in actual fact it was the possibility of naval co-operation between the continental powers that paralysed English policy in 1884 and made the British navy less of a factor than might have been supposed. To be sure, the British fleet was, in point of numbers, the strongest fleet in the world. But the period was one of transition, and the change from the old wooden frigate to the new ironclad, the rapid development of armour and armament, the astounding improvements in machinery, and the invention of new weapons like the torpedo had upset the old standards completely. In the years after 1870 all the leading continental powers, with France in the lead, had made great efforts to build up a modern fighting force. In 1882 England had twenty first-class ships as against thirty-two possessed by France, Germany, Italy, Austria, and Russia. France alone had sixteen, and Germany nine, so that these two powers together outnumbered England.[2] Of course, it does not follow that these two powers could have defeated England on the sea. More than the number of ships, or even their tonnage and armament, must be considered in estimating the relative strength of navies, and even then there is no certain test excepting the test of actual battle, where relative superiority in leadership and personnel can be brought into play.

We cannot say whether France and Germany could have defeated England at sea in 1884 because they did not fight. It should be noted, however, that the British naval authorities had been very hesitant about introducing new designs and armament, and that the government had been slow in increasing appropriations for construction. With England in a very precarious position, internationally speaking, it was quite natural that attention should be given to the fighting power of the nation. In August 1884 a determined agitation was started

---

[1] Bourgeois and Pagès, op. cit., pp. 209–10, 383–6.
[2] Sir Thomas Brassey: *The British Navy* (London, 1882), II, part ii, p. 226.

for increased expenditure on the navy. The movement was led by W. T. Stead, the editor of the *Pall Mall Gazette*. It enjoyed the sympathy of men like Sir Cooper Key, the first sea lord, and Admiral Beauchamp Seymour, chief of the Mediterranean squadron. The country at large was seized by a sort of naval panic, the press followed Stead, and the government was forced to yield to the popular demands. On December 2, 1884 parliament voted the sum of five and a half million pounds as extraordinary expenditure for construction during the following five years.[1]

The Franco-German entente, had it actually issued in a naval combination against England, would have been a very serious threat to the English position. It seems very doubtful, however, whether Bismarck himself had much confidence in the possibility of consummating so close an understanding, or whether he desired to estrange England permanently. He was too great a statesman to delude himself with vain hopes, and he must have foreseen that Ferry and his associates could not go beyond a certain line. Ferry's colonial policy had met with considerable opposition in France from the very beginning. There was a pronounced feeling that it was dangerous to become involved in foreign adventures and unwise to allow antagonism between France and England to develop till France was dependent on the goodwill of Germany. To quote from a letter of Lord Lyons: " The best card in our hand, and it is not a high trump, is the reluctance of the French to be thrown irretrievably into the clutches of Bismarck by a distinct quarrel with us." [2] " Woe to the government which should try to induce the nation to accept the results of 1870 as definitive," wrote the Paris correspondent of *The Times* in October 1884. " It would encounter a latent, perhaps unconscious sentiment, which would never forgive such a betrayal of the national greatness and honour. Curiously enough, the simple rumour of a drawing together and possible alliance between France and Germany has aroused slumbering recollections and revived passions supposed to be allayed or extinct." [3]

Public opinion and pressure were not necessary to hold back Ferry. It is quite clear from what few French documents we have on this period that the premier shared the suspicions of Courcel, the ambassador at Berlin. Courcel could not help feeling that Bismarck aimed at bringing England to her knees, and that he meant to use France as a tool for the attainment of this object. Meanwhile the chancellor would reserve the possibility of making up with the English when the proper time came. The French statesmen therefore evaded

---

[1] See Frederic Whyte: *The Life of W. T. Stead* (London, 1925), Volume I, chapter vii; F. W. Hirst: *The Six Panics and Other Essays* (London, 1913), pp. 41 ff.; Bernard Mallet: *Thomas George, Earl of Northbrook* (London and New York, 1908), pp. 199 ff. Stead's articles were collected and published under the title *The Truth about the Navy and the Coaling Stations*. For statistics on the relative strengths and relative expenditures of the various powers see Brassey, op. cit., and the same author's *Naval Annual, 1886* (London, 1886), *passim*.

[2] Newton, op. cit., II, p. 338.

[3] Quoted by Wienefeld, op. cit., p. 148.

Bismarck's more far-reaching suggestions, while the chancellor, in turn, was constantly trying to force the French to show their hand. " He wants to thrust upon us the glory of regulating the Egyptian question and of regulating it at Paris itself, in a conference over which we should preside and at which Europe would form a triumphal cortège for us," wrote Courcel on December 3, 1884. But, he admitted, this " brilliant tableau " aroused his distrust. If the conference succeeded, Bismarck would claim the credit; if it failed, he would desert France and turn to the victor: " It will be an open market between France and England, and he will sell himself to the highest bidder." But what put the French ambassador on his guard more than anything else was the renewal of Bismarck's seductive suggestions for a closer entente: " I want to induce you to pardon Sedan as you have pardoned Waterloo." That was too much for Courcel. From the beginning of the entente he had specified that Alsace and Lorraine should not be brought into the discussion, because on that point agreement would be impossible.[1]

The wariness of the French statesmen did not prevent them from making the most of the entente with Germany, such as it was. Not only did they work with Germany to bring about the Berlin Conference on African problems, but they accepted German aid in bringing about a French victory in Egyptian affairs. The English were faced with a serious dilemma when the London Conference broke up in August. There was no way of solving the problem of the Egyptian deficit without ignoring the rights of Europe and following an independent policy. Lord Northbrook was sent to Egypt to examine the problem, and advised the Egyptian government to divert funds arbitrarily from the surplus revenue set aside for service of the debt and to use them to meet the shortage in funds for administrative purposes. This the Egyptian government did on September 18, but this rather naïve attempt to cut the Gordian knot was doomed to failure from the very start. The powers refused to be pushed aside in this cavalier fashion. Suit was brought against the Egyptian government in the mixed courts and was decided in favour of the plaintiffs. The Egyptian government, which in this case meant the British government, was obliged to turn to the powers once more and to submit to them new suggestions for meeting the situation.

On November 24, 1884 the British foreign office forwarded to the powers new proposals for solving the Egyptian financial difficulty. The main points of the program were the raising of a loan of nine million pounds, to be guaranteed by the British government; the suspension of the sinking-fund payments; the taxation of foreigners; and the reduction of the land-tax. The cabinet was quite clear in its own mind what the implications of this program were, for Lord Northbrook, in making the suggestions, stated that their effect would undoubtedly be " to substitute the financial control of England for the international control which was proposed by the conference." But the change seemed

---

[1] See Bourgeois and Pagès, op. cit., pp. 386–8.

to him to be advantageous to both the English and the Egyptian governments, and he could not see what objections the other powers of Europe could entertain to this control being exercised by Great Britain after the sacrifices she had made in maintaining the peace and safety of Egypt and the financial liability which she would undertake. Lord Cromer bitterly bemoans the fact that the Gladstone cabinet did not carry these proposals into execution. If it had done so, " internationalism, which had been the bane of Egypt, would have received a heavy blow, and the paramount power of Great Britain, as the guide and protector of Egypt, would have been asserted." [1]

All one can say on this point is what has already been said above in regard to the English attitude towards colonial problems. What incredible lack of appreciation of the international situation was required to suggest that the powers should give up their claims in Egypt in order that England's paramount position might be established! What sublime forgetfulness of these factors in Lord Cromer's criticism of the government! The government was absolutely helpless. Bismarck delayed his reply to the English proposals until Ferry had had an opportunity to submit counter-proposals, on January 8, 1885, and then the German chancellor, followed by the other continental states promptly supported the French plan.

Lord Lyons saw through the game easily enough: " Bismarck and Ferry are *jouant au plus fin* with each other at our expense," he wrote on January 20. " Each seems to think that he can use the other to help in thwarting us, without risk to himself. But Bismarck has the best of the game. He occupies the French thoughts, and to some extent their forces, at a distance from Europe; he keeps up irritation between them and us, and some of the acquisitions he encourages them to make will in all probability be a permanent cause of weakness to them. At the same time he neutralizes opposition from us to his childish colonial schemes, which I cannot help suspecting are founded as much on what, for want of a better word, I must call spite against us, as on any real expectation of advantage to Germany. Ferry hopes, by means of Bismarck and the powers who follow Bismarck's lead, to carry his immediate points in regard to Egypt and other parts of the world, and so increase his reputation at home for the moment; and he trusts to his skill to enable him to stop before he has so alienated us as to be quite at Bismarck's mercy. It is the natural disposition of almost all Europe to side against us, as matters stand, on the Egyptian financial question, which makes this pretty game possible." [2]

It took no diplomatic genius to see this, the more so as both Ferry and Bismarck announced the facts of the situation to the whole world. France, said Ferry, was in accord with the three empires on the Egyptian question and was no longer playing on the European stage the rather effaced role of a parvenu. She was no longer " the Cinderella of European politics." [3] Soon afterwards the

---

[1] Cromer: *Modern Egypt*, II, pp. 370–1.   [2] Newton: *Lord Lyons*, II, p. 341.
[3] Speech of December 11, 1885 (Ferry: *Discours et opinions*, V, p. 485).

German chancellor corroborated the statements of his French colleague: "With France we have not for many years — I may truly say since the time before 1866 — been on so good a footing as now." [1] So far had the entente gone that Bismarck could appeal once more to the French ambassador: "Renounce the question of the Rhine; I will help you in securing all the satisfaction you desire on all other points." [2] He even spoke of arranging a meeting with Ferry.

Unable to withstand the combined pressure that was brought to bear from Berlin and Paris, the British government accepted the counter-proposals submitted by Ferry. The loan was to be under the joint guarantee of the powers, and important changes were made in the disposition of the surplus from the assigned revenues. The details of the agreement, which was signed at London in March 1885, need not detain us. The crucial point from the standpoint of international relations was that the financial control of Egypt retained its international character. The action of England in Egypt was to continue to be hampered by foreign interference. The sword of Damocles was still suspended over the heads of the English statesmen.

By this time the English position had become a really desperate one. The struggle for Africa and the Pacific had been going on apace, and England had not much to show. While the Germans acquired South-west Africa, Togoland, the Cameroons, East Africa, a part of New Guinea, and some of the islands to the north of it; while France had established the French Congo and various smaller possessions on the Guinea coast, to say nothing of a foothold on the Red Sea coast and the great French advance against China in Tonkin, the British government had, in a sudden burst of vigour, occupied St. Lucia Bay and Bechuanaland in December 1884, to keep these areas out of German hands. But the effort to annex New Guinea (apart from the Dutch possessions on the island) had been foiled. Furthermore, England had been obliged to give up the treaty with Portugal regarding the Congo. The Berlin Conference, which concluded its labours in February 1885, was a meeting engineered by Ferry and Bismarck, with little reference to England. By paving the way for the recognition of Leopold's International Association of the Congo as an entity in international law it rang the death-knell of English hopes of controlling either the Congo territory or the navigation of the river through the medium of Portugal. To be sure, the opening of the great Congo basin to freedom of commerce was a move of which England could only approve, and on this point there was more unity of interest between Germany and England than there was between Germany and France. Still, the decisions of the conference, especially the decision that, in future, territorial claims, in order to be recognized, must be supported by effective occupation, made an English monopoly of the colonial field in Africa absolutely impossible. The dream of a Monroe Doctrine for Africa, if

---

[1] Speech of January 10, 1885.
[2] Bourgeois and Pagès, op. cit., pp. 388–91, Courcel's report of January 20, 1885.

such ever existed in the minds of British or colonial statesmen, was completely dissipated.

By the time when the sessions of the Berlin Conference came to an end, on February 26, 1885, the relations between England and Germany had reached a degree of tensity and acrimony that was almost unprecedented. Lord Granville, caught in the Franco-German vise, felt driven by despair to make an effort to break this ominous combination. On February 28, in defending the English policy in Egypt before the House of Lords, he explained that Bismarck disapproved of this policy because the government had not taken his advice, which was " to take Egypt." This revelation was perhaps intended more for the French statesmen than for the English peers and was probably meant to open the eyes of Ferry to the perfidy of the German chancellor. But the experiment was a foolhardy one. It immediately brought down upon Granville's head the wrath of Bismarck. In a Reichstag speech on March 2, 1885 he denied Granville's assertion and indignantly repudiated the suggestion that he had been acting the part of the seducer in order to create confusion in Europe. He had given advice on the Egyptian question only when pressed to do so by the English statesmen, and even then he had urged England to act through the Sultan.

Historians have not been entirely satisfied with Bismarck's reply and have pointed out that in the period from 1875 to 1878 he certainly told English statesmen in almost so many words " to take Egypt." It appears, however, that the speech of March 2 was prepared on the basis of the negotiations of 1882 only, and that Bismarck's statement had reference to his discussions with Granville, not with Granville's Conservative predecessors. However that may be, there is no denying that Granville's revelation was contrary to the accepted rules of international intercourse.[1]

That Bismarck had no intention of driving things to extremes is shown by the fact that within a couple of days of his speech in the Reichstag he sent his son Herbert on a special mission to London.[2] The purpose of this move was clearly to put an end to the Anglo-German feud and establish some sort of truce. The reasons for Bismarck's change of attitude at this critical juncture are not entirely patent. It may well be that he feared the effect of Granville's revelations upon the French, and it may also be that he felt apprehension lest the entente with France should disintegrate, as the fury of the colonial storm was spending itself. At the time there were rumours that Herbert Bismarck was to bring about the resignation of Granville and Derby, if possible, and this story is to be found even in Dilke's notes.[3]

Certainly this is a gross exaggeration. From the evidence at our disposal it appears that while Count Herbert spoke in a very determined fashion to Lord

---

[1] See the detailed discussion in Kleine: *Deutschland und die ägyptische Frage*, pp. 105 ff.

[2] Waldersee: *Denkwürdigkeiten*, I, p. 253, refers to the mission on March 3.

[3] Gwynn and Tuckwell: *Life of Sir Charles Dilke*, II, p. 99. For other rumours see Hagen: *Bismarcks Kolonialpolitik*, pp. 491 ff.

Granville, he made a very favourable impression upon Gladstone. Whether the foreign minister was convinced by the German arguments or not, he yielded on almost every point and even read in advance to young Bismarck the text of the declaration which he made in the House of Lords on March 6, a declaration in which he explained away his revelation of February 28. Gladstone, who had never sympathized with the imperialistic views of some members of his cabinet and had regarded with dislike the theory prevalent in many of the colonies that as much territory as possible should be seized in order to prevent some other power from acquiring it, supplemented Granville's remarks by his own declaration in the House of Commons on March 12: " If Germany is to become a colonizing power, all I say is 'God speed her!' She becomes our ally and partner in the execution of the great purposes of Providence for the advantage of mankind."

With that the truce between England and Germany was concluded. Bismarck had obliged his opponents to yield on the essential points. He had known how to take advantage of the favourable moment. Of course the settlement of the dispute was likely to react upon the entente with France, and the chancellor must have considered this aspect of the problem. Apparently he had concluded from his negotiations with Baron de Courcel that there was a distinct point beyond which the understanding could not go. He could not afford to let the estrangement between Germany and England go too far, the more so as there was no telling how long the Ferry régime would last. France had become involved in war with China over the Tonkin question, and the opposition to the policy of colonial adventure was rapidly spreading in France. On March 26 a great debate started in the Chamber of Deputies, and the French premier was more bitterly assailed than ever before. In the midst of the crisis came the news, on March 28, that the French forces had suffered a reverse and had been obliged to evacuate Lang-Son. Paris became panic-stricken, and Ferry's doom was sealed. Clemenceau in the chamber declared that there could be no further discussion with him, and that he and his ministry were in the position of men accused of high treason. In the streets outside, the mob surged about, shouting: " Down with Ferry! Death to Ferry! To the river with him! Down with the Prussian! " The hour of the famous ministry had struck. On March 31 Ferry, the real founder of the second French colonial empire, was obliged to resign.[1]

Bismarck had come to terms with the English because he was unwilling to stake too much on the friendship of France. That the English would accept his peace offers was a foregone conclusion, for by March 1885 new and even more threatening clouds had appeared upon the English political horizon. It was on January 26, 1885 that Khartoum had fallen into the hands of the Mahdi, and Gordon had lost his life. The relief expedition under Wolseley's command reached the scene too late. The great tragedy had occurred, and when news of the disaster reached London, on February 5, the country was in uproar. Glad-

---

[1] See especially Rambaud: *Jules Ferry*, pp. 362 ff.

stone and his cabinet were covered with obloquy. Even the Queen made no secret of where she placed the responsibility.

The cabinet, under the circumstances, felt obliged to continue the Sudan campaign at least until the fate of Gordon was definitely determined; but before much could be done, the government and the people were alike confronted with an even more serious crisis. On March 30 Russian troops engaged an Afghan force at Penjdeh, on the Afghan frontier, and defeated it.

The clash at Penjdeh was simply the culminating point in the development of the central Asian question, which had been troubling the English for years. Ever since the Crimean War there had been a pretty steady advance on the part of the Russians in Turkestan and towards the frontiers of Afghanistan and India. The gradual conquest of the Tartar tribes and the incorporation of their territory in the empire of the tsars may, in fact, be regarded as the counterpart of the imperialistic drive of the western European powers in Africa, excepting that in the case of Russia there is little evidence at this time of economic urge or pressure. Russian expansion in central Asia was more a matter of prestige and national pride and at the same time a matter of political strategy.

It is fairly clear that the Russian government estimated at their full value the difficulties of actually attacking India, and it is reasonable to suppose that the invasion project was not seriously entertained in St. Petersburg. But the threat of an attack was of supreme value for Russian policy. Pressure in the Near East could always be alleviated by an advance in central Asia. The idea is well expressed in the recently published correspondence that passed at this time between the Russian foreign minister, Giers, and the ambassador at London, Baron de Staal. Writing in June 1884, Giers pointed out that England had always striven to ruin Russian sea-power, especially in the Black Sea and the Mediterranean. The Russian advance was meant as a reply to this policy and as a check on England. At bottom Russian policy was wholly defensive: " Our August Master does not cherish hostile intentions towards England, either in Asia or in Europe." And again, in July 1884: " Our movements in central Asia have been commanded by our own interests, as well as by the necessity of securing a defensive position against the hostility displayed by the English government towards us since the Crimean War and more recently during the war with Turkey. At present we have, through great sacrifices, reached the stage where we can consider our security fully guaranteed. We can, therefore, content ourselves with consolidating this position and awaiting with calm the actions of the English government, firm in the resolution to reply in kind to its proceedings, whether pacific or hostile." [1]

The English government, however, could not be certain of the Russian policy and became more and more uneasy as the Russian advance continued. This was the more natural as the Russian government frequently gave assurances that it

[1] Baron A. Meyendorff: *Correspondance diplomatique de M. de Staal* (Paris, 1929), Volume I, pp. 25 ff., 40 ff.

would not continue its expansion and then failed to keep its promises. Even if due allowance was made for the restless and unsettled character of the territory in question, for the difficulty of communication between the scene of operation and the government offices at St. Petersburg, and for the stormy enthusiasm of the officers on the spot, who frequently exceeded their instructions, it could not be denied that the policy of the Russian government was suspicious and unreliable.

When, in February 1884, the Russian Tsar accepted the allegiance of the Turkoman tribes of Merv, it was clear that some arrangement would have to be made, and that soon. England, as the Duke of Argyll jokingly put it, was afflicted with *Mervousness*. The Russians were rapidly approaching Afghanistan, a client of England, and a state which the English government had repeatedly promised to defend against unprovoked attack. The peculiar danger of the situation arose from the fact that no one knew where the boundary of Afghanistan was. The Ameer himself showed little interest in the insubordinate tribes of the frontiers, and even though the English and Russian governments had, in 1873, come to a general agreement as to what provinces should be regarded as part of the Afghan territory, there was no knowledge of the actual boundaries of the provinces.

The Russian incorporation of Merv led to bitter reproaches on the part of the English government, which thought fit to recall all the promises that had been made and broken by the Russian government. Giers, the Russian minister for foreign affairs, had no desire to precipitate a crisis and agreed in the summer of 1884 that a joint commission should be sent to the scene in order to determine the frontier. The English government sent out General Sir Peter Lumsden in September in the hope that he would be able to join his Russian colleague, General Zelenoi, and start work by November. But Zelenoi failed to put in an appearance. It was said that he was ill and would proceed to the frontier as soon as possible. But the real cause for the delay must be sought elsewhere. In the first place, there was a fundamental difference of opinion between the two governments as to what the commission should really do. The Russians desired that a frontier should be drawn on the basis of geographical and ethnological considerations. They hoped to push back the Afghan frontier to the mountains, leaving all the Turkoman tribes of the plain to the mercies of Russia. The English, on the other hand, were interested merely in defining the limits of the political authority of the Ameer. Tribes that owed him allegiance were to be *ipso facto* recognized as within Afghan territory.

The Russian acceptance of the commission appears, under the circumstances, to have been something of a ruse to gain time. While negotiations proceeded, the Russian commanders on the spot kept pushing their advanced posts forward, with the natural result that the Afghans, too, began to occupy territory which, they claimed, undoubtedly belonged to the Ameer. If these military operations were to continue, a clash between the Russian forces and the Afghans would, sooner or later, be inevitable, and the conflict would almost certainly lead to England's becoming involved. Granville kept urging the need for early action by the boundary commission, but Zelenoi did not appear and the Russian government complicated the situation further by insisting that the two cabinets should first agree on a zone beyond which the deliberations of the boundary commission should not be allowed to go.

The British government felt almost helpless against the obstructionist tactics of the Russians. That Giers desired to avoid friction is certain. But the British suspected, and evidently with some justification, that the nationalist and military groups in St. Petersburg were preventing the government from pursuing a conciliatory policy. There was talk of a Russian advance as far as the important fortified town of Herat and of far-reaching schemes directed against India. A real antagonism had developed between the Russian civil and military authorities.[1] All this served to cause anxiety in London, where it was believed that the Russian attitude enjoyed the approval of Bismarck, if it was not actually due to his encouragement.[2]

This accusation against the chancellor has been frequently repeated. It has been argued that it was part of his general strategy. Just as he wished to perpetuate the antagonism between England and France, so he wished to cause friction between England and Russia. " The Penjdeh incident," says Sir Eyre Crowe in the memorandum which has already been quoted from, ". . . was the outcome of his direct suggestion that the moment was favourable for Russia to act." [3] But these assertions, however comforting they may have been to English sense of pride, cannot be substantiated. No doubt the Russians felt encouraged by the Anglo-German feud, and no doubt Bismarck did not feel called upon to smooth out difficulties for the English when they were throwing all possible obstacles in his own path, but even admitting all this is very different from saying that Bismarck actually worked for a clash between Russia and England. The Russian ambassador at London himself put no credence in these stories, and Bismarck, in a detailed report to the Emperor in June 1885, pointed out that the German government had scrupulously resisted the temptation to sow discord. The German government had no desire to create friction, though there was no denying that from the German view-point it was better for the Russians to occupy themselves on the Indian frontier than on the German-Austrian borders. No encouragement had been given the Russian government, but the German government had abstained equally from using restraint, for fear that this would arouse the suspicions of Russia and would divert her indignation from England to Germany.[4]

By February 1885 the situation began to look very black. The British

---

[1] Meyendorff, op. cit., I, pp. 115, 117, 160 ff.
[2] Fitzmaurice: *Granville*, II, pp. 422; John F. Baddeley: *Russia in the " Eighties "* (London, 1921), p. 212.   [3] *British Documents on the Origins of the War*, III, pp. 397 ff.
[4] *Die Grosse Politik*, IV, No. 777; Meyendorff, op. cit., I, p. 129.

Government, weakened by the conflict with Germany and discredited by the terrible news from Khartoum, barely escaped censure in the House of Commons and seriously debated resignation.[1] It was felt, however, that the time was not yet ripe, and the cabinet decided to take a stronger stand. On February 18 Sir Peter Lumsden, who had been sending the most alarming reports of Russian progress, was ordered, in the event of a Russian advance on Herat, to throw himself into the city and aid the Afghan defence.[2]

The Russians did not proceed to Herat, but on February 21 they established themselves at Penjdeh, one of the crucial points and one on which the whole dispute hinged. The crisis which now ensued was the most acute since that of 1878. It undoubtedly had much to do with the capitulation of the British government in colonial and Egyptian affairs. The government, indeed, desired peace, but public opinion was united in the belief that the dangerous Russian advance must be stopped. The question of central Asia and the future safety of India was put far above the problems of the Sudan, Egypt, or colonial expansion.[3]

The government, acting under public pressure, began to take the necessary military measures. The Indian authorities were notified to prepare an army corps to be marched to Herat in case of hostilities with Russia, and Sir Peter Lumsden was told that the government considered that the advance of the Russians should be resisted by the Afghans.[4] On March 12 the cabinet decided to limit the Sudan operations and make further preparations in India. Twenty thousand men were to be assembled at Quetta, and a Russian march on Herat was to be regarded as a *casus belli*.[5] The question was no longer one of territorial delimitation alone. It had become a test of national strength. The Russian government would give only qualified assurances in regard to further advance of the troops, and the English felt that their position towards the Ameer of Afghanistan would be forever ruined if they allowed him to be despoiled by the Russians. Even Sir Charles Dilke admitted that the Russians were right both in form and in substance, " but," he said, " we cannot have the pill forced down our throats by Russia without inquiry or discussion, on equal terms." [6]

The negotiations between London and St. Petersburg had made almost no progress for several weeks when, on April 8, the news reached London that on March 30 the Russian and Afghan troops had clashed at Penjdeh, and that the Afghans had been beaten. The terrible eventuality that had been expected for some time had at last taken place. Both in St. Petersburg and in London

---

[1] Fitzmaurice: *Granville*, II, pp. 421–2; Gwynn and Tuckwell: *Sir Charles Dilke*, II, p. 111.

[2] Gwynn and Tuckwell, op. cit., II, p. 115.

[3] Meyendorff, op. cit., I, pp. 168 ff.

[4] Lyall: *Lord Dufferin*, II, p. 88; *Central Asia*, No. 2 (*1885*), No. 212; Fitzmaurice: *Granville*, II, p. 423.

[5] Gwynn and Tuckwell, op. cit., II, pp. 115–16; *Letters of Queen Victoria*, III, p. 629.

[6] Gwynn and Tuckwell, op. cit., II, p. 116; *Die Grosse Politik*, IV, No. 762 (Rosebery's utterances to Herbert Bismarck).

war was regarded as unavoidable. On the London Exchange the stocks crumbled and crashed in a panic worse than any since 1870.[1] The cabinet met almost daily, and considered seriously the question of giving up the offensive in the Sudan. The Queen objected vigorously to this suggestion, but the step had to be taken. England was face to face with Russia and had hardly a friend in the world. " It is too dreadful," wrote Granville, " jumping from one nightmare into another. Once at war with Russia we shall be obliged to toady Germany, France, and Turkey." Rosebery explained later to the Queen's secretary that England would have been entirely at the mercy of Russia, France, and Germany if she had kept an army tied up in the Sudan: " Every nation could do as it liked with us. . . . In all probability we should have embarked in one of the greatest wars of the century; and with both our arms bound, one to Afghanistan, the other to Central Africa, we should be exposed to endure what any Power might choose to lay upon us, and be compelled to forgo all voice or share in the destinies of the world. Nothing but a sense of *force majeure,* of greater necessity, could justify the policy. But there *was* this greater necessity; and sad as the necessary course of withdrawal might be, the other course opened an abyss which I do not like to contemplate." [2]

The attitude of the continental powers was certainly of key importance. The Prince of Wales, who was in Berlin in March, had already paved the way for the mission of one of the British ministers, who was to arrange with the German government for common action in the central Asian problem, if possible.[3] Lord Rosebery was sent in April, but evidently accomplished nothing. The English plan of campaign apparently envisaged operations in the Caucasus, but these would have been possible only if the Straits were open to the passage of English warships. It was this that the Russians feared, and they immediately appealed to Bismarck for aid, making reference to the terms of the Alliance of the Three Emperors.

The German chancellor showed no hesitancy in his attitude. He instructed the German ambassador at Constantinople to use his influence to preserve the neutrality of Turkey. In contrast to the English view as expressed at the Congress of Berlin, that the Sultan was free to allow the passage of warships if he saw fit, Bismarck insisted on the international character of the principle of closure. To allow the ships of belligerents to pass the Straits would create a state of war between Turkey and Russia, he pointed out. More yet, he used his influence to induce Austria, Italy, and even France to follow the German lead in this question. The Porte felt sufficiently strengthened to maintain a neutral attitude and determined to defend the Dardanelles against a possible English attempt to force the passage. Whether the British government actually went so

[1] Baddeley, op. cit., pp. 217–19; Schweinitz: *Denkwürdigkeiten,* II, pp. 300–1; Meyendorff, op. cit., I, p. 185; *Letters of Queen Victoria,* III, p. 634.

[2] *Letters of Queen Victoria,* III, pp. 640 ff.; Newton: *Lord Lyons,* II, p. 349.

[3] Lee: *Edward VII,* Volume I, p. 481.

far as to make proposals in this matter cannot be said with certainty. The question is not mentioned in any published contemporary English documents or biographies. All the information we have comes from German sources. From these, however, it appears that soundings were taken. In fact, it is stated in a retrospective survey of the crisis, dated 1890, that the English government offered, in return for the opening of the Straits, to permit the Turks to occupy Egypt and the Suez Canal and to give them a free hand in Bulgaria and a payment of twenty-five million pounds. On the other hand, they threatened to sever completely the connexion of the Porte with Egypt if the English demand were not granted.[1]

Whatever steps the English government may or may not have taken, the activity of Bismarck in this matter is of great interest. His intervention on behalf of Russia shows that he was firmly determined to support the Alliance of the Three Emperors at any cost, and that the recent colonial truce with England did not weigh heavily with him when matters of international alignment were to the fore. He served Russia well on this occasion, as the Russian foreign minister acknowledged, but he also served Europe generally by helping to preserve peace. The German chancellor did not want war. At times, no doubt, he felt that perhaps it would be a good thing if Russia became deeply involved in Asia and were thus distracted from the Austrian frontier.[2] He may also have felt that a second defeat of Russia by England would weaken his eastern neighbour and make the colossal empire of the tsars innocuous for a long time to come. But he never acted on this theory. He always stopped short of putting it into practice. It is perfectly true that Prince William of Prussia, the future William II, at this time wrote a series of extraordinarily inflammatory letters to the Tsar, in which he did his utmost to discredit the Anglophil tendencies of his own parents and to arouse the hatred of the Tsar for the English.[3] But these private letters are material suitable for the psychologist rather than for the historian. There is no evidence that Bismarck knew anything of them, and it is inconceivable that he should have resorted to such clumsy methods to attain an end. Bismarck's object was not to precipitate a conflict, for he regarded any war between two great powers as a menace to Germany. Such conflicts could rarely be localized and it was Germany's interest to avoid them. His ideal was rather to keep the relations between England and France and between England and Russia in a certain state of rivalry or tension sufficient to prevent their uniting against Germany and sufficient to make them look to Germany for support and friendship.[4]

---

[1] *Die Grosse Politik*, VII, No. 1376. The contemporary German documents are in the same collection, Volume IV, chapter xxii. See also Radowitz: *Aufzeichnungen und Erinnerungen*, II, pp. 244 ff.

[2] Hohenlohe: *Denkwürdigkeiten*, II, pp. 358 ff. (June 19, 1885).

[3] These are printed in the *Krasny Arkhiv*, II, pp. 118–29 (1922).

[4] See especially Reuss's dispatch to Bismarck, July 2, 1884, printed in Rothfels: *Bismarcks englische Bündnispolitik*, p. 135.

During April preparations for war were pushed vigorously by both sides. On April 21 the British government announced its intention to ask parliament to vote a credit of eleven million pounds for further preparations. The idea of an attack on Russia in the Pacific was seriously considered. The Russians closed the port of Vladivostok to foreign shipping by laying mines, but on April 26 a British squadron occupied Port Hamilton, off the coast of Korea, threatening Vladivostok.[1] The discussion between the two governments made little progress, especially after the problem had become further complicated by the question of responsibility for the Penjdeh clash. The English blamed the Russian commander, while the Russians attributed the conflict to the encouragement given the Afghans by the English military mission on the spot.

Although war seemed to be drawing nearer and nearer, a turn for the better came during the dark days of late April. The British government suggested that the happenings at Penjdeh should be reviewed by an arbitrator, who should decide whether either side had violated a vague agreement of March 16 providing against further advance by either side. The suggestion to arbitrate marks a distinct change in British policy and may have been due to the certain knowledge that the continental powers would stand together to keep the Straits closed.[2] This we cannot say for certain, though it seems likely, for in the ensuing negotiations the English government scaled down its demands one after another and accepted the proposals of the Russians. By May 4 the most serious phase of the crisis was over. The British government had agreed that the arbitrator should not investigate the conduct of the Tsar's commander, but should inquire only into the misunderstanding and misinterpretation that had arisen from the so-called agreement of March 16. In actual fact the arbitration never took place. Instead the two governments began to negotiate directly regarding the fundamental lines of the frontier delimitation. Even these pourparlers had not been brought to an end when the Gladstone ministry resigned, on June 9, 1885. It was left for Lord Salisbury to conclude the discussions and to sign the agreement of September 10, 1885.

The period of the Afghan crisis coincided with the period of the gradual disintegration of the Franco-German entente. Ferry had been so closely identified with this policy that his fall from power was tantamount to the rejection of the policy by parliament. But the entente did not meet with a sudden death. Freycinet, the new foreign minister, was a circumspect man who preferred to allow the understanding to die a natural rather than a violent death. Bismarck immediately noticed the change and warned the French ambassador that an alteration in the French attitude, especially with respect to Egypt, might necessitate a corresponding change in the German policy. Evidently he was already beginning to consider a definite turn towards England, the more so as

---

[1] Gwynn and Tuckwell, op. cit., II, p. 120.

[2] The matter was bruited in parliament on April 21 and 23 (Hansard, CCXCVII, pp. 314, 485) and was discussed by the continental press (Radowitz, op. cit., II, p. 245).

the serious illness of the old Emperor opened the prospect of a new régime under Frederick III, whose Anglophil proclivities were well known.[1] On May 28 the chancellor discussed these considerations with Baron de Courcel in so frank a fashion that the ambassador reported: "Prince Bismarck returns today to his policy of 1882 in regard to the Egyptian question: namely, to abandon Egypt to England on condition that the latter reach an agreement with Turkey, and to send off France to make her own agreement with England."[2]

This was overdrawing somewhat. From the German documents it is quite clear that Bismarck had no desire to provoke an abrupt break, and in fact the relations between the two governments remained distinctly cordial until the elections in France in the autumn of 1885. But the chancellor had come to see that France was too uncertain an ally to justify Germany's losing English friendship for her sake. On June 1 he told the cabinet: "For us the French will never become even dependable defensive allies. The enmity is too old and will continue to exist. At the same time a war between England and France is for us just as inconvenient as a war between Austria and Russia. If we remained neutral, we should inherit the hatred of both parties, and in the end we could hardly do otherwise than go over to the side of the English."[3]

Freycinet viewed these developments with little concern, evidently quite content that the days of temptation were over. "For a long time," he wrote to Courcel, "I have told myself that circumstances over which France has no control might lead any day to a sudden change in German policy and a rapprochement between the empire and England. I have long known of the sympathy which the future Empress feels for her native land, of the great ascendancy which she exercises over her husband, and of the easy conscience which permits the chancellor to change allies without much ado; I have realized since then how dangerous it would be for France to emphasize a policy by which she risked at any moment finding herself alone and face to face with a hostile England and an indifferent Europe. Hence the extreme circumspection which you have seen since my entrance upon office."[4]

And so the entente gradually faded away. The advent of the conservative government of Lord Salisbury in June made the reconciliation between England and Germany easier. Bismarck seems to have felt some regret at the passing of his system, but little of this was noticeable on the French side. At any rate, the summer of 1885 marks an important turning-point in European relationships. The constellation of the years 1883–5 was vanishing, new problems were arising to overshadow the old, and new combinations between the nations were being devised to meet the new requirements.

---

[1] Busch: *Bismarck, Some Secret Pages*, III, pp. 132, 137 ff.; Lucius: *Erinnerungen an Bismarck*, p. 315.   [2] Bourgeois and Pagès, op. cit., pp. 395 ff.

[3] Lucius, op. cit., p. 316. See also *Die Grosse Politik*, III, Nos. 702 ff.

[4] Bourgeois and Pagès, op. cit., p. 211.

As one looks back on the years discussed in this chapter, the striking feature is the unusual co-operation between Germany and France. Yet the understanding between these two powers, to be properly estimated, must be viewed against the background of the violent outburst of imperialism, for without this the entente is almost unthinkable. Of the strong stream of expansive tendencies that made its appearance in these years nothing more need be said. If one is an idealist, one may condemn both the movement and the methods by which it was furthered. But at bottom the whole thing was a perfectly natural result of the changing conditions of European economic life, the outcome of the greater and greater social pressure in the industrialized parts of the world. That it should have led to a battle that was waged with the most complete ruthlessness is not to be wondered at, for there was something of the life and death struggle about this imperialistic competition, and the world of the 1880's was too much dominated by the brutal concepts of the "struggle for existence" and the "survival of the fittest" to take deep offence at the methods employed.

Gladstone, to be sure, never shared this view-point. But his ministry on this occasion, as on previous ones, was weakened by fundamental disagreement. Neither the prime minister nor Lord Granville was able or willing to challenge the views of the energetic younger men of the party, like Dilke and Chamberlain, nor, for that matter, to ignore the strong trend of public opinion both at home and in the colonies. At the same time it cannot be denied that England's policy, as conducted by Lord Granville, was marked throughout by lack of understanding and absence of tact. "Mr. Gladstone has alienated all other countries from us, by his very changeable and unreliable policy — unintentionally, no doubt," complained Queen Victoria, towards the end of the Liberal administration.[1] This is the key to the whole problem. There was no evil intention on the part of the English government, but there was failure to appreciate the hard realities of the situation. Bismarck, it is perfectly clear, embarked upon the sea of colonial expansion confident that the German land-lubbers could count upon the aid of the English water-rats when they took to the sea. The close relations between the two countries during the preceding years, and the whole policy of Germany during the Egyptian crisis, seemed to warrant the expectation. But the English statesmen completely underestimated the seriousness of the potent urge that was transforming the continental powers into world powers. Far from securing aid from England, the German chancellor found her everywhere in the way. He turned to France as a matter of necessity, not of choice. In Ferry he found an understanding, kindred soul, a man with whom he could work.

Even now, with the documents at our disposal, it is impossible to tell how seriously Bismarck may have meant his suggestions for a wider entente with France. The mere fact that he later scoffed at the idea proves nothing. It is much more important to remember that ever since 1875 Bismarck had pursued

---

[1] *Letters of Queen Victoria*, III, p. 643.

a policy of supporting French aspirations everywhere outside Europe, in the hope of distracting the energies and the thoughts of the French from the sore spot in the Vosges. At first there was no thought of a closer understanding, but the co-operation with Ferry seems to have suggested the possibility of something more than a narrow entente for a specific purpose. If this were not so, it would be hard to explain Bismarck's advances to Courcel. One does not touch a sensitive spot without some hope of giving relief. Of course the idea must not be pressed too hard. Courcel made it clear almost from the start that there was a *noli me tangere* for France, a point beyond which the entente could not go. Ferry and Courcel were both patriots, but even if they had not been, as statesmen they were bound to watch the pulse of the country. No one can doubt that a policy of far-reaching understanding with Germany would never have been accepted by a France still smarting from the wounds of 1870–1. The France of Ferry's day was still so imbued with distrust of Germany that it condemned a colonial policy as a dangerous dissipation of the national forces. " I weep for two lost children, and you offer me twenty domestic servants," Deroulède, the nationalist leader, is said to have told Ferry. The figure is a good one, for it expresses pretty well what many Frenchmen thought.

Even as a temporary expedient Bismarck found the entente with France useful. With the Egyptian question as a lever England could be brought to her knees. The continental coalition was for the moment a reality, and England was helpless. Certainly she was the strongest naval power in the world, but the British fleets could not sail to Paris or Berlin, the more so as they were threatened by a possible coalition of naval forces on their own element. This factor must not be left out of account, for it explains how Bismarck and Ferry, through purely political methods, were able to paralyse British sea-power and establish great colonial empires without having, individually, really powerful navies. The British government that was responsible for this turn of events pursued a policy more disastrous than it could know, for the year 1885 marks the end of England's unquestioned pre-eminence in the colonial field. She was no longer the one real world power. The others had acquired extra-European interests, and the new colonies were born under the evil omen of antagonism to England. With new footings abroad the other powers were in a better position than ever to bring pressure upon England. She was more exposed to attack than before. From this time on, the policy of splendid isolation was already *passé*. For some time yet the policy was maintained, at least in theory, but if the isolation remained, the splendour was gone.

BIBLIOGRAPHICAL NOTE

DOCUMENTARY SOURCES

Accounts and Papers. State Papers. The numerous Blue Books on colonial questions in these years will be found in the *Accounts and Papers* as follows: *1883,* Volumes XLVIII and XLIX (*African Questions*), LXXXII (*Madagascar*), LXXXIII and LXXXIV (*Egypt*); *1884,* Volumes LVI (*Africa*), LXXXVII (*Central Asia*), LXXXVIII and LXXXIX (*Egypt*); *1884–1885,* Volumes LIV (*Pacific Islands*), LV and LVI (*Africa*), LXXXVII (*Central Asia*), LXXXVIII and LXXXIX (*Egypt*); *1886,* Volume XLVII (*Africa*).

Documents diplomatiques. Affaires d'Égypte, 1882–1883 (Paris, 1883). *Affaires d'Égypte, 1884–1893* (Paris, 1893). *Affaires du Congo, 1884–1887* (Paris, 1890). *Affaires du Tonkin,* parts i and ii (Paris, 1883).

Bourgeois, E., and Pagès, G.: *Les Origines et les responsabilités de la Grande Guerre.* Paris, 1921.

German White Books. 1884: *Aktenstücke, betreffend die Unterstellung des Togogebiets . . . unter den Schutz Seiner Majestät des Kaisers. Aktenstücke, betreffend die Unterstellung des Gebiets von Angra Pequena,* etc. *Sammlung von Aktenstücken, betreffend deutsche Interessen in der Südsee.* 1885: *Sammlung von Aktenstücken, betreffend deutsche Land-Reklamationen auf Fidji. Zweite Sammlung von Aktenstücken, betreffend deutsche Interessen in der Südsee. Sammlung von Aktenstücken, betreffend die Kongofrage. Sammlung von Aktenstücken, betreffend Ägypten.*

Die Grosse Politik der Europäischen Kabinette, Volumes III, IV.

MEMOIRS, AUTOBIOGRAPHIES, BIOGRAPHIES, AND LETTERS

Fitzmaurice, Lord Edmond: *The Life of Lord Granville.* Two volumes. London, 1905. One of the most important sources for the study of British policy.

Gwynn, Stephen, and Tuckwell, Gertrude M.: *The Life of the Rt. Hon. Sir Charles Dilke.* Two volumes. New York, 1917. Throws a good deal of light on the history of British policy in the Gladstonian period.

Rambaud, Alfred: *Jules Ferry.* Paris, 1903. An admirable biographical study, though it does not add much factual knowledge.

Meyendorff, Baron A.: *Correspondance diplomatique de M. de Staal, 1884–1900.* Two volumes. Paris, 1929. The Russian correspondence between St. Petersburg and London, essential for the study of Anglo-Russian relations.

Buckle, G. E.: *The Letters of Queen Victoria.* Second series, Volume III. New York, 1926.

SPECIAL STUDIES

MOON, PARKER T.: *Imperialism and World Politics.* New York, 1926. One of the best introductory accounts for the study of modern imperialism.

BODELSEN, C. A.: *Studies in Mid-Victorian Imperialism.* New York, 1925. A careful analysis of the evolution of the new imperialism in England.

ROBERTS, STEPHEN H.: *The History of French Colonial Policy (1870–1925).* Two volumes. London, 1929. Deals more with problems of administration than with the international aspect of colonialism.

HAGEN, MAXIMILIAN VON: *Bismarcks Kolonialpolitik.* Stuttgart, 1923. By far the best treatment, though written before the German diplomatic documents appeared.

ROGGE, HELMUTH: *" Bismarcks Kolonialpolitik als aussenpolitisches Problem "* (*Historische Vierteljahrschrift*, XXI, pp. 304–33, 1923, and pp. 423–43, 1924). An excellent analysis of Bismarck's policy viewed in the light of the German documents.

STUHLMACHER, WALTHER: *Bismarcks Kolonialpolitik.* Halle, 1927. A dissertation which adds nothing.

TOWNSEND, MARY E.: *The Rise and Fall of Germany's Colonial Empire, 1884–1918.* New York, 1930. Easily the best general account in English.

KELTIE, J. SCOTT: *The Partition of Africa.* London, 1893. Still one of the best treatments of the subject.

HARRIS, NORMAN D.: *Intervention and Colonization in Africa.* Boston, 1914. A convenient review of the African problem.

RONZE, RAYMOND: *La Question d'Afrique.* Paris, 1918. Another reliable general account.

DARMSTAEDTER, PAUL: *Geschichte der Aufteilung und Kolonisation Afrikas.* Two volumes. Berlin, 1913, 1920. The best general book in German.

WIENEFELD, ROBERT H.: *Franco-German Relations, 1878–1885.* Baltimore, 1929. A careful and faithful collation of the available material, without much effort at interpretation.

KLEINE, MATHILDE: *Deutschland und die ägyptische Frage, 1875–1890.* Greifswald, 1927.

HAGEN, MAXIMILIAN VON: *Voraussetzungen und Veranlassungen für Bismarcks Eintritt in die Weltpolitik.* Berlin, 1914.

BADDELEY, JOHN F.: *Russia in the " Eighties."* New York, 1921. Reminiscences of an English correspondent who was in close touch with official Russian circles.

CHIROL, VALENTINE: *The Middle Eastern Question.* London, 1903. One of the best general treatments of central Asian problems.

ROUIRE, DR.: *La Rivalité anglo-russe en Asie.* Paris, 1908. A general essay, too general to be of much use.

CHARLES-ROUX, FRANÇOIS: *" Allemagne, question d'Égypte et affaires coloniales de 1884 à 1887 "* (*L'Afrique française,* XXXVIII, supplement, November 1928, pp. 665-77). Primarily an analysis of the German documents.

ROUARD DE CARD, E.: *Le Prince de Bismarck et l'expansion de la France en Afrique.* Paris, 1918. A careful monograph, but out of date since the publication of the documents.

THIMME, FRIEDRICH: *" Das Memorandum E. A. Crowes vom 1 Januar 1907 "* (*Berliner Monatshefte,* VII, pp. 732-68, August 1929).

—: *" Das ' berühmte Schwindel-dokument' E. A. Crowes"* (*Berliner Monatshefte,* VII, pp. 874-9. September 1929). These two articles are essential for a study of the Anglo-German dispute of 1884-5.

IBBEKEN, RUDOLF: *Das aussenpolitische Problem Staat und Wirtschaft in der deutschen Reichspolitik 1880-1914.* Schleswig, 1928. Contains a good chapter on the economic factors in Bismarck's colonial policy.

X

The Bulgarian Problem

I N THE YEARS BETWEEN 1870 AND 1914 PERIODS OF EXTRA-EUROPEAN ACTIVITY
alternated with periods of continental crisis. The remarkable outburst of
colonial enterprise which has just been discussed would have been impossible
had not Bismarck, after securing the German position by the alliances with
Russia, Austria, and Italy, been able to paralyse the two leading naval powers by playing off one against the other to the advantage of his own country.
But it has been pointed out that the Franco-German entente was distinctly a
limited understanding, a convenient combination for the attainment of a specific object. In the same way it must be clearly understood that the Three
Emperors' Alliance of 1881 was by no means a panacea. However it may have
been regarded at Berlin, and whatever hopes may have been centred upon it, in
the Russian and Austrian capitals it was looked upon primarily as a truce. The
fundamental antagonism of the two empires, which hinged on the Near Eastern
situation, had only been temporarily veiled. Neither party felt disposed to make
serious sacrifices in the cause of solidarity. Each continued, as best it could, to
strengthen its position in the Balkans and to watch with suspicious eye the
activities of its opponent.

It should be said at the outset that neither Austria nor Russia seems at this
time to have cherished hopes of territorial aggrandizement in the Balkans. The
problem had become, since the establishment of the new states of the peninsula,
primarily a problem of political and economic influence. Take Austria, for
instance. There is not a shred of convincing evidence that the Viennese statesmen planned territorial expansion in the direction of Salonika. The opposition
of the Hungarians to the inclusion of further Slav territory in the monarchy
was so great that the annexation of Bosnia and Herzegovina, which was confidently expected in the years after the Congress of Berlin, could not be undertaken. It will be remembered that under the terms of the Alliance of the Three
Emperors of 1881 Austria was free to carry through the annexation when she
saw fit. In 1882, therefore, Kálnoky took up the matter. The ambassador at
Constantinople, who had been instructed to sound out the attitude of the Sultan and his ministers, reported that the Grand Vizier returned only evasive
replies. But this was hardly what decided the Austrian government to postpone action. It was a memorandum from the Hungarian minister, Tisza, that
settled the question. Tisza demanded that in the event of annexation the

Hungarians should secure part of the two provinces for incorporation in their part of the empire. This was too much for Kálnoky, and the proposal was dropped.[1]

The opposition of the Magyars to any further acquisition of Slavic territory was so well known that it could not be ignored. It was an insuperable obstacle in the way of territorial expansion by the monarchy in a south-eastern direction. Andrássy, who was a strong advocate of the spread of Austrian influence in the western Balkans and regarded the Sanjak of Novi-Bazar as a port of issue on the road to Salonika, loudly disclaimed any idea of acquiring territory in that region. His successor, Baron Haymerlé, unhesitatingly told an agent of the Italian government in 1881 that "Austria-Hungary had no intention of following a policy of expansion in the East. She would not push forward to Salonika or into Albania, where she would carefully maintain the *status quo*. On this point," he added, "all necessary guarantees would be given to prove Austria-Hungary's firm intention of respecting scrupulously the Treaty of Berlin and of abstaining from all expansion."[2]

But this abstention in matters of territorial expansion by no means precluded the idea of what has come to be known as pacific penetration. Indeed, governing circles in Vienna frankly based their policies on this idea. It was the Austrian expression of the economic urge, which in western Europe found its outlet in overseas enterprise, and in Russia took the form of Asiatic advance. Men like the Crown Prince Rudolf believed firmly in Austria's "civilizing mission" in the Balkans and even envisaged the ultimate formation of a ring of client states, enlarged, perhaps, even at the expense of Austria herself, once the Russian danger had been removed by a successful war.[3] Speaking to the eminent Belgian economist M. de Laveleye, Kálnoky described the Austrian view-point very succinctly: "In the West we are believed to mean conquest, which is absurd. It would be impossible to satisfy the two great parties in the empire, and we have, besides, the greatest interest in the maintenance of peace. Nevertheless, we do dream of conquests, but of such as you, a political economist, will approve. They are the conquests to be made by our manufactures, our commerce, our civilization. But to realize them we must have railways in Servia, Bulgaria, Bosnia, Macedonia; and, above all, a junction with the Ottoman system, which will definitely connect East and West. Engineers and diplomatists are both at work. We shall get to the end soon, I hope. When a Pullman car will take you comfortably from Paris to Constantinople in three days, I venture

---

[1] R. W. Seton-Watson: "Russian Commitments in the Bosnian Question and an Early Project of Annexation" (*Slavonic Review*, VIII, pp. 578–88, March 1930).

[2] Wertheimer: *Andrássy*, III, p. 210; *Documents diplomatiques français*, II, No. 468 (Andrássy's assurances to the French ambassador in 1879); Crispi: *Memoirs*, II, p. 121. Similarly Haymerlé's letter to Kálnoky, May 6, 1880 (quoted in Egon C. Corti: *Alexander von Battenberg*, Vienna, 1920, p. 94).

[3] Oskar, Freiherr von Mitis: *Das Leben des Kronprinzen Rudolf* (Leipzig, 1928), pp. 155, 156, 334.

to believe that you will not be dissatisfied with our activity. It is for you Westerners that we are working." [1]

That these were not empty words can be easily shown by a short digression on the subject of Balkan railways. Prior to 1870 the only railways of European Turkey were the short line from Constanţa, on the Black Sea, to the town of Czernewoda, on the Danube, and the longer line from Varna, on the Black Sea, to Ruschuk, on the Danube. These lines had been built by English concessionaires and illustrate the efforts made by English commercial interests to capture the Balkan trade after the Crimean War. Since the mouths of the Danube still required regulation, it was necessary to reach the lower stretches of that great trade artery by means of railroads from the Black Sea.

The leaders of the reforming, Westernizing influence in Constantinople in the period from 1856 to 1876 were fully aware of the importance of railway connexions and did their utmost to further construction. The Sultan himself, according to Ignatiev, was consumed by a veritable " railroad fever." [2] The English projects having proved unprofitable, the Porte finally accepted a plan for a trunk line to run from Constantinople by way of Adrianople, Philippopolis, Sofia, Nish, Mitrovica, Sarajevo, Banjaluka, and Novi, to connect with the Austrian Southern Railway and so with Vienna. In 1868 Baron Hirsch, a Belgian financier with extensive business connexions in both Paris and Vienna, took over the contracts. It is quite clear that he was determined to make the most of his opportunities, and there was constant friction between the construction company (Société Impériale des Chemins de Fer de la Turquie d'Europe) and the operating company (Compagnie Générale de l'Exploitation des Chemins de Fer de la Turquie d'Europe), both under Hirsch control, and the Turkish government. After some delay the work of construction was actively taken up in 1872, and by 1875 the following stretches were open for operation: Constantinople to Sarambey, in Eastern Roumelia (June 1873); a side-line from Adrianople to Dedeagach, on the Ægean (August 1873); a line from Salonika to Uskub, not in the original plans (August 1873); Uskub to Mitrovica, in the Sanjak of Novi-Bazar (December 1874); and a short branch line from Tirnova-Sejmen to Yambol, in Eastern Roumelia (December 1874).

It will be noticed that these lines all ran from the Turkish end into the Balkans. For this reason they opened up great possibilities for English commerce, which could penetrate the peninsula from Salonika, Dedeagach, Constantinople, and Varna and make great inroads upon the economic preserve of the Austrians, who relied largely upon the Danube. For this reason the Austrian government was extremely anxious to bring about the completion of the trunk line, the plan being to continue both the Roumelian line and the Salonika-Uskub line to Nish and construct Serbian lines from there to Belgrade,

---

[1] Emile de Laveleye: La Péninsule des Balkans (new edition, Brussels, 1888), Volume I, pp. 40-1 (abbreviated English edition: The Balkan Peninsula, New York, 1887, p. 5).

[2] Skazkin: Konets avstro-russko-germanskogo soiuza, p. 259.

where the junction with the Austrian lines could be made at Semlin. Articles X and XXXVIII of the Treaty of Berlin handed over to Bulgaria that part of the Turkish line located in the territory of the new principality, but also required the Bulgarian government to assume the obligation to build the connecting link from Sarambey (Bellova) to Tzaribrod, on the Bulgarian-Serbian frontier. Austria, Serbia, Turkey, and Bulgaria were to make the necessary arrangements by reaching agreements "immediately after the conclusion of peace." In 1880 the Austrian and Serbian governments concluded a convention providing for the construction of the Belgrade-Nish and Nish-Vranja lines within three years, and this work was pushed along as fast as possible. At the same time conferences were opened at Vienna between the Austrian, Turkish, Serbian, and Bulgarian governments. No agreement, however, was reached before April 1883. This provided for the completion of all the connecting lines by October 1886. As a matter of fact, however, the work was delayed, especially by the Turks, so that it was August 12, 1888 before the first through train from Vienna to Constantinople passed over the tracks.[1]

The Orient Railway program was the outward manifestation of the Austrian policy which aimed at the commercial and political control of the Balkan states. In extending her influence, it must be confessed, Austria had an easy time after the Congress of Berlin. Although she had snatched Bosnia and Herzegovina from under the eyes of the Serbs and had established herself in the Sanjak of Novi-Bazar, thus blasting Slavic hopes of an eventual union of Serbia and Montenegro, Austria soon found the Serbs knocking at her gates. For Russia, disgusted and dissatisfied with the Serbs, had concentrated her attention upon the Bulgarians. At the congress the Serbs had been obliged to rely upon the Austrians, through whose good offices they were finally able to secure an extension of territory in the region about Nish and Pirot. This extraordinary generosity on the part of Austria is easily explained. Andrássy told the Serbian statesman Ristič, at the congress, that he would oppose all Serbian territorial claims unless Serbia agreed to a convention providing not only for railway construction, but for an eventual customs union or a commercial and tariff treaty. Ristič signed a preliminary agreement of this general tenor on July 8, 1878.[2]

Ristič was, however, no friend of Austria and probably meant to evade as far as possible the obligations upon which he had entered. He regarded the menace of Austrian domination as a very serious one and centred his hopes on the road to Salonika as the only commercial outlet which promised independ-

---

[1] The history of the Orient Railway is treated by Paul Dehn: *Deutschland und Orient in ihren wirthschaftspolitischen Beziehungen* (Munich, 1884) and *Deutschland und die Orientbahnen* (Munich, 1883); Radoslave M. Dimtscheff: *Das Eisenbahnwesen auf der Balkanhalbinsel* (Bamberg, 1894); Iwan Karosseroff: *Zur Entwicklung der bulgarischen Eisenbahnen* (Erlangen, 1907); Iwan Simeonoff: *Die Eisenbahnen und Eisenbahnpolitik in Bulgarien* (Halle, 1909).

[2] See Bernhard Singer: *Die Verträge mit Serbien* (Vienna, 1882), chapter ii, where Ristič's statements in the Skupshtina are quoted.

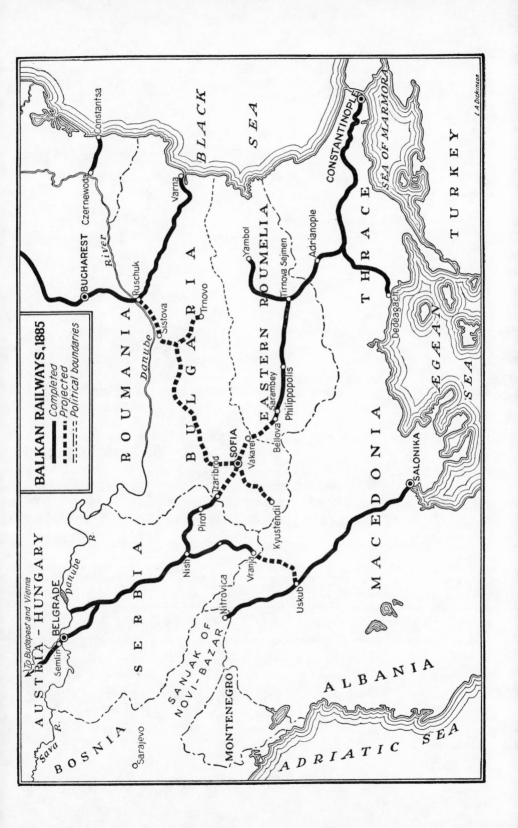

BALKAN RAILWAYS, 1885
— Completed
▪▪▪ Projected
–·–·– Political boundaries

ence. In the years following the congress Ristič succeeded in getting the idea of a customs union rejected by the Serbian assembly by pointing out its possible implications. At the same time he attempted to circumvent economic concessions to the Dual Monarchy by concluding with England a tariff treaty with a most-favoured-nation clause, while he denied the right of Austria to claim similar treatment under the terms of the older agreements with Turkey, which were recognized by the Congress of Berlin. This was too much for the Viennese statesmen, who appear to have brought pressure to bear in Belgrade. Prince Milan was probably glad to get rid of the domineering Ristič, who was obliged to resign. Negotiations for a tariff and commercial treaty were then initiated and led to the conclusion of the agreement of May 6, 1881, which was to remain in force for ten years. This treaty secured for Austria favourable differentiation for several of her products (paper wares, glass, and even iron and steel products and agricultural machinery). Serbia was accorded most-favoured-nation treatment and facilities for the shipment of live cattle into the monarchy. On the whole the Austrians were not given very extensive concessions, and in the following years the treaty seems to have acted to the advantage of the Serbs more than to the benefit of the Austrians. Though reliable statistics are lacking, it appears that, in the years from 1871 to 1875, 93 per cent of Serbia's export and 78 per cent of her import trade was with the monarchy. During the years from 1884 to 1892 reliable statistics indicate that 87 per cent of the export and 66 per cent of the import trade was still in the same direction. What falling off there was of Austrian exports to Serbia was due less to English competition than to the growing trade between the German Empire and Serbia. In any case the differential treatment accorded to Austria by the treaty of 1881 for iron and steel products and machinery evidently reacted very unfavourably upon the development of Serbian industry, and this, in turn, caused considerable dissatisfaction among Serbian industrial and trading classes.[1]

Among the commercial classes of the Dual Monarchy there was much criticism of the treaty with Serbia, the prevalent idea being that the Viennese government had not made the fullest use of its great opportunity to impose its terms upon helpless Serbia. The obscurities of this subject have, however, been removed by the revelation of the political treaty signed between the two governments on June 28 of the same year, 1881.[2] Prince Milan, filled with

---

[1] Laveleye: *La Péninsule des Balkans*, I, pp. 320 ff. The best general account of the economic relations between Austria and Serbia is by Karl Grünberg: *Die handelspolitischen Beziehungen Österreich-Ungarns zu den Ländern an der unteren Donau* (Leipzig, 1902), part ii; but see also Josepf Grunzel: *Die Handelsbeziehungen Österreich-Ungarns zu den Balkanländern* (Vienna, 1892); Ziwojin Janitchijewitch: *Die Entwicklung der serbischen Handelspolitik* (Würzburg, 1911), part iii; Ivan Z. Nestorovič: *Der Aussenhandel Serbiens* (Leipzig, 1913), pp. 16 ff.

[2] First revealed by Stojan Protitch: " The Secret Treaty between Servia and Austria-Hungary " (*Fortnightly Review*, XCI, pp. 838–48, May 1909). Further information may be found in Count Chedomille Mijatovich: *The Memoirs of a Balkan Diplomatist* (London, 1917), chapter iii. The text was published in Pribram's *Secret Treaties of Austria-Hungary*, and the same author has written the history of the negotiations from the Austrian archives (Alfred F. Pribram: " *Milan IV*

resentment against Russia and with hatred against Bulgaria, and requiring financial support for his own personal needs, was very favourably disposed towards an agreement with Austria. After the overthrow of Ristič, in October 1880, he summoned a progressive cabinet under the leadership of Pirochanats and Garashanin, which was disposed to follow his policy of a rapprochement. In June 1881 Prince Milan visited Vienna, Berlin, and St. Petersburg, after which he returned to Vienna and opened discussions with the Austrian ministers. Baron Haymerlé was glad to take up the suggestions made to him. As he explained to the Serbian foreign minister, Mijatovich, Austria was prepared to support a Serbia that was not under Russian influence: " The Dual Monarchy has no objection to the existence of a truly independent Serbia, cultivating good and neighbourly relations with her. We have no objection to the extension of her territories in a southern direction. But if Serbia should turn out to be a ' Russian satrapy' and were herself to abandon her independence and act on orders from Petersburg, then we could not tolerate such a Serbia on our frontier, and we would, as a lesser evil, occupy it with our armies." [1]

Milan accepted the draft treaty submitted to him by the Austrians, evidently without raising objections, and certainly without consulting his ministers. Taking the treaty back with him to Belgrade, he induced Mijatovich, the foreign minister, to sign it on June 28, 1881. Within the next ten days the agreement was ratified, and it was only then that Pirochanats, the prime minister, learned of it, not from Milan, but from the Austrian minister to Belgrade! [2]

Although Pirochanats was himself in favour of close relations with Austria, he objected vigorously to the treaty which Milan had accepted at Vienna. And well he might, for the text provided that Serbia should not tolerate on her territory political, religious, or other intrigues directed against the Austro-Hungarian monarchy, including Bosnia, Herzegovina, and the Sanjak of Novi-Bazar; that Austria should assume the same obligation towards Serbia and her dynasty; and that Austria should recognize and use her influence to induce other powers to recognize the title of king, if Milan should consider it necessary to assume it. There was, in addition, an article (number IV), which was full of dangerous implications. It read, textually: " Austria-Hungary will use her influence with the other European cabinets to second the interests of Serbia. Without previous understanding with Austria-Hungary, Serbia will neither negotiate nor conclude any political treaty with another government, and will not admit to her territory a foreign armed force, regular or irregular, even as volunteers." The two governments promised each other friendly neutrality if either were at war with one or more other powers, and envisaged a military convention to regulate questions of supreme command and the passage

von Serbien und die Geheimverträge Österreich-Ungarns mit Serbien, 1881–1889," in Historische Blätter, I, 1921–2, pp. 464–94).

[1] Mijatovich, op. cit., p. 38.

[2] Pribram, in Historische Blätter, I, pp. 469–70; Protitch, loc. cit.

of troops through their respective territories in the event that active co-operation between them should be deemed necessary. In return for all these concessions Austria promised, in Article VII, that " if, as a result of a combination of circumstances whose development is not to be foreseen at present, Serbia should be in a position to make territorial acquisitions in the direction of her southern frontiers (with the exception of the Sanjak of Novi-Bazar), Austria-Hungary will not oppose herself thereto and will use her influence with the other powers for the purpose of winning them over to an attitude favourable to Serbia." The treaty was to be kept strictly secret and was concluded for a period of ten years.[1]

Pirochanats, when he learned the text of this agreement, declared " that by such a convention Serbia would stand in the same relation to Austria-Hungary as Tunis to France." This can hardly be called an exaggeration. In fact, this treaty was more far-reaching than any concluded between independent European states in the period from 1870 to 1914, and it is hard to understand Mijatovich's defence: that the famous Article IV did not " in any way compromise our liberty to conclude secret political treaties with other powers," and that Serbia was obliged to inform Austria only if she concluded such agreements.[2] Pirochanats was right in maintaining that this article " deprived the Serbian government of its independence of decision and made Serbian policy wholly subordinate to Austria, without in any way limiting the freedom of Austrian policy in the East." He and Garashanin threatened to resign unless some change were made in the agreement, even though it had already been ratified and was legally valid. Milan was in a dilemma, but finally agreed that Mijatovich should go to Vienna to see what could be done.

Haymerlé and his assistant, Kállay, assured Mijatovich that the whole purpose of the article was to prevent Serbia from making agreements directed against Austria. But they regarded this article as their " greatest success " and were unwilling to weaken it. The Serbian minister obtained nothing more than a declaration that the article did not restrict Serbia's right to conclude non-political treaties with other powers. This assurance could not satisfy Pirochanats, so in September 1881 Milan went to Vienna himself to talk the matter over. Attacking the situation from a different angle, he started by sounding a querulous note: " Serbia must decide between Austria and Russia. Russian policy did us no good, but brought us only humiliation. Especially since the creation of Bulgaria, we have lost all value and significance for Russia. We served Russia loyally in the war with Turkey, covered her operations on the right flank, and at the time of the siege of Plevna kept sixty thousand men engaged. But at San Stefano the Russians were deaf to our wishes and claims. . . . Since then Russia treats us as minors or subordinates. But I do not want to be the prefect of Russia." He would, he continued, remain devoted to Austria and

---

[1] A faithful summary was given by Protitch, loc. cit., pp. 843–4; the official Austrian text in Pribram: *Secret Treaties*, I, pp. 51 ff.

[2] Mijatovich, op. cit., pp. 39–40.

stand loyally by the treaty. He would rather resign than act contrary to it. In fact, he would rather leave Serbia today than tomorrow, for his "damned country" caused him nothing but anger.

But Haymerlé avoided giving definite promises. Article IV was too valuable to be lightly cast aside. In the end Milan had to reach a compromise with Pirochanats. Austria was to be asked to accept a declaration that Article IV simply prevented Serbia from concluding agreements contrary to the spirit of the treaty or to the common interests of the contracting powers. At the same time, however, Milan assured the Austrian minister of his readiness to write a letter recognizing the validity of the article so far as he personally was concerned. When Pirochanats came to Vienna, the matter had practically been settled. The Austrian government temporized only until it secured from Milan a letter, dated October 24, 1881, in which, after explaining the situation in detail, he said: "Having it much at heart to prove with the very first steps which I take in the path I have chosen of my own free will how I hold to the faithful execution of my promises, I hereby, Excellency, assume the formal engagement on my honour, and in my quality as Prince of Serbia, not to enter into any negotiation whatsoever relative to any kind of political treaty between Serbia and a third state without communication with and previous consent of Austria-Hungary. I beg Your Excellency to consider the present engagement as having an entirely official character towards the government of His Imperial and Royal Apostolic Majesty." It was only with this declaration in hand that the Austrian government signed the statement desired by Pirochanats "that the aforesaid provision of Article IV cannot impair the right of Serbia to negotiate and conclude treaties, even of a political nature, with another government. It implies for Serbia no other engagement than that of not negotiating and of not concluding any political treaty which would be contrary to the spirit and the tenor of the said secret treaty." [1]

Sir Charles Dilke once described King Milan (he assumed the regal title, with Austrian support, in 1882) as a "third-class sovereign." He was as cynical in political matters as he was immoral in his private life, and it would be hard to find terms strong enough to condemn the methods which he employed to maintain his position in his "damned country." But this is not the place to moralize. What concerns us is that Austria, by her commercial and political agreements with Serbia in 1881, established what was not far removed from a protectorate over her little neighbour, and that control over Serbia was the strongest plank in the platform of Austrian preponderance in the Balkans. We must now turn to another aspect of the same policy: Austrian relations with Roumania.

Here, as with Serbia, the Russian policy as expressed in the Treaty of San Stefano had paved the way for a rapprochement with Austria. The Roumanians

---

[1] Milan's letter and the declaration of October 30 are in Pribram: *Secret Treaties*, I, pp. 56 ff. The negotiations are described in detail in Pribram's article in the *Historische Blätter*, loc. cit.

were profoundly disappointed by the cavalier treatment meted out to them by the Russians, who had been only too glad to secure Roumanian assistance during the critical days of the siege of Plevna. Roumania had been left in the lurch; she had been obliged by the Congress of Berlin to cede Bessarabia to Russia and take the Dobruja in exchange. No one in Roumania considered the exchange a fair one, even though Prince Gorchakov added insult to injury by telling the Roumanian delegates at Berlin that the cession of the Dobruja was "an act of generosity on the part of Russia." The provisions of the Treaty of Berlin regarding the treatment of the Jews in Roumania did not help to raise the spirits of the governing classes at Bucharest. Indeed, they regarded these stipulations as an infringement of the independence of the principality. Public feeling ran high in the years following the Russian-Turkish War, the more so as there were repeated difficulties arising from the execution of the peace treaties — problems of the regulation of the Lower Danube, disputes with respect to the delimitation of the frontier with Bulgaria, arguments about the treatment of the Jews. But the generally prevalent sentiment at Bucharest was that the Russian Orthodox crusade had been a farce, that Roumania's claims had been openly flouted, and that Russia was interested not so much in freeing her co-religionists from the yoke of the infidel as in establishing her domination over the southern Slavs. The non-Slavic Roumanians had been convenient tools for the realization of Pan-Slav aspirations, but once they had done their duty, they could go.

The geographic position of Roumania was such that it was constantly in danger of being annihilated by the pressure of the two great powers Russia and Austria. After 1878 the logical course would seem to have been one of close friendship with Austria, in view of the estrangement between Roumania and Russia and in view of the fact that Roumania, located between Russia and her client Bulgaria, was more seriously menaced than ever before. But the idea of an agreement with Austria did not appeal strongly to the Roumanians, whose intellectual and political inspiration had come from France. Neither could they forget that the Dual Monarchy included a large fragment of the Roumanian people, located in Transylvania. The problem of Roumania Irredenta was not to be sure, so advanced as that of Italia Irredenta, but it was a comparable problem, and agitation against Hungarian oppression of the Transylvanian Roumanians had already been begun.

Then, too, there were economic factors that kept the two governments apart: the question of the Danube and the question of trade relations. The commercial treaty concluded by Roumania and Austria in 1875, though it gave Roumanian grain and cattle free entry into the monarchy, also threw open the door to Austrian products and manufactures. In the period from 1875 to 1882 over 50 per cent of Roumanian imports came from Austria-Hungary and about 32 per cent of her exports went to the Dual Monarchy. As against this it should be noted that only 18 per cent of the import trade and 29 per cent of the export trade was with Great Britain, a remarkable fact, considering the general extent of British commerce in the Black Sea and the easy accessibility of Roumania. In any case, there was in Roumania, as in Serbia, a pronounced uneasiness concerning the economic control of Austria, and a distinct feeling that the flood of Austrian goods was hampering the growth of Roumania's own industry.[1]

Being ill-disposed towards a rapprochement with Austria, the Roumanian statesmen attempted, after 1878, to enlist the friendship of Germany. Between the two countries there were no standing disputes. On the contrary, Prince Carol (King after 1881) was himself a Hohenzollern, and there was some hope that the dynastic connexion might be capitalized. Bismarck appears to have had little use for Carol and to have been always on his guard lest the family ties should create difficulties for Germany. But late in July 1879, when the relations between Germany and Russia were becoming very tense, Bismarck made some effort to establish a closer contact. Speaking to the Roumanian minister Sturdza, he described Roumania as an " iron barrier " lying between Russia and Russia's " province" Bulgaria, a barrier which it was in Russia's interest to break down. Therefore, he suggested, it would be to the interest of Roumania to stand with the Western powers, Germany and France. " You have enemies; you must also secure friends." But in order to win the sympathy and support of the Western powers Roumania, said the chancellor, would have to fulfil the stipulations of the Berlin Treaty. In strong language he insisted that the vexed problem of the Jews should be settled and that the Roumanian government hasten to reach an agreement with respect to certain railway interests in which a number of Silesian magnates and Bismarck's Jewish banker friend Bleichröder were heavily involved. The Roumanian representative could have listened to these words only with mixed feelings. Bismarck's advances were certainly not pressing, and there was little comfort to be derived from them.[2]

For the present, Roumania remained isolated. But the dangers to which the state was exposed continued to exist, and gradually the governing classes came round to a realization that a rapprochement with Austria would have to be sought. In January 1881 Titu Majorescu, the Roumanian party-leader and statesman, published in the *Deutsche Revue* an article reviewing the international position of his country. While stressing the desirability of an understanding with Germany, he aimed chiefly at paving the way for an agreement with Austria, a necessary preliminary step. Owing to her geographic location, he argued, Roumania was practically forced to come into the sphere of interest of either Russia or Austria. The Russian orientation had become utterly impossible; therefore Roumania must turn to Austria. Even the question of the Roumanians in Transylvania should not stand in the way, for there were Roumanians also in Bessarabia, which had been taken by Russia in 1878, and

---

[1] Grünberg: *Die handelspolitischen Beziehungen Österreich-Ungarns,* part i; Cornelius G. Antonescu: *Die rumänische Handelspolitik von 1875–1910* (Leipzig, 1915), chapters i and v.

[2] *Aus dem Leben König Karls von Rumänien* (Stuttgart, 1900), Volume IV, pp. 233 ff.

these nationals under Russian rule were in a much less favourable position than those under the sceptre of the Habsburgs: " The Russian Roumanians are being annihilated, the Austrian Roumanians are flourishing. Russia is a monarchy that devours nationalities, Austria is one that preserves them. Russia is a centralistic, oppressive absolutism, Austria essentially a federative compromise state composed of individual nationalities." Therefore the connexion with Austria was to be greatly preferred, and, said Majorescu, this opinion was held by a large number of Roumanian politicians and statesmen.[1]

The weakness in Majorescu's argument was that he considered the Three Emperors' League definitely a thing of the past and regarded German relations with Russia not only as bad, but as growing steadily worse. As we know, the negotiations for the Alliance of the Three Emperors were taking place at this very time, and consequently there was no possibility that Bismarck would be willing to take up with the Roumanians. It was not until the summer of 1883, when the situation in Bulgaria had become critical and there seemed, for a time, to be real danger that Russia might intervene militarily, that the German chancellor took up the question of the Roumanian connexion seriously. King Carol was expected in Germany on a visit, and Bismarck, in correspondence with the German ambassador at Vienna, raised the question whether the League of Peace could be extended to include Roumania and possibly Serbia and Turkey. Kálnoky received the suggestion with enthusiasm, pointed out that of Serbia Austria was as certain as one ever could be of Balkan affairs, declared that Greece could be brought in at any time, and agreed that Roumania and Turkey would be useful.[2]

Having secured the assent of his Austrian colleague, Bismarck took up the matter with the Roumanian prime minister, Jon Bratianu, who came to visit him at Gastein. He found the Roumanian statesman very Russophobe and very favourably disposed towards Germany. There was much to complain of as far as Austria was concerned, but he was willing to accept the agreement with Austria along with an understanding with Germany. It seemed to Bismarck that he was rather disappointed at the idea of a simple defensive alliance, and that he had had in mind an offensive and defensive treaty with some provision for eventual territorial gain. The chancellor therefore warned him that Germany and Austria were anxious to avoid a conflict with Russia. He advised a purely defensive pact between Roumania and Austria, which Germany would be willing to join.[3]

The actual negotiations for the treaty were taken up at Vienna in September and resulted in an agreement before the end of the month. The question of Germany's relation to the alliance then came up. Bismarck's attitude was that,

---

[1] Titu Majorescu: " Zur politischen Lage Rumäniens " (Deutsche Revue, VI, pp. 12–20, January 1881).

[2] Die Grosse Politik, III, Nos. 583–4.

[3] Ibid., No. 585; Mitis: Kronprinz Rudolf, pp. 278 ff.

even without her signature, Germany would assume obligations under the treaty if she agreed to regard as a *casus foederis* of the Austro-German Alliance any action taken by Austria to ward off an attack upon Roumania. It was clear that the German chancellor disliked the idea of signing a treaty in which Russia was specifically mentioned as the possible aggressor, and he obviously expected opposition on the part of the Emperor to the conclusion of such a pact.

Kálnoky, on the other hand, regarded Germany's adhesion as essential, because, as he said, he was under no illusions regarding the feelings of the Roumanians towards Austria and it was more likely that King Carol would keep his word to the German Emperor than to Austria alone. The Austrian minister therefore agreed to certain minor changes in the text, as requested by Bismarck. The alliance was signed on October 30, 1883. Germany acceded to it on the same day. It provided that the two contracting parties should not enter into alliances or engagements directed against one another, that Austria-Hungary should come to the assistance of Roumania if the latter should be attacked without provocation, and that Roumania should come to the support of Austria if, without provocation, the latter should be attacked in a portion of her states bordering on Roumania. This last phrase was simply a circumlocution to avoid the mention of Russia by name. The remaining clauses provided for the negotiation of a military convention if common action should become necessary, and laid the two governments under promise not to conclude a separate peace. The treaty was made for a period of five years and was to be kept strictly secret. As a matter of fact, it was renewed several times, and continued in existence till the time of the World War. The secret was well maintained and the content of the treaty was known to very few even of the leading Roumanian politicians.[1]

The treaties with Serbia and Roumania gave Austria a very strong hold on the Balkan situation, but the picture of Austrian policy in these years would not be complete without some reference to Greece and Turkey. The Greeks, like the Serbs and the Roumanians, were anything but pleased with the settlement of 1878 or with the territories that had been finally awarded them. The great Bulgaria of the San Stefano Treaty was a nightmare to them, and they looked with alarm upon the Russian policy, which had so frankly accepted the teachings of Panslavism to the detriment of the non-Slavic peoples. It was natural that the Greeks should look to Austria as the great opponent of the Slavic doctrine. As early as 1880 King George of Greece had offered Austria the full support of Hellenism for her policy. In June 1883 the Greek advances were resumed with greater vigour, but negotiations for an agreement dragged. Kálnoky, while denying any Austrian designs on Salonika, refused to give any definite promise for the future and appears to have viewed the Greeks with some suspicion. Bismarck, too, distrusted them, and noted on a report from

---

[1] Text in Pribram: *Secret Treaties*, I, pp. 78 ff. The negotiations are dealt with in *Die Grosse Politik*, III, Nos. 587 ff.

Vienna that Greece had a Russian queen, who was full of French sympathies and could be bribed into committing indiscretions. No actual agreement was signed by either Austria or Germany with Greece, but the relations were close. Kálnoky did not go too far when he said that an agreement with Greece could be had at any time. In fact, the Greek statesman Delyannis, in an instruction to the legation at Constantinople dated June 13, 1885, declared in so many words: " We consider this cabinet [that is, the Austrian] as our most sincere and most natural ally in all questions which at present may arise in the Ottoman Empire." [1]

With the Turks the connexion was much more tenuous and uncertain. The simple fact was that it was hard to entertain close relations with the Porte and at the same time with the Balkan states, most of which cherished designs on Turkish territory. The Austrian government was, therefore, obliged to proceed cautiously and to leave the initiative more or less to Germany. Bismarck certainly appreciated the possible value of Turkish support in the event of a conflict with Russia, but he did not want to jeopardize his relations with Russia for the sake of the unreliable Turkish friendship. When the Sultan, in 1880, requested that Prussian officers be sent to reorganize and train his army, the chancellor first evaded and temporized and finally refused. In January 1882 Abdul Hamid went so far as to express the desire for an alliance with Austria and Germany. This suggestion, too, was rejected, because the two central powers were unwilling to become involved in the standing conflict between Turkey and Russia. Bismarck, however, felt strongly that the Sultan should not be cast adrift entirely, and in the spring of 1882 he allowed German officers to be sent to Constantinople. The mission was not very successful at first, but it served to keep up the connexion, and Abdul Hamid came to look more and more to Berlin for advice and support. The basis for the later German influence at Constantinople had already been laid, and the efforts made by the Russians to draw the Turks to their side were never more than ephermal.[2]

While the Austrians were reaping the benefits of Russia's exaggerated policy, the Russians themselves had staked everything on Bulgaria. Prince Nicholas of Montenegro, it is true, was a faithful trabant, but then, Montenegro was merely an isolated outpost, a forlorn hope, on which too much reliance could not be placed. It was in Bulgaria that Russia hoped to realize her aspirations in the Near East, and all necessary arrangements were made before the country was evacuated. When the Russian troops withdrew from Eastern Roumelia, they left for the inhabitants eighty thousand rifles, with instructions to practise and to help themselves. The ultimate union of Roumelia and Bulgaria

---

1 Edouard Driault and Michel Lhéritier: *Histoire diplomatique de la Grèce*, Volume IV (Paris, 1926), pp. 157 ff., 186 ff., 200. See also *Die Grosse Politik*, III, No. 584.

2 See especially Hajo Holborn: *Deutschland und die Türkei, 1875–1890* (Berlin, 1926), pp. 8 ff.; and Generalfeldmarschall Colmar Freiherr von der Goltz: *Denkwürdigkeiten* (Berlin, 1929), pp. 106 ff.

was still a prime tenet of Russian policy.[1] In Bulgaria itself the Russian governor-general, Prince Dondukov, worked out a fairly liberal constitution, which provided not only for the necessary ministries, but also for a popularly elected assembly (Sobranje), which was to limit the power of the prince and serve as a bulwark of Russian influence. The administration was organized and large numbers of Russian officers and civil servants put in control, on the theory that the Bulgarians lacked the proper experience. In April 1879 the assembly, under Russian direction, elected Alexander of Battenberg as hereditary Prince. The Treaty of Berlin had excluded from the throne members of the Russian ruling family, but Alexander of Battenberg seemed to fill the requirements almost as well. He was a favourite nephew of the Tsar and had fought as a volunteer in the war against Turkey. He was a German prince, his father had served in both the Russian and the Austrian armies, and he was related by marriage to the English royal family. In short, his election could be counted upon to win general approval.[2]

The Russians, however, were to suffer profoundest disappointment in Bulgaria and finally to see the complete collapse of their policy. The reasons for the difficulties that soon arose were not simple; indeed, there were many factors that contributed to complicate the situation. Looking back, it is easy enough to see that the Russians underestimated the ability and determination of the Bulgarians, and that they failed to understand the Bulgarian thirst for independence not only from Turkey, but from any other power. The educated Bulgarians, who had grown up at Constantinople, Bucharest, Odessa, or even Vienna or Paris, resented the monopoly of place which the Russians had taken for granted. The system simply proved to be unworkable, for the Russian officers and administrators, most of them members of the high nobility, looked down on the peasantry as hardly better than serfs, quite ignoring the rugged democracy of the Bulgarian population. On the other hand, the Bulgarians themselves were individualists and, like most newly awakened nationalities, extremely sensitive to foreign interference. The leaders not only fell to fighting each other, but also regarded their Russian mentors with disdain. It was commonly said that the Russians, far from being in advance of the Bulgarians, had received their alphabet, their civilization, and their religion from Bulgaria.[3]

Another cause of trouble for Russia was the lack of unity in her policy. It

---

[1] Egon C. Corti: *Alexander von Battenberg: Sein Kampf mit den Zaren und Bismarck* (Vienna, 1920), p. 58.

[2] The fundamental account in Bulgarian of this period of Bulgarian history is Simeon Radev: *Stroitelite na Sovremenna Blgarija*, Volume I, 1879–86 (Sofia, 1910). The best Russian account is that of S. Skazkin: *Konets avstro-russko-germanskogo soiuza* (Moscow, 1928), Book II, covering the period to 1884 and based on Russian archive material. See also Corti, op. cit., whose book is based on the Battenberg papers; Georges Bousquet: *Histoire du peuple bulgare* (Paris, 1909); N. Staneff: *Geschichte der Bulgaren* (Leipzig, 1917), Volume II; and Eumène Queille: *Les Commencements de l'indépendance bulgare* (Paris, 1910).

[3] See Georges Fillion: *Entre Slaves* (Paris, 1894), pp. 56 ff.; P. F. Kanitz: *Donau-Bulgarien* (Leipzig, 1875–80), III, p. 112.

seems certain that Tsar Alexander II was well-intentioned with regard to the Bulgarians. He really meant to do all he could for the country which his armies had liberated. But the moderate policy pursued by the Russian government was constantly being jeopardized by the actions of the Russians on the spot, many of whom were either Pan-Slavs themselves or completely under the influence of the powerful Slavic Welfare Society. Not only that; there were economic factors to be borne in mind, and business interests were evidently in alliance with the Pan-Slavs. Even the great Russian journalist Katkov is said to have been influenced in his work by very mundane considerations, and it is certain that the Russian representatives in Bulgaria were frequently tools in the hands of Russian financial cliques. All these people regarded Bulgaria primarily as a new field for exploitation, and a field in which no opposition was to be feared.[1]

Lastly the position and attitude of Alexander of Battenberg must be considered. The attractiveness of his appearance and the charm of his manner were proverbial and generally recognized in his own time. But it appeared before long that Alexander lacked real discernment, moderation, and statesmanship. Whatever blame may be placed upon the Russians for the break that took place, it can hardly be denied that part of the responsibility rested with the Prince himself. These personal shortcomings were bad enough, but they were, if anything, encouraged by the peculiarities of the international situation. We may assume that Alexander meant to play the part assigned to him, even though, from the start, he protested that the Bulgarian constitution was far too liberal to be workable. But before he ever went to Bulgaria he made a round of visits to the various European courts and exposed himself to the whisperings of international intrigue. Bismarck encouraged him to go to Bulgaria. He may have considered it useful to have a German prince on a Balkan throne at a time when Russian-German relations were rapidly becoming cold. Alexander was then still somewhat hesitant and asked what would happen if he failed. "You will at all events take away a pleasant recollection with you," replied the chancellor.[2]

Alexander evidently relied heavily on English support in the event of a conflict with the Russians. Soon after his election his father wrote to Queen Victoria assuring her that Alexander was not Russian at heart, and that he was not inclined to act as Russia's marionette. The Prince himself visited England in June 1879 and made a very favourable impression on the Queen, who from

---

[1] The strongest statement of this matter is to be found in an anonymous but very well-informed pamphlet entitled: *Les Causes occultes de la question bulgare* (Paris, 1887). The question is discussed in great detail and with the use of unpublished material by Skazkin, op. cit., pp. 256 ff.

[2] This story may be found in many contemporary books. Bismarck himself denied having said anything of the kind to Alexander (Corti, op. cit., p. 65), but the fact that Alexander himself told the anecdote to Queen Victoria almost immediately afterwards would seem to show its accuracy (*Letters of Queen Victoria*, III, p. 26).

this time on was one of his most faithful champions. She told him to consider himself as " one of the family." At the same time the Prince of Wales did his utmost to counteract the Russian influence. Beaconsfield and Salisbury entertained the young ruler in London, and, we are told by the biographer of Edward VII, " from all his influential English hosts the young man received the counsel to remember that he was a vassal of the Sultan and no puppet of the Tsar." [1]

When Alexander arrived in Bulgaria, he found two ill-defined political groups. One could hardly call them parties, for they were personal followings more than anything else. The one group, known as the conservative, was composed largely of the representatives of the wealthier classes. Its members had, many of them, been educated in central and western Europe, and yet, curiously enough, they were looked upon as the exponents of a close connexion with Russia as well as the advocates of a strong executive power in Bulgaria itself. The other group, the so-called liberal, represented the Bulgarian bourgeoisie and what Mr. Bourchier described as " home-grown philistinism." [2] Most of these men were either home-bred or educated in the Bulgarian schools of Bucharest or Odessa. They were by no means all radicals or revolutionaries, but some of them, like the leader Karavelov, had imbibed the Russian Nihilist teaching and were pretty extreme in their demands. In 1879 the whole group was looked upon as representing an unadulterated Bulgarian nationalism, which implied opposition to foreign influence in general and to autocratic Russia in particular. That these sentiments were not too deeply rooted appeared not long after, when the liberals showed themselves only too ready to sacrifice impractical doctrines in order to secure actual political power.

Alexander began by choosing a ministry composed of conservatives. But this arrangement soon proved impossible. The reasons for the difficulty are not wholly clear, for if the Russian element and the Russian government had supported the Prince loyally, he would not have been obliged to take the liberal opposition to the conservative government very seriously. What seems to have been at the root of the matter was the pressure from speculators and concession-hunters who, so far as one can determine, were connected with the powerful Pan-Slav committees in Moscow and through these were able to make use of the official Russian representatives in Bulgaria. These interests, the Günzburgs, Poliakovs, Muranievs, and others, were especially concerned with the railway problem. Hardly had Alexander landed at Varna when their agents approached him with far-reaching proposals. Their object was to block the infiltration of Austrian influence by preventing the construction of the Bulgarian part of the Orient Railway, and to reinforce the Russian position in the Balkans by work-

---

[1] Lee: *Edward VII*, Volume I, pp. 499–500; *Letters of Queen Victoria*, III, pp. 16, 26–8.

[2] James D. Bourchier: " Prince Alexander of Battenberg " (*Fortnightly Review*, LXI, pp. 103–18, January 1894). There is an excellent discussion of the make-up of the Bulgarian groups in Georges Fillion, op. cit., pp. 58 ff.

ing for the construction of a line from Ruschuk, on the Danube, through Sofia to Kyustendil, on the south-western frontier. This transverse line, which was to be connected with the Roumanian and Russian systems in the north, could be extended in the south to Salonika, thus opening up the whole area to Russian penetration. It may be added that Russia probably did not possess the economic strength to conquer this territory in a business sense, and it is therefore likely that the main objective was to counteract the Austrian *Drang nach Osten*. However that may be, the question of the Ruschuk-Sofia railway runs like a red thread through the whole period of Bulgarian history from 1879 to 1885, and it appears that the unwillingness of the conservative ministry to ignore its obligations under the Treaty of Berlin and its hesitancy about throwing open the door to Russian economic influence led the Russians to turn more and more to the liberal opposition, thus creating an extremely tense and almost impossible situation.[1]

The Prince, relying upon the benevolence of the Tsar, journeyed to St. Petersburg in 1880 to arrange for a change in the Bulgarian constitution which would enable him to get out of the vortex of party conflicts. But the Tsar, under the influence of the Pan-Slavs, advised him to co-operate with the liberals, who were now looked upon as the instruments of Russian policy. Thereupon Alexander summoned a liberal ministry, under the two prominent leaders Zankov and Karavelov. But this solution did not prove satisfactory either, for the liberals, once in power, showed themselves to be true representatives of the clever trading classes and, for that matter, of the parsimonious peasantry. To be sure, they were obliged to do something for the Russian interests which had supplied two hundred thousand francs to help them on to victory. But the assembly only went so far as to recognize the value of the Russian railway project and to instruct the government to undertake surveys and gather estimates. The Russians were not very happy about the situation and redoubled their efforts to build up a satisfactory following in the assembly. The result was that the assembly, already turbulent enough, became a battle-ground for the struggle of all against all. During these first two years of Alexander's rule he was obliged to dismiss seven ministries and three assemblies. Something had to be done.

In March 1881 Alexander again journeyed to St. Petersburg to pay his respects to the new Tsar, Alexander III. The assassination of Alexander II was a great blow to the Prince of Bulgaria, for there had been real affection and confidence between uncle and nephew. Alexander II had generally listened to the Prince's complaints, and had recalled many of the officials who had been obnoxious to him. But the new Tsar did not share this affection. Indeed, he seems

---

[1] The railway problem is well dealt with in the interesting anonymous pamphlet: *Les Causes occultes de la question bulgare* (Paris, 1887). See also Fillion, op. cit., pp. 66 ff.; Queille, op. cit., pp. 94 ff.; Corti, op. cit., p. 90; and the scholarly account of Skazkin, op. cit., pp. 256 ff., which is based on Russian diplomatic correspondence. It might be added that these same Russian interests pressed strongly for the creation of a national bank, which would have given them almost complete financial control.

to have had little sympathy either for the Bulgarians or for their Prince. When asked to permit a change in the Bulgarian constitution, he gave his consent, but grudgingly and with a warning to Alexander that he must not reckon on active Russián assistance. Thereupon the Prince returned to Sofia and announced the dismissal of the liberal ministry, the formation of a new cabinet under his friend the Russian general Ernroth, and the convocation of a grand Sobranje to approve certain changes in the constitution which would strengthen the position of the ruler. The details were easily enough managed, for in spite of all provisions for manhood suffrage and secret ballot the government could always, by the employment of *sopadzis* (cudgellers), induce the population to vote properly. In this instance the use of official pressure almost exceeded the bounds of the credible. The government won a resounding victory.[1]

When the liberal leaders appealed to the Russian Pan-Slavs for assistance in this crisis, they received no encouragement. They had not been faithful enough to the Russian ideas, but it was hoped that Alexander, now that the troublesome assembly was practically suspended, could easily be brought round. General Struve was immediately sent to Sofia to press for the award of the Ruschuk-Sofia railroad concession. It soon appeared, however, that the Prince was no more pliable than the assembly, the more so as the Austrians were loudly demanding the fulfilment of the terms of the Treaty of Berlin. Now began the great crusade against Alexander, who had never been liked by the Russians. The numerous officials whom he had succeeded in getting recalled began to blacken his reputation in St. Petersburg, while the agents on the spot reported him to be entirely under the influence of Baron Hirsch and the Austrians. They made no secret of their hostility and told Alexander to his face that they regarded themselves as advanced outposts of Russian influence. They were fighting purely for Russian interests, and the disfavour of the Prince was their best recommendation at home.[2] The Russian representative Hitrovo, one of the worst intriguers, was already renewing connexions with the liberal opposition when Alexander finally secured his recall. Unfortunately for the Prince, his best friend, General Ernroth, was recalled at the same time, and in his place the Russian government sent Generals Kaulbars and Sobolev to act, respectively, as minister of war and minister of the interior. Like the new Russian consul, Jonin, these gentlemen were vigorous Pan-Slavs, who were determined to brook no opposition from the " German." Jonin made his début by cynically telling Alexander that if anyone had to clear out it would not be the Russian ministers or generals, but the Prince himself.[3]

Kaulbars and Sobolev regarded Bulgaria as a satrapy of the Tsar and ruled it

---

[1] See especially Ellinor F. B. Grogan: "Bulgaria under Prince Alexander" (*Slavonic Review*, I, pp. 561–71, March 1923); Corti, op. cit., pp. 108--12.

[2] Corti, op. cit., p. 89.

[3] A. Kutschbach: *Der Brandherd Europas* (Leipzig, 1929), pp. 295–6.

with the most autocratic police methods. They even went so far as to employ government "secretaries" who were paid from the Bulgarian treasury to write attacks on Alexander. But their position was soon challenged by the assembly, which refused to accept the government projects for the construction of the Ruschuk-Varna railway and voted lack of confidence in the ministry. The struggle between the Russian ministers and the Bulgarian assembly developed rapidly. The Prince was caught between the upper and the nether millstones. An assembly of notables advised him to go to St. Petersburg and request the Tsar to recall the generals, and in the spring of 1883 he set out, travelling over a rather circuitous route, which included Constantinople and the Balkan capitals. Alexander's plan was evidently to see if he could engineer an alliance which could offer a united front to Russian influence. Of the details little is known. The idea of a league was much discussed in the Balkan countries at that time, and there were even suggestions made to include the Turks. Alexander's pilgrimage, however, proved to be unsuccessful, it is said because he found the Greek terms too exorbitant.[1] In any case his activities must have been looked upon at St. Petersburg with the greatest distrust. Most of the Balkan states were under Austrian influence. If Alexander were to identify himself with Serbia and Greece and Roumania, he would be entering the anti-Russian league. So serious did this departure appear to the Russians that it is said the ambassador at Constantinople, Nelidov, began to work for a league under Russian leadership and even for a Russian-Turkish understanding.[2]

Under the circumstances Alexander could not hope to meet with much sympathy when he reached the Russian capital. It is true that the Tsar desired to maintain peace, and that he agreed that the generals should turn over their powers to a new conservative ministry. But on his return to Bulgaria the Prince found everything in confusion, the Russians ruling with a high hand and already resuming their intrigues with the liberal leaders. In fact, Jonin and the generals went so far as to arrange a plot to kidnap Alexander.[3] Finally the contest came to a head when the famous railway project was again brought forward, and pressed with greater vigour than ever before. The result of this move was to close the ranks of the Bulgarians in opposition to foreign exploitation. Zankov and the liberals rallied to the support of the Prince, the generals were dismissed, and something akin to a coalition ministry came into power. In September 1883 the constitution was restored.

The dismissal of Kaulbars and Sobolev was tantamount to a rejection of Pan-Slav influence. The indignation in Russia rose to unheard-of heights and soon became a veritable delirium of animosity against the Prince. The Tsar did not even reply to Alexander's letter of explanation, and Giers, the Russian

---

[1] Corti, op. cit., p. 130; Driault and Lhéritier, op. cit., IV, pp. 178 ff.
[2] *Die Grosse Politik*, III, No. 644.
[3] Radev, op. cit., I, pp. 407 ff.; Fillion, op. cit., p. 77; Bourchier, loc. cit.; Corti, op. cit., p. 143.

foreign minister, declared passionately to the Austrian ambassador: "I am usually a calm person, but the blood mounts to my head when I have to busy myself with this unhappy Bulgarian affair. I spoke to the Tsar yesterday and told him that, in the forty-five years I have been in service, I have never become involved in an affair which was so repulsive to me." Battenberg, he said, seemed to want to become a second Alexander of Macedon, but all Russia needed to do in order to have him ejected in twenty-four hours was to recall the two hundred and thirty Russian officers who were in Bulgaria.[1]

This step, however, the Russians were by no means willing to take at that time. A revolutionary movement had just begun in Serbia, and the Austrian government, after appeals from King Milan for help, had announced to the Tsar's government that, if necessary, Austria would force the restoration of order.[2] This caused some consternation in official Russian circles, where there was probably some knowledge of the Austrian-Roumanian negotiations which were going on at the time. The Tsar and Giers were probably well-advised, under the circumstances, to open negotiations for the renewal of the Alliance of the Three Emperors, though this treaty was not due to expire until June 1884. When Giers visited Bismarck at Friedrichsruh in November 1883, he succeeded in convincing the chancellor that Russia desired peace. At the same time he was told that Germany could not afford to desert Austria, for fear that, once cast adrift, she might conclude an alliance à la Kaunitz with France and Russia. But Germany, said Bismarck, would nevertheless do her utmost to maintain peace between Austria and her neighbour.[3] On arriving at Vienna Giers avoided discussion of the Bulgarian situation. The negotiations for the renewal of the treaty went on without a hitch and resulted in the signature of a protocol (March 27, 1884) extending the alliance for a further period of three years, with only one or two minor changes in the text.[4]

The Russian government was evidently determined to abstain from hasty action in the Bulgarian question and allow Alexander to hang himself, so to speak. As a matter of fact, the Prince realized that he could not go on for ever with the Russians against him. He had appealed to the representatives of the powers for support, but had not received much encouragement. Queen Victoria, to be sure, was very solicitous for his welfare. She tried to bring pressure to bear upon her ministers, urged upon them her conviction that " our object is to *prevent* Russia forcing this Prince to resign, and thus to see a Russian vassal placed there," and complained that the government " do not seem sufficiently alive to the immense danger of Russia getting a hold there, for these Principalities *ought* to be a safeguard for Turkey against Russian influence and encroachment." But Granville, while he agreed with her argument, showed no disposition

[1] Corti, op. cit., pp. 145–8.
[2] Schweinitz: *Denkwürdigkeiten*, II, pp. 241 ff.; Szeps: *Kronprinz Rudolf*, p. 64.
[3] *Die Grosse Politik*, III, No. 611.
[4] The best Russian account is in Skazkin, op. cit., pp. 333 ff.

to challenge Russia, and Alexander never got much more than moral support from London.[1]

If, as Count Corti believes, Alexander took a strong stand against Russia in the hope that England would do something for him, this was a gross error in statesmanship. But it was even worse to hope for support from Germany, as Alexander clearly did. During a visit to Berlin in June 1883, he had met the Princess Victoria, with whom he fell in love. The young lady was the daughter of the German Crown Prince Frederick, and her mother was a daughter of Queen Victoria. Both the mother and the grandmother supported the marriage project with great enthusiasm, but Bismarck succeeded in convincing both the Crown Prince and the Emperor that such an alliance would jeopardize German relations with Russia and imply German support for Alexander. It seemed to him like an attempt on the part of the English royal family to bring about an estrangement between Germany and Russia. Before the matter found its way into the papers, in May 1884, the chancellor had managed to force a decision, and when Prince William went to Russia in the same month, he was able to give the Tsar the most explicit assurances that nothing would come of the project.[2]

Alexander came to Berlin in May 1884, for just what reason is not clear, unless he still hoped to win the support of the German government. His mission was bound to be a failure. The old Emperor told him rather brusquely that he should devote himself to effecting a reconciliation with Russia, while Bismarck was positively brutal in his efforts to clarify the Prince's ideas. After rehearsing the matter of the marriage project and his own efforts to frustrate it, the chancellor continued: " Germany has no interest in Bulgaria; our interest is peace with Russia, and that requires, first and foremost, that the Russians should be convinced that we do not pursue interests of our own in the East. On the day when a Prussian princess becomes Princess of Bulgaria, the Russians will become distrustful and will no longer lend credence to our assurances; besides, this marriage would spoil my circles. This I will not tolerate, and I told His Majesty that so long as I am chancellor this marriage would not take place. . . . As a matter of fact, I cannot understand why you wish to marry a princess; at best, Princess Beatrice of England or Princess Helen of Mecklenburg would be suitable for you. My advice would be to marry an Orthodox heiress. That would strengthen your position in Bulgaria, for to govern in the Orient you must grease the wheels (*im Orient regieren, heisst Schmieren*), and for that you need money. You cannot get anywhere with morality. In any case, it seems to me that you should definitely decide whether you are a German or a Bulgarian. So far you have acted the part of a German, and that must end with

---

[1] *Letters of Queen Victoria,* III, pp. 445, 454; Corti, op. cit., p. 149.

[2] Schweinitz: *Briefwechsel,* pp. 204–5; id., *Denkwürdigkeiten,* II, p. 271; *Die Grosse Politik,* III, Nos. 631–4; Waldersee: *Denkwürdigkeiten,* I, p. 240; William II: *My Early Life* (New York, 1926), pp. 324–5.

your abdication. . . . But if you want to stay in Bulgaria, throw yourself upon Russia's mercy; if necessary, assume even an anti-German attitude. As a matter of fact, I consider the future of Bulgaria problematical. Sooner or later it will become an object of compensation, and certainly some time, sitting by the fireside, you will be thinking back upon your stormy youth. Our view-point is known in St. Petersburg. I advise you to seize every opportunity to return to a good footing with Russia. Your Highness enjoys the full sympathy of German governing circles and I myself have high respect for you, but I am the chancellor of forty-five million Germans, whose interests I cannot sacrifice for the interest of any one German." [1]

It was no wonder that Alexander returned to Sofia deeply discouraged and with a feeling that he was entirely deserted. Kálnoky felt that he at least deserved credit for having opposed Russia, and thought that he ought to be supported for fear lest someone else might be put in his place, but his utterances to this effect simply stirred the ire of Bismarck, who annotated almost every line of the report. Bulgaria, he insisted, was no affair of Germany and Austria, and Alexander should, from the start, have played the part of a Russian *Statthalter*. Replying to Kálnoky's remarks, he stressed the fact that the Alliance of the Three Emperors rested on the supposition that Russia should have a free hand in Bulgaria, while Austria should be free to pursue her own policy in Bosnia and Serbia. Austria, he continued, had tacitly recognized the Russian claims when, in the treaty of 1881, she had left to Russia the decision regarding the union of Bulgaria and Eastern Roumelia. [2]

This theory underlay Bismarck's attitude through the whole crisis which followed, and should be carefully borne in mind. The occasion to develop it still further arose in the summer of 1884, when an acute conflict broke out between Serbia and Bulgaria regarding a small strip of disputed territory on the frontier. It was only with great difficulty that Bismarck succeeded in maintaining the principle of co-operation within the Three Emperors' League. To prevent the two rivals Austria and Russia from flying at each other's throats he urged once again the desirability of dividing the Balkans into two spheres of influence, though he recognized that both sides disliked the idea because each still nourished the hope of bringing the whole area under its own influence. Kálnoky defended himself by arguing that the deposition of Alexander would lead to revolutionary upheavals in both Serbia and Roumania. Subversive movements were already being supported there by Russia. Indeed, the great objection to a division of the Balkans into two spheres arose from the fact that Russian propaganda would transgress the recognized limits of the Russian sphere. Austria had no intention of disputing legitimate Russian influence in Bulgaria, but she could not give Russia a free hand, for fear of the eventual establishment of a huge Slav state which would girdle Austria-Hungary. Besides, Austria had economic interests, such as railways — a statement which Bismarck charac-

---

[1] Corti, op. cit., pp. 165–8.   [2] *Die Grosse Politik*, III, Nos. 635, 636.

teristically annotated with the words: "*hic hæret.*" It was, indeed, the crux of the problem as viewed from the Viennese standpoint.[1]

The German chancellor was obviously very uneasy about Russian-Austrian relations. Now that Russia had lost her hold on Bulgaria, there was no knowing what she might do to regain it. Neither was there any knowing what the Austrians might essay in order to usurp the place from which the Russians had been ejected. For this reason Bismarck was anxious to avoid a meeting between Tsar Alexander and Francis Joseph alone and was glad when a Three Emperors' conference could be arranged for September 1884. The three rulers met at Skierniewice, in Poland, and were accompanied by their foreign ministers. We have no detailed record of the conversations that took place, but we do know that the Balkan situation was entered into. Giers assured his Austrian colleague that in his view Serbia must depend chiefly on Austria, and that Russia would never support the rival Karageorgevič dynasty. Neither would Russia proceed against Alexander of Battenberg. These were valuable assurances. It does not appear that Kálnoky made similar declarations of Austrian good intentions. It is no wonder, then, that Giers came away filled with the conviction that there was a deep antagonism between Russia and Austria. " On that point there can be no illusion," he remarked to the German chargé d'affaires. It was in the same spirit that one of the Pan-Slav leaders wrote after the meeting: "Austria will girdle the Balkan Peninsula with railways, will encircle Montenegro with fortresses, will subject the Serbs and Bulgarians economically speaking, and will flood Bulgaria, Serbia, and Macedonia with Jesuit missions, with educational institutions, with Catholic propaganda, and finally with German colonists — and what is to become of us? "[2]

In the meanwhile Alexander of Battenberg had come to realize the urgent necessity of a reconciliation with the Tsar. In March 1885 he not only formally renounced any idea of asking for the hand of the Emperor's grand-daughter, but actually appealed to William to mediate between him and the Tsar. He was willing, he said, to stand by Russia unconditionally in matters of foreign policy and to represent Russian interests in Bulgaria so far as he constitutionally could. He would obey any commands that came to him directly from the Tsar, though he would refuse to play the role of a phantom ruler (*Scheinregent*).

Whether through the good offices of William or otherwise, it was arranged that Alexander should meet Giers in August 1885 at Franzensbad, where the Russian minister was taking a cure. The meeting took place as scheduled and was an unqualified success. Giers was ready to further a reconciliation, but declared strongly in favour of the maintenance of the *status quo* in the Balkans. Russia did not desire the union of Bulgaria and Eastern Roumelia at this time. In reply to which Alexander stated that no immediate trouble was to be

---

[1] Ibid., Nos. 637–44.
[2] Ibid., Nos. 645–9; Schweinitz: *Denkwürdigkeiten*, II, pp. 283 ff.; id., *Briefwechsel*, p. 210.

expected. Whether anything in the form of a definite assurance was given may be doubted, though it cannot be denied that Giers was justified in thinking that Alexander could be relied upon, especially as he had talked for four hours and had begged Russia's forgiveness.[1]

But the desires and intentions of Giers and Alexander had no bearing on the situation. The revolutionary movement in Eastern Roumelia was already beyond their control, and the demand for union with Bulgaria had become well-nigh irresistible. Through the efforts of the powers the province of Eastern Roumelia had been endowed with a constitution. This Organic Statute was an elaborate document of four hundred and ninety-five articles. It provided for a Christian governor-general, appointed for five years by the Sultan, with the consent of the powers; for a partly elected assembly; and for a separate militia. The administration was admittedly efficient. Both governors-general, Aleko Pasha Vogorides, a Bulgaro-Greek (1879–84), and his successor, Gavril Pasha Krestovich, a Bulgar (1884–5), carried out their duties in a satisfactory manner. In spite of all this, however, the revolutionary movement developed rapidly. No doubt the Russians had much to do with fomenting it, both through financial aid and through the supply of weapons. In like manner the Bulgarians carried on a systematic propaganda, and it is said that the Roumelian committee in Sofia had several million francs at its disposal.[2] After the suspension of the Bulgarian constitution, in 1881, many of the liberal leaders fled into Eastern Roumelia, where they took a prominent part in the preparation of the revolution.

Russia's attitude towards the question of union had, in the meantime, undergone a decisive change. Since the break with Alexander of Bulgaria the Russian government had become very anxious that no action should be taken until the Prince had been removed. The union, if it was to be effected at all, was to be the work of Russia, not of Alexander.[3] This was the official view, and the stand of the Russian representative at Sofia conformed to it. On the other hand, the Russian agent at Philippopolis, as well as the Russian military attaché, was undoubtedly kept fully informed of what was being planned. They were present at a secret meeting in June 1885 when it was decided to start the revolution in September, and it is said that they reported the news home. This may explain why Giers took the matter up with Alexander at the Franzensbad meeting. The statement sometimes made that Alexander had himself fomented the movement, and that he had wilfully deceived Giers, is certainly not provable.[4] Evidently the

---

[1] Corti, op. cit., pp. 181–8; Schweinitz: *Denkwürdigkeiten*, II, p. 299; Toutain: *Alexandre III et la République française*, p. 36; *Letters of Queen Victoria*, III, p. 698.

[2] N. Iorga: *Histoire des états balkaniques* (Paris, 1925), p. 409.

[3] *Die Grosse Politik*, III, No. 612 (November 16, 1883).

[4] A. G. Drandar: *Les Événements politiques en Bulgarie* (Brussels, 1896), p. 78. For the complicity of the Russian agents see Adolf Koch: *Fürst Alexander von Bulgarien* (Darmstadt, 1887), p. 233; Radev, op. cit., I, p. 565; Corti, op. cit., p. 190; Richard von Mach: *Aus bewegter Balkanzeit, 1879–1918* (Berlin, 1928), pp. 32–3.

first information received by the Prince came early in September, when agents of the revolutionary group informed him at Shumla and then at Varna and attempted to secure his approval and leadership. Rumours of coming action had been anything but rare and Alexander refused at first to take the matter seriously. When his prime minister, Karavelov, realized the extent of the danger, the Prince tried to dissuade his visitors and urged the impossibility of taking action so soon after the assurances he had given Giers at Franzensbad.[1]

The revolutionary leaders, however, decided that further delay would be fatal. On September 18 the movement began, when mutinous troops marched upon Philippopolis. No resistance was encountered. In fact, the whole incident had more or less of a light-operatic tinge. Having read French history, one of the commanders took the precaution of bringing with him a Joan of Arc in the shape of a somewhat superannuated village school-teacher. After Gavril Pasha, the governor-general, had been surprised in his house, and the German general von Drygalski Pasha had been quietly arrested, the revolting soldiers placed the old governor in a carriage and sent him to the Turkish frontier under guard of the heroine, who held a dangerous-looking naked sword in her hand.[2]

Their success once assured, the revolutionary leaders again called upon Alexander to take the lead, but the Prince, knowing full well what international complications might result, still hesitated. Karavelov urged him to act, and the rising young Bulgarian politician Stambulov was insistent. " Sire," he said, " the union is made — the revolt is an accomplished fact, past recall, and the time for hesitation is gone by. Two roads lie before Your Highness: the one to Philippopolis and as much farther as God may lead; the other to Sistova, the Danube, and Darmstadt. I counsel you to take the crown the nation offers you." [3] The dilemma was clear. If the Prince assumed the leadership, he would surely bring the wrath of the Russians upon his head. If he refused, he would unquestionably become impossible in Bulgaria, and his ejection would be merely a matter of time. Alexander did the natural thing; he defied the dangers of the future in order to avoid the dangers of the present. A few days later he arrived at the Roumelian capital.

In the European chancelleries the news from the Balkans was received with consternation, for the threat of an acute crisis was immediately scented. Lord Salisbury, the head of the new Conservative cabinet in England, had been one of the exponents of a small Bulgaria at the Congress of Berlin and feared the reopening of the whole Near Eastern question. " Action of Prince of Bulgaria

---

[1] Koch, op. cit., p. 230; Bourchier, loc. cit., p. 111; Fillion, op. cit., pp. 107 ff.; Corti, op. cit., pp. 191–2; British Blue Book, *Turkey*, No. 1 (*1886*), No. 267.

[2] One of the best accounts of the proceedings is given by the German journalist von Mach, op. cit., chapter i; see also Spiridion Gopčević: *Bulgarien und Ost-Rumelien* (Leipzig, 1886), p. 312; James Samuelson: *Bulgaria, Past and Present* (London, 1888), p. 80; Fillion, op. cit , pp. 107 ff.; A. Hulme Beaman: *Stambuloff* (London, 1895), p. 58.

[3] Beaman, op. cit., p. 59. Corti, op. cit., p. 193, minimizes Alexander's hesitation.

very ill advised," he telegraphed to Queen Victoria. "Rising of Macedonia is almost certain; Greece will take the field; there will be great difficulty in keeping the war from spreading and perhaps Turkish Empire itself may be endangered. If he succeeds, he would be only plucking fruit for Russia to eat." In a letter he explained that the whole movement gave Russia a very good weapon against Alexander. It might be doubted whether the German powers would try to save him. England could do little, since Bulgaria was hardly accessible to the English fleet. England should uphold the Treaty of Berlin and discourage the use of force and should, besides, act conjointly with Austria.

The Queen, who was undoubtedly influenced largely by her affection for Alexander, queried whether, since the Bulgarian people desired the union, it would not be best to protest against the violation of the treaty and then accept the accomplished fact. But the prime minister pointed out that England, after insisting on the division of Bulgaria in 1878, could not now take the lead in tearing up the treaty. The wishes of the Bulgarians for union were as well known then as they were now, and the danger of a large Bulgaria had not been diminished, either. If the powers insisted on maintaining the separation, England would have to agree. Still the Queen was not satisfied. She was convinced that the hand of Alexander had been forced by a popular movement, and that the movement could not be in favour of Russia. Besides, in 1878 Bulgaria had been regarded as very pro-Russian. Now all that had been changed.[1]

That the Queen's surmise was correct became clear on September 23, when Tsar Alexander abruptly recalled all Russian officers from the Bulgarian army. This meant that all soldiers above the rank of lieutenant were withdrawn. It will be remembered that Giers had on an earlier occasion expressed the opinion that such action on Russia's part would lead to the immediate downfall of the Prince. For the moment the Tsar's spectacular action served as a notice to the world that Russia thoroughly disapproved of the union, and that Alexander could not count upon Russian support or sympathy. This was, in effect, what the Tsar personally told a Bulgarian delegation which had been sent to him at Copenhagen: "There can be no question whatever of dissolving the union, but as long as you keep your present government, expect from me nothing, nothing, nothing." [2]

The first move of the Russian government was to suggest the meeting of an informal conference of ambassadors at Constantinople to draw up a protest against the violation of the treaty and to consider ways and means of solving the question. This suited even the English cabinet, which, since the Russian attitude had become clear, was gradually adopting a less uncompromising

---

[1] *Letters of Queen Victoria,* III, pp. 690–3.

[2] Beaman, op. cit., p. 75; Corti, op. cit., p. 196. It seems to me very likely that the Russians, from the start, were less interested in revoking the union than in getting rid of the Prince.

stand. Already the ambassador at Constantinople had been instructed that the changes of the Treaty of Berlin should be limited to the personal union and the appointment of the Prince as governor-general of Eastern Roumelia. All attempts to depose Alexander should be resisted.[1]

If the Turks had immediately dispatched troops to Eastern Roumelia, they could probably have driven out the Bulgarians with relative ease, especially while the Bulgarian army was, figuratively speaking, decapitated by the loss of its officers. Von Drygalski had warned the Sultan over and over again of what was coming, but his warnings had been ignored. Now General von der Goltz, head of the German military mission, pressed upon the Sultan the necessity of sending troops immediately. The Grand Vizier approved this policy, and on September 22 the Sultan ordered the troops to march. But the decision was almost at once revoked and the ministry dismissed. Abdul Hamid had changed his mind, apparently thinking that, whatever occurred, the Turks would lose territory, or else believing that England and Austria would save for him what he was unwilling to save for himself.[2] The attitude taken by the Porte in the following weeks was that any solution would be satisfactory if only it retained Turkish suzerainty over Eastern Roumelia.[3]

Prince Alexander was entirely engrossed by the danger of a Turkish invasion during the first few weeks after the revolution. The result was that he failed to appreciate the much greater danger that threatened from Greece and especially from Serbia. The three states Serbia, Bulgaria, and Greece had already become rivals for the Macedonian legacy, which had been snatched from Bulgaria by the Treaty of Berlin. Despite vigorous claims advanced by the Serbs and Greeks to the contrary, the majority of the population was Bulgarian, though much of it was still subject to the Greek Patriarchate and was therefore frequently referred to as Greek. De Laveleye, who made a careful study of the problem at the time, quoted with approval the estimates made by the German geographer Ritter, who reported 1,125,000 Bulgars, 360,000 Turks, 422,000 Serbs, Albanians, and Wallachians, and 60,000 Greeks in the territory. In the period after the Congress of Berlin the Bulgarians had initiated a vigorous propaganda in the whole region. They had been staunchly opposed by the Greeks, co-operating with the Turks, but had, nevertheless, made considerable progress. In both Athens and Belgrade it was assumed that the revolution in Eastern Roumelia would be followed shortly by another rising in Macedonia.[4] Neither the Greeks nor the Serbs were willing to tolerate such an enlargement of

---

[1] *Letters of Queen Victoria*, III, p. 694.

[2] Von Mach, op. cit., p. 14; von der Goltz: *Denkwürdigkeiten*, pp. 126–7.

[3] Radowitz: *Aufzeichnungen*, II, p. 253.

[4] The Macedonian situation is thoroughly discussed in E. de Laveleye: *La Péninsule balkanique*, II, pp. 201 ff. and Annexe 6. The Serbian claims are set forth in Spiridion Gopčević: *Makedonien und Alt-Serbien* (Vienna, 1889), *passim;* and in James G. C. Minchin: *The Growth of Freedom in the Balkan Peninsula* (London, 1886), pp. 94 ff. See also Yvan Koucheff: *Les Conséquences balkaniques du Traité de Berlin et la Bulgarie* (Toulouse, 1928), chapter i.

Bulgaria, which, they maintained, would disturb the balance of power in the Balkans.

The Serbian government mobilized its forces almost immediately and expressed to the Greek representative a desire to co-operate with the government at Athens. King Milan was simply swept away by the popular demand for an advance into Old Serbia and Macedonia. All parties were at one in demanding satisfaction, and this meant not only the conservative Pan-Slav group which followed Ristič, but also the government party, the progressives, with their pro-Austrian program, and even the radical party, whose leader, Pasič, was in exile, preaching the sermon of southern Slav unity and advocating the idea of a Balkan league. No doubt a great many of the younger men, especially the students at Belgrade, accepted the teachings of Pasič, which aimed particularly at blocking any further advance by the Austrians.[1]

The Austrian government was greatly embarrassed by the attitude of the Serbs. Milan had proved to be a loyal, but withal a restless and troublesome, ally. His pro-Austrian policy was unpopular in Serbia and he felt constantly exposed to the danger of a return of Ristič to power. At the same time the growing strength of the radical party was a menace to him. In 1883 a serious revolt had broken out that was put down only with difficulty. Milan himself was evidently convinced that his days were numbered. In his usual cynical manner he wrote to Alexander of Bulgaria in November 1884: "We must support each other, for the peoples of this peninsula have a tendency to change their rulers like their shirts. If you ever have to pack your trunks, you can pass through Belgrade and I will give you part of my luggage, and *vice versa.*" "Don't rely on your Bulgarians; don't believe that they are good and naïve, as you say. They are Slavs, and that explains everything. My Serbs are worth no more, and it is in spite of them and against their will that one must do one's duty." [2]

This correspondence, though illuminating, was innocent enough, but when Milan began to press the Austrian government for financial aid if he were forced to leave Belgrade, the situation became embarrassing in the extreme. Milan came to Vienna in June 1885 and offered to add five articles to the treaty of 1881. These were to provide that the treaty should continue till Milan's son Alexander had attained his majority (in 1894), and that Milan should not abandon the throne until that time, unless the Austrian government desired to put Alexander in his place or take over the principality itself or establish some other dynasty. In effect, Milan was offering to put the whole country under Austrian tutelage. No wonder that Kálnoky could hardly believe what he heard. In any case, he refused to become so deeply involved. Austria did not

---

[1] Driault and Lhéritier, op. cit., IV, pp. 202–6; Fillion, op. cit., pp. 3 ff.; British Blue Book, *Turkey,* No. 1 (*1886*), No. 194.

[2] Corti, op. cit., pp. 174, 177–8.

want to occupy Serbia, but she did want to see Milan maintained on the throne as long as possible.[1]

This awkward matter had hardly been disposed of when the Near Eastern problem was reopened by the Philippopolis revolution. Under the terms of her treaty with Serbia Austria had promised that if Serbia were in a position to make territorial gains in the direction of her southern frontiers, Austria would not oppose such acquisitions, but would use her influence with the other powers to create an attitude favourable to Serbia. Now the Serbs were loudly demanding compensation. What was Austria to do? Kálnoky felt the danger keenly, for, as he wrote to the Austrian ambassador at Berlin, any step that Austria took would be regarded as evidence of an advance to Salonika and would create great excitement in Montenegro, Albania, and Macedonia. In reality it was less the excitement in these countries that Kálnoky feared than the fact that an advance by Serbia into Old Serbia or Macedonia might cut off the Austrian connexion with the Turkish provinces. It was Austria's interest to divert the attention of the Serbs from Turkish territory to Bulgarian territory. If the union with Eastern Roumelia were recognized by the powers, Bulgaria could compensate Serbia by ceding to her the small block of territory about the town of Vidin. If this led to war between the two Balkan states, Austria would not mind. Of course, if Russia supported Bulgaria, the situation would be serious. But Kálnoky seemed to think that Russia could be brought to agree. In any case, he felt that it was essential for Austria to support Milan for fear that otherwise he would be overthrown and succeeded by a Karageorgevič prince who would take up again the Serbian claims to Bosnia.[2]

Milan had immediately hurried to Vienna and urged upon the Austrian goverment the need for doing something. He was not quite clear as to whom he wanted to march against, but he was convinced that the Serbs must march. Kálnoky evidently directed his attention to Bulgarian territory and persuaded him to hold his hand until it had been decided whether or not the Bulgarian union would be recognized by the powers. Milan was told that Austria would not lose Serbia's interests from sight, and that he could count on the friendship of the imperial government. This was enough for the Serbian King, who did not take too seriously the warnings of Kálnoky that Austria would support him only in the attainment of " sensible, justifiable, and realizable wishes " by pacific means, that he would undertake a *coup de tête* on his own responsibility, and that Austria could not " approve " separate military action by Serbia. The Serbian government actually took this as a veiled encouragement and

[1] Pribram: "*Milan IV von Serbien*" (*Historische Blätter*, I, 1921–2), pp. 478–94; Mitis: *Kronprinz Rudolf*, pp. 301 ff.

[2] Corti, op. cit., pp. 198–9; *Die Grosse Politik*, V, Nos. 956, 957; Széchenyi's report, October 2, printed in Bismarck: *Gesammelte Werke*, VIII, pp. 529 ff.

determined to take action as soon as the outcome of the ambassadorial conference at Constantinople was known.[1]

In view of the fact that action by Serbia might lead to far-reaching complications and possibly to war, Kálnoky felt obliged to inform Bismarck of the situation. The chancellor had not taken the Bulgarian business too tragically and had urged the German ambassador at Constantinople to try to drown the whole matter in a flood of ink.[2] When he heard of the Austrian determination to back Serbia at all costs, he became genuinely alarmed. The Austrian attitude he rightly described as a " free pass to the most insane and dangerous Serbian undertakings," and as likely to lead to war with Russia. The Austrian ambassador attempted to deny that Austria had given such encouragement, and assured the chancellor that Austria placed peace with Russia above her interests in Serbian friendship. But Bismarck was sore and warned his interlocutor in a prophetic way: " With the Balkan states no lasting bond can be established. You will suffer the same ingratitude and the same bitter disappointments from Serbia that Russia has suffered in Bulgaria and Roumania. As soon as King Milan, that unreliable, flighty, and sensual man, has enlarged his country through Austria's aid, he will suddenly reveal himself as a Pan-Serb and will fearlessly cast his eyes over your frontier." Perhaps he would lose his throne if he yielded to Austrian pressure and abstained from action. But would not a new dynasty or an anarchical republic so weaken the country that Austria would have less to worry about? The argument was an irrefutable one, but the chancellor knew that the Austrians were too deeply committed. He ended by saying that if the Serbs had to fight, they should fight against Bulgaria and they should do so " en champs clos " without involving other powers.[3]

Bismarck did not underestimate the dangers of the situation and seems, for a moment, to have thought of seeking a rapprochement with England by adopting the program of a personal union between Bulgaria and Eastern Roumelia, which was being put forward by Lord Salisbury. This solution, he thought, would avoid the establishment of a great Bulgaria and would thus circumvent many of the problems which had arisen.[4] There is some indication that the chancellor may have been willing to go even further in establishing contact with London. Since the fall of the Gladstone ministry, in June, the relations between the two governments had become cordial once more. Salisbury and Bismarck had exchanged friendly letters and had returned to a policy of co-operation in colonial matters.[5] It is unlikely that Bismarck intended to go much further in the direction of an understanding with England so long as German relations with Russia continued close and the Three Emperors' Al-

---

[1] Corti, op. cit., pp. 200–1; Die Grosse Politik, V, No. 956; Bismarck: Gesammelte Werke, VIII, pp. 529 ff.

[2] Radowitz: Aufzeichnungen, II, p. 252.

[3] Bismarck: Werke, VIII, pp. 529 ff.; Corti, op. cit., pp. 204–5.

[4] Die Grosse Politik, V, No. 958.

[5] Ibid., IV, Nos. 779–83.

liance was unshaken. But there is a letter of Queen Victoria dated October 6, 1885 in which there is reference to a "most curious, important and secret memorandum," evidently setting forth Bismarck's views. The Queen writes: "It is doubtless very desirable that we should cultivate the most friendly relations with Germany, but Prince Bismarck's views are peculiar and will frequently not accord with ours. For instance, to allow Russia to go to Constantinople is *out* of *the question*. This country would never stand that." [1] These utterances are cryptic and are not a sufficient foundation for the construction of an imposing theory. There is no other evidence as to what passed between Berlin and London at this time. But it is clear that Bismarck was keeping the door open, and that he was probably setting forth an argument that he used frequently later: namely, that Russia should be allowed to advance, not only to Bulgaria, but to Constantinople. Once established there, she would be more vulnerable than ever.

While the international situation was gradually taking shape, the ambassadors at Constantinople were endeavouring to find a formula to meet the needs of the situation. A protest against the violation of the Treaty of Berlin and a condemnation of the revolution was finally worked out and submitted to the Turkish and Bulgarian governments, but when it came to discovering some method of solving the question, difficulties immediately arose. The English had now definitely decided not to allow the dissolution of the union. They advocated personal union as the least objectionable arrangement and stood by their program even under the greatest pressure from the other powers. The Russian view was quite different, for though the Tsar sympathized with the union, he thoroughly disapproved of the methods by which it had been effected, and objected to the union under Prince Alexander. This could not be said officially in so many words, so the Russian minister, Giers, argued that the demands of the Serbs and the Greeks placed the powers before the alternatives of either returning to the *status quo ante* or facing a complete overturn in the Near East and perhaps in Europe. [2] Bismarck was very anxious to avoid any such disaster. He gave up his earlier preference for a personal union and assured Giers at Friedrichsruh that Germany would approve any program agreed to by Russia and Austria. He himself recommended the return to the *status quo ante,* and Kálnoky accepted it. During the conference at Constantinople the representatives of the three empires stood together in their demands and thus came into conflict with the British view. Under the circumstances not much was to be hoped from the efforts of the powers, who were so completely at odds. [3]

---

[1] *Letters of Queen Victoria,* III, p. 698.

[2] Meyendorff: *Correspondance diplomatique de M. de Staal,* I, pp. 262 ff.

[3] *Die Grosse Politik,* V, No. 959; Meyendorff, op. cit., I, pp. 265–73. A detailed account may be found in Joseph V. Fuller: *Bismarck's Diplomacy at its Zenith* (Cambridge, 1922), pp. 28–36.

This was evidently the view of the Serbs. By the middle of October it had become clear that they were meditating an attack on Bulgaria rather than on Turkey. All efforts made by Prince Alexander to come to an agreement with his " friend " Milan had proved vain and the Bulgarians themselves began to concentrate troops on the Serbian frontier. The Serbs had completed all their preparations. They had secured a loan of twenty-five million francs from the Länderbank at Vienna and had concentrated upwards of forty thousand men about Nish and Pirot, opposite the Bulgarian frontier. As soon as it had become clear that the Constantinople Conference would not lead to an agreement, Serbia declared war on Bulgaria (November 13). Milan and Garashanin had no hope of getting compensation through the pacific efforts of Austria and were determined to take care of their own interests. The proclamations which referred to the disturbance of the balance of power in the Balkans, the violation of the Treaty of Berlin, and the asylum granted to Serbian agitators in Bulgaria were meant primarily as camouflage and did not convince anyone.[1]

At the outbreak of the war all the chances of success seemed to be on the side of the Serbians, who were ready to invade Bulgaria and march on Sofia in full force. The Bulgarians, to be sure, were better equipped with rifles and artillery, but their forces were scattered. At Constantinople there had been much talk of inducing the Turks to invade Eastern Roumelia as the best method of restoring the *status quo*. This policy was, as a matter of fact, supported by the Russian ambassador.[2] For this reason Alexander had been obliged to keep the bulk of his forces on the Turkish frontier. Only weak detachments had been sent to defend Sofia. They were, however, able to hold off the Serbians long enough at Slivnitsa, about twenty-five miles from the capital, to enable Alexander and a large part of the army to come up from Roumelia in a series of forced marches. On November 19 a decision was reached after three days of fighting. The Serbs were completely defeated and began to stream back through the Dragoman Pass and across the frontier. On November 26 and 27 the Serbs were again defeated at Pirot, and the advance on Nish was begun. The Serbs were now completely demoralized. They were pursued by overwhelming numbers of the enemy and were practically out of ammunition. Whatever may have been said later, the fact is that they could not possibly have continued. The Bulgarian officers, who had been suddenly promoted from lieutenants to captains, majors, and colonels, had done credit to their former Russian instructors.

Ever since the defeat at Slivnitsa King Milan had been appealing to Kálnoky to bring about a cessation of hostilities through an intervention by the powers. As he suffered further reverses, he became mad with desperation and tearfully begged the Austrian minister, Count Khevenhüller, for Austrian intervention. Kálnoky had urged moderation on Alexander and had pressed the Porte to

---

[1] Mijatovich: *Memoirs of a Balkan Diplomatist*, pp. 52–3.
[2] Edwards: *Sir William White*, p. 232; Baddeley: *Russia in the " Eighties,"* p. 261.

propose an armistice. Since nothing had come of these attempts, the Austrian minister was obliged to intervene, in view of what had gone before. Count Khevenhüller was therefore sent to pursuade the Prince of Bulgaria that, in order to avoid Austrian intervention, which might lead to action by the powers, he should desist from advancing further. Khevenhüller was not to threaten, but in a postscript to his instructions he was told that, if necessary, he was to declare categorically to Alexander that he would become involved in conflict with Austria if he did not follow what was still friendly advice.[1]

Khevenhüller arrived at the Bulgarian headquarters on the morning of November 28. After an hour's argument he failed to convince Alexander that an armistice should be granted unconditionally. It was then that he resorted to extreme measures, telling the Prince " that if he intended to wage a war of conquest, he would be able to do so only at an enormous sacrifice of life, and, he added, in that case Austrian troops would enter Serbia, which would be the signal for the occupation of Bulgaria by the Russians, a step which would cost him his throne." Thereupon Alexander, naturally enough, agreed to a cessation of hostilities.[2]

The Austrian démarche certainly relieved the tension between Serbia and Bulgaria for the time being, but it had serious effects on the international situation. The Russians were very much irritated by Khevenhüller's reference to a possible Russian occupation of Bulgaria, for which he had no authority. They feared that the Austrian threat to march into Serbia might be only a preliminary to the invasion itself. Kálnoky gave assurances that no such action was contemplated, but it remained to be seen whether the Austrian declarations were sincere or, assuming that they were, whether Austria could stand by her decision. In Vienna there was still much apprehension lest the Bulgarians should resume the campaign and lest the Serbians could not be induced to accept their defeat as definitive. Men like the Crown Prince Rudolf were convinced that in the end the Austro-Russian antagonism could be settled only by war. Austria should vigorously support the Bulgarian union and induce Bulgaria to make a cession of territory to Serbia. The Greeks should be promised something and the Roumanians should be baited with the prospect of acquiring Bessarabia. With the Balkan states friendly, Austria would be able to devote herself wholeheartedly to the Russian problem. Kálnoky's reply stressed the uncertainty of Balkan friendships and emphasized the fact that in a conflict with Russia the position of Germany would be of key importance. But Germany would not approve a sudden change of the policy thus far pursued by the three empires. Austria might find herself isolated, and, said Kálnoky in closing: " One thing

---

[1] Corti, op. cit., pp. 222–8.

[2] Khevenhüller's own account to Mr. Wyndham, the British minister to Belgrade (*Turkey*, I, *1886*, No. 560); see also Corti, op. cit., pp. 228–9; *Die Grosse Politik*, V, No. 966; A. von Huhn: *The Struggle of the Bulgarians for National Independence* (London, 1886), pp. 252–3; Fillion, op. cit., pp. 300 ff.

the monarchy would not be able to survive, and that would be defeat at the hands of Russia, a Slavic power." [1]

Kálnoky was certainly right in thinking that a forward policy would not meet with approval in Berlin. Bismarck was enraged with the action of the Austrians, which, he feared, might lead to trouble with Russia. In violent terms he castigated the blindness, obstinacy, and insanity of the Austrians for allowing the Serbs to make war, when it was clear that their enterprise would lead to disaster. When Kálnoky explained his position and pointed out that the mission of Khevenhüller was necessary to stop the shedding of blood, the German chancellor noted cynically that this sentiment would be fine for the British parliament, but was not in keeping with the Austrian tradition. The intervention, he insisted, was a great mistake, for the Bulgarians, lacking provisions, exposed to the cold, and menaced by guerrilla warfare, could not have gone much farther in any case. Both sides would have worn each other out, Serbia would then have been more dependent than ever on Austrian support, and Bulgaria would not have been estranged.[2]

Bismarck, while condemning the Austrian policy during the war, was quite as staunchly opposed to all suggestions that Austria march into Serbia in case of necessity. He could not see why Austria should desire a strong and enlarged Serbia, which would exert an ever greater magnetic influence over the Slavs within the monarchy. Besides, such action on Austria's part would undoubtedly bring Russia upon the scene. He reminded Kálnoky that under the terms of the Three Emperors' Alliance Austria was obliged not only to keep Russia informed of her plans, but to reach a special agreement with Russia before taking action. Kálnoky argued that Austria was not planning a change in the *status quo territorial* or a permanent occupation of Serbia, to which Bismarck replied that even a temporary occupation would be a breach of the *status quo*. He asked whether Austria would be willing to permit a temporary Russian occupation of Roumania, Bulgaria, Serbia, or Constantinople. Once again he urged upon Kálnoky the desirability of a demarcation of spheres of influence. But above all he warned Austria that she must not reckon on German support for her forward policy.[3]

Bismarck's strong stand removed the danger of Austrian action and gave the Near Eastern situation an opportunity to calm down. Kálnoky refused to accept the chancellor's repeated suggestions for the delimitation of spheres, but agreed that it would be better to await developments and to allow the English to take the lead. In the meanwhile Alexander, after another vain attempt to conciliate

---

[1] Mitis: *Kronprinz Rudolf*, pp. 312 ff.; Corti, op. cit., p. 230; *Die Grosse Politik*, V, Nos. 967, 968.

[2] Karl Schünemann: " *Die Stellung Österreich-Ungarns in Bismarcks Bündnispolitik* " (*Archiv für Politik und Geschichte*, VII, pp. 118–52, 1926), pp. 120–4, quoting unpublished German documents.

[3] *Die Grosse Politik*, V, Nos. 969–72; Corti, op. cit., p. 233; Mittnacht: *Erinnerungen*, pp. 43 ff.; Schünemann, loc. cit.

the Tsar, opened negotiations with the Turks for a settlement of the Roumelian problem. Even Russia had come to see that a simple return to the *status quo* would be impossible. Negotiations on the basis of a personal union were resumed at Constantinople. The Sultan was willing to invest Alexander with the governor-generalship of Roumelia every five years, but the Prince insisted on a hereditary or at least lifelong investiture. Russia demanded that Alexander should not be mentioned by name in any case, and insisted that the investiture should be in the name of the Prince of Bulgaria. Finally, in April 1886, an agreement was signed by which the Prince of Bulgaria was named governor-general of Eastern Roumelia for five years. Since the Salisbury cabinet had given way to another Gladstone cabinet (February 6, 1886), the British government had not pressed the Bulgarian claims with the same vigour, but had tried to conciliate the Russians. The result was that the Russians secured the recognition of the union on their own terms.

There was a very good reason why the St. Petersburg government desired to avoid the mention of Alexander by name in the agreement with the Turks. The Russians had by no means become reconciled to him and were as determined as ever to get rid of him if possible. The settlement of the Roumelian question supplied an excellent opportunity, for there was much dissatisfaction with the terms in Bulgaria, and the Russian nationalist press spared no pains to point out that Alexander had accepted the overlordship of the infidel. " The protocol of April 5 was my political death-warrant," wrote Alexander himself, after his fall.[1] Prince Nicholas of Montenegro was warmly received in St. Petersburg, and there were rumours that, after the expulsion of Alexander, he was to become the head of a large Slavic state in the Balkans.[2] For a time it was feared in Berlin that the Russians would go so far as to invade Bulgaria themselves, and Bismarck was already facing the question of how Austria could be made to remain quiet until the English took the lead. Evidently, however, both the Tsar and Giers were opposed to so radical a solution.[3]

Alexander tried to counteract these intrigues by working for an understanding with Roumania. In fact, it is said that he offered King Carol the Dobruja if Roumania would help Bulgaria to acquire Macedonia. This agreement was to be the first step towards the organization of a Balkan league.[4]

It may be doubted whether the Bulgarian political leaders were initiated into these schemes and whether they approved of them if they were. Alexander was not so popular as one might have expected after his victories. A number of the officers were at odds with him, the more so after he had upbraided one of them for engaging the Serbs against orders, despite the fact that the action

[1] *Letters of Queen Victoria,* Third Series, Volume I (New York, 1930), pp. 208 ff.

[2] Corti, op. cit., pp. 250–2.

[3] Ponsonby: *Letters of the Empress Frederick,* p. 205; Schweinitz: *Denkwürdigkeiten,* II, pp. 315, 319.

[4] Radowitz, op. cit., II, p. 264; Bourchier, loc. cit.

resulted in victory. Even those who had no personal grudge to nurse had, many of them, come to feel that Russia must be reconciled and that this result could be attained only by getting rid of the Prince. Karavelov and Stambulov went to the Russian agent in July 1886 to see if they could prepare the ground for a resumption of friendly relations, but they were met with the usual definite reply: no reconciliation was possible so long as Alexander remained on the throne.[1]

It was then that a large number of officers organized a conspiracy to get rid of Alexander. The complicity of the Russian government cannot be proved, but the Russian minister Kojander and the military attaché Sacharov are said to have been among the chief promoters.[2] On the plea that the Serbians were rearming, these officers, including some of the most prominent military leaders of the country, induced Alexander to send several loyal regiments from the capital. The plotters then had a free hand. Their secret was marvellously well kept and it was not until the last minute that Alexander was warned of what was going on. The Prince ignored the warnings, for he was convinced that the activity of the Russian intriguers was rather letting up.[3]

On the night of August 20 the Struma regiment, the chief support of the conspirators, marched more than twenty miles in a pouring rain to the capital. It was after midnight when the mutineers arrived. They surrounded the palace and announced their presence by firing off a salvo. In the palace everything was in commotion, the Prince and his attendants running about, half-dressed, with candles in their hands. After slipping hastily into his uniform Alexander met the leaders of the revolt in the lower hall. He noticed that several of the soldiers and cadets who crowded about him and pushed their pistols into his face were more than slightly intoxicated. They demanded his abdication, which one of them scribbled off so carelessly that he could hardly read it himself for all the blots. Alexander signed the paper on the back of a stooping officer and added the words: " God save Bulgaria." He was then taken to the ministry of war and from there was transported under guard to the Danube, put aboard his yacht, and landed, several days later, at Reni, in Russian territory. There he was liberated. He took train and on August 28 arrived at Lemberg in Galicia.[4]

---

[1] Radev I, p. 790; Kutschbach, op. cit., pp. 303 ff.

[2] Radev, op. cit., I, p. 811; Bourchier, loc. cit.; R. Léonoff: *Documents secrets de la politique russe en Orient 1881–1890*, pp. 100 ff.; *Letters of Queen Victoria*, I, pp. 191–2.

[3] Fillion, op. cit., pp. 319 ff.; Corti, op. cit., p. 261; British Blue Book, *Turkey*, No. I (*1887*), No. 261; Alexander's letters in *Letters of Queen Victoria*, I, pp. 199, 208 ff.

[4] The best accounts of the kidnapping are those given by Alexander himself at Lemberg to his friend Koch (Adolf Koch: *Fürst Alexander von Bulgarien*, Darmstadt, 1887, pp. 268 ff.), and soon afterwards to Queen Victoria (*Letters of Queen Victoria*, Series III, I, pp. 199, 208 ff.), and to the Earl of Carnarvon (Sir Arthur Hardinge: *Life of the Earl of Carnarvon*, [London, 1925], III, p. 237). An almost identical account is given by the German correspondent A. von Huhn: *The Kidnapping of Prince Alexander of Battenberg* (London, 1887), pp. 29 ff. See also an anonymous article: " The Kidnapping of Prince Alexander " (*Quarterly Review*, October 1886), and the ac-

The military leaders of the revolt evidently had no very definite plan as to what should be done after Alexander had been got rid of. The civil authorities were loath to take the responsibility, and it was only after a demonstration before the legation and assurances from the Russian representative that Bulgaria could rely on the Tsar's continued sympathy that an extremely Russophil provisional government was formed under the Metropolitan Clement and the liberal leader Zankov. Even this government showed little stability. In Eastern Roumelia there was much discontent with the proceedings at Sofia, and when the nationalist leader Stambulov began to organize a counter-revolution at Trnovo, the troops at Philippopolis immediately joined and most of the provincial regiments followed suit. The loyal soldiers began to march on the capital. Only the surrender of the revolutionists prevented the outbreak of civil war.

For many days the Prince's whereabouts were completely unknown. It was only at Lemberg that he was reached by Stambulov's message asking him to return. His decision was easily made, though even then he did not intend to stay in Bulgaria more than a short time. The situation with regard to the army made everything uncertain.[1] As he said later to the British representative, he returned to Bulgaria " in order that he might be able to leave it by the light of day, instead of being dragged like a malefactor through the streets in the dead of night, and also that he might leave as a friend rather than as an enemy of the country." [2]

Alexander arrived at Ruschuk on August 28 and was surprised to find the Russian consul awaiting him. A few hours later Shatokhin asked to be received in audience. He came in full evening dress, and said that he had been sent by his government to inform the Prince that Prince Dolgoruki was already on his way to take over the government of Bulgaria and Eastern Roumelia in the name of the Tsar. This was a veiled declaration of war on Alexander. In view of the uncertainty in the country and the unreliability of the army, Dolgoruki would have had an easy time. " The populace would have grovelled in the dust before the Imperial Envoy; it would have been an ignominious end of everything," reported Alexander's brother to Queen Victoria. Action was urgent, and Alexander finally decided to appeal directly to the Tsar. He drew up a telegram, which he asked the Russian consul to send in cipher. In it he thanked the Tsar for his intention to send a high official to report on the situation and then threw himself on the Tsar's mercy: " Russia gave me my crown; I am ready to return it into the hands of her sovereign."

But the Prince made a fatal mistake in hoping to soften the heart of the

count of the French correspondent Fillion: *Entre Slaves* (Paris, 1894), pp. 319 ff., and Kutschbach: *Der Brandherd Europas*, pp. 306 ff. The report of the acting British representative is very similar (*Turkey*, No. I, *1887*, No. 261).

[1] Koch, op. cit., p. 275; *Letters of Queen Victoria*, I, pp. 204–5.
[2] *Turkey*, No. I, *1887*, No. 298.

Tsar by this appeal. The reply, when it came, was uncompromising: "Cannot approve your return to Bulgaria, foreseeing disastrous consequences to the country, already so severely tried." It was practically an ultimatum, an invitation to Alexander to leave the country before he was ejected. The Prince was convinced that the appearance of Shatokhin and the story of the Dolgoruki mission was all part of a ruse to make him withdraw. Of the Tsar's unalterable hostility there could be no further doubt. The situation in Bulgaria itself left no hope for the future without Russian support. The army was largely disaffected, the clergy was on the side of the Russians, the civilians were not dependable, and there was, so the Prince thought, real danger of a Russian occupation of the country. He was convinced that if he stayed, he would be assassinated. He therefore rejected the efforts made by Stambulov and others to induce him to remain. On September 7 he formally abdicated and left Bulgaria. With his abdication the first stormy chapter in the history of the new Bulgaria came to a close. A new phase of the Near Eastern question began.[1]

It is difficult to see how Alexander could have acted differently. Partly through his own shortcomings and mistakes, but chiefly because of the hostility of Russia, his position had become an utterly untenable one. The Russians were convinced that Bulgaria was a legitimate sphere of influence for them. It was one of the few advantages that had been derived from the abominable Treaty of Berlin. On the other hand, Alexander devoted himself to the interests of Bulgaria, and these interests, clearly, were not always in consonance with those of Russia. The conflict was inevitable, but so was its outcome, for the Prince could not hope to resist the weight and power of Russia for any length of time. His efforts to maintain himself only made him the object of greater hatred. "That unfortunate young man," said Giers to the British ambassador on the very day of Alexander's abdication, "has become, in the eyes of the Russian people, the incarnation and embodiment of everything which most deeply stirs the national indignation. He represents, in the first place, the untold ingratitude of the Bulgarians for their deliverers, and reminds them of the losses of blood and treasure incurred in a war which yielded no other results but disappointments. In the second place, he reminds them of all the humiliations submitted to in the Constantinople Conference and since. Lastly, he represents the hopes and desires of Russia's enemies. Never, therefore, could there be peace between him and the Russian people."[2]

The ambassador replied that the English people took a very different view. They "regarded His Highness as a Prince who had striven to the best of his abilities to create a free and orderly community in the territories committed to

---

[1] I have followed closely the account given Queen Victoria by Alexander's brother, who was with him at the time (*Letters of Queen Victoria*, I, pp. 204–5). See also Alexander's explanations to the British representative (*Turkey*, No. I, *1887*, Nos. 277, 278, 280, 284, 298), and to Valentine Chirol, who accompanied him as he left Sofia (Chirol: *Fifty Years in a Changing World* [London, 1928], pp. 123 ff., and Corti, op. cit., pp. 272 ff.).

[2] *Turkey*, No. I, *1887*, No. 295.

his charge, and they had throughout wished him success in his arduous under-taking." This statement was but a mild reflection of the sentiments of Queen Victoria and Lord Salisbury. The Queen, when she heard of the kidnapping, was beside herself. She wrote to the prime minister of " these Russian fiends," and about " the monstrous revolution brought about by Russian villainy." To Alexander himself: " My horror and rage against your barbarous, Asiatic-minded, tyrannical cousin [the Tsar] are so great that I cannot trust myself to write about it." From the beginning she insisted that " England must speak out and be firm." " This is the stepping stone to getting Constantinople." " Rus-sia is intriguing right and left and we must not tamely swallow everything with a mere protest. Russia sets us at defiance." " Russia must be unmasked."

Lord Salisbury shared the Queen's indignation. He considered the conduct of Russia " simply piratical." But he was a cautious man and pointed out to Victoria that, after all, there was no proof of the complicity of the Russian gov-ernment. England, he explained, was always at a disadvantage in a case of this sort, because, without adequate secret-service money, without a large army, with a rigid diplomatic régime, she could not compete with Russia in the field of subterranean activity and could not back up her policy with the threat of military action. The government was therefore obliged to restrain its desire to act. Efforts were made to induce the Austrians to take a strong stand against a Russian occupation of Bulgaria, while the English cabinet itself warned Russia that an invasion might lead to the mission of the English fleet to the Black Sea. The other powers were invited to enter upon an exchange of views as to what should be done. Bismarck, however, discouraged these plans. Even within the British cabinet there were dissentient voices, and so this policy was dropped. But the events of August 1886 drove England into a more clearly defined antagonism to Russia. It was hoped that Austria would stand by. On the other hand, Bismarck insisted on leaving the Russians a free hand. The setting was complete for the crisis of 1887.[1]

BIBLIOGRAPHICAL NOTE

DOCUMENTARY SOURCES

Accounts and Papers. 1886, Volume LXXV. *Turkey*, No. 1 (*Correspondence respecting the Affairs of Eastern Roumelia and Bulgaria*); *Turkey*, No. 2 (*Further Correspondence, etc.*). *1887*, Volume XCI. *Turkey*, No. 1 (*Further Correspondence, etc.*). These British Blue Books are very extensive and are of great value for a study of events in Bulgaria and Eastern Roumelia from the time of the union.

---

[1] *Letters of Queen Victoria*, I, pp. 178 ff., 191–8; Corti, op. cit., pp. 266, 271–2.

Documents diplomatiques. Affaires de Roumélie et de Grèce, 1885–1886. Paris, 1886.

Documenti diplomatici presentati al parlamento. Rumelia Orientale. Serie I (1885); serie II (1886).

Die Grosse Politik der europäischen Kabinette. Volume III: chapter xvi (Renewal of the Austro-German Alliance, 1883), xvii (Treaty with Roumania), xviii (Renewal of the Three Emperors' Alliance), xix (German-Russian Relations, 1884). Volume V: chapter xxx (Eastern Roumelian Question and the Serbian-Bulgarian War), xxxi (German-Russian Relations, 1886).

Documents secrets de la politique russe en Orient, 1881–1890. Published by R. Léonoff. Berlin, 1893. Stolen documents from the Russian consulate at Ruschuk, throwing light on the activities of the Russian agents. The documents appear to be genuine.

MEMOIRS, AUTOBIOGRAPHIES, BIOGRAPHIES, AND LETTERS

The Letters of QUEEN VICTORIA. Edited by George E. Buckle. Series II, Volume III; Series III, Volume I. Of great interest.

Denkwürdigkeiten des Botschafters GENERAL VON SCHWEINITZ. Two volumes. Berlin, 1927. A valuable supplement to the German documents.

Correspondance diplomatique de M. DE STAAL, *1884–1900.* Edited by Baron A. Meyendorff. Two volumes. Paris, 1929. Contains relatively little of interest, as Staal was not at his post during the most critical moments.

MITIS, OSKAR: *Das Leben des Kronprinzen Rudolf.* Leipzig, 1928. Based upon unpublished papers, this volume throws much light on the political views of the Crown Prince.

FRIEDJUNG, HEINRICH: " *Graf Kálnoky* " (*Biographisches Jahrbuch,* III, 1900, pp. 359–80; reprinted with some changes in the author's *Historische Aufsätze,* Stuttgart, 1919). The best biographical study of Kálnoky.

MIJATOVICH, COUNT CHEDOMILLE: *Memoirs of a Balkan Diplomatist.* London, 1917. The reminiscences of the Serbian foreign minister.

KOCH, ADOLF: *Fürst Alexander von Bulgarien.* Darmstadt, 1887. The author was very close to Alexander, and his book is still one of the best accounts.

KLAEBER, HANS: *Fürst Alexander I von Bulgarien.* Dresden, 1904. A careful scholarly work, with emphasis on the military side.

CORTI, COUNT EGON C.: *Alexander von Battenberg. Sein Kampf mit den Zaren und Bismarck.* Vienna, 1920. This volume is based upon Alexander's private papers and is one of the most important contributions to the subject.

Aus dem Leben KÖNIG KARLS VON RUMÄNIEN. Four volumes. Stuttgart, 1900. The papers of King Carol, covering the period to 1881 and containing interesting information on the first stages of the rapprochement with the central powers, as well as on the course of events in Bulgaria.

BOURCHIER, JAMES D.: " Prince Alexander of Battenberg " (*Fortnightly Review,* Volume LXI, pp. 103–18, January 1894). Written by a famous English correspondent in the Near East.

SPECIAL STUDIES

RADEV, SIMEON: *Stroitelite na Sovremenna Blgarija.* Two volumes. Sofia, 1910–11. A standard work, based upon the extensive use of Bulgarian official and unofficial material.

SKAZKIN, S.: *Konets avstro-russko-germanskogo soiuza.* Moscow, 1928. The best account from the Russian side, based on all published material and on unpublished Russian documents.

KOJOUHAROFF, CONSTANTINE: *Istochniyat Upros u Blgarija, 1875–1890.* Sofia, 1929.

FILLION, GEORGES: *Entre Slaves.* Paris, 1894. One of the most interesting and best-informed accounts, written by a French journalist.

HUHN, MAJOR A. VON: *The Struggle of the Bulgarians for National Independence.* London, 1886.

—: *The Kidnapping of Prince Alexander of Battenberg.* London, 1887. Written by a German correspondent.

DRANDAR, A. G.: *Les Événements politiques en Bulgarie.* Brussels, 1896. Very hostile to Alexander. A rather racy book that is not wholly reliable.

MACH, RICHARD VON: *Aus bewegter Balkanzeit, 1879–1918.* Berlin, 1928. The experiences of a German in Alexander's service.

PROTITCH, STOJAN: " The Secret Treaty between Servia and Austria-Hungary " (*Fortnightly Review,* Volume XCI, pp. 838–48, May 1909). The first revelation of the secret treaty, written by a Serbian statesman. Substantially correct.

PRIBRAM, ALFRED F.: " *Milan IV von Serbien und die Geheimverträge Österreich-Ungarns mit Serbien, 1881–1889* (*Historische Blätter,* Volume I, 1921-2, pp. 464–94). An article of fundamental importance, based upon the Austrian archives.

FULLER, JOSEPH V.: *Bismarck's Diplomacy at its Zenith.* Cambridge, 1922. A very thorough-going and detailed study of Bismarck's diplomacy from 1885 to 1888, based upon all the material then available.

BENNECKE, HEINRICH: *Bulgarien in der Politik Bismarcks bis zur Thronbesteigung Ferdinands von Coburg.* Dresden, 1930. A conventional doctoral dissertation.

XI

The Crisis of 1887

〜

BEFORE THE NEWS OF THE KIDNAPPING OF PRINCE ALEXANDER REACHED the European capitals, the situation had been fairly quiet. The difficulties between Serbia and Bulgaria had been ironed out, at least for the time being. Under pressure from the powers the two Balkan antagonists had been induced to conclude one of the briefest peace treaties of which there is record: " Peace is restored between Serbia and Bulgaria " (March 3, 1886).[1] Soon afterward the problem of the Greek claims was settled by an international blockade of the Greek coast, instituted after repeated though futile attempts had been made by the powers to induce the Greeks to disarm and desist from further preparations for a campaign against Turkey.[2]

The startling reports of the happenings at Sofia brought the relative calm of the summer months to an abrupt close. Liberal opinion throughout Europe, which had no sympathy whatever for the Russian autocracy or its designs, felt outraged by the abominable treatment meted out to Alexander, for no doubt was felt that the Russian government was the power behind the plot. Queen Victoria's sentiments were shared fully by the governing circles of Vienna, though the personal element was not, with the Austrians, the decisive one.[3]

It was not to be expected, however, that even the powers which resented most the Russian policy in the Balkans would provoke a conflict for the sake of Alexander alone. At the moment the logical policy was to await further developments. Nor did they have to wait long, for the Tsar had been prepared to send his friend Prince Dolgoruki to Bulgaria ever since the news of the kidnapping had reached him. Because of Alexander's return nothing had come of this projected mission, but the Prince had hardly abdicated when General Kaulbars, brother of the notorious Bulgarian war minister of 1883, arrived in Sofia to advise the three regents and to ascertain the wishes of the Bulgarian people. It appears that the mission was the idea of the Tsar himself,

---

[1] See the account of the protracted negotiations by the Serbian delegate in Chedomille Mijatovich: *The Memoirs of a Balkan Diplomatist*, pp. 58 ff.

[2] Driault and Lhéritier: *Histoire diplomatique de la Grèce*, IV, pp. 212–26; Sir Horace Rumbold: *Final Recollections of a Diplomatist* (London, 1905), chapters iv–vi; Comte Charles de Moüy: *Souvenirs et causeries d'un diplomate* (Paris, 1909), chapter vi; *Letters of Queen Victoria*, Series III, Volume I, pp. 45 ff., 77 ff., 111, 123, 140.

[3] Corti, op. cit., pp. 277, 286; Alfred E. Gathorne-Hardy: *Gathorne-Hardy* (London, 1910), Volume II, p. 262; Meyendorff, op. cit., I, pp. 304 ff.

who was evidently convinced, as were most Russians, that the Bulgarians were at heart thoroughly Russophil and had merely been led astray by the intrigues and machinations of Battenberg.

The very opposite proved to be the truth, for the attitude of Stambulov, the leader of the regency, was much more uncompromisingly hostile to the Russian influence than Alexander's had ever been. Ignoring the advice of Kaulbars and the pressure brought to bear by him, the Bulgarian government arranged for the convocation of the national assembly and made efforts, in secret, to induce Alexander to return once more to the uncomfortable throne. At the same time the Russian emissary made a tour of the country, attempting to arouse the population in Russia's favour. He declared in advance that his government would not recognize the legality of the national assembly or any of its decisions, and, as the tension grew greater yet, he summoned two gunboats to Varna, on the plea that those who sympathized with Russia needed protection. In spite of all, the assembly met at Trnovo on October 27 and elected to the throne Prince Waldemar of Denmark, a relative of the Tsar. After consultation with the Russian government the Prince rejected the offer. Soon afterwards, on November 17, Kaulbars and all the Russian consuls left the country. Diplomatic relations were ruptured and the tension between Russia and Bulgaria reached the highest pitch.

In Vienna and London the activities of Kaulbars were watched with the greatest uneasiness. Here, it was felt, was irrefutable proof of the extent and aggressive character of Russian policy. Both powers felt strongly on the subject, and it was only natural that they should make some effort to reach an agreement for common action if the occasion arose. Even before the abdication of Alexander the Austrian ambassador at London had suggested to the British foreign minister that any proposal for a secret Anglo-Austrian understanding would be favourably received at Vienna. At the same time he suggested that the British position in these matters was freer than that of Austria, and that therefore England should take the initiative. The British minister replied that taking the initiative would be of little use if no one followed. The subject of an accord was, however, broached again and again during September and October, though no positive result was obtained. No wonder Sir Charles Dilke found it laughable that Austria should declare " that she would be delighted to take the first step, as Lord Salisbury proposes, if Lord Salisbury will begin by taking the second." [1]

The project of an Anglo-Austrian accord was bound to meet with these difficulties, just as in 1877–8, for the fact that both these powers wished to block the Russian advance was not sufficient to establish a policy of co-operation. The Austrians were interested chiefly in checking the spread of Russian influence in

---

[1] Sir Charles Dilke: *The Present Position of European Politics* (London, 1887), p. 23; on these earlier negotiations see W. N. Medlicott: " The Mediterranean Agreements of 1887 " (*Slavonic Review*, V, June 1926, pp. 68 ff.); *Letters of Queen Victoria*, I, pp. 220–2.

the Balkans. If their policy were to lead to a conflict with Russia, the attack would come on the Galician front, where the British navy would be of very little use. On the other hand, the English were more concerned with Russia's ultimate designs on the Straits, control of which would involve the closing of the Black Sea and a threat at England's connexions with India. The Austrian armies could be of immense value to the English in any conflict with Russia, and for that very reason the Austrians were bound to be cautious; they could not afford to be sent into the fire for British interests, the more so as they were never able to free themselves from the idea that "perfidious Albion" would leave them in the lurch. Bismarck was an ardent advocate of an Anglo-Austrian understanding, as he had been in 1878, but his unchanging view was that Austria must leave the initiative to England and wait patiently until the Russians were engaged in the Balkans, after which the great advantages of Austria's geographical position would make themselves felt automatically.[1]

Queen Victoria complained constantly that the English government was doing too little, and that it ought to come out much more strongly in behalf of dear "Sandro." This opinion, however, was not shared entirely by the cabinet. Even Lord Salisbury, the heir to the Beaconsfield tradition, was unwilling to go too far in supporting the Bulgarians against the Russians. He was determined to act if Constantinople were actually threatened, but excused himself from undertaking anything more. "We are fish," he declared to the German ambassador. It would be up to Austria to defend interests in regions inaccessible to the British fleet. The Chancellor of the Exchequer, Lord Randolph Churchill, went even further and believed that England should work for an understanding with Russia which would secure the Indian frontier at the expense of the Balkans. He told the Russian ambassador as much and objected loudly to an active policy of England on behalf of the Bulgarians. The English could not afford to "rush in where Bismarck feared to tread," and should avoid becoming involved unless Austria not only took the lead, but brought in German support as well: "Our action with Austria means war with Russia; our action with Austria and Germany means peace. We can perfectly defend Constantinople by going in for the independence of Bulgaria, and we can best obtain that independence by persuading Austria to take the lead," he wrote Lord Salisbury. His remarks to the German ambassador came to the same thing. It goes without saying that Bismarck received these disclosures with the greatest scorn. Clearly there was nothing to be expected from England. The important thing for him was to prevent the Austrians' being led astray. It would not do for Austria to try to bell the Russian cat alone, for if a conflict resulted, Germany might very well find herself involved.[2]

---

[1] Schweinitz: *Denkwürdigkeiten*, II, p. 319; *Die Grosse Politik*, IV, Nos. 861 ff.; *Letters of Queen Victoria*, loc. cit.

[2] See *Die Grosse Politik*, IV, Nos. 863 ff.; Winston S. Churchill: *Lord Randolph Churchill*

Kálnoky had no intention of being stampeded into difficulties with Russia. He had come to know Bismarck's attitude only too well and realized that German support would not be forthcoming for any Austrian policy that aimed at contesting Russia's preponderance in Bulgaria. The advice he received from Berlin was the advice he had heard for a long time: to come to an agreement with Russia based on the demarcation of spheres of influence in the Balkans. But for Kálnoky this solution was simply impossible. The opposition to his policy had been growing stronger and stronger, and now, since the abdication of Prince Alexander, the Hungarian element in the monarchy was loudly demanding vigorous action. It was assumed throughout that Germany would support Austria, under the terms of the alliance of 1879. When it was hinted that this was not so, the feeling of dissatisfaction with the alliance became widespread. Germany, it was argued, had held back Austria from occupying Serbia, on the plea that such action would be intolerable to Russia. Now, however, Bismarck's argument was that a Russian occupation of Bulgaria should in no way disturb Austria. What sort of alliance was it in which two of the partners were always united against the third? " Germany has two allies," they complained, " while Austria has only half a one." Kálnoky tried to explain in the council of ministers that Austria, unable to count on the help of either Germany or England, was forced to pursue a dilatory policy, but Tisza, the Hungarian premier, was profoundly irritated. Kálnoky was obliged to promise that if Russia occupied Bulgaria, Austria would take action. Tisza made the most of this concession and proclaimed in the Hungarian parliament on September 30 that " the government stands firmly by its repeatedly expressed opinion that, under the existing treaties, unless Turkey should assert her rights, no power is entitled to undertake any single-handed armed intervention or to set up any protectorate in the Balkan Peninsula." [1]

The strong language of Tisza no doubt encouraged the English to think that, after all, the Austrians would relieve them of the initiative. This belief was clearly reflected in the great speech made by Churchill at Dartford on October 2, and in Salisbury's Guildhall speech of November 9, in which he referred to the conspiracy against Alexander of Bulgaria as a plot of officers " debauched by foreign gold," and spoke of Russia's " encroachment upon the rights of a free and independent people." England, he declared, would perform the duties which devolved upon her as a member of the European confederation in concert with the other powers, " but she will not accept the duty of maintaining these obligations on behalf of others who do not think it necessary to maintain them for themselves." This reference was clearly to Austria and Turkey, for Salisbury went on to state that " the opinion and judgment of

(London, 1906), Volume II, pp. 155 ff.; Corti, op. cit., p. 285; *Letters of Queen Victoria*, I, pp. 201 ff.

[1] Quoted by Joseph V. Fuller: *Bismarck's Diplomacy at its Zenith* (Cambridge, 1922), p. 87. This is the fullest treatment of the international relations of this critical period.

Austria must weigh in the councils of Her Majesty's Government, and the policy which Austria pursues will contribute very largely to determine the policy which England will also pursue." [1]

It was to Austria's interest not to be drawn into complications by these English utterances, and Kálnoky would probably have liked to avoid an extreme stand in his relations to Russia. But the Hungarian opposition, under the leadership of Count Andrássy, was strong and noisy. In the Delegations the Austrian foreign minister was obliged to reply to vicious attacks upon the alliance with Germany and upon the policy of the government. On November 13 he spoke in defence of the alliance of 1879, pointing out that, though Austria and Germany might have certain divergent interests, in fundamentals the connexion of the two countries was sound and unshakable. In regard to the Bulgarian situation, he hoped that England would join Austria if it came to a question of intervening for the maintenance of the Berlin Treaty and the legal status created by it. As for Russian policy, " even a temporary single-handed occupation of Bulgaria by foreign troops, without the previous consent of Turkey and the other powers, would be a violation of the treaties which, in our opinion, is not admissible." As to the extent of Russian control which might be permitted in the final settlement, he could only say " that any appropriation of the self-governing powers of the autonomous principality, or anything approaching a protectorate, would not be admissible." [2]

The declarations of Kálnoky, taken together with the Russophobe utterances of Andrássy, brought on the most acute phase of the Austro-Russian tension. At St. Petersburg deep indignation was felt at the insinuations of Salisbury, but the Austrian speeches were so extreme that everything else was forgotten. The Tsar, who was directly responsible for the mission of Kaulbars, felt personally insulted. Russian opinion was humiliated and enraged to find that, even after the removal of Battenberg, Russia was helpless in Bulgaria. The diplomats went even further and talked of " displacing the Bulgarian question." Like the Austrians, they complained of Bismarck, arguing that Austria would never have dared to take such a stand unless certain of ultimate German support. " It is absolutely necessary that we should make Austria disappear from the map of Europe," said the Russian ambassador at Berlin. That the Three Emperors' Alliance was a thing of the past was an opinion on which all Russians were agreed. [3]

Bismarck's position in the dispute was a very uncomfortable one. Just because he had always feared the clash of Russian and Austrian interests in the

---

[1] Fuller, op. cit., pp. 93, 107.

[2] Ibid., pp. 108–9. The conflict between Andrássy and Kálnoky is discussed in Wertheimer: *Andrássy*, III, pp. 329 ff.; and in Heinrich Friedjung: " *Graf Kálnoky* " (*Biographisches Jahrbuch*, III, 1900, pp. 359–80).

[3] *Die Grosse Politik*, V, Nos. 989 ff., 1021–2; Meyendorff, op. cit., I, pp. 319–24; Schweinitz: *Denkwürdigkeiten*, II, p. 325.

Balkans, he had made a special point of constructing and maintaining the Alliance of the Three Emperors. Now everything was in jeopardy, and Germany, in Bismarck's words, was standing between Austria and Russia like a man between two vicious dogs, who would fly at each other as soon as they were unleashed.[1] With his idea of a demarcation of spheres of influence nothing more could be done, but he was still determined to act as mediator between his two allies and to hold the balance between them. To the Austrians he repeated over and over again that the alliance of 1879 was a defensive one, and that he would not allow the power of Germany to be enlisted by Austria for a provocative forward policy in the Balkans, where Germany had no interests of her own: "We have no intention of allowing ourselves to be bound by the alliance to the tail of the Hungarian comet, but to establish a regular orbit of calculable dimensions."[2] Austria, according to the German chancellor, had no reason to oppose a Russian occupation of Bulgaria, for the Alliance of the Three Emperors had at least tacitly assigned Bulgaria to the Russian sphere. In any case, under the terms of this agreement Austria was obliged to consult her allies before taking action.

While doing his utmost to hold back the Austrians, Bismarck devoted his efforts to reassuring the Russians. He put aside the suggestions which came to him from Russian diplomats and refused to abandon Austria to the mercies of the Tsar. On the contrary, he kept insisting that Germany must stand behind Austria if the position of the latter as a world power were seriously menaced. At the same time he was willing to recognize the Russian claims in Bulgaria *sans phrase* and to approve in advance any action which the Russians decided to take. He hoped that they would not attempt an occupation of the country, because this would strain their relations with Austria to the breaking-point. But if an occupation were decided upon, Russia could reckon on the goodwill of Germany. In fact, Germany would even support Russian designs which aimed at the control of the Straits.[3]

There was nothing novel about Bismarck's attitude. He had always devoted himself to the problem of avoiding a conflict with Russia, partly because he dreaded the shock to the monarchical principle, in part because he realized that such a clash would lead inevitably to the reopening of the Polish question, and because he could not see that anything worth while was to be gained even from a victory over Russia, but especially because he was firmly convinced that France would strike just as soon as Germany was deeply engaged in the

---

[1] Lucius von Ballhausen: *Bismarck-Erinnerungen* (Stuttgart, 1920), p. 359.

[2] *Die Grosse Politik*, V, No. 1022. The Austro-German relation is discussed in Fuller, op. cit., and in Heinz Trützschler von Falkenstein: *Bismarck und die Kriegsgefahr des Jahres 1887* (Berlin, 1924), pp. 19–23, as well as in the special studies of Eduard Heller: *Das deutsch-österreichische Bündnis in Bismarcks Aussenpolitik* (Berlin, 1925), pp. 90 ff., and Karl Schünemann: " *Die Stellung Österreich-Ungarns in Bismarcks Bündnispolitik* " (*Archiv für Politik und Geschichte*, VI, pp. 549–94, 1926, and VII, pp. 118–52, 1926).

[3] *Die Grosse Politik*, V, Nos. 992 ff., 1015; VI, Nos. 1206–7.

East. Consideration for the position of France was all the more urgent in the autumn of 1886 because relations between Germany and her neighbour, which had been at least cordial in the time of the Ferry ministry, had begun to cool soon after his overthrow and had become distinctly critical before the end of the year. To make matters worse, from the German view-point, a strong nationalist current in Russia was beginning to demand the severance of the connexion with Germany and the establishment of an understanding with France.

It will be recalled that Ferry's fall from power was due to opposition to his colonial policy, which, it was felt by the royalists and the radicals alike, simply served to weaken France and make her a tool of Germany. That the dissatisfaction of the chamber was shared by the country at large came out clearly in the elections of October 1885, when the royalists and Bonapartists polled 3,500,000 votes as against 1,700,000 in the election of 1881. The new chamber contained about 180 monarchists and about the same number of radicals, while the moderate republicans had only about 220 seats. Freycinet, "the little white mouse," "the silver-tongued serpent," a cautious, quiet little man, but a clever parliamentary tactician, formed the new cabinet, and, at the suggestion of the radical leader, Clemenceau, appointed as minister of war General Georges Boulanger, because he was "the only really radical republican general." [1] The appointment was one of great importance, for before long, Boulanger was to become the symbol of the French revival.

Freycinet began with a ministerial declaration in which he said: "If there is one point on which the ballot-boxes have expressed themselves without ambiguity, it is on the direction to be followed in foreign affairs. It is understood that France is to have a policy of dignity and peace, and that her forces are to be concentrated on the continent, respected by all and menacing none. France desires no more of these distant expeditions, which are a source of sacrifice without any obvious compensation." [2] This utterance was rather ominous, but in no sense threatening. If Freycinet had been able to pursue his policy without opposition, friction would probably have been avoided. As a matter of fact, however, the government was weak, and the country was stirred up. For a period of fully three years there was no knowing how long the existing republican régime would last. Either a monarchical restoration or a radical dictatorship seemed to most people the logical outcome of the situation.

There is no need to discuss here the problems of French domestic politics. It is enough to note the fact that the government was shaky and to stress the fact that the uncertainty of French internal politics had a distinct relationship

---

[1] Freycinet: *Souvenirs,* pp. 329 ff., says that General Campenon, who had resigned from Ferry's cabinet because of disagreement with his foreign policy, recommended Boulanger, but this is not the version given by others concerned. See, e.g., Henri Rochefort: *Les Aventures de ma vie* (Paris, n. d.), Volume V, pp. 3 ff.; Gabriel Terrail: *Les Coulisses du Boulangisme* (Paris, 1890), p. 4.

[2] Quoted by G. P. Gooch: *Franco-German Relations 1871–1914* (London, 1923), p. 24. See also Pierre Albin: *L'Allemagne et la France en Europe, 1885–1894* (Paris, 1913), pp. 23–5.

to the problem of foreign policy. From the very beginning of the Freycinet ministry the government was subjected to strong pressure from the side of the radical patriots, who championed the idea of revenge. Since Gambetta's death their leader was Paul Deroulède, the poet agitator who, after being wounded and captured in the war with Germany, had devoted himself almost entirely to the cause. His first volume of poems, *Chants au soldat,* published in 1872, went through one hundred and fifty-eight editions and was crowned by the French Academy. In 1881 Gambetta, while prime minister, appointed his friend Deroulède to a commission on military and national education, the idea of which was to develop patriotic spirit and military aptitude among the young. Deroulède was convinced that the memory of defeat must be kept alive in order to further the idea of revenge. When his work was discouraged by the Ferry ministry, he came into conflict with the advocate of an understanding with Germany. " I have lost two children, and you offer me twenty domestics," he said bitterly to Ferry.

It was during these years — in May 1882, to be exact — that Deroulède founded the League of Patriots, which was to serve as a connecting link for the numerous gymnastic, rifle, and patriotic societies which had grown up.

The constitution of the league stated explicitly that it existed for the purpose of bringing about the revision of the Treaty of Frankfurt and the return of Alsace and Lorraine. Deroulède afterwards explained in a speech that this end could be attained only by the use of force, and the official organ of the league, *Le Drapeau,* showed no hesitation in saying the same thing over and over again. In fact, the medal of the society showed on one side a gleaming French flag between figures of Metz and Strassburg, with the inscription: " *Qui vive? France,*" and on the reverse the figure of an Alsatian woman supporting a dying soldier and handing his rifle to a figure representing France. The inscription on this side was: " *1870/18 . . . Quand même.*"

It has often been said that Deroulède was a crazy agitator and a fool, but this was certainly not so. Maurice Barrès, the great apostle of modern French nationalism, described him as " a magnificent exciter of men, not one who works in salons and academies, but in the street." [1] The truth of the description is borne out by the record of his activities. In an official report of the league it is stated that by the end of 1885 no less than nine hundred rifle clubs and six hundred gymnastic societies in France were associated with it. A report of April 1885 fixed the membership of the league at eighty-two thousand and summed up the activity of the organization since its foundation as follows: three hundred meetings organized in more than sixty cities; fifty-two regional committees established in the departments; more than 250,000 francs distributed to associated organizations for presents and subsidies; more than 200,000 pamphlets printed; more than 100,000 maps distributed; more than 150,000 medals show-

---

[1] Maurice Barrès: *Scènes et doctrines du nationalisme,* pp. 262–71.

ing Alsace-Lorraine presented. In July 1886 the league was said to have 130,000 members. And the stronger it grew, the more outspoken it became. In January 1885 Deroulède wrote in *Le Drapeau* of the " hole in the Vosges, which hypnotizes us," and asked the pertinent question: " What good is all this formidable military apparatus which is crushing us, if it is not the instrument of victory and liberation? " In a poem of the same year he declared: " France and the French have but one object: to defeat Prussia and the Prussians." No question, Deroulède and his league were a force which could not be ignored, especially by a weak government.[1]

Modern French historians no longer deny that the idea of revenge, the idea of recovering the two lost provinces, existed in France, but they still disclaim all thought of taking the offensive. " French public opinion," says General Franchet d'Esperey, " wished the army to be ready so that when Germany gave the signal, it could not only defend itself, but also efface the shame of defeat." [2] That this was not the case with Deroulède and the active League of Patriots is patent to anyone who examines *Le Drapeau* and other publications of the organization. Deroulède, it is true, was not at this time a member of the government or even of the Chamber of Deputies, but many of the leaders of the league were active in French politics, and Deroulède himself polled 105,000 votes in the elections of October 1885, though he announced his candidacy in Paris at the last minute.[3] Furthermore, he attempted to bring pressure on the new government from the very beginning and had much to do with the spread of Boulanger's reputation. He had known the general since 1883 and had, we are told, talked over with him " the governmental anarchy and the slumber which had fallen upon patriotism." When Boulanger became minister of war, Deroulède immediately went to him and urged him to make the best of his position: " A *coup d'état* must be tried," even though not immediately. He promised the support of the three hundred thousand (!) members of the League of Patriots, who would act as the leaven to the loaf: " The presidency of the republic will be yours in a year, if you know how and if you really desire to will it." Boulanger was duly cautious about committing himself, but the league worked for him nevertheless and, as aforesaid, had much to do with the spread of his popularity throughout France.[4]

In the summer Deroulède made an extensive tour of Europe, concentrating

---

[1] On Deroulède see Jean and Jérôme Tharaud: *La Vie et la mort de Deroulède* (Paris, 1914); Florent Matter: *Paul Deroulède* (Paris, 1909); Camille Ducray: *Paul Deroulède* (Paris, 1914); Chenu: *La Ligue des Patriotes* (Paris, 1916); Anonymous (Moritz Busch): " *Die Patriotenliga* " (*Die Grenzboten*, 1887, II, pp. 280–90); Joachim Kühn: *Der Patriotismus im Leben der dritten Republik* (Berlin, 1922), pp. 20 ff.

[2] Franchet d'Esperey: *Histoire militaire* (in Gabriel Hanotaux: *Histoire de la nation française* [Paris, 1927], Volume VIII), pp. 448–9. See also A. Lajusan, in Henri Hauser: *Histoire diplomatique de l'Europe* (Paris, 1929), Volume I, p. 229.

[3] Ducray, op. cit., p. 159.

[4] Ibid., pp. 162–5.

his attention upon Russia. The object of the tour was to prepare European opinion " for the probable and early rise of a popular chief, destined to regain for France her due rank and rights." In practice it came to a vigorous agitation on behalf of a Franco-Russian alliance against Germany. In an interview published by the *Novoie Vremia,* one of the leading Russian organs, he stated that Germany had inflicted on Russia a moral defeat comparable to the material defeat inflicted on France in 1870. An alliance should be made between the two afflicted powers, " for now, militarily and morally, we are ready for war against Germany." [1]

While Deroulède was attempting to prepare the world for the coming of the French saviour, Boulanger was not idle. He was a man of " indisputable soldierly qualifications, indefatigable energy, quick perceptions, and a bold and inventive mind." But these characteristics were offset by his lack of judgment in political matters, by his want of moderation and tact, and by his inordinate passion for popularity.[2] From the outset he devoted himself to the strengthening of the army, in part by recalling many of the troops engaged in colonial campaigns, in part by various projects of reform. At the same time he joined Clemenceau in his attacks upon royalism, removed royalist regiments from Paris, issued proclamations against the interference of the army in politics, and played a prominent part in the move to expel the princes from France (June 1886). These measures, together with his efforts to improve the lot of the common soldier, made a profound impression on the population. By the summer of 1886 he was the talk of France. At the great review at Longchamps on July 14, he appeared in gorgeous uniform, mounted on a splendid black charger with a circus record. He pranced before the spectators, an elegant military figure, with well-brushed and carefully pomaded hair, parted with precision, a short, pointed blond beard, and luxuriant mustachios. No attention was paid to the drab-looking President of the Republic and his civilian friends. The crowd was carried away with enthusiasm for the man of the hour. The man who mounted the horse had completely overshadowed the men who mounted the tribune.[3]

After the great review Boulanger was a made man. Paulus, one of the most popular café singers of Paris, produced a song entitled *En revenant de la revue,* with which he brought down the house night after night. The song became more popular than the *Marseillaise.* Soon the enthusiasm of the capital took yet other forms: " Boulanger five franc pieces (in paper) were sold in the street, along with Boulanger pins, Boulanger ties and Boulanger pipes

[1] Edmond Toutain: *Alexandre III et la République française* (Paris, 1929), pp. 102 ff.; Ducray, op. cit., pp. 165–6.

[2] Gabriel Monod: " Contemporary Life and Thought in France " (*Contemporary Review,* September 1887, pp. 428–47).

[3] Freycinet, op. cit., p. 350; Newton: *Lord Lyons,* II, pp. 367 ff.; W. H. Gleadell: " General Boulanger " (*Fortnightly Review,* September 1887, pp. 360–71).

with a figure-head of him carved on the bowl. Prose narratives and songs innumerable were devoted to telling the story of his life and recording his triumphs in the future. In all these publications he appears as the hero of the Retribution, the Liberator of Alsace-Lorraine, the terror of Germany, the hope of France." [1] Boulanger had, indeed, become Général Revanche. Sir Charles Dilke declared him to be more popular than any man since Napoleon at the height of his power, with the possible exception of Lafayette in the revolution of 1830. Even though the circus element was not lacking, he became a symbolic figure: "In the minds of the mass of his countrymen he has secured the invaluable honour of seeing his individual and personal cause confounded with the cause of the nation at large," says one observer; and Maurice Barrès, himself one of his adherents, says succinctly: "The natural traits of Boulanger no longer counted; by the strength of the popular desire he had just undergone a transformation. . . . Although he made no express proposal that could be criticized, all the politicians understood that he could be used to re-establish unity of sentiment. Unity of sentiment, in France, is a danger for Germany; it is also the negation of parliamentarism." Boulanger was vain enough to allow himself to be made the symbol of a dangerous movement, and even though he drew strength from the general dissatisfaction felt in France in matters of domestic politics, it cannot be denied that the idea of revenge was uppermost in the minds of his followers. General Franchet d'Esperey admits this when he remarks that "the thought of an early struggle was the bond which united the partisans of the general of the black horse; it alone can explain the confidence blindly accorded to a man who appears to have been a mediocrity and a weakling." [2]

The popular enthusiasm aroused by Boulanger and systematically fomented by the League of Patriots soon gave rise to a militaristic literature. The most noteworthy example was H. Barthélemy's *Avant la bataille,* which was published in April 1886 and was very widely discussed. The author was a close friend of Gambetta, and his book was prefaced by an introduction written by Deroulède, in which the latter said: "The battle is inevitable, the army is ready." The book itself pictured the French army as superior to the German and regarded the chances of success as very favourable. Other writers advocated peaceful means to recover Alsace and Lorraine, but agreed that if such methods were not soon successful, war would be inevitable. In general, the military writers were optimistic: "France may be confident, for the day of victory is near." [3]

[1] Monod, loc. cit., pp. 430–1.

[2] Sir Charles Dilke: *The Present Position of European Politics,* pp. 58–9; Gleadell, loc. cit., p. 365; Maurice Barrès: *L'Appel au soldat* (Paris, 1900), p. 58; Freycinet, op. cit., pp. 331–2; Franchet d'Esperey, loc. cit., p. 449. See further Joseph Reinach: *Le Cheval Noir* (Paris, 1890), Arthur Meyer: *Ce que mes yeux ont vu* (Paris, 1911); Francis Laur: *L'Epoque boulangiste* (Paris, 1912–4); Alexandre Zevaes: *Au temps du Boulangisme* (Paris, 1930).

[3] General L.: *Manière de combattre et battre les Prussiens* (Paris, 1886), quoted by Matthias

From beyond the Rhine the activities of the French patriots and the career of the new war minister were viewed with great misgiving. The German military authorities recognized the danger almost immediately, and from February 1886 onwards the military attaché at Paris reported on the rising spirit of revenge, at the same time warning his government of Boulanger. General von Waldersee, the assistant of Field-Marshal von Moltke, was inclined to regard the agitation as mere bluff, but Bismarck took the matter seriously from the beginning and expressed the fear that France was drifting towards war.[1]

These earlier fears were greatly enhanced as Boulanger's popularity grew, and especially when the abdication of Alexander of Battenberg opened a new phase of the Eastern question. For, after all, it was not a Franco-German war that Bismarck dreaded. The military men were quite convinced that, whatever the opinion the French held of their own prowess, the German military machine would still be able to repeat the victory of 1870-1. The great problem was not France alone, but France and Russia combined. In Berlin it was regarded as certain that if Russia became involved in war with Austria and Germany, France would immediately strike.[2] What made the situation so critical in the autumn and winter of 1886 was that a Russian-French combination really appeared upon the horizon.

The idea of such a coalition was one which was at the back of the mind of almost every French statesman. Even Gambetta, who hated the Asiatic-Russian autocracy, is said to have seen the necessity of cultivating the goodwill of tsarism. And Jules Ferry, representative of the policy of conciliation towards Germany, claimed to have done his share in that direction.[3] The same was true of Freycinet, who says in his memoirs that he had, as far back as 1880, advocated " carefully cultivating all opportunities for developing sympathy between the two governments," even though it would not be wise to " trumpet it from the roof-tops." [4] After becoming premier he scrupulously followed the lead of Russia in the Bulgarian question, despite the fact that many Frenchmen thought the struggling little nation rather than the Russian autocrat ought to enjoy the sympathy and support of France. During the spring and summer of 1886 the relations between Paris and St. Petersburg were strained, partly on account of the lenience of the French government towards the Russian nihilists in Paris and the harshness with which the French princes were treated, partly

Salm: " Der Angriffsgedanke in der französischen Militärliteratur seit 1871 " (in Joachim Kühn: Der Nationalismus im Leben der dritten Republik), pp. 305 ff.

[1] Die Grosse Politik, VI, Nos. 1223, 1224; Waldersee: Denkwürdigkeiten, I, pp. 270, 277, 280-1; Briefwechsel (Stuttgart, 1928), Nos. 12, 15, 20, etc.; Lucius von Ballhausen, op. cit., p. 341; Bourgeois and Pagès: Les Origines et les responsabilités de la Grande Guerre, p. 220.

[2] Bourgeois and Pagès, op. cit., p. 217; Waldersee: Denkwürdigkeiten, I, pp. 280-1.

[3] Rambaud: Jules Ferry, pp. 398 ff.

[4] Freycinet, op. cit., p. 110.

because of the recall of General Appert, the ambassador at St. Petersburg, who was a particular favourite with the Tsar.[1]

The French efforts to win the sympathy of Russia would probably not have led to any serious problem unless a strong current in the same direction had set in in Russia itself. For some time dissatisfaction had been felt with the Alliance of the Three Emperors, on the ground that the text of the alliance left Germany a free hand in the West while it bound Russian action in the East and made it dependent on previous consultation among the allies. Saburov, the man who had originally negotiated the treaty, took this stand and in 1884 wanted to make the renewal of the treaty conditional on some fundamental changes in the text. He was not, however, supported by Giers. Yet Bismarck found it desirable to give assurances at that time that Germany would never attack France unless provoked.[2] Saburov was, soon after, recalled from Berlin, but he continued his agitation and succeeded in winning over to his view Michael Katkov, the editor of the *Moscow Gazette*. Katkov was a brilliant writer and a very influential leader of the Russian nationalist party. Through his unswerving championship of the principles of autocracy he began to play an important role in Russian politics and to gain the ear of the Tsar himself, until by 1886 his paper could be described as the "most powerful paper in the world, because it is all-powerful or nearly all-powerful in one great empire."[3]

Katkov had, until 1885, been a supporter of the Three Emperors' Alliance, largely in the interest of monarchical solidarity. But after the great disappointment of the Bulgarian crisis and after learning the actual terms of the treaty he veered suddenly. In a famous article in the *Moscow Gazette* on July 31, 1886 he bitterly compared the visits of Giers to Bismarck to the pilgrimages of the Russian princes to the Golden Horde of the Tartars and argued that the advantages of the alliance were all on the side of Germany: "If Germany stands so high, it is because Germany stands on Russia." He did not advocate an alliance with France, but desired the continuance of good relations with Germany. Only they should be on a basis of equality. Russia should retain a free hand.

Katkov himself never became a warm advocate of an alliance with France,

[1] See Kurt Koerlin: *Zur Vorgeschichte des russisch-französischen Bündnisses, 1879–1890* (Halle, 1926), pp. 110 ff.; Toutain, op. cit., chapter iv.

[2] *Die Grosse Politik*, III, chapter xviii, *passim;* Serge Goriainov: "The End of the Alliance of the Emperors" (*American Historical Review*, Volume XXIII, January 1918, pp. 324–49); S. Skazkin: *Konets avstro-russko-germanskogo soiuza* (Moscow, 1928), pp. 333 ff.

[3] Sir Charles Dilke: *The Present Position of European Politics*, p. 131. English readers will find good accounts of Katkov's spectacular career in the articles of H. Sutherland Edwards: "Mr. Katkoff and the Moscow Gazette" (*Fortnightly Review*, September 1887, pp. 379–94), and of An English Resident in Russia: "Michael Katkoff" (*Contemporary Review*, October 1887, pp. 504–22). See also the account of his collaborator Elie Cyon: *Histoire de l'entente franco-russe* (Paris, 1895); S. Nevedenski: *Katkov i ego Vremia* (St. Petersburg, 1888); Irene Grüning: *Die russische öffentliche Meinung, 1878–1894* (Berlin, 1929), introduction.

but the demand for a free hand for Russia became a slogan which he used consistently until his death, in the summer of 1887. In the last days of December 1886 he handed in to the Tsar a long memorandum, which has never been published, but of which we have summaries and extracts. In this document the great publicist argued eloquently against a policy which bound Russia to neutrality in the event of a clash between France and Germany. A neutral attitude under such circumstances would be the equivalent of an attitude hostile to France, for an assurance against attack on her eastern front would enable Germany to throw three hundred thousand more troops against the French. Since it could not be to Russia's advantage to see France defeated again and perhaps annihilated, she must avoid any binding engagement given in advance.[1]

The ideas expounded by Katkov were supported and developed by other newspapers, many of which went further and called for an out and out understanding with France. Nationalist circles were well-nigh unanimous on this matter and were able to bring sufficient pressure to bear to effect the resumption of normal relations between France and Russia. Some went even further and took unofficial soundings in Paris and in Rome, towards the end of August or the beginning of September. Giers was certainly no party to these manœuvres, and it seems more than doubtful that the Tsar himself should have had any connexion with them. But they were symptomatic of a strong current of opinion, to which the Tsar himself could not remain indifferent. When the new French ambassador, M. de Laboulaye, arrived in November, Alexander remarked to him that the times were hard and might bring tribulations. It was necessary, then, that Russia should be able to count on France, and France on Russia. What Russia needed was a strong France. Even Giers hinted at a future Franco-Russian connexion before the year was out.[2]

None of these doings escaped Bismarck. He had, from the start, recognized the implications of French willingness to support Russia in her Bulgarian policy and had got wind of the Russian feelers in Paris almost immediately. Eventually Freycinet himself, realizing the dangers of the situation, confessed to the German ambassador.[3] Taken together with the spreading Boulanger agitation in France, the situation looked serious. The assurances of the German ambassador that the French desired peace made no impression on Bismarck. Count Münster had shown, during his tenure of the London post, that he was not a great diplomat. His aristocratic bent made it quite impossible for him to gauge the strength of a popular movement or to get below the surface of ministerial declarations. Herbette, the new French ambassador at Berlin, was

---

[1] Cyon: *Histoire de l'entente franco-russe*, pp. 195 ff.; Toutain, op. cit., pp. 164 ff.
[2] Toutain, op. cit., pp. 140–1, 154.
[3] *Die Grosse Politik*, IV, No. 903; V, Nos. 1001, 1004, 1007; VI, Nos. 1200–4, 1210, 1211; Schweinitz: *Denkwürdigkeiten*, II, pp. 324 ff.; Waldersee: *Denkwürdigkeiten*, I, p. 303; Bernhard Schwertfeger: *Amtliche Aktenstücke zur Geschichte der europäischen Politik, 1885–1914* (Berlin, 1925), Volume I, p. 13, note.

also full of words of peace, which the German chancellor accepted coolly. He did not doubt that the French government wished to avoid a conflict, but he could not ignore the danger of Boulanger and the movement which he represented. In October a new journal, *La Revanche,* had begun to appear, bearing Boulanger's picture. Boulanger himself pressed forward along the road towards military reform and reorganization. More and more troops were concentrated on the eastern frontier, and barracks were hurriedly constructed. Indeed, work on these new structures was done even at night, by electric light. Even French writers are agreed that Boulanger's activities were suspicious and that he showed " too much chauvinistic zeal." Emile Bourgeois, who takes good care to stress the pacific reports which Münster sent from Paris, and attempts to show that Bismarck pursued a provocative policy, is ready to admit that Boulanger was constantly alarming his colleagues with sensational reports of German plans, and that his activities " contradicted and compromised the pacific intentions of his colleagues and of the country." Another recent French writer is quite ready to understand Bismarck's uneasiness and condemns the Boulangist measures, which, viewed from abroad, " seemed like preparations for an eventual offensive." [1]

The German general staff did not believe that the French were actually preparing an attack for any specific time. The whole system of fortifications and the concentration of troops on the frontier seemed to indicate an intention of awaiting the German attack. But it was agreed that if complications should break out elsewhere, the French would "seize the opportunity to take revenge. Indeed, some of the German military men advocated a preventive war, on the theory that the clash was inevitable sooner or later. Bismarck's attitude, on the other hand, was perfectly consistent. He saw the Franco-German problem in a larger setting. There was no doubt in his mind that the mass of the French people and the French civil government desired peace. But he feared that an extremist group, under the leadership of Boulanger, might seize control of power and precipitate a conflict, especially if a favourable opportunity were supplied by a Russian-Austrian war. For that reason he kept urging the Austrians to avoid provocation of the Russians. [2]

Bismarck's reply to the French preparations was to bring before parliament, on November 25, 1886, a new military bill. The German appropriations were

---

[1] Münster's reports are in *Die Grosse Politik,* VI, Nos. 1238 ff. The reports of the German military attaché were diametrically opposed, and so were those of Hohenlohe (*Denkwürdigkeiten,* II, pp. 400, 403). For French opinions see Emile Bourgeois: " *L'Allemagne et la France au printemps de 1887* " (*Revue des sciences politiques,* Volume XLVII, pp. 5–17, January-March 1924), and the effective reply by Heinz Trützschler von Falkenstein: " *Kontroversen über die Politik Bismarcks im Jahre 1887* " (*Archiv für Politik und Geschichte,* VI, 1926, pp. 269–81); also Emile Bourgeois: *Manuel historique de politique étrangère,* Volume IV (Paris, 1926), pp. 32 ff.; and L. Cahen, in Hauser: *Histoire diplomatique de l'Europe,* I, p. 274.

[2] See especially Eduard Heller: " *Bismarcks Stellung zur Führung des Zweifrontenkrieges* " (*Archiv für Politik und Geschichte,* VII, 1926, pp. 677–98); Waldersee: *Denkwürdigkeiten,* I, pp. 298–301, 308; Graf Moltke: *Die deutschen Aufmarschpläne, 1871–1890* (Berlin, 1929), pp. 122 ff.

made for periods of seven years, and the arrangement of 1881 was not due to expire until April 1888. The premature demands of the government were, therefore, intended to indicate the existence of an emergency. The demands of the ministry were not, however, extreme. Under a previous law the number of troops under arms was to constitute one per cent of the population. That figure would not be met even by the new bill. The German army was to be raised from 427,000 to 468,000 men. In proportion to population the French had a larger force under arms. In any case, the new German bill was the result of the increased armaments of the French, as even French writers admit.

It was only natural, therefore, that in the first debates on the projected increase the existence of a French danger was stressed. But just how much value is to be attached to these utterances it is very hard to say. Almost from the beginning it was fairly certain that the bill would not be passed, for the Reichstag, elected in 1884, contained a strong progressive and Catholic opposition, which had already embittered Bismarck's life. He wanted to get rid of this Reichstag if possible and secure a parliament more amenable to the wishes of the government. We know that he did not look forward with regret to the failure of the military bill, and that he was determined to dissolve the Reichstag several times until a satisfactory body was returned by the electorate. In the event of continued disappointment he even considered a revision of the constitution which would have involved a fundamental modification of the suffrage.[1] On the other hand, it would be erroneous to overemphasize this aspect of the problem and to say that the military bill was brought in for reasons of domestic policy rather than for military reasons. As aforesaid, Bismarck was genuinely nervous about the developments in France and wanted the military bill to go through, no matter what constitutional steps it might necessitate. Nothing shows this more clearly than the fact that he appealed to the Pope to use his influence with the Catholic leaders to induce them to vote for the bill, which the Pope did.[2]

By the beginning of the new year war was generally expected to break out in the immediate future. In Germany and in France the newspaper press had entered upon violent alarmist campaigns. On each side of the Rhine an attack from the other was feared. As a matter of fact, the crisis was not so acute as many people thought. In France the government was pacifically inclined; of

---

[1] Lucius von Ballhausen, op. cit., p. 359. See the discussion in Johannes Ziekursch: *Politische Geschichte des neuen deutschen Kaiserreiches,* Volume II (Frankfurt, 1927), pp. 392–5; and in Egmont Zechlin: *Staatsstreichpläne Bismarcks und Wilhelms II* (Stuttgart, 1929).

[2] Bismarck: *Werke,* VIII, p. 548. On this much discussed intervention of the Pope in a purely domestic matter, see Lefebvre de Béhaine: *Léon XIII et le Prince de Bismarck* (Paris, 1898); Kurd von Schlözer: *Letzte römische Briefe* (Stuttgart, 1924), pp. 88 ff.; C. Crispolti and G. Aureli: *La Politica di Leone XIII* (Rome, 1912), pp. 99 ff.; F. Mourret: *Les Directions politiques, intellectuelles, et sociales de Léon XIII* (Paris, 1920), pp. 168 ff.; E. L. Woodward: " The Diplomacy of the Vatican under Popes Pius IX and Leo XIII " (*Journal of the British Institute of International Affairs,* May 1924, pp. 113–39). The texts of the correspondence are in Mgr. de T'Serclaes: *Le Pape Léon XIII* (Paris, 1894), I, p. 427.

that there can be no doubt. There is even some indication that Boulanger and his followers were seriously frightened by the German army bill. At any rate, they kept quiet for the time being, in order to avoid provocation. But Boulanger stayed on as minister of war even after the fall of the Freycinet cabinet, on December 3, and the organization of a new ministry under Goblet, with Flourens as minister for foreign affairs. No doubt some of the more moderate French statesmen who had come to recognize the danger of a man like Boulanger would have liked to exclude him from the government, but they did not dare. He was too popular. Henri de Rochefort, the leader of yellow journalism in Paris, threatened the government with a popular mob if any attempt were made to get rid of the great general. While the ardour of the French nationalists was, therefore, dampened, the danger of a *coup de tête* was still there.[1]

Bismarck had refused to consider any plan to reduce the number of men asked for the army and had rejected proposals to grant the necessary number of men for three years instead of seven. It was quite clear that the bill would not be passed, but in the final debates the chancellor himself rose to speak, on January 11, 1887. It was one of his oratorical masterpieces, one of his most brilliant reviews of the European situation. From the very beginning he made it clear that the increase of the forces was desired because of the possible threat from France. The governments of Europe were pacific, he said, but popular passions, the ambitions of party-leaders, public opinion misled by writings and speeches, might be stronger than the governments. Germany herself was a saturated state and desired no further conquests. Relations with Austria were very close and left nothing to be wished for. To be sure, Bismarck pointed out in the discussion following the speech, the Austro-German Alliance should not be misinterpreted. While each of the contracting powers had an interest in the continued existence of its partner as a great power, each had interests for which the other could not be expected to risk everything. As for Russia, the friendship between that power and Germany was above all question and doubt. The difficulty of maintaining the Three Emperors' League arose, not from any obstacle to German friendship with the other two powers, but from the difficulty of reconciling the interests of Austria and Russia. But Germany expected no hostile action from Russia and did not believe that Russia would seek alliances against Germany. The military bill was not designed with the thought of a Franco-Russian alliance in mind. There would be no trouble with Russia unless Germany went to seek trouble in Bulgaria.

The great danger, as Bismarck saw it, came from France and from Franco-German relations, for here there was an antagonism that went back for centuries and was kept alive by an outstanding boundary dispute. Since 1870 Germany had done all she could to conciliate France and to help her in every way excepting in the matter of the lost provinces. Germany had possession of the

---

[1] René Goblet: " *Souvenirs de ma vie politique* " (*Revue Politique et parlementaire*, October 10, 1929, pp. 5–29).

object in dispute and had nothing more to desire from France. The idea of waging a preventive war was one to which he could not at all adhere. He had always opposed it and could give the assurance that if the French would maintain the peace until the Germans attacked, peace would be secured for ever. Germany would not attack under any circumstances. But the danger from France was none the less real because the existing French government wanted peace. It was clear from French history that the decisions in difficult moments were made by energetic minorities, not by majorities or by the whole people. And a minority in France was constantly stirring the " sacred fire " of revenge. Germany must, therefore, fear a French attack, whether it be in ten days or in ten years, the duration of peace depending on the permanence of the French government. In the ministerial crisis of December 1886 no one could have anticipated the course of developments. For eight days or more no one knew who Freycinet's successor would be. It might just as well have been someone less pacifically inclined than Goblet. It was possible at any time that a government might come into power which drew its strength entirely from the " sacred fire." No French government since 1870 had ever dared to renounce publicly the idea of regaining the lost provinces. It was likely that France would attack as soon as she had reason to think that she was stronger than Germany, either because of alliances or because of superiority in number of men or in the quality of her armaments. If she were successful, no one knew how severe the peace terms would be. She would try to bleed Germany white, and Germany, if successful, would do the same thing; she would try to render France helpless for thirty years. The war of 1870 would be child's play compared to the war of 1890 or later.

Then, coming back to the subject in the subsequent discussion, Bismarck developed the theme further yet. It was, he said, quite conceivable that the French might attack even before they felt stronger than Germany. They might, if their domestic affairs sank too deeply into the morass, engage in war as a safety-valve for home troubles, as Napoleon III did. This danger might arise especially if a military government came into power. For example, why might not General Boulanger, if he formed a ministry, attempt that course? Bismarck would not even blame him, for he was willing to believe that any high French officer would act in good faith and with the idea of serving his country.[1]

Even this brilliant survey of the situation was not sufficient to secure the passage of the bill. The Catholic leaders, ignoring the repeated request of the Pope, rejected the government's demand for a seven-year appropriation, and the Reichstag was dissolved on January 14, 1887. The period of the new elections which followed was perhaps the most critical of all, for the German press went the limit in its recriminations and attacks on France and on Boulan-

---

[1] Horst Kohl: *Die politischen Reden des Fürsten Bismarck* (Stuttgart, 1894), Volume XII, pp. 173–226. See Bismarck's utterances to his friends at this same time, which bear out the assertions in the speech (Mittnacht: Erinnerungen pp. 49 ff.; Hohenlohe, op. cit., II, p. 404).

ger. Papers which drew their inspiration from the government snatched up every bit of information regarding French preparations and exploited it to the full. As a matter of fact, Boulanger as war minister did his share in supplying material for alarmist articles. In 1885 Germany exported to France 32,700 kilograms of picrin, which was needed in the manufacture of the new French explosive known as melanite. In 1886 the figures rose to 53,300 kilograms; in January 1887 no less than 7,400 kilograms were sent over the border. In addition extensive purchases of horses and especially of lumber for barracks were made in Germany on behalf of the French government.[1] Towards the end of January it was reported that the German chancellor would demand explanations of the French, and on January 31 the Berlin *Post*, which in 1875 had published the famous "War in Sight" article, came out with another article, evidently inspired, entitled "On the Razor-blade," which hinged on the argument that Boulanger was now all-powerful in France and that there was for him no turning back. He would have to make war.

The German opposition press refused to take all this agitation seriously, and declared roundly that all the noise was due to the shameless electioneering manœuvres of Bismarck. This opinion was widely held outside Germany, even in France, and there is undoubtedly more than a grain of truth in it. Bismarck, using his so-called " reptile press," was playing with fire. The student of public opinion can find here a superabundance of material to illustrate how public opinion, so called, can be manufactured to serve the ends of the government. On the other hand, this argument must not be pressed too far, for it is clear that Bismarck himself was fully convinced of the inherent danger of the Boulangist movement, and the methods he pursued in the election campaign of 1887 are eloquent proof of his conviction that the military bill must be passed if peace was to be maintained. That he stopped at nothing cannot be denied. In reply to the activities of the French war office he decided, early in February, to summon seventy-two thousand reservists to Alsace and Lorraine, for practice with the new infantry weapon. He let it be known, further, that the government planned to ask the Prussian parliament for an appropriation of three hundred million marks for military purposes. The demand was never made, but these measures were enough to cause a panic on the Berlin stock exchange and many people believed that war would break out in a short time. The country was thoroughly stirred up, and in the elections of February 21 fully seventy-seven per cent of the electorate voted, as against sixty per cent in the elections of 1884. The government secured a large majority, and the famous military bill was passed with little difficulty on March 11.[2]

Of course, in the Europe of that day the actual military preparations were

---

[1] Statistics quoted in Karl Wippermann: *Deutscher Geschichtskalender 1887*, part i, p. 148.

[2] See extracts from the opposition press in Wippermann, loc. cit., pp. 148 ff.; see also Fuller, op. cit., p. 136 ff.; Trützschler, loc. cit., pp. 42 ff.; Albin, op. cit., pp. 71 ff.; Bourgeois and Pagès, op. cit., pp. 222 ff.; Gooch: *Franco-German Relations 1871–1914*, p. 29; Goblet, loc. cit.

only one consideration. All the governments took steps to strengthen their forces, in the firm belief that in order to maintain peace one must be prepared for war. It would, in fact, be difficult to prove that armaments necessarily make for war. Certainly the British navy has always been regarded by modern Englishmen as a defensive rather than an offensive weapon. The Germans in 1887 looked upon their forces as a guarantee of peace, and Pope Leo held the same opinion, else he obviously would not have favoured the passage of the military bill. During the whole agitation the French and German governments remained on cordial terms and exchanged very positive assurances. If the French leaders entertained the fear of a German attack at all, it was only momentarily.[1] But, as aforesaid, the question of armaments was only part of the problem. What the statesmen were most concerned about was the question of international alignments, for it was practically a foregone conclusion that the struggle between France and Germany, if it broke out, would not remain localized.

Boulanger and those who supported him were strong advocates of an alliance with Russia and certainly pressed upon the foreign minister, Flourens, the desirability of supplementing French armaments with Russian assurances of sympathy and support. Laboulaye, the ambassador at St. Petersburg, was anxious to do all he could. On or about January 12, 1887, acting evidently on his own initiative, he asked Giers whether, if France were attacked by Germany, Russia would maintain her liberty of action. Giers replied that in such an event Russia would certainly have a word to say, always on condition that France was not the aggressor. But it appears that there was little faith in Bismarck's supposed aggressive plans among the officials of the Russian foreign office, and that even Flourens wished to avoid anything that might be regarded as provocatory in Berlin. Writing to Laboulaye, he pointed out that France desired peace and would not be the aggressor if war broke out. Bismarck had given similar assurances to the French ambassador. Laboulaye should avoid and evade definite commitments towards Russia. All France desired was that Russia should maintain her freedom of action: " If Germany suspected that we were trying to estrange her from Russia and take her place in the alliances of the future, I have reason to fear that this attitude would be of the very nature to bring about the dangers it is our object to avoid." [2]

During the last days of January, however, when the situation became particularly acute, both sides made serious efforts to secure support from other powers. Count Hatzfeldt, the German ambassador at London, came to Lord Salisbury on January 24 to discuss the situation. He seemed to assume that war was near, though he insisted that the Germans did not want it. Again and again he asked the English prime minister if England would be able to look

---

[1] Newton: *Lord Lyons,* II, p. 383; Bourgeois and Pagès, op. cit., pp. 222–5.
[2] Toutain, op. cit., pp. 171 ff.; Ernest Daudet: *Histoire diplomatique de l'alliance franco-russe* (second edition, Paris, 1898), p. 212.

quietly on, especially if Austria and Turkey became involved. " He pointed out the advantage we enjoyed from the position of Germany towards France, in that France could not do us any mischief because of the fear of Germany; and he pressed for ' reciprocity,' " reported Salisbury to the Queen. Hatzfeldt suggested further that the best thing for England would be to become engaged in a "good war." Salisbury replied that his personal opinion was that Austria and Turkey could not be abandoned if seriously pressed. But he could not tell what attitude parliament would take. To the Queen he wrote, referring to the Irish question, that England, "torn in two by a controversy which almost threatens her existence, cannot, in the present state of public opinion, interfere with any decisive action abroad. . . . We have absolutely no power to restrain either France or Germany; while all the power and influence we have will be needed to defend our influence in the South-east of Europe." [1]

There was nothing to be hoped for from England, that was clear. Bismarck, if it actually came to war, would have to rely on his allies and on the good German sword. Still, England's neutrality was almost certain. But the situation required caution.

Flourens had no better luck with the advances he made to Russia. During the last days of January he himself approached Baron Mohrenheim, the Tsar's ambassador at Paris. He too gave assurances of the most pacific intentions, but he asked for support if the Germans attempted to check French armaments. Rumours that some such demand would be made by Bismarck were rife at the time. Still the Russian government refused to commit itself. The Tsar was willing to promise moral support, but Giers wrote that the French fears were exaggerated, since Bismarck had given repeated assurances that Germany would not attack. Suspicion that France and Russia were concluding an agreement hostile to Germany would embitter Franco-German relations more than anything else. The French suggestion that a special mission be received at St. Petersburg to discuss the situation was put off.[2]

Flourens was certainly doing all he could to draw closer the ties between Russia and France and to induce Russia not to allow herself to become involved in a war in the Near East. What he wished was that she should maintain freedom of action for possible complications in the West. But he did not want to go too far or too fast. When, early in February, Boulanger attempted to go over his head and write directly to the Russian minister of war, or, as some say, to Alexander himself, Flourens threatened to resign and forced Boulanger to give up the plan.[3]

---

[1] *Letters of Queen Victoria*, I, p. 262.

[2] Emile Flourens: *Alexandre III* (Paris, 1894), pp. 312 ff.; Goriainov, loc. cit., pp. 331–2; Anonymous: " *La Russie et le Quai d'Orsay* " (*Nouvelle Revue*, LXXVI, May 1, 1892, pp. 5–20).

[3] Newton, op. cit., II, p. 387; *Die Grosse Politik*, VI, No. 1252; Schwertfeger, op. cit., I, No. 17; W. H. Gleadell: " General Boulanger " (*Fortnightly Review*, September 1887, p. 369); Toutain, op. cit., pp. 189 ff., 216.

The freedom of action which Flourens desired Russia to reserve for herself was exactly the thing that Katkov had been clamouring for; it was the key argument of the memorandum which he had handed to the Tsar late in December. Alexander, who was heartily sick of the connexion with Austria and felt disgusted with the way in which affairs had developed in Bulgaria, was certainly impressed with Katkov's argument. This is shown clearly enough by his willingness to lend the French moral support and by his expression of dislike not only for the Alliance of the Three Emperors, but even of a separate Russian-German agreement.[1]

But the policy advocated by Katkov, Mohrenheim, Ignatiev, and Saburov was vigorously opposed by the foreign minister, Giers, who was supported by Paul Shuvalov, the ambassador at Berlin, and the latter's brother Peter, formerly ambassador to Great Britain. Towards the end of December Giers was still speaking of a possible renewal of the Alliance of the Three Emperors, provided Russia and Austria could come to some agreement on the Bulgarian question.[2] Early in January Count Peter Shuvalov came to Berlin to explore the possibility of securing from Emperor William a definite declaration against the restoration of Battenberg, which was feared in Russia. He found Bismarck very well-disposed, and, on his own initiative, he began to discuss with Count Herbert Bismarck the terms of a possible Russian-German treaty. He would stake his head, he said, that the Tsar would never attack Germany, least of all in alliance with France. He was convinced that a written treaty could be secured from the Tsar in twenty-four hours stating that he would never intervene in Franco-German complications, no matter whether France attacked Germany or whether Germany attacked France, defeated her, and levied an indemnity of fourteen billion francs or even sent a German governor to Paris. In return all Russia wanted was the repetition of Bismarck's promise not to hinder Russia's securing the closure of the Straits, the only matter which really meant much to the Tsar. Shuvalov then worked out a draft agreement, dated January 10, in which these ideas were expressed. Germany was to recognize Russia's exclusive right to exercise her influence in Bulgaria and to promise friendly neutrality " if solicitude for the interests of Russia should oblige His Majesty the Emperor of Russia to assure himself of the closure of the Straits and thus to retain (*garder en ses mains*) the key to the Black Sea." Germany, on the other hand, could count on Russia's friendly neutrality in any conflict that might arise between her and France. Both were to recognize that the existence of the Austrian Empire was necessary to the maintenance of the European equilibrium and to agree to undertake no action directed against Austria's territorial integrity, unless Austria herself attacked. Both were also to recognize the

---

[1] Goriainov, loc. cit., pp. 331–2; *Dnievnik V. N. Lamsdorfa, 1886–1890* (Moscow, 1926), pp. 35–40 (see Hans Uebersberger: "*Abschluss und Ende des Rückversicherungsvertrages,*" in *Die Kriegsschuldfrage,* V, October 1927, pp. 933–66).

[2] *Die Grosse Politik,* V, Nos. 1061 ff.

necessity for maintaining the independence of Serbia so long as it remained as it was and under the sceptre of King Milan.[1]

Bismarck, naturally enough, was delighted by Shuvalov's disclosures. He could not know that they were not official. Therefore he took them at face value. His very friendly references to Russia in the great speech of January 11 are to be attributed to the great promise of these negotiations. But Shuvalov, on his return to St. Petersburg, had no success. The Tsar refused to consider the terms he had worked out for a Russian-German agreement. Katkov had come to the capital from Moscow, and his influence was supreme. The whole problem seems to have been gone over in a great council about January 20. The Tsar rejected the idea of a warlike policy in company with France, but at the same time refused to follow Giers's policy of the German alliance. It was expected that the foreign minister would resign. The struggle continued for some weeks longer. In the meanwhile the Russian attitude remained uncertain and unaccountable.[2]

As Bismarck received no reply from St. Petersburg regarding the negotiations opened by Peter Shuvalov, he began to realize that he had been over-optimistic. He spoke to his friends of having painted Russian-German relations too rosily in his speech of January 11 and warned the federated German governments not to overestimate the cordiality between the two countries. If trouble developed between France and Germany, he told his friend Busch, the strong national current in Russia would become so influential that Germany would be obliged to leave a hundred thousand men on the eastern frontier as a precaution. Even if France were defeated by Germany, Russia would not permit an exploitation of the victory sufficient to weaken France for thirty or forty years. Besides, in the event of a Franco-German war Russia would probably attack Austria, and then Germany would have to come to the assistance of the latter. All these reasons contributed to make Bismarck more than ever averse to war with France.[3]

"Russia," says Sir Charles Dilke in his remarkable survey of the European situation in the spring of 1887, "is the one power which is a comet of eccentric orbit rather than a planet in the European system. The power of Russia is wielded by a single man, or shall I say by two — the Emperor, and the Moscow newspaper emperor, Katkoff."[4] It was this uncertainty as to Russia's policy that caused Bismarck more uneasiness than anything else. Because of it he was obliged to cultivate the other friendships of Germany with greater care than ever. His efforts to enlist the support of England for Austria had been frustrated by the unwillingness of the English to take the initiative and by Churchill's

---

[1] Ibid., Nos. 1062-3.
[2] Cyon: *Histoire de l'entente franco-russe*, p. 234; Lamsdorf: *Dvievnik, 1886-1890*, pp. 50 ff.; Schweinitz: *Denkwürdigkeiten*, II, p. 332; Corti: *Alexander von Battenberg*, p. 293.
[3] Busch: *Bismarck*, III, p. 160. See also *Die Grosse Politik*, V, No. 1006.
[4] Dilke: *The Present Position of European Politics*, p. 32.

attitude of indifference in matters touching the English position in the Balkans and at Constantinople. The German chancellor now changed his tactics and attempted the great task of drawing the English into association with the central powers by exploiting the French aspect of the international situation. This comes out very clearly in the negotiations for the renewal of the Triple Alliance.

The treaty between Germany, Austria, and Italy was due to expire in May 1887. It had not been taken very seriously by the two German powers, which had consistently refused to read into the alliance any obligation on their part to support Italian colonial projects in the Mediterranean or the Red seas. In 1884 Bismarck had flatly rejected the suggestion that Germany should support the Italian policy in Morocco against France.[1] Both he and Kálnoky thoroughly disapproved of the Italian colonial activity, which led to the occupation of Massawa in the spring of 1885. In the summer, when Kálnoky visited Bismarck, the two statesmen agreed that Italy "could not be regarded as a significant factor in any possible combination."[2]

Under the circumstances the Italians were disappointed in the fruits of the alliance. They had based their policy more and more on close co-operation with England. With the greatest consistency they supported the British policy in Egypt, and in return the English gave encouragement to Italian colonial aspirations. Lord Cromer denies that England instigated the occupation of Massawa or used Italy as a cat's-paw to extricate the English from the difficulties of the Sudan problem. He goes so far as to say that he told the Italian consul-general at Cairo, de Martino, that in his opinion the Italians were making a mistake. Nevertheless, it is a fact that the English gave the Italians every encouragement, for they feared that otherwise the French would occupy the region. Professor Salvemini told me that he had seen the reports of de Martino, in which he states that Lord Cromer proposed that the Italians occupy Massawa. This seems to have been as early as October 1884.[3] The point is a minor one, for even Lord Cromer does not deny that the British were benevolently disposed towards the Italian action. Besides, the Italian minister Mancini was enthusiastically in favour of a colonial policy. To the Italian parliament he announced that the keys of the Mediterranean would be found to lie in the Red Sea. Italy proceeded to the occupation and in this way embarked upon a colonial enterprise which was to prove disastrous in itself, while at the same time causing a further estrangement from France.

In October 1885 Count Robilant, the Italian ambassador at Vienna, became foreign minister in a Depretis cabinet. He had, it will be remembered, opposed the helter-skelter fashion in which the government had rushed into the alliance with the central powers in 1882, and had taken the view that much more could

---

[1] *Die Grosse Politik*, III, Nos. 678–9.

[2] Pribram: *The Secret Treaties of Austria-Hungary*, II, p. 45.

[3] Cromer: *Modern Egypt*, II, pp. 56–7. See also Gaetano Salvemini: "*L'Italia a Massaua*" (*L'Azione*, January 6, 1924).

have been obtained. He was willing enough to renew the alliance when it expired, but not in the original form. There were two important changes that he wished to see introduced into the treaty. One should provide adequate support of Italian colonial policy, while the other should pave the way for the safeguarding of Italian interests in the Balkans. So far the treaty had been " sterile " from the Italian standpoint, and there was no advantage in renewing it in its " unproductive " form, which secured the central powers against Italian hostility and secured Italy nothing.[1]

The first hints thrown out by Robilant as to his attitude met with no satisfactory response. Kálnoky received them with the utmost coolness, declared that Austria could not be expected to act in regions where she had no interests, and complained that, despite the alliance, the irredentist agitation had been allowed to continue in Italy. There the matter was dropped, not to be resumed until the summer of 1886, when Robilant realized that in view of the complicated situation in the Balkans and the danger of a Russian-Austrian clash, the connexion with Italy might have greater value for Austria and Germany. But Bismarck, when he was approached with the suggestion of a renewal of the treaty with additional provisions for the maintenance of the *status quo* in the Mediterranean and Adriatic, was no more encouraging than Kálnoky had been a year before. In conference with Kálnoky he decided that the Italian proposals could not be entertained. Robilant was much mortified by this attitude and used strong language about the alliance in writing to the ambassadors. The truth was that he had been somewhat premature in coming forward with his desiderata.[2]

Yet hardly a month later Bismarck showed himself much more inclined to discuss the matter with the Italian ambassador. The reason for this change of heart is evidently to be found in the fact that at this very time the first reports of Russian soundings in Paris reached the Berlin foreign office. In communicating with Vienna Bismarck stressed the danger of losing the connexion with Italy. At the same time he instructed the German ambassador at Rome to find out just what Robilant wanted. The Italian minister pointed out that the alliance was of no value to Italy unless it secured her against the danger of a French occupation of Tripoli. In the same way Italy could not afford to be surprised by a partition of European Turkey between Russia and Austria without her interests being considered. The German chancellor listened to the arguments of the Italians with considerable interest, the more so as the Italian ambassador fortified his remarks by a story of extensive alliance offers which Freycinet had been making to the Italians. In accordance with his past policy, however, Bismarck referred the Italians to Vienna.[3]

---

[1] Luigi Chiala: *Pagine di Storia Contemporanea,* III, p. 471.

[2] Pribram, op. cit., II, pp. 47–9; Chiala, op. cit., III, pp. 471, 474; *Die Grosse Politik,* IV, No. 822.

[3] Pribram, op. cit., II, pp. 48–50; *Die Grosse Politik,* IV, Nos. 833 ff.

Although Kálnoky would have preferred to reject the Italian demands out and out, he, too, was impressed with the seriousness of the international situation and realized that Bismarck attached greater value to the treaty than he had previously done. He was willing to promise the Italians moral and diplomatic support in the Tripolitan question, but could not see how Austria could possibly risk becoming involved in war over such a matter. So far as the Balkans were concerned, he pointed out that Austrian policy did not aim at the partition of Turkey, and that Italy could depend upon being informed if anything came up. At the same time he attempted to counteract the Italian demand by raising the question whether Italy could not be asked to lend Austria support if it came to war with Russia. In short, Kálnoky was trying to evade the serious demands which came from Rome. Bismarck, however, did not relish this procedure. For him the situation was becoming precarious. He informed Kálnoky that the Emperor William took the view that Germany could not remain neutral in a Franco-Italian war, no matter what the cause of it might be, for Germany could not allow Italy to be subjected or annihilated by France. The danger of Italy's being seduced into a French alliance by promises of Tripoli was not to be taken lightly.[1]

Kálnoky could not afford to antagonize Bismarck still further, for the question of the extent of German obligations under the alliance of 1879 had already caused friction and tension. He therefore agreed reluctantly to listen to the details of the Italian project. The whole matter was handled dilatorily. It was not until the last week of November 1886 that Robilant came forward with the draft of a new treaty, and this he wisely communicated to Berlin, not to Vienna. He proposed that the three powers should agree to work for the maintenance of the *status quo* on " the coasts and islands of the Adriatic and Ægean seas belonging to the Ottoman Empire." In the event that another power should attempt to bring about a change, Italy and Austria should consider joint action. Germany should be obliged only to favour the operations of her two allies. The latter would take steps temporarily or permanently to occupy such territories as might be menaced by a third power. Before beginning operations, however, they should reach an understanding as to the reciprocal compensation by which the legitimate claims of both parties should be equally satisfied. In another article Robilant asked for freedom of action in the Egyptian question and for the whole matter of Italy's relations with England. Finally he came to the Tripolitan question. After stressing the danger of French advances in Morocco and Tripoli and declaring that Italian opinion would regard such advances as " a wound inflicted on the national integrity," he went on to explain the Italian view: " We do not ask our allies to give us armed assistance in preventing a French inroad in Tripoli or Morocco; neither do we ask their help if we seek compensation for French conquests in Morocco by a gain of territory in Tripoli,

---

[1] Pribram, op. cit., II, pp. 50 ff.; *Die Grosse Politik*, IV, Nos. 831 ff.

if unopposed by France. What we do ask of them is this: if we should proceed to oppose by armed force a French advance against Tripoli, or if, as the result of French action in Morocco, we should prepare an advance on Tripoli in the face of French resistance; or if, in either of these events, a formal declaration of war should be followed by an outbreak of hostilities between us and France, either in Tripoli or in a part of the French possessions in Europe, then, and only then — after we had taken the initiative in armed action against France — should we invoke the aid of both our allies and enjoy all the consequences of *casus fœderis.*[1]

Bismarck had no hesitation about accepting these proposals and recommending them to Vienna. The more acute the tension between France and Germany became, the more anxious was the chancellor to make sure of Italy. Robilant even talked of being prepared to send two hundred thousand men across the Alps to fight by the side of the Germans. But there seems to have been another thought in Bismarck's mind. Robilant wanted to reserve freedom of action in his dealings with England and stated that what he was asking was "a tacit sanction by the two empires of the combinations which a regard for our interests would oblige us to effect with the English government." It seems that negotiations between Rome and London were already under way, and that Bismarck saw here the possibility not only of burdening the English with the support of Italy's colonial aspirations, but of creating a nexus between England and the central powers. The common hostility of Italy and England to French expansion in the Mediterranean could be used to weaken France's position generally and perhaps enlist the help of the English for Austria against Russia. In a memorandum Bismarck pointed out (and he asked that the Italian ambassador be informed of his thought) not only that Italy, in alliance with England, would be secured against a landing by the French on the Italian coasts, but that, under protection of the British fleet, the Italians might undertake a landing themselves, near Marseilles: "In brief, to complete the picture and to enhance the position of Italy as it deserves to be enhanced, an alliance with England or at least the closest possible connexion (*Anlehnung*) is urgently to be desired."[2]

Kálnoky, on the other hand, did not feel that the Italian demands were defensible. Austria was being asked for more and more concessions, without herself making any gains. The fact was that the Austrian government was always opposed to being drawn into a conflict with France. This had come out only too clearly in the negotiations for the alliance of 1879. The attitude taken in Vienna was the exact counterpart of that taken in Berlin, where the foreign office was anxious not to become involved in war with Russia over Balkan affairs.[3] It was necessary, then, for Bismarck to bring pressure to bear. Again

---

[1] *Die Grosse Politik,* IV, No. 836; Pribram, op. cit., II, pp. 54–8.
[2] *Die Grosse Politik,* IV, No. 841.
[3] The point is well developed in Eduard Heller: *Das deutsch-österreichische Bündnis,* pp. 94–6.

and again he stressed the danger of a possible Franco-Italian-Russian alliance, which would be as much of a menace to Austria as to Germany. At other times he told the Austrians that if they were going to maintain their uncompromising attitude towards Russia, they would have to rely upon their own strength. Germany would be occupied chiefly with France, and it would therefore be advisable for Austria to find other allies. He even went so far as to threaten to conclude a separate agreement with Italy.[1]

The hint that Germany could not be depended upon to give much assistance in a conflict with Russia certainly made a profound impression upon Kálnoky. If such was the situation, it would be of greater importance for Austria to be secured from attack in the rear. Italy could not be put off without further ado. But the Austrian minister tried to scale down Robilant's demands. The *status quo* should be maintained not only on the coasts and islands of the Adriatic and Ægean belonging to Turkey, but in "the Balkans and their coasts"— that is, in the interior as well as on the seaboard. The idea of reciprocal compensation in the event of a change in the *status quo* he wished to eliminate completely. Furthermore, if the Italian interests in the Balkans were to be admitted in the new treaty, Kálnoky insisted that Italy's obligations should be extended and that it should be provided that she should come to the assistance of Austria if the latter were attacked by Russia. This would be all the more necessary if the bulk of the German forces was to be directed against France.[2]

Kálnoky's counter-proposals met with the approval of neither Bismarck nor Robilant. Bismarck refused to undertake the maintenance of the *status quo* in the whole Balkans, because he was determined to leave Russia a free hand in the eastern part of the peninsula. Furthermore, he feared that if Austria were assured of Italian support in case of a Russian attack, she might provoke Russia, relying on her own military strength, together with the aid of Italy, Serbia, and Roumania. As for Robilant, he rejected the wide extension which Kálnoky wished to give the Italian project. If Italy was to aid Austria in a war against Russia, it should be only on condition that the two powers conclude at a suitable time before the beginning of hostilities "a special agreement intended to regulate, on the basis of just indemnification, the territorial changes which might eventually result from a war waged in common."

Such was the situation at the opening of the new year. Bismarck continued to support the Italian proposals and to urge their acceptance at Vienna. Kálnoky, on the other hand, was becoming more and more opposed to concessions. Bismarck's great speech of January and the repeated hints from Berlin that Austria would have to depend chiefly on herself in case of war with Russia had profoundly irritated and disappointed the Austrian statesmen, including the

---

[1] *Die Grosse Politik*, IV, No. 837; Pribram, op. cit., II, pp. 58–9; Heller: "*Bismarcks Stellung zur Führung des Zweifrontenkrieges*" (*Archiv für Politik und Geschichte*, VII, 1926, p. 683).

[2] Pribram, op. cit., II, pp. 60–2.

Emperor Francis Joseph himself.[1] On January 16 Kálnoky told the German ambassador that he could not accept Robilant's counter-proposals. As a matter of fact, he could not go beyond the simple renewal of the treaty of 1882, for since Bismarck had declared that Germany could not support Austria's Balkan policy it behoved Austria to watch the more keenly over her interests in the East. Under the circumstances she could not expose herself to the danger of becoming involved in war with France as the result of Italian aspirations and activities in Tripoli or Morocco. Kálnoky and other Austrian statesmen were convinced, in the latter part of January, that war between France and Germany would soon break out. Under the terms of the treaty Italy would be obliged to help Germany, and then, if Robilant's proposals were accepted, Austria would have to help Italy. This would leave Austria's interests in the East to the tender mercies of the Russians.[2]

Although the German ambassador at Vienna and some of the officials of the German foreign office were panic-stricken by Kálnoky's sudden change of front, Bismarck himself appreciated the force of the Austrian argument, particularly the desire of Kálnoky to avoid becoming involved in war with France. The chancellor then hit upon an ingenious way of solving the dilemma. He proposed to Robilant that the old treaty be renewed as it stood, but that it be supplemented by new German-Italian and Austro-Italian agreements. Germany should take over the obligation to support the Italian Mediterranean policy, while Austria should accept Robilant's demand for consideration in Balkan problems. Robilant accepted this proposal, and Kálnoky also agreed to it, though evidently with some reluctance. By the first of February the understanding was complete, and the discussion narrowed down to a few details. Kálnoky wanted it specifically stated that the eventual annexation of Bosnia and Herzegovina should not be regarded as a change of the *status quo,* and that Italy, in that case, should not be entitled to compensation. He wished it also to be understood that if Italy came to the assistance of Austria in a war with Russia, the Italians should not be permitted to demand compensation in the Trentino. The first of these reservations was accepted by Robilant, but in regard to the second he claimed that he had been misunderstood. Italy had not agreed to support Austria militarily if she were attacked by Russia. This view rested on a rather flimsy foundation and there was some acrimonious debate about it, but the Germans and Austrians finally allowed the matter to drop, making, incidentally, some rather cynical remarks about the value of Italian military aid and the force of treaties.[3]

The new treaties of the Triple Alliance were signed at Berlin on February

---

[1] *Die Grosse Politik,* V, Nos. 1026, 1027; Pribram, op. cit., II, pp. 66–7; Edmund Glaise-Horstenau: *Franz Josephs Weggefährte* (Vienna, 1930), pp. 283–95.

[2] *Die Grosse Politik,* IV, No. 845; Pribram, op. cit., II, pp. 67–9. On the Austrian fear of a Franco-German war, see *Die Grosse Politik,* VI, Nos. 1246 ff., 1256; Schwertfeger, op. cit., I, No. 16; Heller, loc. cit., p. 683.

[3] Pribram, op. cit., II, pp. 69 ff.; *Die Grosse Politik,* IV, Nos. 846 ff.

20, 1887. The old treaty was renewed for five years (till May 30, 1892). In addition there were the two new agreements concluded by Italy with Austria and Germany. The essential clause of the Austro-Italian pact provided for the maintenance of the *status quo* in the Orient, but went on to say that if the maintenance of the *status quo* " in the regions of the Balkans or of the Ottoman coasts and islands in the Adriatic and in the Ægean Sea should become impossible, and if, whether in consequence of the action of a third power or otherwise, Austria-Hungary or Italy should find themselves under the necessity of modifying it by a temporary or permanent occupation on their part, this occupation should take place only after a previous agreement between the two powers aforesaid, based upon the principle of a reciprocal compensation for every advantage, territorial or other, which each of them might obtain beyond the present *status quo,* and giving satisfaction to the interests and well-founded claims of the two parties."

The separate Italian-German treaty was more elaborate. It, too, provided for the maintenance of the *status quo* in the East, but only " on the Ottoman coasts and islands in the Adriatic and the Ægean Seas," not " in the regions of the Balkans." Furthermore, there was no provision made for the event that the *status quo* should, after all, be disturbed. In Article II both powers reserved liberty of action in the Egyptian question. But Articles III and IV were the really important ones. The former read: " If it were to happen that France should make a move to extend her occupation, or even her protectorate or her sovereignty, under any form whatsoever, in the North African territories, whether of the Vilayet of Tripoli or of the Moroccan Empire, and that in consequence thereof Italy, in order to safeguard her position in the Mediterranean, should feel that she must herself undertake action in the said North African territories, or even have recourse to extreme measures in French territory in Europe, the state of war which would thereby ensue between Italy and France would constitute *ipso facto,* on the demand of Italy and at the common charge of the two allies, the *casus fœderis* with all the effects foreseen by Articles II and V of the aforesaid treaty of May 20, 1882, as if such an eventuality were expressly contemplated therein." Article IV went on to state: " If the fortunes of any war undertaken in common against France should lead Italy to seek for territorial guarantees with respect to France for the security of the frontiers of the kingdom and of her maritime position, as well as with a view to the stability of peace, Germany will present no obstacle thereto; and, if need be, and in a measure compatible with circumstances, will apply herself to facilitating the means of attaining such a purpose." [1]

The terms of the new treaties undoubtedly represented a great victory for Robilant, who had succeeded in making the best of the difficult international situation and the enhanced value of Italy's friendship to extract substantial concessions from the central powers. The separate agreement with Austria

---

[1] Texts in Pribram, op. cit., I, pp. 104 ff.

signified the recognition of Italy's right to be heard in Balkan affairs and to participate in the Turkish heritage if the sick man should pass away or meet with a violent end. As for the Italian-German pact, it changed the very nature of the alliance, for it transformed what was a strictly defensive treaty into one with a distinct offensive tinge. In addition, of course, it secured Italy the support she had long desired for her colonial policy in north Africa.

The far-reaching nature of the German concessions has given rise to some controversy, the more so as there is some evidence that, in the discussion preceding the agreement, actual mention was made of Nice, Corsica, Tunis, and even Albania as possible "territorial guarantees" to be taken by Italy after a successful war with France. The difficulty here arises from the fact that almost no documents are available touching on the separate German-Italian negotiations. One thing, however, seems certain, and that is that these negotiations concerning possible guarantees took place in the last week before the signature of the treaty. In his instructions to the Italian ambassador at Berlin on February 15, Robilant authorized him to demand the insertion of a clause concerning compensations, to apply to any war of Italy and Germany against France, even if it did not originate in the Mediterranean. The suggestion may very well have come from Bismarck, who was, above all, interested in satisfying the Italians and who evidently made no objection to the demands advanced by the cabinet at Rome. To be sure, the provision as we see it in Article IV is extremely vague, and it may well be that Bismarck regarded it as a pious wish rather than a definite engagement. But there it is, and the only explanation that can be offered for it is that Bismarck, as we know, regarded the origins of an eventual Franco-Italian conflict as immaterial. It was to Germany's interest to prevent the annihilation or subjection of Italy by France. He probably did not take these vague promises too seriously. As he himself remarked, if one wants to evade even the clearest specifications of a treaty, one can always find ways and means to excuse oneself.[1]

It is quite important to note that Article IV of the German-Italian agreement was negotiated in the last days before the signing of the treaty, because by that time an exchange of notes had taken place between the British and the Italian governments, and this so-called First Mediterranean Agreement is closely bound up with the new treaty of the Triple Alliance. It will be remembered that during the autumn of 1886 repeated efforts had been made by the English statesmen to effect an understanding with Austria. These advances had been

---

[1] *Die Grosse Politik*, IV, No. 850; Waldersee: *Briefwechsel*, No. 37. Nice, Corsica, and Tunis were mentioned by Bismarck in conversation with Crown Prince Rudolf in March 1887 (Pribram, in *Österreichische Rundschau*, 1921, pp. 57–68; Mitis: *Kronprinz Rudolf*, pp. 359 ff.) and are referred to in a later document (*Die Grosse Politik*, IX, No. 2018). For discussion of the question, see Emile Bourgeois: "*L'Allemagne et la France au printemps de 1887*" (*Revue des sciences politiques*, January–March 1924, pp. 5–17), and the reply by Heinz Trützschler von Falkenstein: "*Kontroversen über die Politik Bismarcks im Jahre 1887*" (*Archiv für Politik und Geschichte*, VI, 1926, pp. 269–81). Trützschler publishes the instructions of Robilant to Launay, hitherto unknown.

looked upon with suspicion by Kálnoky, while Bismarck had explicitly warned his Austrian colleague against allowing himself to be pushed forward by the English. Repeated statements by Lord Randolph Churchill made it clear that the English thought Austria ought to take the initiative. The English would support the Austrian action provided Germany did likewise.

Since there was little prospect of an English-Austrian understanding, Bismarck began, in the last days of December, to urge upon the Italians the desirability of an agreement with England, which would greatly strengthen their position with respect to France. He pointed out that the relations between England and France were not good, and that there were people who thought the next war would be one between these nations.[1] In other words, the chancellor saw the possibility of establishing contact with England by way of the French rather than the Russian channel. The relations between England and France were certainly such that there was reason to suppose that the English would listen to approaches of this sort. Leaving aside the tension that had arisen from conflicting interests in Madagascar, the New Hebrides, Indo-China, etc., it was, as usual, the Egyptian question that served as an index for relations between the two powers. To extricate itself from the difficulties of the situation the British government had, in October 1885, concluded an agreement with the Turkish government envisaging the evacuation of the country as soon as the questions of military and administrative organization should have been settled. Since that time Sir Henry Drummond Wolff and a Turkish commissioner, Muktar Pasha, had been in Egypt studying the problems at issue. But in the autumn of 1886 the French press had become very rabid on the subject of the Anglo-Turkish negotiations, arguing that these should be replaced by Anglo-French conversations. The whole agitation was characteristic of the Boulangist movement, which was as hostile to England as to Germany. Freycinet continued to be cautious, but he sought the support of Russia and even Germany and opened up negotiations with London. At the same time the French ambassador at Constantinople, supported by his Russian colleague, brought pressure to bear on the Sultan to induce him to accept a proposal that Turkish troops or officers should be used to form the cadres of the Egyptian army. According to Sir Charles Dilke, the Franco-Russian understanding was already so complete that it had the " effect of an alliance," and pressure of the two powers at the Porte was " immensely strong." [2] The climax was reached when Freycinet declared in the French chamber on November 27: " He who is master of Egypt is, in large part, master of the Mediterranean. It is certain that if a

---

[1] *Die Grosse Politik*, IV, No. 841.

[2] Dilke: *The Present Position of European Politics*, p. 70. The French advances to Germany, in *Die Grosse Politik*, VI, Nos. 1227, 1231, 1233. On this phase of the Egyptian question see Freycinet: *La Question d'Égypte*, pp. 356 ff.; Sir Henry Drummond Wolff: *Rambling Recollections* (London, 1908), Volume II, chapters lix–lxii; Newton: *Lord Lyons*, II, pp. 375 ff.

great power established itself definitively in Egypt, that would be a very serious blow at the influence of France in the Mediterranean, so much so that, in my opinion, France can never entertain the idea that Egypt should pass definitively into the hands of a great European power."

The tension between France and England which arose from the Egyptian question was so great in the winter of 1886–7 that Lord Salisbury went so far as to write to Lyons that, in view of the irritation resulting from this and other questions, "it is very difficult to prevent oneself from wishing for another Franco-German War to put a stop to this incessant vexation." [1] The atmosphere was evidently favourable for negotiations dealing with Mediterranean questions. But the success of the negotiations was undoubtedly furthered by the fact that Lord Randolph Churchill, proponent of the view that England's interest in the Near East was no longer of crucial importance, had resigned from the cabinet during the last days of December. In other words, when Bismarck urged upon the Italians the desirability of an agreement with England, it was likely that Salisbury would listen more appreciatively. In fact, Germany and England had already drawn together and were discussing possible co-operation in the Egyptian question. [2]

During the autumn of 1886 Bismarck had made every effort to evoke a more vigorous attitude on the part of the English in Near Eastern affairs. He had forwarded to London reports from von der Goltz, head of the German military mission at Constantinople, in which the danger of Russian influence was strongly presented. If Russia succeeded in securing control of the Porte, it would be hopeless for England to get her ships through the Straits. The emphasis on this aspect of the international situation made a real impression on Lord Salisbury, who sent Sir William White, one of the ablest English diplomats, to Constantinople. [3]

All these efforts reflect Bismarck's desire to induce the English to take a more active part in meeting the Russian danger. The chancellor's interest was to enlist the support of England on behalf of Austria. But the negotiations with Italy in December 1886 showed that Germany would have to promise support for Italy in her Mediterranean policy, and for that reason Bismarck became more eager than ever to bring the English to the side of the central powers. On January 1, 1887 the German Crown Princess wrote to Queen Victoria a letter which bears all the indications of having been inspired by Bismarck. The Princess stressed the desire of the Germans that England should re-establish her influence over Turkey. Bismarck, she said, feared Austria's weakness and England's inertia. Turkey, under English guidance, with Italy and Austria and the Balkan states, would indeed be strong enough to resist Russia and overcome

[1] Newton: *Lord Lyons,* II, p. 386.
[2] *Die Grosse Politik,* IV, Nos. 805 ff.
[3] Hajo Holborn: *Deutschland und die Türkei, 1878–1890* (Berlin, 1926), pp. 51 ff.

her. Germany would then be able to fight both France and Russia without fear, and the Eastern question would be solved once and for all.[1]

This letter contained the very germ of the idea of a Mediterranean coalition. Evidently Salisbury received the suggestion with favour. We do not know when actual negotiations with Italy were started, but on January 17, 1887 Salisbury expressed to the Italian ambassador his readiness to enter upon an exchange of views, with the object of making the relations between the two countries more intimate and useful. He desired to know more specifically what interests of Italy in the Mediterranean and in the Orient it was expected to protect by an entente. To this Robilant replied with a memorandum in four points, dated January 26. The first provided for the maintenance of the *status quo* in the Mediterranean, including the Adriatic, the Ægean, and the Black seas, and the prevention, if necessary, of any change which might be to the detriment of the two powers. The second point stated that if the *status quo* could not be maintained, the two powers should see to it that a modification took place only after previous agreement between them. In point three it was stated that Italy was prepared to support the work of England in Egypt, and that Great Britain in turn should support, against eventual invasion by the French, the action of Italy at every other point on the North African coast, and especially in Tripoli and Cyrenaica. Finally, point four: " Italy would be ready to range herself by the side of England in the Mediterranean in any war which this power might have with France, on the condition of reciprocity, on England's part, in any war between Italy and France." [2]

We have very little material bearing on these negotiations, particularly as they touched English policy. But in the recently published correspondence of Queen Victoria there is a letter of Lord Salisbury written a few days before the submission of the Italian proposals. This letter throws a flood of light on the considerations which moved the British prime minister. Germany, he argued, had made it clear that she would not help in resisting Russian pretensions in the East. She would not even promise to rescue Austria. All her attention was centred upon France. This made any conflict in the East more hazardous for England. Her own interests she could protect: "We can prevent Russia acquiring any foothold on the Ægean and on the Straits." But a conflict would menace Austria too, " and we can do nothing effective to save Austria. Yet it is of great importance to us that Austria should not succumb." Hence it was very necessary to avoid a conflict in the East. This did not mean that Russia should be given a free hand in Bulgaria. But time must be gained until the Franco-German tension was relaxed.[3]

Bearing these considerations in mind, Lord Salisbury was ready to entertain the Italian suggestions sympathetically when they were presented to him by the Italian ambassador on February 1. The proposal of an alliance with Italy in case

---

[1] *Letters of Queen Victoria*, I, p. 246.   [2] *Die Grosse Politik*, IV, No. 887
[3] *Letters of Queen Victoria*, I, pp. 264 ff.

of war with France could not, of course, be seriously discussed by a parliamentary government like the English, but the other points in the Italian note were not objectionable. Count Corti was told that England never promised material assistance in view of an uncertain war, of which the object and cause were unknown. Furthermore, any promise even of diplomatic assistance could not be directed against any single power such as France. But England would be glad to co-operate in the maintenance of the *status quo*. In any case the matter would have to be discussed in the cabinet.

The cabinet, when it met on February 2, approved the reply given by Salisbury. In the meanwhile Bismarck had been informed of the negotiations. He promptly began to use his influence to bring them to a successful close. Hatzfeldt was instructed to take the matter up with Salisbury, and Bismarck himself took the unusual step of calling personally on the British ambassador. He spent an hour urging the need for an agreement between England and Italy. In his instructions to Hatzfeldt he pointed out that a great power like England could not hold itself aloof from the problems of European politics without exposing itself to the danger of coalitions, which would be incompatible with England's own interests. Germany, for example, could not afford to oppose the French desires in Egypt or the Russian designs in the East unless England could be depended upon to support the treaty settlements and the *status quo*. Germany had nothing to gain by war with France or Russia, and, since she herself had no interests in Egypt or the East, she would have to purchase peace by concessions to these two powers, even at the expense of the Sultan. Austria was hardly strong enough to protect her own interests against Russia. The friendship of Italy would help her and give her greater confidence. This would be even more true if England stood behind Italy and if the latter had the assurance that the British fleet would fight by the side of the Italian. Unless the English supported Italy, the Italian fleet would not be strong enough against the French to enable Italy to take upon herself the dangers which threatened Austria. Germany could hardly do more than keep France in check, but so long as she fulfilled this function, England and Italy would have greater freedom of action. In combination with Austria they would be able to prevent a breach of peace by Russia. Thus the balance of power would be restored.[1]

Salisbury recognized the force of these arguments, but he pointed out to Hatzfeldt that, even though the assistance of England might be confidently looked for to maintain the *status quo* in the Mediterranean and might very probably be looked for if France were to attack Italy, it was very unlikely to be given if Italy made an aggressive war on France, even if Italy attacked in order to anticipate an attack from France. England, said Salisbury, had an earnest horror of the possible calamities of war. To which Hatzfeldt replied by renewed asseverations of Germany's pacific intentions. The prime minister, however,

---

[1] *Die Grosse Politik*, IV, Nos. 883, 889.

felt that there was great anxiety in the tone of the ambassador's remarks, and
that he betrayed a disposition to press the idea that the beginner of actual
operations was not necessarily the aggressor.[1]

The negotiations now proceeded apace. Robilant raised no objections to
Salisbury's reservations. The form of the agreement was a matter of indifference
to him, and he did not press the idea of an offensive and defensive alliance
against France. Bismarck argued that if the agreement were consummated,
France could by that very fact be kept in order. Salisbury's request for an assurance that the agreement would in no way be aimed at Austria was readily
granted by Robilant. By February 10 the English draft was complete and
was approved by parliament. The actual exchange of notes took place on
February 12.

Curiously enough, the English note was not drawn in exactly the same
terms as the Italian. The latter was practically in the form of the original
draft, excepting that the important fourth article had been modified to meet
the English objections. The final Italian version of this article read; " In general,
and to the extent that circumstances shall permit, Italy and England promise
one another mutual support in the Mediterranean in every difference which
may arise between one of them and a third power." The English reply began by
discussing this last article of the Italian note: " The statement of Italian policy
which is contained in Your Excellency's despatch of the 12th of February has
been received by H. M.'s Government with great satisfaction, as it enables them
to reciprocate cordially Count Robilant's friendly sentiments and to express
their own desire to co-operate generally with the Government of Italy in matters
of common interest to the two countries. The character of that co-operation
must be decided by them, when the occasion for it arises, according to the
circumstances of the case."

The whole wording of the English reply was more informal than that of
the Italian note. Salisbury was anxious to avoid high-sounding and impressive
terminology, and to save himself from constitutional difficulties in the future.
But it must not be supposed that he was trying to evade the issue. He wrote
to Queen Victoria that the English reply was so drawn " as to leave entirely
unfettered the discretion of your Majesty's Government, as to whether, in any
particular case, they will carry their support of Italy as far as ' material co-
operation.' But, short of a pledge upon this subject, it undoubtedly carries very
far the *relations plus intimes* which have been urged upon us. It is as close an
alliance as the Parliamentary character of our institutions will permit. Your
Majesty's advisers recommend it on the whole as necessary in order to avoid
serious danger. If, in the present grouping of nations, which Prince Bismarck
tells us is now taking place, England was left out in isolation, it might well
happen that the adversaries, who are coming against each other on the Continent, might treat the English Empire as divisible booty, by which their dif-

---

[1] *Letters of Queen Victoria*, I, pp. 268–70.

ferences might be adjusted; and, though England could defend herself, it would be at fearful risk and cost." [1]

The phrase promising support " to the extent that circumstances shall permit," or " according to the circumstances of the case," is found in similar form in Article IV of the separate Italian-German Treaty signed on February 20 and discussed above. There the German government promised support for Italy's desire for territorial guarantees after a war with France, " in a measure compatible with circumstances." It is a phrase of the greatest utility in diplomacy, for it always leaves a loop-hole. Promises conditioned by this reservation are likely to be of little or no value. They are there merely to give vague agreements an appearance of substantiality which they do not really possess. The English assurances to Italy could always be evaded. Take the passage in the English note which says that " the character of that co-operation must be decided by them." To the average reader the " them " refers to the English government. Yet Salisbury admitted that the Italian reading, by which it referred to both governments, was justifiable. The uncertain phraseology was allowed to stand because it would enable the English ministers to put their own construction upon it when pressed for information by parliament. [2]

In other words, the effort to read this or that into the terms of agreements of this sort is a mistaken effort. It was not intended that the provisions of these engagements should ever lead to action. They were meant as a deterrent. For the English and Italians the First Mediterranean Agreement was intended to check in advance any French designs in Tripoli or Morocco and to present a united front in the Egyptian question. At the same time it represented a connecting link between England and the Triple Alliance, which might, eventually, be extended. That Salisbury had this idea in mind is clear from the documents, and his apologist tells us of his great interest at that time in assuring the stability of the Triple Alliance and preventing Italy's withdrawal from it. [3]

The same attitude was taken by Italy, which had, even in the Triple Alliance Treaty of 1882, indicated anxiety to associate England with the continental grouping. In 1887 Robilant expressed the desire that this Mediterranean Agreement should be added to the renewed Triple Alliance. This Bismarck refused, because he was unwilling, on account of Russia, to associate Germany too obviously with the anti-Russian group. [4] But Depretis was right when he told the Italian cabinet in February 1887 that Robilant had attained what no cabinet had dared hope for from England, security for the Italian position on land and on sea. [5]

---

[1] *Letters of Queen Victoria*, I, pp. 271-2. On the negotiations see, further, *Die Grosse Politik*, IV, chapter xxvi, *passim*. The texts of the notes are in Pribram, op. cit., I, pp. 95-7.

[2] *Die Grosse Politik*, IV, No. 890.

[3] Ibid., No. 892; Anonymous: " The Marquis of Salisbury " (*Quarterly Review*, CXCVI, October 1902, pp. 663-4).

[4] *Die Grosse Politik*, IV, No. 890.

[5] Chiala: *Pagine di Storia*, III, p. 703.

For Bismarck himself the moral value of the connexion was of considerable importance, and for that reason he had furthered it to the best of his ability. In the first place it enabled him to make far-reaching promises of German support for Italy's North African policy in order to effect the renewal of the Triple Alliance. Furthermore, the association of England with the Triple Alliance gave him a certain contact and control over English policy, which was now definitely committed to the anti-French direction. But, above all, it seems that Bismarck had the East in view. The agreement was intended, by him, to furnish "a basis of defence upon which Austria could stand in case of necessity." [1] He had here a combination that would serve as a check on France, but could, so he hoped, be extended to serve as a check against Russia. England was relieving Germany of part of her obligations to support Italy, and he hoped that she could be brought to do the same with respect to Austria. And all the time Germany could manage to avoid out and out hostility to Russia. Bismarck was playing with the finesse of an expert chess-player. There was certainly a tinge of duplicity in the whole procedure, but this was redeemed by the fact that the great chancellor was working for European peace.

Even before the signature of the English-Italian agreement the English government had again approached Austria, asking how it could help in the event of a war between Russia and Austria. Kálnoky was evasive, as on earlier occasions. He feared that the English were trying to put Austria forward. But Salisbury, though discouraged, did not give up hope. The agreement with Italy was communicated to Vienna on February 19. Bismarck had already informed Kálnoky in great confidence some days earlier and had made clear the desirability of cultivating the connexion with England. Kálnoky therefore wrote to London expressing Austrian approval of the engagements and stating that there was no obstacle to a similar agreement between England and Austria, "if circumstances demanded it." He was evidently not very enthusiastic and would have preferred an arrangement by which Austria would be definitely assured of British military support, an arrangement, too, which would bind any British government. Salisbury, however, pointed out that such a pact would be impossible without consulting parliament. Italy had not been promised material support either. The thing to do would be to make an agreement concerning political aims and to effect unity of policies. It was true that in order to help Austria against Russia in the Black Sea it would be necessary for England to be able to get there. This would make an arrangement with Turkey in regard to the passage of the Dardanelles and Bosporus desirable. [2]

Nothing seems to have been done about the proposed agreement with the Porte, or about any project of military co-operation, though Bismarck urged the need for some action. But on March 5 Salisbury invited the Austrian

---

[1] *Die Grosse Politik,* IV, No. 885, marginalia, and 893.

[2] W. N. Medlicott: "The Mediterranean Agreements" (*Slavonic Review,* V, pp. 66–88, June 1926); *Die Grosse Politik,* IV, chapter xxvii; *Letters of Queen Victoria,* I, p. 276.

government to adhere to the English-Italian agreement. Bismarck gave his approval, though he was anxious not to put himself forward unless absolutely necessary to induce the Austrians to accept: "We must try to keep our hands free for the time being, so that we shall not be drawn in at once if it comes to a break with Russia in matters of the East, for we need all our forces against France. If we can stand aloof in a war of Austria and her allies against Russia, we can spare ourselves a war with France, because France will not be able to go to war, so long as we remain neutral and are not drawn into the struggle. If we make Russia distrustful by participating in the English-Italian-Austrian negotiations, it will hardly be possible for us not to become involved in a war with Russia, and then we shall be putting France in a very favourable position. It cannot be doubted for a moment that France will attack as soon as we get into armed conflict with Russia. . . . If we maintain the political attitude I have sketched, it is very likely that each of the two wars with which Europe is threatened can be fought separately." Austria should not forget that, if England were turned away, Salisbury would be likely to seek support against Russia among the Balkan states and encourage them in designs that would be to the detriment of Austria.[1]

In the meanwhile Kálnoky himself had followed up the English offer. The difficulty with a simple acceptance of the English-Italian agreement, he pointed out, lay in the fact that it gave greater assurances to Italian than to Austrian interests. England promised to " act " in Mediterranean affairs, but with respect to the Black Sea and the Ægean she simply expressed a "wish" that they should remain in the same hands as before. Austria had little interest in the problems of the Mediterranean, but great interest in the Near East. Salisbury had foreseen this objection and was prepared to meet it with concessions, for he agreed with Kálnoky that England had an equal interest in the Near East. In fact, Salisbury's object was to establish a common policy with Austria on just this question. The agreement with Italy was meant merely as a starting-point. There was no further obstacle to the Austrian adhesion, which took place on March 24, 1887. The wording brings out the important extension of the agreement so far as England was concerned. In the Austrian note it is stated: "Although the questions of the Mediterranean in general do not primarily affect the interests of Austria-Hungary, my government has the conviction that England and Austria-Hungary have the same interests so far as concerns the Eastern question as a whole, and therefore the same need of maintaining the status quo in the Orient, so far as possible, of preventing the aggrandizement of one power to the detriment of others, and consequently of acting in concert in order to ensure these cardinal principles of their policy."

To this the English cabinet replied: The British government " are fully

---

[1] *Die Grosse Politik*, IV, Nos. 900–1; Holborn: *Deutschland und die Türkei*, pp. 53 ff. Salisbury, at the time, was really encouraging the formation of a Balkan league (Driault and Lhéritier, op. cit., IV, p. 248).

convinced that, in respect to the political future of the territories which are washed by the Mediterranean and the adjacent seas, the interests of Austria-Hungary are closely related to those of Great Britain and Italy. It is rather, however, with the Euxine and the Ægean than with the western portion of the Mediterranean that the policy of Austria is engaged. But in respect to the territories on those seas whose political status more specially affects the interests of the Austro-Hungarian Empire, the objects of English and Austrian policy are the same, and the principles which ought to guide it are clearly indicated in the communications to which Count Kálnoky has expressed his willingness to adhere. Without determining beforehand the character which the co-operation of the two powers ought in any particular contingency to take, the efforts of H. M.'s Government in harmony with those of the Austro-Hungarian Government will be constantly directed to secure in these regions the maintenance, so long as it shall be possible, of the *status quo,* and, should that unhappily cease to be possible, the prevention of the growth of any novel domination hostile to the interests of the two countries." [1]

While the negotiations for the adherence of Austria to the English-Italian agreement were under way, discussions were also taking place between Rome and Madrid. In September 1886 the Spanish government had expressed the desire for an understanding, but these approaches had been coolly treated by Robilant, who was suspicious of Spain's designs in Morocco. Then, on November 29, the Spanish foreign minister, Señor Moret, came forward with the suggestion that Spain be admitted to the Triple Alliance. When the question was raised in Berlin, Bismarck referred the Spanish government to Rome. Little is known of these negotiations, which do not appear to have become serious until March 1887. On March 11 the Italian government drew up a projected agreement which envisaged the adhesion of Spain to the Triple Alliance. This idea was rejected by Bismarck, who considered the situation in Spain to be too uncertain and recommended a simple agreement between Madrid and Rome. An exchange of notes between these two cabinets took place on May 4, 1887. The Spanish note stated, among other things, that " Spain will not lend herself as regards France, in so far as the North African territories among others are concerned, to any treaty or political arrangement whatsoever which would be aimed directly or indirectly against Italy, Germany, and Austria, or against any one of these powers," and that " Spain will abstain from all unprovoked attack, as well as from all provocation."

The Italian government accepted these provisions and pledged reciprocity, but at the same time reserved the right to examine, in full agreement with Germany and Austria, whether and to what extent " there might be need, according to circumstances, to enter into further concert with the cabinet of Madrid in order the better to assure the purpose which it too has in view." The notes were communicated to Vienna and Berlin, and both Austria and Ger-

---

[1] Texts in Pribram, op. cit., I, pp. 98 ff.; *Die Grosse Politik,* IV, Nos. 905–6.

many acceded to the agreement on May 21, 1887. On June 13 the British government was informed of what had taken place, and Salisbury expressed his full sympathy with the agreement.[1]

The upshot of these numerous agreements was that they aimed at the preservation of the *status quo* in the Mediterranean and made a French forward policy there almost impossible. Bismarck has been called the spiritual father of the whole policy, and no doubt he was. For him the connexion of the powers whose interest it was to check French colonial enterprise was of value, for in case of need the same combination could be used to bring pressure upon France if she attempted to stir even upon the continent.

An interesting indication of this possibility is to be found in the discussion regarding England's stand towards a violation of Belgium's neutrality. As the danger of a Franco-German war became acute, the Belgian government, which had been very lax in its military preparations, was greatly concerned at the prospect of the violation of its territory by either France or Germany. That an invasion would take place seemed almost a foregone conclusion, for both the Germans and the French had fortified their frontiers so strongly that neither could hope to get past the forts of the other. The Belgians had relied upon eventual English aid, the more so as in 1870 Lord Granville had demanded from both the German and the French governments a promise that Belgian neutrality would be respected. On January 4 and again on the 13th Bismarck had instructed the minister at Brussels to secure from the Belgian government a statement as to how, where, by what time, and by what means Belgium intended to defend her neutrality. A high official of the Belgian foreign office thereupon approached the British minister, Lord Vivian, on January 27. The latter assured him that in case of war Belgium could count on English support, even though England had few forces at her disposal and the Belgians would, at the start, have to defend themselves.

Then, quite unexpectedly, there appeared in the London *Standard,* on February 4, a letter signed "Diplomaticus," and a leading article dealing with the subject of England's attitude towards the eventual violation of Belgian neutrality. The *Standard* was regarded as the mouthpiece of the Salisbury government, and for that reason great significance was attached to its utterances. "Diplomaticus," after reviewing the general situation, stated with undiplomatic bluntness that, "however much England might regret the invasion of Belgian territory by either party to the struggle, she could not take part with France against Germany (even if Germany were to seek to turn the French flank by pouring its armies through the Belgian Ardennes), without utterly vitiating and

---

[1] Texts in Pribram, op. cit., I, pp. 116 ff. Of the negotiations little is known, but see the account in Trützschler: *Bismarck und die Kriegsgefahr vom Jahre 1887,* pp. 70–2, which is based on unpublished German papers. See also Albert Mousset: *L'Espagne et la politique mondiale* (Paris, 1923), pp. 66–72; Conde de Romanones: *Las Responsabilidades políticas del antiguo Régimen* (Madrid, 1924), pp. 15 ff.; Angel Marvaud: "*La Politique extérieure de l'Espagne*" (*Revue des Sciences politiques,* I, pp. 41–74, January–March 1927).

destroying the main purposes of English policy all over the world." After all, he argued, " the temporary use of a right of way is something different from a permanent and wrongful possession of territory." The writer of the leading article subscribed to this view-point and concluded that " it would be madness for us to incur or assume responsibilities unnecessarily, when to do so would manifestly involve our participation in a tremendous war." Other newspapers and periodicals joined in, the Liberal *Pall Mall Gazette* even maintaining that there was no English guarantee to Belgium. Sir Charles Dilke, who himself believed that England should stand in support of Belgian neutrality, was obliged to admit, in the *Fortnightly Review*, in June, that it had become clear that if Belgium was to be saved, it was not by England: " My question whether we intend to fight for Belgium according to our treaty obligations, or to throw treaty obligations to the winds under some convenient pretext, is already answered."

The Belgian government was greatly alarmed by the view-point set forth in the *Standard* and supported by so much of the English press. It therefore approached the British minister again, but found that his attitude, too, had changed. His view now was that Belgium would do best to prepare as though she would have to act alone. Considering all this, it is hardly possible to take the denials of the British government during the World War very seriously. The Belgian government straightway initiated measures to strengthen the army and especially to refortify the strong places of the Meuse, like Namur and Liége. Bismarck welcomed these measures of preparation. It is absolutely certain that the German military authorities did not, at this time, include the invasion of Belgium in their plans of campaign, just as Bismarck had no intention whatever of taking the offensive against France. The Belgian government was assured by Bismarck that Belgian neutrality would not be violated, and the Berlin *Post* on February 24 stated, in what was clearly an inspired article, that Germany would not wage a preventive war, neither would she start a conflict with the violation of a European treaty. Since no war resulted, the whole incident is of rather academic interest, excepting as it bears on the English attitude in 1914. Here the matter has been brought up chiefly to show how the connexion of England with Italy and indirectly with the Triple Alliance was bound to colour her attitude towards the Franco-German problem.[1]

To return to the Mediterranean agreements. Apart from the effect which these engagements might have had on the European situation they contained a

---

[1] The Belgian problem is well discussed by Trützschler, op. cit., pp. 52–5, who makes use of some unpublished documents. The articles in the *Standard* are reprinted in full in C. P. Sanger and H. T. J. Norton: *England's Guarantee to Belgium and Luxemburg* (New York, 1915), pp. 99–107. Material published from the Belgian archives during the World War may be found in Bernard Schwertfeger: *Der Geistige Kampf um die Verletzung der belgischen Neutralität* (Berlin, 1919), pp. 104–13. On the German plans of campaign see H. von Kühl: *Der deutsche Generalstab in Vorbereitung und Durchführung des Weltkrieges* (Berlin, 1920), pp. 152 ff.; Graf Moltke: *Die deutschen Aufmarschpläne, 1871–1890* (Berlin, 1929), pp. 122 ff.

valuable promise for the future. The exchange of notes between London and Vienna had already brought the Near Eastern possibilities of the new grouping prominently to the fore. If the policy involved could be further developed in the same direction, so much the better, for the really important thing was to build up a barrier against Russia. Germany alone could hold France in check, and, besides, France would not be likely to move unless Russia stirred. Pending the completion of this highly complex but extraordinarily interesting international system Bismarck was anxious to maintain good relations with Russia. For that reason he kept out of the Mediterranean Agreement. He acceded to the Italian-Spanish understanding only with reluctance, regretting the complication of the system in this way. But this was a relatively unimportant aspect of the problem. In the major operations the German chancellor acted behind the scenes. By May 1887 France was completely hedged about. Had she attempted to move, she would have found herself entirely surrounded by the members of a coalition determined to maintain the *status quo* and prevent her taking action.

BIBLIOGRAPHICAL NOTE

DOCUMENTARY SOURCES

Accounts and Papers. 1887, Volume XCI. *Turkey,* Nos. 1 and 2 (*Further Correspondence respecting the Affairs of Bulgaria and Eastern Roumelia*). *1888,* Volume CIX (*Further Correspondence respecting the Affairs of Bulgaria and Eastern Roumelia*).

Die Grosse Politik der europäischen Kabinette. Volume IV: chapter xxiii (German-English Relations, 1885–8, with special references to colonial matters), xxiv (The Renewal of the Triple Alliance), xxv (Anglo-Austrian negotiations during 1886), xxvi (The Negotiations between England and Italy in 1887), xxvii (Austrian adherence to the Anglo-Italian entente). Volume V: chapter xxxi (German-Russian Relations, 1886), xxxii (Austria and the Bulgarian Crisis), xxxiii (Continuation of the Bulgarian Crisis). Volume VI: chapter xxxix (Franco-Russian Soundings, 1886–90), xl (The Franco-German Crisis and its Aftereffects, 1886–90).

MEMOIRS, AUTOBIOGRAPHIES, BIOGRAPHIES, AND LETTERS

The Letters of QUEEN VICTORIA. Edited by G. E. Buckle. Third Series. Volume I. New York, 1930. Contains valuable material on English policy.

CHURCHILL, WINSTON S.: *Lord Randolph Churchill.* New York, 1906. Two volumes. A source of first-rate importance for the study of British foreign policy in the autumn of 1886.

NEWTON, LORD: *Lord Lyons*. Two volumes. London, 1913. Contains some interesting reports from Paris for the winter of 1886–7.

DUCRAY, CAMILLE: *Paul Deroulède*. Paris, 1914. The best general study of the political aspect of Deroulède's activity.

TOUTAIN, EDMOND: *Alexandre III et la République française*. Paris, 1929. These reminiscences of a French diplomat throw considerable light on Franco-Russian relations in this period. Toutain frequently refers to unpublished French correspondence.

FREYCINET, CHARLES DE: *Souvenirs, 1878–1893*. Paris, 1913. The French statesman's memoirs are of great interest for the whole subject of French domestic and foreign affairs in these years.

FLOURENS, EMILE: *Alexandre III, sa vie, son œuvre*. Paris, 1894. In this biography of the Tsar the French foreign minister has taken the opportunity to reveal something of his own policy towards Russia.

SCHWEINITZ, GENERAL LOTHAR VON: *Denkwürdigkeiten*. Two volumes. Berlin, 1927. In this period, too, these recollections of the German ambassador to Russia serve as a useful supplement to the German documents.

LUCIUS VON BALLHAUSEN, ROBERT: *Bismarck-Erinnerungen*. Stuttgart, 1920. The diary of a German minister and close friend of Bismarck. One of the most revealing and intimate sources for these years.

WALDERSEE, ALFRED GRAF VON: *Denkwürdigkeiten*. Three volumes. Stuttgart, 1922–3. *Briefwechsel*. Berlin, 1928. These very detailed diaries and correspondence of the German quartermaster-general and first assistant to Moltke at the general staff give the most complete picture of the last years of the Bismarck régime.

CORTI, EGON C.: *Alexander von Battenberg*. Vienna, 1920. Valuable for the history of the attempts made to restore Alexander to the Bulgarian throne after his abdication.

MEYENDORFF, BARON A.: *Correspondance diplomatique de M. de Staal*. Two volumes. Paris, 1929. The correspondence of the Russian ambassador at London, surprisingly sterile for the study of this period.

LAMSDORF, COUNT VLADIMIR: *Dnievnik, 1886–1890*. Moscow, 1926. The diary of one of the high officials of the Russian foreign office. It is not a complete record and contains many lacunae, but is of first-rate importance.

NEVEDENSKI, S.: *Katkov i ego Vremia*. St. Petersburg, 1888. The best general study of Katkov's career, based upon the great journalist's articles in the *Moscow Gazette* and other publications.

SPECIAL STUDIES

DILKE, SIR CHARLES: *The Present Position of European Politics*. London, 1887. This volume consists of articles published monthly in the spring of 1887 in the

Fortnightly Review. They are of the utmost interest, full of discernment and understanding.

FULLER, JOSEPH V.: *Bismarck's Diplomacy at its Zenith.* Cambridge, Mass., 1922. The most detailed study of Bismarck's policy in the years 1885 to 1888, and fully abreast of the material available at the time of publication; but characterized throughout by deep distrust of the chancellor's aims and methods.

TRÜTZSCHLER VON FALKENSTEIN, HEINZ: *Bismarck und die Kriegsgefahr des Jahres 1887.* This must be read in conjunction with Fuller. It is perhaps the best single study of the critical year 1887.

ALBIN, PIERRE: *La Paix armée. L'Allemagne et la France en Europe, 1885–1894.* Paris, 1913. Though in some respects now out of date, this is still one of the best books to read on the period, for it is well-informed and well-balanced.

GOOCH, GEORGE P.: *Franco-German Relations 1871–1914.* London, 1923. This is the best general account of Franco-German relations in the period.

HALLER, JOHANNES: *Tausend Jahre deutsch-französischer Beziehungen.* Stuttgart, 1930. An excellent survey of the same subject.

PINON, RENÉ: *France et Allemagne, 1870–1913.* Paris, 1913. A standard French account, but far inferior to Albin for this period.

ZEVAES, ALEXANDRE: *Au Temps du Boulangisme.* Paris, 1930. The latest systematic account of the movement, stressing the domestic aspect.

BOURGEOIS, EMILE and PAGÈS, GEORGES: *Les Origines et les responsabilités de la Grande Guerre.* Paris, 1921. Contains some documents on Franco-German relations in these years.

PRIBRAM, ALFRED F.: *The Secret Treaties of Austria-Hungary.* Two volumes. Cambridge, 1920–1. By far the best single account of the renewal of the Triple Alliance. Based on the unpublished papers of the Austrian foreign office.

CHIALA, LUIGI: *Pagine di Storia Contemporanea.* Volume III: *" La Triplice e la Duplice Alleanza."* Second edition. Turin, 1898. Though it must be corrected in the light of Pribram's book and the German documents, this is still the standard Italian account.

BOURGEOIS, EMILE: *" L'Allemagne et la France au printemps de 1887 "* (*Revue des sciences politiques,* XLVII, pp. 5–17, January–March 1924). A bitter attack upon the German policy, based upon the German documents.

TRÜTZSCHLER VON FALKENSTEIN, HEINZ: *" Kontroversen über die Politik Bismarcks im Jahre 1887 "* (*Archiv für Politik und Geschichte,* VI, 1926, pp. 269–81). An effective reply to the preceding.

MEDLICOTT, W. N.: *" The Mediterranean Agreements of 1887 "* (*Slavonic Review,* V, pp. 60–88. June 1926). The only monographic study of these important agreements, especially valuable because based in part upon unpublished Austrian material.

Mousset, Albert: *L'Espagne et la politique mondiale.* Paris, 1923. The best general account of Spanish foreign policy in these years, though now somewhat out of date.

Marvaud, Angel: " *La Politique extérieure de l'Espagne* " (*Revue des sciences politiques,* L, pp. 41–74, January–March 1927). Reviews the more recent literature on Spanish foreign policy.

Heller, Eduard: *Das deutsch-österreichische Bündnis in Bismarcks Aussenpolitik.* Berlin, 1925.

Schünemann, Karl: " *Die Stellung Österreich-Ungarns in Bismarcks Bündnispolitik* " (*Archiv für Politik und Geschichte,* VI, pp. 549–94, 1926; VII, pp. 118–52, 1926). This and the preceding title supplement each other. The two writers take different views of the problem of German-Austrian relations in these years.

Heller, Eduard: " *Bismarcks Stellung zur Führung des Zweifrontenkrieges* " (*Archiv für Politik und Geschichte,* VII, pp. 677–98, 1926). An interesting contribution to the strategical problems of the war on two fronts.

Goriainov, Serge: " The End of the Alliance of the Emperors " (*American Historical Review,* XXIII, pp. 324–50, January 1918). An article of great importance, dealing with the Russian-German negotiations in these years and based upon the Russian documents.

Uebersberger, Hans: " *Abschluss und Ende des Rückversicherungsvertrages* " (*Die Kriegsschuldfrage,* V, pp. 933–66, October 1927). Chiefly an analysis of the Lamsdorf diaries.

Koerlin, Kurt: *Zur Vorgeschichte des russisch-französischen Bündnisses, 1879–1890.* Halle, 1926. A thorough but conventional account of the relations between France and Russia.

Daudet, Ernest: *Histoire diplomatique de l'alliance franco-russe.* Paris, 1894. Still the best general account of the making of the alliance from 1873 onwards.

Hansen, Jules: *L'Alliance franco-russe.* Paris, 1897. Hansen was a French secret agent and there is much of interest in his book.

Cyon, Elie de: *Histoire de l'entente franco-russe, 1886–1894.* Paris, 1895. Though in many respects unreliable, this book will always have to be read in connexion with Franco-Russian relations. Cyon was a collaborator of Katkov and throws much light upon the activity of the Russian nationalist group both in Moscow and in Paris.

Grüning, Irene: *Die russische öffentliche Meinung und ihre Stellung zu den Grossmächten, 1878–1894.* Berlin, 1929. A valuable study of the evolution of the Russian press, with special reference to Katkov and his policies.

XII

The League of Peace

◈

ON FEBRUARY 20, 1887, THE VERY DATE OF THE RENEWAL OF THE TRIPLE Alliance, there appeared in the *Nord,* a Russian official paper published in Brussels, an article purporting to define the policy of the Russian government. "Russia," it said, "will henceforth watch the events on the Rhine and will relegate the question of the East to the background. Russia's interest forbids her observing the same benevolent neutrality as in 1870 in the event of another Franco-German war. The St. Petersburg cabinet will, under no circumstances, permit a further weakening of France. In order to preserve her liberty of action, Russia will avoid all conflict with Austria and England and will allow events in Bulgaria to take their course."

This was an accurate definition of the policy which Katkov had been advocating for the past several months. Its official adoption would have meant the victory of the journalist over the foreign minister. As a matter of fact, however, the article was a ruse, for which the foreign minister, Giers, disclaimed all responsibility.[1] And in any case even a victory for Katkov would have come too late. There was not going to be a Franco-German war. The elections for the German Reichstag indicated that the army bill would be passed, and the conclusion of the Triple Alliance and the Mediterranean Agreement had completely altered the complexion of international affairs. Though the texts of these agreements were kept rigorously secret, the fact of the renewal of the Triple Alliance had been published almost at once, and rumours of the Mediterranean Agreement had leaked out in the Paris press, probably through indiscretions at London. It appears, in fact, that the French government was pretty well-informed of what was going on and had a fairly accurate idea of the terms of the Triple Alliance.[2]

Whatever information the government may have had, it certainly served to dampen its ardour for an agreement with Russia. Flourens became rather uncomfortable about the violence of the Pan-Slav affection for France and especially for Boulanger.[3] It was probably this anxiety that led the cabinet to send the famous builder of the Suez Canal, Ferdinand de Lesseps, to

---

[1] Schweinitz: *Denkwürdigkeiten,* II, p. 335; Cyon, op. cit., p. 239.

[2] Charles de Moüy: *Souvenirs et causeries d'un diplomate,* pp. 228–9. Moüy was French ambassador at Rome. See also Newton: *Lord Lyons,* II, pp. 390, 398–9.

[3] Toutain, op. cit., p. 216.

Berlin in March. Ostensibly his mission was to award the French ambassador at Berlin a high order in the Legion of Honour. But a meeting with Bismarck was arranged for. The chancellor told him that he was glad to see him, since "the great cloud" had now been dispelled. No one wanted peace more than he did. But for a moment he had thought it would be necessary to take up arms to resist a French attack.[1] His attitude towards the French situation had not really changed, for he still felt that trouble might arise if Boulanger remained in office. This is well brought out by his conversation with Crown Prince Rudolf of Austria, who came to Berlin in March to attend the jubilee of the old Emperor.

Rudolf was known to cherish distinct sympathies for France and to look upon Germany with some suspicion. Like many prominent Austrians he believed that Bismarck was seeking a pretext for war with France, and that war was inevitable for that reason. If war broke out, it was to be expected that Russia would attack Austria, and the great question in the minds of all Austrian statesmen was how much support could be expected from Germany. They had been warned by Bismarck that it would not be much, and for that reason Rudolf was an ardent advocate of a close understanding between Austria, Germany, England, and Italy. The great problem was how to restrain Russia, for there was no denying that at the moment "Russia played the first fiddle in Europe, and was the strongest power and imposed her will on the rest; and that this would remain a constant danger, as she could get France to join her whenever she liked." Only the alliance of the four powers could keep her in check.[2]

The chancellor began by assuring his interlocutor that he did not desire war and that Germany was not a predatory state. The military men were trying to force action upon him, but he was insisting on peace. Germany would attack no one, and if France and Russia did not begin a war, peace would be maintained for a long time. So far as France was concerned, everything depended on whether Boulanger succeeded in acquiring more influence and power. If he did, war would be almost certain, and Germany would need most of her forces in the West. For that reason Austria should strive to establish a strong coalition so that she could shoulder the war with Russia even without much German help. Time and again he referred to the Mediterranean Agreement. Then, turning to Russia, he remarked that he was not at all certain what her attitude would be. In the beginning of a Franco-German war she would probably remain neutral, but if things took a bad turn for France, the nationalists in Russia would probably force the Tsar to save France from annihilation. It might also be that Russia would, from the start, direct her efforts against Austria. But it was more likely that she would try to utilize

---

[1] Bismarck: *Werke*, VIII, p. 556.

[2] Ponsonby: *Letters of the Empress Frederick*, pp. 210–11 (remarks of Rudolf to the German Crown Prince before his interview with Bismarck).

the opportunity to advance in the East, to occupy Bulgaria or approach Constantinople. In that case his advice to Austria would be to let the Russians enter the "mouse-trap" and embroil themselves with the Roumanians and Bulgarians. The Turks also would come in and England would have to act to protect her interests, whether she liked it or not. The Austrians should be well prepared and then wait until the English fired the first shot. If Austria acted first, there would be always the danger that the English would remain idle spectators. In Italy he had little confidence, but she must be made reliable and must be bound to the central powers with presents such as Nice, Corsica, Albania, and the North African coast. Peace, he thought, was secure for the year 1887, but there was always danger, and Austria ought to strengthen her military forces, for a strong army was a guarantee of peace.[1]

In other words, Bismarck still looked with uneasiness towards Paris. Boulanger was still the great menace, for, as the chancellor said to a friend, the French minister of war was like a leashed dog. The other ministers were holding him back and he could not get loose from the chain. But if he did succeed in tearing himself loose, he could no longer take his tail between his legs and retreat. He would have to leap forward and attack.[2] Germany, as he repeated over and over again, would not attack.

The so-called Schnaebele incident of April 1887 has always received a good deal of attention from writers on Franco-German relations, some of whom go so far as to describe it as marking the height of the international tension. This is a great exaggeration. The episode is of secondary importance and interesting chiefly for the light it throws upon the policies of the French and German governments. Schnaebele was an Alsatian who had opted for France in 1871 and who had been made a French frontier official at Pagny-sur-Moselle. There is no question whatever that he utilized his position to organize and supervise an elaborate system of espionage in the two lost provinces, and that his reports went not only to the French ministry of the interior, but also to the ministry of war. For these activities the German high court at Leipzig had, in February 1887, ordered his arrest as soon as he appeared on German territory. This decision was taken with the knowledge and approval of Bismarck.[3] Schnaebele was evidently regarded as a very dangerous character.

It seems that the French official was warned of the steps to be taken against him, and that he ceased making his usual little excursions to Metz and other places. But on April 20 he crossed the frontier to consult with his German colleague about local matters. He was set upon by two men and arrested.

---

[1] A. F. Pribram: "Zwei Gespräche des Erzherzogs Rudolf mit Bismarck" (Österreichische Rundschau, 1921, pp. 8–19). See also Eduard von Wertheimer: "Kronprinz Erzherzog Rudolf und Fürst Bismarck" (Archiv für Politik und Geschichte, IV, pp. 349–63, April 1925); Mitis: Kronprinz Rudolf, pp. 359 ff.

[2] Ferdinand Philipp: Bismarck-Gespräche (Dresden, 1927), pp. 86–7. See similar statements in Lucius von Ballhausen, op. cit., p. 373.

[3] Die Grosse Politik, VI, No. 1258 and foot-note.

According to the French version, he had, in the struggle, carried his two attackers some feet over the frontier line into French territory. But Schnaebele himself does not appear to have been absolutely certain of this point, and the Germans have always insisted that the arrest took place on German territory. The incident created a great stir on both sides of the frontier, the French being generally convinced that the whole affair was a ruse by which the chancellor hoped to provoke the French government into rash actions which could be taken as a pretext for war. Fortunately President Grévy and the foreign minister, Flourens, as well as the ambassador at Berlin, were anxious to avoid friction and settle the matter in an amiable way. It was their good luck that among Schnaebele's papers were found invitations from his German colleague, Gautsch, to cross the frontier to discuss official matters.[1] These papers gave the whole incident a different setting. Thus far Bismarck had maintained that Schnaebele's arrest had taken place on German territory and that he must be tried for his subversive activities. This view-point the chancellor maintained throughout, but he admitted immediately when photographs of the invitations were shown him by the French ambassador that these documents gave Schnaebele what amounted to safe-conduct. The German officials had, on this point, been in the wrong. On April 30 Schnaebele was released.[2]

One thing came out very clearly in the negotiations for the settlement of this untoward incident, and that was Bismarck's readiness to give the French their due. French writers like Albin remark on the extreme cordiality and reciprocal goodwill with which the pourparlers were carried on, and impartial recent writers like Cahen have completely discarded the old thesis that Bismarck was seeking a pretext for war. Certainly at the time neither Grévy nor Flourens took a tragic view of the situation. The President especially insisted that the thing could and should be settled in a pacific way. Goblet, the prime minister, however, favoured a firm stand against such provocation by Bismarck. After the affair had blown over, he is reported to have expressed the opinion that perhaps it would have been preferable to settle all these quarrels with the Germans by war.[3]

Boulanger, it seems, desired to concentrate troops in the newly built barracks on the Franco-German frontier and took some steps in the direction of military preparation. Goblet denies absolutely that the war minister wished to precipitate a war, but on the other hand President Grévy himself told the German ambassador somewhat later of Boulanger's demands and insisted that Goblet had supported them. However this may have been, Grévy and

---

[1] The facsimiles of these letters are now printed in the microscopic articles of Camille Vergniol: " L'Affaire Schnaebele " (La Revue de France, II, pp. 406–25, 645–68, April 1 and 15, 1929).

[2] Die Grosse Politik, VI, Nos. 1257–64; Albin, op. cit., chapter ii; Fuller, op. cit., chapter viii; Vergniol, loc. cit.

[3] Bourgeois and Pagès, op. cit., p. 229; see also Goblet's memoirs (René Goblet: " Souvenirs de ma vie politique; L'Affaire Schnaebele," in Revue Politique et parlementaire, CXXXVII, pp. 177–97, November 10, 1928).

Flourens managed to exclude Boulanger from the crucial discussions and to put their own policy into effect. After the crisis Herbette, the ambassador at Berlin, came to Paris. He evidently urged once again the necessity of getting rid of the war minister if peace was to be secured. Grévy had reached the same conclusion some time before. With the aid of Ferry, who was one of Boulanger's most consistent opponents, a cabinet crisis was brought about. The Goblet ministry fell on May 16, but it was almost two weeks before anyone could be found with sufficient courage to form a cabinet without Boulanger. Finally Rouvier took over the formation of a government, in which General Ferron was minister of war, while Flourens remained at the foreign office. The first critical phase of the Boulangist period was over.[1]

Bismarck welcomed the formation of a new French cabinet without Boulanger, because he regarded it as an added guarantee of peace. He had been careful to avoid trouble with France, because he was uncertain of the Russian attitude, despite the fact that the Three Emperors' Alliance was not due to expire until June 1887. He knew perfectly well that this agreement was practically defunct and had already made up his mind to replace it by a separate Russian-German alliance if that were possible. What would actually happen depended entirely upon whether or not Katkov would be able to win over the Tsar to his point of view. The German chancellor watched the Giers-Katkov struggle with the greatest interest, and when the famous article was published in the Nord on February 20, he hastened to give assurances to the Russian government that Germany would not attack France, and that if she were drawn into war through the provocation of France, she would not, in case of victory, "bleed her white," but would treat her leniently, as she had treated Austria in 1866. "We need a counter-weight to England on the sea," said Bismarck in this statement which was to be shown to the Tsar, "for the changing governments of England afford us no security over a long period." An entente with France, even closer than in the time of Ferry, would, he asserted, not be out of the question.[2]

Bismarck's assurances with respect to France were the negative side of his policy. They were intended to convince the Russians that there was no need for anxiety in the West. The positive side of the policy is expressed in Bismarck's efforts to interest the Russians once more in the Near East, for there, he believed, they would immediately feel the need for German support and would come to realize again the value of German friendship. After the conclusion of the Mediterranean Agreement the chancellor instructed the German ambassador at Constantinople not to support the Russian policy so

---

[1] See *Die Grosse Politik*, VI, Nos. 1263, 1267, 1275, for Boulanger's attitude during the Schnaebele crisis. On his overthrow see Freycinet: *Souvenirs*, pp. 372 ff.; Rambaud: *Jules Ferry*, pp. 430 ff.; Goblet, loc. cit.

[2] Schweinitz: *Briefwechsel*, p. 234; *Die Grosse Politik*, VI, No. 1253; Waldersee: *Denkwürdigkeiten*, I, pp. 317 ff.

actively as in the past. On the other hand, he was to assist England in the Egyptian question more actively than before.[1] Hardly a week later the ambassador at St. Petersburg was instructed to say that Germany had no objection to offer even if Russia extended her influence south of Bulgaria, to the Straits. Speaking to a friend at this time, the chancellor asserted that it would suit him very well if Russia were to make an agreement with Turkey regarding the occupation of several points on the Dardanelles, for this "would give Germany the opportunity to mobilize England."[2] When, early in April, the Turks came forward with the suggestion that they be admitted to the Triple Alliance, Bismarck rejected the idea, but encouraged England and Austria to follow it up. Nothing came of the soundings, but they illustrate the aim which the German chancellor was pursuing.[3] The policy, as aforesaid, was simply this: to encourage the Russians to resume their activity in the East, but at the same time to mobilize the new Mediterranean coalition against Russia and thereby prove to the Tsar that his only hope of success lay in obtaining German support. There is no evidence that Bismarck was himself involved in various projects to restore Alexander of Battenberg to the Bulgarian throne in March and April, and Lord Salisbury was certainly wrong in supposing that the German statesman's game was to involve Russia deeply in Bulgaria in order to get a free hand for a reckoning with France. The policy was much more subtle. Bismarck's eye was not fixed on the West, but on the East, for in his opinion "the decision on war or peace depends exclusively upon the feeling and decision of the Emperor of Russia."[4]

By this time the tide of battle in the Giers-Katkov conflict had already begun to turn. The Tsar was outraged by a violent article in the *Moscow Gazette* of March 7, in which Katkov delivered an uncompromising attack on the Three Emperors' Alliance and demanded once more that Russia retain a free hand. Alexander insisted that the famous journalist be warned, and declared roundly that he would not accept dictation in foreign policy. The warning as originally planned was toned down somewhat, but the Tsar himself remonstrated with Katkov when the latter came to St. Petersburg at the end of March. The Moscow influence was clearly waning and the stormy period of Russian politics drew to a close when Saburov was called to account for having communicated the text of the Three Emperors' Alliance to Katkov.[5]

---

[1] *Die Grosse Politik*, V, No. 1007; IV, No. 808; Radowitz: *Aufzeichnungen*, II, p. 267.

[2] Trützschler: *Bismarck und die Kriegsgefahr des Jahres 1887*, p. 62; Waldersee, op. cit., I, p. 317.

[3] Trützschler, op. cit., pp. 87–8.

[4] Schweinitz: *Denkwürdigkeiten*, II, p. 339. The Bulgarian projects and Lord Salisbury's suspicions are discussed, on the basis of unpublished material, in Corti: *Alexander von Battenberg*, pp. 295–301. See also the *Letters of Queen Victoria*, Third Series, Volume I (New York, 1930), pp. 294–5; and the able criticism in Trützschler, op. cit., pp. 91–4.

[5] See especially Grüning: *Die russische öffentliche Meinung*, pp. 110 ff.; Pobiedonostsev: *Mémoires*, pp. 410 ff., 466 ff.

The victory of the Russian foreign minister over his attackers was a matter of supreme significance for the shaping of international relations, for Giers had no use whatever for the idea of a Franco-Russian alliance, which was so popular in Russian society and in the army. He did not even believe in Katkov's theory that Russia should retain a free hand and direct her attention to the development of the situation in the West. He had no faith whatever in the current belief that Bismarck was planning a preventive war against his French neighbour. Quite the contrary, if Giers had had his way, he would have proceeded with the renewal of the Three Emperors' Alliance; that is, he would have tried to patch up the differences between Russia and Austria in order to maintain the "triangular rampart" of the three empires against all subversive tendencies. In the middle of March he spoke to the German chargé d'affaires of the desirability of continuing the agreement between the three powers, though he realized fully the difficulties presented by the inclusion of Austria. Evidently this broaching of the question was due to Giers's desire to do something to regulate the Bulgarian problem. Without the support of Germany little was to be done, but Bismarck had made it clear by repeated statements that he was only too ready to assist the Russians in the execution of any plans they might advance. The Russian scheme was to replace the Bulgarian regency with a single regent designated by the Russian government. Efforts to convince the Sultan of the advantages of such an arrangement had failed completely, and in the middle of April Giers approached the Germans with a request that they use their influence. Bismarck seized the opportunity to indicate his sincere goodwill towards Russia. All he asked was that Giers should bring forward a concrete proposal. After that Germany would support it to the utmost. Indeed, the chancellor even offered to send his son Herbert to London to persuade the English government of the Russian view-point.[1]

With this projected co-operation in the Bulgarian affair as a background the negotiations between the two governments were begun. On April 23 the Russian ambassador at Berlin, Count Paul Shuvalov, and Giers himself went over the matter with the Tsar. Alexander flatly refused to consider the renewal of the agreement with Austria and was evidently supported in his view by Shuvalov. Soon afterwards the Austrian ambassador was politely told that there could be no thought of continuing the connexion. But the Tsar agreed that an alliance with Germany was desirable and authorized the beginning of negotiations. For two weeks Giers and Shuvalov went over the situation. Apparently Shuvalov wished to start where his brother Peter had left off in January, but Giers, as usual, was moderate in his desires. The instruction with which Shuvalov went to Berlin in the first week of May set forth as Russia's objects: (1) to surround the maintenance of peace with solid guarantees, indispensable to the development of Russia's military, naval, and financial strength, and to guard Russia against the danger of European coalitions by sincere

---

[1] *Die Grosse Politik*, V, Nos. 1034 ff.

and firm alliance with the most powerful of the neighbouring states, whose influence was at the time decisive in most questions arising in Europe and even in the Orient; (2) to prevent any arbitrary alteration of the territorial *status quo* in the Balkan Peninsula and to cause it to be recognized that a preponderant influence on Russia's part in the two Bulgarias was legitimate; (3) to guarantee as far as possible the inviolability of the Straits by assuring Russia of the firm support of Germany in proclaiming in decided terms, and in case of need enforcing, respect for this principle on the part of Turkey and of all the powers signatory to the treaties in which it had been embodied.[1]

These points, with the exception of the second, which would cause no difficulty, were essentially the same as those pursued by the Russian government in negotiating the agreement of 1881. The discussions, therefore, should have run smoothly. In reality they were very trying. Not that Bismarck objected to the exclusion of Austria. On the contrary he seems to have regarded this matter with great equanimity, probably because he had come to realize the danger of Austria's efforts to extend German obligations under the treaty of 1879 to include support for Austria's Balkan policy. He was already pressing upon Kálnoky the desirability of publishing the text of the Austrian-German Alliance in order to put an end to exaggerated notions regarding its scope.[2] The difficulties in the negotiations with Shuvalov arose rather from the efforts of the latter to sell Russia's friendship dearly and extract additional concessions.

The conferences between the two men began on May 11 and lasted until May 18. Shuvalov began by recalling to Bismarck his oft-repeated statements that Germany would not attack France, and then pointed out that, in his understanding, what Germany wanted was an assurance of Russian neutrality in the event of a French attack upon Germany. He then brought forward and read a complete Russian draft for a treaty. Article I read: "If one of the High Contracting Parties should find itself at war with a third great power, the other would maintain a benevolent neutrality towards it and would devote its efforts to the localization of the conflict." This was an exact reproduction of the first clause of the Alliance of the Three Emperors, excepting that it was arranged for two powers instead of for three. It will be noted that in both instances Russian neutrality was provided for a Franco-German conflict, no matter which side was the aggressor. It gave Germany an entirely free hand in the West and contained no indication of Russia's desire to restrict her neutrality to the case of a French attack upon Germany. It seems that Giers was willing to let this stand as it had stood since 1881, but that Shuvalov on his own initiative meant to attempt to limit the Russian obligation in order to strengthen his bargaining power.[3]

---

[1] Goriainov, loc. cit., pp. 334–5.

[2] *Die Grosse Politik*, V, Nos. 1012, 1101 ff.

[3] Shuvalov's reports of these conversations have been published in *Krasny Arkhiv*, I (1922), pp. 92–135. Goriainov's account is based on these papers. The German documents contain almost no material on the negotiations.

Bismarck made no comment as Shuvalov read, but he evidently saw from the beginning what the Russian diplomat was aiming at. The second article presented no difficulty. It read: "Germany recognizes the rights historically acquired by Russia in the Balkan Peninsula, and particularly the legitimacy of her exclusive influence in Bulgaria and in Eastern Roumelia. The two courts engage to admit no modification of the territorial *status quo* of the said peninsula without a previous agreement between them, and to oppose, as occasion arises, every attempt to disturb this *status quo*." Bismarck merely suggested the substitution of the phrase "preponderant and decisive influence" for "exclusive influence," pointing out that, after all, Turkey was the suzerain power. In the same way he suggested that it would be better to say the "legal territorial *status quo*," rather than merely the "territorial *status quo*" because the conditions at the moment were distinctly not legal according to the Treaty of Berlin. Shuvalov accepted these suggestions, admitting, incidentally, that Giers would have been satisfied with the phrase "preponderant influence," and that it was he who had argued for a stronger word.

Coming to the third article, this was taken word for word from Article III of the Alliance of the Three Emperors, excepting that the term "three courts" was changed to "two courts." Since its importance is very great, it may be well to repeat it here: "The two courts recognize the European and mutually obligatory character of the principle of the closure of the Straits of the Bosporus and Dardanelles, founded on international law, confirmed by the treaties, and summed up in the declaration of the second plenipotentiary of Russia at the session of July 12 of the Congress of Berlin (Protocol 19). They will take care in common that Turkey shall make no exception to this rule in favour of the interests of any government whatever, by lending to warlike operations of a belligerent power the portion of her empire constituted by the Straits. In case of infraction, or to prevent infraction if such should be in prospect, the two courts will inform Turkey that they would regard her, in that event, as putting herself in a state of war towards the injured party, and as depriving herself thenceforth of the benefits of the security assured to her territorial *status quo* by the Treaty of Berlin."

It was this clause that gave Bismarck his opening. He repeated statements he had made before, to the effect that he was prepared to see Russia installed in the Straits and at Constantinople, the key to her house. Shuvalov said that the Russians counted on this attitude of the German government, and that this matter had not been included in Article III because it was feared that it might obscure the provisions regarding the closure of the Straits. Bismarck admitted the contradiction, but restated his position more forcefully than ever: "Germany would have no objection to seeing you masters of the Straits, possessors of the entrance to the Bosporus, and of Constantinople itself." This declaration, he said, could be registered in a separate protocol, under double seal and the utmost secrecy.

Why was the German chancellor so free with other people's property? Why was he so anxious to press these far-reaching concessions upon the Russian negotiator? The reason is not far to seek. Article I was the crux of the whole matter. So long as the agreement with Russia had been a tripartite one in which Austria was included, it had presented no difficulties. Now, however, its general form could not be accepted because Germany's obligation to defend Austria against a Russian attack (alliance of 1879) was incompatible with the proposed obligation to remain neutral in any war in which Russia might become involved with a third power. Bismarck wanted the assurance of Russian neutrality in the event of any Franco-German conflict, because he knew how elusive a term the word " aggression " was and feared that if the Russian obligation were limited to the case in which France was the attacker, a very dangerous loop-hole would be left and evasion would be almost certain. At the same time he was forced to ask for just this limitation of German neutrality in a Russian-Austrian war. In order to prepare the way for this demand he tried to distract Shuvalov by dangling before his eyes the attractive prospect of a Russian occupation of the Straits and Constantinople. Shuvalov, who was no fool, seems to have sensed the chancellor's strategy, for he immediately added that decisive action on Russia's part in the Bosporus was theoretical rather than probable and that therefore he could not consider the advantages to be derived from Bismarck's friendly assurances as of very great weight in Russia's favour.

There was no further use in trying to evade the issue. Bismarck came back to Article I. This, he said, provided for Russian neutrality in a Franco-German conflict and for German neutrality in a war between Russia and a third power: England, Turkey, Austria. But the eventuality of a war between Russia and Austria would greatly embarrass Germany, because of the Austro-German Alliance. Shuvalov replied that Russia had no hostile intentions towards Austria, but valued the continuance of the conservative understanding between the three empires. Russia, however, could not engage to respect the integrity of the Dual Monarchy under all circumstances, especially in view of Austria's attitude in Balkan affairs. Bismarck appreciated the pacific intentions of Russia, he said, but there was no getting round Germany's obligations, and in order to prove it he drew out a copy of the text of the Austro-German Alliance, which he read to Shuvalov from beginning to end. It was the first time the Russians learned the actual provisions, and particularly the fact that the agreement was directed against them exclusively. Bismarck explained in detail how he had been forced into this alliance by the hostile demonstrations of the Russians, but insisted that there was no longer anything to be done about it. Shuvalov on his part refused absolutely to consider the addition of a saving clause to Article I of the projected treaty which would relieve Germany of the obligation to remain neutral and allow her to aid Austria if Russia attacked. This, said the Russian negotiator, would reverse the whole sense of Article I.

Though Russia harboured no hostile intentions towards Austria, if unexpected complications in the Balkans were to arise to trouble the relations of the two powers, who would be able to decide which party was the aggressor? This was certainly the root difficulty of the whole matter. The first conference ended without an agreement.

The two statesmen devoted several more meetings to the discussion of the troublesome Article I. Bismarck explained once more the nature of the alliance with Austria and stated very categorically that if Austria embarked upon a policy of adventures in the Balkans, she would do so at her risk and peril. But he refused to entertain the suggestion that the alliance should be given up when it expired in 1889, for, he pointed out, the attitude of the Russian press and public opinion was such that Germany could not afford to cut loose from Austria. Shuvalov on his part refused to consider a reservation to Article I saving Germany's obligations to Austria, unless Germany were willing to accept the limitation of Russia's obligation to maintain neutrality to the case of a French attack upon Germany. Russia, he said, could not afford to see a mortal blow delivered at France. This approach to the problem irritated Bismarck considerably. He did not want to accept the limitation of Russia's obligation if he could help it. It was not that he was planning to attack France. If he had, he could have done so while the Alliance of the Three Emperors was still in force, for this gave Germany, at least on paper, a free hand in the West. His anxiety is to be explained rather in terms of Shuvalov's anxiety. The difficulty would be in defining what was aggression. Bismarck feared this dilemma in the event of a Franco-German conflict just as Shuvalov feared it in the case of a Russian-Austrian clash.

Various drafts were made in an effort to find a satisfactory solution, and finally Bismarck proposed that Article I should be made strictly defensive: each side should remain neutral only if the other were attacked by a third power. This did not suit Shuvalov at all, for, he argued, of what advantage would it be to have the benefits of benevolent neutrality only in case of attack by some third power? Was it Russia's fault that she had several enemies while Germany had only one? Could Russia bind herself, with respect to Austria or Turkey, to remain impassive in the face of every threat, perhaps even of having to meet the hostility of Germany if she were obliged to act in a direction which Germany might judge to be aggressive? To this Bismarck replied by pointing out that Russia was offering "half-neutrality" in a Franco-German war, in return for Germany's "half-neutrality" in an Austro-Russian war, plus her full neutrality in any conflict between Russia on the one hand and Turkey, England, or Italy on the other. Shuvalov could not answer this argument, and fell back on his instructions: "I do not feel strong enough to contend with you. I set things before you as they are. . . . If I insist on the clause concerning France, it is because I know that it is a condition *sine qua non.*" He produced his instructions to prove the point, and the chancellor realized that further debate would be futile. Together the two men worked out a reservation to Article I which read, in the final version: " This provision would not apply to a war against Austria or France if this war should result from an attack directed against one of these two latter powers by one of the High Contracting Parties."

Shuvalov returned to St. Petersburg with the draft agreed upon. Evidently Giers and the Tsar were satisfied with it, but Shuvalov himself hoped to extract more concessions yet. Germany was to be enlisted in support of Russia's policy in Bulgaria, or, better yet, she was to act as vanguard for the Russian advance. Bismarck was to engineer the removal of the Bulgarian regency and induce the powers as well as the Bulgarians themselves to accept the Russian candidate. It goes without saying that Bismarck rejected these suggestions with considerable warmth. Even so, when Shuvalov finally returned to Berlin on June 12, he came with a proposed addition to Article II of the draft treaty. This stated: " Germany will, as in the past, lend her aid to Russia in order to re-establish a regular and legal government in Bulgaria. She promises in no case to give her consent to the restoration of the Prince of Battenberg."

So much Bismarck agreed to, but the rest of it he rejected out of hand, for it provided that Germany should eventually oppose Battenberg's return if he were re-elected. Furthermore, in order to prevent any conflict of interest in the Balkans, Russia, in agreement with Germany, was to recognize the position acquired by Austria by virtue of the Treaty of Berlin. But in case of encroachment (*empiètement*) Germany would warn the Vienna cabinet that it would be acting at its own risk and peril and would announce that any interference with the action of Russia in Bulgaria, in Roumelia, or at Constantinople could never lead to the *casus fœderis* between Germany and Austria-Hungary.

Bismarck's patience was at an end. He warned the Russians not to overestimate the value to Germany of the treaty and indicated that if the old relationship with Russia were to come to an end, Germany would replace it by arrangements with other powers, not excluding Turkey. This was enough to frighten Giers, whose heart was evidently not in the policy pursued by Shuvalov. On June 15 the ambassador was instructed to drop the new Russian demands and sign the treaty. This was done on June 18. The text consisted of the three articles already discussed above, and three others which fixed the duration at three years, provided for secrecy, and set down the conditions of ratification. The " additional and very secret protocol " consisted of the German promises to aid in re-establishing a regular and legal government in Bulgaria and not to consent to the restoration of Battenberg. The second point dealt with Bismarck's assurances in regard to the Straits and Constantinople: " If His Majesty the Emperor of Russia should find himself under the necessity of assuming the task of defending the entrance of the Black Sea in order to safeguard the interests of Russia, Germany engages to accord her benevolent neutrality and her moral and diplomatic support to the measures which His Majesty may deem it necessary to take to control (*garder*) the key of his empire." [1]

This so-called Reinsurance Treaty was the most famous and easily the most disputed agreement ever concluded by Bismarck. Its existence was made known in 1896 and caused considerable discussion. Since the publication of the actual text, in 1918, an impressive controversial literature has grown up about it. Almost every aspect of the treaty has been minutely examined and analysed, and the German historical profession has been divided into a Bismarckian and an anti-Bismarckian group as a result of endless attacks and vindications. [2]

This is hardly the place to enter upon a microscopic analysis of the arguments that have been advanced pro and con. Criticism has centred very largely upon the compatibility of this agreement with Germany's obligations to Austria. It has been said that Bismarck in promising support for the Russian policy in the Balkans was acting disloyally towards his Austrian ally. This argument will hardly hold water, for Bismarck had proclaimed to the world, over and over again, that Germany had no interests in the Near East and would not be drawn into a conflict concerning the Balkans. He had told the Austrian government time and again, he had announced in the Reichstag on January 11, 1887, that Germany could not support the Austrian policy in those regions. And besides he had repeatedly urged upon his neighbours the division of the Balkans into a western and an eastern part, one to be an Austrian, the other a Russian sphere of influence. As late as May 1887 he had told General Kaulbars in Berlin that this would be the best solution. It is true that neither Russia nor Austria accepted the proposal, but it is equally true that Bismarck made this division of spheres the guiding principle in determining Germany's attitude. Then, too, it should be noted that in the Reinsurance Treaty Russia was left a free hand in Bulgaria, Eastern Roumelia, and Constantinople, all of them areas which Bismarck considered to lie in the eastern zone. Under the circumstances it is hard to see how he can be accused of having betrayed Austrian interests.

It would be more to the point to argue that England on the one hand and Russia on the other were the powers that were misled. In sponsoring the Mediterranean Agreement the German chancellor was encouraging the formation of a group which he hoped would serve as a check on Russian action in the East. Less than six months later he signed an agreement which tended to encourage the Russians in their aspirations. There is no getting round these facts. But there is this to be said: Bismarck sponsored the Mediterranean Agreement, not for the protection of German interests, but for the protection of Austrian, English, and Italian interests. He would have been the last to entertain the

---

[1] The later negotiations may be followed in *Die Grosse Politik*, V, Nos. 1082 ff. The text of the treaty was first published by Goriainov, loc. cit., and is now printed in *Die Grosse Politik* and the *Krasny Arkhiv*.

[2] The most important controversial literature is listed in the bibliographical note at the end of the chapter.

idea that this combination was for Germany of value comparable to the good relationship to Russia. He purchased this good relationship by giving Russia freedom of action in an area where Germany herself had no interests. The Russians asked nothing more. They never expected that the treaty would remove the antagonism of England and Austria. What Bismarck had really done was to establish a sort of balance of power, a system under which Russia would be held in check by the Mediterranean coalition, and the peace of Europe preserved.

That the German chancellor was in no way conscious of committing trickery is shown most clearly in his attitude towards the question of publicity. The Russians had stipulated from the start that the whole matter be kept rigorously secret. Bismarck consented, because he knew that the Tsar would never dare conclude such an agreement in the face of the violent anti-German feeling in Russia. But he would have preferred an open agreement. He was not in favour of mystification in any case and was not ashamed of the arrangements he made. Had he had his way, the Austro-German Alliance of 1879 would have been a public treaty approved by the parliaments of the two countries. At the very time when the negotiations for the Reinsurance Treaty with Russia were under way, he was urging upon the Austrian government the desirability of publishing the Austro-German Alliance and also the Austro-Russian agreements of 1876 and 1877. Later on he always maintained that the Austrians, had they known of the Reinsurance Treaty, would not have objected, for there was nothing in the provisions to which they could have justly demurred, and at the same time it was a matter of consequence to the Austrians themselves that the German connexion with Russia should be kept intact. In this way Germany could act as mediator between the two Balkan rivals and prevent the differences between the two countries from ending in a catastrophe. This same argument he advanced in discussion with Shuvalov. Kálnoky, at the time, appreciated the difficulties of Bismarck's position more than have some later historians.[1]

On the surface the advantages to be derived from the treaty seem to be very unevenly divided between Germany and Russia, and some objection has been made to it on this account. The objection can easily be met, however, by recalling the fact that in practice many of the concessions made to Russia were illusory, while it was unlikely that England or Austria, if not supported by Germany, would actually attack Russia and thus oblige Germany to remain neutral. On the other hand, Bismarck placed a very high value on the Russian promise of neutrality if Germany were attacked by France. Even though there was nothing in the agreement to prevent the formation of a Franco-Russian alliance, the terms of the agreement did preclude a Franco-Russian combination designed for offence against Germany. The German chancellor was not given to delusions. From the beginning he realized that an agreement with Russia might go to pieces as a result of a revolution in the Tsarist Empire. But

---

[1] See his dispatch of August 18, 1887, quoted by Medlicott, loc. cit., p. 78, note 4.

he thought that the better is the enemy of the good. Relations with Russia had a better chance of running smoothly with a treaty than without. It could, of course, be argued that in the event of a Franco-German conflict the Tsar might not be able to withstand the pressure of Russian public opinion and the military circles, and that he might be forced to intervene on the side of France despite the agreement with Germany. On the other hand, it was fairly clear that the French would not attack Germany unless they were certain of Russian support. That they should receive promises of such support from the Tsar was practically out of the question after the signature of the Reinsurance Treaty. The more one studies this famous document, the more one becomes convinced that it was the very keystone of the Bismarckian structure. With it the great chancellor had succeeded in completing the intricate system of checks and balances which was intended to preserve the peace of Europe. That Bismarck controlled this balance is perfectly true, but was anyone better fitted to hold the decisive power?

With the signature of the Reinsurance Treaty Bismarck's system of alliances reached its completion. On paper at least, Germany's security was provided for. Yet it must not be supposed that the formation of the League of Peace led to a marked diminution of the international tension. The Reinsurance Treaty was kept rigorously secret and its existence could not, on that account, influence the movement of European opinion or allay the prevalent fears of the uninitiated. Though Boulanger had been excluded from the French government formed in May, and though the great Russian journalist Katkov died on August 1, the agitation in both countries continued. In Paris fully half the press took the side of Boulanger against his opponents, and many of the leading provincial newspapers protested against his exclusion from the ministry.[1] The extreme nationalists continued to organize anti-German demonstrations, and when Boulanger left the capital in July to take over a command at Clermont-Ferrand, a tremendous crowd assembled at the Gare de Lyon. For a time it seemed as though the affair might have serious consequences. The leaders of the movement, men like Deroulède, regretted that no adequate preparations had been made to exploit the situation. From this incident arose the organization of a Boulangist party.[2] For a while less was heard of the general, but in October the government was shaken by an unedifying affair. It turned out that one of the high officers of the general staff had been making a business of selling the decoration of the Legion of Honour, and that the son-in-law of President Grévy, M. Wilson, was implicated. This scandal led to the fall of the cabinet and to the resignation of the President (December 2). In the struggle for the succession the moderate republicans tended to support Ferry, but the royalists and the radicals combined against him. He was defeated and Sadi-Carnot became President. A few days later an attempt was made to assassinate Ferry,

[1] Francis Laur: *L'Époque Boulangiste* (Paris, 1912), pp. 317–8.
[2] Ducray: *Deroulède*, p. 169; Freycinet: *Souvenirs*, pp. 375–6; Albin, op. cit., p. 125.

" *le Prussien.*" The incident is of special interest because, during the days before the election, Boulanger came to Paris. He was approached by the royalists as well as by the radicals and there was some talk of a *coup d'état*. But the time was not yet ripe, and the second great wave of Boulangism was to come only during the year 1888.[1]

In the meanwhile Deroulède was still busy preparing the way for the chosen one of the nationalists. He went to Russia in the summer of 1887 to attend the funeral of Katkov and took the opportunity to make a political tour. His reception this time was much more enthusiastic than the year before. Military circles received him with open arms, and at Nizhni-Novgorod the Russian governor spoke with great fervour of Deroulède's efforts to effect a Franco-Russian alliance. The same theme was taken up again and again by the newspaper press, for Katkov's death, far from entailing the collapse of the movement, had made it more extreme. The great journalist had asked only for a policy of the free hand, but his successors came out openly for an alliance with France.[2]

The German government protested vigorously against these excesses, but the foreign minister insisted that there was nothing he could do. It was the truth, for the agitation was supported or connived at by many of the most prominent members of the ruling caste, men like Count Tolstoi, the powerful minister of the interior; Constantine Pobiedonostsev, the influential adviser of the Tsar; General Obruchev, the chief of the general staff; and Vishnegradski, the minister of finance. Giers did, however, affirm and reaffirm his conviction that the Tsar would never consider an alliance with France, despite the fact that the French, as he put it, kept running after him with eau de cologne in their hands, begging for the honour of rubbing his back.[3]

The Russian love for all things French, and the outspoken hostility displayed towards all things German, were so striking that it could escape no one. This surge of public emotion was deeply rooted and hard to define, but Bismarck continued to take the view that, so long as the autocracy lasted, the final decision in matters of war and peace would always rest with the ruler. He relied upon the treaty with Russia and the Tsar's word, but at the same time he appreciated the fact that the Tsar himself might be carried along by popular pressure. Was it not a well-known fact that Alexander II had in 1877 been carried into war with Turkey by the pressure of the Panslavists?

The German chancellor hoped to allay the suspicion and hostility of the Russians by affording them full support in their Bulgarian policy. The question had entered upon a new period of crisis when, on July 7, the Bulgarian assembly elected to the throne Prince Ferdinand of Saxe-Coburg-Koháry. The move was intended to frustrate the efforts of the Russians to set up a new regency under General Ernroth, and it succeeded. Ferdinand, a member of the great Coburg

---

[1] Mermeix (Gabriel Terrail): *Les Coulisses du Boulangisme* (Paris, 1890), pp. 56 ff.
[2] Toutain, op. cit., pp. 264 ff.; *Die Grosse Politik,* VI, Nos. 1215–16.
[3] *Die Grosse Politik,* V, Nos. 1117 ff.; VI, Nos. 1216 ff.

family and a grandson of Louis Philippe of France, was an officer in the Hungarian army. For some time he had been angling for the Bulgarian throne in the hope of finding a larger field of activity, but he seems to have been chosen by the Bulgarian assembly simply as a last resort, after many efforts to secure the return of Prince Alexander had failed. Ferdinand, before accepting the throne, had asked the Tsar for his approval, arguing that his election would be the best safe-guard against the establishment of a republic in Bulgaria or the recall of Alexander of Battenberg. The Tsar's reply, however, had been very unfriendly: let the Bulgarians do what they liked; the question was whether the powers would tolerate their high-handedness.[1] In his view the Bulgarian assembly had no legal standing and therefore its acts were illegal. As for Ferdinand, the Russians evidently regarded him as an Austrian agent. They had been opposed to his candidacy from the very start.

But Ferdinand went to Bulgaria nevertheless. He had the permission of Francis Joseph to accept the election. Whether he received approval or support from Vienna it is impossible to say.[2] In any case he seems to have regarded the odds as just about even, and remarked in a cynical way that even though he were only the flea in the ear of the (Russian) bear, the experience ought to be amusing.[3] None of the powers recognized him, and even the statesmen who were favourably disposed towards him had doubts whether he would be able to maintain his position. The Russian government simply ignored him at first and continued its efforts to establish an Ernroth regency that might arrange for a new assembly and the election of a satisfactory candidate. Bismarck gave the Russians his full support, though he refused, as ever, to take the initiative and thus expose himself to the danger of being disavowed if he failed. When there appeared to be some danger that the Russians would settle the question by military action in Bulgaria, he urged upon the Austrians the necessity for abstention, pointing out to them that the Russians, once they were engaged in Bulgaria, would be much more exposed to Austrian pressure than ever before. It goes without saying that this view was not accepted in Vienna.[4]

The repeated efforts made by the Russian government to induce its German ally to take the initiative in proposing and pressing a solution of the Bulgarian question is sufficient indication that at St. Petersburg more had been expected from the Reinsurance Treaty than was actually provided for by the letter of the agreement. The hostility of Russian public opinion and the patent dissatisfaction of the government caused the German chancellor not a little uneasiness. Clearly it would not have been wise to stake everything on a scrap of paper or even on the good intentions of an autocrat who might be carried along

---

[1] The letters are printed in Meyendorff: *Correspondance diplomatique de M. de Staal*, I, pp. 353–4.

[2] See the cryptic letter of Ferdinand to Crown Prince Rudolf in Mitis: *Kronzprinz Rudolf*, pp. 376 ff.

[3] Sir Valentine Chirol: *Fifty Years in a Changing World*, p. 129.

[4] *Die Grosse Politik*, V, Nos. 1044 ff.

at any time by the tide of popular pressure. Bismarck therefore continued the policy he had already initiated in the spring. While supporting the Russians *sans phrase* in the Bulgarian question, he lent what encouragement he could to all projects for strengthening the Mediterranean combination, a coalition that would serve to hold the Russians in check and at the same time keep open for Germany a safe refuge if the alliance with Russia collapsed.[1]

To understand the working of this policy in the latter part of 1887 it is necessary to recur to the troublesome Egyptian question. Sir Henry Drummond Wolff had been carrying on negotiations at Constantinople since February and had succeeded, by dint of great patience, in concluding with the Porte on May 22 the convention which bears his name. The agreement hinged on Article V, which provided that the English troops should be withdrawn from Egypt in three years. But " if, at that time, the appearance of danger in the interior or from without should necessitate the adjournment of the evacuation, the English troops will retire from Egypt immediately after the disappearance of this danger, and two years after the aforesaid evacuation the stipulation of Article IV [authorizing the provisional presence of British troops] will cease completely to have any effect." Furthermore, if at any time subsequent to the evacuation, " order and security in the interior were disturbed, or if the Khedivate of Egypt refused to execute its duties towards the Sovereign Court [Turkey], or its international obligations," both the Turkish and the British governments would have the right to occupy the country with troops.

This convention was to be ratified within one month. The British government promptly sent its act of ratification, but at Constantinople the storm broke. The French immediately assumed a position of uncompromising opposition, partly because they had always objected to direct negotiations between England and the Porte, but especially because the convention did not really fix a definite date for the evacuation. On the contrary, it threatened to establish " a political condominium with Turkey, and without Europe, in place of the financial condominium with France, under the control of Europe." [2] The Turks were between the devil and the deep sea, but eventually they yielded when the protests of the French were supported by the objections of the Russians. The two ambassadors resorted to threatening language, telling the Sultan that if he ratified the convention, " France and Russia would thereby be given the right to occupy provinces of the Empire, and to leave only after a similar convention had been concluded. France might do so in Syria, and Russia in Armenia." [3] Abdul Hamid attempted time and again to postpone the ratification, until Sir Henry left Constantinople on July 15 and the whole projected agreement failed.[4]

---

[1] Radowitz: *Aufzeichnungen*, II, p. 274.

[2] Freycinet: *La Question d'Égypte*, p. 369.

[3] *Egypt*, No. 8 (*1887*), Nos. 45, 50, 54.

[4] The correspondence in *Egypt*, No. 8 (*1887*): *Further Correspondence respecting Sir H. Drummond Wolff's Mission*. See also Freycinet: *La Question d'Égypte*, pp. 367 ff.; Sir Henry Drummond Wolff: *Rambling Recollections*, II, pp. 317 ff.

It is pretty clear that Lord Salisbury from the beginning expected the failure of the Wolff mission. The negotiations had been opened because of French pressure to get something done. Now the English could claim to have made the effort, which had failed because of the intransigence of the French themselves. Sir William White, the ambassador to the Porte, was so elated that he told his French and Russian colleagues that he had written to his government suggesting that the two ambassadors be awarded the Grand Cross of the Bath for the immense services they had rendered England.[1]

But there was another aspect of the problem, and a more serious one. The English efforts had been defeated, not by France alone, but by France supported by Russia. It was the first striking instance of Russian assistance to the republic. This is not to be wondered at, for the French had consistently supported the Russian policy in Bulgaria, and, besides, the Egyptian question was for Russia an excellent means of bringing pressure on England and perhaps making her more amenable in the Bulgarian affair. It was England, then, rather than Germany, that first felt the impact of the Franco-Russian combination. This point must be kept in mind.

The German attitude was no less interesting than the Russian. Efforts had been made by the French to enlist the aid of Germany, but without avail. The French ambassador was told that the Boulangist agitation had completely undermined the German government's confidence in the French people. As Bismarck himself put it: " Germany could never secure a sufficient measure of goodwill in France to compensate for estrangement from England." [2] Throughout the duration of the crisis the German ambassador, like the Austrian and the Italian, gave Wolff the firmest and most steadfast support. Here was the Mediterranean combination in action, flanked by Germany.[3] Bismarck even went so far as to cover the English retreat, suggesting that it would be best for Lord Salisbury to drop the whole thing rather than attempt to force its acceptance on the Sultan. Since this was clearly what the English statesman preferred to do, he accepted the idea with alacrity.[4]

Bismarck's support of the English in Egypt and of the Russians in Bulgaria is the best illustration of his policy of holding the balance between the two and preventing the formation of a Franco-Russian combination directed against Germany. Salisbury, however, must have looked upon the Franco-Russian coalition with considerable anxiety. His feelings towards France are well reflected in a dispatch to Lord Lyons, written shortly after the failure of the Wolff Convention. After listing six places where England and France were at odds, the prime minister remarked: " Can you wonder that there is, in

---

[1] Chirol: *Fifty Years*, p. 37; *Letters of Queen Victoria*, I, pp. 272–3 (February 10, 1887).

[2] *Die Grosse Politik*, VI, No. 1269.

[3] *Egypt*, No. 8 (*1887*), Nos. 24, 56, 58, 61; Wolff, op. cit., II, p. 317; Radowitz: *Aufzeichnungen*, II, pp, 267–9. See also Mathilde Kleine: *Deutschland und die ägyptische Frage, 1875–1890* (Greifswald, 1927), pp. 150 ff.

[4] *Die Grosse Politik*, IV, No. 817.

my eyes, a silver lining even to the great black cloud of a Franco-German War?"[1]

But mere speculation on the possibility of a Franco-German war could hardly meet the needs of the situation, and Salisbury could hardly expect the Germans to do the fighting for England. Another solution might be found in an arrangement with Russia, which Lord Randolph Churchill had so eloquently advocated. The prime minister decided to sound out the possibilities of this approach. On August 3 he had a most interesting conversation with Count Hatzfeldt, the German ambassador. The real and dangerous enemy of both England and Germany, he said, was not Russia, but France. Everything pointed to the fact that Russia would abstain from all action until the ever-threatening conflict between France and Germany should break out. This attitude of the Russians simply served to strengthen the French in their hostility to England and Germany. After this preface the prime minister passed to a discussion of the Turkish situation, and the ambassador gathered from his rather general and cryptic utterances that he believed conditions in Turkey would in time become intolerable for the powers. Churchill had always maintained that England had no interests on the Bosporus of so vital a nature as to justify war against Russia. In any case, an understanding with Russia would have to take full account of Austrian interests. But he wished to know Bismarck's reaction to the whole question, if the chancellor was willing to express an opinion.

The whole conversation was carried on by Salisbury in a very guarded fashion. Just what did it mean? Was Salisbury really intending to come to an agreement with Russia at the expense of Turkey, in order to shatter the threatening Franco-Russian combination in the Mediterranean? Would he actually be prepared to throw overboard the Turcophil policy of Disraeli and abandon Constantinople to the Russians? Only in October 1886 he had written to Churchill: "I consider the loss of Constantinople would be the ruin of our party and a heavy blow to the country; and therefore I am anxious to delay by all means Russia's advance to that goal."[2] A fundamental reversal of policy was here in question if Salisbury was sincere.

That Bismarck was not convinced of the sincerity of the prime minister's intentions is indicated by his marginal notes on Hatzfeldt's report: "French and English policy are again waiting till we are in trouble with Russia, and English like Russian policy is waiting till France has been engaged by us." In other words, in his opinion Salisbury was trying to deflect the impetus of the Franco-Russian coalition and to bring the Germans to the side of the English by conjuring up the spectre of an Anglo-Russian agreement.

Bismarck was the man not only to penetrate the minds of his opponents, but to turn the tables upon them. In his reply he spoke with some enthusiasm about the project of an Anglo-Russian agreement, for, he said, Germany was the friend of both and did not expect that either would exploit the situation

---

[1] Newton: *Lord Lyons*, II, p. 409.   [2] Churchill: *Lord Randolph Churchill*, II, p. 161.

to her detriment. Germany had even fewer interests in the Near East than England and could not devote her strength to support the Austrian plans for expansion in that region. If England and Russia reached an understanding in the Near East, Austria would have no other course open to her than to come to an agreement with Russia. Bismarck himself would be only too glad to help in bringing about an agreement between Russia, England, and Austria. Even Italy might be drawn into it. The key to the whole situation would be found in Bulgaria. Germany's policy had been to support the Austrian position in Serbia, the Russian in Bulgaria, and the English in Egypt. If England were prepared to make concessions to Russia in the Bulgarian question, it might be possible to get Austria to accept the Russian view. Italy could be compensated, perhaps in Abyssinia. Such a combination would greatly make for peace: " The most bellicose state in Europe is France, and with the isolation of France the peace of Europe would be assured." There was no danger of a German-Russian war and not much probability that Austria and Russia would clash. Germany would be even less likely to attack Russia than France, and if France attacked Germany, the latter would have to be completely deserted by Providence not to be able to win. France in such an event would certainly not have the support of Russia, but even if she did, Germany could throw a million good soldiers on each frontier, and with Austrian help her position would be by no means desperate: " I repeat to Your Excellency the expression of my firm conviction that a Russian-French alliance against us is quite beyond the range of probability." [1]

It was a Franco-Russian alliance *against Germany* that Bismarck discounted. He certainly exaggerated the security of the empire, but he wished to discourage all speculation on a war between Germany and her neighbours and to evade the attempt made by Salisbury to enlist aid against the threatening coalition in the Mediterranean. If there were to be a Franco-Russian alliance, it would be infinitely better from the Berlin standpoint if it concentrated its efforts on the Near East rather than on the German frontiers. In the meanwhile the chancellor quietly transformed the English approaches and tried to use them to effect a settlement of the crucial Bulgarian problem.

Staal, the Russian ambassador at London, was at this very time reporting home that Salisbury seemed to be much less interested in the Bulgarian problem than he had been a year before, but that he seemed most eager to reach an understanding with Germany and Austria.[2] This would indicate that the prime minister had really only been trying to frighten the Germans by the suggestion of an agreement with Russia. This view is borne out further by the fact that Salisbury, as soon as he had Bismarck's reply, began to beat a retreat, urging the danger of estranging Italy and asserting that he had been moved from the beginning by the fear that a war of France and Russia against Germany and Austria was imminent, that Germany would be entirely taken up with fighting France, and that Russia would, in the meanwhile, annihilate Austria. The

---

[1] *Die Grosse Politik*, IV, No. 908.   [2] Meyendorff, op. cit., I, pp. 357-8.

Balkan states would then have fallen upon Turkey, and England would have been alone with the thankless job of protecting the Sultan. The German ambassador rightly described these statements as "logical confusions," and they are not to be taken seriously. Bismarck seized the opportunity to state categorically that Germany did not wish to press for an agreement between England and Russia and was willing to support it only if Salisbury "gravitated" to it himself and if Austria and Italy could be included: "We desire first and foremost the maintenance of the Anglo-Austrian-Italian understanding." This was the line of approach now followed by the chancellor, and on the further history of the Mediterranean coalition the interest then centred.[1]

As Bismarck was faced by the growing hostility of Russia, he turned naturally to Austria, Germany's ally in the event of a Russian attack. The Emperor William met Francis Joseph at Gastein in August. In the course of the discussion the aged monarch made no secret of his ebbing confidence in the Tsar and his policy. The natural corollary was his stressing of the Austrian-German relationship, which he spoke of in stronger terms than ever before. "I can only say," wrote Francis Joseph to Kálnoky, "that I have never brought back from a meeting with Emperor William an impression so favourable to us." [2]

But the close alliance between Germany and Austria was not sufficient, in the eyes of Bismarck, to meet the needs of the situation. Being unwilling to support the Austrian policy in the Balkans, he had to find for Austria adequate backing elsewhere. It will be remembered that the Mediterranean Agreement of February 12, 1887 was essentially an Anglo-Italian agreement. Austria had only joined later, and the understanding had then been given a somewhat more pronounced Near Eastern turn. The next step was to develop this theme further and give the Mediterranean coalition the same potentiality for action in the Near East that it had in the western Mediterranean.

The moment seemed a propitious one, for early in August Francesco Crispi took over the Italian premiership left vacant by the death of Depretis. The fiery Sicilian and ex-Garibaldian, who reserved for himself the portfolio of the ministry for foreign affairs, brought about a complete change in the conduct of Italian foreign relations. The cynical indifference of Depretis and the cautious calculation of Robilant were things of the past. Crispi's purpose was to secure for Italy her rightful place among the powers, to activate the Triple Alliance, and, if possible, to strengthen the position of his country through new connexions.[3] While still minister of the interior in the Depretis cabinet, he had attempted to reach a settlement of the Roman question through negotiations with the clerical leaders

---

[1] The later negotiations in *Die Grosse Politik*, V, Nos. 909–13, especially Bismarck's marginal notes.

[2] Mitis: *Kronprinz Rudolf*, pp. 374–5. See also Kálnoky's dispatch to Constantinople, August 18, quoted by W. N. Medlicott: "Austria-Hungary and the War Danger of 1887" (*Slavonic Review*, VI, pp. 437–41, December 1927); Radowitz: *Aufzeichnungen*, II, p. 274.

[3] The best study is by Gaetano Salvemini: *La Politica Estera di Francesco Crispi* (Rome, 1919), which is based on a critical reading of Crispi's memoirs.

of the conciliation movement, but had seen these well-intentioned efforts ruined by the pressure brought to bear upon the Pope by the French representative.[1] From this time on he became more and more convinced that France was moved by a deep and dangerous hostility to Italy. A shipping treaty, which had been concluded after years of negotiation between the two governments, had been thrown out by the French chamber in July 1886, after the Italian parliament had already accepted it. The reply from Rome was the threat to abrogate the tariff agreement between the two countries. Temporary arrangements had to be made, but serious economic tension was rapidly developing, and to this was added the conflict of interests in the Red Sea, where the French raised all possible obstacles to the establishment of the Italian colonies.[2]

Crispi, who was deeply interested in the expansion of Italy in the Mediterranean and had for years been preaching the necessity for establishing a "greater Italy" in keeping with the teachings of modern imperialism, was determined to abandon the pusillanimous policy followed by the Italian government at the Congress of Berlin and at the time of the English occupation of Egypt.[3] The Italian claims were vigorously maintained and every effort made to secure the support of Italy's allies. More especially did Crispi devote himself to the cultivation of close friendly relations with England, for British sea-power was of far greater value for colonial enterprise than the huge land-forces of Germany.

During the negotiations for the ratification of the Drummond Wolff Convention the Italian government had given the English unreserved support. But the election of Ferdinand to the Bulgarian throne opened up broader vistas and greater opportunities for Italian activity. Nothing could be done so long as Depretis remained at the helm, but when Crispi took over the premiership, on August 8, he promptly assumed the lead. Without recognizing the legality of Ferdinand's position, he insisted that, until conclusive proof were offered to the contrary, the election must be regarded as the expression of the Bulgarian national will, and that in any case it promised to be at least the beginning of a settlement. To the Russian scheme of setting up a regency under General Ernroth he was immovably opposed. For a time, at the end of August, there seemed to be some danger that the Russians would try to force their solution by sending an expedition to Varna or a force to Erzerum. Salisbury was distinctly worried by the prospect, and Crispi seized the opportunity to propose

[1] Francesco Crispi: *Politica Interna* (Milan, 1924), pp. 97 ff.; Salvemini, op. cit., pp. 49 ff.; A. A. di Pesaro: "*La Diplomazia Vaticana e la Questione del Potere Temporale*" (*Rassegna Nazionale*, May 1, 1890, pp. 3–129); Waldersee: *Briefwechsel* (Berlin, 1928), pp. 87–8, 141–3; Hubert Basthgen: *Die römische Frage* (Freiburg, 1919), III, pp. 43 ff.; and especially Vergilio Procacci: *La Questione Romana: le vicende del tentativo di Conciliazione del 1887* (Florence, 1929).

[2] Giacomo Curàtulo: *Francia e Italia* (Turin, 1915), chapter viii; Charles de Moüy: *Souvenirs*, chapter vii; Albert Billot: *La France et l'Italie* (Paris, 1905), I, chapter iii; Auguste Gérard: *Mémoires* (Paris, 1928), chapter viii.

[3] G. Palumbo Cardella: "*Crispi e la Politica Mediterranea e Coloniale*" (*Politica*, XXIX, pp. 150–79, April 1928; 387–431, June–August 1928; XXXI, pp. 350–80, June–August, 1929).

the conclusion of a military convention between England and Italy. This was a little too much for the English statesman, who seems to have been rather suspicious of his Italian colleague's superabundant energy. He explained to the Italian chargé d'affaires that, until war actually threatened, the political constitution of England and the accepted traditions of the country made it impossible for him to enter upon engagements of this kind.[1]

In the meantime the Austrian government had initiated discussions that were to have more fruitful results. Baron Calice, the ambassador at Constantinople, consulted with his English and Italian colleagues concerning a " basis of ideas " designed to preserve the interests of the three powers in the East. On hearing of this, Crispi approached Kálnoky with the suggestion that arrangements be made for practical co-operation. The Austrian minister, like Salisbury, evaded these dangerous proposals and pointed out that nothing could be done so long as England was undecided. The negotiations progressed only when Calice forwarded to Vienna, on September 17, the first draft for an understanding. The eight points of the draft provided for the maintenance of peace and the *status quo* in the East, based on the treaties, to the exclusion of all policy of compensation, and the maintenance of local autonomies and the independence of Turkey from all foreign preponderating influence. Turkey should not be allowed to cede or delegate her suzerain rights over Bulgaria to any other power, or intervene in order to establish a foreign administration there, or tolerate acts of coercion undertaken to that end, either in the form of a military occupation or of the dispatch of volunteers. The three powers desired to join with Turkey in the common defence of these principles and, if Turkey resisted hostile enterprises, to come to an immediate agreement with her concerning the support to be given her. Should the Porte, however, be in connivance with an illegal enterprise of the character indicated, or should the Porte fail to oppose it seriously, the three powers would agree to occupy provisionally, by military or naval forces, certain points of Ottoman territory in order to re-establish the political and military equilibrium necessary for safe-guarding the principles already mentioned.[2]

This draft agreement must be read in the light of the rumours current at the time that Russia was planning military action against Bulgaria or Turkey. It is clear that the projected agreement was intended, in the words of Kálnoky, " to prevent Turkey from joining Russia," and that the original plan was to inform the Turks of the agreement, if not actually to make them parties to it. This idea seems to have been suggested by Bismarck, who thoroughly approved of the rapprochement between the three powers. Still, Kálnoky took no further steps, thinking that the object in view could be more easily attained if Austria put up a show of reluctance and allowed Crispi to assume the lead.[3]

---

[1] Crispi: *Memoirs*, II, chapter v; *Die Grosse Politik*, IV, No. 915.

[2] W. N. Medlicott: " The Mediterranean Agreements " (*Slavonic Review*, V, pp. 66–88, June 1926), which is based on unpublished Austrian documents.

[3] Ibid., p. 78; *Die Grosse Politik*, IV, Nos. 914, 916.

The Italian minister was only too ready to do so. Bismarck had indicated to the Italian ambassador at Berlin that if " some favourable breeze should waft Crispi in the direction of Friedrichsruh, Varzin, or Berlin," he would receive him with great pleasure. Crispi lost no time in accepting the invitation and on October 2 and 3 conferred with the chancellor at his Friedrichsruh estate. Bismarck stressed his desire to preserve peace, but confessed that he had failed to gain the friendship of Russia. Still, he was not afraid of war, for Germany had large and well-trained forces. He did not think that the Tsar desired a conflict. In any case it would not do for him to carry operations into Bulgaria, where he would be exposed to an Austrian attack in the rear. If he proceeded against Constantinople, the chancellor would care little. Russia would only be weakened by such a conquest.

Bismarck's approach was a very clever one, for he elicited from Crispi an immediate and emphatic statement that Italy could not allow Russia to go to Constantinople: " Once there, Russia would be mistress of the Mediterranean." For that reason Italy had sought to prevent any act on the part of either Russia or Turkey which might lead to a European war. The disorder existing in Turkey might be to Russia's advantage, for the latter was on the look-out for the chance of giving Turkey a death-blow. But this state of things could not suit the great powers, who could not allow Russia to possess herself of that territory.

This declaration gave Bismarck the opening he desired. He replied by saying that he entirely approved of this group of three powers, and that he hoped it would become still more closely united and make its authority felt: " Should a breach of peace occur in the East, Germany would join her allies, but would keep in the background." [1]

It seems highly probable that Bismarck invited Crispi to Friedrichsruh with the primary purpose of strengthening him in his desire to establish closer relations with Austria and England in matters pertaining to the Near East. The turn given the conversation by Bismarck is sufficient indication of this. It is true that Crispi brought forward also his favourite idea of putting teeth into the international agreements by the negotiation of military conventions. Bismarck showed himself favourably disposed towards the suggestion of such agreements between Italy on the one hand and Germany or Austria on the other. But he avoided a definite commitment, and it appears from the material we possess that the whole subject of Franco-German relations was brought into the discussion without much motivation.

Before Crispi had an opportunity to begin discussions with Austria and England, the course of events obliged Kálnoky to take the initiative himself. On October 1 Herbert Bismarck submitted to the Austrian chargé d'affaires a series of proposals by which the Porte hoped to effect a settlement of the Bulgarian problem. The plan was to send Russian and Turkish commissioners into Bulgaria with joint authority to hold new elections for an assembly to which

---

[1] Crispi, op. cit., II, pp. 211 ff.

the Russian government would then submit the names of three acceptable candidates for the throne. Bismarck urged upon Kálnoky the necessity of definite assurances being given to the Sultan by the representatives of the three powers to prevent this scheme from materializing. On October 10 the projected agreement in eight points was communicated to Crispi.[1]

At Rome the proposals were accepted at once, the only question in Crispi's mind being whether the last article should not be amplified by a secret Italian-Austrian agreement providing for the eventual break-up of Turkey. This suggestion was rejected by Kálnoky, who communicated the draft agreement to Berlin, asking for German support in pressing the scheme at London. Bismarck gave unhesitating approval to the project, at the same time lending unqualified support to Kálnoky's decision to reject Crispi's suggestion for a further understanding with regard to the eventual break-up of Turkey. Such an agreement, he argued, would be premature and dangerous. Evidently his idea still was that Turkey should be informed of the entente between the three powers, and in his mind the primary purpose of the accord should be to strengthen Turkey in an anti-Russian policy. The danger, he said, lay, not so much in a war of Russia against the Turk, as in a peaceful arrangement by which Russia would receive the right to occupy and fortify the Straits in return for a guarantee of the integrity of the rest of the Ottoman Empire. *Militarily* speaking, an agreement with Turkey, which could put a hundred thousand men into the field in a short time, would be of greater value for Austria and Italy than would be the agreement with England. It was in accord with this view-point that Bismarck had already instructed the German ambassador at Constantinople to inform the Sultan that a close accord existed between England, Austria, and Italy for the purpose of maintaining the *status quo* in the Balkans and the integrity of Turkey, and that Germany was in full sympathy with this accord.[2]

The draft of the projected agreement was now submitted to Lord Salisbury, who accepted it in a general way, but insisted on referring the matter to the cabinet. Kálnoky, who took the lead in the scheme, explained in a covering letter that collective action at Constantinople had hitherto been hampered by the pro-Russian policy of Bismarck in matters concerning the Near East. He had now given up the ungrateful task of supporting Russia and was placing himself by the side of the powers in opposition to Russia. This favourable change should be taken advantage of.

Salisbury had no objection to the proposed text, excepting that he wished the agreement to apply also to Asia Minor, but he did wish to know more definitely what Germany's attitude would be. Count Hatzfeldt was hurriedly recalled from leave, summoned to Friedrichsruh, and then dispatched to London. His instructions seem to have been to do all he could to bring about the con-

---

[1] Medlicott, loc. cit., pp. 79–80. Crispi had already learned of these points from the ambassador at Vienna (Crispi, op. cit., II, p. 223).

[2] Medlicott, loc. cit., pp. 80–1. Most of the documents are in *Die Grosse Politik*, IV, Nos. 918–21.

summation of the agreement, but to leave Germany as much as possible in the background. This is clear from the efforts he made to dissuade Salisbury from asking special assurances from Bismarck.[1] He did not succeed, however, in satisfying the English minister. Salisbury insisted that several of his colleagues were uneasy about an agreement that might give umbrage to France, the more so as the French were making efforts to improve their relations with England. Above all, the serious illness of the German Crown Prince, and the well-known pro-Russian sympathies of his son, Prince William, opened up the prospect that German policy might, in the not too distant future, undergo a transformation in the direction of a closer understanding with Russia, which would be in contradiction to the purposes of the proposed *entente à trois*. Hatzfeldt's argument that Germany would hold France in check and that the fundamental bases of German policy rested upon unalterable principles was admitted by Salisbury, but the English prime minister still insisted that his colleagues desired Germany's " moral approbation " for the projected accord, and a " certain reassurance " with respect to the future development of German policy. In writing to Bismarck Hatzfeldt suggested that the Austrian-German Alliance should be communicated to Salisbury, and that possibly some assurance could be attached to the treaty.[2]

The text of the Austrian-German Treaty was submitted to Salisbury on November 13, in the form of the three articles, but without the clause determining the time limit. To make doubly sure, Bismarck announced his intention of communicating with the English prime minister by letter, an unusual though not unprecedented procedure. The letter was drawn up with the greatest possible care and dispatched to London on November 22. It must certainly be reckoned as one of the greatest of Bismarck's state papers, for the very nature of the case required a frank declaration on his part of the basic principles of German policy. The letter began by stressing the fact that Prince William, when he came to the throne, would not be able to follow a pro-Russian policy any more than his father could follow a pro-English policy when he succeeded to the title. German rulers would not and could not be inspired by other interests than those of Germany, and " the road to follow in the safeguarding of these interests is traced in so rigorous a fashion that it would be impossible to depart from it." A country of fifty million inhabitants could not be led into war unless public opinion were convinced of its necessity. This was the more true of a country like Germany, where the army was recruited from all classes of the population and was literally the nation in arms. The millions of German

---

[1] *Die Grosse Politik*, IV, Nos. 923–4.

[2] Ibid., Nos. 925–6. On October 24 England and France had signed an agreement regarding the neutralization of the Suez Canal, and this Flourens hoped to make the starting-point for an eventual Anglo-Russian-French entente, as envisaged by Gambetta. Nothing came of it, as Salisbury did not follow up the French advances. See Hansen: *L'Ambassade du Baron de Mohrenheim*, pp. 56 ff.; Chaudordy: *La France en 1889* (Paris, 1889), pp. 229–32; Anon.: " *La Russie et le Quai d'Orsay* " (*Nouvelle Revue*, May 1, 1892, pp. 5–20).

soldiers would hasten to the colours if the independence and integrity of the country were menaced, but not otherwise.

This did not mean, Bismarck went on, that only a direct attack on German territory would justify an appeal to arms. With three great powers on her frontiers Germany was exposed to the danger of coalitions directed against her. If Austria were defeated, weakened, or hostile, Germany would be isolated between Russia and France, both of them inimical and dissatisfied with the actual status of Europe. "The existence of Austria as a strong and independent great power is a necessity for Germany which the personal sympathies of the ruler cannot change." Germany must seek to maintain the alliance of nations which were likewise menaced by France and Russia. If the alliance failed, Germany's position in a war on two fronts would still not be desperate, but, whatever the outcome, it would be so great a calamity that she would try to avoid it by a friendly arrangement with Russia. "But so long as we are not certain that we shall be left in the lurch by the powers whose interests are identical with ours, no German emperor will be able to follow any other policy than that of defending the independence of friendly powers which, like ourselves, are satisfied with the present state of Europe and are ready to act unhesitatingly and without weakness if their independence is threatened. . . . We desire that the friendly powers having interests to safeguard in the Near East which are not our interests also should make themselves strong enough by union and militarily to keep the Russian sword in its scabbard or to resist Russia if circumstances bring about a rupture. So long as no German interest is involved, we should remain neutral; but it is impossible to admit that a German emperor could ever support Russia militarily to help her strike down or enfeeble one of the powers on whose support we reckon either to prevent a war with Russia or to assist us in facing such a war. From this standpoint German policy will always be obliged to enter the line of battle if the independence of Austria-Hungary were to be menaced by Russian aggression, or if England or Italy were to be exposed to invasion by French armies."[1]

Just what was the purport of this document? The theory advanced by some writers that it contained a veiled offer of alliance to England seems quite untenable and need not detain us. What Salisbury had been trying to do since August was to enlist the support of Germany for the anti-Russian group. As he explained to Bismarck in his reply, Russia would probably, in the event of a war between Germany and France, not attack Germany, but would compel the Sultan to assent to proposals which would make Russia the mistress of the Bosporus and the Dardanelles, by occupying positions in the Balkans or in Asia Minor. England and Italy alone would not be sufficient to deter her, and everything therefore would depend on the attitude of Austria. But Austria, unless certain of assistance from Germany, might not feel strong enough to hazard a war and the consequent invasion of her north-east frontier. Instead she might

---

[1] *Die Grosse Politik,* IV, No. 930.

accept compensation from Russia. She would be able to carry out the policy laid down in the eight points only if she were certain of German support. Now that Bismarck had shown him the text of the Austro-German Treaty, Salisbury understood that " under no circumstances could the existence of Austria be imperilled by a resistance to illegal Russian enterprises." [1]

Now, this was certainly stretching the point. Salisbury could not possibly have read such an interpretation out of the text of the alliance. In his letter Bismarck had assured England of German support if England were in danger of invasion by French armies. This was a concession, but it had been given informally before and it lay in Germany's interest just as much as support of Austria against Russian attack. But Bismarck's promise to take action if Austria's independence and position as a great power were threatened could only be taken by derivation to mean that Austria might herself jeopardize her position by resisting Russian policy in the Near East. In his negotiations with Austria Bismarck had repeatedly insisted that Austria must not expect German aid if she embarked on this course. It is not at all unlikely, however, that Bismarck aimed at vagueness on this point in writing to Salisbury. He raised no objection to the English interpretation as it appeared in the prime minister's reply. The fact probably was that he never expected the problem to be raised in a practical way. From his marginal notes it is clear that in his opinion what Austria needed was, not the assurance of German support, but the assurance of English support. The solution of the Near Eastern problem depended, not on Germany's attitude, but on the position taken by England and Turkey. Speaking to a friend in these very days, he described the situation as he saw it in a picturesque but forceful way: " The possibility of war depends upon the attitude England takes towards Russia; whether she takes the part of a charging bull, or that of an asthmatic fatted ox. . . . If England plays the charging bull, not only will the French fleet be neutralized, but even Turkey will then join against Russia." [2]

Whatever interpretation may be placed on the Bismarck-Salisbury correspondence, it was decisive in determining the English policy. The prime minister was now ready to enter upon an exchange of notes with Austria and Italy, though he suggested a few minor changes and insisted that the agreement should be kept secret, even from Turkey. This was not the original idea of either Kálnoky or Bismarck. Even in London it was recognized that the purposes of the entente would be best served if the Russians learned of it and took warning. But the parliamentary situation in England was so delicate that Salisbury feared a storm of protest, not only from the Liberals, but also from the Liberal-Unionists, who had taken places in his cabinet. Bismarck and Kálnoky saw the reasonableness of the argument and raised no further objection. The exchange of notes took place in London on December 12, while the

---

[1] *Die Grosse Politik*, IV, No. 936.

[2] John Booth: *Persönliche Erinnerungen an den Fürsten Bismarck* (Hamburg, 1899), p. 72.

notes between Italy and Austria were exchanged by these governments on December 16.

In their final form the points agreed upon by the three governments were as follows: (1) The maintenance of peace and the exclusion of all policy of aggression. (2) The maintenance of the *status quo* in the Orient, based on the treaties, to the exclusion of all policy of compensation. (3) The maintenance of the local autonomies established by these same treaties. (4) The independence of Turkey, as guardian of important European interests (independence of the Caliphate, the freedom of the Straits, etc.), of all foreign preponderating influence. (5) Consequently Turkey can neither cede nor delegate her suzerain rights over Bulgaria to any other power, nor intervene in order to establish a foreign administration there, nor tolerate acts of coercion undertaken with this latter object, under the form either of a military occupation or of the dispatch of volunteers. Likewise Turkey, constituted by the treaties guardian of the Straits, can neither cede any portion of her sovereign rights nor delegate her authority to any other power in Asia Minor. (6) The desire of the three powers to be associated with Turkey for the common defence of these principles. (7) In case of Turkey's resisting any illegal enterprises such as are indicated in Article V, the three powers will immediately come to an agreement as to measures to be taken for causing to be respected the independence of the Ottoman Empire and the integrity of its territory, as secured by previous treaties. (8) Should the conduct of the Porte, however, in the opinion of the three powers, assume the character of complicity with or connivance at any such illegal enterprise, the three powers will consider themselves justified by existing treaties in proceeding, either jointly or separately, to the provisional occupation by their forces, military or naval, of such points of Ottoman territory as they may agree to consider it necessary to occupy in order to secure the objects determined by previous treaties. (9) The existence and the contents of the present agreement between the three powers shall not be revealed, either to Turkey or to any other powers which have not yet been informed of it, without the previous consent of all and each of the three powers aforesaid.[1]

The *Second Mediterranean Agreement* is somewhat of a misnomer when applied, as it generally is, to the understanding of December 12, 1887. It would be much better to refer to the combination of powers involved as the *Near Eastern Triplice,* and to the agreement as the *Near Eastern Understanding or Entente,* for it was much more specific than the earlier one and dealt exclusively with the Near Eastern situation. The text is so clear that it requires no elucidation. The three powers, whose common interest was to prevent Russian action in Bulgaria or Russian pressure upon Turkey which might secure for Russia a special position in the Straits, had done the obvious thing in drawing up a program of opposition. To be sure, no definite plan of action was

---

[1] Pribram, op. cit., I, pp. 124 ff. On the final negotiation see *Die Grosse Politik,* IV, Nos. 932–40; Medlicott, loc. cit., pp. 84–6.

included and further negotiation would have been necessary before actual operations could be undertaken. This was probably due to the anxiety of Salisbury to avoid awkward questions in parliament, but there seems to have been no eagerness on the part of Austria, at least, to make the arrangement more forceful. After all, the expectation was that the agreement would serve as a deterrent and that actual military operations would never become necessary. The expectation was fulfilled.

During the very days when Bismarck was working on his famous letter to Salisbury Tsar Alexander appeared in Berlin for a short visit. It was just at this time that the relations between Russia and her two western neighbours were in a particularly strained condition. The Tsar had been visiting his Danish relatives at Copenhagen since August, but German expectations that he would come to see the old Emperor at Stettin or elsewhere had been disappointed. When Alexander finally did come to Berlin, it was only because the illness of his children had delayed the return of the imperial family until it was too late to go by sea. In the meanwhile the nationalist agitation in Russia had become more and more outspoken against Germany, as against Austria, especially after the election of Ferdinand to the Bulgarian throne and the failure of the projected Ernroth regency had shown the Russians how helpless they were in the Bulgarian affair. In October news began to seep through to the German capital that the concentrations of Russian troops in Poland were being accelerated. A cavalry division was to be moved from the interior to the frontier area, obviously to hinder the German mobilization in the eastern provinces if war should take place. In August the French chamber had passed a new military law, which definitely established a national army with a total of twenty years' service.

The international tension was becoming very great, especially when Crispi, Kálnoky, and Salisbury, in important speeches between October 25 and November 9, proclaimed their sympathy with the Bulgarians and hinted that the three powers would stand together in defence of the treaties. The Russians felt outraged, and hastened their preparations. Their policy seemed to be to provoke the Austrians into action, in which case they expected that Germany, under the terms of the Reinsurance Treaty, would remain neutral, especially if the French assumed a hostile attitude. Bismarck replied in a rather spectacular manner.

Ever since a Russian ukase of May had forbidden the holding of land in the border provinces by foreigners, there had been a demand in Germany for reprisals, because the Russian measures affected chiefly German subjects in Poland. A newspaper campaign had been started against Russian securities, and this campaign seems to have had the approval if not the support of the chancellor. It culminated on November 10 when a government decree forbade the Reichsbank to accept Russian securities as collateral for loans. The measure itself was of no very great significance, but it was taken in Germany as a declaration of lack of confidence in Russian credit, and it had, therefore, a very serious effect upon Russian financial operations. At this time more than half of the Russian securities held abroad were held in Germany, and this share is said to have amounted to more than two billion marks in valuation. Germans began to get rid of these securities as fast as they could. The international money-market became glutted and the prices fell. In view of the fact that the Russian minister of finance had been doing his utmost to convert the outstanding loans and to re-establish the value of the ruble, it will be readily understood that the so-called *Lombardverbot* of November 10, 1887 was a matter of some importance and created much ill feeling in official Russian circles. Just why Bismarck resorted to these means and just why he chose this particular time are questions which it is impossible to answer with certainty. There is some indication that he lacked faith in the permanence of the tsarist régime in Russia and was genuinely anxious about the heavy German investments in Russian securities. It may also be that he wished to show his neighbours that Germany had methods of retaliation, and that he hoped to undermine the position of the finance minister, Vishnegradski, one of the tools of Katkov, and an ardent worker in the cause of the Franco-Russian alliance.[1] But the most likely explanation is that the German chancellor hoped to discourage the military party in Russia by raising financial difficulties. In any case his action was one of far-reaching consequences, which many writers have criticized as a serious blunder, because the result of it was the transfer of Russian financial connexions to Paris and the development of a close economic bond between the two countries.[2]

The moment was not propitious for the visit of the Tsar. Bismarck, receiving constant reports of further Russian troop movements and being told by the highest officers of the general staff that to all appearances Russia was preparing for war in the spring, was very much irritated. Just before the arrival of Alexander he spoke to the Russian ambassador without mincing words: "You forced us into closer relations with Vienna and last year with Rome; now we shall go to Constantinople, and finally we shall stir up the Chinese against you."[3] He was determined to speak quite as openly to the Tsar himself and drew up a memorandum for the old Emperor's discussion with his nephew in which emphasis was to be placed on the dangerous effects of war, even victorious war, upon the stability of the monarchies in Europe. It almost seemed, the Emperor was to say, that the Reinsurance Treaty had been intended by the

---

[1] See especially S. M. von Propper: *Was nicht in die Zeitung kam* (Frankfurt, 1929), p. 143.

[2] *Die Grosse Politik*, V, Nos. 1137 ff.; good accounts of the problem in J. V. Fuller: *Bismarck's Diplomacy at its Zenith*, pp. 255 ff.; Jacob Viner: "International Finance and Balance of Power Diplomacy 1880–1914" (*Southwestern Political and Social Science Quarterly*, IX, pp. 1–45, March 1929); Herbert Feis: *Europe the World's Banker 1870–1914* (New Haven, 1930), pp. 212 ff.; and especially Rudolf Ibbeken: *Das aussenpolitische Problem Staat und Wirtschaft in der deutschen Reichspolitik 1880–1914* (Schleswig, 1928), chapter ii.

[3] Waldersee: *Denkwürdigkeiten*, I, pp. 333–4.

Russians primarily as a means of gaining time for the completion of Russian and French armaments. Emperor William himself, despite his preference for the Russian connexion, was evidently shaken in his confidence. He approved of Bismarck's policy in the matter of the Near Eastern combination without raising objection and is said to have spent restless nights repeating in his sleep the words which he was to use to the Tsar.[1]

Alexander arrived in Berlin on the morning of November 18 and left the city the same evening. During the day he granted Bismarck an audience which lasted over an hour. It appears to have been a very spirited interview. According to Bismarck's account, the Tsar smoked one cigarette after another and was much agitated. In the course of the conversation it turned out that Alexander's suspicions of Bismarck and his policy were due to a number of letters supposedly written by Ferdinand of Bulgaria to a relative, the Countess of Flanders. From these it was clear that Bismarck, far from supporting the Russian policy in Bulgaria, had encouraged the Coburg candidacy and secretly backed it. The complete story of these letters has never become known, but there can be no doubt that they were forgeries — crude forgeries, in fact. They had been supplied to the French foreign office by a secret agent named Mondion and had been forwarded to the Tsar by the French foreign minister Flourens, who made use of various subterranean channels to accomplish his purpose. Bismarck convinced the Tsar that these papers were forgeries, and that Germany did, in actual fact, support the Russian claims in Bulgaria. But the attitude of the Russian press and military circles, he said, made it very hard to maintain a friendly policy. Under the circumstances it was inevitable that Germany should seek everywhere for allies. Alexander hastened to say that he had no alliance with France or with that " animal " Boulanger, but he spoke very bitterly of Austria and remarked that the existing tension might some day lead to a catastrophe. Thereupon Bismarck reminded him of the terms of the Austro-German Alliance. What the Tsar's reply to this was we do not know.[2]

Both parties seem to have been satisfied with the conversation, though Bismarck was on his guard and insisted, in speaking to his friends, that one must wait and see what the effect of this exchange of views would be. He certainly desired to maintain good relations with Russia, but his confidence had been badly shaken and he was not sanguine. As a matter of fact, the immediate results of the visit were not very impressive. The Russian press was instructed to desist from its attacks upon Germany, and the foreign minister, Giers, was

---

[1] Fürst Philip zu Eulenburg-Hertefeld: *Aus 50 Jahren* (Berlin, 1923), p. 146; *Die Grosse Politik*, V, No. 1127.

[2] Lucius von Ballhausen, op. cit., pp. 404–5; Waldersee: *Denkwürdigkeiten*, I, pp. 335–6; *Die Grosse Politik*, V, Nos. 1128 ff. On the Bulgarian documents see *Die Grosse Politik*, V, chapter xxxvi, appendix ii; Charles de Maurel (pseud.): *Le Prince de Bismarck démasqué* (Paris, 1889), written by Mondion; H. Galli: *Dessous diplomatiques* (Paris, 1894), chapter ii. Ferdinand himself denied the authenticity of the papers and has recently done so again (Karl F. Nowak: *Kaiser and Chancellor*, New York, 1930, p. 151, foot-note).

full of friendly sentiments, but attacks on Germany still continued to appear and there was no cessation of military preparations. To be sure, the troop concentrations were on the Austrian rather than on the German frontier, but that did not improve matters from the German view-point, for the danger of a clash between Russia and Austria was a matter of supreme moment to the Berlin government.

German military men had long since become impatient. General von Waldersee, the quartermaster-general and first assistant to Moltke at the general staff, complained of Bismarck's tergiversations and his unwillingness to break completely with Russia. Russia was not to be trusted and Germany should come out openly on the side of England, Austria, and Italy. These three powers together with Germany could look forward with full confidence to a struggle with France and Russia.[1] Convinced that Russia was making all preparations for war in the spring, he drew up a memorandum which he wished Moltke to submit to the Emperor. The memorandum was sent to both Bismarck and the Emperor on November 30. It stressed the tremendous increase of Russia's armed forces since the war with Turkey and called attention to the construction of railways and forts in Poland. Moltke subscribed to the view that Russia was directly arming for war and progressively mobilizing her forces. In a covering letter to Bismarck the old field-marshal elaborated this idea, saying that the Russians evidently wished to take advantage of Austria while she was rearming her forces, and that they hoped that Germany would allow an attack. In that case Austria would undoubtedly be defeated. But even if Germany aided Austria, most of the German troops would be tied up in the West: "Only if we take the aggressive in company with Austria and at an early date will our chances be favourable." There would be no obstacle to a winter campaign, for the frost would be a help more than a hindrance.[2]

Bismarck's notations upon this document are interesting. He doubted whether the Russians were actually mobilizing, pointed out that a Russian attack upon Austria would not be allowed by Germany, and insisted that neither the Reichstag nor the Austrian government would agree to an offensive war against Russia. When he forwarded the memorandum to Vienna, he added the remark that in his opinion Moltke's conclusions were premature. Far from subscribing to the theory that Germany and Austria should take the initiative and engage in a preventive war against Russia, he urged the Austrian government again and again to abstain from all action that might be interpreted as provocative. At the same time, however, he kept putting pressure upon the

---

[1] Eduard von Wertheimer: "*Ein K. und K. Militärattaché über das politische Leben in Berlin, 1880–1895*" (*Preussische Jahrbücher*, September 19⁓⁓, pp. 264–82), p. 268 — November 5, 1887; Waldersee: *Denkwürdigkeiten*, I, p. 334; id., *Briefwechsel*, No. 64.

[2] Moltke: *Die deutschen Aufmarschpläne*, pp. 137 ff., 143 ff. See also: *Waldersee in seinem militärischen Wirken* (Berlin, 1929), pp. 299 ff.; Waldersee: *Denkwürdigkeiten*, I, p. 339.

Austrians to induce them to bring their armaments up to date and make every preparation for war, in order to be ready for a Russian attack.

This policy, it must be admitted, was open to misunderstanding, especially if it was not clearly expounded. The Austrians, though they confidently expected war in the spring, were not ready, could not possibly have carried through mobilization before the middle of February, and disliked the idea of a winter campaign on the wind-swept plains of Galicia.[1] But the German military attaché at Vienna, Major von Deines, who believed in the advisability of a preventive war, and thought that Germany ought to stand by Austria from the beginning in any conflict with Russia, apparently gave the impression that the German government would like to see war break out, and that it would lend support. At any rate, a number of war councils were held under the presidency of Francis Joseph, and it was decided to ask the German government to enter upon discussions with the object of defining more closely the *casus fœderis* and the exact distribution of forces in the event of war. Archduke Albert, veteran commander of the Austrian armies, went so far as to draw up a plan for a military convention regulating German aid in case of a Russian attack and at the same time providing for a joint attack upon Russia in the spring of 1888. To this suggestion neither Francis Joseph nor Kálnoky would agree.[2]

This development of the situation was not at all to Bismarck's liking. The military attaché was severely reprimanded for engaging in conversations of a political nature, and it was pointed out to the Austrians again and again that Germany did not desire war and would not support Austria unless she were the victim of Russian aggression. In a very important dispatch of December 15 the chancellor redefined his attitude: " So long as I am minister, I shall not give my consent to a prophylactic attack upon Russia, and I am far removed from advising Austria to make such an attack, so long as she is not absolutely certain of English co-operation. If this co-operation were secure, the whole picture of the European situation would be changed. Through the superiority of the Anglo-Italian fleets the whole Italian army would be free for offensive purposes, and the Porte would probably be carried along to break with Russia. Without the certain prospect of English co-operation in a war against Russia, I consider it my duty to advise Austria against any offensive action." Germany would support Austria if she were attacked, but not if Austria took the offensive for reasons of Balkan policies. For this latter case Germany had tried to strengthen Austria by securing the friendship of England and Italy. If support from these powers could be absolutely relied on, Bismarck himself, if he were Austrian minister, might be tempted to risk a campaign, but otherwise not. Germany would not be involved in any case, for she could not fight for

---

[1] Waldersee: *Briefwechsel,* pp. 67, 73; Glaise-Horstenau: *Franz Josephs Weggefährte,* pp. 306 ff.; Radowitz, op. cit., II, p. 277.

[2] Eduard Heller: " *Bismarcks Stellung zur Führung des Zweifrontenkrieges* " (*Archiv für Politik und Geschichte,* VII, pp. 677–98, 1926); Glaise-Horstenau, op. cit., pp. 312 ff.

Balkan interests. If Austria attacked Russia, Germany's interest would lie in attacking France, in order to prevent an almost certain assault from that quarter.[1]

This dispatch lacks nothing in the way of clarity. It cannot be interpreted as meaning that Bismarck would have liked to see Austria declare war with the support of England and Italy. All that was intended was the expression of the opinion that an Austrian-Russian conflict over Balkan affairs would be inevitable sooner or later, and that for such an event Austria must be strong herself and must be sure of Anglo-Italian co-operation. But the decision lay with Austria, and she should not count on Germany.

Despite this reiteration of Germany's stand, the Austrian military men pressed for the initiation of discussions with their German colleagues, and pourparlers were actually opened. Fortunately, Moltke accepted Bismarck's view that matters of political import, like the definition of the *casus fœderis,* could only be decided by the foreign offices. He carefully avoided any definite statements in regard to the allocation of German troops or eventual German action.[2] Waldersee, on the other hand, told the Austrian military attaché that Germany would leave in the East four army corps, in addition to reserve divisions and cavalry, and that four more divisions would probably be added. Bismarck himself promised, on January 24, 1888, that if the Russian preparations in Poland went so far that there could be no further doubt of Russia's aggressive intentions, Germany would mobilize, in order to be ready to ward off an attack upon Austria; such mobilization, he said, would be sufficient to divert the Russian forces proportionately from Austria.

From Waldersee's notes it appears that he considered this concession to indicate a complete change of attitude on Bismarck's part, but there is no evidence of such a change. Bismarck wanted to reassure Austria that Germany would be on hand to join in repulsing a Russian attack. Furthermore, he was trying to induce the Austrians to permit Italian troops to be transported through their territory for use on the Rhine in case of war with France. It is clear that he thought the Russians would be deterred by prompt action on Germany's part. As a matter of fact, he doubted that the Russians would attack, knowing as they did that Germany would support Austria. The danger as he saw it lay in the possible Russian plan of provoking Austria to take the initiative. Certainly throughout the crisis of December and January he stated and restated his own attitude often enough. Under no circumstances would he consider a preventive war. Despite reports of discouragement and disappointment in Vienna he refused categorically to enter upon an academic discussion of what represented aggression. He would not for a moment entertain the theory advanced by the military men on both sides that even in a war of defence against Russia

---

[1] *Die Grosse Politik,* VI, No. 1163.
[2] Ibid., No. 1183; Moltke: *Die deutschen Aufmarschpläne,* pp. 147 ff.; Trützschler: *Bismarck und die Kriegsgefahr des Jahres 1887,* p. 141.

military considerations demanded that Austria and Germany proceed offensively, and that, after all, the party that first takes action is not always the aggressor. Such theories, Bismarck held, would lead into all sorts of difficulties and were therefore unfruitful. He could not negotiate as to the meaning of phrases, and Austria must rely on the good faith of her ally rather than upon the letter of the engagements. Without good faith the alliance would be worthless anyway.[1]

While advising the Austrians to make all necessary preparations for war, but to avoid all provocation, Bismarck pursued the same policy. The government, late in November, brought in a new military bill, in reply to the French bill of August. The new German bill provided for the extension of service in the reserve to the age of forty-five, thereby increasing the number of men liable to service by about six hundred thousand, equal to the forces of another ally.[2] At the same time Crispi's suggestion of a military convention was taken up. The military men had little confidence in the efficacy of Italian help, and this feeling may well have been shared by Bismarck. But Crispi was anxious, and it was felt that he must be humoured. Besides, if Italian troops could be engaged by the side of the German or Austrian forces, there would be added security of Italy's loyalty.

The problem confronting the military men was this: The Italian plan of campaign, as worked out by the chief of the general staff, General Cosenz, recognized the difficulty of waging war with France in the Alps, excepting at the most favourable season. Even then the French fortifications were so strong that a decision could hardly be hoped for. Instead of tying up the whole Italian army in the Alps, it would be far better to send part of the forces to Germany or Austria, where the decisive conflicts would probably take place.

After some preliminary negotiation, the purpose of which was to define the nature of Italian co-operation, two Italian officers were sent to Berlin towards the end of December 1887. In the course of the discussions it was decided that five Italian army corps and two or three cavalry divisions should be sent to the Rhine, where they should operate as the third Italian army, in the event of a war against France and Russia. The simple case of a war of Germany and Italy against France alone could not be considered, for in such a conflict Austria would remain neutral, and yet the transport of the Italian troops to Germany could take place only through Austrian territory. For this reason the Austrians were associated in the conversations, and the Austrian delegate joined in signing the memorandum of January 28, 1888, which laid down the terms of Italian co-operation. The Italians even went so far as to offer to send troops to the aid

---

[1] See, in general, *Die Grosse Politik*, VI, chapters xxxvii and xxxviii; Waldersee: *Denkwürdigkeiten*, I, pp. 340–56; id., *Briefwechsel*, Nos. 71 ff. See also Heinz von Trützschler: " *Bismarcks Stellung zum Präventivkrieg* " (*Europäische Gespräche*, I, pp. 185–94, August 1923), and Heinrich Ulmann: " *Störungen im Vertragssystem Bismarcks Ende 1887* " (*Historische Zeitschrift*, CXXVIII, pp. 92–104, 1923); Heller, loc. cit.; Glaise-Horstenau, op. cit., p. 321.

[2] See Rudt von Collenberg: *Die deutsche Armee von 1871–1914* (Berlin, 1922).

of the Austrians, and Kálnoky favoured the idea of transporting them over the less congested southern railway lines to the Roumanian frontier. One hundred thousand Italians on that front might, in Moltke's opinion, enable the Roumanians to take the offensive in the direction of Odessa. This, in turn, would oblige the Russians to leave three more army corps on the Roumanian front and thus correspondingly relieve the Galician front. Nothing seems to have come of these negotiations, but the discussions concerning the use of the Austrian railways for the transport of Italian troops to southern Germany led to consideration of the use of German railways in Upper Silesia for the transport of Austrian troops from Bohemia to Galicia. It seems that this suggestion was not followed up and that the matter rested in abeyance. But on April 14, 1888 a railway convention, regulating the transport of Italian troops through Austrian territory, was concluded at Vienna.[1]

By that time the acute danger of war had already passed. Giers and the Russian foreign office were probably opposed from the beginning to the military measures taken, but they had no control over the war office or the general staff. It was late November before the Tsar returned to Russia. There is some doubt whether he himself was kept informed of the preparations being made in Poland. It may be taken for granted that the foreign minister, who had to hear the complaints of the Germans, lost no time in enlightening him. Giers could no longer be blind to the fact that Russia's position was a very dangerous one. In September the British fleet had made a demonstrative visit to Austrian and Italian harbours. Salisbury, Kálnoky, and Crispi had, in their speeches in October and November, made a special point of stressing the community of interest of England, Austria, and Italy so far as the Near East was concerned. Though the Russian ambassador at London persisted in disbelieving all rumours of England's connexion with the powers of the Triple Alliance, Giers had no doubt of it. He feared that the immediate outcome would be an initiative by these powers in the Bulgarian question and pressure on their part on behalf of the recognition of Ferdinand. The active interest of England in the Mediterranean situation caused him great uneasiness.[2]

In view of the threat of an imposing coalition Giers did his utmost to reduce friction. While the *Russki Invalid,* organ of the war office, published a statement on December 15 in which the Russian preparations were explained

---

[1] *Die Grosse Politik,* VI, chapter xli, *passim;* Pribram, op. cit., II, p. 85, note 173; Waldersee: *Briefwechsel,* Nos. 55, 59, 61, 84, 94, 95; id., *Denkwürdigkeiten,* I, pp. 347, 357; *Waldersee in seinem militärischen Wirken,* II, pp. 306 ff.; Moltke: *Die deutschen Aufmarschpläne,* pp. 128 ff.; Glaise-Horstenau, op. cit., pp. 317 ff. See also Angelo Gatti: " *La Rottura Militare della Triplice Alleanza* " (*Rassegna Italiana;* XII, pp. 755–67, December 1923); François Charles-Roux: " *Les Conventions militaires italo-allemandes sous la Triple Alliance* " (*Revue de Paris,* IV, pp. 608–31, August 1, 1926); Graf Waldersee: " *Von Deutschlands militärpolitischen Beziehungen zu Italien* " (*Berliner Monatshefte,* VII, pp. 636–64, July 1929); Georg Graf Waldersee: " *Über die Beziehungen des deutschen zum österreichisch-ungarischen Generalstabe vor dem Weltkriege* " (ibid., VIII, pp. 103–42, February 1930).

[2] Meyendorff: *Correspondance de M. de Staal,* I, pp. 360–71.

as a necessary reply to German and Austrian armaments and concentrations, Giers gave assurances at Vienna on December 18 that Russia had no intention of attacking Austria. At the same time he began to retreat on the Bulgarian problem. To the British ambassador he said that Russia would never do anything rash in this matter for the sake of the Bulgarians: " They may do anything they please, from cutting each other's throats to declaring themselves an empire. We shall not move a finger to prevent them. We wash our hands of the whole concern." [1] All Russia still asked for was that Ferdinand be declared a usurper, and that he be expelled. Bismarck was appealed to, and as usual offered to support any Russian proposal, provided German support were formally requested. [2]

For some time the matter was left undecided, while Bismarck had the old Emperor William write the Tsar a New Year's letter explaining the situation and affirming his profound desire for the maintenance of peace. Alexander was in a sober mood, as the French ambassador discovered when the Tsar received him on December 24. The audience was an unusual one, for Laboulaye and the other French ambassadors were not given new credentials after the election of Carnot. It was evidently this circumstance that led the ambassador to expect something of importance, for he told the Russian ruler that France now considered him as the guardian and arbiter of peace in Europe. In the furtherance of this work he could count on the energetic and devoted assistance of the French government. It was a good lead, but Alexander did not follow it. His reply was that he saw the best guarantee of peace in the continuance of the excellent relations between the two countries, but when Laboulaye began to talk of a possible Anglo-Russian rapprochement, in which Italy might be included, Alexander said nothing, except that he did not expect Germany to break the peace while the old Emperor lived. On the other hand, there was always the chance that Austria might be pushed into a conflict, he added. [3]

Laboulaye's suggestion of an Anglo-Russian understanding was made in anticipation of a visit which Lord Randolph Churchill was about to pay to Russia. He stayed for some weeks and spoke to the leading persons in diplomatic circles, but it was clear from the start not only that he came without the approval of his government, but that Salisbury was opposed to this independent move on his part. Under the circumstances Churchill's long talk with the Tsar about the possibility of an understanding between the two countries was purely academic and could have no practical importance. [4]

---

[1] *Turkey*, No. I, p. 169 (quoted by Fuller, op. cit., p. 285). The Russian assurance to Austria in *Die Grosse Politik*, VI, No. 1170.

[2] Trützschler: *Bismarck und die Kriegsgefahr des Jahres 1887*, pp. 144 ff.

[3] Toutain, op. cit., pp. 309 ff.

[4] Winston Churchill: *Lord Randolph Churchill*, II, pp. 359 ff.; Lee: *Edward VII*, Volume I, pp. 682 ff.; Meyendorff, op. cit., I, pp. 376–7, 382–4, 388–9; *Letters of Queen Victoria*, Third Series, Volume I, pp. 367–9, 379, 383.

Whether Giers awaited the outcome of Churchill's visit before coming forward with proposals regarding Bulgaria cannot be determined. It is more likely that the Russian action was the result of two other factors. The first of these was the publication of the Austro-German Alliance of 1879, which took place on February 3, 1888. Renewed interpellations in the Hungarian parliament as to whether Austria-Hungary could count on German support in a war with Russia led Bismarck to insist on the publication of the treaty, so that all the world might be convinced of its defensive character. It undoubtedly had a sobering effect in Austria-Hungary and caused the greatest dejection in Russian circles. It must be remembered that the Russian government had been informed during the preceding summer of the terms of the treaty, but that the public had not known that it was directed against Russia. All thought of settling the Balkan difficulty through a war with Austria now had to be given up, unless a conflict with Germany was to be faced at the same time. The treaty was a great blow to the Russian nationalists and increased their dislike of Germany. It is a debatable question whether it was advisable for Bismarck to cause further estrangement from Russia in order to disillusion the Hungarians.

Some uneasiness about the reaction of the publication of the treaty in Russia appears in the great address which Bismarck delivered on February 6. The resounding words which occur towards the end of the speech: " We Germans fear God and nothing else in the world! " have given the impression that the chancellor was breathing defiance. Nothing is further from the truth, for the address, while characterized by self-assurance and confidence, was distinctly conciliatory. After pointing out that the danger of conflict with France was decidedly less than it had been a year before, Bismarck entered upon a long historical review of German relations with Russia, which had always been good until, in 1875 and 1879, they were embittered through the policy of Gorchakov. He explained in detail how Germany, embedded in the heart of Europe, must have one reliable friend, and how therefore he had been driven into alliance with Austria. The alliance rested upon common interests and did not represent an effort on Germany's part to pursue a policy of prestige or force towards her neighbours. It was erroneous to speak of the revelation of the treaty as an act of defiance or menace, for the Russian government had been informed some time before of its content. Relations with Russia were still good, and Germany was perfectly willing to acknowledge Russia's claim to a special position in Bulgaria. Let the powers which were directly interested in the Near Eastern situation take the lead, either to agree with Russia or to fight her. It was not up to Germany to act. Despite all the press campaigns and even the concentrations of troops in Poland, Bismarck himself did not believe in the danger of a Russian attack. The newspaper polemics meant only so much printer's ink to him, and the concentrations of troops could be explained in a variety of ways. What he relied upon was the word of the Tsar, and the Tsar had declared that he had no intention of attacking Germany or of waging any offensive war. As against these assurances everything else weighed light as a feather.[1]

This great speech, full of assurance and confidence in Germany's strength, which, as the chancellor said, made all attempts to threaten seem ridiculous, was characterized throughout by goodwill towards Russia and the desire to maintain friendly relations. Giers seized the opportunity and on February 13 asked for German support to induce the Sultan to declare the régime of Ferdinand illegal. Bismarck accepted the task and pressed it upon the Porte, pointing out that even though the other powers rejected the proposal, it was still the duty of the Porte to make the declaration. The chancellor then went even further and urged acceptance of the Russian proposal both at Vienna and at Rome. But both the English and the Italian governments used their influence at Vienna to bring about the failure of the Russian move. The proposal was rejected on the theory that it would be unwise to ruin the existing régime before knowing what was to happen next. Nevertheless the Porte, on March 4, issued the declaration of illegality which Giers had desired. The situation had begun to clear. It was evident that German support of the Russian policy could be relied upon, but it was also patent to the Russians that the coalition which they had suspected really existed. They had won a victory in getting the Porte to declare Ferdinand a usurper, but they had also seen that it would be futile and dangerous to attempt to go further. From this time on, the tension began to relax and the Bulgarian question began to lose its acute character. The great powers knew what to expect and could make their arrangements accordingly. Bismarck's diplomacy had been wholly successful, for without drawing upon Germany's head the wrath of Russia for her failure in Bulgaria the chancellor had evolved a triple combination of powers which, operating in a pacific way, served as a counter-weight to Russia's aspirations in the East, aspirations which might threaten the common interests of these three powers, but did not touch German interests.[2]

A more complicated chapter of diplomacy than that dealing with the year 1887 could hardly be found in the history of European international relations. And yet, though the clouds of war lowered on all horizons, the general peace was maintained. This fact alone is a tribute to the statesmen of the continent, most of whom desired to avoid conflict and showed but little sympathy with the violent outbursts of national sentiment or the pressure for action exerted by the military men. But it may well be doubted whether the statesmen could have held their own against such pressure had it not been for the mastery with which Bismarck guided the course of diplomacy. It is easy enough to understand that many political and military writers of the time regarded him as an evil spirit, a demon, an intriguer, a bully. They could not know what was going on behind

[1] Kohl: *Die politischen Reden des Fürsten Bismarck*, XII, pp. 440–78.
[2] See especially Trützschler: *Bismarck und die Kriegsgefahr des Jahres 1887*, pp. 144 ff.

the scenes, for the agreements made in this eventful year were secret. Had the chancellor had his way, they would probably have been public, as public as his great speeches, in which he reviewed the situation with the greatest bluntness, not to say brutality. Bismarck believed in an open diplomacy supported by strong national forces. He did not allow the military power of Germany to fall behind that of her neighbours, but he did not intend to use Germany's power for aggressive purposes. For him Germany was a " saturated " nation, forced to maintain a strong military establishment because of her dangerous geographical location.

As for his diplomacy, it was really simple in its underlying principles, and anyone might have understood it. Threatened on two fronts, Germany's interest was to prevent the formation of a Franco-Russian coalition by showing herself amenable to Russian desires in Bulgaria, where Germany had no direct interests. The difficulty with this solution, however, arose from the fact that the Austrians and the Russians would not agree to a peaceful partition of the Balkans into spheres of influence. They threatened to go to war over the Bulgarian question. Now it was clear that in a Russian-Austrian conflict one of two things would happen. Either Russia would attack, in which event Germany would be brought in on Austria's side under the terms of the alliance of 1879; or Austria would attack and most likely be defeated unless Germany came to her assistance. But Germany could not afford to see the position of Austria as a great power jeopardized by a Russian victory. How was the dilemma to be solved? The Reinsurance Treaty is the key to the whole situation, for in it Bismarck, while securing Germany against the danger of a Franco-Russian alliance, checkmated the two eastern powers: Germany would stand by the party attacked. Thereby, as Bismarck put it, he had set a premium upon the preservation of peace.

There was only one great danger that haunted Bismarck after the conclusion of the Reinsurance Treaty, and that was that Russia, counting on German neutrality if Austria were the aggressor, would provoke the latter into taking the initiative. What would Germany's position then be? This difficulty was to be solved by the Mediterranean coalition, which in its earlier form was to ensure the three powers, England, Austria, and Italy, against the disturbance of the *status quo* in the Mediterranean. The agreement of December 12 represented a great reinforcement of the earlier understanding and made Russian action in the East almost impossible. She could no longer provoke Austria without coming to blows with the Near Eastern Triplice. Quite naturally, she chose to retreat in the Bulgarian question.

In all this there was no question of loyalty or disloyalty on Bismarck's part, any more than there was a question of his siding with one power as against another. Historians who attempt to make out a case of this sort in one way or the other are bound to find themselves in a blind alley. The German chancellor repeatedly distinguished between a policy of interests and a policy of

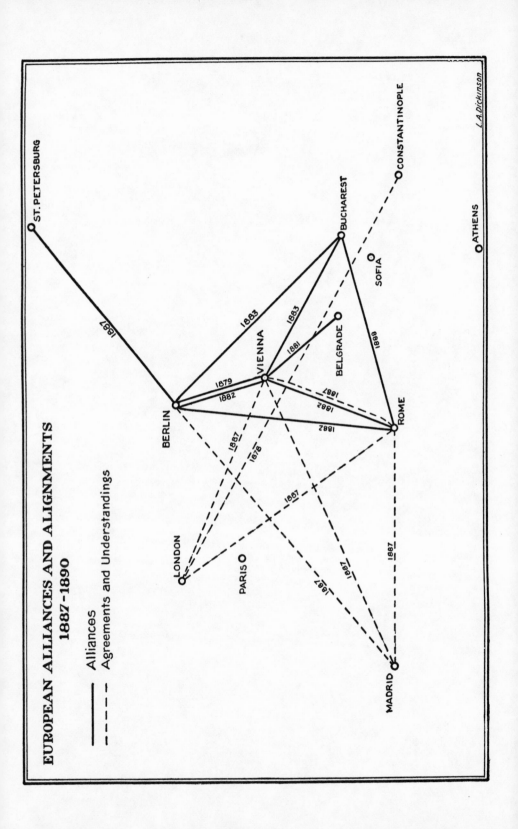

EUROPEAN ALLIANCES AND ALIGNMENTS
1887-1890

——————— Alliances
- - - - - - - Agreements and Understandings

ST. PETERSBURG

BUCHAREST

CONSTANTINOPLE

ATHENS

SOFIA

1887

1883

1883

BELGRADE

1888

1881

VIENNA

1879

1882

1887

1882

1882

ROME

BERLIN

1887

1878

1887

LONDON

PARIS

1887

1887

1887

1887

MADRID

L.A.Dickinson

prestige. He was following the interests of Germany, nothing more, nothing less. But above all he based his policy upon real factors in European relations. He did not expect others to act contrary to their own interests. Just as he would not engage Germany in a quarrel with Russia over Bulgaria or take the side of Austria in a Balkan policy which did not concern Germany, so he avoided unreasonable demands upon other powers. If the Austrians wished to fight because of Bulgaria, well and good, but let them first assure themselves of the proper support. Did the English wish to smash the Franco-Russian coalition in the Egyptian question and resist the Russian policy in the East at all costs? Let them do so, but let them first make the necessary arrangements with Austria and Italy, countries which had similar interests. In the same way the Italians should enlist the aid of the other Mediterranean powers if they hoped to check the French policy in North Africa.

One can hardly escape the conviction that Bismarck throughout this critical year, while doing his utmost to liberate Germany from the danger of a Franco-Russian alliance, at the same time maintained a careful balance between the other powers. He deluded and disappointed some and enraged others, Austrians as well as French and Russians, but he preserved the peace. Had he not been there, the nations would have had it out in the good old way. They had often fought on less pretext. But for Germany's sake Bismarck desired to avoid any conflict in Europe. He would not fight himself, no matter how favourable the situation might be for Germany, but at the same time he would not let the others fight if he could help it. As the situation stood at the end of 1887, no power could move without involving itself in endless difficulties and dangers. The sanctions of peace lay in the great alliance system which spread over Europe like a huge web. Bismarck was denounced and misunderstood, but for him the preservation of peace was worth it.

BIBLIOGRAPHICAL NOTE

(SUPPLEMENTARY TO THE BIBLIOGRAPHICAL NOTE TO CHAPTER IX)

DOCUMENTARY SOURCES

Accounts and Papers. 1887. Volume XCII. *Further Correspondence respecting Sir Henry Drummond Wolff's Mission.*

Documents diplomatiques. Affaires d'Égypte 1884–1893. Paris, 1893.

Die Grosse Politik der europäischen Kabinette. Volume IV: chapter xxviii (The Entente between England, Austria, and Italy, 1887). Volume V: chapter xxxiv (The Reinsurance Treaty), xxxv (The Publication of the Austro-German Treaty), xxxvi (The Tsar's Visit to Berlin, with appendices on the prohibition of Russian securities and the forged Bulgarian documents). Volume VI: chapter xxxvii

(The Russian-Austrian Crisis), xxxviii (Austrian-German negotiations concerning the *casus fœderis*), xli (Italian co-operation in a Franco-German war).

"*Russko-Germanskie Otnoshenia.*" Edited by M. N. Pokrovski. (*Krasny Arkhiv*, I, 1922). Includes a number of documents reporting Shuvalov's negotiations with Bismarck in the spring of 1887.

MEMOIRS, AUTOBIOGRAPHIES, BIOGRAPHIES, AND LETTERS

WOLFF, SIR HENRY DRUMMOND: *Rambling Recollections.* Two volumes. London, 1908. Contains some material on the author's mission and the agreement which bears his name.

RADOWITZ, JOSEF MARIA VON: *Aufzeichnungen und Erinnerungen.* Two volumes. Berlin, 1925. Throws some light on the German policy at Constantinople, with special reference to the Wolff Convention.

GOBLET, RENÉ: "*Souvenirs de ma vie politique; L'Affaire Schnaebele*" (*Revue Politique et parlementaire*, CXXXVII, pp. 177–97, November 10, 1928). Adds somewhat to our knowledge of the Schnaebele crisis and the attitude of the French ministry.

CRISPI, FRANCESCO: *Memoirs.* Three volumes. New York, 1912–14. A very important source for the period under discussion, but one which requires comparison with other material.

MOÜY, CHARLES DE: *Souvenirs et causeries d'un diplomate.* Paris, 1909. The author was French ambassador at Rome. He discusses the Franco-Italian difficulty without adding much.

BILLOT, ALBERT: *La France et l'Italie. Histoire des années troublées, 1881–1899.* Two volumes. Paris, 1905. An elaborate history of Franco-Italian relations, by a French ambassador at Rome. There is not, however, much in the way of revelations.

GÉRARD, AUGUSTE: *Mémoires.* Paris, 1928. The writer was secretary of the French embassy at Rome in this period, but does not reveal many new facts in connexion with the Franco-Italian problem.

GLAISE-HORSTENAU, EDMUND: *Franz Josephs Weggefährte. Das Leben des Generalstabschefs Grafen Beck.* Vienna, 1930. Contains much valuable material on military problems.

SPECIAL STUDIES

PRIBRAM, ALFRED F.: "*Zwei Gespräche des Erzherzogs Rudolf mit Bismarck*" (*Österreichische Rundschau*, 1921, pp. 8–19). Contains the report of the highly interesting conversation of March 1887.

WERTHEIMER, EDUARD: "*Kronprinz Rudolf und Fürst Bismarck*" (*Archiv für Politik und Geschichte*, IV, pp. 349–63, April 1925). Supplements the preceding through the use of some unpublished material in the Vienna archives.

—: *" Ein K. und K. Militärattaché über das politische Leben in Berlin, 1880–1895"* (*Preussische Jahrbücher*, September 1925, pp. 264–82). Based on the reports of von Steiniger, the Austrian military attaché at Berlin.

MOLTKE, GRAF: *Die deutschen Aufmarschpläne 1871–1890.* Berlin, 1929 (*Forschungen und Darstellungen aus dem Reichsarchiv*, No. 7). The strategical plans and more important memoranda of the chief of staff, of great interest in connexion with the crisis of December 1887–January 1888.

WALDERSEE, GRAF ALFRED: *General-Feldmarschall Alfred Graf von Waldersee in seinem militärischen Wirken.* Edited by Hans Mohs. Two volumes. Berlin, 1929. Contains the military writings of Moltke's first assistant.

TRÜTZSCHLER, HEINZ VON: *" Bismarcks Stellung zum Präventivkrieg"* (*Europäische Gespräche*, I, pp. 185–94, August 1923). Collates and reviews Bismarck's utterances on the subject of preventive war.

ULMANN, HEINRICH: *"Störungen im Vertragssystem Bismarcks Ende 1887"* (*Historische Zeitschrift*, CXXVIII, pp. 92–104, 1923). Discusses the relations between Austria and Germany and the problems connected with the terms of the alliance.

IBBEKEN, RUDOLF: *Das aussenpolitische Problem Staat und Wirtschaft in der deutschen Reichspolitik 1880–1914.* Schleswig, 1928. The best general treatment of the economic side of German-Russian relations.

MEDLICOTT, W. N.: *" Austria-Hungary and the War Danger of 1887"* (*Slavonic Review*, VI, pp. 437–41, December 1927). Prints an unpublished memorandum of Kálnoky of January 1888, in which he stresses the general aspects of the international tension.

VERGNIOL, CAMILLE: *" L'Affaire Schnaebele"* (*Revue de France*, II, pp. 406–25, 645–68, April 1 and 15, 1929). A microscopic review of the Franco-German crisis, using some new material.

FREYCINET, CHARLES DE: *La Question d'Égypte.* Paris, 1905. Contains the best presentation of the Wolff Convention as seen from the French side.

KLEINE, MATHILDE: *Deutschland und die ägyptische Frage, 1875–1890.* Greifswald, 1927. An excellent account of the German policy in the Egyptian question, with due emphasis on the international aspects of the problem.

CURÀTULO, GIACOMO E.: *Francia e Italia, 1849–1914.* Turin, 1915. A reliable though conventional account of Franco-Italian relations.

SALVEMINI, GAETANO: *La Politica Estera di Francesco Crispi.* Rome, 1919. An excellent critical essay, though now somewhat out of date.

CARDELLA, G. P.: *" Crispi e la Politica Mediterranea e Coloniale"* (*Politica*, XXIX, pp. 150–79, April 1928; 387–431, June–August 1928; XXXI, pp. 350–80,

June–August 1929). A very detailed account, but based chiefly on Crispi's memoirs.

GATTI, ANGELO: "*La Rottura Militare della Triplice Alleanza*" (*Rassegna Italiana*, XII, pp. 755–67, December 1923).

CHARLES-ROUX, FRANÇOIS: "*Les Conventions militaires italo-allemandes sous la Triple Alliance*" (*Revue de Paris*, IV, pp. 608–31, August 1, 1926).

WALDERSEE, GRAF GEORG: "*Von Deutschlands militärpolitischen Beziehungen zu Italien*" (*Berliner Monatshefte*, VII, pp. 636–64, July 1929).

—: "*Über die Beziehungen des deutschen zum österreichisch-ungarischen Generalstabe vor dem Weltkriege*" (*Berliner Monatshefte*, VIII, pp. 103–42, February 1930). These last four titles deal primarily with the military relations between the powers of the Triple Alliance in the period just before the World War, but they all contain some discussion of the earlier negotiations which are mentioned in this chapter.

HELLER, EDUARD: "*Bismarcks Stellung zur Führung des Zweifrontenkrieges*" (*Archiv für Politik und Geschichte*, VII, pp. 677–98, 1926). Very important discussion of the military problem, based in part on unpublished material.

SPECIAL LITERATURE ON THE REINSURANCE TREATY

DANIELS, EMIL: "*Der Rückversicherungsvertrag vom 18 Juni 1887*" (*Preussische Jahrbücher*, October 1919, pp. 178 ff.).

FERENZ, JOSEPH: "*Der bismarcksche Rückversicherungsvertrag zwischen Deutschland und Russland*" (*Vergangenheit und Gegenwart*, XVII, pp. 477–84, 1927).

GORIAINOV, SERGE: "The End of the Alliance of the Emperors" (*American Historical Review*, XXIII, pp. 324–50, January 1918). Deals as much with the making as with the breaking of the treaty. The text was first published in this article, which is of prime importance.

HARTUNG, FRITZ: "*Der deutsch-russische Rückversicherungsvertrag von 1887 und seine Kündigung*" (*Die Grenzboten*, 1921, pp. 12–17).

RAAB, GERHARD: *Der deutsch-russische Rückversicherungsvertrag in dem System der bismarckschen Politik, vornehmlich des Jahres 1887*. Wetzlar, 1923. The most elaborate study of the making of the treaty and its implications.

RACHFAHL, FELIX: "*Der Rückversicherungsvertrag, der ' Balkandreibund' und das angebliche Bündnisangebot Bismarcks an England vom Jahre 1887*" (*Weltwirtschaftliches Archiv*, XVI, pp. 28–81, 1920). A pioneer and fundamental discussion of the treaty in its general international setting.

RASCHDAU, LUDWIG: "*Der deutsch-russische Rückversicherungsvertrag*" (*Die Grenzboten*, April 12, 1918, pp. 25–32).

—: *" Zur Vorgeschichte des Rückversicherungsvertrages "* (*Deutsche Rundschau,* CXCIX, pp. 113–26, May 1924). Raschdau is the last surviving member of the staff of the German foreign office in the last days of Bismarck.

ROTHFELS, HANS: *" Zur Geschichte des Rückversicherungsvertrages "* (*Preussische Jahrbücher,* CLXXXVII, pp. 265 ff., March 1922). One of the soundest estimates of the treaty and its significance.

UEBERSBERGER, HANS: *" Abschluss und Ende des Rückversicherungsvertrages "* (*Die Kriegsschuldfrage,* V, pp. 933–66, October 1927). Based primarily upon Russian source material.

XIII

The End of the Bismarckian System

～

WHATEVER ELSE MAY BE SAID OF THE INTRICATE ALLIANCE SYSTEM evolved by the German chancellor, it must be admitted that it worked and that it tided Europe over a period of several critical years without a rupture. The powers were so enmeshed in an elaborate scheme of insurance treaties, reinsurance treaties, agreements, and understandings that it was almost impossible for any one of them to act without bringing all the others upon the scene. Under the circumstances there was, as Bismarck himself said, a premium upon the maintenance of peace.

But this delicately adjusted system of balances could not be worked without difficulty. The very secrecy of the agreements upon which it was based gave rise to misapprehensions and dissatisfaction. Among the military men in Berlin and Vienna there were not a few who regarded all this diplomatic quibbling as utterly futile. The facts of the case seemed obvious: the central powers were exposed to hostile action on both flanks. War would come sooner or later. Would it not be better to cut the Gordian knot while the military advantage still lay with the Triple Alliance? It was the old theory of the preventive war, and it was by no means confined to the allied capitals. In Russia and in France, too, pressure was being constantly brought to bear upon the governments in favour of military action. From all sides the German chancellor was being attacked, at home as well as abroad. During his last years of power the complaints of his weakness and vacillation became more and more frequent and discontent with the course of events grew with every month. During the last two years of his régime he was, more or less, on the defensive. He was fighting for a system which few really understood, though it aimed directly at the preservation of peace.

It must be confessed that the historian is confronted with a very serious problem of presentation in attempting to unravel the tangled skeins of European diplomacy in this period. The guiding thread through the labyrinth must not be lost sight of. Bismarck had made Berlin the focal point of international relations. Bound on the one hand by his agreement with Russia and on the other hand by his connexion with Austria and Italy, and indirectly with England, he was obliged to share his favours equally and to avoid partiality to either group. To lean too far in one direction would almost inevitably lead to disaster. To desert the Mediterranean powers would result in the break-up of the Mediterranean Triplice and possibly end with an arrangement between Russia and England. To desert Russia would almost certainly mean the formation of a Franco-Russian alliance. The problem was difficult enough to test even the greatest genius.

Bismarck's refusal to join either camp without reservations led to considerable ill feeling in all of the major countries. The Austrian government could not swallow its resentment at the German attitude. When Queen Victoria, in April 1888, spoke with Francis Joseph, who had come to Innsbruck to greet her as she passed through on her way to Berlin, she found that he was much pleased with Anglo-Austrian relations, because in war the two countries could co-operate. But he considered Russia to be incomprehensible and thought Bismarck much too weak and yielding in his relations with the Tsar.[1] There was, indeed, a strong government group in Austria which was opposed to the alliance with Germany and Italy and favoured an agreement with Russia. This group drew its strength from the clerical elements and from the Czech and Polish leaders, who supported the Emperor's favourite, the prime minister, Count Taaffe. It was, therefore, not far removed from the throne and threatened to influence the foreign policy of the government as it had already determined the line of domestic affairs.

When the young German Emperor, William II, came to pay a visit to Vienna in August 1888, Francis Joseph was anxious lest it should be too much of a success.[2] Soon afterwards a violent newspaper campaign began in Vienna, directed in part against the Crown Prince Rudolf, but also against the alliance with Germany. Bismarck viewed the situation with great earnestness, for, as he had often said, the alliance with Austria depended upon the goodwill of the Austrian Germans and upon the anti-Russian attitude of the Magyars in Hungary. If the Slavophil policies of Taaffe were victorious in Austria, the defeat of the German element would be complete, and the very basis of the alliance would be shaken. To create a demonstration the chancellor sent his son Herbert to Budapest in October to bestow upon the Hungarian prime minister, Count Tisza, the Order of the Black Eagle, while the Austrian minister Taaffe was ostentatiously passed by. From utterances made by Bismarck to his friends at this time it is clear that he feared for the unity of the Austrian army if the nationalist movements were allowed to progress, and that he considered the eventuality of not renewing the alliance if matters continued on the same course.[3]

The Emperor Francis Joseph refused to take any notice of the German

[1] George E. Buckle; *Letters of Queen Victoria*, Third Series, Volume I (New York, 1930), p. 400.

[2] Mitis: *Kronprinz Rudolf*, pp. 144 ff.

[3] Schweinitz: *Denkwürdigkeiten*, II, p. 370; Lucius von Ballhausen, op. cit., p. 480; Eduard von Wertheimer: "*Erzherzog Rudolf und Fürst Bismarck*" (*Archiv für Politik und Geschichte*, IV, 1925, pp. 349–63), and especially Eduard von Wertheimer: *Bismarck im politischen Kampf* (Berlin, 1930), pp. 503–18.

attitude and continued to stand by Taaffe, with the result that a pronounced strain of dissatisfaction crept into the alliance, a point that must be borne in mind in discussing these critical years. And the same factors served to colour the relations between Austria and Italy, for Crispi objected as much to the clerical trend of Austrian policy as Bismarck did to the racial bias, and there was, besides, the friction constantly arising from the activities of the irredentists in Italy. Crispi was a loyal supporter of the Triple Alliance, but the developments in Austria did not make the connexion more popular in the peninsula. Even the alliance between Italy and Germany was attacked by the Francophil radicals, and Bismarck, while he cultivated the friendship of Crispi with great assiduity, was evidently anxious lest the Italian statesman's well-known irascibility and hot-headedness should lead to international complications.

Throughout the year 1887 the danger of a Franco-German war had been ever present. The governments had repeatedly proclaimed their pacific intentions and there was no real danger that either would take the initiative and provoke a conflict. The real menace at this time had lain in the instability of the French government and in the possibility that the unpopular régime of the moderate republicans would be overthrown by a popular leader like Boulanger. This danger had once more become acute in the winter of 1887-8, for the famous general, though holding an army command at Clermont-Ferrand, continued to come to Paris in disguise and kept in close touch with politics. Though he was ineligible for election to the Chamber of Deputies, his name had been submitted in five by-elections in February 1888 and he had polled some fifty thousand votes. The government decided to proceed against him, relieved him of his command, placed him on half pay, and finally, on March 27, retired him from the army.

The wisdom of this procedure may well be questioned, for Boulanger now became eligible for election to parliament. His supporters, especially Deroulède and the League of Patriots, organized a committee of protest and secured a campaign fund of several million francs from the royalist Duchesse d'Uzès. A program calling for the dissolution of the legislature and the revision of the constitution was brought forward. On March 30 the Tirard cabinet fell after it had refused to consider the revision which was demanded. A few days later Boulanger was elected deputy from Dordogne, but he rejected the office on the ground that he had promised to stand for the department of Nord. There he was elected with 172,000 votes on April 15. Of his popularity there could no longer be the slightest doubt. The republicans, even his original sponsors like Clemenceau, withdrew their support and organized the Society of the Rights of Man to put an end to the agitation and defend the republic. But Boulanger's followers were even more active. They adopted the motto of the League of Patriots and enlisted the support of the Bonapartists and Orleanists. Even the Church threw its influence into the scales in his favour.

In the summer of 1888 civil war in France appeared almost certain. In the chamber bitter words passed between the leaders of the two groups, Boulanger declaring that the country was tired and disgusted with a régime "which is nothing but empty agitation, disorder, corruption, lies, and sterility," while the prime minister, Floquet, accused the general of having passed from the sacristies into the antechambers of princes, and asked by what right he spoke like Bonaparte returning from his victories: "At your age, General Boulanger, Napoleon was dead, and you will never be more than the Sieyès of a constitution stillborn." On July 12 the general submitted a motion calling for the dissolution of the chamber. There followed another heated conflict between the popular leader and the prime minister, in which the lie was passed. The two men fought a duel with rapiers the next day, and the aged statesman wounded the general severely in the neck. Boulanger had resigned his seat, and it might have been reasonably expected that the outcome of the duel would completely discredit him.

Exactly the contrary happened. His supporters redoubled their efforts and determined to secure as many elections as possible, evidently with the idea of holding an indirect plebiscite in this way. The country was flooded with portraits and pamphlets and re-echoed with innumerable Boulangist songs: *General Revenge; Frenchmen, Let's drink to Boulanger; See him and die; Down with Bismarck,* etc., the latter with the characteristic verse:

> *Par tout le sang de la France entière,*
> *Par le passé, par les morts à venger,*
> *Avec le Tsar, pour Dieu, France, pour la patrie,*
> *Mort aux Prussiens, et vive Boulanger!*

Mr. Belfort, the general's secretary, has given a vivid description of these stirring events: "During our electoral tournaments throughout France I noted that his popularity was amazing; poets sang his praises, musicians composed hymns in his honour, the Press devoted to him and his campaigns daily attention, the cables of the world vibrated with interminable despatches recording his exploits and his triumphs. Wherever he went the people applauded him with frenzied enthusiasm: daily I saw men weep with joy at shaking him by the hand; women stormed his guard and kissed him with patriotic fervour; his portrait was found in the cottages of the poor as in the mansions of the rich. At some Paris houses he was entertained as a monarch. . . . At the most aristocratic houses in Paris the ladies were presented to the General, and curtseyed as to an emperor or prince of the blood." [1]

Lest it be thought that the Boulangist agitation was merely an artificial demonstration, it must be pointed out that in August 1888 the general was elected deputy in the departments of Nord, Somme, and Charente Inférieure. The autumn was filled with campaigns and celebrations, and in January 1889 the general stood for election in the department of Seine, the very stronghold of

---

[1] Roland Belfort: "General Boulanger's Love Tragedy" (*Nineteenth Century*, CV, pp. 413–27, March, 1929).

French radicalism and republicanism. To be sure, Boulanger denied his hostility to the republic as a form of government and disclaimed all ideas of a dictatorship. Nevertheless, his election was regarded by all political experts as quite impossible because all the republican groups had united against him, and his opponent was a prominent radical and president of the general council of the department. It was with consternation, then, that the news spread on the evening of January 27 that Boulanger had been elected with 244,000 votes. The cabinet met in hurried session at the Élysée Palace to discuss ways and means of meeting the crisis, for it was generally expected that Boulanger would seize the opportunity and overthrow the government. The enormous crowds that surged about the Café Durand, where the general was staying, certainly expected some such action. The rank and file of the army were favourable, the police were on his side. The government was helpless. Even so prominent a statesman as Freycinet believed that if Boulanger had acted promptly, he might have swept aside all obstacles. But the general failed to act. Instead of placing himself at the head of the crowd he slipped out the back door and went to his mistress, who was anxiously awaiting him.

Many attempts have been made to explain this extraordinary conduct. The question need not detain us here. Suffice it to say that Boulanger, who evidently thought his position so strong that illegal methods were unnecessary, failed at the crucial moment to fulfil the expectations of his followers. The government was not slow to take advantage. After restoring the uninominal system of voting the cabinet resigned and a new government was formed, in which the energetic and ruthless Constans was minister of the interior. He promptly dissolved the League of Patriots and instituted proceedings against Boulanger himself. The government's plans were purposely allowed to leak out, and in April Boulanger fled to Brussels. Though the agitation continued for some time, the peak of the crisis had been passed. In the general elections in the autumn of 1889 the Boulangist party was overwhelmingly defeated. When, in 1891, Boulanger committed suicide on the grave of his mistress, at Brussels, he had long ceased to play any political role whatever.[1]

It is quite true that in the course of the year 1888 the Boulangist movement assumed the form of an acute domestic conflict and that the duel between the republicans on the one hand and the royalists and imperialists supporting Boulanger on the other diverted the attention of the French from foreign affairs and concentrated all efforts on the struggle nearer home. Nevertheless, this same movement continued to influence European international relations and to affect the position of France in a number of ways. Bismarck, who had long since considered the desirability of instituting a rigorous system of passports in

---

[1] Good accounts of the Boulangist movement may be found in Mermeix (Gabriel Terrail): *Les Coulisses du Boulangisme* (Paris, 1890), the most important source; Freycinet: *Souvenirs*, chapter xii; Alexandre Zevaès: *Histoire de la Troisième République* (Paris), 1926, chapter xii; idem: *Au Temps du Boulangisme* (Paris, 1930).

Alsace-Lorraine, overruled the objections of the Statthalter, Prince Hohenlohe, and introduced the new regulations in May 1888. It was provided that no foreigner should be allowed to enter the provinces without a visa granted by the German embassy at Paris. These arrangements were certainly very vexatious, not only for Frenchmen having relatives in the provinces, but for all foreigners. The reason given for their introduction was the maltreatment of Germans in France and the constant propaganda being carried on by emissaries of the League of Patriots. But it can hardly be doubted that Bismarck intended the new régime to be a warning to the French government. It was just after the first resounding victories of Boulanger, and the chancellor most probably feared a recrudescence of the former agitation against Germany.[1]

In speaking to the French ambassador about the relations between France and Germany Count Herbert Bismarck is said to have expressed the wish that the great wall of China stretched between the two countries and that there were no reason for intercourse and discord.[2] This solution of the Franco-German problem was hardly possible in the modern world, but the passport system came as near realizing it as was feasible. Under these conditions the chances of friction were reduced, to be sure at the expense of the inhabitants and their French relatives. But at any rate the likelihood of further Schnaebele incidents was diminished. There was relative calm on the Franco-German frontier from the spring of 1888 till the time of Bismarck's fall.

But the Boulangist movement, which might at any time have resulted in international complications, exercised a profound effect on French relations with Russia. The Tsar's dislike of parliamentary democracy and the instability that seemed to be inseparable from it was notorious. The uncertainty of French politics in 1888 was bound to reduce Russian interest in the connexion between the two countries.[3] Furthermore, Flourens, one of the ablest foreign ministers France had had for some time and one of the foremost advocates of the understanding with Russia, left office when the Tirard cabinet fell, in March 1888. Great efforts had been made by Baron Mohrenheim, the Russian ambassador, to secure his retention, but they were unsuccessful. The new prime minister, Floquet, had for many years been a *bête noire* to the Russians, because of his reputed "*Vive la Pologne!*" flung in the face of Tsar Alexander II during his visit to Paris in 1867. Foreseeing the inevitability of Floquet's leadership, the Russian government had instructed its ambassador to effect a reconciliation with him, but it stands to reason that his cabinet was not regarded with enthusiasm by the Tsar or his ministers.[4]

---

[1] See Hohenlohe: *Denkwürdigkeiten*, II, pp. 432 ff.; *Die Grosse Politik*, VI, Nos. 1283 ff. Good discussions may be found in Frédéric Eccard: *L'Alsace sous la domination allemande* (Paris, 1919), and in Wilhelm Seydler: *Fürst Chlodwig zu Hohenlohe-Schillingsfürst als Statthalter im Reichslande Elsass-Lothringen* (Frankfurt, 1929), pp. 99 ff.

[2] Crispi: *Memoirs*, II, pp. 301–2.

[3] Toutain, op. cit., pp. 354 ff.

[4] Hansen: *L'Ambassade à Paris du Baron de Mohrenheim*, pp. 86 ff.; Toutain, op. cit., p. 358.

As a matter of fact, the attitude of the French government towards the idea of an alliance with Russia had undergone considerable change. Not that there was a cooling of popular enthusiasm. On the contrary, the agitation for such an alliance assumed ever greater proportions as the Boulangist movement spread. But the government had got wind of various international agreements which made it realize how complete was France's isolation and the danger of an adventurous policy. Through an indiscretion at the Italian court the French government learned almost immediately of the conclusion of the German-Italian military convention.[1] Then the publication of the Austro-German Alliance on February 3 led to much discussion in the European press concerning the terms of the Triple Alliance. The *Neue Freie Presse* of Vienna on February 11 gave a pretty accurate summary of the terms of the Triple Alliance, and on the following day the *Kölnische Zeitung,* which frequently published articles inspired by the German foreign office, stated that in diplomatic circles the terms as given in the Vienna paper were regarded as substantially correct, if not perhaps quite complete.

At much the same time there was a good deal of debate about the reputed arrangement between England and Italy and Austria regarding the Mediterranean, an agreement which had been suspected for some months. The article of the *Neue Freie Presse,* mentioned above, stated that the treaties between the central powers were " supplemented by special arrangements between Italy, Austria, and Great Britain, having for their object the defence of the Austrian and Italian coasts against a hostile country." On the preceding day the English radical Labouchère had interpellated the government, asking "whether any engagement, contingent or otherwise, was entered into by Her Majesty's Government with Italy or with any other Foreign Power last year which has not been made known to the House." He received an evasive answer, but after the article of the *Neue Freie Presse* became known, he returned to the charge, on February 14, asking that any diplomatic correspondence bearing on the question be laid before parliament. Once again Sir James Fergusson, the under-secretary of state for foreign affairs, declined to give a direct answer.[2]

The London *Times* strongly deprecated the attempts of Labouchère to force information from the government in a matter of supreme importance, but the question was not allowed to come to rest. On February 15 the newspapers reported that Admiral Hewett, who was visiting the Mediterranean with the Channel fleet, had made an address at Genoa in which he said that " the bonds which unite us [to Italy] may hereafter receive a practical application by the union of the Italian and English fleets." A few days later the Paris correspondent of *The Times* revealed correspondence which he had had with the late Count Corti, who had been recalled from the Italian embassy at London just

---

[1] Salvemini: *La Politica Estera di Francesco Crispi,* pp. 59–60.
[2] Hansard: *Parliamentary Debates,* Third Series, Volume CCCXXII, pp. 153, 377.

before his death. It appeared from this correspondence that Crispi had recalled the ambassador because the latter had expressed scepticism of the possibility of coming to a positive understanding with England. In view of these revelations Labouchère announced his intention of again interpellating the government. Once again *The Times* denounced such tactics, but at the same time the great London newspaper, which was read in every foreign office and embassy in the European world, made a significant statement: "If there should be any danger of a blow struck at Italy which would destroy the Italian navy and give France an undisputed ascendency in the Mediterranean, it would be the duty of England, for the security of her own empire and commerce as well as for the maintenance of the European equilibrium and the preservation of a state to which we are bound by ties of sympathy and friendship, to exert all her power to avert the disaster." [1]

Labouchère questioned the government for the third time on February 16, and, failing to get a satisfactory reply, he moved an amendment to the address in reply to the speech from the throne, stating that it would conduce to the House's understanding of various questions if it could be assured that no correspondence had been exchanged between the English and the Italian governments containing "any assurance of a contractual character, which would constitute a binding pact upon Her Majesty's Ministers in the unfortunate event of a war breaking out during their tenure of office between the French Republic and the Kingdom of Italy," or that, if such assurances had been given, they should be brought to the knowledge of the House. [2]

The debate on the amendment took place on February 22. Labouchère, after adducing the evidence from the newspapers, attacked bitterly the policy of continental entanglements. Leagues of Peace, he said, ordinarily ended in war, and England should not, as in the past, resort to arms for "that mirage, the European equilibrium." Sir James Fergusson's statement that no assurances had been given to Italy was a mere play upon words and was not satisfactory. The truth was that Lord Salisbury's policy had always been the same — a policy of hatred of France and jealousy of Russia.

Sir James Fergusson spoke in reply, and we know from the letters of Queen Victoria that his statement was a "very carefully prepared speech," drawn up under the direction of Lord Salisbury himself. The burden of the argument was that some of Labouchère's statements were of a nature that was most mischievous in their tendency and reckless in their particulars. The government would always be ready to give the House all the information that the safety of the country and its interests would allow. After all, Labouchère's remarks were based merely upon newspaper statements and rumours, which could not be confirmed. The statement attributed to Admiral Hewett, for instance, was denied by a telegram from the admiral which the speaker read. Besides, the government had already stated on various occasions that "we

---

[1] London *Times*, February 15, 21, 22, 23, 1888.   [2] Hansard, op. cit., pp. 557–8.

were under no engagements pledging the employment of the Military and Naval forces of this country, except such as are already known to the House," said Sir James. For all practical purposes this gave a negative answer to La-bouchère's charges. Of course there had been correspondence with other powers during the crisis of the past year and a half, but clearly this correspondence could not be published to the whole of Europe. For that reason the " government do not feel themselves justified in answering, or even discussing further, the questions which the honourable member asks as to this correspondence, and we must oppose a simple negative to any motions which he or his honourable friends may make for the purpose of eliciting information upon this question at the present time." [1]

While this discussion was going on, the Paris *Temps,* generally looked upon as the organ of the French government, remarked, on February 15, that there might not be a treaty between England and the central powers, but there might very well have been an exchange of notes or something similar. This was certainly a reflection of the opinion of the French foreign office, for the Russian ambassador at Paris reported the disgust felt in official circles at the discovery that England was bound to Italy " for the event of war in the Mediterranean and the Straits," and even Waddington, the French ambassador at London, who had refused to believe in anything more than vague promises exchanged between England and Italy, came round to the view that memoranda had been signed dealing with the common interests of England and Italy in the Mediterranean and in Turkish waters.[2]

This news, which was fairly accurate, must have had a profound influence on the further course of French policy. It is clear that ideas such as Flourens had entertained of an agreement between England and France and Russia would have to be given up. Indeed, even the project of an alliance with Russia would have to be treated with considerable circumspection. On February 29 the Marquis de Breteuil, a warm advocate of the Franco-Russian alliance, who had just returned from St. Petersburg, where he had been received by the Tsar, made a significant statement in the French chamber. Reviewing the international situation, he said: " The alliance of France with Russia cannot at present be carried out, and at the present time it is not even desirable. It would, in fact, have the disadvantage of unduly hurrying on events. It is enough to be convinced that Russia has an interest in our existence." This declaration made a deep impression upon governing circles, the more so as the same attitude was taken by such influential papers as the *Temps* and the *Journal des Débats.* In the *Revue des deux mondes* the eminent French economist Anatole Leroy-Beaulieu, a relative of Flourens, published an anonymous article which came to the same conclusion as that of the Marquis de Breteuil. It is evident that the

---

1 Hansard, op. cit., pp. 1172–94; *Letters of Queen Victoria,* I, p. 386.
2 Meyendorff: *Correspondance de M. de Staal,* I, pp. 404, 408–9, 412–13.

French government had been frightened into a policy of severe caution and discretion.[1]

Just as the French government became aware of the implications of the new international alignments, the Russian government, which had been much more suspicious for a much longer time, decided to retreat in the Bulgarian affair. Relations with France were viewed with circumspection. " Whatever may be the affinities which have grown up between ourselves and France," Giers wrote to the Russian ambassador at Berlin, " they cannot be of a practical nature in view of the chronic anarchy with which the French Republic is struggling." The French government, he continued, was maintaining a reserved attitude, and Russia would certainly not egg it on. The same view-point was expressed in the Russian press, which stressed the uncertainty of the Boulangist movement and pointed out that " an alliance with France at this moment is a complete absurdity, not only for Russia, but for any other country." [2]

Under these circumstances it was not to be wondered at that the Tsar should have received with gratitude any suggestion for an agreement with England. A settlement of the Anglo-Russian antagonism would revolutionize the whole European scene. The view of Lord Randolph Churchill that Russia should be allowed to advance in the Near East and find her way to the Mediterranean on condition that she desist from further pressure upon the Indian frontier was one which the Tsar could appreciate, and the reception which Churchill had received in Russia had been a very cordial one. But the English government had made it so obvious that Churchill had no official mission and that his suggested policy could not be entertained for a moment that the projected understanding was still-born. Despite this set-back, however, the Tsar, in May 1888, received W. T. Stead, the editor of the Pall Mall Gazette, and a well-known advocate of good relations with Russia. Stead, on his arrival in the Russian capital, found a certain M. Millevoye there, evidently acting as an emissary of General Boulanger. What he attempted to accomplish and what he did accomplish is not known. As for Stead himself, he began his conversation with Alexander by begging pardon for all the harm England had done to Russia. The Tsar replied by saying that Russia wanted nothing: " We do not want to make Bulgaria a Russian province. Of course, M. Ferdinand of Coburg, he will have to go. But he will go very soon, I hope." Stead then tried to draw the Tsar out in regard to the Russian plans in the Straits. He pointed out the prevalent fear in England that the Black Sea would become a Russian lake and the base for a Russian attack, in conjunction with France, upon the English position in the Mediterranean. Alexander insisted that these were not at all the ideas of the Russian government, but he admitted that the suggestion sometimes advanced that Russia should hold the forts of the Bosporus while England controlled those

---

[1] Schwertfeger: Die belgischen Dokumente zur Vorgeschichte des Weltkrieges, I, pp. 227 ff.
[2] Meyendorff, op. cit., I, pp. 427 ff.; Grüning: Die russische öffentliche Meinung, pp. 148–9.

of the Dardanelles would be impossible. On the other hand, a solution based upon Russian control of both straits and an English occupation of some island such as Mytilene might be feasible. In any case, Stead's idea of a Russian-German-English combination met with his entire approval: "Germany, Russia, England, these together can keep the peace. . . . Austria I look upon as a lost empire."[1]

Stead had no influence beyond what he could exert through his newspaper, but his pilgrimage to Russia created some discussion, and the results of the mission were reported in detail to the English government by Sir Robert Morier, the ambassador at St. Petersburg. So far as known, Lord Salisbury was unimpressed. The Russian ambassador at London felt obliged to report home that Stead had exaggerated the importance of his reception by the Tsar. Clearly the English government was not disposed to consider any serious reconstruction of its international policy.[2] For Russia direct action had become impossible, and when the Tsar spoke about the early expulsion of Ferdinand from Bulgaria, he was expressing a pious wish and a fond hope rather than a policy. The same may be said of numerous articles appearing during the next eighteen months in the Russian press which dealt with the Tsarist aspirations in the Straits. Tatishchev, the editor of the *Russki Viestnik,* was the author of most of them. His object was to prove that these aspirations were not "an urge to conquest, but a fateful inheritance of immutable necessity." "When the last hour of the Ottoman Empire strikes, Russia will have no right to permit, and she never will permit, the Straits to fall into the hands of any other power."[3]

Tatishchev criticized the Russian government severely for its passivity in this matter. He could not appreciate the difficulties of the international situation and the total impossibility of Russia's embarking upon an active policy. With a potential coalition aligned against her, she could act only indirectly, if at all. During the years 1888 and 1889 great efforts seem to have been made to undermine the position of Ferdinand of Bulgaria by strengthening the Russian influence in Serbia and Roumania and building up a Balkan combination to isolate Bulgaria. During the spring of 1888 the situation in Roumania threatened to become serious, for the Russian minister Hitrovo was reported to be supporting Prince Bibesco or Prince Cuza as possible candidates for the throne. The conservative, pro-Russian party was constantly gaining strength, and the Hohenzollern dynasty was in a precarious position. It was probably on this account that Bismarck suggested to the Roumanian statesman Sturdza, when the latter came to Berlin in January 1888, that steps should be taken to bring about Italy's adherence to the alliance of the central powers with Roumania.

---

[1] Frederic Whyte: *The Life of W. T. Stead* (New York, 1925), Volume I, pp. 259 f.; W. T. Stead: *The M. P. for Russia. Reminiscences and Correspondence of Madame Olga Novikoff* (London, 1909), Volume II, pp. 242 ff.

[2] Meyendorff, op. cit., I, p. 437.

[3] Grüning, op. cit., pp. 151, 154–5.

Negotiations to this end were entered upon, and led to a favourable result on May 15, 1888.[1] Nevertheless, the situation in Roumania continued to be critical. Most of the Roumanian statesmen were left in ignorance of the treaty by King Carol, and it was probably due chiefly to these questionable tactics that the agreements could be maintained at all.[2]

In Serbia the situation was no less confused and the King, Milan, was constantly exposed to the attacks and intrigues of a pro-Russian opposition, exactly as in Roumania. The ill-fated campaign against Bulgaria in 1885 had undoubtedly shaken the position of the dynasty and had discredited the Austrophil policy of the King. The liberals, under Ristič, and the radicals, under Gruič and Pasič, were steadily gaining strength at the expense of the progressives, under the leadership of Garashanin. Both the liberals and the radicals were strongly Russian in their sympathies, and it is said, though it would be hard to prove the statement with specific facts, that plans were on foot to depose Milan and proclaim either his rival Peter Karageorgevič or Prince Nicholas of Montenegro king in his stead. Whatever may have been the truth in regard to these dark machinations, it is perfectly clear that Milan's position was becoming more and more untenable and that the opposition parties were not in favour of the foreign policy which had been pursued since the Congress of Berlin. During the year 1888 Milan ruled with a strong-arm ministry led by Christič, a progressive, but he could not hold out for ever against the radical majority in the assembly. In March 1889 he abdicated in favour of his thirteen-year-old son, Alexander, after endowing the country with a more liberal constitution. For years Milan had desired to abdicate, but it is not clear what the purpose of the constitutional revision at this time was. In any case, the regency appointed by Milan was headed by Ristič. It governed with a radical cabinet under General Gruič. In September 1889 Queen Nathalia, the divorced wife of Milan, whom he had attempted to keep out of Serbia, was received with enthusiasm in the capital. She was herself a champion of close connexions with Russia, and with her return to Belgrade the victory of the pro-Russian elements seemed to be complete. It goes without saying that these events were looked upon with great misgiving in Vienna, while at St. Petersburg they aroused considerable jubilation.[3]

In Greece the Russians were no less active. Nelidov, the Russian ambassador at Constantinople, came to Athens in April 1888 to discover, if he could, what connexion there might be between Greece and the Mediterranean Triplice. He opened up pleasant vistas to the Greek statesmen if they would stand by Russia. At the same time the Russian government, acting apparently upon rumours of Austrian efforts to draw Turkey into the Triple Alliance, enlisted the aid of

---

[1] *Die Grosse Politik*, VII, No. 1464, foot-note; Pribram, op. cit., I, pp. 84 ff.

[2] Waldersee: *Briefwechsel*, Nos. 171, 176; id., *Denkwürdigkeiten*, I, p. 380; Crispi: *Memoirs*, II, pp. 282, 380 ff.

[3] Waldersee: *Briefwechsel*, No. 156; Meyendorff, op. cit., II, pp. 21 ff.

France to bring pressure to bear at Constantinople, threatening to reopen the question of the Turkish-Greek frontiers. During the Cretan troubles of 1888–9, which caused considerable tension between the Turkish and Greek governments, the Russians regularly supported the Greek view, and only the cautious policy pursued by the Greek premier, Tricoupis, prevented serious complications.[1]

The efforts of the Russian government to undermine the position of Austria in the Balkans and in this way to prepare for the expulsion of Ferdinand from Bulgaria found their counterpart in western Europe in the policy of the French government towards Italy. Ever since Crispi, by his journey to Friedrichsruh, had advertised to the world the Italian connexion with (the French said subserviency to) German policy, the relations between France and Italy had gone from bad to worse. Crispi, at least, was convinced that from this time on, the French embassy at Rome was the centre of an active republican propaganda, and that the Italian republicans were financed from Paris.[2] Reports like these, of subtle intrigue, can rarely be substantiated, but there is abundant material to illustrate other aspects of French policy equally hostile. The most extraordinary of these aspects was the French activity at the Vatican.

It seems fairly clear that Leo X, when he exercised his influence on behalf of the German military law of 1887, still hoped that Bismarck might be induced to take up the matter of the restoration of the temporal power of the Papacy. The appointment of Cardinal Rampolla as papal secretary of state in the spring of 1887 and the failure of the move for a settlement of difficulties with Italy were evidences of the growing influence of the French ambassador at the Vatican, but the Pope still adhered to his previous policy. In February 1888 Cardinal Galimberti, the leading advocate of close relations with Germany, was sent to Berlin, on the occasion of the funeral of William I. He was instructed to take up with Bismarck the possibilities of a settlement of the Roman question, but the German chancellor once again returned evasive replies: " You are right, but you must wait." The restoration of Rome to the Pope would mean revolution in Italy, would result in the downfall of the dynasty and lead to an alliance with republican France. But if Italy should turn into a republic anyway, Bismarck would, he said, support the papal claims for a restoration of Rome.[3]

There could no longer be any reasonable doubt of Bismarck's attitude. Neither could the Pope deny that the closeness of the connexion between

---

[1] Driault and Lhéritier: *Histoire diplomatique de la Grèce*, IV, pp. 255, 272–80.

[2] Crispi: *Memoirs*, III, p. 184; *Ultimi Scritti* (Rome, 1913), pp. 88, 101, 106, 147; *Die Grosse Politik*, VII, No. 1395; X, No. 2369; Waldersee: *Briefwechsel*, p. 408.

[3] Crispolti and Aureli: *La Politica di Leone XIII* (Rome, 1922), chapter vii; Kurd von Schlözer: *Letzte römische Briefe* (Stuttgart, 1924), p. 123; E. L. Woodward: " The Diplomacy of the Vatican under Popes Pius IX and Leo XIII " (*Journal of the British Institute of International Affairs*, May 1924, pp. 113–39); Maximilian Claar: " *Kardinal Rampolla als Staatssekretär und Papstwerber* " (*Europäische Gespräche*, VII, pp. 465–82, September 1929).

Germany and Italy made German action on behalf of the Papacy extremely unlikely. At the time it was generally supposed that the German-Italian Alliance
involved a guarantee to Italy of the possession of Rome. In short, there was
nothing to be hoped for from Berlin. On the other hand, the French government had been making attractive offers. Flourens, for example, had told an
emissary of the Church that he desired the restoration of the temporal power
as a support for the religious authority of the Church, on condition that it
should not be to the detriment of France. "What we do in the interest of the
universal Church must not be turned to the exclusive profit of Italy, which is
allied to our enemies," he remarked in a discussion of the possibility of a reconciliation between the Church and the Italian government.[1] At the same time,
in the autumn of 1887, the French foreign office had done its utmost to pave
the way for the resumption of diplomatic relations between the Vatican and
the Russian government, evidently not only with the object of doing Russia
a good turn and furthering the policy of Leo XIII, but also with an eye to
securing the moral support of the Pope for the projected Franco-Russian
alliance.[2]

Through the exploitation of the Roman question the French cabinet could
cause the Italian government endless embarrassment. So could any other nation. In 1882 it had been Italian fear of German action on behalf of the
Pope that had driven the Italians into the alliance with the central powers.
It may well be that in 1887 Crispi was led to stress the alliance more strongly
because of the same danger. But when he averted the danger of German action,
he simply opened the door to French influence. Of course the French government had no intention of waging war to restore the temporal power of the
Pope, but it had an interest in holding the threat of eventual action over the
head of the Italians. To quote an obviously inspired French article: "The
restoration of pontifical royalty can no longer be the *cause,* but it can be
the *consequence* of a war. . . . No power would embark upon war to replace
Rome under ecclesiastical domination; but any state, once engaged in war with
Italy, would be forced to play the papal card against her. . . . Catholic, Protestant, schismatic, atheistic, any government provoked by Italy would seek to
strike her in a vulnerable spot, and that spot is Rome.[3]

Italy had indeed a very vulnerable spot, and Crispi knew it only too well.
He began to regard the Papacy with hatred and distrust and to make no secret
of his hostility. The Pope, on the other hand, felt that efforts were being made
to force him to abandon the Holy See. In June 1888 he instructed the nuncio at
Vienna, Cardinal Galimberti, to inquire whether, if obliged to leave Rome, he

---

[1] Crispolti and Aureli, op. cit., p. 375.

[2] Ibid., chapter ix; A. A. di Pesaro: "*La Diplomazia Vaticana e la Questione del Potere
Temporale*" (*Rassegna Nazionale,* May 1, 1890), pp. 89, 114–18; Toutain, op. cit., pp. 360 ff.

[3] Anonymous: "*La France, l'Italie et la Triple Alliance* (*Revue des deux mondes,* July 15, 1889,
pp. 277–318).

could find an asylum in Austria. The question was an awkward one, and Kálnoky, after consulting Francis Joseph, decided to send a special agent to Rome. Count Hübner, the well-known Austrian diplomat, now a man of almost eighty, was asked to go once again to the Vatican, in the heat of midsummer. He arrived at Rome in August, armed with a letter from Francis Joseph, in which His Holiness was urged not to leave Rome excepting in an extremity, in which case he would be received in Austria. The Austrian emissary, after discussions with the Pope and with Cardinal Rampolla, thought the fears of the churchmen exaggerated. Leo declared Crispi capable of anything and was very bitter against the German and Austrian Emperors for having renewed the alliance with Italy. Hübner explained that the alliance was of a transitory character and intended only to make use of Italy as part of " a gigantic barrier, from the Baltic to Sicily, to separate Russia from France, in the interests of European peace." It appears that Bismarck also had given the Pope assurances of this kind, and that Leo still had confidence in the German chancellor. Hübner got the impression that it was Rampolla and the French influences that were precipitating matters. Rampolla had a scheme by which the powers were to be called upon to guarantee the Pope's personal security and that of the Vatican palace, by means of an international convention. It was only with difficulty that the Austrian diplomat dissuaded the Pope from following up this idea.[1]

Although Hübner had succeeded in shelving the question of the Pope's departure from Rome for the time being, the matter was brought up several times during the winter of 1888-9. But the great crisis in the Roman question came in June 1889, when the erection of a statue in commemoration of Giordano Bruno, the sixteenth-century victim of papal intolerance, led to monster demonstrations in Rome. On June 30 an important consistory was held at the Vatican. At the moment the relations between France and Italy were very tense and the Pope seems to have expected that war would break out soon. If war actually came, he was determined to leave Rome. He could go to Monaco, Malta, or Spain. Apparently Spain had been definitely decided on and the Queen Regent had already been induced to send an invitation. If the Italian government offered resistance to the Pope's departure, it was hoped that the Catholic powers would intervene on behalf of the Holy Father. As a matter of fact, Crispi had no intention of offering such resistance. On the contrary, he seems to have warned the Pope that he might leave when he wished, but that his return later would be out of the question. This warning, taken together with the arguments of the Austrian ambassador, probably determined the Pope to do nothing, though it appears that considerable pressure was brought to bear upon him from the French side.[2]

---

[1] Francesco Salata: *Per la Storia Diplomatica della Questione Romana* (Milan, 1929), pp. 180-226.

[2] Crispi: *Memoirs*, II, pp. 393 ff., 407 ff.; *Ultimi Scritti*, chapter ii; *Politica Interna* (Milan,

The French pressure upon the Pope, and the threat of raising the dangerous Roman question, were a most serious menace as seen by the Italian government. From the French standpoint it must, however, be regarded as an error, for it drove Italy only further and further into the arms of Bismarck. Of greater immediate effect was the French economic policy, which ran parallel to the papal policy just discussed. It will be remembered that in December 1886 the Italian chamber, under the influence of the rising protectionist sentiment in the country, had denounced the tariff treaty with France, concluded in 1881. Negotiations had been opened for a new treaty, and during the period of discussion the old agreement had been several times extended for short periods of a few months. The negotiations were taken up seriously in December 1887, both sides realizing the need for some sort of *modus vivendi*. Suddenly, in February 1888, the pourparlers were abruptly broken off. Last-minute efforts to reach an agreement proved abortive, and on March 1, 1888 a famous tariff war between the two countries was begun. It cannot be denied that the growing demand for protection in all the western European countries had a good deal to do with the failure of these negotiations. Neither side dared to confront the chambers with suggestions for sacrifices. On the other hand it is quite clear from the sources that the break was due to political as much as to economic causes. The French broke off the discussions when they learned of the existence of the German-Italian military agreement and the Mediterranean pacts. When the French negotiator left Rome, he said to his Italian colleague: "As long as you remain in the Triple Alliance, no commercial agreement between Italy and France will be possible." [1]

For Italy the rupture of commercial relations was a very severe blow, for a large part, some thirty per cent, of the entire Italian trade was with France. As a result of the break Italian exports dropped forty per cent, the export of cheap wines ceasing almost completely. At the same time French bankers, who in 1884 had held about eighty per cent of the Italian consolidated debt, began to unload their securities upon the market and to withdraw their support for Italian public works, such as railroads and housing projects. It has been estimated that in one year French bankers withdrew no less than seven hundred million francs from Italy. The result was a severe economic crisis. Failures in business rose from about 1,300 in 1887 to almost 2,200 in 1888. The government was faced with a staggering deficit, numerous banks failed or were on the verge of failure, the agricultural population, especially in the south, suffered acute want, and emigration from the peninsula assumed unprecedented proportions.

1924), pp. 120–3; Salata, op. cit., pp. 227–32; G. Pietro Sinopoli di Giunta: *Kardinal Mariano Rampolla* (Hildesheim, 1929), pp. 154 ff.; G. Giolitti: *Memorie della mia Vita* (Milan, 1922), I, pp. 47–8; Monsignor de T'Serclaes: *Le Pape Léon XIII* (Paris, 1894), II, p. 154; Giuseppe Manfroni: *Sulla Soglia del Vaticano* (Bologna, 1920), II, pp. 175 ff.; Humphrey Johnson: *The Papacy and the Kingdom of Italy* (London, 1926), pp. 55–9.

[1] Crispi: *Memoirs,* II, p. 254; Albert Billot: *La France et l'Italie* (Paris, 1905), I, chapters iv and viii; Charles de Moüy: *Souvenirs,* pp. 248 ff.; Auguste Gérard: *Mémoires,* pp. 140 ff.; Crispi: " *L'Accordo franco-italiano* " (*Rivista d'Italia,* February 1899).

At the same time Crispi demanded ever larger expenditures for armaments, for he believed that an attack was imminent. Finally German and English banking interests had to come to the rescue in order to prevent the total collapse of the currency. Taken by and large, the effect of this tariff war upon the international situation can hardly be over-stressed, for the trials through which Italy passed led to increasing criticism of Crispi, to a growth of anti-monarchical sentiment, and to a general spread of the agitation against the Triple Alliance, which was made responsible for the strained relations with France and especially for the staggering outlays for armaments. Nowhere could one find a better illustration of the methods of modern warfare in times of peace. To all the intrigue and military preparations was added the deadly weapon of economic reprisal.[1]

This period of French pressure upon Italy was punctuated by a number of serious incidents of a political nature which threatened on various occasions during 1888 and 1889 to lead to actual war. Crispi has been bitterly criticized by some recent Italian historians, like Salvemini and Croce, for the hot-headed alarmism of his policy. Undoubtedly he exaggerated the dangers of the situation and was quite wrong in ascribing plans for an attack to the French government. There is no evidence whatever that the statesmen in Paris, fully cognizant of France's isolation and taken up, as they were, with the problem of Boulangism, had any intention of precipitating a crisis. On the other hand it must be confessed that the non-military pressure being brought to bear was very heavy and that Flourens's successor at the French foreign office, Goblet, was hardly less irascible and passionate than Crispi himself. It is scarcely necessary to enter into the details of all these incidents or to discuss them excepting in their effects upon the international alignment. The first came in the crucial months of January and February 1888 and arose from the violation of the French consulate at Florence by Italian officials, who demanded the papers of a Tunisian subject who had died in the city. While Flourens handled the matter from the French side with considerable skill, it was noticed, in the early days of February, that the French were concentrating their ironclads at Toulon, leaving only a few cruisers in the Channel ports. The Italian authorities had some knowledge of the French war plans and believed that hostilities would open with a French offensive against Italy, while on the German frontier the French would stay on the defensive. At the same time a naval attack would be made upon the important base at Spezia.[2] How accurate this information may have been it is not possible to say, but curiously enough there appeared at Paris in 1888 a

---

[1] Percy Ashley: *Modern Tariff History* (new, third edition, New York, 1926), pp. 326 ff.; H. Geffcken: "The Economic Condition of Italy" (*Contemporary Review*, October 1890, pp. 609–25); Testis: "*La Crise économique de l'Italie*" (*Nouvelle Revue*, February 15, 1891); A. Plebano: *Storia della Finanza Italiana 1888–1901* (Turin, 1902), III, pp. 131 ff.; Benedetto Croce: *A History of Italy 1871–1915* (New York, 1929), pp. 180 ff.; Feis: *Europe, the World's Banker*, pp. 233 ff.

[2] Waldersee: *Briefwechsel*, No. 96; Crispi: *Memoirs*, II, pp. 285–6, 293.

military study of an imaginary war between France on the one hand and
Germany and Italy on the other. The war was supposedly to break out during
the last days of March, and one of the first moves of the French was to be a
surprise naval attack upon Spezia.[1]

Whatever the facts may have been, the German government learned, evidently from Cardinal Galimberti, that the French were planning to seize
Spezia, which would lead to war with Italy. In the meanwhile Germany would
be taken up with Russia. The object of the French would be to secure for the
Pope a part of his temporal possessions. Austria, as a Catholic state, would
hardly feel inclined to fight with Italy against the interests of the Pope, and
even the Catholics of Germany would not be ready to stand enthusiastically by
Italy in such an event.[2] The German government, genuinely alarmed, it seems,
appealed to the British government and suggested that the British fleet go to
Toulon and threaten the French base with bombardment. According to the
first lord of the admiralty, this proposal was ignored, as the danger was not
viewed seriously at London.[3] Nevertheless a strong English squadron, under
Admiral Hewett, appeared at Genoa at the crucial moment, and important
Italian newspapers at the time reported that he asked, when he landed, for news
of the French declaration of war.[4] At any rate, it was at this time that he was
reputed to have made the statements which stirred up so much discussion in
t. e British parliament. At Berlin and Rome it was thought that the appearance
of the British fleet, whether intentional or accidental, had saved the situation.

Despite the statements of Lord George Hamilton it is clear that the scare of
February 1888 was genuine. The German government urged the Italians to
complete the defences of Spezia, which they did without loss of time. Italian
expenditures on naval affairs, which had been 44,000,000 lire in 1878, reached
the appalling figure of 158,000,000 in 1888, coming to almost ten per cent of the
entire budget. The Italians concentrated on the construction of monstrous ships,
seven of which carried twenty-eight cannon of over one hundred tons each
and were far larger than any French or English ironclads of the time.[5] The
English, too, appear to have been alarmed. They arranged for a demonstration
of the English, Italian, and Austrian squadrons, which visited Barcelona together in March 1888 to greet the Queen Regent of Spain.

At the same time the question of English sea-power was subjected to a
careful study. Despite the increased expenditure brought about by the naval
scare of 1884 the problem was still a very urgent one. All the accepted ideas of

---

[1] Charles Rope: *Rome et Berlin. Opérations sur les côtes de la Méditerranée et de la Baltique
au printemps de 1888* (Paris, 1888).

[2] Hohenlohe: *Denkwürdigkeiten*, II, pp. 434–5.

[3] Lord George Hamilton: *Parliamentary Reminiscences and Reflections 1886–1906* (London,
1922), p. 139.

[4] Salvemini: *La Politica Estera di Francesco Crispi*, pp. 59–60.

[5] Joannès Tramond and André Reussner: *Eléments d'histoire maritime et coloniale contemporaine, 1815–1914* (Paris, 1924), p. 647.

construction had been invalidated by the development of the ironclad and the breech-loading gun. Technical improvements came so rapidly that warships were out of date in ten or a dozen years. Until 1878 the position of the English was, however, a relatively safe one, for the French, always the chief rivals of England on the sea, were so taken up with the reconstruction of their army that there was little interest left for the navy. After 1878 all this changed. The French and the Russian governments, as well as the Italian, embarked upon extensive building projects which threatened to shake British supremacy. In France, especially, the so-called *Young School,* under the leadership of men like Admiral Aube, advocated the construction of numerous cruisers and destroyers rather than of huge warships, their theory being that the principal object of naval war must be to destroy the wealth of the enemy by cruiser warfare and the bombardment of fortified places. In France, as in England, public opinion, which theretofore had generally regarded naval affairs as a matter for experts, began to take a lively interest in sea-power and to bring pressure to bear upon the government in the interest of more extensive construction. In the early 1880's the French spent almost as much on their fleet as did the English, and when Admiral Aube became minister of marine, in January 1886, he brought through the French parliament a vote for the construction of sixteen new cruisers, twenty scouts, and forty-two torpedo-boats. Believing that the decision in war must be sought in European waters, he effected the concentration of the fleet at Brest and Toulon.[1]

The British navy had hardly kept abreast of these extensive increases and improvements in foreign fleets. In 1885 one of the leading squadrons of the navy possessed no breech-loading gun of more than six-inch calibre, while all the new Russian ships, for example, were equipped with this type. In the decade from 1878 to 1888 the English had launched sixteen new battleships as against twelve launched by the French and five launched by the Russians. When the annual manœuvres were first instituted, in 1885, the results were pathetic. It was found that there was no real system of preparation for war. The dockyards were inadequate, and it took them about five years to build a ship. Guns were difficult to obtain, and not infrequently a completed ship had to wait many months before the proper armaments were ready. There was no uniformity of type in construction, and handling a large number of ships was almost impossible. To quote Lord George Hamilton, the first lord of the admiralty in the Salisbury administration: " All idea of homogeneity had vanished, and effective or simultaneous manœuvring was impossible with such a variety of ships, differing so much as they did in tonnage, speed, armament and armour." [2]

---

[1] Tramond and Reussner, op. cit., pp. 650–65; S. Eardley-Wilmot: *The Development of Navies* (London, 1892), pp. 255 ff.

[2] Lord George Hamilton: *Parliamentary Reminiscences and Reflections 1868–1885,* pp. 292–3; *1886–1906,* pp. 80 ff.; Lord Thomas Brassey: Letter to *The Times,* May 25, 1888 (reprinted in his

Ever since the autumn of 1886 Bismarck had appreciated the growing weak-ness of British sea-power and had taken this fact into consideration.[1] In the spring of 1888 he urged the English government to strengthen the Mediter-ranean squadron. The German naval authorities were genuinely alarmed at the prospect of a French attack upon the Italian coasts, and Bismarck would have liked the English to warn the French government that such an attack would bring England upon the scene.[2] Nothing seems to have come of this last suggestion, but investigations were made as to the strength of the Medi-terranean squadron. The Duke of Edinburgh, who was in command, reported that he had told the admiralty that the squadron " was insufficient in case of a sudden attack or outbreak of war," the more so as France had concentrated almost the whole of her ironclad fleet in the Mediterranean. The government therefore decided that some of the ships of the Far Eastern squadron should be sent as temporary reinforcement. Because of the great difficulty of getting the necessary guns, it was not possible to send permanent reinforcements until after the manœuvres in July. About a dozen ships were practically paralysed for want of cannon, and it took about two years to manufacture this equipment.[3]

Not content with emergency measures, the government now seriously un-dertook a complete survey of the status of the navy and its needs. A committee examined in detail the danger of a Franco-Russian combination on the sea and looked into the requirements of the British navy to meet such a force. It found the fleet inadequate in numbers and insufficiently manned, while it was equally critical of the value of individual ships. It recommended that the British forces should be kept at least as strong as the fleets of the next two naval powers com-bined; that is, it accepted the so-called two-power standard as a guide to further construction. On the basis of this report the government worked out the provi-sions of the famous Naval Defence Act, which was laid before parliament in March 1889 and was passed without serious opposition. The measure involved a credit of 21,500,000 pounds to be expended over a period of five years. The admiralty was to lay down eight first-class battleships larger than any previ-ously built, two second-class battleships, nine large cruisers, twenty-nine smaller cruisers, four gunboats, and eighteen torpedo-boats. It was a pretentious pro-gram, but it was received with enthusiasm by the country. The most serious criticism directed against it was that it was not pretentious enough. And yet with this famous act it may be said that the modern race for naval armaments began. While Europe was lining the frontiers with enormous masses of men, and pouring funds into military expenditures, England now set the pace for

---

Papers and Addresses, London, 1894, Volume I, pp. 175 ff.); Sir William Laird Clowes: The Royal Navy, Volume VII (London, 1903), pp. 47, 82.

    [1] See the unpublished reports in Trützschler: Bismarck und die Kriegsgefahr des Jahres 1887, pp. 80-1.

    [2] Die Grosse Politik, VI, No. 1281.

    [3] Letters of Queen Victoria, Third Series, I, pp. 399, 409-10, 413, 415.

extravagant naval construction. Under pressure of modern technical developments the problem of security on land and on sea was becoming ever more
difficult to solve.[1]

During these years the immediate danger of war continued to arise from
the relations of France and Italy, which were characterized throughout by
distrust, suspicion, and exasperation. In June 1888 a serious conflict arose regarding the validity of the capitulations in Massawa. It appears that the French
government purposely raised this question in order to extort from the Italians
their consent to certain educational measures projected for Tunis.[2] In any
case, the French government attempted to ignore Italian rights in pro-
mulgating new school regulations, and the dispute dragged on through the
rest of the year. Crispi, as usual, appealed to his allies and friends for support,
and the position of the Italian government was defended by Germany, Austria,
and England. But Bismarck always urged his Italian colleague not to precipitate
trouble and impressed upon him the need of cultivating the friendship of
England. This was the substance of his remarks when the Italian statesman
came to Friedrichsruh for the second time, in August 1888. Even Goblet, who
was French foreign minister at the time, has admitted that Bismarck attempted
to cool the ardour of Crispi.[3]

There was no need for urging upon Crispi the importance of the connexion with England. Fear for the safety of their coasts kept the question
of sea-power constantly before the Italian statesmen. In the spring of 1889
Crispi approached the Austrian government with the suggestion that the
two powers conclude a naval convention regulating the action of their fleets
in the event of a French attack upon Italy. Kálnoky refused to enter upon this
path, pointing out that " events in the eastern basin of the Mediterranean would
have a much more profound and direct significance for Austria-Hungary than
those which might take place off the western coasts of the Mediterranean. This
difference between the scenes of action, as well as between the interests in
question, would offer an almost insuperable obstacle to any attempt to realize
in concrete form the idea of co-operation between the two fleets." [4] The force
of the argument was inescapable, but the matter was of great importance to
Crispi and he tried repeatedly during the summer of 1889 to conclude a naval
and military agreement with Austria. At the same time he attempted to enlist
the aid of Bismarck in order to bring Austria to terms. The German chancellor

---

[1] On the Naval Defence Act see Lord George Hamilton, *Parliamentary Reminiscences, 1886–
1906*, pp. 105 ff.; Frederic Manning: *The Life of Sir William White* (New York, 1923), pp. 234,
243–4; Lord Charles Beresford: *Memoirs* (London, 1914), Volume II, pp. 360 ff.; Lord Brassey:
The Naval Annual, 1890, chapter x.

[2] René Goblet: " *Souvenirs de ma vie politique* " (*Revue politique et parlementaire*, January
1929).

[3] Goblet, loc. cit., January and February 1929. See also *Die Grosse Politik*, VI, No. 1287;
Crispi: *Memoirs*, II, pp. 307 ff., 327 ff., 349 ff.

[4] Pribram, op. cit., II, p. 85, foot-note.

was evasive and, like Kálnoky, continued to stress the fact that even if Italy secured the support of the Austrian fleet, the combined forces would be barely a match for the French squadrons. On the other hand, if the aid of the British fleet were obtained, the French naval forces would be completely immobilized. Suggestions that Germany should come into a naval convention with her allies Bismarck rejected, because, as he said quite rightly, the German fleet could never get by the French squadrons in the Channel, and, besides, what ships the Germans had would have to be employed to protect the coasts against French and Russian raids. He was willing to exchange naval attachés and to keep in touch with the Italian admiralty; indeed, he was willing to have an Italian naval mission come to Berlin by way of a demonstration; but, for the rest, he insisted that the essential thing was to make sure of English assistance.[1]

In the meanwhile the great crisis of July 1889 had come up and the departure of the Pope from Rome was momentarily expected. To Crispi an attack by France seemed imminent. He therefore sent a special emissary, a certain Signor Cucchi, to Bismarck and summoned the Italian representatives at London and Vienna to Rome. Cucchi found the officials of the German foreign office incredulous. They had no indications of French preparations and did not believe that France wanted war. Bismarck shared this view and declared that a surprise attack such as Crispi feared would be an act of brigandage which would cost France dearly. Furthermore, he expressed great faith in English support if the French provoked the war. In that case the English, Italian, and German fleets could completely paralyse the French naval forces, and this in turn would facilitate the operations by land.[2]

The Italian premier had had little success in his efforts to enlist the aid of his allies for possible naval operations. It was therefore necessary for him to do the very utmost to secure some definite assurance from the British government. Signor Catalani, the chargé d'affaires at London, who had been called to Rome, was of the opinion that England would not wait for Italy to be attacked, but would send a powerful fleet into the Mediterranean. He was sent back to London to give assurance to Lord Salisbury that Italy would not be the first to attack. In his reports, so far as we know them, he stated that Salisbury, like Bismarck, did not share the apprehensions of Crispi, but that strong reinforcements would be sent to the British Mediterranean fleet.[3] A few days later, on August 5, when the German ambassador once again pointed out the desirability of securing promises from England, Crispi said triumphantly that he had already done so and that he had a clear understanding with England. The statement was a veiled one, and the German ambassador took it to mean, not that a treaty had been signed, but that the British government had given a definite promise. He had learned some weeks before that Admiral Hoskins,

[1] *Die Grosse Politik*, VI, Nos. 1318–26.   [2] Crispi, op. cit., II, pp. 407 ff.
[3] Ibid., II, pp. 393 ff.

commanding the Mediterranean fleet, had received orders to attack the French fleet immediately if it made any move to attack Genoa or any other coastal city, provided the French squadrons were weaker than the English. If they were stronger, he was to withdraw to Gibraltar and wait for reinforcements.[1]

The question whether an English assurance was given to the Italian government cannot be answered with certainty. It may well be that Crispi exaggerated, or that the assurance, if it was given, applied only to a specific case, not to the English policy in general. There is, for example, some evidence of a promise to protect the Italian coast against French attack and of secret orders given to the fleet in the summer of 1888.[2] In any case, King Humbert seems to have been convinced by his minister, for in January 1890 he is reported to have said to Prince Napoleon: " I have nothing to fear for the security of the Italian coasts, for I have had a formal promise from the cabinet of St. James's that the British fleet will ally itself with mine, should the necessity arise, in order to protect Italy against all maritime operations." The promise, he continued, had been laid down in an exchange of dispatches, " which contain certain definite engagements."[3] On the other hand, Crispi's successor, Marchese di Rudini, when he took over the Italian foreign office, in 1891, could find no trace of these documents, and Crispi would not show him the "private letter from Lord Salisbury" which was supposed to contain the assurance. Furthermore, Sir James Fergusson stated categorically in the House of Commons on several occasions in 1891 that England had no engagements involving the use of military or naval forces beyond those of which the House knew, and that the government had "entered into no agreement or understanding with any power pledging us to the employment of Her Majesty's forces in any contingency." It must be concluded therefore, that Crispi's assertions, if they were not a pure figment of the imagination, could have referred only to the moral obligation which arose from the Mediterranean Agreement of 1887.[4]

Bismarck's effort to enlist English support for Italy was simply a continuation of the policy which had taken form in the Mediterranean agreements. In fact, the acute tension in Franco-Italian relations was a direct effect of the discovery, by the French, of the existence of a coalition potentially hostile. The great problem of German policy in the last years of the Bismarckian period was to maintain the balance between England and her friends on the one hand and Russia and France on the other.

The German chancellor managed this difficult and delicate situation with consummate skill, but his task was made unspeakably complex by the changes which took place in Germany through the death of the old Emperor William

---

[1] *Die Grosse Politik*, VI, No. 1327.

[2] Crispi, op. cit., II, p. 349.

[3] London *Times*, June 4, 1891.

[4] The question is discussed in detail in William L. Langer: *The Franco-Russian Alliance, 1890–1894* (Cambridge, Mass., 1929), pp. 161–2, 166–7, 171.

in March 1888 and the death of his successor, Frederick III, in June of the same year. Frederick III, who was known to be deeply influenced by his English wife, was generally reckoned a member of the group of military men who favoured German support of the Austrian policy against Russia, but he was mortally ill when he came to the throne and was determined not to embark upon a new course. When Bismarck explained, in the first crown council, that Austria must not take action until the English cannon boomed on the Bosporus as they had in the Crimean War, he nodded assent, the more so as Bismarck admitted that if Austria became involved in war with Russia despite German efforts to prevent such a conflict, Germany might at first " play dead," but in the end would be obliged to intervene to prevent the annihilation of her ally and her disappearance as a great power.[1]

Yet, with all the good intentions of the sick Emperor, his brief reign of three months was stormy enough and threatened to upset the balance of German foreign policy. Trouble arose when the Empress Frederick insisted on resuming her plans for the marriage of her daughter Victoria to Prince Alexander of Battenberg, the former ruler of Bulgaria. One of her first successes was to secure from her husband an invitation to the Prince to come to Berlin. Alexander himself was opposed to the reopening of the question and had, it seems, already fallen in love with the actress whom he later married. But the Empress would not be denied and Alexander was obliged to follow her lead.

When Bismarck learned of what had been done, he immediately protested, and threatened to resign if the affair were pursued. This whole matter, he pointed out, would hopelessly compromise Germany's relations with Russia. The Tsar would hardly go to war on account of Battenberg, but he would be justified in regarding the marriage as a preliminary step to the Prince's return to Bulgaria with German support and would never trust Germany again. In view of the serious implications of the question, the chancellor threatened to resign if his advice were ignored. On April 9 he had a long talk with the Empress, in which he evidently induced her to postpone the project. At any rate the Empress was very well satisfied with the result of the conversation and persuaded her husband to express a wish in his will that the marriage should take place.[2]

The family aspect of this affair need not detain us. The important thing was its effect on the international situation. Bismarck was, from the start, convinced that the whole thing was an English intrigue, engineered by Queen Victoria and her daughter the Empress, with the express purpose of bringing about a permanent estrangement between Germany and Russia and then enlisting German services in the pursuit of purely English interests. The very thought

---

[1] Lucius von Ballhausen, op. cit., pp. 442–3; *Die Grosse Politik*, X, p. 216, foot-note.

[2] See especially Corti: *Alexander von Battenberg*, pp. 313 ff. Other important sources are *Die Grosse Politik*, VI, Nos. 1328 ff.; Ponsonby: *Letters of Empress Frederick* (London, 1928), pp. 295 ff.; *Letters of Queen Victoria*, I, pp. 397, 404–5, 409.

of being victimized in this fashion sent him into one of his " raging moods," as the English ambassador reported. He even went so far as to accuse Queen Victoria in the newspapers, through the use of inspired articles, and wrote to Lord Salisbury warning him that the marriage would force Germany into taking a much more Russian line of policy than otherwise she would be inclined to do. As a matter of fact, Queen Victoria, though she had been ardently in favour of the marriage at an earlier date, had come to see the inadvisability of it and had urged her daughter to let the matter rest. Both the Queen and her prime minister were therefore fully justified in regarding Bismarck's attitude and action as " very impertinent."

It had been suggested from Berlin that it would be unwise for Queen Victoria, who was spending some time at Florence, to visit her sick son-in-law on her way back to England. But the Queen was not to be deterred and insisted on following her own inclinations. She arrived in the German capital on April 25 and received Bismarck in a rather long audience. With respect to the marriage project there was no difference of opinion between them. The chancellor then went over the whole international situation, explaining his desire to prevent war and discussing the undependability of Russia. If Austria should be attacked, he said, Germany was bound by treaty to come to her assistance. The danger would then arise of France's joining Russia. In that case England could be of great use with her fleet. The Queen pointed out that France did not wish for war. To this Bismarck agreed, but he in turn pointed out that the French government was so powerless that it might be forced into anything. The Queen recognized the force of the argument and expressed her full sympathy with the policy pursued by Germany. Lord Salisbury, she said, shared her view, and she would do what she could to throw the weight of English influence on the side of the conservative and pacific powers. These words delighted the chancellor, who made no effort to conceal his satisfaction. Referring to the Queen's visit to Italy and her brief conversation with Francis Joseph at Innsbrück, he said that she was " like an officer going the round of the outposts and seeing that the pickets were all doing their duty, and that it would have an excellent effect in strengthening and encouraging the league of the central powers." [1]

The Queen had shown herself to be above any petty resentment on account of Bismarck's hasty accusations. The Battenberg marriage project blew over without detrimental effects upon Anglo-German relations. The same was true of Germany's relations with Russia. In the critical days of early April Bismarck had appealed to Giers to come to his support and express the aversion of the Russian government to the proposed visit of the Prince to Berlin. To the

---

[1] Sir Frederick Ponsonby: *Letters of the Empress Frederick*, pp. 302 ff.; Sir James Rennell Rodd: *Social and Diplomatic Memoirs, 1884–1893* (London, 1922), pp. 138 ff. The Queen's account of the interview in the *Letters of Queen Victoria*, I, pp. 404–5; Bismarck's account in *Die Grosse Politik*, IV, No. 819.

German ambassador, General von Schweinitz, it seemed that the Russian foreign minister was not wholly sorry to see Bismarck embarrassed. At any rate Giers did not appear to take the matter too tragically, and this attitude caused Bismarck not a little irritation. From Russian documents, however, it is clear that both Schweinitz and Bismarck were unnecessarily nervous about the Russian stand. The Tsar had become reconciled, at least for the present, to the impossibility of doing anything further in the Bulgarian question and could not refuse to recognize the fact that Bismarck had stood by Russia in this matter while the other powers had been uncompromising. Both Alexander and Giers wished for the continuance of good relations with Germany and were anxious that Bismarck should remain in office. Furthermore, they were firmly opposed to the Battenberg marriage project, whatever Giers may have said to Schweinitz concerning the proposed visit of Battenberg to Berlin.[1]

Despite the Empress's plans and her attempts to force them through while her husband was still alive, Bismarck's greatest problem during the brief reign of Frederick III was not to manage the Emperor, but to lead the Crown Prince William in the proper path. The young man had never got on well with his parents and had been systematically shut out from all contact with foreign affairs, so far as possible. His education had been largely military and his connexions were chiefly with army circles. Yet he was ambitious and active, and if he did not have clearly formulated views on international affairs, he had some firmly rooted prejudices. After his visit to Russia in 1884 he had been passionately Russophil and very deeply opposed to English policy. It will be remembered that Lord Salisbury, in his correspondence with Bismarck in November 1887, had expressed the anxiety of the British government about the future course of German policy when William should have ascended the throne. The same uneasiness came out in connexion with Queen Victoria's visit to Berlin in the spring of 1888. Acting on a hint from the German ambassador, Lord Salisbury wrote to the Queen asking her to be very careful in what she said to the Prince: " The two nations are so necessary to each other, that everything that is said to him must be very carefully weighed." [2] Victoria spoke to Bismarck about the Prince and mentioned his inexperience in foreign affairs, to which the chancellor replied that while William knew nothing of civil matters, " should he be thrown into the water he would be able to swim," as he was certainly clever.[3]

What the English did not realize was that Prince William had already recovered from his Russophilism. He had come back from a second visit to the Tsar, in September 1886, deeply impressed with the hostility of the Russians and very dubious about Bismarck's policy. To be sure, he had an unbounded

---

[1] Meyendorff: *Correspondance de M. de Staal,* I, pp. 409, 413 ff., letters of Giers. On the German side see *Die Grosse Politik,* VI, Nos. 1328 ff.; Schweinitz: *Denkwürdigkeiten,* II, pp. 363–4.

[2] *Letters of Queen Victoria,* I, p. 398.

[3] Ibid., pp. 404–5.

admiration for the great chancellor, but by the autumn of 1887 he had come under the influence of Count Waldersee, who, like most of the military men, was in favour of German support for Austria and the waging of a preventive war against Russia if need be.[1] In commenting upon a report from Vienna in April 1888, the Prince made it quite clear that he regarded Bismarck's diplomatic combinations with the greatest scepticism and that he did not believe that Russia could be successfully checkmated in that fashion. These remarks were so ominous that they caused Bismarck considerable anxiety. He replied to the Prince's comments at great length, pointing out that it was futile to talk of destroying the military power of a state like Russia. Germany had not succeeded in permanently disabling France in 1871, despite the completeness of her victory. The destruction of Russia's power would be even more difficult, owing to geographical considerations. Even after a successful war Germany would gain nothing, for Russia would be filled with hatred and desire for· revenge, and Germany would be in a hopeless position between two defeated states of great potential military strength. Italy and England could hardly be counted upon for support under such circumstances, and if Germany were to become dependent upon Austria, the Habsburg influence in German affairs would be what it was before 1866. But if the Prince meant to change German policy so radically, a different attitude towards Russia would have to be adopted immediately, and Russia would have to be provoked into making an attack, either upon Germany or upon Austria. As a matter of fact, if war was to be waged, it would be better to seek it in the West than in the East. It would be easier to pick a quarrel, a war with France would be regarded in Germany as a necessary sacrifice in the interest of permanent peace, and the conflict could probably be brought to a decision earlier. Besides, it might be assumed that war could be waged against France without Germany's being necessarily forced into war with Russia at the same time. On the other hand, it was certain that France would act at once if Germany became involved in the East.[2]

Prince William talked the matter over with his friend Count Waldersee before he replied. The burden of his argument was that he had not intended to express disagreement with the chancellor's policy. On the contrary, he thoroughly approved of it and had always defended it. The point of his comments had simply been that, militarily speaking, the wise thing perhaps would be to wage war if it was inevitable and if the situation was particularly favourable. He still maintained that it was the duty of the army authorities, not only to examine the situation from this view-point, but to keep the foreign office posted on its ideas. The letter was an able one and betrays the helping hand of Waldersee.[3]

[1] Wilhelm II: *Ereignisse und Gestalten* (Leipzig, 1922), pp. 12–15; Radowitz: *Aufzeichnungen*, II, p. 274; Fürst Philipp zu Eulenburg-Hertefeld: *Aus fünfzig Jahren* (Berlin, 1923), pp. 139, 150.
[2] *Die Grosse Politik*, VI, Nos. 1339 ff.
[3] Bismarck: *Gedanken und Erinnerungen*, III, pp. 136 ff. The draft of the Prince's reply in Waldersee: *Denkwürdigkeiten*, I, pp. 395 ff.

Bismarck's letter to William was dated May 9 and the reply May 10. Soon afterwards the rigorous passport regulations were introduced in Alsace-Lorraine, despite the objections of the Statthalter. Furthermore, the chancellor told his fellow ministers on May 13 that a war with France was not to be so ardently avoided as before, and he mentioned the warlike proclivities of the Crown Prince. On May 16 Waldersee noted that William had told him confidentially that the chancellor had now decided not to shy at war any longer. He would try to anger the French to induce them to attack. He thought he could be sure of the Russians for some time. On the following day the war minister told Waldersee officially that Bismarck was inclined to bring about a war with France, and that he believed he was certain of Russian neutrality, at least for the beginning of the conflict. Waldersee was told to observe secrecy, but otherwise to make his preparations.[1]

It might be deduced from these cryptic references that Bismarck, who for years had devoted himself to the preservation of the peace, had now suddenly changed his mind and decided to seek a decision by the sword. There are, however, various objections to this interpretation. In the first place, these are the only indications we have of such a decision. In the second place, Bismarck told the ministers explicitly that Germany " would neither provoke nor attack, but if one allowed matters like the Schnaebele case to take their course, war would be the result." Then, too, he told Prince William that " of course the death of Emperor Frederick would have to be awaited." Waldersee was himself rather doubtful of the finality of the decision and suspected that the chancellor might be trying to make himself agreeable to the Prince in order to exert greater control over him. This explanation has been accepted by a number of German historians. No others have interested themselves in this rather intriguing point.

But there may be yet another explanation. On May 28 Waldersee himself discussed the situation with Count Herbert Bismarck, at that time secretary of state for foreign affairs. He explained that the French showed very little desire for war, partly because they were afraid of the Germans, partly because they did not yet feel prepared. Count Herbert replied that, according to recent reports, the Russians, too, were very pacific. The war minister had been unable to put through large demands for money, and the Tsar desired a quiet summer. Waldersee came away with the impression that German policy would once again switch from the line just decided upon. It seems not at all unlikely that Bismarck had seized upon the comments of the Prince in order to force the issue — that is, to lay before William all the arguments in favour of the policy pursued thus far, but also to adopt, seemingly, the arguments of the military men like Waldersee. The Prince's reply and Waldersee's own efforts to emphasize the peaceful intentions of the French government appear to indicate that he was not himself ready to accept the consequences. In any case it would

---

[1] Lucius von Ballhausen, op. cit., p. 452; Waldersee: *Denkwürdigkeiten*, I, pp. 399, 401.

be foolhardy to convict Bismarck of the charge of having wished to provoke a war in his old age after he had spent years in overcoming innumerable obstacles to peace. Certainly the evidence available is not sufficient to warrant such a conclusion.

In connexion with the discussions which took place between the chancellor and Prince William the latter was evidently informed of the terms of the Rein-surance Treaty, if he was not shown the actual text. The former Emperor has recently denied that he knew of the agreement before Bismarck's dismissal, in March 1890, but contemporary documents leave little room for doubt that he was initiated at this time, though it does appear that the Emperor Frederick died without ever having been informed.[1] Bismarck's object clearly was to prove to the Prince that the maintenance of good relations with Russia was desirable and feasible. William was not convinced, as his letter to Bismarck shows. To quote his own words, published long afterwards, the value of the treaty had been greatly exaggerated; it " had no significance save as a device of the great chancellor to assist him in his complicated game of juggling with the five balls." [2] It was probably for that reason that Bismarck tried to persuade the future Emperor that Russia, if left alone and not deterred by Austria, would go into the Balkan " trap " and in this way be forced to divert attention from the German-Austrian frontier. It was always his contention that Russia would be weakened by the possession of Constantinople, for she would then be more exposed to the hostility of England and much more easily attacked. No doubt he would have been glad to have the Russians embark upon the adventure, for Germany would in that case have been relieved of pressure without effort on her part. Surely it would have been insane for Germany to take action against Russia so long as there was a prospect that the Russians would turn to the south and that England and her friends would assume the burden of stopping their advance. That William finally recognized the cogency of the argument is shown by the fact that he told Waldersee, as the latter left for Vienna to announce William's accession, in June 1888, that Germany's hope was that Russia could be induced to take energetic action, and that Austria should allow Russia to do so in Bulgaria. Waldersee was firmly convinced that Bismarck wished to see Russia embroiled in war with Turkey.[3]

When William II ascended the throne, in June 1888, he was regarded with some suspicion in France and Russia, for warlike plans and the desire to

---

[1] The Emperor's assertion in Karl F. Nowak: *Kaiser and Chancellor* (New York, 1930), pp. 80–1, 201; but see the report of Schweinitz, May 23, 1888, which Nowak himself prints on pp. 211–12, and, above all, Nowak's heated controversy with Siegfried von Kardorff, reprinted by the latter under the title *Im Kampfe um Bismarck* (Berlin, 1930). The essential contemporary document is in *Die Grosse Politik*, VI, No. 1341.

[2] William II: *My Early Life* (New York, 1926), p. 279.

[3] Waldersee: *Briefwechsel*, Nos. 108, 149; id., *Denkwürdigkeiten*, I, p. 407; Crispi, op. cit., II, p. 327 ff.

emulate Frederick the Great were attributed to him. As a matter of fact, the situation was far too uncertain to admit of any far-reaching projects. The new Emperor, perhaps by way of reaction to the Anglophilism of his parents, had little sympathy for English policy or for his English relatives. In the spring of 1888 this latent antipathy had been fanned by ill-advised remarks made by the Prince of Wales during several visits to Berlin. He seems to have suggested that the Emperor Frederick intended to return to France some part of Alsace or Lorraine, and to Denmark northern Schleswig. He certainly made some effort to bring about the restoration of the property of his brother-in-law the Duke of Cumberland. These efforts, however well-intentioned, were indiscreet. Quite naturally they aroused the anger of Bismarck, who strongly resented all attempts to interfere with German affairs. Queen Victoria's letter to her grandson suggesting that he postpone all visits for some months out of respect for his father's memory only heightened the friction. The Queen received General Winterfeld, who came to announce William's accession, with studied coolness, and the Emperor replied by letting it be known that he did not desire to meet the Prince of Wales during the visit which he expected to make to Vienna in October. The estrangement between the two families was complete and a visit of the Emperor to England was, for the time being, at least, quite out of the question.[1]

Lord Salisbury, and, for that matter, the Queen, were very anxious that the political relations between England and Germany should not suffer from the cool relations between the ruling families. Victoria thought it desirable that the prime minister should, if possible, arrange for meetings with Bismarck, Kálnoky, and Crispi, but Salisbury did not believe that the danger of isolation was, for the moment, acute: " The alliance with Austria covers the only weak point in the English position," he wrote the Queen. " No foreign power (setting aside France for the moment) is in a position to threaten England's interests, except Russia by striking at Constantinople. If Austria — that is to say Hungary — could be induced to view with equanimity the seizure of the Bosphorus by Russia, the English position would be very difficult; as England would have to defend the Bosphorus by herself; for Russia can always purchase the complicity of Italy and Germany by consenting to allow them to do what they like with France. But, so long as Austria stands firm upon this point, Germany, and consequently Italy, must go with her. To England, therefore, for the moment, the most important question is — What is the disposition of Austria? As far as we can form a judgment, her disposition was never more favourable. If this view be correct, there is nothing to disquiet England in the meetings of emperors or ministers. . . . France is, and must always remain, England's greatest danger. But that danger is dormant, so long as the present strained relation exists between France and her two Eastern neighbours. If ever France should

---

[1] Lee: *Edward VII*, Volume I, pp. 262, 365, 484, 643–53; *Letters of Queen Victoria*, I, pp. 421–33, 438–41; Ponsonby: *Letters of the Empress Frederick*, pp. 335–7.

be on friendly terms with them, the Army and Navy estimates would rise very rapidly." [1]

This long passage has been quoted in full because it is almost the only authoritative statement of the motives behind English policy in this period. The Queen was uneasy because she and her son had fallen out with the new Emperor and because German policy seemed to be swerving off in a Russian direction. It may be that the Tsar was filled with an insurmountable suspicion of Bismarck, as the Grand Duke Vladimir admitted during a visit to Berlin in April. But the Tsar and his minister saw that their hands were shackled so far as Bulgaria was concerned, and they realized that everything depended on keeping up friendly relations with Berlin. Otherwise the German Alliance with Austria, "the black point" in German-Russian relations, might be interpreted as the Austrians wished — that is, as giving them a free hand for expansion in the East, not only in Bosnia and Herzegovina and Serbia, but in Bulgaria. The opening of the railroad from Vienna to Constantinople at this very time was an ominous event as seen from St. Petersburg. With England and Italy standing behind Austria, Germany was the only obstacle in the way of the realization of the Austrian aspirations. [2]

For these reasons the Tsar was eager to cultivate the goodwill of the young Emperor, just as Bismarck was eager to cure William of his antipathy for the Russian connexion. It must be admitted that the chancellor showed consummate skill in dealing with his new master. He raised no objection to the exchange of warm letters between William and Francis Joseph, and when he had persuaded the Emperor to pay his first state visit to St. Petersburg, he drew up long instructions in which particular emphasis was laid upon the need for upholding the alliance with Austria. It might not be so strong a connexion militarily speaking, he said, but it was a more reliable connexion than one with Russia. Germany could not promise Russia concessions in the East that would be to the detriment of Austria. But Germany could allow Russia a free hand in directions which were not of vital interest to Austria — that is, in Asia, in the region of the Black Sea, the Straits, and even Constantinople. If Austria wished to oppose the Russian advance in those regions, she must find other allies. Russia would only weaken herself by going to Constantinople and would call forth the hostility of England and perhaps of France. The Emperor's visit to Russia should be non-political, in the sense that Germany offered nothing beyond what she had always offered, and that, in return, Germany asked for nothing. Count Herbert Bismarck was to accompany the Emperor on his journey, evidently in order to assure the observance of the chancellor's instructions. [3]

Emperor William's sojourn in Russia took place during the last ten days of July. Viewed from the angle of personal relations, the visit was undoubtedly a

---

[1] *Letters of Queen Victoria*, I, pp. 436–8 (August 25, 1888).

[2] *Die Grosse Politik*, VI, No. 1338; Meyendorff, op. cit., I, pp. 427 ff.

[3] *Die Grosse Politik*, VI, No. 1343.

success. Politically speaking, it led to nothing. In his conversations with the Tsar and Giers, Herbert Bismarck listened patiently to long and bitter complaints of the Austrian policy in Bulgaria and the Near East generally, but all efforts made by the Russians to elicit suggestions from the Germans were carefully evaded. Count Bismarck simply took the view that if the situation in Bulgaria was so intolerable from the Russian standpoint, the Russians should do something about it. If the Austrians invaded Serbia, let the Russians invade Bulgaria. The German standpoint in the Bulgarian question was perfectly well known, but Germany could not be expected to take the lead. Under the circumstances it was natural that Giers should have been somewhat disappointed, and that he made no mention from the Russian side of any aspirations or designs on the Straits, though this matter was clearly in the forefront of discussion in the Russian foreign office at this time.[1]

During the autumn of 1888 Emperor William followed up his visit to Russia by visits to Vienna and Rome, in October. No new problems were raised by these journeys, and no new view-points were expressed. But the visit to Rome was interesting as being the first paid by a foreign ruler to the Italian capital since the abolition of the temporal power of the Papacy, in 1870. William combined the visit to King Humbert with a visit to Pope Leo, but he found His Holiness completely wrapped up in hopes for a favourable turn of affairs in France. Evidently to prevent a discussion of the Roman question it was arranged by Herbert Bismarck that the Emperor's conversation with the Pope should be interrupted at the proper moment by the entry of the Emperor's brother, Prince Henry. This procedure caused considerable indignation and irritation in Vatican circles and led to a definite rupture of the close relations that had been established in preceding years. The Pope's expectations of support from Germany had been blasted and he turned his attention more and more towards France.[2]

The general international situation during these months was fairly quiet, at least outwardly. The Emperor himself was evidently not cured of his suspicions of Russian policy and seems to have feared that the Russians would, before long, attempt an advance in the Balkans by land as well as by sea.[3] Before the end of the year he felt certain that war might come at any time, from either the Russian or the French side. The military men shared these apprehensions, and Bismarck himself became uneasy, for the Tsar, evidently disappointed by the unwillingness of the Germans to lead Russian policy in Bulgaria, resumed the transfer of troops from the Caucasus and other interior

[1] See especially Baron Jomini's utterances just before the visit (*Die Grosse Politik*, VI, No. 1344). On the visit itself see *Die Grosse Politik*, VI, Nos. 1345 ff.; Schweinitz: *Denkwürdigkeiten*, II, p. 368; Nowak: *Kaiser and Chancellor*, pp. 214 ff.; Meyendorff, op. cit., I, pp. 434–5; Hohenlohe, op. cit., II, pp. 445, 446, 449.

[2] See especially Nowak: *Kaiser and Chancellor*, p. 61; Schlözer, op. cit., pp. 131–2; Basthgen: *Die römische Frage*, III, pp. 4–5.

[3] *Die Grosse Politik*, VI, No. 1350.

regions to the Austrian frontier. At the same time the commercial relations between Germany and Russia were becoming steadily worse as a result of increasing tariffs on both sides and the apparent unreadiness of the Germans to negotiate a tariff treaty.[1]

More disquieting yet was the development of the situation in France and the opening of new connexions between St. Petersburg and Paris. Freycinet, who was minister of war in various cabinets from April 1888 until January 1893, had embarked upon the great work of reorganization and development, which was estimated to cost some eight hundred million francs. The greatest emphasis was laid on the completion of the fortifications, on the perfection of high explosives and smokeless powder, and on the rearming of the infantry with the new Lebel rifle.[2] The progress of these reforms was startlingly rapid, and the Germans did not fail to appreciate it.[3] They did not know that at this very time, in November 1888, the Grand Duke Vladimir, supposedly the best friend of the Germans in the Russian imperial family, was negotiating with Freycinet concerning an examination of the new French rifle, with a view to placing a large order for the Russian army. Freycinet acted in this matter with the knowledge of the French cabinet, though Goblet, the foreign minister, thought the Russian request rather strong and resented the Russian policy of fine words with no action. At last, in January 1889, the negotiations were successfully closed and the order placed, after the Russian government had given definite assurance that the rifles would never be used against the French.[4]

Even more serious than these transactions were the budding financial connexions between the French and the Russian governments. It will be remembered that in November 1887 the German government had issued a decree forbidding the Reichsbank to accept Russian securities as collateral for loans. Even before this time efforts had been made by men like Cyon, the friend of Katkov, to open the French market for Russian purposes. Bismarck was simply playing into the hands of these men, and there can be no denying that he seriously miscalculated in his attempts to weaken Russian credit. What happened was that the Germans hurriedly rid themselves of their Russian securities, frequently at a considerable loss, while the French bought them at an attractive price, realizing, it is said, a profit of some five hundred million francs. Besides, the German measure enabled the Russian government to buy back its securities at a low figure and thus to effect conversion operations which had been contemplated for some time. In the long run Bismarck, far from crippling Russia's

---

[1] V. Wittschewsky: *Russlands Handels, Zoll und Industriepolitik* (Berlin, 1905), pp. 135 ff.; A. Zimmermann: *Die Handelspolitik des deutschen Reiches* (Berlin, 1901), pp. 162 ff.

[2] Freycinet: *Souvenirs*, pp. 396 ff., 404 ff.

[3] Waldersee: *Denkwürdigkeiten*, II, pp. 17, 19; *Waldersee in seinem militärischen Wirken*, II, pp. 317 ff.

[4] Freycinet, op. cit., pp. 415 ff.; René Goblet: *"Souvenirs de ma vie politique"* (*Revue politique et parlementaire*, February 10, 1929, pp. 183–208).

financial position, made it possible for her to secure greater sums of money for the same rate of interest. Most important of all was the fact that the Russian ministry of finance, after the closure of the Berlin market, was practically obliged to accept the offers of French syndicates and to float its future loans in Paris. Negotiations to this end were begun in October 1888 and led to the flotation of a loan of five hundred million francs at four per cent in Paris early in December. The French government did not conceal from the bankers the interest it took in the success of the loan, but its anxiety was unfounded, for the loan was oversubscribed and passed into the hands of more than 110,000 persons. It was the beginning of a long series of operations which built up the huge indebtedness of Russia to France in the period before the World War and established a very strong financial tie between the two countries. Indeed, it may be said that during these last years of the Bismarckian period a veritable financial revolution was taking place in Europe, as the French unloaded their Italian securities and took over the Russian, which the Germans were discarding in favour of the Italian.[1]

Bismarck did not fail to realize the danger of these financial connexions and brought pressure to bear upon German bankers to prevent their participation. The Emperor, too, took a very pessimistic view of the situation.[2] It was under the influence of this renewed danger that Bismarck decided to draw more closely to England. The connexion had, of course, never been broken, and even in August 1888, in a dispatch to the ambassador at London, the chancellor had pointed out that, in view of England's military and naval unpreparedness, her sole assurance against French attack lay in good relations with Germany. Germany could effectively hold France in check, but only if she were certain that England would stand by the League of Peace in the event of Russia's supporting France. These same ideas he developed in conversation with Hatzfeldt during the latter's stay at Friedrichsruh from January 5 to 7, 1889. They were worked out in the instructions sent to the ambassador after his return to London. Hatzfeldt was to communicate to Salisbury the chancellor's conviction that peace, even if only for a period sufficient to complete the armaments of Germany and England, could be most safely attained by a treaty between the two countries, by which they should accept the obligation for a definite period to ward off a French attack in common. A secret treaty of this sort, if it were possible, would afford them both considerable security for the outcome of a war, but the prevention of war could be expected only from a public treaty. Bismarck then pointed out that England was exposed to attack only from France, as no other powers would act against her unless sure of French support.

---

[1] The best source is Ernest Daudet: *Histoire diplomatique de l'alliance franco-russe* (Paris, 1894), chapter vi. The best discussion is in Ibbeken: *Staat und Wirtschaft,* chapter ii. See also Goblet, loc. cit., and Georges Michon: *The Franco-Russian Alliance* (New York, 1929), chapter i, *passim.*

[2] Waldersee: *Denkwürdigkeiten,* II, pp. 17, 19.

A defensive alliance for one, two, or three years would, therefore, meet the English needs completely.[1]

It will be recalled that Lord Salisbury, in the survey of British policy written for the Queen in August 1888, had made exactly the point that Bismarck made: namely, that "France is, and must always remain, England's greatest danger." At that time he had considered the danger dormant because it was overshadowed by the strained relations of France with her two eastern neighbours. But in his speech at the Lord Mayor's banquet on November 10 he had given clear expression to his uneasiness. He believed that the governments were pacifically inclined, he said, but they might at any time be carried away by popular pressure. Furthermore, the five continental powers were reported to have no less than twelve million men for use in war. The terrible pressure of armaments was increasing all the time. Where, he asked, would all this lead? But instead of answering, he indicated that Britain herself must build up her armaments. In speaking to the Russian ambassador he made no secret of the fact that his fears centred on France, with her excessive military expenditures and the growing Boulangist agitation.[2]

The moment, therefore, was favourable for Bismarck's step, and Salisbury received it with great interest and seriousness. He promised to speak to his closest associates and sound out the political leaders. He did not inform Queen Victoria, so far as we know. Indeed, in this matter we have not a single scrap of evidence from the English side. Even in the German foreign office there are only a few documents dealing with the subject. All we know is that every effort was made in the spring of 1889 to improve relations between the two countries. Bismarck, disappointed by the results of Germany's colonial experiment, was determined not to allow serious friction to arise from colonial questions. To the explorer, Eugen Wolf, he said in December: "My map of Africa lies in Europe. Here lies Russia, and here " — pointing to the left — "lies France, and we are in the middle; that is my map of Africa." [3] It is said that he even considered giving up some of the German colonies. At any rate, in a Reichstag speech on January 26, 1889 he spoke warmly of England as Germany's "old and traditional ally, with whom we have no conflicting interests." This did not mean, he explained, an "ally" in the diplomatic sense, for Germany had no agreements with England. But he wished to keep up the old friendship.

In March Count Herbert Bismarck came to London, primarily to discuss colonial affairs, especially the troubles in Samoa and in East Africa. He reviewed the general situation in conversation with Lord Salisbury, stressing the Franco-Italian tension and pointing out the necessity that England and Germany appear friendly before the world. "It was a great object with Germany," he continued, "that war, if it was to come, should not come for eighteen months,

---

[1] *Die Grosse Politik,* IV, Nos. 942–3.   [2] Meyendorff, op. cit., I, p. 443.
[3] Bismarck: *Gesammelte Werke,* VIII, p. 646.

as their rifles would not be ready till then." The conversation turned to the matter of a defensive treaty. Evidently Salisbury had not yet given a reply to Bismarck's overture, since he had been told that an immediate reply was not expected. He now explained that he had consulted with his colleagues and had found that they all agreed with him that an Anglo-German alliance would be very beneficial for both countries and for the peace of Europe; but they had all felt that the time was inopportune, for action in this matter would lead to the break-up of the parliamentary majority. He appreciated Bismarck's initiative and wished to leave the matter open: "Meanwhile we leave it on the table, without saying yes or no; that is unfortunately all I can do at present."[1]

Despite Lord Salisbury's unwillingness to follow up the German proposal at this time, the relations between the two countries continued to grow closer during the spring and summer. Herbert Bismarck paved the way for the settlement of outstanding colonial questions in East Africa and Samoa. He even discussed with Joseph Chamberlain the possibility of an exchange of German South-west Africa for the little island of Heligoland, which lay off the German coast: Bismarck, however, did not think the time ripe for raising so important a problem, and the matter was hardly touched upon in conversation between Salisbury and the German ambassador.[2] On the other hand, a reconciliation between the Emperor and the Prince of Wales was effected and arrangements were made for William to visit England in the summer. Every effort was made on the English side to make a good impression upon the young ruler. In consideration of his great interest in naval affairs it was decided to name him Admiral of the Fleet. This decision was communicated to the Emperor in June, though the visit did not take place until August. Its effect was instantaneous. William wrote to the English ambassador that he was "fairly overwhelmed. . . . Fancy wearing the same uniform as St. Vincent and Nelson; it is enough to make one quite giddy."[3] So enthusiastic was he that it was only with difficulty that Bismarck dissuaded him from broaching anew the subject of Heligoland during his visit.[4]

The visit itself was in every way a success. In a sense it was a naval demonstration, for the Emperor went to England accompanied by a German squadron and during his stay was present at a great review of the British fleet. After returning to Germany he wrote the Queen: "I now am able to feel and take interest in your fleet as if it were my own; and with keenest sympathy shall I watch every phase of its further development, knowing that the British ironclads, coupled with mine and my army, are the strongest guarantees of peace; which Heaven may help us to preserve. Should, however, the will of Providence

---

[1] Die Grosse Politik, IV, No. 945; Letters of Queen Victoria, I, pp. 483 ff.

[2] Die Grosse Politik, IV, Nos. 946–9; Maximilian von Hagen: Geschichte und Bedeutung des Helgolandvertrages (Munich, 1916).

[3] Letters of Queen Victoria, I, p. 504.

[4] Die Grosse Politik, IV, Nos. 950 ff.

lay the heavy burden on us of fighting for our homes and destinies, then may the British fleet be seen forging ahead side by side with the German, and the 'Red Coat' marching to victory with the 'Pomeranian Grenadier'!"[1]

Though Bismarck was undoubtedly gratified by the improvement of relations with England, he certainly did not desire to see German policy orientated exclusively in that direction. In explaining to General von Schweinitz the German offer of an alliance to England, Count Herbert Bismarck said explicitly that this in no way touched Russia.[2] It was directed against France. And yet the Russians quite naturally watched the course of the Anglo-German rapprochement with anxiety. The visit of Herbert Bismarck to London caused suspicion, and the Emperor's visit was looked upon with even greater uneasiness. The Tsar himself felt certain that Bismarck was again engaged upon some intrigue directed against Russia. He would hardly hear of Giers's suggestion that he visit Berlin to repay the visit of the Emperor in 1888.[3] In May, during the festivities connected with the marriage of a Russian Grand Duke with a daughter of the Prince of Montenegro, Alexander spoke, in a toast, of the Balkan Prince as his only true and faithful friend.

General von Schweinitz took a very pessimistic view of the situation, and the military men in Berlin once more advanced the argument that Russian activities in the Balkan countries and the resumption of troop concentrations on the Austrian and German frontiers was sufficient proof that the Tsar was planning action and that it would be the part of wisdom to anticipate him. Bismarck himself was not certain of the future and was uneasy about the progress of the pro-Russian parties in the Balkan countries. He admitted that Russia could not be counted upon as of yore, but he refused to draw the conclusion suggested by the military men that this meant war. Germany, he said, must still try to preserve the peace and must not seek a quarrel.[4] In other words, the German chancellor was unwilling to throw in the lot of Germany with either the English or the Russian side. His object was to maintain a careful balance between them and to allow the antagonism between the two groups to paralyse all efforts to disturb the peace. It is perfectly true that after 1878 Bismarck relied less and less upon Russian friendship and kept the door open for advances and connexions with other powers. After the crisis of 1886–8 he was more inclined than ever to lean towards the English side. But he never, even for a short time, lost sight of the power of Russia or discontinued his efforts to maintain the best possible relationship with her.

The Emperor William, on the other hand, sympathized strongly with the anti-Russian views of the military men. As he was drawn into the sphere of

---

[1] *Letters of Queen Victoria*, I, p. 526; Lee: *Edward VII*, Volume I, p. 656.

[2] Schweinitz: *Denkwürdigkeiten*, II, p. 374.

[3] Lamsdorf: *Dnievnik*, pp. 114, 164, 166, 172 ff., 195, 201; Meyendorff, op. cit., II, pp. 17–26, 42–4.

[4] See especially Radowitz: *Aufzeichnungen*, II, p. 296.

the English influence, this attitude became more and more outspoken. In August 1889 the Emperor told the Austrian chief of staff, in the presence of Francis Joseph, that, no matter what the reason for Austrian mobilization, be it the Bulgarian question or some other, the day of Austrian mobilization would be the day for German mobilization too, whatever the chancellors might say. This was the very negation of Bismarck's policy. Such a difference of view led inevitably to friction with the old chancellor, whom personally William so much admired.[1] In the summer, when the Russian government proposed to float a loan in Berlin, the two men found themselves in open conflict. Bismarck, who had evidently come to realize the danger of the Franco-Russian financial connexion, was anxious to have the matter go through. The Emperor, on the other hand, supported by Waldersee, took the view that the German people must not be allowed to supply the enemy with money for additional armaments, which, it appeared to him, were destined for use against Germany and Austria. Bismarck argued that good relations be maintained at least until the rearming of the German troops should be complete in the spring of 1890 and until England could be counted upon with certainty. But it was all of no avail. The old chancellor was given to understand that his policy was too "Russophil." [2]

From this time on, the chancellor's hold upon the Emperor relaxed more and more. Friction developed between them on matters of domestic policy and they drifted further and further apart on questions of foreign affairs. In his memoirs Bismarck says that "the uniform of Admiral of the Fleet may be regarded as the symbol of a new chapter in the foreign policy of the empire," and he was not far from the truth. William was through with Russia and was drifting more and more into the course of the Mediterranean coalition. Though the chancellor disapproved, the Emperor insisted on going to Athens to attend the wedding of his sister and Prince Constantine of Greece, and he intended to go on from the Greek capital to Constantinople. The Russians naturally put a political construction on these plans, and when the Tsar finally came to Berlin, in October, he made no secret of his suspicions. The Emperor's visit to England and his projected trip to the Near East had, to quote a letter of William to Francis Joseph, led Alexander to believe " that I had joined with you, Humbert, and the Queen of England — the Sultan ought to come in too, in order very soon to unite in suddenly falling on the Tsar, destroying his empire, and annihilating himself and his house! " Alexander complained, furthermore, of the military influences in Berlin, mentioning especially Waldersee. His expression of doubt as to whether Bismarck would long continue in office showed that he

---

[1] Radowitz, op. cit., II, p. 297; Glaise-Horstenau: *Franz Josephs Weggefährte*, p. 338.

[2] Wilhelm Schüssler: *Bismarcks Sturz* (Leipzig, 1921), p. 38; Georg von Eppstein: *Bismarcks Entlassung* (Berlin, 1920), pp. 95–118; Ernst Gagliardi: *Bismarcks Entlassung* (Tübingen, 1927), I, pp. 245 ff. See also Bismarck: *Gedanken und Erinnerungen*, III, p. 142; Waldersee: *Denkwürdigkeiten*, II, pp. 54–60.

was well-informed with respect to the course of affairs in Berlin. Bismarck did his utmost to reassure Alexander, reiterating his indifference to Balkan affairs, stating that there were no written agreements between the Triple Alliance and England, and declaring most positively that the Emperor's visit to the East had no political import whatever.[1] The Tsar left Berlin with his mind set at rest.

The visit of the Tsar led only to new friction between the Emperor and Bismarck, for the chancellor, fearing lest the two rulers, with their very different temperaments, might see too much of each other, thoroughly disapproved of William's hasty action in inviting himself to Russia for the following summer. The Emperor, on the other hand, undoubtedly expected that Bismarck would be pleased by this well-intentioned effort to establish closer relations.[2] He was irritated and disgusted by an attitude which he could not understand, and on his trip to the Near East he went his own way. The visit to Athens and Constantinople really had no political object and led to no new alignments, but the Emperor took the opportunity to show his interest in the British navy. He inspected the fleet at the Piræus and discussed with the Prince of Wales the entire problem of sea-power in the Mediterranean. The whole demonstration caused irritation at St. Petersburg, and the Tsar is said to have spoken very disparagingly of the Emperor, describing him as " an ill-bred and faithless youngster." [3]

It seems that the Tsar's confidence in Bismarck grew as his estrangement from the Emperor developed. The chancellor now appeared as the representative of the old policy of good Russian-German relations, deterring the young ruler from enterprises advocated by the military men. To avoid Germany's going over entirely into the course of the Mediterranean coalition it was essential to maintain the policy of the Reinsurance Treaty. This treaty was not due to expire until June 1890, yet in December 1889 the Tsar decided that negotiations for its renewal might be opened, when the time came in April.[4] But in February, when rumours got abroad of a new conflict between the Emperor and the chancellor, and Bismarck's continuance in office became more and more problematical, Count Shuvalov, the ambassador at Berlin, took up the matter with Bismarck, evidently on his own initiative. Bismarck was quite ready to renew the treaty indefinitely, for, he said, the text is " the expression of a fixed

---

[1] *Die Grosse Politik*, VI, No. 1358; Radowitz, op. cit., II, pp. 300–7; Meyendorff, op. cit., II, pp. 51 ff.; Lucius von Ballhausen, op. cit., p. 504; Brauer, Marcks, Müller: *Erinnerungen an Bismarck* (Stuttgart, 1915), p. 59; Otto Gradenwitz: *Bismarcks letzter Kampf* (Berlin, 1924), pp. 64–6; Nowak: *Kaiser and Chancellor*, pp. 225–6; Waldersee: *Denkwürdigkeiten*, II, pp. 70–3.

[2] Bismarck: *Gedanken und Erinnerungen*, III, pp. 144–5; Hermann Hofmann: *Fürst Bismarck 1890–1898* (Leipzig, 1914), I, p. 16; Waldersee: *Denkwürdigkeiten*, II, p. 72; Eulenburg, op. cit., p. 286; Schweinitz: *Denkwürdigkeiten*, II, p. 392.

[3] Bismarck: *Gedanken und Erinnerungen*, III, pp. 83–5; Waldersee: *Denkwürdigkeiten*, II, pp. 116–17.

[4] Lamsdorf: *Dnievnik*, pp. 226, 239, 247 ff.; Serge Goriainov: " The End of the Alliance of the Emperors " (*American Historical Review*, January 1918, pp. 340–1); Schweinitz: *Denkwürdigkeiten*, II, p. 397.

and unchanging situation." He informed the Emperor of his conversation with Shuvalov and secured his consent to the renewal.

The Emperor's attitude in this matter is remarkable, considering his well-known views regarding Russia. Evidently he agreed to the continuance of the treaty either because he rated its value very low and saw no harm in it, or else because he had no coherent plan to offer as a substitute for the policy followed by Bismarck.[1] In a letter written in 1929 the former Emperor asserts that on this occasion Bismarck simply spoke of Shuvalov's coming journey to Russia and the desirability of taking advantage of it "to underline our good intentions." It was not out of the question — in fact, the chancellor hoped — that perhaps in time this might lead to some tangible result. He asked permission to speak to Shuvalov of the "renewal and eventual strengthening of our friendly relations with Russia." The former Emperor denies that he knew the actual text of the treaty or that he approved its renewal. But he was not the type of man who could be kept in ignorance of so important a matter if he knew of its existence, and it is not possible for a historian to accept the validity of a statement made forty years after the event when that statement is in direct contradiction to official contemporary documents.[2]

The tension in the relations of the Emperor and Bismarck came to a head about March 15. The questions involved dealt primarily with matters of domestic policy, but the problem of international relations was not without bearing on the crisis. Military circles were, if anything, more uneasy about Russia's intentions than ever. News had just come that the latest Russian loan in Paris had been oversubscribed seven or eight times, and that the Russian ministry of finance had on hand large sums of ready cash. Russia had a numerical superiority of ninety thousand troops on the German and Austrian frontiers and was massing forces on the Roumanian front as well. The presence of the Serbian statesman Nikola Pasič at St. Petersburg was taken as evidence of a Russian scheme to organize a Balkan league against Austria and Roumania. So serious were some of the reports from Russia that Bismarck thought best not to submit them to the Emperor for fear of increasing his irritation. This turned out to be a fatal mistake on the part of the chancellor, for one of the high officials of the foreign office, Baron von Holstein, of whom much will have to be said later, worked in collusion with Waldersee to keep the Emperor well supplied with correspondence and newspaper clippings of the right sort.[3]

On March 15 a bundle of twenty reports reached Berlin from the German consul at Kiev, who was one of the government's most reliable reporters. Bis-

---

[1] *Die Grosse Politik*, VII, No. 1367; Goriainov, loc. cit., p. 342; Wilhelm Mommsen: " *Bismarcks Sturz* " (*Archiv für Politik und Geschichte*, I, 1923, pp. 481 ff.).

[2] See Kardorff: *Im Kampfe um Bismarck*, pp. 37 ff.

[3] Waldersee: *Denkwürdigkeiten*, II, pp. 85-9; Schweinitz: *Denkwürdigkeiten*, II, p. 402; Eulenburg, op. cit., pp. 224, 286, 289. See also my *Franco-Russian Alliance*, pp. 39 ff., which is based upon unpublished documents and contemporary newspaper material.

marck sent several of them, which dealt with military matters, to the Emperor. Some of them were of earlier date and William concluded that they had been withheld from him. From the news they contained he was convinced that the menace from Russia was very serious and that the Tsar was on the point of declaring war. It was high time, he wrote Bismarck, that Austria should be warned and counter-measures taken. The chancellor replied immediately, pointing out that the Russian concentrations had been going on for years, that the Austrians had taken counter-measures, and that the Russian willingness to renew the treaty with Germany indicated that there was no immediate danger. He thought that he had convinced the Emperor, but the fact that the reports were handed over to the general staff, and copies sent to Vienna, shows that no attention was paid to his representations.[1]

The break was now complete; Bismarck could no longer subscribe even to the Emperor's foreign policy. In his resignation he pointed out that disagreement regarding Germany's policy towards Russia made it impossible for him to retain charge even of the ministry of foreign affairs. As a matter of fact, the Emperor had no clear-cut ideas about Germany's future policy. He told his generals that Russia was about to occupy Bulgaria and desired the neutrality of Germany, that he had promised Francis Joseph that he would be a faithful ally, and that he meant to stand by his promise. Bismarck, he said, intended to give up Austria and the Triple Alliance and effect an understanding with Russia. On the other hand, the diplomats were informed that foreign affairs had nothing to do with the chancellor's dismissal and would in no way affect Germany's relations to foreign powers.[2] In other words, he appreciated the possible reaction of Bismarck's disappearance upon the international situation and wished to gloss over the difference of opinion which undoubtedly existed. He made the greatest efforts to retain the services of Count Herbert Bismarck as secretary of state for foreign affairs, because he feared the initiation of a new policy.

Shuvalov reached Berlin from St. Petersburg on March 17, at the very height of the crisis. He had full powers to negotiate a renewal of the Reinsurance Treaty for six years, with the idea that it should become permanent. When he learned of the impending resignation of the chancellor, he declared that before opening negotiations he must wait for further instructions from home. It seems that he also expressed some doubt whether the Tsar would want to conclude the agreement with a new chancellor. At any rate, that is what Herbert Bismarck reported to the Emperor on March 20.[3]

---

[1] *Die Grosse Politik*, VI, Nos. 1360–2; Bismarck: *Gedanken und Erinnerungen*, III, pp. 88 ff., 100; Eppstein, op. cit., pp. 183 ff.; Eulenburg, op. cit., p. 236; Gradenwitz, op. cit., pp. 61, 160–1.

[2] Hohenlohe, op. cit., II, pp. 465–6, 469; Schweinitz: *Denkwürdigkeiten*, II, p. 399; Waldersee: *Denkwürdigkeiten*, II, pp. 117–19; Radowitz, op. cit., II, pp. 315 ff.; Crispi: *Memoirs*, II, p. 431.

[3] *Die Grosse Politik*, VII, Nos. 1366–7; Bismarck: *Gedanken und Erinnerungen*, III, pp. 90, 101, 105–6; Hofmann, op. cit., I, p. 113; Schweinitz, op. cit., II, p. 400; and the important quota-

Now, if the Emperor really wished to break the connexion with Russia, if he really had plans for a reorientation of German policy, here was a golden opportunity to withdraw gracefully from the treaty. What he actually did was to express astonishment at Shuvalov's attitude and indicate his readiness to renew the treaty. If the Bismarcks, in turn, had taken advantage of the situation, they might have seen the treaty safely renewed. But Herbert Bismarck insisted that Shuvalov was unwilling to negotiate with the new chancellor and insisted further on handing in his resignation. He was clearly attempting to utilize the question of renewing the treaty to force the Emperor to retract and recall Prince Bismarck to office.[1]

But events took a different turn. The Emperor had Shuvalov waked at one o'clock in the morning and invited to breakfast at the palace at eight. He was determined to clear up the situation himself. When Shuvalov, alarmed by these extraordinary tactics and fearing that bad news had arrived from Russia, appeared promptly on the morning of March 21, he was received " with a kindness and cordiality beyond all expression." The Emperor asked the ambassador to sit down and then explained that he had been obliged to part with the old chancellor because of the wretched state of his health and the excitable condition of his nerves. It was an explanation of which he made liberal use in discussions with foreign representatives. Then he continued: " Herbert Bismarck told me last evening that you were authorized by your sovereign to pursue negotiations respecting the renewal of our secret treaty, but that at present you had abandoned them. Why? I beg you to tell His Majesty that on my part I am entirely disposed to renew our secret treaty, that my foreign policy remains and will remain the same as it was in the time of my grandfather. That is my firm resolve. I shall not depart from it." Assured by Shuvalov that he was merely awaiting new instructions, the Emperor concluded: " Nothing has changed, then, and I rely on your friendship to lay the situation before your Emperor, assuring him that nothing has changed either in my personal sentiments towards him or in my policy towards Russia." [2]

This conversation is irrefutable proof that the Emperor, having got rid of Bismarck, feared to discontinue the policy which he had denounced, and that he dreaded lest the chancellor's dismissal should lead to international complications which, while Bismarck was at the helm, he had regarded with equanimity. But there were powers in the foreign office who were more determined than the Emperor. Baron von Holstein, who for fifteen years had been regarded as one of Bismarck's right-hand men, had joined hands with Waldersee and his group and had worked for Bismarck's fall. He disliked the Bismarcks,

---

tion from the unpublished diary of Herbert Bismarck in Kardorff, op. cit., p. 13, foot-note, which has led me to modify somewhat the opinion expressed in my *Franco-Russian Alliance*, p. 46.

[1] Shuvalov saw through these tactics. See Lamsdorf, op. cit., p. 302.

[2] Goriainov, loc. cit., pp. 343–4; *Die Grosse Politik*, VII, No. 1373; Lamsdorf, op. cit., pp. 283 ff.; Schweinitz, op. cit., II, p. 400; Meyendorff, op. cit., II, p. 75–6.

father and son, and he disagreed with the policy of grovelling before Russia. In his opinion the Berlin Congress and Bismarck's efforts to prevent war between Russia and England in 1885 were serious mistakes. He disapproved of the Reinsurance Treaty, which appeared to him as a betrayal of the alliance with Austria.[1]

Holstein, who evidently hoped to secure control of the foreign office, though he shunned the externals of power, was determined to keep the Bismarcks out of office if he could. He may have had something to do with the appointment of the new chancellor, General von Caprivi. The new minister for foreign affairs, Baron Marschall von Bieberstein, was undoubtedly his nominee. Both were men who lacked experience in foreign affairs and who would be dependent on his judgment. His first move was to induce the new chancellor to call a conference at the foreign office on March 23 to reconsider the question of the treaty with Russia. Besides Caprivi and Holstein there were present the under-secretaries Berchem and Raschdau, who had evidently been instructed beforehand. All were unanimously opposed to the renewal of the treaty, not so much because of the policy which it represented as because all the advantages of the agreement accrued to Russia. It was dangerous to have the German promises on paper, they claimed, for Russia might at any time reveal them to Austria or England and thus disrupt the Triple Alliance. Bismarck himself might divulge them. Furthermore, the treaty was not compatible, at least not in spirit, with the obligations of Germany under the terms of other alliances. At the same time Germany gained nothing by the pact, for there was nothing in it to prevent Russia from concluding an alliance with France. All told, it was a dangerous thing, more likely to lead to war than to preserve the peace, a product of Bismarckian ingenuity which so complicated Germany's international relations that no one lacking Bismarck's genius and prestige could hope to make the intricate system function.[2]

These considerations, embodied in a memorandum drawn up by Berchem, decided Caprivi, who had assumed his position with reluctance and who appears to have been genuinely frightened by the complexity of the problems which confronted him. Thus far Holstein's plans had worked perfectly. Herbert Bismarck, who had handed in his resignation in the expectation that his friend Alvensleben would be appointed, was not informed of what took place, though he was technically secretary of state for foreign affairs until his

---

[1] Maximilian Harden: *Köpfe* (Berlin, 1910), pp. 89–147; G. P. Gooch: " Baron von Holstein " (*Cambridge Historical Journal*, I, pp. 61–84); Hohenlohe, op. cit., II, p. 507; Julius von Eckardt: *Aus den Tagen von Bismarcks Kampf gegen Caprivi* (Leipzig, 1920), p. 24; R. C. Muschler: *Philipp zu Eulenburg* (Leipzig, 1930), p. 232.

[2] *Die Grosse Politik*, VII, No. 1368; Ludwig Raschdau: " *Das Ende der russischen Rückversicherung* " (*Der Tag*, October 17, 1920); Eckardt, op. cit., p. 53. See also the studies of Conrad Bornhak: " *Das Rätsel der Nichterneuerung des Rückversicherungsvertrages* " (*Archiv für Politik und Geschichte*, II, pp. 570–82, 1924) and Richard Frankenberg: *Die Nichterneuerung des deutschrussischen Rückversicherungsvertrages im Jahre 1890* (Berlin, 1927).

resignation was accepted by the Emperor, on March 26. The Bismarcks evidently had no inkling of the intrigues of Holstein. They liked Caprivi and had no doubt that he could be persuaded to continue the old policy. But when, on the very day of the foreign-office conference, Bismarck went over the situation with the new chancellor, he received only evasive answers.[1]

In the meanwhile Holstein had succeeded in persuading General von Schweinitz, who happened to be in Berlin, of his view. The ambassador had for some time entertained doubts as to the advisability of renewing the treaty and on March 27 joined Caprivi in advising the Emperor to drop it. William accepted the advice, apparently with not much regret, though on the following day he tried to sugar the pill by leading Shuvalov to believe that negotiations would be continued at St. Petersburg and that the matter might be arranged at a later date by some alterations in the text. Holstein's victory was complete and he telegraphed the good news to his friends.[2]

It was for General von Schweinitz to break the news at St. Petersburg. He arrived there on March 31 and immediately looked up Giers. The Tsar and his minister had been very uneasy about Bismarck's dismissal, and felt that they were before the unknown. After all, the great chancellor had been an advocate of peace. Could the same be said of the young Emperor and the men in his entourage? Under the circumstances Shuvalov's report of his conversation with the Emperor on the morning of March 21 was received with great satisfaction at St. Petersburg. Giers set to work on instructions for the ambassador, but before they were ready, word came that the negotiations had been suspended. Yet the Russian minister was still in a hopeful frame of mind when the German ambassador tactfully informed him that the treaty could not be renewed.[3]

The Russian foreign minister was struck with consternation on hearing the ambassador's message. He could hardly believe it and recalled to Schweinitz what the Emperor had said to Shuvalov on March 21. The Tsar, however, received the news with greater equanimity. He certainly distrusted Emperor William, as appears from his notation on Giers's report: " The new chancellor's views about our relations are very significant. It appears to me that Bismarck was right when he said that the policy of the German Emperor would alter from the day when he, Bismarck, retired." [4] This did not satisfy Giers, who felt that his entire policy was bound up with this treaty; and his policy, it must

---

[1] Eckardt, op. cit., pp. 52, 59; Radowitz, op. cit., II, pp. 314, 321, 323; Bismarck: *Gedanken und Erinnerungen*, III, p. 114; Waldersee: *Denkwürdigkeiten*, II, pp. 199, 202; Karl Alexander von Müller: " *Die Entlassung* " (*Süddeutsche Monatshefte*, XIX, pp. 138–78, December 1921).

[2] Johannes Haller: " *Warum der russische Draht zerriss* " (*Der Tag*, November 4, 1920); Muschler, op. cit., p. 242; *Die Grosse Politik*, VII, Nos. 1369, 1370, 1391, 1392; Schweinitz, op. cit., II, pp. 392, 404, 406; Radowitz, op. cit., II, p. 323.

[3] *Die Grosse Politik*, VI, Nos. 1364, 1365; Schweinitz, op. cit., II, pp. 396–405; Lamsdorf, op. cit., pp. 272 ff.; Goriainov, loc. cit., pp. 343–4; and unpublished material in my *Franco-Russian Alliance*, pp. 54–5.

[4] *Die Grosse Politik*, VII, No. 1371; Goriainov, loc. cit., p. 344.

be remembered, had been maintained only at the expense of a bitter conflict with Katkov and his circle. Twice during the next two weeks he raised the subject again, pointing out to Schweinitz that the Russians would be content with any scrap of paper — an exchange of notes or of imperial letters. On May 15 he even suggested that Russia would be willing to renew the treaty without the secret protocol and without the German recognition of Russia's preponderant and decisive influence in Bulgaria. Schweinitz, who had never been more than half converted to the new course, reported to his government in favour of acceptance of the Russian offers.[1]

The whole matter was gone over again at Berlin, and various memoranda were drawn up by officials of the foreign office. The tenor of these was that even without the protocol and without the recognition of Russia's claims in Bulgaria the treaty would bind Germany to insist on the principle of the closure of the Straits. This would be detrimental to English interests, and the English, who had never entirely forgiven Germany's action in maintaining the principle in 1885, would be estranged if she persisted in supporting the Russians in this matter. The argument that the treaty was incompatible with Germany's other agreements was also disinterred, but special stress was laid on the possibility and danger of divulgence by Russia and the consequent disruption of the Triple Alliance. Russia, it was pointed out, was evidently preparing for action in the Near East and was therefore anxious to prevent Germany from siding with England and Austria. With the treaty in her hands Russia could, at the crucial moment, reveal the terms to Austria and thus throw the whole anti-Russian coalition into confusion.[2]

Schweinitz was therefore instructed to explain the German attitude to Giers, saying that Caprivi intended to maintain the existing good relations with Russia and to pursue a " simple and transparent " policy, which would " give no occasion for misunderstanding." But there could be no treaty. On hearing this Giers was disconsolate. His first impulse was to attempt to renew negotiations through the Emperors themselves, or through Shuvalov at Berlin, but he was finally convinced of the futility of such action. Nothing more was done, and on June 18, 1890 the famous Reinsurance Treaty automatically lapsed.[3]

The great chancellor was gone, and with him went one of the pivotal agreements of his system. His had been a great career, beginning with three wars in eight years and ending with a period of twenty years during which he worked for the peace of Europe, despite countless opportunities to embark on further enterprises with more than an even chance of success. No other states-

---

[1] *Die Grosse Politik*, VII, No. 1372; Schweinitz, op. cit., II, p. 412.

[2] *Die Grosse Politik*, VII, Nos. 1374 ff.; Ludwig Raschdau: " *Zur Vorgeschichte des Rückversicherungsvertrages* " (*Deutsche Rundschau*, May 1924, pp. 113–26).

[3] *Die Grosse Politik*, VII, Nos. 1380, 1382; Goriainov, loc. cit., pp. 344–6; Lamsdorf, op. cit., pp. 310 ff., 322 ff.; Schweinitz, op. cit., II, pp. 405–6.

man of his standing had ever before shown the same great moderation and sound political sense of the possible and the desirable. Of course much had changed since the time when he first took over the control of Prussian policy, and it cannot be said that he succeeded entirely in estimating the new forces at their full value. In the last years of his régime the old cabinet diplomacy had become quite impossible, for the dissemination of education and more liberal representative institutions had made public opinion a force in foreign affairs. Bismarck himself had not been much influenced by this new factor, for the German Reichstag had little to say in matters of international relations, and the chancellor, with his " reptile fund," was able to mould press opinion to suit his needs, especially in cases of army appropriations. He had a very keen appreciation of the strength and danger of popular passions in other countries, but he was often unwise and unscrupulous in the way in which he manipulated German opinion and aroused the feelings of other nations.

It might also be said that the great chancellor failed to understand all the implications of the great economic changes that were taking place in Europe. The technical advances in armaments he saw clearly enough and he had no hesitation in joining the race for military power without making any serious effort to check the disastrous development of a Europe armed to the teeth. But his advocacy of a colonial policy was hardly more than reluctant and half-hearted. Even though he realized the growing importance of overseas sources and markets, he was, to the end, primarily a continental statesman. In the same way he allowed himself to be carried away by the wave of protection that swept Europe towards the end of the century, yet without seeing the great importance of close economic connexions between Germany and her allies, let alone countries like Russia. The force of international finance escaped him almost completely until the very last years of his chancellorship, and by that time it was almost too late to check the course of events.

It must be remembered, of course, that no other statesman of his time was able to grasp the full significance of these tremendous changes. Bismarck at least deserves full credit for having steered European politics through this dangerous transitional period without serious conflict between the great powers. Paradoxically enough it may be said that by preserving the peace of Europe the great chancellor made possible the phenomenal development of forces which made peace more and more difficult to maintain in the future. As for his own diplomacy, its methods changed while its purposes remained the same. In 1871 he was certainly an advocate of the free hand in international relations. To bind oneself beforehand for certain eventualities that might never occur seemed to him contrary to the fundamental principles of good statesmanship. And yet when he laid down his offices, he had built up the most complicated system of alliances that Europe had ever known in peace times. It was, of course, the product of circumstances, the resultant of the new forces and the new pressure in international relations.

What his alliances came to in the aggregate was a series of security pacts designed to protect the German Empire from any conceivable attack so far as human foresight and ingenuity could do so. With the exception of a slight nuance in the German-Italian treaty of 1887 these agreements were all strictly defensive and were intended to secure the European centre from aggression by the wings. To say that Bismarck's object was to isolate France is only a simplification of his policy and a half-truth. His object was to reduce the pressure upon the German frontiers as much as possible by diverting the European powers to colonial fields and by building up a system of protective agreements that made action difficult and dangerous. Realizing full well that the ferment and urge for expansion in a nation like Russia could not be wholly suppressed, he was willing to protect the Russian rear while the Russians were busy in Asia. He was willing even to allow them a reasonable field for expansion in the eastern Balkans. It was only because Austria, which was absolutely necessary to Germany to complete the central European dike against Russia, objected to Russian activity even in Bulgaria that the German chancellor was led into the policy of the Mediterranean coalition. This combination, as viewed from Berlin, was designed for the simple purpose, not of checking the Russian advance in the Near East, for which Bismarck cared nothing, but of securing for Austria the support of England and Italy in protecting interests for which Germany was unwilling to fight. It was the classic illustration of Bismarck's uncanny sense for the objects and interests of other nations as well as of Germany. The Mediterranean coalition was a tool in Bismarck's hand, but it was not based on unfair exploitation of the other powers. Quite the contrary, the chancellor simply brought together powers like England and Austria who had been for years groping in the dark to join hands.

This careful system of checks and balances was thrown into the discard by Bismarck's successors without much compunction or hesitation. The young Emperor certainly never understood the working of the Bismarckian policy. Perhaps it was a mistake on the chancellor's part not to have initiated him fully. Holstein, of all the men in the foreign office, was alone fully informed and conversant with affairs. He disapproved of the policy and disliked the Bismarcks. He manœuvred to get them out of office and he worked hard to scrap the treaty because he wanted to keep them out of office. Whether Holstein sincerely believed, like Caprivi, that the system was too complicated for anyone but Bismarck to manage is a question that cannot be settled. Certainly, however, it would have been wise for the new men to have gone to the master for advice and information. But Bismarck was practically thrown out of office, and his policy was thrown after him. Holstein carefully avoided consultation with the former chancellor or his son. He wanted to get rid of the policy as well as of the man, and in the end the two went out together.

Considering this aspect of the question, it is hardly worth while to analyse in detail the specific arguments advanced against the renewal of the treaty by

Bismarck's successors.[1] It may be true that the text of the treaty was not wholly compatible with the text of the treaty with Roumania, but it is certain that Bismarck was unaware of this, and these difficulties could easily have been straightened out. Of fundamental disloyalty there can be no serious thought, especially so far as the Austrians are concerned. At Vienna some sort of German-Russian agreement was suspected, but Bismarck had so frequently explained to the Austrians his attitude on the matters in dispute between them and Russia that Kálnoky could take no umbrage. For the same reason it is doubtful whether the revelation of the text by the Russians, which the new men in Berlin seem to have feared as much as anything, would have had any real effect. Bismarck was never partial to secret agreements and he never objected to the publication of this one, though his willingness to see it published may have been due to the fact that he knew that the Russians would not dare publish it. Some point was made in the course of the discussions in Berlin of the fact that the advantages under the treaty were all on the Russian side. It will be remembered, however, that Bismarck himself had offered many of the far-reaching concessions embodied in the protocol, and that Giers attached little value to them.

But even if these arguments were advanced seriously by the officials of the foreign office, Giers's offer to strike out the protocol and accept a simple exchange of notes would have removed almost every objection. In the discussions that followed the proposal it came out clearly enough that the fundamental objection in Berlin was not so much to *the* treaty with Russia as to *any* secret treaty with her. The men of the new course were unwilling to continue the Bismarckian policy, they were afraid to jeopardize German relations with Austria and England, they were frightened by the complexity of the whole thing. They asserted and repeated that no change in Germany's policy towards Russia was intended, but by refusing even to discuss the continuance of the old treaty relation they gave Russia every reason to think that a thorough-going revision of German international relations was intended.

BIBLIOGRAPHICAL NOTE

DOCUMENTARY SOURCES

Die Grosse Politik der europäischen Kabinette. Volume IV: chapter xxix (Bismarck's Offer of an Alliance to England in 1889); Volume VI: chapter xlii (Emperor Frederick III and the Battenberg Marriage Project); xliii (Emperor

---

[1] These are discussed in the preceding chapter and at some length in my *Franco-Russian Alliance,* pp. 58–68. See also Erich Pürschel: "*Das Ende des Rückversicherungsvertrages*" (*Vergangenheit und Gegenwart,* XV, pp. 144–59, 1925); Richard Frankenberg: *Die Nichterneuerung des deutsch-russischen Rückversicherungsvertrages* (Berlin, 1927).

William II and German foreign policy, 1888–90); Volume VII: chapter xliv (The Non-Renewal of the Reinsurance Treaty).

MEMOIRS, AUTOBIOGRAPHIES, BIOGRAPHIES, AND LETTERS

The Letters of QUEEN VICTORIA. Edited by George E. Buckle. Third Series. Volume I. New York, 1930. One of the most important sources for the study of English policy.

Letters of the EMPRESS FREDERICK. Edited by Sir Frederick Ponsonby. London, 1928. Of great interest in connexion with the Battenberg marriage project.

LEE, SIR SIDNEY: *King Edward VII, a Biography.* Two volumes. New York, 1925–7. Contains much interesting material on the early years of William II and his relationship with the Prince of Wales.

MEYENDORFF, BARON A.: *Correspondance diplomatique de M. de Staal.* Two volumes. Paris, 1929. One of the most useful sources for the study of Russian policies.

LAMSDORF, COUNT VLDIMIR N.: *Dnievnik V. N. Lamsdorfa, 1886–1890.* Moscow, 1926. The diary of one of Giers's chief assistants, and the most important source for the study of Russian policy.

CRISPI, FRANCESCO: *Memoirs.* Three volumes. New York, 1912–14. Contains much information not only on the problems of Italian policy, but on the European situation generally.

MOÜY, CHARLES DE: *Souvenirs et causeries d'un diplomate.* Paris, 1909. The memoirs of the French ambassador to Rome in the days of the rupture of trade relations.

BILLOT, ALBERT: *La France et l'Italie.* Two volumes. Paris, 1905. The most complete account of Franco-Italian relations as seen from the French side.

WALDERSEE, GRAF ALFRED VON: *Denkwürdigkeiten.* Three volumes. Berlin, 1922–3. In view of Waldersee's high position and close connexion with the young Emperor William, these diaries are of the greatest value for the student of this period.

—: *Briefwechsel.* Berlin, 1928.

RADOWITZ, JOSEPH MARIA VON: *Aufzeichnungen und Erinnerungen.* Two volumes. Berlin, 1925. The reminiscences of the German ambassador to Constantinople, containing much of interest on the first years of William II.

SCHWEINITZ, LOTHAR VON: *Denkwürdigkeiten.* Two volumes. Berlin, 1927. For this period, as for the preceding ones, this work is of prime importance.

BISMARCK, PRINCE OTTO VON: *Gedanken und Erinnerungen.* Volume III. Stuttgart, 1921. The famous suppressed third volume of Bismarck recollections, giving a detailed account of his conflict with the young Emperor and of his dismissal.

WILLIAM II: *Ereignisse und Gestalten aus den Jahren 1878–1918.* Leipzig, 1922. The former Emperor's autobiography, useful as a check on the Bismarckian account.

EULENBURG-HERTEFELD, PRINCE PHILIPP ZU: *Aus fünfzig Jahren.* Berlin, 1923. Eulenburg was one of the closest friends of the Emperor and of Holstein. His notes, though not complete, are of the greatest interest for this period.

HAMILTON, LORD GEORGE: *Parliamentary Reminiscences and Reflections, 1886–1906.* London, 1922. Contains an important chapter on the Naval Defence Act.

FREYCINET, CHARLES DE: *Souvenirs, 1878–1893.* Paris, 1913. Of great value for the history of the Boulangist movement and for the story of the French army reforms.

HOHENLOHE-SCHILLINGSFÜRST, FÜRST CHLODWIG ZU: *Denkwürdigkeiten.* Two volumes. Stuttgart, 1907. Contains important notes on this period.

LUCIUS VON BALLHAUSEN, ROBERT FREIHERR: *Bismarck-Erinnerungen.* Berlin, 1920. One of the most illuminating sources.

SPECIAL STUDIES

SALATA, FRANCESCO: *Per la Storia Diplomatica della Questione Romana.* Milan, 1929. Based upon unpublished material from the Austrian archives.

JOHNSON, HUMPHREY: *The Papacy and the Kingdom of Italy.* London, 1926. A good survey.

WOODWARD, E. L.: " The Diplomacy of the Vatican under Popes Pius IX and Leo XIII " (*Journal of the British Institute of International Affairs,* May 1924, pp. 113–39).

CURÀTULO, GIACOMO: *La Questione Romana da Cavour a Mussolini.* Rome, 1928.

SALVEMINI, GAETANO: *La Politica Estera di Francesco Crispi.* Rome, 1919. A valuable antidote to Crispi's memoirs.

LEROY-BEAULIEU, ANATOLE: *La France, la Russie et l'Europe.* Paris, 1888. These essays are among the best criticisms of the Franco-Russian connexion.

TRAMOND, JOANNÈS M., and REUSSNER, ANDRÉ: *Éléments d'histoire maritime et coloniale contemporaine.* Paris, 1924. The only general history of European navies in the nineteenth century.

LANGER, WILLIAM L.: *The Franco-Russian Alliance, 1890–1894.* Cambridge, Mass., 1929. Based in part upon unpublished material from the Austrian archives. Takes up in detail the conflict between Bismarck and William II.

NOWAK, KARL FRIEDRICH: *Kaiser and Chancellor.* New York, 1930. Based in large part upon conversation with the former Emperor. A book that must be used with caution.

KARDORFF, SIEGFRIED: *Im Kampfe um Bismarck.* Berlin, 1930. A reprint of the controversial articles exchanged between the author and Nowak, containing some new material of importance.

SCHÜSSLER, WILHELM: *Bismarcks Sturz*. Leipzig, 1921. One of the best studies of Bismarck's fall.

EPPSTEIN, GEORG FREIHERR VON: *Fürst Bismarcks Entlassung*. Berlin, 1920. Based upon unpublished papers.

GORIAINOV, SERGE: "The End of the Alliance of the Emperors" (*American Historical Review*, XXIII, pp. 324–50, January 1918). A fundamental contribution, based upon unpublished Russian material.

UEBERSBERGER, HANS: "*Abschluss und Ende des Rückversicherungsvertrages*" (*Die Kriegsschuldfrage*, V, pp. 933–66, October 1927). Based primarily upon the German documents and the memoirs of Lamsdorf.

BORNHAK, CONRAD: "*Das Rätsel der Nichterneuerung des Rückversicherungsvertrages*" (*Archiv für Politik und Geschichte*, II, pp. 570–82, 1924).

FRANKENBERG, RICHARD: *Die Nichterneuerung des deutsch-russischen Rückversicherungsvertrages im Jahre 1890*. Berlin, 1927. One of the most exhaustive studies.

HAAKE, PAUL: "*Der Neue Kurs*" (*Zeitschrift für Politik*, XV, pp. 320–47, 1925). An admirable analysis of the non-renewal of the Reinsurance Treaty.

HARTUNG, FRITZ: "*Der deutsch-russische Rückversicherungsvertrag von 1887 und seine Kündigung*" (*Die Grenzboten*, 1921, I, pp. 12–17).

PÜRSCHEL, ERICH: "*Das Ende des Rückversicherungsvertrages*" (*Vergangenheit und Gegenwart*, XV, pp. 144–59, 1925).

Index

i